Benn Pitman

The Trials for Treason at Indianapolis,

disclosing the plans for establishing a north-western confederacy

Benn Pitman

The Trials for Treason at Indianapolis,
disclosing the plans for establishing a north-western confederacy

ISBN/EAN: 9783337288761

Printed in Europe, USA, Canada, Australia, Japan

Cover: Foto ©ninafisch / pixelio.de

More available books at **www.hansebooks.com**

THE

...S FOR TREASON

AT

INDIANAPOLIS,

...NG THE PLANS FOR ESTABLISHING

A

...estern Confederacy.

Trials before the Military Co...
...t Brevet Major General ...
...ILAS COLGROVE, Presiden...
...Northern Department, ...
...ents, Finding and Senten...
...REYS, HORACE HEFFRE...
...History, Extent, Nam...
...Golden Circle, the Cir...
...and Order of the Sons ...
...ials, Passwords, Grips, ...
...alties; their ostensibl...
...Greek Fire Shells, Han...
...pirators, introduced in...
...f Judge Advocate Ge...
...; a Western Conspi...

EDI...

...NN...

NTRODUCTORY.

DOUBLE interest attaches itself to the records contained in the following pages: first, they contain the exposure of a plot to overthrow the National Government—a more perfidious, and, perhaps, more gigantic conspiracy than is found in the annals of any nation; and, secondly, the fact and incidents of its suppression by Martial law.

The Northern sympathizers with the Southern Rebellion sought to give it aid, and insure its success, by designs both daring and malignant; and with no other purpose than to perpetuate an institution at once a reproach and an outrage to civilization. These designs were checked, and a great calamity averted, by the strong arm of military power. The chief criminals were seized by military authority, and tried and condemned by a military tribunal.

For the first time in the history of the world, this mighty power, heretofore but too frequently used by kings and despots for the purpose of aggression, or personal aggrandizement, has been exercised in a spirit of wise beneficence, to conserve the liberty of a great and free people. But, it is asked, is not this the attainment of a right by doing a great wrong? Such is the argument of the enemies of the Government.

Has, then, the military power been unlawfully exercised? Has the supremacy of the Constitution been questioned, or have its wise provisions been ignored? Has Liberty—the priceless jewel for which the wisest and noblest have died—been confided to faithless hands? These are among the vital questions discussed and decided in the able arguments contained in this volume.

Thanks to the institutions that have so ordained, and to the progress that has prepared us, the People are now the makers and directors of this potent, and necessarily despotic arm! It is for the people, then, to determine whether they or a faction shall rule; whether freedom shall continue to be the privileged birthright of our children, or whether an oligarchy shall plot to destroy this Great Republic, and erect a barbarism upon its ruins. These are questions upon which every one desiring or deserving to live under the shield of a free and great nation, should satisfy himself; and he can not fail to be instructed, as well as deeply interested, in the developments contained in this volume.

TABLE OF CONTENTS.

Explanation of Illustrations.............. 7
Illustrations...................................... 8
Commission, Special Order for............ 9
Jurisdiction of the Commission, Plea
   to the.. 9
Jurisdiction of the Commission, Argu-
   ments in support of the Plea........... 10
Judge Advocate's Reply to Argument
   of Counsel.................................... 12
Charges and Specifications preferred
   against H. H. DODD........................ 17
FELIX G. STIDGER, Testimony of............ 19
GEORGE E. PUGH,   "   " 37
JOSEPH KIRKPATRICK, "   " 38
WILLIAM CLAYTON,   "   " 39
WESLEY TRANTER,   "   " 47
ELLIOTT ROBERTSON,   "   " 49
Affidavit of Counsel on the escape of
   H. H. DODD.................................... 50
Report of Colonel WARNER on the escape
   of H. H. DODD............................... 50
Argument of Judge Advocate, on pro-
   ceeding to findings and sentence in
   absence of the accused................... 50
J. W. GORDON, Reply of...................... 53
"   "   "   Argument of, on the Ju-
   risdiction of the Commission............ 55
M. M. RAY, Argument of..................... 64
Judge Advocate, Reply of.................. 67
Commission, Special Orders for............ 73
Counsel, Introduction of..................... 74
Charges and Specifications preferred
   against WILLIAM A. BOWLES, ANDREW
   HUMPHREYS, HORACE HEFFREN, L. P.
   MILLIGAN, and STEPHEN HORSEY......... 74
Severance, Motions for....................... 77
Judge Advocate, Reply of on Severance. 78
WILLIAM M. HARRISON, Testimony of..... 80

Circular of the O. S. L. to County
   Temples....................................... 83
Letter of L. P. MILLIGAN to General H.
   H. DODD....................................... 88
EDWIN A. DAVIS, withdrawal of as Coun-
   sel.. 89
WESLEY TRANTER, Testimony of........... 93
STEPHEN TENEY,   "   " 96
JOSEPH J. BINGHAM, "   " 97
FELIX G. STIDGER,   "   " 106
THOMAS R. COBB, Introduction of, as
   Counsel for STEPHEN HORSEY............ 114
Colonel A. J. WARNER, Testimony of..... 118
C. L. V. (Vallandigham), Letter from... 119
ELLIOTT ROBERTSON, Testimony of......... 119
HENRY L. ZUMRO,   "   " 120
HORACE HEFFREN, Charges and Specifi-
   cations canceled........................... 123
HORACE HEFFREN, Testimony of........... 123
CYRUS L. DUNHAM, Counsel for HEFFREN,
   Statement of................................ 128
Colonel J. T. WILDER, relieved............ 137
JAMES L. MASON, Testimony of............ 141
HARRISON CONNELL, "   " 141
ELISHA COWGILL,   "   " 141
JAMES B. WILSON,   "   " 143
WILLIAM S. BUSH,   "   " 150
Speech of L. P. MILLIGAN, Argument on
   admissibility of newspaper report of. 151
Speech of L. P. MILLIGAN, loyal or dis-
   loyal character of.......................... 153
NICHOLAS COCHRANE, Testimony of........ 156
Testimony on the part of the Govern-
   ment closed................................. 157
WILLIAM G. MOSS, Testimony of........... 157
Argument on the admissibility of state-
   ments made by the accused in his
   own favor.................................... 157

	PAGE.
Character for loyalty, etc., of A. Humphreys	163
D. O. Dailey, Testimony of	165
Rev. Richard A. Curren, Testimony of	166
Argument on admissibility of statements not expressed to any public assembly	166
John J. Scotton, Testimony of	169
William Sayler, " "	169
George Bailey, " "	169
William Allen, " "	169
William Wolf, " "	170
W. M. Swasey, " "	170
Geo. Bailey (recalled) " "	170
William Wines, " "	171
William Johnson, " "	171
William C. Kocher, " "	172
Joseph Johnson, " "	172
Samuel Winters, " "	173
G. R. Corlew, " "	176
Samuel F. Day, " "	177
Ochmig Bird, " "	177
B. F. Ibach, " "	179
Captain Samuel Place, " "	180
G. R. Corlew (recalled) " "	180
Moses W. Milligan, " "	180
Edward Price, " "	180
S. G. Burton, " "	181
Speech of A. Humphreys, Argument on the admissibility of what he said as to right of secession, etc.	181
Willis G. Neff, Testimony of	185
John Roach, " "	186
Wilson B. Lockridge, " "	186
Samuel McGaughey, " "	187
Cutter S. Dobbins, " "	187
Harrison Connell, " "	187
William N. Ranney, " "	187
Gen. Alvin P. Hovey, " "	188
M. B. Brant, " "	188
W. J. Smith, " "	188
Samuel Chandler, " "	189
D. Garland Rose, " "	189
Edward Harrison, " "	189
John Nave, " "	189
W. C. Smock, " "	189
David Stockman, " "	189

	PAGE.
Jacob Farling, Testimony of	189
Wm. R. Taylor, " "	190
R. C. Bocking, " "	190
Wm. H. Chapman, " "	191
William Johnson, " "	191
Samuel D. Price, " "	191
Thurston W. Ritting, " "	191
Borzillai Messler, " "	191
Thomas G. Smith, " "	192
Mrs. Elizabeth T. Simons, Testimony of	192
Impeaching of the Testimony of Richard A. Curren, Argument on	192
Jonathan W. Gordon, Argument of	195
M. M. Ray, " "	224
J. R. Coffroth, " "	238
Judge Advocate Burnett, Reply of	240
Explanation of Initials employed in the Rituals	295
Knights of the Golden Circle, Ritual of	297
Sons of Liberty, First Degree (I)	299
Sons of Liberty, Vestibule Lesson, (S. L.)	302
Sons of Liberty, First Degree (O. S. L.)	303
Sons of Liberty, First Conclave or Second Degree (I)	306
Sons of Liberty, Second Conclave or Third Degree (II)	308
General Laws of the Order of Sons of Liberty	308
Constitution of the Grand Council of S. L. of Indiana	311
Constitution and Laws of the Supreme Grand Council	314
Proceedings of the Grand Council State of Indiana	315
Address of the Grand Commander State of Indiana	316
Resolutions of the Grand Council State of Indiana	319
Report of the Grand Secretary State of Indiana	319
Holt, Judge Advocate General, Official Report of	323
Letter from General Heintzelman to Major General Halleck	339
H. H. Dodd, Letter of, to the Cincinnati Enquirer	340

EXPLANATION OF THE ILLUSTRATIONS.

No. 1 is a seemingly harmless portmanteau.

No. 2 exhibits its internal arrangement. An alarm-clock, with the bell removed, set to any given time, springs the lock of a gun, the hammer of which, striking and exploding a cap, placed upon a tube filled with powder, fires a train connected with a bottle of Greek fire. The explosion of these combustibles ignites the tow, saturated with turpentine, with which the remainder of the portmanteau is filled.

No. 3 is a conical shell, three and a half inches in diameter.

Nos. 4 and 5 exhibit the same unscrewed.

No. 7 is a case to contain powder, with a nipple for a cap at its upper end. No. 7 screws into 6, the space between the two being filled with Greek fire. Nos. 6 and 7 make an interior shell, fitting loosely in No. 3, and which, on striking any object, explodes the cap on the top of 7.

No. 8 is a spherical shell, or hand-grenade.

Nos. 9 and 10 exhibit the same unscrewed.

No. 11 is an interior shell, with nine nipples for caps, fitting loosely so as to leave space for concussion. No. 11, also, is made to unscrew, in the center, to hold No. 12, a small vial containing Greek fire.—the space between the two being filled with powder. The dropping of this shell a quarter of a yard from the floor, invariably explodes one or more of the caps. The string attached to No. 8 enables a person to throw it a greater distance, as a sling, with less danger of explosion in his own hand.

No. 13 is a letter in secret cipher, sometimes employed by the Order of Sons of Liberty in their communication with each other, upon matters requiring secrecy.

" Headquarters, 10th District, }
Grand Marshal's Office.   }

" *Dept. Marshal:*

"We have 40 rifles and 100 pistols for your township. It is necessary that they are placed in the hands of our brothers immediately. Inform your company that the arms will be ready on Wednesday night.

"Yours,

"A. A. D. C.

"F—— W."

APPROVAL OF THE SECRETARY OF WAR, ETC.

CINCINNATI, O., Nov. 7, 1864.

Major H. L. Burnett, Judge Advocate Department of the Ohio and Northern Department:

Messrs. Moore, Wilstach & Baldwin, of this city, will publish in permanent and respectable book shape, and I will edit, the official reports of the trial of H. H. Dodd, also of W. A. Bowles, and others, adding thereto the report of the Judge Advocate General, if I can obtain your sanction and co-operation, and the approval of the Military authorities.

I am, very respectfully and obediently,

(Signed)   BENN PITMAN,

Recorder to the Military Commission.

INDORSEMENT OF H. L. BURNETT, JUDGE ADVOCATE DEPARTMENT OF THE OHIO AND NORTHERN DEPARTMENT.

JUDGE ADVOCATE'S OFFICE,
Department of the Ohio and Northern Department,
Cincinnati, O., Nov. 7, 1864.

Respectfully referred to Brigadier General J. Holt, Judge Advocate General, U. S. Army.

The within application of Mr. Pitman receives my approval, and, in the enterprise which he proposes to undertake, I will give him such assistance as I am, from time to time, able to render. I think the publication of these treason trials will be of great public service in showing the people the contemplated anarchy and bloodshed from which they have been delivered, and, as a result, confirming them in their patriotic resolves to support the Government in its efforts to maintain law, order and civilization. It will tend to unite the Northern people more completely in their support of the Government in its efforts to maintain the integrity of the Republic as the only means of establishing a permanent peace.

(Signed)   H. L. BURNETT,

Judge Advocate Department of the Ohio
And Northern Department.

INDORSEMENT OF BRIGADIER GENERAL J. HOLT, JUDGE ADVOCATE GENERAL.

BUREAU OF MILITARY JUSTICE, Nov. 11, 1864.

Approved.

(Signed)   J. HOLT,

Judge Advocate General.

INDORSEMENT OF ASSISTANT SECRETARY OF WAR, C. A. DANA.

WAR DEPARTMENT, Nov. 15, 1864.

Approved.

By order of the Secretary of War.

(Signed)   C. A. DANA,

Assistant Secretary of War.

PROCEEDINGS

MILITARY COMMISSION,

Which convened at Indianapolis, Indiana, by virtue of the following Special Orders, to wit:

Special Orders No. 129.

A Military Commission is constituted to meet at the United States Court Rooms, in the city of Indianapolis, on the nineteenth (19th) day of September, 1864, at 10 o'clock, A. M., or as soon thereafter as practicable, for the trial of Harrison H. Dodd, and such other prisoners as may be brought before it.

DETAIL FOR THE COMMISSION.

1. Brevet Brigadier General Silas Colgrove, United States Volunteers.

2. Colonel William E. McLean, 43d Infantry, Indiana Volunteers.

3. Colonel John T. Wilder, 17th Infantry, Indiana Volunteers.

4. Colonel Thomas I. Lucas, 16th Infantry, Indiana Volunteers.

5. Colonel Charles D. Murray, 89th Infantry, Indiana Volunteers.

6. Colonel Benjamin Spooner, 83d Infantry, Indiana Volunteers.

7. Colonel Richard P. DeHart, 128th Infantry, Indiana Volunteers.

Major Henry L. Burnett, Judge Advocate Department of the Ohio and Northern Department, Judge Advocate.

The Commission will sit without regard to hours.

By order of Brevet Major General Alvin P. Hovey.   AND. C. KEMPER,
Assistant Adjutant General.

Special Orders No. 131.

2. Colonel Ambrose A. Stevens, Veteran Reserve Corps, is appointed a member of the Military Commission, constituted by Special Order No. 129, of the 17th of September, instant, from these Headquarters.

By order of Brevet Major General Alvin P. Hovey.

[Signed]   AND. C. KEMPER,
Assistant Adjutant General.

The Commission met pursuant to the foregoing orders.

All the members present.*   Also, the Judge Advocate.

The Commission then proceeded to the trial of Harrison H. Dodd, a citizen of Indiana, who was present before the Commission, and who, having heard read the order appointing the Commission, also the order detailing Colonel Ambrose A. Stevens as a member, was asked by the Judge Advocate if he had any objection to any member named in the orders, to which he replied, " I have none."

The members of the Commission and the Judge Advocate were then duly sworn in the presence of the accused.

Benn Pitman and W. S. Bush were duly sworn by the Judge Advocate, as Recorders to the Commission, also in the presence of the accused.

The accused applied to the Commission to be permitted to introduce J. W. Gordon, Esq., and M. M. Ray, Esq., as his counsel, which application was granted, and they appeared as counsel for the accused.

The accused, through his counsel, then offered the following plea to the jurisdiction of the Commission:

The defendant, Harrison H. Dodd, protests and objects to the jurisdiction of the Commission appointed to try him upon the aforesaid charges and specifications thereunder, and claims the right, as a citizen of the United States, and of the State of Indiana, to have the said charges and specifications presented by a grand jury of the

---

*If a member of the Commission was, in any case, absent from sickness, or other unavoidable cause, the case was proceeded with, on the consent of the accused being given in open Court, and such member took his seat again on the Commission only with the consent of the accused being given in open Court, after having first heard read all the testimony taken during his absence.

district wherein said several offenses are alleged to have been committed, to the proper District Court thereof; and to be tried by a jury of the said district, duly elected and sworn according to the Constitution and laws of the United States of America. This he claims as a citizen of the United States, and of the State and District of Indiana, and as being in no wise connected with the army or navy of the United States, as a member thereof, or as attached thereto.

Respectfully submitted,

HARRISON H. DODD.

The Commission adjourned, to meet on Friday, September 23, at 10 o'clock, A. M.

COURT ROOM, INDIANAPOLIS, INDIANA,
September 23, 1864, 10 o'clock, A. M.

The Commission met pursuant to adjournment.

All the members present. Also, the Judge Advocate, the accused, and his counsel.

The proceedings were read and approved.

The accused, through his counsel, submitted the following brief in support of his plea to the jurisdiction of the Commission:

Mr. President and Gentlemen of the Commission:

In support of his objection to the jurisdiction of the Commission to try him upon the charges preferred against him, the defendant respectfully submits the following considerations:

I. These charges involve capital and infamous crimes, and the Constitution of the United States expressly provides that "no person shall be held to answer for a capital or otherwise infamous crime, unless on a presentment or indictment by a grand jury, except in cases arising in the land or naval forces, or in the militia, when in actual service in time of war or public danger." (*Amend. Const. Art.* 5.) And again: "In all criminal cases the prisoner shall enjoy the right of a speedy and public trial, by an impartial jury of the State and district where the crime shall have been committed," etc. (*Amend. Const. Art.* 6.)

These provisions were adopted after the organization of the Government of the United States under the Constitution, and for the purpose of placing the trial by jury entirely beyond the power of Congress, and of all other branches of the Government. The Constitution, as originally adopted, contained the following provision on the subject: "The trial of all crimes, except in cases of impeachments, shall be by jury; and such trial shall be held in the State where such crime shall have been committed." (*Article* 4, *section* 2.) So jealous were the people of the right in question, that they required the amendment quoted, notwithstanding the original provision.

The defendant is a citizen of the United States, and of the State of Indiana, not in the land or naval forces, or in the militia in actual service. He is, therefore, not within the exception of Article 5 of amendments above cited. That exception does not affect his right any more than if it did not exist. These several provisions of the Constitution are absolute as to him; and if any constitutional provision can protect a right, it would seem that he ought to be protected from a trial not in conformity with them. It seems that he can not, in fairness, be tried without first being presented by a grand jury; or tried without a petit jury of the district wherein his alleged offenses were committed.

II. But it may be said that we are in a state of war; that the writ of *habeas corpus* is suspended; and the provisions in question are under similar suspension. But there is no provision for the suspension of any branch of the Constitution. The Constitution, indeed, authorizes the suspension of the *habeas corpus* act—a law of the land, generally adopted in the States prior to the adoption of the Constitution. The right of trial by jury, however, is placed on a different and higher ground. It is secured by these several absolute provisions of the Constitution, against all chances, and under all circumstances. The fiat that suspends it must be potent enough to abolish every principle of the Constitution, and all those primordial rights that existed before the Constitution, and so far as human foresight could provide against their invasion, protected by plain constitutional provisions.

If it should be contended, then, that the power necessary for the suspension of the *habeas corpus* involves in its exercise the suspension of the right of trial by jury, he begs leave to say that, in his opinion, it can not for the following reasons:

1. The trial by jury is placed by the Constitution among the original reserved rights of the people, and must, in favor of natural liberty, be held safe as against the exercise of any doubtful power, upon the principle of construction applied to constitutions, that grants of power are to be construed strictly as against the power, and in favor of liberty.

2. But, being last in point of time, and of equal authority with the provision in relation to the suspensions of *habeas corpus*, the amendments must be held to restrain that provision so far as may be necessary to the perfect enjoyment of the rights asserted in the amendments.

3. Simply, however, because they are amendments to the Constitution, every thing contained in that instrument that may, in any view, be held to impair rights therein asserted, must give way to them. To that extent they change and modify the powers conferred on the Government, in the original instrument. The right of trial

by jury in the cases referred to, can not be impaired, much less taken away, by a suspension of the *habeas corpus*, nor, indeed, by any order of the Executive, or law of Congress. To this effect see *2d Story on Const., section* 1778 *to* 1795, *inclusive.*

III. But not only may this right of trial by jury be regarded as affirmatively asserted, and secured to the citizen, by the provisions of the Constitution, but any and every other mode of trial must be taken to be excluded and prohibited. Thus: "No person shall be held to answer for any capital or otherwise infamous crime, unless in case of presentment and indictment by grand jury," etc., clearly precludes the notion of any other form of trial. The old common law, and great statutes of England, brought over with them by the founders of the English colonies, and in force at the time of the adoption of the Constitution of the United States, excluded all other modes of trial of any citizen, not in the military service, and expressly that by military commission. Mr. Justice Story, as already cited, expressly appeals to and quotes *Magna Charta* upon this point, and in support of this position. The 39th chapter of that great act is as follows: "No freeman shall be taken or imprisoned, or disseized, or outlawed, or banished, or in any way destroyed; nor will we pass upon him, unless by the lawful judgment of his peers, or by the law of the land." "The judgment of his peers, here alluded to," says Story, "is the trial by jury, who are called the peers of the party accused, being of the like condition, and equal." He also expressly says: "When our more immediate ancestors removed to America, they brought this great privilege with them, as their birthright and inheritance, as a part of that admirable common law, which had fenced round and interposed barriers on every side against the approaches of arbitrary power." (*Section* 1779.) But this denial of any other form of trial, and especially that by military commission, was asserted in the "Petition of Right," passed in the third year of Charles I. It is therein enacted and established, "that no man, of what estate or condition that he be, should be put out of his land or tenement, nor taken, nor imprisoned, nor disherited, nor put to death, without due process of law;" and in speaking of the commissions aforesaid, the act employs the following terms: "Which commissions, and all others of like nature, are wholly and directly contrary to the said laws and statutes of the realm." Similar language was employed in the Bill of Rights, passed at the time of the revolution of 1688, and it may safely be stated that since that time no proceeding of this nature has taken place in England, against any person not a member of the army or navy, or in the militia in actual service. Indeed, a distinguished English Judge has said that "martial law, as of old, does not exist in England at all," and is contrary to the Constitution, and has been for a century exploded. (*Grant* vs. *Gould,* 2 *H. Bl.,* 69; 1 *Hale P. C.,* 364; *Hale Com. Law C.,* 2, 36.) This, it has been remarked by a learned Judge, "is correct as to the community, both in war and peace."

IV. By an act of Congress, approved July 31, 1864 (*Vol.* 12, *Statutes at large, p.* 2184), conspiracies are defined, and the mode of punishment prescribed, namely, by trial in the Circuit or District Courts of the United States, of the proper circuit or district. Can these parties be tried before any other tribunal? The defendant holds not. By the President's proclamation of September 24, 1862, suspending the privilege of the writ of *habeas corpus,* it was ordered, "That during the existing insurrection, and as a necessary measure for suppressing the same, all rebels and insurgents, their aiders and abettors, within the United States, shall be subject to martial law, and liable to trial and punishment by court-martial or military commission." Without stopping to inquire whether this proclamation was authorized, and if so, whether it embraced persons charged with committing a substantive offense, within a State not in insurrection, and where the United States Courts were in the full exercise of their powers, the defendant claims that it has been superseded by the act of Congress of the 3d of March, 1863 (*Vol.* 12, *Statutes at large,* 755), relating to the writ of *habeas corpus,* and the President's proclamation based thereon, of September 15, 1863. The first section of the act of 1863, authorizes the President to suspend the writ of *habeas corpus.* The second requires the Secretaries of State and War to report to the Judges of the United States Circuit and District Courts the names of all persons held in military custody, by order of the President, in their respective districts, and if the grand juries of the proper districts fail to find bills, it is made the duty of the Judges to have all such persons discharged on taking the oath of allegiance and giving bond, if required. The third section provides that all persons so held and not reported, shall be entitled to a discharge in the same manner as is provided in the second section, after a failure on the part of the proper grand jury to indict them. Here are all the sections of this act which bear on the question, and it will be seen that while they contemplate and sanction military arrests, they do not countenance or authorize military trials. On the contrary, they fairly discountenance them.

The President's proclamation, based on this act, limits the suspension of *habeas corpus* to persons amenable to military law, or to the rules and articles of war. No order is contained in the proclamation in regard to trial, and the inference is irresistible that the proper courts are left to act under the rules of law upon that subject, and these are too well defined to require comment. Civil courts try offenses against the law committed by citizens—military courts and commissions try such as are subject to the rules and articles of war, and the defendant claims that he does not fall within that class.

V. The recent act, giving military courts jurisdiction of offenses against the civil laws when committed by soldiers, excludes citizens, by its silence, from any such provision, and leaves them to be tried by the civil courts, for all such offenses. (*Revised Reg.*, 1863, *p.* 544.)

VI. The defendant further desires the Commission to consider this question, in determining that of jurisdiction, namely: Can the sentence of the Commission be pleaded in bar to a prosecution upon indictment for the offenses charged in the civil courts? It would seem not, in view of the recent legislation of Congress already cited. That legislation clearly gives the jurisdiction of the case to the civil courts, and upon the failure to try or convict him, entitles him to be discharged, either upon terms, or absolutely.

In view of these considerations, the defendant respectfully submits that he is not triable by this Commission, not being within the jurisdiction thereof, or of any other military tribunal whatever.

All of which is respectfully submitted,

HARRISON H. DODD.

JUDGE ADVOCATE'S ANSWER.

The Judge Advocate, Major Burnett, then made the following reply:

To support the jurisdiction of the Commission appointed to try this case, I submit:

1. The proclamation of the President of the United States, published in General Orders No. 141, dated September 25, 1862.

2. The general principles of the laws of nations, and the laws and customs of war—the military *lex non scripta* of every land.

The proclamation of the President is as follows:

War Department, Adjutant General's Office, }
Washington, September 25, 1864. }

General Orders No. 141.

The following proclamation by the President is published for the information and government of the army, and all concerned:

BY THE PRESIDENT OF THE UNITED STATES OF AMERICA—
A PROCLAMATION.

Whereas, It has become necessary to call into service not only volunteers, but also portions of the militia of the States by draft, in order to suppress the insurrection existing in the United States, and disloyal persons are not adequately restrained by the ordinary process of law from hindering this measure, and from giving aid and comfort in various ways to the insurrection; now, therefore, be it ordered,

First. That during the existing insurrection, and as a necessary measure for suppressing the same, all rebels and insurgents, their aiders and abettors, within the United States, and all persons discouraging volunteer enlistments, resisting militia drafts, or guilty of any disloyal practice, affording aid and comfort to rebels against the authority of the United States, shall be subject to martial-law, and liable to trial and punishment by courts-martial or military commission.

Second. That the writ of *habeas corpus* is suspended in respect to all persons arrested, or who are now or hereafter during the rebellion shall be imprisoned in any fort, camp, arsenal, military prison or other place of confinement, by any military authority, or by the sentence of any court-martial or military commission.

In witness whereof, I have hereunto set my hand, and caused the seal of the United States to be affixed.

Done at the city of Washington, this, twenty-fourth day of September, in the year of our Lord one thousand eight hundred and sixty-two, and of the independence of the United States the eighty-seventh.

ABRAHAM LINCOLN.

By the President:

William H. Seward, *Secretary of State.*

By order of the Secretary of War:

L. Thomas, *Adjutant General.*

In determining the action of the Commission, this is sufficient, but in support of the position held, I submit:

That it is an admitted principle in ethics, that self-preservation is the first law of nature; that self-preservation, or self-defense, is the right of every unity or community. This nation is engaged in suppressing a gigantic rebellion, to which end it has brought into the field a vast army. Every fiber of this great nation is quivering in its effort to sustain this army in its present vast proportions. That army being organized and put into the field, becomes a living, sentient, and, to a certain extent, independent body. A blow is sought to be struck at that body—at that great army of the Republic—to sever it, and render it powerless—a blow all the more mischievous and malignant, because it is covert and concealed. To preserve itself, to maintain its integrity when it finds itself thus secretly attacked, it does not wholly fall back on its Government to protect it, but it protects itself by seizing the antagonistic force. It is one of the innate principles of every existing thing, that it is endowed with the right to meet and overcome the force that seeks to destroy it. Here, then, is a power being organized—it is true, in a loyal State, but with the purpose of moving into a semi-disloyal State, a portion of which is occupied and held by forces seeking to destroy this army, and with the intent to co-operate with those forces to render powerless our army, and, if possible, to destroy it and the Government. This army, therefore, without waiting for its Government to move, through the slow machinery of civil law, against this military force that is being arrayed against it, seizes it, and says to it, " You are not meeting us in open battle, but you steal upon us in the night time, and attempt, assassin-like, to stab us in the back while we are facing the common enemy in the front. You are not fighting us according to the recognized military law of nations, but by the secret arts of the assassin. We, therefore, wheel upon you, and grapple you, from an instinct of self-preservation."

It is as though a stealthy foe should creep into a camp or garrison at night, and seek to ignite the magazine, and destroy the lives of the entire garrison. If caught, would that garrison hesitate to convene a court, and try the offender as a secret, military assassin? In like manner, when foes, cunningly avoiding all show of open hostility, secretly arm themselves, not as enemies particularly of the General Government, but as enemies of the military power of the Government, the military laws of the land give power to seize the persons of these secret foes, and hold them responsible for their acts to the common law military.

Take the case in hand, as it is claimed to be, that there was an organized, formidable conspiracy, military in its character, and created and held in existence for the purpose of aiding the enemies of the. country and destroying the armies of the nation, numbering in the States of Ohio, Indiana and Illinois, as claimed by its leaders, one hundred thousand men, the avowed purpose of these conspirators being to release the rebel prisoners held in those States, numbering between forty and fifty thousand veteran soldiers, arm them with guns to be seized from the arsenals of these States, and then to move into Kentucky, seizing all the large cities by the way, take possession of the Louisville and Nashville road, and, intrenching at Nashville or Chattanooga, cut General Sherman's communications, thereby placing him between two large armies, severing him from his base of supplies, and thus effectually, as they thought, destroying this great South-western wing of our army—this right arm of the Republic—thereby giving to the rebels the power to dictate to the United States terms of peace and separation. It was a far-reaching, villainous scheme, and had in it many of the elements of success. The Government stood on the brink of a precipice. But the conspirators were foiled by the military power of the Government. Will it be said that when the

military authorities discovered this plot, they should have waited for affidavits, for an arrest and hearing before a United States Commissioner, and then have released these conspirators upon bail, permitting them to again take the lead of their hosts to work out their schemes of treason against the Government? Such a course might have involved the destruction of the nation. Self-preservation demanded that these men should be seized by the military power. Foreseeing this danger, martial law had been declared by the President, and military courts given jurisdiction.

In support of the powers of the Government, in cases of insurrection, or in case of great public danger, to suspend the operations of the civil law, I cite the opinion of Chief Justice Taney, in a case before the Supreme Court, where the Government of the State had declared martial law in Rhode Island. In rendering an opinion on that case, he says: "Unquestionably a State may use its military power to put down an insurrection too strong to be controlled by the civil authority. The power is essential to the existence of every government—essential to the preservation of order and free institutions, and is as necessary to the States of this Union as to any other government. * * * Without power to do this," he again says, "martial law and the military array of the Government would be mere parade, and rather encourage attack than repel it."

Justice Woodbury, dissenting, said that "a *State* could not declare martial law, inasmuch as the war power, of which it forms a part, was lodged exclusively in the General Government." Certainly no one will deny that if the Government of a State can declare martial law for suppressing an insurrection within that State, with much stronger reason can the General Government, when an insurrection exists against it, declare and enforce martial law, either in part or in whole.

The main question raised by the defense in their argument, is, whether the legislative branch of this Government, or the President, has the power of suspending the writ of *habeas corpus*, and declaring martial law throughout the land. In reply to the argument of the counsel for the accused, I propose to cite a few quotations applicable to this case:

Martial law is the suspension, for the time being, of all constitutions and civil laws, the closing of common law courts, and the forcible inauguration of a new, temporary, arbitrary system of administering justice; and is only to be justified by the overwhelming necessities of the case.

I propose, first, to examine English authorities upon this subject; and then refer to American jurisprudence as to the right to proclaim martial law.

It may be premised that martial law in England as completely violates and suspends the Magna Charta as in this country it does our own Constitution.

Section 39 provides: "No freeman shall be taken or imprisoned, or disseized, or outlawed, or banished, or in any way destroyed; nor will we pass upon him, unless by the lawful judgment of his peers, or by the law of the land."

The Mutiny Act of 1689, which has been re-enacted at every session of Parliament for more than one hundred and seventy years, contains the following declaration:

"Whereas, no man may be forejudged of life or limb, or subjected to any kind of judgment by martial law, or in any other manner than by the judgment of his peers, and according to the known and established laws of this realm," etc.

It is impossible to conceive of any doctrine more irradically graven upon the Constitution and civil polity of England, than this right of *habeas corpus*, and exemption of the subject from the operation of martial law. But notwithstanding this clear provision of the Magna Charta, as often as it is necessary, martial law is proclaimed. In the riots of 1780, after the mob had insulted a majority of Parliament, and the residence of the Chief Justice, the King in council issued his proclamation:

"We have, therefore, issued the most direct and effectual orders to all our officers, by an immediate exertion of their utmost force, to suppress the same."

After which the Adjutant General issued orders to the army as follows:

"In obedience to an order of the King in council, the military are to act without awaiting the direction of the civil magistrate, and to use force for dispersing the illegal and tumultuous assemblies of the people."

In subsequent debates in Parliament, the conduct of the King was approved. Lord Mansfield and Lord Thurlow claimed that it was not a prerogative of the King to declare martial law, or to use the military to suppress riots; but they defended the act on the ground of necessity.

During the Irish rebellion in 1798, Lord Camden, Lord Lieutenant of Ireland, proclaimed martial law, which existed a year without any legislative action, and after that the Irish Parliament sanctioned the act. In 1801, after the union, this subject was discussed, and a bill was introduced to continue martial law in Ireland. In this debate, both those who approved, and those who opposed the bill, conceded the right of the Executive Government to proclaim martial law when necessary.

Sheridan, opposing the bill, said:

"In case of rebellion or invasion, His Majesty has, by virtue of his prerogative, a right to martial law."

Lord Castlereagh, in defense of the bill, said:

"I perfectly understand that the prerogative of the crown authorizes those acting under its authority to exercise martial law. I maintain that it is a constitutional mode for the Executive Government to exercise martial law in the first instance, and to come to Parliament for indemnity afterward, and is preferable to applying to Parliament first. * * * * *

"The only circumstance in mind is whether, if the necessity exists, this is the proper remedy? If it be so, we ought not to take alarm at a departure from principle, which is necessary for the preservation of the Constitution itself."

Sir L. Parsons, opposing the bill, said:

"He thought the measure unnecessary. The Executive Government could resort to martial law, if it was necessary to suppress rebellion."

Mr. Gray, who also opposed it, said:

"It was better that the Executive Government should resort to what has been called (he thought, not legally) its prerogative of proclaiming martial law. That was no prerogative of the crown, but rather an act of power sanctioned by necessity, martial law being a suspension of the King's peace. But it was better that martial law should proceed from the Executive Government in urgent moments, than to be the work of the Legislature, on every slight pretense."

In the rebellion in Ceylon, in 1848, the Governor proclaimed martial law, and tried and executed many rebels. His conduct was severely criticised in England, upon the ground that it was unnecessary; and in an able review in the *Quarterly*, volume 83, page 127, it is said:

"We shall define martial law to be the law of necessity, or defense. The right which a Governor of a colony has to proclaim martial law over subjects, may be said to bear a close analogy to the right which an individual, in absence of legal protection, has to slay an assailant. In both cases, the evil must be grave. In both cases, all regular means of defense must be exhausted, or beyond reach, before the aggrieved party resorts to extremities. In both cases, the burthen of proof lies on him who has ventured on such an expedient, and, if he fails to vindicate himself, he is liable to severe punishment."

Hallem 1, *Const. Hist., p.* 240, says:

"There may, indeed, be times of pressing danger, when the conservation of all demands a sacrifice of the legal rights of a few; there may be circumstances that not only justify, but compel the temporary abandonment of constitutional forms. It has been usual for all governments, during an actual rebellion, to proclaim martial law, or the suspension of civil jurisdiction.

And this anomaly, I must admit, is very far from being less indispensable at such unhappy seasons, in countries where the ordinary mode of trial is by jury, than where the right of decision rests in the Judge."

Coming now to our own country, the same doctrine is laid down even more explicitly, and by higher sanctions than in England. In the debate in Congress upon the subject of martial law proclaimed by General Jackson in New Orleans, Robert J. Walker, in the Senate, submitted a report upon this subject, in which he said:

"The law which justified this act, was the great law of necessity; it was the law of self-defense. This great law of necessity—of defense of self, of home, and of country—never was designed to be abrogated by any statute, or by any constitution."

Mr. Payne, of Alabama, also speaking upon this subject, said:

"I shall not contend that the Constitution or laws of the United States, authorize the declaration of martial law by any authority whatever; on the contrary, it is unknown to the Constitution or laws."

And, commenting on the argument that if the Constitution did not authorize it, the General ought not to declare martial law, he says:

"Who could tolerate this idea? An Arnold might, but no patriotic American could. I may be asked, upon what principle a commander can declare martial law, when it is so evident that the Constitution or laws afford him no authority to do so? I answer, upon the principle of self-defense, which rises paramount to all written laws; and the justification of the officer who assumes the responsibility of acting on that principle, must rest upon the necessity of the case."

Mr. Livingston, in a written document submitted by General Jackson to the Court, gave his opinion as follows:

"On the nature and effect of the proclamation of martial law by Major General Jackson, my opinion is, that such proclamation is unknown to the Constitution and laws of the United States; that it is to be justified only by the necessities of the case," etc.

During the Dorr revolution in Rhode Island, when an attempt was made to array a military force against the old State Government, and supplant it with a more democratic form, the State Government proclaimed martial law throughout the State. A house was broken open to make an arrest without warrant, under martial law; and subsequently an action of trespass was commenced to try the legality of the act. It was taken to the Supreme Court of the United States, and is reported, *Luther vs. Borden*, 7 *Howard*, 1.

It is to be noticed that this case presented the precise question at issue now before this Court, for the determination of the highest Court in the land. The case was not the suspension of the *habeas corpus*, but it was for trespass, by breaking into houses without warrant, which was clearly illegal, unless the existence of martial law could be recognized as affording a defense.

Chief Justice Taney says:

"Unquestionably, a State may use its military power to put down an armed insurrection too strong to be controlled by the civil authority. The power is essential to the existence of every government, essential to the preservation of order and free institutions, and is as necessary to the States of this Union as to any other Government. The State, itself, must determine what degree of force the crisis demands; and if the Government of Rhode Island deemed the armed opposition so formidable and so ramified throughout the State as to require the use of its military force, and a declaration of martial law, we see no ground upon which this Court can question its authority. It was a state of war, and the established Government resorted to the rights and usages of war to maintain itself, and to overcome the unlawful opposition. And in that state of things, the officers engaged in its military service might lawfully arrest any one who, from the information before them, they had reasonable grounds to believe was engaged in the insurrection, and might order a house to be forcibly entered and searched, when there were reasonable grounds for supposing he might be there concealed. Without power to do this, martial law and the military array of the Government would be mere parade, and rather encourage attack than repel it."

Justice Woodbury dissented upon the ground that a State could not declare martial law, inasmuch as the war power, of which it formed a part, was lodged exclusively in the General Government.

The question, then, for this Commission to determine, is, whether, with this armed force threatening the life of the nation, the leaders here among you, secretly and covertly, as it is claimed—for this is to be a matter of proof—attempting to strike at your camps, destroy the military forces that are guarding them, release the rebel prisoners there confined, then to move into a State, partly occupied by rebels, seize your supplies and munitions of war at Louisville and other points throughout the country—the question, I say, is, whether these men shall be dealt with by the civil or by the military law; whether in this crisis they shall be permitted to avail themselves of the slow process of civil justice, to be released upon bail, again to take the lead of these disloyal forces, and move again in their work of treason and anarchy—or whether the Government shall use the power rightfully belonging to it for its self-preservation? I repeat the language I have quoted, and say, that only an Arnold would, in such a case, hesitate in the course he would recommend. No officer who is faithful to his trust, who respects his Government, who loves his home, and desires the peace and prosperity of the citizens of that home, would desire to wait till it was too late to save the Government, and, with it, all he holds dear. Seeing this necessity for action, the military arm of the Government moved. It seized this man, believed to be one of the leaders—whether he be or not, will be a matter of proof before this Commission—and of the power of this Commission to try him there can be no more doubt, than of the power of the Government to declare martial law. As to the question of the power of the Government to declare martial law throughout a part or the whole of this land, there can be no doubt, that having been decided by the mightiest tribunal of the land—the Court of last resort. It only remains for this Commission to take up the facts of the case, and determine whether or not they are as presented in the charges and specifications.

In conclusion, I submit, that while the rights and liberties of the citizen are in all cases to be held most sacred and inviolate, we are not, in our admiration of that general principle, to lose sight of that higher and still more sacred duty of protecting the life and liberty of the nation; I might say of the lives and liberties of the millions who compose that nation. Let us not, in our attempt to protect the forms of the Constitution, sacrifice its life. What is that Constitution worth to this land if the nation, which is its life, be destroyed? Shall we, in our fear of interfering with the forms of that Constitution, hesitate to stop the wound that is bleeding its life away? There is something beyond the rights of a single individual—something more sacred than his personal liberty, when that liberty can be shown to have been used to imperil the life of the nation—and that is, the life and liberty of the millions of loyal citizens for whom this Government was established, and by whom, with God's help, it will ever be upheld.

The court-room was then cleared for deliberation. On being reopened, the Judge Advocate announced that the plea was overruled, and that the Commission would proceed to the trial of the accused.

The Commission adjourned, to meet on Tuesday, September 27, at 2 o'clock, P. M.

Court Room, Indianapolis, Indiana, }
September 27, 1864, 2 o'clock, P. M.}

The Commission met pursuant to adjournment.

The same members present as on Friday, September 23d; also the Judge Advocate, the accused, and his counsel.

Colonel C. D. Murray being in Court, and having heard read the Order convening the Commission, the accused was asked if he had any objection to Colonel Murray taking his seat on the Commission, to which he replied, "I have not."

Colonel Murray being then duly sworn by the Judge Advocate, in the presence of the accused, took his seat on the Commission.

The accused was then arraigned on the following charges and specifications:

CHARGES AND SPECIFICATIONS

PREFERRED AGAINST

HARRISON H. DODD,

A Citizen of the State of Indiana, United States of America.

CHARGE FIRST.—Conspiracy against the Government of the United States.

SPECIFICATION FIRST.—In this, that the said Harrison H. Dodd did, with William A. Bowles, of Indiana, Joshua F. Bullitt, of Kentucky, Richard Barrett, of the State of Missouri, and others, conspire against the Government and duly constituted authorities of the United States, and did join himself to, and secretly organize and disseminate, a secret society or order, known as the Order of American Knights, or Order of the Sons of Liberty, having a civil and military organization and jurisdiction, for the purpose of overthrowing the Government and duly constituted authorities of the United States. This at or near the city of Indianapolis, Indiana, on or about the 16th day of May, 1864.

SPECIFICATION SECOND.—In this, that the said Harrison H. Dodd, during an existing rebellion against the Government and authorities of the United States, said rebellion claiming to be in the name and on behalf of certain States, being a part of and owing allegiance to the United States, did combine and agree with one William A. Bowles, to adopt and impart to others the creed or ritual of a secret society or order, known as the Order of American Knights, or Order of the Sons of Liberty, denying the authority of the United States to coerce to submission certain citizens of said United States, designing to lessen thereby the power and prevent the increase of the armies of the United States, and thereby did recognize and sustain the right of the citizens

2

and States then in rebellion to disregard and resist the authority of the United States. This at or near the city of Indianapolis, Indiana, on or about the 16th day of May, 1864.

SPECIFICATION THIRD.—In this, that the said Harrison H. Dodd, then a citizen of the State of Indiana, owing true faith and allegiance to the Government of the United States, and while pretending to be a peaceful and loyal citizen of said Government, did secretly and covertly combine, agree, and conspire with one William A. Bowles, of the State of Indiana, Joshua F. Bullitt, of the State of Kentucky, Richard Barrett, of the State of Missouri, and others, to overthrow and render powerless the Government of the United States, and did, in pursuance of said combination, agreement, and conspiracy with said parties, form and organize a society or order, and did assist in extending said secret order or organization, known as the Order of American Knights, or Order of the Sons of Liberty, whose intent and purpose was to cripple and render powerless the efforts of the Government of the United States in suppressing a then existing formidable rebellion against the Government of the United States. This on or about the 16th day of May, 1864, at or near the city of Indianapolis, Indiana.

SPECIFICATION FOURTH.—In this, that the said Harrison H. Dodd did conspire and agree with William A. Bowles, David T. Yeakle, L. P. Milligan, Andrew Humphreys, John C. Walker, and J. F. Bullitt—these men at that time holding military positions and rank in a certain secret society or organization known as the Order of American Knights, or Order of the Sons of Liberty—to seize, by force, the United States and State Arsenals, at Indianapolis, Indiana, and Columbus, Ohio; to release, by force, the rebel prisoners held by the authorities of the United States, at Camp Douglas, Illinois; Camp Morton, Indiana; and Camp Chase, Ohio; and at the Depot of Prisoners of War, on Johnson's Island; and to arm those prisoners with the arms thus seized; that then said conspirators, with all the force they were able to raise from the secret order above named, were, in conjunction with the rebel prisoners thus released and armed, to march into Kentucky, and co-operate with the rebel forces to be sent to that State by the rebel authorities, against the Government and authorities of the United States. This on or about the 20th day of July, 1864, at or near the city of Chicago, Illinois.

CHARGE SECOND.—Affording aid and comfort to rebels against the authority of the United States.

SPECIFICATION FIRST.—In this, that the said Harrison H. Dodd, being then a member of a certain secret society, or order, known as the Order of the American Knights, or Order of the Sons of Liberty, the United States then being in arms to suppress a rebellion in certain States against the authority of the United States, and said Dodd, then and there acting as a member and Grand Commander, so styled, of said secret society or order, did design and plot to communicate with the enemies of the United States, and did communicate with the enemies of the United States, with the intent that they should, in large force, invade the territory of the United States, to-wit, the States of Kentucky, Indiana, and Illinois, with the further intent that the so-called secret society, or order aforesaid, should then and there co-operate with the said armed forces of the said rebellion against the authority of the United States. This at or near Indianapolis, Indiana, on or about the 16th day of May, 1864.

SPECIFICATION SECOND.—In this, that the said Harrison H. Dodd, while the Government of the United States was attempting by force of arms to suppress an existing rebellion, and while guerrillas and other armed supporters of said rebellion, were in the State of Kentucky, did send a messenger—then a brother member with him of a secret society or order, known as the Order of American Knights or Sons of Liberty—into said State of Kentucky, with instructions for J. F. Bullitt, Grand Commander of said secret society or order in said State, and other members of said secret society or order in said State, to select good couriers or runners, to go upon short notice, and for the purpose of assisting those in rebellion against the United States, to call to arms the members of said secret society or order, and other sympathizers with the existing rebellion, whenever a signal should be given by the authorities of the said secret society or order. This at or near Indianapolis, Indiana, on or about the 16th day of May, 1864.

SPECIFICATION THIRD.—In this, that the said Harrison H. Dodd, during an existing rebellion against the authority of the United States, he knowing that in Kentucky there were various armed forces in the interest of said rebellion, and that said State was in constant danger of invasion by further rebel forces, did attempt therein to organize and extend a secret society or order, known as the Order of American Knights, or Order of the Sons of Liberty, having for its object to aid and assist said rebellion, and to treat the United States Government, in its efforts to suppress said rebellion, as a usurpation. This at or near Indianapolis, Indiana, on or about the 16th day of May, 1864.

SPECIFICATION FOURTH.—In this, that the said Harrison H. Dodd, being a citizen of the State of Indiana, United States of America, owing true allegiance to the said United States, did join himself to a certain secret society or order, known as the Order of American Knights, or Order of the Sons of Liberty, the object of which society or order was hostile to, and designed for the overthrow of, the Government of the United States, and to compel terms with the citizens or authorities of the so-called Confederate States, the same being portions of the United States in rebellion against the authority of the United States, and did communicate the designs and intent of said order to those in rebellion against the Government of the United States. This at or near Indianapolis, Indiana, on or about the 16th day of May, 1864.

CHARGE THIRD.—Inciting Insurrection.

SPECIFICATION FIRST.—In this, that the said Harrison H. Dodd did, during a time of war between the United States and armed enemies of the United States, organize, and attempt to arm, a portion of the citizens of the United States, through a secret society or order, known as the American Knights, or Order of the Sons of Liberty, with the intent to induce them, with him, to throw off the authority of the United States, and co-operate with an armed insurrection, then existing against the legally constituted authorities of the United States. This at or near Indianapolis, Indiana, on or about the 16th day of May, 1864.

SPECIFICATION SECOND.—In this, that the said Harrison H. Dodd did, by public addresses, and by secret circulars and communications, and by other means, endeavor to and did arouse sentiments of hostility to the Government of the United States, and did endeavor to induce the people openly to revolt against said Government, and to secretly arm and organize themselves, for the purpose of resisting the laws of the United States and the orders of the duly elected President thereof. This at or near the city of Indianapolis, Indiana, on or about the 16th day of February, 1864.

CHARGE FOURTH.—Disloyal Practices.

SPECIFICATION FIRST.—In this, that the said Harrison H. Dodd, during an armed rebellion against the legally constituted authorities and Government of the United States, did counsel and advise citizens of, and owing allegiance and Military service to, the United States, to disregard the authority of the United States, and to resist a call or draft, designed to increase the armies of the United States. This at or near the city of Indianapolis, Indiana, on or about the 16th day of May, 1864.

SPECIFICATION SECOND.—In this, that the said Harrison H. Dodd did accept and hold the office of Grand Commander, or Commander-in-Chief, of the Military forces, for the State of Indiana, in a certain secret society or order, known as 'the Order of

American Knights, or Order of the Sons of Liberty, which said officer and order were unknown to the Constitution or Laws of the United States, and were not in aid of, but opposed to, the constituted legal authorities thereof. This at or near the city of Indianapolis, Indiana, on or about the 16th day of February, 1864.

SPECIFICATION THIRD.—In this, that the said Harrison II. Dodd did appoint, and aid to appoint, and did recognize, within the State of Indiana, and within the jurisdiction of the United States, and while acting as Grand Commander, or Commander-in-Chief, of certain Military forces, in the State of Indiana, a certain secret society or order, known as the Order of American Knights, or the Order of the Sons of Liberty, certain persons by the title and grade of Major General, the same being unknown to the Military Laws of the United States, or to the Military Laws of the State of Indiana, and did treat and accredit them as such, subordinate to him as Grand Commander, for the purpose of creating and perfecting a military organization within the United States, hostile to, and designed to overthrow, the Government and the legally constituted authorities of the United States. This at or near the city of Indianapolis, Indiana, on or about the 16th day of May, 1864.

SPECIFICATION FOURTH.—In this, that the said Harrison II. Dodd did, while assuming to act as Grand Commander, or Commander-in-Chief, of certain Military forces in the State of Indiana, and within the jurisdiction of the United States, of a certain order, known as the Order of American Knights, or Order of the Sons of Liberty, recognize as the highest Military authority in the United States an officer unknown to the Constitution and Laws of the United States, styled Supreme Commander, or Commander-in-Chief of all Military forces belonging to the order in the various States, for the United States, said officer being recognized by said Dodd as clothed with authority over all the military forces of said order within the United States when called into active service, and holding his, the said Dodd's, obligation of obedience to said Supreme Commander to be absolute and unlimited, and paramount to the laws of the land, or orders emanating from the authorities or President of the United States. This at or near the city of Indianapolis, Indiana, on or about the 17th day of February, 1864.

SPECIFICATION FIFTH.—In this, that the said Harrison II. Dodd did attempt to prevent the further enlistment of citizens in the armies of the United States, declaring the Government thereof to be a usurpation, and to be expelled by force of arms; and did take, and cause other citizens to take, a solemn oath, inconsistent with and in violation of their duties as citizens of the United States, and did attempt to arm certain disloyal citizens of the United States, for the purpose of resisting the laws and duly constituted authorities of the United States, and for the purpose of establishing, or assisting to establish, a separate and independent government within the limits of the United States. This at or near the city of Indianapolis, Indiana, on or about the 17th day of February, 1864.

CHARGE FIFTH.—Violation of the Laws of War.

SPECIFICATION FIRST.—In this, that the said Harrison II. Dodd did, while the United States were carrying on war against the enemies of the United States, and while pretending to be a peaceable, loyal citizen of the United States, violate his allegiance and duty as a citizen of said Government, and did attempt to introduce said armed enemies of the United States into the loyal States of the United States, thereby to overthrow and destroy the authority of the United States. This at or near the city of Indianapolis, Indiana, on or about the 16th day of May, 1864.

SPECIFICATION SECOND.—In this, that the said Harrison II. Dodd did, during a war between the United States and the enemies of the United States, and while pretending to be a peaceable, loyal citizen of the United States, organize and extend a certain secret society or order, known as the Order of American Knights, or Sons of Liberty, having for its purpose the same general object and design of the said enemies of the United States, and with the intent to aid and insure the success of said enemies in their resistance to the legally constituted authorities of the United States, This at or near the city of Indianapolis, Indiana, on or about the 16th day of May, 1864.
H. L. BURNETT,
Judge Advocate Department of the Ohio and Northern Department.

To which Charges and Specifications, to all and severally, the accused pleaded NOT GUILTY.

FELIX G. STIDGER, a witness for the Government, was then introduced into Court, and being duly sworn by the Judge Advocate, testified as follows:*

Question by the Judge Advocate. State your name and place of residence.

Answer. Felix G. Stidger. I resided all the summer in Louisville till the first of September; I am now living in Illinois. I resided four months and a half in Louisville before going to Illinois.

____

* The admirable manner in which Mr. Stidger acted the part of a United States Detective, was shown by the fact, that up to the moment of his appearance as a witness, the accused had no suspicion of his being other than a co-conspirator. At the instant of Stidger's appearance on the witness stand, Dodd stared at him in bewildered surprise, as though he found it difficult to admit the evidence of his own senses.

Q. Where did you live previous to that time?

A. I was in Taylorsville, Kentucky, thirty-one miles south-east of Louisville, for ten months previous to that.

Q. Are you a native of Kentucky?

A. I am, sir.

Q. Please to state to the Commission where, if ever, you had any knowledge of the existence of a secret society, or order, known as the Order of American Knights, or Order of the Sons of Liberty; when your attention was first directed to it, and how.

A. On the 6th day of May I started from Louisville, Kentucky, and went to Dr. Bowles and conversed with him on the subject of the Order of the Sons of Liberty. He gave me the first information on the subject.

Q. State how you came to go to Dr. Bowles' to converse upon that subject.

A. I was sent there by Captain S. E. Jones, Provost Marshal of the District of Kentucky, to converse with Dr. Bowles upon the subject of this secret order.

Q. Did you, in that conversation, learn of the existence of any such order?

A. Yes, sir, I did.

Q. State what was your next step in obtaining information upon the subject.

A My next information was in a second interview I had with Dr. Bowles at his house at French Lick Springs. That was about the 20th of May, I think. For the first interview I started on the 6th, and arrived there on the 9th of May, 1864.

Q. State whether you were ever initiated into any secret order; if so, state when and where?

A. I was regularly initiated in the First Temple Degree of the Order of the Sons of Liberty only, the Vestibule. The first degree was given me in Louisville. The second degree I heard, but did not take. The third degree I was instructed in, in this city, by Mr. Harrison.

Q. When was that?

A. It was about the 5th or 6th day of June, 1864.

Q. Who is this Mr. Harrison?

A. He represented himself as the Secretary of the Grand Council of this State.

Q. State where, if ever, you have come in contact with Harrison H. Dodd, the accused, in connection with this organization.

A. I have. I saw him on the same day that Harrison instructed me in the third degree. That was on the first Sunday in June.

Q. Where did you first meet Mr. Dodd?

A. I first saw him in the office of Mr. Bingham, editor of the Indianapolis *Sentinel*.

Q. Who was present?

A. Mr. Bingham was there—at least I received an introduction to a gentleman as such.

Q. What conversation, if any, took place between you and Mr. Dodd at that time?

A. I presented a letter of introduction from Judge Bullitt, and was recognized by Mr. Dodd as the person referred to in the letter.

Q. What became of that letter?

A. I gave it to Mr. Dodd.

Q. Was that any thing more than a letter of introduction, or did it accredit you as a member of the order?

A. Here is the letter. [The witness here produced the letter.]

Q. Do you know it to be Judge Bullitt's signature?

A. I saw him sign it. I got the letter this morning at General Carrington's head-quarters. How it got there, I do not know.

[The letter referred to was then offered in evidence by the Judge Advocate.]

Q. You may now state what your conversation with Mr. Dodd was, when you delivered that letter.

A. I was sent to Dr. Bowles and Mr. Dodd by Judge Bullitt, in reference to Mr. Coffin, who was living in this city, and who was then employed as a Detective officer by the Government. My instructions were, that Coffin was to be put out of the way at all hazards.

Q. What do you mean by being "put out of the way?"

A. I understood he was to be murdered. I stated my instructions to Mr. Dodd.

Q. From whom did you receive those instructions?

A. They were from Judge Bullitt to Dr. Bowles and Mr. Dodd, and whoever else I might think well to communicate it to.

Q. Who did that message relate to?

A. To Mr. Coffin, United States Detective.

Q. What was said by Mr. Dodd in reference to that message?

A. I do not remember distinctly, except that Coffin and such men were to be disposed of.

Q. What injury had Coffin done to Dodd, or to Bullitt, or Bowles?

A. I do not know of any, except that he was acquainted with their secrets; I mean the secrets of the Order of the Sons of Liberty.

Q. What was done by Dodd in this matter?

A. There was nothing in particular done, but he expressed himself in favor of Coffin being disposed of, and that he agreed with Judge Bullitt.

Q. Do you know if Dodd was a member of the Order of American Knights, or of the Order of the Sons of Liberty?

A. He did not say in so many words that he was. I found it out afterward, from what he said, and from what others said.

Q. State if any thing was done in reference to the contemplated assassination of Mr. Coffin.

A. Not at that time.

Q. How long were you present in your interview with Mr. Dodd?

A. Probably an hour, or more.

Q. Was that the only subject under discussion?

A. Nothing particular do I recall now, except some outside matters.

Q. Was any thing said at that interview respecting the Order?

A. Not a word.

Q. When did you next see Dodd?

A. On the 14th day of June. It was the 5th or 6th of June that I first saw him. It was the first Sunday in June.

Q. How are you able to fix the dates of these interviews with exactness?

A. By knowing the date of the meeting of the Grand Council of the Order of the Sons of Liberty, which was on that day.

Q. Where did they meet?

A. In the fourth story of the building occupied by Mr. Dodd, as printer.

Q. Were you present at that time at that meeting?

A. I was.

Q. State how many persons you met at that time, and mention their names.

A. I can recollect Mr. Dodd, Mr. Harrison, Dr. Bowles, Mr. Milligan, Mr. Humphreys, and Dr. Gatling,* and there were others whose names I do not remember.

Q. What process had one to go through to gain admission to those meetings?

A. It was by a password. The password was the word of the order. On the day referred to, the password was "America."

Q Was that the word by which you gained admission to the meeting?

A. No, sir; I was in the room when the meeting commenced. I was known as a third degree member, and the word was given after I got into the room. It was given to every person in the room by Mr. Dodd.

Q. Did you at the time hold any office?

A. Yes, sir; I was Secretary of the Grand Council for the State of Kentucky. At that time we had no organized Grand Council. I was appointed by the Chief Officer of the State.

Q. Who was that?

A. Judge Bullitt.

Q. Do you still hold that position in Kentucky?

A. I do not know if such an office now exists; but if it does, I may still be considered as holding that position.

Q. Do I understand that you were at that meeting on the 14th or 15th of June, 1864?

A. Yes, sir, I was; and Mr. Dodd was there too.

Q. State, as nearly as you can, what took place at that meeting.

---

* The inventor of the gun, with revolving rifle barrels, mounted on wheels, known as the Gatling gun, and exhibited in many Northern cities during 1861.

A. Mr. Dodd opened the meeting by remarking that they wanted to define the politics of the order; if they had any, he wanted to know what they were. Committees were appointed to consider the military organization of the order. There was also a Committee on Education, and one to examine into a secret discovery of a member of the order; and there were other committees, the objects of which I do not now recollect. Then the case of Coffin was brought up before the Council and discussed at length.

Q. Do you mean before the whole meeting?

A. Yes, sir, before the whole Council.

Q. What was the nature of that discussion?

A. About various things Coffin had done as a detective for the benefit of the United States Government; and it was finally decided that he should be murdered.

Q. Was that the decision of the order?

A. Yes, sir. It was known that there was to be a meeting at Hamilton, Ohio, on the next day, and it was supposed Coffin would be there. Mr. Dodd called on the meeting to know what members would volunteer to go to the meeting with him, to put Coffin out of the way. There was a man by the name of McBride, from Evansville, Ind., who said he knew Mr. Coffin well, but he was sorry he was so situated he could not go. That closed the proceedings of the morning, and is all I remember of it now. We met from 10 to 12 o'clock. In the evening the committee reported; they reported in favor of a military organization of the order, and of organizing and equipping as rapidly as possible. That committee was composed of Dr. Bowles, Mr. Milligan, Dr. Gatling, and other names I do not remember. I distinctly remember that they wished the military organization should be completed as quickly as possible. Some proposed to raise means by taxing the members of the Order; some by subscriptions; and others voted that the members should individually arm themselves. They finally decided that each sub-district should arm as they could. The subject of education was discussed, and a resolution was offered on the subject, recommending the establishment of Democratic schools. I do not remember whether the resolution was overruled or not.

Q. Was any thing further done respecting Coffin, at the morning meeting?

A. His case was put off till the evening. It was discussed both morning and evening. Mr. Dodd volunteered to go to Hamilton, and, if Coffin was there, to dispose of him; and he wanted to know who would go with him, as I have before stated.

Q. What was the final arrangement for disposing of Coffin, at Hamilton?

A. I met Mr. Dodd and Dr. Bowles. They

asked me if I had seen Coffin. I told them that I did not know the man. They said they did not believe he was there; they hunted for him, but could not find him at the meeting, and nothing further was determined upon with respect to the day, or place of rendezvous.

Q. State, if you know, how far the organization of this order partook of the nature of a military organization, and whether they had drills, and officers, and reports, similar to those appertaining to the organization of an army.

A. I can not say any thing more than what I was told. Dr. Bowles told me that he had his command organized, and divided into regiments and companies, and officers appointed, except in one district, and he told me that he was going to organize that district, and that they were drilling at any snatch times they could get.

Q. When was this told to you?

A. Previous to that meeting.

Q. Do you know, of your own knowledge, any thing of the military organization of the order?

A. No, sir.

Q. Did you ever see them drilling?

A. No, sir, and know of none, except what Dr. Bowles and other members of the order told me.

Q. Did Mr. Dodd tell you any thing at any time about drilling?

A. No, sir.

Q. State when next you saw Dr. Bowles or Mr. Dodd, and where—that is, after the meeting on the 14th day of June, 1864.

A. I next saw Dr. Bowles in Louisville, at the Louisville Hotel. I think I never saw Mr. Dodd any-where except here, and once in Hamilton.

Q. What was Bowles doing at Louisville?

A. He was getting up and superintending the Greek fire arrangement. He had a chemist there, and was experimenting and explaining it to the members who were present. This Greek fire, as it was called, was invented by a man named R. C. Bocking.* The members of this order were to use it for the purpose of destroying Government property.

Q. Did you see Bowles there with this man Bocking?

A. Yes, sir, I did; he was experimenting and explaining.

Q. Had you any further talk with Bowles about the military organization of this order at that time?

A. Yes, sir. It was in substance the same as the conversation we had had before, namely, that they were completing their military organization as fast as possible.

Q. Did he say that they were drilling?

A. No, sir.

Q. Did he say any thing about opposing the draft and enlistments?

A. I do not remember that any thing was said about that. They did not seem to care about the draft.

Q. Was any thing said about it at the meeting?

A. No, sir.

Q. What was their avowed purpose then?

A. Their organization was for the general purpose of opposing the Government in every possible way, and by force of arms, and they expected to co-operate with the rebel forces.

Q. Who told you so?

A. Mr. Dodd and Dr. Bowles both told me so.

Q. What further passed between you and Dr. Bowles at Louisville?

A. He was present at the experiments. He introduced us to the company, and this man Bocking went to work to explain the hand grenades, and the machine for setting boats and Government buildings on fire. This machine will set a building on fire at a given time; it is something like a clock. It is wound up, and at a certain time it will set any boat or building on fire, in which it may be left. It is put in a box or trunk, and might be put on board a boat or left in a house without exciting any suspicion. Mr. Bocking also had a muster-roll of rebel prisoners, that were designed to be turned over to the rebel army. He said a part of them who had enlisted in an Indiana Battery had deserted in Tennessee, and had carried over a portion of a battery with them.

Q. Did Bowles inform you that any Government stores had been destroyed by this invention you have described?

A. He did not at that time, but he did before. He said that those two boats that were destroyed at the wharf, at Louisville, were burned by this Greek fire arrangement. He said that there had been fires before, and that they had been caused by this Greek fire, and had been done by this Order of the Sons of Liberty.

Q. Did that close your interview at Louisville?

A. Yes, sir.

Q. State what your next connection with the order was, whom you saw, and what was said.

A. I was in constant communication in Louisville with Dr. Bullitt and some other members of Kentucky, and also when I was up here.

Q. Can you name the next time you saw Mr. Dodd or Dr. Bowles?

A. The next time I saw Dr. Bowles was at his own house, about the last of July.

Q. What was said and done there?

A. At that time I had the whole programme of the uprising of the order, and every thing they were to do respecting the

---

* A resident of Cincinnati; formerly a commission merchant. Subsequently a captain of artillery, United States Volunteers.

seizing of the United States arsenals, the liberation of the rebel prisoners, and the concentrating of the members of the order.

Q. From whom did you get this programme?

A. From Mr. Dodd.

Q. Was it given to you in writing?

A. No, sir, it was given verbally. He pressed upon me the importance of secrecy, and reduced nothing whatever to writing.

Q. Where was he when he gave you this information?

A. At his business place in this city.

Q. Did any one else hear the conversation?

A. There were others in the room, but no one else heard the conversation?

Q. How was it that you came to be in this city?

A. There was to be a meeting in Chicago on the 20th day of July, and Judge Bullitt left Louisville in time to be here. He was expected back in five days from a meeting in Chicago. Dodd had been to New York. I came to Indianapolis on no particular business, but arrived here on the day of Dodd's return. I learned from him that the programme had all been decided on. He told me to get him twenty or thirty good runners. They were to notify our men and have them ready when Judge Bullitt got back. I went down to get on to the train, and pretty soon I saw Bullitt come on board. He looked as though he had been traveling, and he told me that he had just come to town on the Bellefontaine train. We went into the cars, and he told me that the programme was all arranged. We talked only a few minutes, and did not get together again during the ride. We kept apart for prudential reasons. In the evening, when he got to Jeffersonville, Indiana, he hired a buggy, and I was to take him across the river. He did not want to go through the town. He did not wish his acquaintances to know that he was there. He gave me the names of A. O. Brannan and Dr. Bayless, to send them to his house, to whom he would impart this programme, and next morning I was to send to Dr. Kalfus and Mr. W. R. Thomas; and then he said he did not care 'much if he was arrested. These men, he said, could carry on the organization, and in the uprising they could release him. Mr. Thomas was the jailor in Louisville. Immediately on the landing of the boat at the Louisville side, he was arrested, and taken to Colonel Farleigh's headquarters.*

Q. How did that arrest occur?

A. It was caused by an order from this city. The order said Judge Bullitt would be down on the train that day, and that he was to be arrested immediately on his arrival there.

Q. Did he have an interview with the four men named?

A. No, sir: he did not get to see them.

Q. Did these men belong to the order?

A. Dr. Kalfus and Mr. Thomas were members of the order. The other two I did not see.

Q. How do you know they were members of the order?

A. By having met Thomas in the Grand Council, and from Dr. Kalfus giving me the signs and secrets, and from seeing him give them to others.*

Q. State, as nearly as you can, what was the plan that Mr. Dodd and Dr. Bowles informed you had been arranged at the meeting in Chicago, and who were the leaders.

A. I was sent back here on Monday night by Kalfus and Thomas, Bullitt being arrested. I told them of Bullitt's arrest, and mentioned the programme to them that Bullitt had spoken of—that two gentlemen should be sent out there on Saturday, and two on Sunday, that Bullitt might impart to them the programme. Bullitt did not impart it to me, and did not intend to. Kalfus made arrangements with Dr. Helm, who said he was personally acquainted with Mr. Dodd, that he was to come up here if he could, but as he did not come up, they directed me to come here on Monday night. Kalfus and Thomas approved of this order, and sent me here to learn from Dodd the arrangement and plan agreed upon at Chicago. I came here and told Dodd of Bullitt's arrest. He asked me if Bullitt was searched. I said not. He appeared very much excited, and said he hoped they treated him like a gentleman, and not search him; that he had drafts on Montreal for money. He said he told Bullitt, when he left Chicago, that he had better not go to Canada; that it would create suspicion, and that he might have known he would be arrested. Mr. Dodd was so much excited that he gritted his teeth.

Q. Where was it you saw Dodd, when you informed him of Bullitt's arrest?

A. It was in Dodd's office, at his business house in this city, about nine o'clock in the morning. It was Tuesday, and about the last of July. I have a memorandum by which I can fix the date; it is the report I made to General Carrington at the time.

Q. You may produce the memorandum.

A. I have not the report made at that time. I gave it to General Carrington in person. It was on Tuesday; either the last Tuesday in July, or the first Tuesday in August.

Q. State what Dodd told you was the plan agreed on at Chicago.

A. Dodd said they had agreed to seize the camps of rebel prisoners here—Camp

---

* Judge Bullitt, on his arrest, was sent to Fort Lafayette.

* Mr. Stidger, during a portion of the time he was United States Detective, was a "student of medicine" in the office of Dr. Kalfus, Louisville.

Morton; Camp Chase, in Ohio; Camp Douglas, at Chicago, and the Depot of Prisoners, at Johnson's Island. They were going to seize the arsenals here, and at Springfield and Chicago, Illinois. They were going to arm these prisoners with the arms thus seized; raise all the members of the order they could, and arm them, and organize as many men as they could on the 15th or 16th of August; for that was fixed as the day of the uprising. Each commander was to move all his men toward, and concentrate them in, Louisville. They were to get the co-operation of Colonel Syphert and Colonel Jesse, of the rebel army, who were then in Kentucky, and who were to seize Louisville, and hold it until their forces could co-operate. They were to seize Louisville and Jeffersonville and New Albany, and the rebels were to hold them until these forces could come to Louisville to assist in holding these places.

Q. Was there any difference of opinion at Chicago as to the course to be taken?

A. At Chicago there was a difference about whether they were to wait until after they were sure of the co-operation of rebel forces, or go ahead without waiting for the rebels.

Q. How was the matter finally fixed?

A. Dodd sent Harrison to see Milligan, Humphreys, and Walker, and get them here before that day. They did not come. Dodd read me letters from them, which were not signed, but which, he said, were from them. They said they were to go ahead at the time designated to release and arm the prisoners and members of the order, and eventually to unite at Louisville. Harrison was a messenger who went to see these men, and have them come here. I left on Saturday. He did not send to Walker, for he was in New York, and expected to be here that week. He also sent a messenger to Dr. Bowles.

Q. From whom did Dodd read letters to you?

A. He read letters purporting to come from Milligan and Humphreys; but I am not sure whether there was one from Dr. Bowles or not.

Q. Did you see the signatures or handwriting?

A. I saw the handwriting.

Q. Did you recognize it?

A. I did not.

Q. If Dodd told you who were at Chicago, state who they were?

A. I did not learn of any one being there but Judge Bullitt, Dr. Bowles, Dick Barrett [afterward corrected to James A. Barrett], Dodd, and Walker.

Q. How did you learn that they were there?

A. From Dodd. He told me they were there. He arranged this plan. There were other persons there from Illinois and from this State.

Q. What day did they meet at Chicago?

A. The meeting was to have been on the 20th of July, and was called about that time.

Q. Was it first arranged to have a meeting earlier than that?

A. It was first arranged to have a meeting of the Supreme Council of the Order on the first day of July.

Q. Why did that meeting not take place?

A. It was postponed on account of the postponement of the National Democratic Convention.

Q. Did it take place on the 20th of July?

A. Yes, sir.

Q. Did you learn from Dodd what rank these men had in the order?

A. Yes, sir.

Q. What rank did Dodd hold in the order?

A. He was Grand Commander of the State of Indiana.

Q. What rank did Bowles have in the order?

A. Major General of the order, commanding one of the districts of the State.

Q. What rank did David T. Yeakle hold?

A. He had held the same rank as Bowles; but was thrown out on the 14th day of June, and Walker elected in his place.

Q. What rank did Milligan hold?

A. The same as Bowles.

Q. What rank did Walker hold?

A. The same as Bowles.

Q. What was the rank of J. F. Bullitt?

A. Grand Commander of the State of Kentucky.

Q. How do the Grand Commanders rank in the order, compared with Major Generals?

A. Grand Commanders rank over Major Generals.

Q. Who composed the meeting at Chicago?

A. They were Major Generals and Grand Commanders of the order.

Q. What day was set for the uprising to take place?

A. The first time was set in Illinois, which was to be the 3d or 17th of August. Dodd told me at the last meeting, the 15th or 16th was the day set.

Q. Why do you say it was on the 3d or the 17th of August?

A. That was the day given me by Piper, of Springfield. The day was to be as Vallandigham chose. That is what Piper told me.

Q. Who is Piper?

A. He said he had an appointment on Vallandigham's staff.

Q. What is Vallandigham's rank in the Order of the Sons of Liberty?

A. Supreme Commander of the United States.

Q. Did you learn if his orders were to be supreme—above all other orders or laws?

A. I learned from members of the order,

that his orders were to be obeyed above all other orders, and the books of the order taught as much.

Q. Did you meet Piper as a member of the order?

A. I met him in the Grand Council of the State of Kentucky.

Q. Was the time of this uprising to be as Vallandigham should determine?

A. That was the first programme. The day had been set from the 3d to the 17th, and if they were sufficiently ready, he was to decide on which day they should rise.

Q. Where was this uprising to be?

A. It was to be general in Ohio, Indiana, Illinois, Missouri, and as much of Kentucky as could be worked.

Q. Did you know of Dodd, or any members of the order, taking steps to communicate to rebels any thing about the order?

A. I know of members of the order doing so. A rebel colonel was given the secrets of the order, and requested to disseminate them at the South. Judge Bullitt admitted to me that he had tried to have a conference with Colonel Jesse.

Q. Who else did he communicate with?

A. He also sent a man to have a conference with Colonel Syphert, of the rebel army, to ascertain when he could best co-operate with him, or whether he could use his forces in the capture of Louisville.

Q. With what forces did Bullitt propose to co-operate with him?

A. He proposed to co-operate with the forces in this order.

Q. Was any rebel colonel initiated into this order, and given particular instructions?

A. Yes, sir.

Q. When and where?

A. In the city of Louisville, in July; about the last of July.

Q. How did he happen to be in Louisville?

A. He was there on parole. He tried to get the military authorities to banish him to Canada; and he told me that he would then go South, and take up arms again; and if they did not banish him to Canada, he said he would go to Canada any way. From there he would go to Mexico, and take the oath of allegiance to the Mexican Government, which would release him from his oath to the United States Government. He would then come back to the South and take up arms again for the Confederacy. I so reported to Colonel Farleigh, and the papers were not given him. He did go to Canada. I saw a letter afterward from him at Winchester. He sent back for the ritual and the unwritten work of the order, which was to be written in secret cypher and sent to him.

Q. Did he get it?

A. He did not, because the military authorities had seen the letter before the officer to whom it was written got it, or had an opportunity of seeing it.

Q. State whether in any of the meetings of these lodges of which Mr. Dodd was a member, and at which he was present, he there used any language, or performed any acts which denied the authority of the General Government to suppress the rebellion by force of arms. If so, what?

A. He used language which strongly denied that power to the Government. There were no acts performed to my knowledge, except what I have already detailed.

Q. Was there any such language used as that this Government was a usurpation, and ought to be set aside?

A. The word usurpation was used. Also the statement that this Government was a "tyrannical usurpation," was used in the meeting that day.

Q. Was it said that the Government should be resisted because it was a usurpation?

A. Yes, sir.

Q. Was the doctrine inculcated that they were to resist the draft?

A. It was not.

Q. Was it inculcated, as a general doctrine, that they were to oppose coercion on the part of the Government?

A. Yes, sir.

Q. Did they, in this order, say that force might yet be of use, on the principle of overthrowing this Government, and establishing independent republics or governments within the States now belonging to the United States?

A. Their design was to carry a portion of the States now composing the United States into the Southern Confederacy.

Q. Was any thing said about establishing a North-western Confederacy?

A. Not in their lodges. It was discussed by Dr. Bowles himself, privately.

Q. What was the general purpose of the order?

A. Its general purpose was to assist the rebellion.

Q. You may state whether, at the first meeting on the 14th of June, any address was made by Dodd to the order. If so, what it was.

A. He made no remarks except about the purpose of the meeting.

Q. Was there any written address delivered by him?

A. The address, which is printed as that of the Grand Commander, was made in February. I was given copies of it, and was told Dodd was Grand Commander at that time.

The Judge Advocate here handed the witness a pamphlet containing an address by the Grand Commander to the Grand Council of the State of Indiana, and asked: Is that one of the addresses.

A. The address in this pamphlet is Dodd's.

The pamphlet is the proceedings of the Grand Council of the State of Indiana, at a session held the 16th and 17th of February, 1864. The first time I was here, one of them was given me to give to Judge Bullitt, and which I gave to him. It was about the 5th of June.

Q. Who gave it to you?

A. It was given to me by Mr. Harrison. All the books of the order I ever received were given me by Harrison.

A pamphlet, entitled "Proceedings of the Grand Council," etc., was here introduced in evidence by the Judge Advocate.

The Judge Advocate here read extracts from the address referred to, that "Lincoln's Government was a usurpation," etc. He then passed to the witness a number of pamphlets, from which he requested him to select and specify to the Commission the ritual, constitution, by-laws, etc., of the Sons of Liberty, and state how he knew them to be such.

A. These pamphlets contain the obligations of the Vestibule and other obligations of the Order of American Knights, and the ritual of the Order of American Knights, which has now given way to the Order of the Sons of Liberty. This order was exposed, and they made some slight changes in the ritual, and called it the Order of Sons of Liberty. These books contain three parts of the ritual. They contain what is known as the ritual and proper work of the order given in all the lodges.

The pamphlets containing the ritual and obligations of the order "O. A. K.," were here introduced in evidence by the Judge Advocate.

Q. Do you recognize that pamphlet, entitled "S. L.," as the ritual of the first degree?

A. This book contains what is known as the Vestibule, or First Temple degree of the Order of the Sons of Liberty.

The pamphlet, entitled "S. L.," was here introduced in evidence by the Judge Advocate.

Q. Do you recognize the pamphlet entitled "I." "K. O. S. L.," as the ritual of the second degree?

A. That book contains the second and third degrees of the order. They are known as the conclave degrees, or second and third degrees of the order, which are given men initiated into the county temples. Responsible men are given the three degrees contained in these books, and in each voting precinct of a county where there is a county temple, branch temples are organized, in which the Vestibule and first degrees are given, but the members are not given all the degrees of the order. Influential men are given the three degrees.

The pamphlet, entitled "I." "K. O. S. L.," was here introduced by the Judge Advocate in evidence.

Q. What is the specific difference between the three degrees?

A. In the books, there is no particular distinction. The members are as much bound in the first as in the second or third degree. More trust is reposed in the members of the second and third degrees, and they are given more of the secrets and ultimate designs of the order.

Q. Are any but members of the second and third degrees permitted to attend meetings of the Grand Council?

A. If any delegates are elected, who are not members of those degrees, they are given the second and third degrees at the session of the Grand Council—if they are not given in the county temple.

Q. Was the plan for the attack upon the arsenals and the camps of prisoners, imparted to any but third degree members?

A. It might have been imparted to other members whom they had confidence in.

Q. Do you recognize the pamphlet entitled "General Laws of the S. L." as pertaining to the order?

A. This pamphlet is the constitution of the county temple; which governs the workings of the county temples, and is regulated by the State Council.

The pamphlet, entitled "General Laws of the S. L.," was here introduced in evidence, by the Judge Advocate.

Q. Do you recognize the pamphlet, entitled "Constitution of the Grand Council of S. L. of Indiana," as pertaining to the order?

A. That is the Constitution of the State Council of Indiana, made by the State Council. Each State Council of the order makes its own constitution in accordance with its own views, but it must not, in any particular, be in violation of the Constitution of the Supreme Council of all the States.

The pamphlet, entitled "Constitution of the Grand Council of S. L. of Indiana," was here introduced in evidence by the Judge Advocate.

Q. Do you recognize the pamphlet, entitled "Constitution and Laws of the S. G. C.," as pertaining to the order?

A. This pamphlet is the Constitution of the Supreme Council of all the States.

The pamphlet, entitled "Constitution and Laws of the S. G. C.," was here introduced in evidence by the Judge Advocate.

The Judge Advocate here handed the witness a book entitled "Roll of Prisoners," and asked:

Q. Do you recognize that book? *

A. Harrison had a series of these books, which he showed to me and explained the

---

* A small account book, containing a list of the members of the Order of the Sons of Liberty, in Indianapolis; also lists of several companies of rebel prisoners, confined in Camp Morton.

manner of keeping them. He told me all the names in this list, (witness pointing out the list of names, with numbers "1" and "3" opposite in parallel column) were those of members of the order. Those numbered "1" at that time had taken the first degree, and those marked "3" had taken the third degree. He had a number of other books in which he kept the accounts with the county temples—the amount they had paid in for organization fees, for books, for regular monthly dues, and for annual dues. They also gave the names of the officers of all the county temples which had reported to him, the amount due from them, the amounts paid, and what for. I have seen this book before. It was kept by Harrison, and contained the names of the members of the order here.

The book entitled the "Roll of Prisoners," was here introduced in evidence by the Judge Advocate.

Q. Does that book contain the names of officers of the county temples?

A. Harrison had other books which contained the names of officers of the county temples.

The Commission then adjourned, to meet on Wednesday, September 28, at eight o'clock.

———

Court Room, Indianapolis, Indiana,
September 28, 1864, 8 o'clock, A. M.

The Commission met pursuant to adjournment.

All the members present; also the Judge Advocate, the accused, and his counsel.

The proceedings of yesterday were read and approved.

Felix G. Stidger, a witness for the Government, then proceeded with his testimony, as follows:

Question by the Judge Advocate. State to the Commission what interviews you had with Mr. Dodd at his house, or otherwise.

A. I was at Mr. Dodd's house twice, but only saw him there once. It was on a Friday night. Mr. Harrison was there also, and in speaking of the uprising of the Sons of Liberty, said something about their being rather dilatory. It appeared they had not enough arms to be of service. Mr. Dodd remarked, that if they did not rise he would leave the country, for he would be damned if he would live under such a Government as the present Administration.

Q. Was or was not that in the contingency of the order not rising to destroy the present Administration?

A. It was.

Q. About what date was that?

A. That was on the Friday night before Judge Bullitt was arrested on the Saturday. It was probably the last Friday in July, though I will not be sure. Mr. Harrison, Grand Secretary of the State of Indiana, was present at the convention.

Q. Was any plan determined upon at the meeting of the order on the 14th of June, as to the manner of disposing of Mr. Coffin, and how it was to be brought about?

A. Mr. Dodd expected to find him at Hamilton, Ohio, the next day, pick a quarrel with him, if possible, and shoot him.

Q. How do you know that?

A. Dodd so expressed it at that meeting.

The roll of the members of the order for Indianapolis was here handed to the witness.

Q. Please to look at that roll, and designate any of the names you know belonging to the Order of the Sons of Liberty.

A. W. M. Harrison, H. H. Dodd, Joseph Ristine. I conversed with him on the subject of the order, but never met him at any lodge.

Q. Did he display any knowledge that he could not have acquired outside the lodge of the order?

A. He did.

Q. Who is Joseph Ristine?

A. Auditor of the State. I have seen him in his office.

Q. Do you recollect the purport of any conversation you have had with him?

A. I do not recollect any, except something that was said about a letter which was supposed, at the time, to have been written by Dick Bright.

The counsel for the accused objected to the witness relating any conversation of Mr. Ristine, as it had not been shown that he was a member of the order, the witness having said that he never saw him at any lodge of the order.

The Judge Advocate, in reply, said that it had been proved that the book or roll in question was kept by an officer of this secret society; the witness also testified that the names on the roll were members of the order. The evidence, therefore, furnished by the book was more reliable than if Stidger, the witness, had seen Ristine at the lodge.

The Court was then cleared for deliberation. On being re-opened, the Judge Advocate announced to the accused that the objection was overruled.

Answer of the witness continued:

The conversation was in relation to a letter written to Dodd, Bowles and Ristine, and signed "Dick," and supposed to have been written by Dick Bright. The letter was a warning against Coffin as a United States Detective; that he was watching them, and reporting every thing they did. I was kept at Ristine's office nearly all day, for young Ristine to point Coffin out to me, in case he should pass the office.

Q. Did you ever meet in the Grand Council, persons from other parts of the country, besides those here named?

A. I have. There was an old gentleman by the name of Oty, Dr. Lemans, a Judge Borten, from Allen county. He was a large, fleshy man. A Mr. Everett, of Vanderberg county; Mr. Leech, of Burnt District, Union county; Mr. Myers, of Laporte county, and Mr. A. D. Kaga of New Amsterdam. These were some I became acquainted with on the 14th of June.

Q. Did you ever meet in any of their lodges, or as a member of the order, a Mr. Lassalle?

A. I do not think I met him. On the 14th of June, he was elected a member of the Supreme Council of the United States. Mr. Lassalle resides in Cass county.

Q. State who else was elected that day?

A. John G. Davis.

Q. Did you ever meet a Mr. Heffren?

A. Yes, sir, I met him in Salem, Indiana, twice.

Q. Was he a member of the order?

A. Yes, sir, he was. He was recognized as such. I was told by the order that he was Deputy Grand Commander of the State of Indiana. His name was called on that day, but he was not present. He was formerly a Lieutenant Colonel of an Indiana regiment. He told me himself that he and Dodd had a right to call the order together at any time they might think proper.

Q. Did he ever explain, in detail, the nature and object of the organization?

A. He told me that they were to co-operate with the Confederate forces. The first time I saw him, he supposed I was a Commissioner, sent by the Confederate forces. I saw him in Salem, Indiana, on the 6th day of May.

Q. How are you able to fix that date?

A. By its being the first day I left Louisville to join Bowles.

Q. Did you know Heffren before?

A. I never saw him before. There was a man there by the name of John Drom, who pointed him out to me; he is a clothier. He took Heffren out and told him that I was from Kentucky. This man told me that Heffren was one of the leaders of the order. Heffren then came to me, supposing I was a Commissioner sent to him from the rebel force.

Q. Did he approach you as a member of the order, making any signs?

A. No, sir, he did not. When he first approached me, he asked if I came on that business. I told him I did not. I then mentioned to him about some regiments of Forrest's being disbanded in Kentucky. He said he knew it, and that they were to have four more, who were to remain at home for a time and to concentrate when necessary.

Q. For what purpose were they disbanded?

A. He did not tell me for what particular purpose, but, he said, he was expecting a commissioner from three of those regiments, and he thought I was the person.

Q. What was that commissioner to arrange with him?

A. I do not know, sir.

Q. What else was said?

A. I do not remember any thing particular. A gentleman on the street asked him why a certain lady was sent to Salem, Indiana, and he said they expected trouble in Kentucky very soon, and it would be safer in Salem than it would be in Kentucky.

Q. Did Heffren inform you then that this organization was for the purpose of co-operating with the rebels?

A. Yes, sir, he did.

Q. Did you ever meet at Louisville a man by the name of Piper, that you say was on Vallandigham's staff; if so, was he a member of the order?

A. Yes sir. I met him there, and he was a member of this order. He told me he resided in Springfield, Illinois. I do not know his first name.

Q. What was he at Louisville for?

A. He had been traveling in the eastern part of the State, initiating men into the order. He was present at the meeting of the Grand Council in Kentucky, and assisted in opening the meeting.

Q. What rank did he claim to have on Vallandigham's staff?

A. He told me he was on his staff, but he claimed no particular appointment. He told me that James A. Barrett, formerly of St. Louis, now of Chicago, was Chief of Staff to Vallandigham, and that Captain Hines, of the rebel army, who also was on Vallandigham's staff, had charge of the releasing of the rebel prisoners on Johnson's Island.

Q. Was this the man you referred to yesterday?

A. It was, and by mistake I gave his name as Dick Barrett. It was James A. Barrett I referred to in my testimony yesterday. Piper said he had a communication from Vallandigham and Bowles, giving him charge of the releasing of the rebel prisoners at Rock Island, and which was to be effected at the same time.

Q. Where was Hines at that time?

A. He was in Canada, waiting for the time to come. Hines was the same man that was afterward captured with Morgan.

Q. Do you know where this man Piper is now?

A. I do not.

Q. Did you learn of any specific action that the branch of the order in Illinois had resolved upon, in case Kentucky should resist the enlistment of negroes?

A. Piper told me that he had attended a meeting of the Grand Council of Illinois, and that they had passed a resolution, unanimously, that if Kentucky considered it advisable to resist the enlistment of negroes, that the members of the order in Illinois would see that none of the State Militia or Loyal Leaguers, as they were called, should be allowed to be sent by the Government to enforce the measure.

A shell about the size of a 32-pounder, of conical shape, was here handed to the witness. The butt of the shell being screwed off, showed an interior shell, which contained an iron case for the charge of powder.

Q. Have you ever seen this instrument before? If so, state where, and what it is.

A. I saw an instrument of that kind at Bocking's room, at the Louisville Hotel, about the 29th or 30th of June. Bowles was present, also Dr. Kalfus and Charley Miller, and a number of other gentlemen. Bocking explained it. The space between the innermost case and the inner shell was to be filled with liquid Greek fire. The space between the inner and outer shell was to give room for it to move, so as to explode the percussion cap, on its being thrown and striking any object.

Q. What was it to be used for?

A. It was contemplated to be used for the destruction of Government property.

Q. Is this the same thing that was exhibited there at that time?

A. Yes, sir, and it was for the use of these conspirators.

Q. Was any thing said about their using such an instrument?

A. Yes, sir; they said it was just such a thing as they wanted.

A spherical shell was here handed to the witness, which unscrewed in the center and showed a smaller spherical shell inside.

Q. Have you seen this before?

A. Yes, sir; I saw it at Bocking's room; he explained the working of it. The inner shell was to be filled with powder, and a cap placed on each of the nine nipples to be seen on its surface; and round a glass vial, which this inner shell contained, was placed the powder. The glass vial contained the Greek fire. On its being thrown against any object, and striking, it would explode and ignite and set on fire whatever it touched. It was designed to be used by the hand, and it would require very careful handling to prevent its exploding, as the least blow might explode it. Bocking mentioned its weight and probable expense.

Q. Did you learn that this instrument had been used in the destruction of Government property; if so, state when and where.

A. I was told by Dr. Bowles that the Greek fire had been used for the destruction of Government property. Two boats had been destroyed at Louisville, in the spring, and a number of boats, down the river, by the same means, in April or May.

I am not sure that he did not say some boats loaded with Government stores in St. Louis. Bocking explained the manner in which this Greek fire could be used outside of the shells. It might be kept in a thin glass vial, and when you wanted to destroy any object, all you had to do was to throw the glass vial against it, by which the liquid would be scattered about, and it would set on fire every thing it touched. Bocking said it might be made so as to ignite instantly it was scattered, or some time afterward. Bowles said it might be arranged with the clock contrivance, to take fire some hours afterward.

Q. Did you learn of the change of the name of this order from American Knights to the Order of the Sons of Liberty; if so, state what time that change was made in the different States.

A. When I was here, I saw Dodd the first of June; he told me that Judge Bullitt and Dr. Kalfus had gotten some new work of the order. He told me that the order had been changed. The work on the American Knights had been distributed over the State, and he wished me to assist in distributing the new work. I had seen the first degree of the Order of American Knights, but had never read it. I only saw what kind of a looking book it was.

Q. Was this a new order, or merely a continuation of the old one, with changes?

A. It was a continuation of the old order, but the name was changed to the Sons of Liberty. Those of the Order of American Knights were not admitted into the Order of the Sons of Liberty, unless they were considered worthy.

Q. Do you know any thing of Dodd's attempt to extend and increase this order, by disseminating the sentiments of the order?

A. No, sir; I do not know that he did in this State. He urged the extension of it in Kentucky, and organizing it as quickly and as thoroughly as possible.

Q. Do you know of his issuing an address, to be sent to the different members of the order?

A. Yes, sir; I know of the circulation of the address exhibited here yesterday. I know there were some of them given to me to take to Kentucky, and I saw Harrison give some of them to persons, whom he told me were members of the order in this State.

Q. Was it inculcated in this meeting and elsewhere, to the members of this order, that in case this order should be called into the field, its members were to obey their chiefs, and that their orders were to be unquestioned, and their commands supreme?

A. The orders of the chiefs of this organization were to be above all orders, and above all laws of the United States. They were to pay no respect to the orders of the civil authorities, or orders of the General Government, but were instructed that the orders of their chief were supreme.

[Close of the examination in chief.]

CROSS-EXAMINATION.

Became a member of the Order of the Sons of Liberty on the 5th of May, 1864. Was instructed in the Vestibule degree by a United States Detective. Took the first degree, in the city of Louisville, about the 12th of May; did not take the second degree at all, and was instructed in the third degree by Harrison, the Grand Secretary of Indiana, in Indianapolis, about the 1st of June. In taking these degrees, witness participated as a *bona fide* member of the order; but acted in the character of a detective from the beginning. Was employed by Captain Stephen E. Jones, of Louisville, Provost Marshal of the District of Kentucky, at witness' request, but not in that particular service. Was shown a letter, written by General Carrington to Captain Jones, requesting him to send a Kentuckian to Dr. Bowles. Witness was sent in accordance with that request. Did not at the time know of the existence of such an order as the Sons of Liberty. Received the Vestibule degree before going to Dr. Bowles. There were three Temple degrees besides the Vestibule degree.

The meeting at Indianapolis, on the 14th of June, was a meeting of the delegates of county temples and chiefs of the order. Heard the roll of names called; but not being personally acquainted with the members, could not recall them.

Respecting the contemplated assassination of Coffin, the United States Detective, I was sent from Louisville to give Dodd and Bowles the opinion of Judge Bullitt, namely: that it was necessary for the interests of the order that Coffin should be put out of the way. The matter was discussed in Council. Dodd did not discountenance the project; but, on the contrary, considered it necessary. Was taken to the State Auditor's office by Mr. Dodd, who requested Mr. Ristine's son to show him Coffin should he pass. Was there, off and on, in Mr. Ristine's front office nearly all day. About sundown Coffin was pointed out to him. Did not express a wish to meet him and kill him; the words used were, he hoped to meet Coffin hereafter "under more favorable circumstances." This was after the Hamilton meeting, which was on the 15th of June, the day after the meeting of the Council in Indianapolis. Did not, in that meeting, insist on going to Hamilton, in order to kill Coffin: did not speak in the Council that day. Did not know of the Hamilton meeting till it was brought up in the Council. Went with Dodd and Bowles to the meeting at Hamilton. Was appointed Grand Secretary of the order, of the Grand

Lodge of Kentucky, by Judge Bullitt, until an election, and was afterward told that he had been elected at a meeting of the Grand Council. Never met Mr. Coffin at any meeting of the Council, nor in any of the lodges; knew he was a United States Detective, but did not act in concert with him, nor communicate any thing to him. Became acquainted with Coffin about the 1st of June. The pretense of not knowing him was a sham, to cover up ulterior objects.

Met Dr. Gatling at Mr. Bingham's office, when he (Stidger) first saw Dodd. Gatling was at the Grand Council, and was present at the discussion of the assassination of Coffin. Do not know Mr. Humphreys personally. A gentleman they said was Andrew Humphreys, was present at the Council: he was a fleshy gentleman—fine-looking—about forty years old. Saw Mr. Milligan also that day, for the first time. He was a tall, bony, tolerably slender man; and was an active participant in the proceedings of the meeting. He was there morning and evening. A man by the name of Thompson was there; he was appointed on a committee. Mr. McBride, of Evansville, also was present; he was a very active member, and was on the military committee.

Did not know positively that the order was a military organization, never having seen the members drill, or with arms in their hands; but had heard members of the order say that it was a military organization. The Order of the Sons of Liberty extended over Ohio, Kentucky, Indiana, Illinois, Missouri, Wisconsin, New York, Pennsylvania, Delaware and Maryland. From the North-eastern States they expected money, but not men—those States were theoretically organized, as far as the military phase was concerned.

Dodd told him of the meeting at Chicago on the 20th of July, and of the plan of action determined on; did not remember whether Dodd said he was present at the meeting or not; but he was at Chicago at the time. In speaking of the meeting, he used the words, "We came to such and such conclusions."

In conversations with members of the order, he learned that they did not intend Indiana and Illinois to be invaded by the rebels, if they could help it. The war was to be confined to Kentucky and Missouri. Indiana and Ohio were to co-operate with Kentucky, and Illinois with Missouri. The order expected the co-operation of the rebel forces, and were to rise at their advance. The order was to organize and join the rebel forces on the border. The point settled on was Louisville.

Dr. Bowles said he cared nothing about the draft, or the politics of the Government—he said they were engaged in a scheme of rebellion against the Government of the United States. In speaking of the movements of the order, Dodd and Bowles expressed themselves confident of success. Dr. Athon, of this city, counseled caution and delay, till they were more thoroughly organized, and until they could see what could be done at the polls. He was present at the meeting on the 14th of June. He also said they should use their military power at the polls, if the Government attempted to control the elections by bayonets; and that there would be a time when it would be proper to use their military power against the Government, but that time had not yet come. He said it would not be changed after election; that an outbreak would come after the election to resist the Government, both as to its political and military policy. The usurpation of the Government, such as the suspension of the writ of *habeas corpus*, freeing of the negroes, and the general tyrannical acts of the Government, they deemed sufficient to warrant military operations against the Government. Dr. Athon expressed this opinion to witness, in his office, in private conversation; Judge Bullitt and Mike Bright had given the same opinion to him before. Did not know that Mike Bright was a member of the order. Bright thought twenty thousand men could be raised in the State of Indiana to further insurrectionary movements, but that the State would not furnish more. This expressed opinion of Bright was an exception to that of the chiefs of the order, so far as witness had heard them express themselves.

Piper professed to have official orders, from Vallandigham, of a military character. Vallandigham had been represented to witness as the Supreme Grand Commander of the United States; elected on the 22d day of February, in New York. Understood from Piper that Vallandigham had knowledge of this insurrectionary movement, and had given his sanction to it; that he had supreme control of it, and the particular day for the rising was left to his discretion. Witness understood that Vallandigham knew of the action of the meeting at Chicago, and approved of it. Heard Vallandigham speak at Hamilton, on the 15th of June, but had no interview with him.

In addition to the rituals, etc., there was the unwritten work of the order, which could not be gathered from the printed books. The unwritten work of the order was mainly confined to the third degree members. It consisted of signs, colloquies, etc., by which members make themselves known to each other, and gained admittance to lodges where they were not known. There were also instructions as to the designs of the order, imparted to members who were thought worthy of the three degrees, that were not considered suitable to be known to less reliable members of the order. The printed works did not say any thing about the military character of the order, or about co-operation with the South, or resistance to the Government by force of arms; but to a third degree member they gave that instruction and information. To second degree members, who were considered worthy, they imparted the same instructions. First degree members were not considered worthy to receive these instructions. If they got them at all, it would be through the friends who were considered worthy.

Did not know the relative proportion of first, second and third degree members. As a general rule, first degree members were more numerous than second degree members ; while second and third degree members were about equal. In Indianapolis township, the second and third degree members numbered only about sixty odd men; but Mr. Harrison said one thousand or twelve hundred could be got into the order. They thought it advisable to take in only responsible men, who would influence others to join when the proper time came.

As to the available means of the order, in arms and ammunition, Dr. Bowles said he knew a man who would furnish any amount of arms and powder, at any time and place the order might designate. Did not know that the order had any storehouses, arsenals, or depots for arms, or that the members had arms beyond what citizens usually have. Did not know of any funds raised to purchase arms, though that question was discussed at length at the meeting of the Council in this city, on the 14th of June.

At that meeting, a committee of thirteen was appointed, to act for the Council in any emergency, during the recess of that body, and whose acts were to be as legal as though the Grand Council had passed them.

Had not been under arrest. Witness' testimony was not given to save him from prosecution. Resided now at Matoon, Illinois. Was raised in Kentucky, and had lived in different parts of the State for eleven years; principally engaged in carpentering, and in the dry goods business. Had been in the army, in Company E, 15th Kentucky; but was detailed as clerk from the first. Left the army on the 14th of February, honorably discharged for disability. Went into the detective service on the 5th of May. Applied for business generally, and was appointed to this particular duty.

Never saw Bocking before meeting him at his room in the Louisville Hotel, when he explained his infernal machines. Bowles, Kalfus and Miller were there, and others, who were members of the order. Had heard that Bocking had brought the conical shell to the notice of the Government, but did not know that he had offered the spherical hand grenade. Dr. Bowles invited these members to Bocking's room, to see whether these instruments could not be made available in carrying out the schemes of the order against the Government. Bowles said Bocking was a member of the order. The project of assisting the South was discussed that day in his room and in his presence, and Bocking said these shells, with the clock arrangement, and the Greek fire, were the very things that should be used, as I understood, for the destruction of Government property. Bowles further said, that he had tested Bocking well before they initiated him; that he had been sent by the order to Canada, and made to spend his own money in experimenting and testing this thing for the benefit of the order. Bowles also said that he, Bullitt, Dodd, a chemist, and one or two others, had spent one Sunday in a basement in this city, experimenting with the Greek fire, when people thought they were at church.

Had been at Dr. Bowles' house three times. Had seen him once at Paoli, once at Louisville, and once in Indianapolis, at the meeting of the Council of the order.

The Commission then adjourned, to meet on Thursday, September 29, at 2 o'clock, P. M.

———

Court Room, Indianapolis, Indiana,
September 29, 1864, 2 o'clock, P. M.

The Commission met pursuant to adjournment.

In consequence of the absence of a member, the Commission adjourned, to meet on Friday, September 30, at 8 o'clock, A. M.

———

Court Room, Indianapolis, Indiana,
September 30, 1864, 8 o'clock, A. M.

The Commission met pursuant to adjournment.

All the members present; also the Judge Advocate, the accused, and his counsel.

The proceedings were read and approved.

The cross-examination of Felix G. Stidger, a witness for the Government, was then resumed.

The witness, after replying to questions of counsel, relative to his particular occupation, by whom employed, and places of abode, for the past eleven years, testified as follows:

Introduced himself to Dr. Bowles, and registered his name at French Lick Springs, as J. J. Grundy. Dr. Bowles asked him if he knew any thing about the Democratic organization in the State of Kentucky? Told Bowles that he did; that he was a first degree member of it; on which Bowles told him that he was Military Chief of the order, and that a man by the name of Wright, of New York, was the Civil Chief. He also gave witness the plans and designs of the Order of the Sons of Liberty up to that time.

The Order of the Sons of Liberty was a continuation of the Order of American Knights, though all the members of the former were not, in all cases, deemed worthy to become members of the Sons of Liberty. Could not give the exact nature and extent of the change, never having been a member of the Order of American Knights. Had been told by members that the Order of American Knights was changed to the Order of Sons of Liberty, and that an addition had been made to the colloquy of recognition between members of the order. The colloquy, "Resistance to tyrants is obedience to God," was said to have been added by Mr. Vallandigham, after the work had been revised by the committee in New York. Mr. Piper also said the ritual had been somewhat changed in other respects.

In witness' conversation with Dr. Bowles, he gave a programme of the operations of the order. Illinois was pledged to forward fifty thousand men, to concentrate at St. Louis, and to co-operate with Missouri, which was pledged to furnish thirty thousand, and these combined forces were to co-operate with Price, who was to invade Missouri with twenty thousand, and more, if possible, by the assistance of Jeff Davis. These one hundred thousand men were to hold Missouri against any Federal forces that could be brought against them. Indiana was to furnish forty thousand to sixty thousand men, to co-operate with other forces that might come from Ohio, and all were to be thrown on Louisville, to co-operate with whatever force Jeff Davis might send into Eastern Kentucky, under Buckner or Breckinridge, as Davis might deem best. Dr. Bowles gave him this, in the first conversation, as the programme of the war at that time.

On leaving Louisville, on the 26th of May, witness stopped at Salem, Indiana; registered his name at the Forsyth House as J. J. Grundy. Had a conversation with Mr. Heffren. First became acquainted with him on witness' first visit to Dr. Bowles. Heffren was formerly a Lieutenant Colonel of an Indiana regiment. Thought witness was a commissioner from some rebel forces in Kentucky. Heffren was looking for a commissioner, so he said, to tell him about some rebel regiments that had disbanded in Kentucky, after Forrest's raid and massacre at Fort Pillow.

Heffren told witness that he had been to Indianapolis a few days before, and had seen H. H. Dodd; that they had consulted together about the time of calling a meeting of the Grand Council of the State, and that it would be between the 15th and 17th of June. Told witness that he and Dodd were the only two men who had the right of calling the members of the order together, and that it would number between seventy-five and eighty thousand men, and that the organization was about complete.

With this information witness went to Dr. Bowles a second time. He had been away from home, but no one appeared to know where. Bowles said, he had been at Indianapolis, and at a meeting there he had met some of the chiefs of Illinois. Judge Bullitt, of Kentucky; Barrett, of Missouri; and the heads of Indiana were there. Their occupation on Sunday, during the time they were here, was down in the basement of a building, testing their Greek fire. They had a chemist there whom Bowles said he had known for some time, and that now they had nearly brought this Greek fire to perfection. Bowles said that, at the meeting, Barrett pledged Missouri for thirty thousand men, and Illinois pledged fifty thousand to co-operate with Price, and Indiana would furnish forty thousand men. Before, he had said that Indiana would furnish more.

Became acquainted with Judge Bullitt, from Dr. Bowles giving him a message to take. Saw Judge Bullitt about the 31st of May. The message was, that Mr. Humphreys was willing to take a Brigadier Generalship, and to remain in the rear. The arrangement had been talked of in Indianapolis, and Bowles told witness to tell Bullitt that it was satisfactory. Bullitt approved, and went on to say, that he had spent a great deal of money in the affair, and that he was willing to spend every cent he had, but that he hoped soon to be able to steal a good living from the d——d sons of b——s. Witness gave his correct name to Judge Bullitt, while to Bowles he was still J. J. Grundy; they, however, seemed to understand each other in the matter.

A conference respecting the murder of Coffin, was held on the 1st or 2d of June. Judge Bullitt, Mr. Piper, Chambers, of Gallatin county, Tennessee, D. C. Phipps, of Louisville, Dr. Kalfus and witness, were present. Immediately after he was sent to Dr. Bowles, on which occasion he revealed his true name. The reason he gave for his assumed name was, that he had been watched by a United States Detective officer—which was true—and that he changed his name to avoid being followed. The message witness took to Bowles was that Coffin should be murdered, or, as he said, as he had been instrumental in getting him into the order, he ought to assist in getting him out. The message to Bowles about Coffin was verbal; it was not deemed prudent to commit such things to writing. Bowles told witness to tell Dodd, that he should set two men on Coffin's track, and that Dodd was to get him out of the way. Bowles did not say murder him; it was to get him out of the way, or make away with him. Witness then came to Indianapolis

and saw Coffin; was introduced to him by Mr. James Prentice, a United States Detective. Had sent word to Mr. Coffin previously by Prentice, that he was to be murdered.

Saw H. H. Dodd on the 5th of May. Had the conversation about the murder of Coffin. Dr. Gatling was in Dodd's office, but did not know that he heard the conversation about Coffin. Dodd, in reply to the message from Bullitt and Bowles, said, if Coffin had betrayed the secrets of the order, he ought to be disposed of, or made way with. Witness stayed in Indianapolis all day, and went to Governor Morton's in the evening. The Governor understood his business. From there he went to General Carrington's.

Returned to Indianapolis on the 13th of June, at the instance of Dr. Bowles. Dodd also said, he would like witness to be present at the meeting of the Grand Council on the 14th. It was at that meeting that the murder of Coffin was discussed. No vote was taken, but all present seemed unanimous. There was no dissenting voice, of the forty or fifty who were present. Dr. Gatling was present at the meeting. Dodd said he should go to Hamilton, and wanted to know who would go with him. McBride said, he was sorry that circumstances prevented his going. McBride was a heavy set man, rather fleshy, medium hight, probably about forty years of age. Dodd, Bowles and witness went to Hamilton. Milligan was there, but did not know that he went on the same train. After Vallandigham had done speaking, witness went up to bid Dodd and Bowles good-by. They asked him if he had seen any thing of Coffin; witness said he did not know him, when they remembered that he had told them so before.

Was in Indianapolis about a week after. Witness believed that was the time when we watched in Mr. Ristine's office for Coffin. Dodd took him there, and mentioned the circumstance about Coffin before Mr. Ristine. Dodd then took witness to young Ristine, and desired him to point out Coffin in the event of his passing the office.

Q. Had Dodd explained to young Ristine the purpose for which he wanted you to see Coffin?

A. No, sir; he did not.

Q. Then you do not know that young Ristine knew that you wanted to kill Coffin, if you saw him?

A. No, sir; he did not.

Question objected to by the Judge Advocate, on the ground that the counsel for the accused was assuming as a fact what had not been asserted by the witness.

Question and answer withdrawn by counsel for the accused.

Q. Did you not pretend and assume to those men that you yourself would make way with Coffin, if a suitable opportunity occurred?

A. I do not know that I said any thing more than that I hoped to meet him under more favorable circumstances, not referring in any way to what those circumstances might be, friendly or otherwise.

Q. What impression did you intend to make upon their minds, by what you said?

A. I left them to draw their own inference?

Q. What was your avowed purpose in watching for him?

A. To see him, because they wished me to see him, to know him when I saw him.

Q. For what purpose?

A. I do not know, except it was their intention that I should kill him; but I do not know what their intention was.

Q. Was not the drift of your actions and conduct that day to give these men the idea that you wished to kill him?

A. I do not know what construction they put upon my conduct?

Q. Was it not your intention to mislead them into the belief that you wished to kill him?

Question objected to by the Judge Advocate, and withdrawn.

Q. Then young Ristine did not know that your intentions were hostile toward Coffin, did he?

A. No, sir, none of them knew that I had any hostile intentions toward Coffin at that time.

Q. Had you done nothing to lead them to that conclusion?

A. Not that I know of.

Q. Then your intention, in sitting in the Auditor's office, so far as you had any intention, or confided any intention, was lawful and legitimate?

A. It was. Simply to see Coffin and know him.

Q. Then they, so far as you knew, understood that to be your intention?

The question was objected to by the Judge Advocate, and withdrawn.

Q. You knew Coffin perfectly well at that time, did you not?

A. Yes, sir.

Q. It was not, then, a *bona fide* intention to know Coffin that induced you to sit there?

A. No, sir, for I knew him already.

Q. What was your object in going there to see him?

The Judge Advocate objected. I object to the question. The witness need not state what his object was, as that is not competent evidence.

The counsel for the accused replied: I submit to the Court, that, while it is not strictly competent evidence, I desire that the witness state what his object was, and leave its competency to be decided by the Court.

The Judge Advocate replied: With that understanding, I have no objection to the question.

Q. What was your object in going there to see him?

A. That they might have the satisfaction of pointing Coffin out to me.

Q. Is Coffin still alive?

A. He was yesterday.

Did not know why the uprising of the order did not take place on the 15th or 16th of August. He got the programme from Dodd, on the Tuesday following Bullitt's arrest, which was on Saturday. On Thursday of the same week he went to Dr. Bowles, who at first hesitated about telling witness, but when he found that witness already knew of the contemplated uprising, he told him that they had agreed at Chicago to wait for the co-operation of the rebels, but after they came from Chicago, Dodd and others determined not to wait for their co-operation. Witness understood that Bowles had received a message from Dodd, announcing that the military commanders of the order had had a meeting, and a change of the original programme had been decided on. On going to Dr. Bowles, witness met Dodd's son on horseback, coming away. He was a boy of thirteen or fourteen years of age. Had seen the boy in Dodd's office, and heard him call Dodd father. Bowles told him the boy had been there.

Bowles said he would call a meeting of the Grand Commanders and Major Generals in a few days. He would probably have them meet at his house, and he would give me the result of their deliberations afterward. The uprising would take place or not, as the military chiefs determined. Bowles said he might consent to it at the appointed time, with the co-operation of the rebel Colonels Syphert, Jesse and Walker, who were then said to be in Kentucky.

Did not know to what members of the order this insurrectionary scheme had been confided, but Dodd remarked to Harrison and witness, that he suspected the propriety of confiding the scheme to Dan. Voorhees. Harrison, too, thought it best not to communicate it to Voorhees. Dodd replied, "You are the only two persons I communicate all my plans to." The knowledge of the insurrectionary scheme, witness knew, extended to the members of the Grand Council, but he believed the exact time determined on was confined to the Grand Commander and his Major Generals. Voorhees was not wholly confided in by Dodd, but he seemed to be in the confidence of the organization, and they were perfectly free with him about it.

Colonel Anderson, a rebel officer of the 3d Kentucky Cavalry, who was on parole in Louisville, and had given bond about the 1st of July, was initiated as a member of the order by Dr. Kalfus. Kalfus gave him the vestibule and first degree, and witness gave him the second and third degrees, at the instance of Dr. Kalfus. Witness reported the fact to Colonel Farleigh, Commander of the Post at Louisville, and an order of banishment was issued, though it never reached Anderson, who left for Canada. Anderson said that had he received his order of banishment for breaking his parole, he would go to the Southern army again.

Had some conversation with Dr. Bowles about the establishment of a North-western Confederacy. Bowles said that Republican leaders had told him that the Government would acknowledge the independence of the Southern Confederacy, provided they were certain that no attempt would be made to establish a North-western Confederacy.

The two gentlemen who went to see Bullitt, on the Saturday afternoon, were A. O. Brannan, and Dr. Bayliss; and Dr. Kalfus and Mr. Thomas, the jailor, went to see him on Sunday morning.

Had a conversation with Ristine and Dodd, in Ristine's office, about the letter from Dick Bright. They said the letter was addressed to all three of them. Dr. Chambers, of Warsaw, Gallatin county, said he had directed Jesse D. Bright to write that letter, but he supposed Jesse had directed Dick Bright to write it. Mr. Chambers was a member of the order.

Piper said he had a communication from Mr. Vallandigham to Dr. Bowles, which referred to the release of rebel prisoners at Johnson's Island, as part of the insurrectionary programme. Captain Hines, a rebel officer, who was captured, imprisoned, and escaped with Morgan, was to have charge of the duty of releasing the prisoners at Johnson's Island. Piper told witness, while in Dr. Kalfus' office, at Louisville, that Captain Hines was on Vallandigham's staff.

Dodd also told Judge Bullitt that he would get together the men he could, and undertake the release of the prisoners at Camp Morton, Indianapolis; and in the event of his not succeeding, he would make his escape.

The counsel for the accused here objected to the witness' voluntary statements not asked for, and to his giving hearsay testimony. Counsel desired that the last statement of witness might be stricken from the record.

The Judge Advocate, in reply, said, that a statement once upon the record could not be stricken from it. At the final deliberation, the Commission would determine what was evidence, and the reliability or otherwise of the witness' statements.

The counsel for the accused assented to this view, and withdrew his objection.

Witness, of his own knowledge, did not know that the Order of American Knights and the Order of the Sons of Liberty were the same order, but Dr. Kalfus, Harrison, Bowles, Piper, and other members of the order, had so informed him. Harrison had told witness that the Order of the Sons of Liberty had had four different names.

The members of the order were sworn to obey the orders of their Commanders, irrespective of the orders or laws of the Government.

The attention of the witness was here called to the book, already in evidence, containing the list of members of the order in Indianapolis; also the roll of rebel prisoners.

Witness first saw the book in Harrison's office. Harrison showed him the list of members of the order, but not the other names.

The counsel for the accused objected to the introduction of the whole book in evidence.

The Judge Advocate replied, that the book, as a whole, had been introduced in evidence, though the attention of the witness had been called only to the names of the members of the order. It was for the Commission to determine what relation, if any, one list in the book bore to the other. There was nothing to preclude the whole book from being received in evidence by the Commission.

The objection of the counsel was then withdrawn.

RE-EXAMINATION.

Question by the Judge Advocate:

I wish you to state whether any thing has been said to you, on the part of the authorities or by me in their behalf, of any promises, or intention on the part of Government, to reward you for any testimony given by you before this Commission?

A. Not a word.

Q. Did I, or did I not, expressly state, that the only way in which you could come as a witness before this Commission, was, to make a full, free and truthful statement of what had occurred, within your knowledge, in connection with this order?

A. Yes, sir.

Q. Has there ever been any intimation, or hint, of any intention on the part of the Government, to waive any arrest, or process for arrest, as a reward for any thing you might say or do in this trial?

A. No, sir.

Q. Will you state who it was that first revealed to you, or to the order, that Coffin was a detective?

A. Dr. Chambers.

Q. Where did he first announce it?

A. In Dr. Kalfus' office, in the city of Louisville.

Q. Had he known Coffin before?

A. He said he knew him previously.

Q. Who were present when he spoke of Coffin as a detective?

A. Judge Bullitt, Piper, T. C. Wips, Kalfus, and myself.

Q. Was this Captain Hines, you mention as on Vallandigham's staff, appointed before or after his capture?

A. After his escape from prison in Ohio.

Q. Then it was after Hines' capture, imprisonment, and escape, that he accepted a commission on Vallandigham's staff, and was assigned to the releasing of the prisoners at Johnson's Island.

A. Yes, sir.

Q. You stated that this order has had four different names. Did you learn them?

A. I learned only the names, Order of American Knights and Sons of Liberty. Nothing was said to me about the Knights of the Golden Circle.

Q. In your examination, I understood you to say that you had a conversation here with certain parties on the 5th or 6th of May. Did you mean to say May or June?

A. June. I was not here in May, nor until the 5th of June.

Q. I will now ask you, as it has been asked you on the part of the defense, whether there was not an unwritten work of the order, which contains or contemplates a military organization, and also signs, grips, passwords, colloquies, and modes of recognition?

A. There is.

Q. You may now give to the Commission what you mean by the unwritten part of the work of the order.

A. There are, in the unwritten work, certain signs, grips and colloquies, used in the recognition and testing of members, as follows: If you are a member of the Vestibule degree, and you meet a stranger whom you suppose to be a member of the order, you test him in the sign of the degree, thus: You place the heel of your right foot in the hollow of the left, with the right hand under the left arm, bringing the left hand under the right arm, thus folding the arms, and placing the four fingers of the left hand over the right arm. The stranger, or person addressed, if a member of the order, will take the same position. That is as far as you go in public. You then retire to some place, where you will not be observed, and continue to test him. You advance your right foot, and he will advance his right foot to meet yours. The two then take an ordinary grip with the right hands, at the same time placing the left hand on the right breast. If you find him incorrect, you stop. If correct, you proceed with the following colloquy, which is given in alternate syllables by the parties, first the password of the order for that degree, which is the word Calhoun spelled backward, thus: "Nu—oh—lac"—"S.—L." —"Give me liberty—or give me death." Then you give one shake of the hand. [The dashes indicate that the syllables or phrases are alter-nately pronounced by the parties.] In this Vestibule degree there is also a signal of distress. This is given by placing the left hand on the right breast, and raising the right hand and arm to their full hight once, if it is in the day-time. If at night, when that could not be seen, you give the word oak-oun three times, thus: "Oak-oun, oak-oun, 'oak-oun." Oak is the tree of the acorn, which is the symbolical emblem of the order, and "oun" is the last syllable of the password as it is usually pronounced. In the first degree, the same position of the feet and arms is taken, except that in place of four fingers over the right arm, the first two fingers are so placed, and they are separated. This position of the fingers is taught to have reference to the sovereignty of States. The feet being in the same position as in the other degree, they are advanced as before mentioned. In taking the grip, each one runs his first finger upon the wrist of the other, taking the ordinary grip with the other three fingers, running the thumbs as nearly straight as possible. This grip is taught to be as near the shape of the acorn—the universal emblem of the order—as can be made with the hand. The left hand is to be placed on the breast as before. The colloquy is repeated thus: "If you go to the East—I will go to the West. Let there be no strife—between mine and thine—for we—be brethren—O—S—L—Resistance to tyrants—is obedience to God." [All colloquies are pronounced alternately, as indicated by the dashes.] Great care is taken to say "be brethren," the word "be" being a test of membership. The part of this colloquy, given after the initial "O. S. L.," is said to have been added by Mr. Vallandigham, when the work of the order was sent to him for revisal, after the committee at New York had finished their part. This is the first temple degree.

In the second degree, the hands are crossed on the abdomen, the right hand outside to represent the belt of Orion; the thumbs pointing upward, represent the point of the star Arcturus. The feet are placed and advanced as before. The colloquy is given thus: "What—a star—Arc—turus—what of the night—morning cometh—Will ye inquire—inquire ye—Return—come—password of degree—Orion." This colloquy is taken mostly from the 11th and 12th verses of the 21st chapter of Isaiah. The grip of this degree is the ordinary grip; the thumbs of the joined hands pointing upward, representing the point of the star Arcturus.

The sign of the third degree is given thus: the arms are crossed on the breast, with the fingers pointing to the shoulders, the right arm outside. This sign is said to represent the Southern cross, as seen in the heavens south of the equator. The feet are placed and advanced as before. The collo- quy is thus given: "Whence—Seir—How— by the ford. Name it—Jaback. Thy pass- word—Washington—Bayard." Washington is the password of the degree. If as a stranger, and you visit any lodge, you give three knocks at the door. You then send in your name, residence, rank, and the temple where you belong. If you are known, you are admitted. If not, a com- mittee is sent out to examine you. They test you, and if they find you perfect in every particular, they admit you. If you fail in any respect, they know you no more. The grip is given by locking the thumbs crosswise, the palm of the hands being downward, and the hands being held hori- zontal. It is a grip of the thumbs alone.

The sign of the Grand Councillor's de- gree is given by placing the right arm in the same position as in the third degree, the left hand being placed under the right elbow. The feet are in the same position, and advanced as in the other degrees. You then take the ordinary grip with the right hand, and with the left hand you take hold of the right elbow of the person you are testing—he doing the same. You then come to the exact position of folding the arms in the Vestibule degree, with the arms folded; then each turns one-fourth around to the right, facing in opposite directions, when the colloquy is given thus: "Whence— America—North—South." America is the password of the Grand Councillor's degree.

What I have gone through with, is part of the unwritten work of the order. There is a reference in the ritual to a passage of Scripture given in the initiation as part of the charge—Isaiah lix: 14–19. This pas- sage, as well as the "Invocation," are said to have been added to the ritual by Val- landigham. The passage reads:

"And judgment is turned away back- ward, and justice standeth afar off: for truth is fallen in the street, and equity can not enter. Yea, truth faileth; and he that departeth from evil, maketh himself a prey; and the Lord saw it, and it dis- pleased Him that there was no judgment. And He saw that there was no man, and wondered that there was no intercessor; therefore His arm brought salvation unto Him; and His righteousness, it sustained Him. For He put on righteousness as a breast-plate, and a helmet of salvation upon His head; and He put on the garments of vengeance for clothing, and was clad with zeal as a cloak. According to their deeds, accordingly He will repay, fury to His ad- versaries, recompense to His enemies; to the islands, He will repay recompense. So shall they fear the name of the Lord from the west, and His glory from the rising of the sun. When the enemy shall come in like a flood, the Spirit of the Lord shall lift up a standard against him."

Q. Is this part of the instruction given in any book?

A. The passwords, signs and colloquies are not given, but are communicated by members of the order, in instructing ini- tiates. This is the portion of the unwrit- ten work Colonel Anderson applied for, to be sent from Kentucky to him in Canada, in secret cypher.

Q. Did I not understand you to say Judge Bullitt was searched at the time he was arrested?

A. He was not searched in my presence. I understood he was searched afterward. When we were going to the cars he carried a satchel with him, and handled it as though it was very heavy. He carried it with him wherever he went, and remarked it was God damned heavy. Afterward I understood he had gold in it: that he had cashed one of his checks on Montreal, and that the other was found on his person when he was arrested. Dodd said that Bul- litt had two checks on his person, on Mon- treal, and that he hoped those who arrested him had not searched him, but had acted the gentleman with him. He hoped he had had an opportunity to destroy them, after taking the numbers, so that he might du- plicate them.

George E. Pugh, a witness for the Gov- ernment, was then introduced; and, being duly sworn by the Judge Advocate, testi- fied as follows:

Question by the Judge Advocate. Please to state to the Commission your name and place of residence.

A. George Ellis Pugh. I reside in the city of Cincinnati, Ohio.

Q. I will ask you whether you have had any knowledge of the existence of the Order of American Knights or Order of the Sons of Liberty?

A. None, except what I have gathered from the newspapers.

Q. Are you acquainted with the hand- writing of C. L. Vallandigham?

A. Yes, sir.

Q. Please to look at these letters, and state to the Commission whether they are his signatures, and whether they are in his handwriting?

[The Judge Advocate here handed the witness four letters, one dated "Windsor, C. W., October 8, 1863," to "My dear Vor- hees," and signed "C. L. Vall.;" another da- ted "Windsor, C. W., May 12, 1864," to "Dr. Sir," signed "C. L. V.;" another dated "May 31, 1864," to "H. H. Dodd, Esq.," signed "C. L. Vall.;" the fourth dated "Dayton, Ohio, June 28, 1864," with the ini- tials of the order, "O. S. L.," under the date, giving the letter an official character, as connected with the order, addressed to "Dr. Sir," and signed "S. C."]

A. I believe they are all in his handwri- ting.

The Judge Advocate handed the witness a letter, dated "Windsor, C. W., 1st May, 1864," addressed to "H. H. Dodd, Esq.," and signed "Friend," and asked:

Q. Will you state whether that is Mr. Vallandigham's handwriting?

A. It is not.

The letter, dated "May 31, 1864," addressed to "H. H. Dodd, Esq.," and signed "C. L. Vall.," was here introduced in evidence by the Judge Advocate.

CROSS-EXAMINATION.

Question by the accused. Mr. Pugh, you have stated that these letters are in Mr. Vallandigham's handwriting. Will you state how you know his handwriting?

A. I have had an intimate personal acquaintance with him; I have seen him write a great many letters, and have received a great many letters from him.

TESTIMONY OF JOSEPH KIRKPATRICK.

Joseph Kirkpatrick, a witness for the Government, was then introduced, and being duly sworn by the Judge Advocate, testified as follows:

Question by the Judge Advocate. State to the Commission your name, residence and business.

A. My name is Joseph Kirkpatrick. I reside in the city of New York, where I have lived since 1858. I am a merchant, and have dealt in fire-arms for the last three years.

Q. State if any arms were sold by you in New York city, to a party purporting to be Mr. Parsons, of Indianapolis? If so, state what they were, and describe them?

A. I sold two hundred and ninety pistols to a man in New York, who represented himself not as Parsons, but as L. Harris.

Q. Did you make any contract to sell him other arms?

A. I made a contract to sell him about two thousand five hundred revolvers.

A. Any ammunition?

A. Yes, sir; one hundred and thirty-five thousand pistol cartridges.

Q. Have you seen these arms since your arrival in this city? If so, state where?

A. I saw them at the Arsenal, near this city.

Q. How were they boxed?

A. In the same boxes in which they were packed in New York, and they are the same arms.

Q. How were the boxes marked?

A. They were marked "J. J. Parsons, Indianapolis, Ind."

Q. Had you any directions about the marking of these boxes, at the time they were shipped from New York?

A. I had nothing to do with marking the boxes. Harris marked them himself in my presence, "J. J. Parsons Indianapolis, Ind." but did not state any reason for marking them thus.

Q. Did he state that his name was Parsons?

A. He did not.

Q. Was your attention called to the marking of the boxes, by any thing said about charges on the arms?

A. No, sir. He paid for the arms at the time.

Q. Did you learn from the conversation at the time of purchase, where the arms were to be shipped to?

A. He spoke of the shipment of arms to California, and to Mexico, and said that the Government seemed to be very willing to permit arms to be shipped to California, and thence to Mexico, if their attention was not called especially to it.

Q. Did you infer from that, that they were to be shipped to the California market?

A. Yes, sir.

Q. How many revolvers did he ship then?

A. Two hundred and ninety. He paid for them at the time.

Q. How many more did he contract for?

A. About two thousand five hundred revolvers.

Q. How many rounds of ammunition were purchased?

A. Thirty-five thousand rounds to fit the same pistols, which were shipped at the same time.

CROSS-EXAMINATION.

Question by the accused. Do you say that the arms found in the boxes in this city, marked "J. J. Parsons," are the same you sold to Harris?

A. Yes, sir.

Q. Did you know Harris before the purchase?

A. I never saw him before, nor have I seen him since.

Q. What was his personal appearance?

A. He had a full form; was about six feet high; quite a large man; weighed about two hundred pounds, and had heavy black whiskers.

Q. Was there any other person with him?

A. Once, when he called on me, quite a tall young man, whom he introduced as his brother, came with him, and he said if he did not call again himself, this young man would represent him.

Q. When did he pay for the arms?

A. He paid for the first order when they were shipped. He said in a few days he would pay for the others and give shipping directions.

Q. Did any person call on you afterward, about the arms contracted for?

A. No, sir.

The counsel here directed the attention of the witness to the accused, H. H. Dodd, and asked:

Q. Was the accused at your place of business at any time with this party, or alone, in connection with the purchase of arms?

A. I never saw him there at all.

Q. You only inferred then, that these arms were to be shipped to Mexico, on account of the willingness of the Government?

A. That was my inference from what Mr. Harris said.

Q. In what part of the city is your place of business?

A. No. 1 Park Place.

Q. What is the name of your firm?

A. Joseph Kirkpatrick. I have no partner.

RE-EXAMINATION.

Question by the Judge Advocate. In the statement Harris made to you about the willingness of the Government to permit shipments of arms to Mexico, if their attention was not called directly to it, you inferred that these arms were to be so shipped?

A. That was the inference, or the conclusion I arrived at, and I think what he stated involved that inference.

The Commission then adjourned to 2 o'clock, P. M.

AFTERNOON SESSION.

Court Room, Indianapolis, Indiana,
September 30, 1864, 2 o'clock, P. M.

The Commission met pursuant to adjournment.

All the members present; also the Judge Advocate, the accused, and his counsel.

TESTIMONY OF WM. CLAYTON.

Wm. Clayton, a witness for the Government, was then introduced, and being duly sworn by the Judge Advocate, testified as follows:

Question by the Judge Advocate. State your name, residence and occupation.

A. Wm. Clayton. I reside in Roseville township, Warren county, Illinois, where I have lived since the fall of 1841. I am a farmer.

Q. Have you ever been admitted to the lodges of a certain order known as the Order of American Knights, or Order of the Sons of Liberty; and if so, are you a member of such an organization?

A. I suppose I am.

Q. Have you been admitted as a member of this organization?

A. Yes, sir.

Q. Into how many degrees?

A. Three.

Q. Have you now or ever been employed in any way as a detective for the Government?

A. No, sir.

Q. Did you join this order, and continue a member of it, in good faith?

A. I did, sir.

Q. Have you volunteered to give evidence in this matter?

A. The first I knew of it was when an officer came after me to attend this Court.

Q. State when you were first admitted to the Order of American Knights, and where.

A. I think it was about the 1st of July, 1863, I was initiated in the congregation formed in the timber at a place called Pearce's Grove, Warren county, by a man by the name of Griffith, and by a Dr. McCartney. They resided at Monmouth, Illinois.

Q. Can you give to this Commission the obligation you took upon yourself?

A. I could not repeat it by heart.

Q. Can you remember the substance of that obligation?

A. I remember some of it; it was in print.

Q. Have you a copy of the ritual or obligation about you?

A. [After a pause.] Yes, sir.

The witness here produced a pamphlet from his pocket, which he handed to the Judge Advocate.

Q. What does this capital letter V., on the title, mean?

A. I don't like to tell, sir.

Q. But you must tell this Commission, sir?

A. "Vestibule," sir, I suppose.

The pamphlet or ritual referred to, was then introduced in evidence by the Judge Advocate.

Q. Turn to the obligation or oath taken by those initiated into the order.

A. It is on page 7.

The obligation was here read to the Court by the Judge Advocate, and is as follows?

I ——, in the presence of God, and many witnesses, do solemnly declare that I do herein freely, and in the light of a good conscience, renew the solemn vows which I plighted in the V——. I do further promise that I will never reveal nor make known to any man, woman or child, any thing which my eyes may behold, or any word which my ears may hear within this sacred T—— [temple], or in any other T——, nor in any other place where the brotherhood may be assembled. That I will never speak of, nor intimate, any purpose or purposes of this order, whether contemplated or determined, to any one, except to a brother of this order, whom I know to be such. That I will never exhibit any or either of the emblems or insignia of the order, except by express authority granted to that end, and that I will never explain their use or signification to any one not a brother of this order, whom I know to be such, under any pretense whatsoever, neither by persuasion nor by coercion. That I will never reveal nor make known to any man, woman or child, any or either of the signs, hails, passwords, watchwords, initials, nor initial letters, belonging to this order, neither by voice nor by gesture, attitude, or motion of the body, nor any member of the body; nor by intimation through the instrumentality of any thing animate or inanimate, or object in the heavens or on the earth, or above the earth, except to prove a man if he be a brother, or to communicate with a brother whom I shall have first duly proved or know to be such. That I will never pronounce the name of this order, in the hearing of any man, woman or child, except to a brother of this order, whom I know to be such. I do further promise that I will ever have in most holy keeping, each and every secret of this order, which may be confided to me by a brother, either within or without the T——, and rather than reveal which, I will consent to any sacrifice, even unto *death by torture*. I do further promise that I will never recommend for membership of this order, any man who is not a citizen of an American State, except by dispensation to that end, by the competent authority of the order—citizenship always resulting from nativity, or from due process of law in such case provided—neither any person who has not attained the age of twenty-one years, neither a man unsound or infirm in body or in mind—such as a cripple or an idiot; neither any one of African descent, whether slave or free man; neither an avowed and acknowledged atheist; neither a person of bad repute. I do further promise that I will ever cherish toward each, and every member of this order, fraternal regard and fellowship; that I will ever aid a worthy brother, in distress, if in my power to do so; that I will never do wrong, knowingly, to a brother, nor permit him to suffer wrong at the hand of another, if it shall be in my power to warn him of danger, or prevent the wrong. I do further promise that I will, at all times, if need be, take up arms in the cause of the oppressed—*in my country first of all*—against any monarch, prince, potentate, power or government usurped, which may be found in arms and waging war against a people, or peoples, who are endeavoring to establish, or have inaugurated, a government for themselves, of their own free choice, in accordance with, and founded upon, *the eternal principles of Truth !* which I have first sworn in the V——, and now in this presence do swear to maintain inviolate, and defend with my life. *This I* do promise, without reservation or evasion of mind, without regard to the name, station, condition, or designation of the invading or coercing power, whether it shall arise within or come from without! I do further promise that I will always recognize and respond to the hail of a brother, when it shall be made in accordance with the instructions and injunctions of this order, and not otherwise. I do further promise that, with God's help, I will ever demean myself toward my fellow men, and especially toward the brotherhood, as becometh a *true man*. I do further promise that, should I cease to be a member of this order, either of my own volition, or by expulsion, I will hold and preserve inviolate my solemn vows and promises herein declared, as well as while I am in full fellowship. All this I do solemnly promise and swear sacredly to observe, perform, and keep, with a full knowledge and understanding, and with my full assent, that the penalty which will follow a violation of any, or either, of these my solemn vows *will be a sudden and shameful death!* while my name shall be consigned to infamy, while this sublime order shall survive the wrecks of time, and even until the last faithful brother shall have passed from earth to his service in the Temple not made with hands! Divine Essence! and ye men of earth! witness the sincerity of my soul touching these my vows! Help me, God! Amen! Amen! Amen!

Q. Was this the obligation of the members of the Order of American Knights?

A. Yes, sir; of the first degree. I took the second degree some time during the fall or winter, and the third degree in the spring of 1864, I believe.

Q. What was the name of the order into which you were initiated?

A. I took one degree in the Order of American Knights, and also the second degree, and before I took the third degree it was changed to the Order of the Sons of Liberty.

Q. When and by whom was that change made?

A. I was informed by the officers of the order that the change was made in New York, about the 22d of last February.

Q. Did you learn at whose instigation the change was made?

A. The ancient brother of the Grand Temple stated to me, that it was made by Mr. Vallandigham, or in consequence of a suggestion from him.

Q. Were you then initiated into the Order of the Sons of Liberty?

A. Only into the third degree. The other vows in the Order of American Knights were considered binding in the Order of the Sons of Liberty.

Q. Did all these members who belonged to the Order of American Knights, become members of the Order of Sons of Liberty, by virtue of taking the obligations of the former order?

A. Yes, sir. All who had taken the third degree. They moved right along with the same officers, and were controlled by the same orders.

Q. When did you take the third degree and become a member of the Sons of Liberty?

A. It was in the spring; about March.

Q. Have you continued, up to the time of

receiving the summons to attend this Commission, to be a member of good standing?

A. Yes, sir, I am so considered. I have never been expelled.

Q. When and where did you meet?

A. We had a tolerably poor temple; we met in the woods generally; we had meetings once a month.

Q. When did you last meet with them?

A. I guess it was two weeks ago to-morrow.

Q. What meeting was that?

A. It was a meeting of the township temple.

Q. Did you ever meet in the Grand Council?

A. I never did.

Q. Did you ever hold any office in the organization?

A. I was lecturer of the Vestibule.

Q. What was the general principle and aim of the organization?

A. In the first place it was organized—at least it was so reported to us—for the purpose of bringing the Democratic party together, shoulder to shoulder, so that, by such an organization, they might defeat the other party, if possible. It was at first reported to be a political organization. Afterward we were informed by the officers, that it was a military organization.

Q. What service were they going to perform?

A. They mentioned a great many different purposes—one of them was that the authorities who have control of our Government were tyrannical; that we were being trampled under foot; and that we should have to stand in defense of our rights.

Q. Was it in contemplation to resist the Government authorities?

A. No time was set to my knowledge.

Q. Was it talked of?

A. It was reported frequently by the officers, that if they did not work right, when we got regularly organized, that there would be a time set to rise, and maintain our rights.

Q. What was the plan?

A. I can not say that the plan was ever developed to me; but so far as it was developed, and I understood it, it was, that force of arms was to be resorted to, and that we should have to fight for our rights.

Q. Did not these "rights" contemplate the overthrow of the Government by force of arms?

A. I would rather consider it that way.

Q. Did the order have any drilling?

A. Yes, sir.

Q. Did you ever drill?

A. Frequently, sir.

Q. How often?

A. I could not state the number of times.

Q. How many times in a month did they drill?

A. Sometimes once, sometimes twice a month.

Q. How long is it since you commenced to drill?

A. About a year ago, in June. We have been drilling on and off for a year.

Q. Did you get pretty well drilled?

A. Pretty well, sir; but we had no great drill master.

Q. To what extent was this organization that you belonged to armed?

A. I could not tell exactly. Most of the arms we had were pistols.

Q. In your township, to what extent were the members of the organization armed?

A. I guess about two-thirds were armed?

Q. Is that a fair average of the arming of the organization, as far as you know?

A. I think it is, sir.

Q. How many members were there in your township?

A. The muster roll numbered one hundred and odd. Two-thirds of that number were armed with revolvers, shot-guns or rifles.

Q. Do you know how extensive the organization in Illinois was?

A. I could only learn through the officers of the Grand Lodge, in their returns to the Grand Council, and according to their reports it was over one hundred thousand in that State.

Q. Did you learn how many could be relied upon, in a military point of view, in case of insurrection?

A. Mr. McCartney, who was the Grand Seignior, informed me that there were forty thousand in the State well armed, and they could depend upon eighty thousand in the State of Illinois.

Q. Did you learn the strength of the organization in the State of Indiana?

A. I learned from the reports of officers of our temple, that they were about eighty thousand in the State of Indiana, but I did not learn how many were armed here?

Q. Did you learn the strength of the order in Missouri?

A. That there were between thirty and forty thousand. Twenty thousand of them were in St. Louis and the vicinity.

Q. Did you ever hear of any plans, or discussions of any plans, among members of the order, or of the officers, to assist the rebels in case of the invasion of Missouri, or of assisting them by moving into Kentucky?

A. I heard some talk of that kind. We were informed in the vicinity where I live, that sometime between May and June, probably, that there was to be an invasion at three different points. One was to be into Ohio, one into Indiana, and another into Illinois.

Q. By whom?

A. If I mistake not. Forrest was to lead the one in Illinois; Wheeler or Morgan, or some of those men, in Indiana; Longstreet was to make for Ohio while Marmaduke or Price (some said one and some another) was to come into Missouri. It was early in the spring that this news reached us.

Q. Was it in contemplation that the order should rise and assist these men, when they invaded these States?

A. I think the understanding was that in case the rebels came over into Illinois, they and the brethren of this organization were to shake hands and be friends.

Q. Were they to receive aid and assistance from this order?

A. I should consider it that way, sir.

Q. Do you know of any assessments upon this order for money, with which arms were to be purchased for the organization?

A. I do not know of any assessments made by the Grand Council; but I know an assessment was made by the temples. An assessment was to be made by all the county temples, and an assessment was made by our lodge to the amount of $200.

Q. Was it paid?

A. Yes, sir.

Q. Do you know what was done with the money?

A. A man who passed by the name of J. A. Barrett, or Colonel Barrett, of St. Louis, was appointed to receive the money. He stated that he was traveling round through the State to receive money to pay transportation on the arms that were engaged for the order.

Q. What arms were engaged for the order, and where were they to come from?

A. The arms were to come from Nassau to Canada, and the understanding was that they were to be brought to the line in Canada by the authorities of the Confederate States, and we were to pay the cost of transportation on them from Nassau to that point, where we were to receive them. If we got them home, it would be all right, and if we lost them, we were to lose what we had advanced.

Q. Do you know any thing of an arrangement, in which Mr. Vallandigham was to give the signal for the rising of this order?

A. I heard in this way, that all the orders would be issued from the Head Department, of which he was Supreme Commander, and that orders would be issued when all things were ready; in other words, we were not to do any thing till the command was given by Vallandigham, who was Supreme Commander. The next highest in command was a man by the name of Holloway. In case the command was not given by Vallandigham, the word would be given by Holloway. He lives in Mercer county, Illinois, and I have often talked with him.

Q. Did you ever talk to him respecting the order?

A. I talked in regard to the movements of the order with Mr. Griffith. The substance of it was that I had my doubts in regard to the order being able to stand up and maintain what they were undertaking. He did not seem to have any doubt about being able to gain their point—that is, as to whether they would be successful or not.

Q. Was this order both civil and military?

A. Yes, sir.

Q. Had you captains, colonels and generals in your organization?

A. Only captains and colonels that I knew of. There was an act passed, that there should be a colonel to each county, and a brigadier general for each Congressional district. That act was passed by the Grand Council of the State: the, made the laws for the order.

Q. What did you understand we.e to be the penalties for divulging the secrets of the order?

A. The obligation there says *death*, and that was understood to be the penalty.

Q. Did you ever know any person who divulged, or who was reported to have divulged the secrets of the order?

A. I do not know of any myself, but there were some who were said to have divulged them.

Q. What was done in the matter?

A. They probably decided that it was a compulsory move, and they did not attempt to do any thing. I heard that there were a number who had joined the order arrested at Richmond, Indiana, on their way to Ohio, and that the Provost Marshal, or some Government officer, got the secrets out of two of them, but it was claimed that force of arms had been used and weapons drawn upon them, and they concluded that they had to tell.

Q. Were any inquiries made into the matter, or any court convened?

A. I do not know that they convened a court, or that any inquiries were made by the order to find out the particulars, but it was understood that if a man was guilty of exposing the secrets of the order, he would be tried by court-martial, and if found guilty he would pay the penalty.

Q. Do you know of any court-martial being held?

A. No, sir. But if they foun' a man guilty of betraying the secrets of the order, if the court decided that he should suffer death, they were to be governed by that entirely.

Q. Do you know of this order having any connection or communication with the rebel authorities?

A. I saw a man from their country, and I heard from members of the order, as well as outside the order, that he belonged to the rebel government.

Q. What did they come there for?

A. I could not positively state their business. But there were many who came over backward and forward from Missouri, whom I saw, living as I did near the Missouri line, and many that came over, I guess, had been in the rebel army.

Q. Was there any communication between these men and the members of the order?

A. Yes, sir.

Q. Did the members or officers of your organization learn of the contemplated rebel movements from these people who crossed from Missouri?

A. Yes, sir.

Q. And did events turn out as your order had been informed?

A. I believe they did. They were informed that Price would invade Missouri.

Q. Prior to his coming, were the members of the order informed of his coming?

A. I was informed by members from Henderson county that he was coming. A person, who professed to be one of Quantrell's men, I think, informed them that Price would be in Missouri toward the first of October, and remain there till after the fall election, or as much longer as he deemed proper, or as he could.

Q. Was any effort made on the part of these emissaries to organize and assist the rebels when they should come into the State, as you have detailed?

A. I think not, sir.

Q. Was it not part of their general plan to assist the rebels, whenever they invaded these States?

A. Yes, sir, and if it has been given up I do not know it.

Q. Then why did they not assist Price when he came into Missouri?

A. I can not tell; but the order is not doing much business in that State of late, from the exposures made in this State.

Q. Had the exposures in St. Louis any thing to do in stopping the operations of the order in Missouri and Illinois?

A. I think, sir, it had a great deal.

Q. Are they still keeping up their organizations, notwithstanding these exposures?

A. The military organization remains the same, but they have not drilled any since.

Q. How do these men that come from the South cross the river to get into Illinois?

A. I have been informed by men who had lived in that State, that they had crossed at different points. One point was near Louisiana, Missouri.

Q. How do they cross?

A. They told me that when they wanted to cross, and they could not hook a skiff, that they had oil-cloth so fixed, that by cutting willows and running poles into them, they could soon fix up a skiff. When they crossed, they would hide the oil-cloth till they wanted to return.

Q. Did you ever belong to the Order of the Knights of the Golden Circle?

A. Yes, sir, I did.

Q. When did you join that order?

A. I joined that before this Order of the Sons of Liberty. It was in 1862, I guess.

Q. Where did you join that order?

A. In Jefferson county. I was down there on a visit, and I heard a great deal of talk about it, and a gentleman proposed to give me the organization to bring up home and start it, but I did not.

Q. Was the Order of the Sons of Liberty, or Order of the American Knights, a continuation of the Order of the Knights of the Golden Circle?

A. I never understood that it was so. The Order of American Knights was introduced in our county in June, 1863. It was at the time of the mass meeting of the Democratic convention at Springfield, Illinois, that it was inaugurated at that place. The Grand Council was inaugurated there, and the Grand Council appointed two officers to each county to promulgate the order, and to set up temples. P. C. Wright, who now, I believe, has an interest in the New York *News*, inaugurated the order.

A lithographed circular was here produced by the witness.

Q. Where did you get this circular?

A. It was first showed to me by Dr. McCartney, in our temple, some time last winter.

The circular, signed P. C. Wright, was here introduced into evidence by the Judge Advocate. It reads as follows:

NEW YORK DAILY NEWS,
Office, 19 City Hall Square,
NEW YORK, January 18, 1864.

Dear Sir: I have this day connected myself with the editorial department of the "New York *News*." You will remember that the *News* has, from the first, advocated the principles inculcated by Jefferson and his illustrious compeers, and has fearlessly and openly denounced the usurpations of power which have wrested from the citizen his cherished rights, and thrown down the last barrier between him and irresponsible despotism.

The *News* will be *our especial organ*, and will be a medium for the interchange of sentiments and opinions of the friends of peace, touching the momentous concerns involved in the existing crisis.

I entreat your kind offices and influence in extending the circulation of the *News* throughout the entire field of our labor.

Yours sincerely,   P. C. WRIGHT.

Q. Who was McCartney?

A. He was the Grand Seignior in the county temple.

Q. Do you know P. C. Wright, and what part he took in organizing the Order of American Knights?

A. He organized the first Grand Council

at Springfield, and he appointed Grand Seignior and Ancient Brethren to organize the counties. It was the same P. C. Wright, so Dr. McCartney represented, who is now connected with the New York *News*.

Q. Can you give to this Commission the unwritten part of the order up to the third degree?

A. I suppose I could, but I do not like to undertake it.

Q. What is the password between the members?

A. Each county has its own passwords. The password of our county was Washington.

Q. How was it given, by syllables or otherwise?

A. It was spoken right out.

Q. How did you recognize each other on the street?

A. We would generally challenge him, that is by placing myself in a proper position.

Q. Give to this Commission the position by which you challenged a member.

The witness here gave some of the challenges and tests described at length by the witness Stidger.

The Commission then adjourned, to meet on Monday, October 3, at 2 o'clock, P. M.

COURT ROOM, INDIANAPOLIS, INDIANA,
October 3, 1864, 2 o'clock, P. M.

The Commission met pursuant to adjournment.

In consequence of the absence of a member, the Commission adjourned, to meet on Tuesday, October 4, at 10 o'clock, A. M.

COURT ROOM, INDIANAPOLIS, INDIANA,
October 4, 1864, 10 o'clock, A. M.

The Commission met pursuant to adjournment.

Present—Brevet Brigadier General Silas Colgrove, Colonel McLean, Colonel Thomas J. Lucas, Colonel John T. Wilder, Colonel Charles D. Murray, Colonel Richard P. De Hart, Major H. L. Burnett, Judge Advocate; also the accused and his counsel.

Absent—Colonel Benjamin Spooner, Colonel Ambrose A. Stevens.

The Judge Advocate then read a medical certificate, excusing Colonel A. A. Stevens from attendance on the Commission. Also, a telegram from Colonel Spooner, stating his inability to be present at the Commission; both of which were ordered to be attached to the record.

By consent of the accused, given in open Court, it was agreed that the record of proceedings should be read, and any nominal business transacted, and that the absent members should take their seats on the Commission when they arrived.

The proceedings of Friday, September 30, were read.

Pending the reading of the record, the Commission adjourned, to meet at 2½ o'clock, P. M.

AFTERNOON SESSION

COURT ROOM, INDIANAPOLIS, INDIANA
October 4, 1864, 2½ o'clock, P. M.

The Commission met pursuant to adjournment.

The same members present as at the morning session; also the Judge Advocate, the accused, and his counsel.

The proceedings were read and approved.

The Commission then adjourned, to meet on Wednesday, October 5, at 10 o'clock, A. M.

COURT ROOM, INDIANAPOLIS, INDIANA,
October 5, 1864, 10 o'clock, A. M.

The Commission met pursuant to adjournment.

All the members present; also the Judge Advocate, the accused, and his counsel.

The proceedings were read and approved.

William Clayton, a witness for the Government, continued his testimony as follows:

Question by the Judge Advocate. State whether or not the league to which you belonged, sent delegates to the Chicago Convention, or to the Chicago Grand Council, that met in that city in July last.

A. The temple to which I belonged was subordinate to the county temple. I belonged to the organization in Roseville township. The Warren county temple sent delegates to the Grand Council for the State of Illinois.

Q. Did you learn any thing of the doings or designs of the Grand Council, or the return of the delegates?

A. Not a great deal. I was at the Warren county temple at Monmouth, and Mr. Griffith and McCarthy, who were officers of that temple, had been to the Chicago Grand Council. They spoke of the Military Committee. The Grand Commander of the State, they said, had the selecting and appointing of the Military Committee in the State. That committee was not known to any person whatever, except to the Grand Commander.

Q. Did you learn what that was?

A. No, sir; I did not. The committee reported to the Grand Commander all their proceedings, and such a part as he thought proper he reported to the Grand Council.

Q. Did you, after the Chicago Convention, hear any thing about the obligation of secrecy being removed?

A. No, sir, I did not; I never heard any thing of it till I saw it in the newspapers.*

Q. Was that the first time you, as a member of the order, heard of the obligation of secrecy being removed?

A. It was.

---

* The Indianapolis *Sentinel* had stated, a few days previous, that the obligation of secrecy was removed during the session of the Grand Council, at Chicago

Was initiated a member of the Order of American Knights on the 17th day of June, 1863. The first knowledge witness had of the order, was at the time of the meeting of the Grand Council, at Springfield, Illinois. It was organized at the mass convention, at which he was present. Mr. Griffith and Mr. McCartney were appointed to organize the county temple. The township temple was organized shortly after. It was organized in the timber, about two and a half miles from his residence; about thirty, or more, were present at the first meeting. There was no drilling at the first meeting, but was not positive but that there was some drilling before the organization of the order; such drilling as there might have been, was not under the laws of the State of Illinois. The only object in drilling, witness knew of, was that the knowledge acquired was to be used for any thing that might come up. They had been informed that the Government was resorting to tyrannical measures, and there might probably come a time when they would have to stand in defense of their rights. They were afraid the Government might crowd them, and there had been talk of conscription, and they were arming, organizing, and drilling, to resist the conscription, or any thing else that pushed them too hard. The company to which witness belonged, numbered one hundred and upward. They generally carried their arms to drill. One of their drill masters was William F. George. He lived in Roseville township, Warren county. There were also one or two men, officers, who were present at one or two drills. One was a captain, and the other a colonel. The colonel was said to live in Knox county, near Augusta. They had been in the army, but were discharged. Supposed they were loyal. Four or five companies were present at the drill, which took place in an open prairie bottom. They did not become very well drilled. Witness was a private, and Mr. Johnson or Mr. Riggs was first lieutenant.

Did not know, of his own knowledge, that the purpose of the organization of the order in other States was resistance to the Government. Was informed by officers of the Warren county temple, that Missouri, Illinois, Indiana and Ohio were so organized; and at first it was reported, that several of the Eastern States had gone into the organization with the same object, and could be relied on, but that afterward it was found that only the four States named had gone thoroughly into the organization, and that those only could be relied upon.

There was a meeting of the Supreme Council of the United States, in New York, on the 22d of February, and it was after this meeting that the Grand Seignior of the Warren county temple said he was afraid that the States east of Ohio could not be depended upon, in case of an outbreak against the Government.

Question by the accused:

Was it the purpose of those who crossed over from the South, as you have stated, that you should help the rebels in case of an outbreak?

A. I considered it that way.

Q. From whom did you learn this?

A. From a member of the Order of the American Knights or Sons of Liberty.

Q. Did you ever talk with any man from the South in regard to helping the Southern rebellion?

A. I do not wish to answer that question. I will answer or not, as the Judge Advocate decides.

The Judge Advocate informed the witness that he must answer every question put by the counsel for the accused, if the answer did not criminate himself.

A. I have been asked by men, who said their homes were in the South or in Missouri, if we had any intention to assist them in case they came over into Illinois.

Q. Well, and what did you tell them?

A. That I presumed a great many would, and some would not assist them.

Q. What did you say you would do?

A. I did not tell them whether I would help them or not.

Q. Now, I wish to ask you what you would have done if the rebels had come into Illinois?

Question objected to by the Judge Advocate, and withdrawn.

Q. What did your society or temple resolve to do, in case of an invasion from Missouri by the rebels?

A. I do not think that our temple ever passed any resolution that they would assist the South; we only talked of it at our meetings.

Q. What did you consider you had sworn to when you took this obligation?

The counsel then read the following from the obligation of the first degree of the Order of American Knights:

"I do further promise, that I will, at all times, if need be, take up arms in the cause of the oppressed—in my country first of all—against any monarch, prince, potentate, power, or government usurped, which may be found in arms, and waging war against a people or peoples who are endeavoring to establish, or have inaugurated a government for themselves of their own free choice, in accordance with and founded upon the eternal principles of truth, which I have sworn in the V——, and now in this presence do swear, to maintain inviolate, and defend with my life."

Q. What did you consider you had sworn to maintain inviolate?

A. I considered that obligation bound us to assist the South, as they were trying to free themselves and form a government of their own free choice.

Q. Do you still hold that this obligation is binding on you?

A. I have taken it on myself, and I consider that it is.

Q. You are sworn to help the South, then, are you?

A. That is the way I read the obligation.

Q. Were the army, then, that you were organizing, and the men under the control of the order, all bound by this obligation?

A. I do not know, of my own knowledge, that they were.

Q. Had all these men who were drilling taken the Vestibule degree obligation?

A. I do not think they had, sir. Some of those who were drilling, were not members of the order.

Q. Did they know of the general purpose of the organization drilling, and that it was in pursuance of this obligation?

A. I think they did not.

Q. How did you come to permit these men to drill with you?

A. We took every man who was disposed to fall in and drill with us, and said nothing about our ulterior purposes.

Q. Did you not consider that portion of the obligation which speaks of "the oppressed," to refer to the negroes enslaved?

A. I did not put that construction on it.

Q. What did you consider the phrase, "the oppressed—in my country first of all"—to imply?

A. I understood it that the people of the South were oppressed, and were trying to establish a government of their own choice.

Q. What was meant by the phrase "power and Government usurped, which may be found in arms?"

A. I will tell you how I understood it. It referred to the Government and the army of the United States.

Q. It was against them, then, that you were organized to wage a war?

A. We were to wage war upon them, of course, if they took up arms against the South.

Q. Did you think that the government referred to, was the government of the whole South?

A. That was the opinion where I lived.

Q. Do you swear that that it was the intention of the order generally?

A. I don't know as it was, and I have never traveled over other States to learn how they considered it, nor conversed with members elsewhere about it.

Q. Did you not state the other day, in your examination-in-chief, that you were to meet the Southern army if they invaded the North, and shake hands with them?

A. It was the understanding, where I lived, that in case of an invasion, we were to shake hands with them and be friends.

Q. Was that the understanding as to the relations of the order to them?

A. It was, as far as my knowledge extends, in our section.

Q. You were willing, then, to shake hands with the invaders of the North, and be friends with them?

A. This was the sentiment in the section where I lived.

Q. Did this sentiment extend beyond the order?

A. I think some outside of the order felt the same way.

Q. You did not think it wrong, then, to welcome them as friends?

A. I never understood any thing about the right or wrong of the case. Of the two evils we were to choose the least.

Q. What two evils did you consider it the least of?

A. The independence of the South or submission to the oppression of the Administration. In our section we considered the success of the South the least evil.

Q. Were you in favor of it against the Government of the United States?

A. Yes, sir.

Q. Do you still maintain that feeling in your lodges there?

A. Yes, sir. At the meeting I attended three weeks ago, we were pledged to that faith.

Q. How did you come to leave home and come here?

A. I was brought here by the Provost Marshal. A subpœna was served on me, instructing me to come here.

Q. Were you arrested, and then subpœnaed?

A. No, sir. I was brought here, and was ignorant as to what I was subpœnaed for.

Q. Did the Government promise you that you would be protected against prosecution, if you testified against the order?

A. I have received no assurances of that kind, except what I had here to-day in court from the Judge Advocate.

Q. Did you testify without fear or favor?

A. I had fears, but not of this court.

Q. What were you in fear of?

A. I have had fears that I would be arrested when I got home, on the strength of the testimony I have given here; and also have had fears about the dealings with me of the organization to which I belong.

Q. Did you not tell General Carrington that you would be ruined at home on account of your testimony?

A. I may have told him so.

Q. Why did you expect it would ruin you?

A. I supposed it would so far as the order extends; for its members are all under the same obligation that I have taken.

Q. Why do you make this exposure of

the order, after taking that obligation to keep it a secret?

A. I have testified before this Court voluntarily, because the law makes it my duty to tell the truth; and as an honest and truthful man, I mean to tell the truth, and nothing else.

Q. You preferred telling the truth, then, and exposing the order, rather than keeping your obligation not to reveal the secrets of the order?

A. I considered this a lawful tribunal, and have spoken the whole truth.

Q. Do you not consider the order a lawful organization?

A. No, sir, I do not.

Q. Then you regard the laws of the land and of this Government as preferable to assisting the Confederacy?

A. I regard my obligations to the laws of the land first of all, to speak the truth, and I wish, so far as in me lies, to respect and obey the laws.

Q. Have you had any inducement held out to you to expose this order?

A. No, sir.

Q. What made you do it?

A. Because I was brought before this Court, and I could not refuse to tell the truth without being false to the oath I took here.

Q. Could you not back up on your rights?

A. Had I been a lawyer, I might have done so.

Q. Did you not do so this morning?

A. I said that I would not answer unless I was so directed by the Judge Advocate.

Q. Do you not know that if you had been asked any question that would lead you to criminate yourself, that you could not be compelled to answer it?

A. I have never been before a military court before; I am no lawyer, only a farmer, and a poor one at that; and I don't know the custom of military courts.

Question by the Judge Advocate:

When I saw you in my room, did I, or did I not, inform you that you were to speak the exact truth, and that without any fear, favor or affection?

A. You did, sir.

Q. And without any hope of fee or reward, or offer of any, in any way whatever; and that all the truth must be spoken without any swerving or prevarication?

A. You did, sir. I felt considerably embarrassed, and when I saw you at your office, you spoke to me as you did here.

Q. Was there any thing said except as to the desire of the Government to get at the clear, unvarnished truth?

A. That was all, sir.

Q. And what brought you here to-day?

A. The subpœna from this Commission was served upon me, and I had to come and testify as I have done.

Wesley Tranter, a witness for the Government, being duly sworn, in answer to interrogatories by the Judge Advocate, testified as follows:

My home is at Shoal's Station, Martin county, Indiana, and am a miller by trade. I have not lived at Shoal's Station since I informed on this Butternut organization in March last.

In the spring of 1863, I joined a secret society, called the Circle of Honor; that was directly after I was discharged from the army for disability. I was a private in the 17th Indiana Volunteers, and was with Sherman's army. I joined the order at the solicitation of a man by the name of Stephen Horsey. There were about forty or fifty in the organization at the time I joined. John W. Stone was the head man, as far as speaking was concerned. He came round to make speeches to the order, and Stephen Horsey assisted him. Horsey resides at the Shoals still, but Stone, who had some difficulty with the boys of the 17th Indiana, in which he had his fore-finger shot off, went away, with his wife, to Kentucky.

Mr. Horsey, who induced me to join the order, said if I would join, he would show me the elephant, and if I did not like it after I was in, he would get me out. He gave the name of the order as the Circle of Honor. He said they wanted to find out how strong the Democratic party was. As I had been a Democrat all my life, I joined the order.

About two months after joining, they gave us the Morgan signs, which they said would, in the event of our being taken prisoners, and making ourselves known, secure us better treatment.

[The witness, at the request of the Judge Advocate, gave the signs, positions, etc., which were similar to those described by the witness Stidger, as belonging to the Vestibule degree of the Order of American Knights.]

We had a little book, or ritual, which a little fellow, whose name I do not remember, and who said he went backward and forward to Richmond, brought there. It was said that the book had been got up by Jeff Davis for the use of the lodges.

About January, 1864, Horsey came to me and said they were going to have a very important meeting. A man by the name of T. Baker also asked me to go. I attended the meeting. They taught us more of the signs of recognition used by the members, and swore us into Jeff Davis' service; and we were to support him, North or South, at all hazards. That was no part of the oath we took, but if we revealed the secrets of the order, we were to suffer our hearts to be torn out, and our bodies to be cut into pieces, and the four quarters to be scattered north, south, east and west.

It was said by members that Dr. Bowles and H. H. Dodd were connected with this organization. Bowles was said to be in New York, and would meet Stone here at Indianapolis about the 26th of March. It was said in the order that H. H. Dodd was to be Governor of the State, in Morton's place; that Governor Morton was to be put out of the way, and Dodd was to be set up in his place. Stone said we were to have arms, and were to resist the draft. Lincoln, he said, had been scared once into putting off the draft, but now they would show him something that would scare him more than that. Lincoln was afraid, he said, of the arming going on here in the North. This was said at a meeting of the Temple of Honor, held about a mile east of the Shoals, at a house belonging to a man by the name of Gaddis, on a Saturday night, toward the latter part of the month of January. They said we must have our old rifles and shotguns fixed up as best we could, and that they would have revolvers shipped to them. Two boxes of revolvers came there, and a man by the name of Coffin, a blacksmith, helped to carry them. The boxes were passed off as jewelry. I was told this by Horsey.

The arms were to be used to assist the rebels, and against the blue coats, as they called the United States soldiers, and they said: " We will show them how to fight." They expressed their intention to resist the United States Government, and to support the South. Stone said, in his speech, that about five days from the first of April, they were to take this place (Indianapolis); the members of the order in Illinois were to take Springfield; while those of Missouri were to take St. Louis. Bragg was to do all he could in Tennessee; Morgan was to advance his force into Kentucky; Forrest was to cross the Ohio to Illinois, and we were to aid. The Indianians were to seize this place and the arsenal, and distribute the arms to those members of the order who had none. The arsenal, it was said, would be seized when there were but few soldiers here.

At that meeting, Stone said Governor Morton was to be put out of the way; that he had but a short time to live after the visit here to the arsenal. Stone read a letter at the meeting, signed M. D., in which this was said about Governor Morton.

At the same meeting, something was said about organizing and drilling. I never drilled with them, but an old man, by the name of Woody, asked me to drill them, as I had been in the army, and was supposed to know something about it; but I would not.

Among the signs of recognition they had in January, 1864, besides that I have mentioned, was the sign O. A. K., spelling the word *oak*. The letters composing the word were to be pronounced alternately by the parties meeting. There was also the sign of distress. In case of the arrest of a member of the Order, he was to halloo *oak-oun* three times, when any member of the order who heard would come to his assistance at all hazards.

I first revealed the designs of the order to Captain Henley, in March of this year, when I wrote out a statement of the matter, giving the signs, signals, etc., substantially as I have given them here. I have not seen, read, or heard any thing in connection with this matter testified to by the witness Felix G. Stidger. I have not attended a meeting of the order since January, 1864, nor have I conversed with a member of the order since that time. The reason why I did not continue to attend was, that the avowed principles of the order did not suit me. I had a brother in the United States army, and I told my father that I should report on them, and they might do just what they liked with me.

Stone said that communication was kept up between the order and the rebels, and that the only way to save the Government was to elect Jeff Davis the next President. That Jeff Davis had three times offered to compromise, and that Lincoln's Government would not do it, and that now something would have to be done to make them yield.

I did not join the order as a detective, nor have I ever acted as such. I joined it in good faith, supposing it to be a legitimate organization. I have received no fee or offer of reward for my testimony, and no promise of any kind has been made to me to induce me to testify.

The Commission then adjourned, to meet on Thursday, October 6, at 10 o'clock, A. M.

Court Room, Indianapolis, Indiana, }
October 6, 1864, 10 o'clock, A. M. }

The Commission met pursuant to adjournment.

All the members present; also the Judge Advocate, the accused, and his counsel.

The proceedings were read and approved.

Wesley Tranter, a witness for the Government, resumed his testimony as follows:

John Stone said, at the meeting in January I have referred to, that, of the Western States, Indiana, Illinois and Missouri would join the Southern Confederacy, and that they would lick out "Old Abe" and his blue coats.

CROSS-EXAMINATION.

I first made up my mind to expose the order the next day after I was sworn into the Knights of the Golden Circle. When I told my father what my intentions were, he was a little scared, and told me to tell my uncle at Washington, Davis county, which I did, and he advised me to come here and report. I came here to Indianapolis about the 10th of March, and Captain Henley wrote out my statement.

The cause of John W. Stone's leaving was: a Lieutenant of the 17th Indiana, with some of the boys, were going to arrest him, to find out if he knew who killed some of our soldiers. When Stone saw them coming, he tried to make his escape, when they fired, and his fore-finger was said to have been shot off.

The name of the order I joined, was the Circle of Honor; I met with them some four or five times, when it was reorganized as the Knights of the Golden Circle. The obligation taken in the Knights of the Golden Circle was to support Jeff Davis, either North or South.

The soldiers who went to take Stone, also went after Horsey, but I think I saved him, and Dr. Bowles too. Dr. Bowles was to be our general to lead us South to support Jeff Davis. Bowles sent for some of us boys to go down to French Lick Springs, where he lived. I was not alarmed at receiving the Morgan signs, and the prospect of serving under Bowles. I knew we had the right sort of man to lead us, and that he would run if there was danger, as he did in Mexico, and that we would be safe.

RE-EXAMINATION.

We had a hailing sign in the order, or sign of distress; it was the word "oak-oun" pronounced three times.

The statement which Captain Henley wrote out from my dictation at the Bates House in this city, was sent to General Carrington.

TESTIMONY OF ELLIOT ROBERTSON.

Elliot Robertson, a witness for the Government, being duly sworn, in answer to interrogatories by the Judge Advocate, testified as follows:

I am a farmer, and live in Randolph county, Indiana. I joined the Order of the Knights of the Golden Circle in Green Fork township, Indiana, about the 1st of June, 1863, or a little later. I joined at the solicitation of a man by the name of John D. Burkebyle, who was the chief of the order at that place. A person named Nathan Brown, who was understood in the order to have been sent from the leaders here in Indianapolis, organized the order in our township. I do not recollect the obligation I took, except the penalty for disclosing the secrets of the order, which was death; the body being cut into four quarters, one part to be cast out at each gate, north, south, east and west. They had grips and signs, etc., by which members of the order could recognize and test each other. First we

4

stood in a military position, with the heel of the right foot in the hollow of the left, arms folded, with the two first fingers of the left hand apart. This position was answered, when it was recognized, by passing the right hand across the face, as though stroking the mustache. Another sign was a grip, in which each party held the forefinger so that it should reach as far as it could up the wrist.

The order was understood to be organized for military purposes, and about one-half of the members were armed. The intention of the order was to oppose the Administration in its attempts to put down the rebellion.

The name of the order was changed to American Knights about September, 1863. I was invited to join the new order, but did not. I was instructed in it by the captain of the Knights of the Golden Circle. Nearly all who belonged to the Knights of the Golden Circle became members of the new order.

I passed into a lodge of the American Knights in Gratis township, Preble county, Ohio, about two months ago. A friend of mine took me, but nothing particular was done. I have not attended any regular meeting of the order since September, 1863.

One purpose of the organization was to oppose the draft and arbitrary arrests, and by force of arms, if need be; but the understanding was, that our operations were to be confined to Indiana.

Burkebyle and Brown said that it was only in part determined what should be done in case of the draft. It was said at a meeting of the order, that should a draft be made, they would know in time whether we were to resist or not.

The captain said he had orders from Indianapolis to arm the members of the order. The question was discussed as to how we should get arms. Some were in favor of buying their own arms, but the captain said there were plenty of arms here in Indianapolis, and we were not to be uneasy about that. I do not know of any arms being distributed, except from hearsay.

I joined the order more out of curiosity than any thing else. I never acted in any capacity as a United States Detective. My testimony before this Commission is voluntary, and no offer or promise of reward, in any way, has been made to me to induce me to testify in this case.

CROSS-EXAMINATION.

I volunteered as a soldier in the 16th Indiana, on the 22d of August last, and made a statement to General Carrington respecting the order soon after I volunteered. Have not joined my regiment yet, or been on particular duty. I should have made a statement of the objects of the organization to the authorities before, if I could have received protection for so doing. I made a statement to 'Squire Hough, I think in October, which was sworn to by me. I met with the order after making this statement to 'Squire Hough, but only to learn their intentions more fully. I was formerly a Republican, but had become a Democrat before joining the order. When I made the statement to 'Squire Hough, I was a Union man, and did not want to favor the order.

I only know of one attempt to resist what was called arbitrary arrests. Burkebyle thought he was going to be arrested, and I and some of the members of the order met at his house to resist it. Burkebyle said to me, that it had become known that he was a member of the Order of the Knights of the Golden Circle. We met at his house two nights. I was armed with a gun. Burkebyle's two boys, Henry Woodin, Henry Robinson, and another man, were there.

J. D. Burkebyle was our captain, Abram Platt was treasurer, and Francis Burridge was secretary; Amos Crew was lieutenant, and Henry Woodin sergeant. There were between sixty and seventy-five members in the order at Green Fork township.

The Commission then adjourned, to meet on Friday, October 7, at half-past 8, A. M.

Court Room, Indianapolis, Indiana,
October 7, 1864, 8½ A. M.

The Commission met pursuant to adjournment.

All the members present, except Colonel Benjamin Spooner. Also present the Judge Advocate, and the counsel for the accused.

It was then announced by the Judge Advocate that the accused, Harrison H. Dodd, had escaped, and could not be present; he therefore asked for an adjournment of the Commission till 11 o'clock A. M., at which time he proposed to submit the case to the Commission, that they might proceed to the finding and sentence.

The counsel for the accused, Jonathan W. Gordon, Esq., and Martin M. Ray, Esq., then submitted to the Commission an affidavit touching the escape of the accused:

United States of America
vs.
Harrison H. Dodd. } Before Military Com.

Be it remembered, that on this 7th day of October, 1864, personally came before me H. L. Burnett, Judge Advocate Department of the Ohio and Northern Department, Jonathan W. Gordon and Martin M. Ray, the counsel for Harrison H. Dodd, in trial before a Military Commission, in the city of Indianapolis, and being by me duly sworn according to law, depose and say jointly and severally, each for himself, that they have this morning heard with surprise of the escape of their client, H. H. Dodd, from his prison, in this city.

They further declare, as an act due from them to this Commission, that never by word, act or intimation, did they, or either of them, counsel, prompt, suggest or intimate to said Dodd, or to any friend or acquaintance of said Dodd, or any one else, his escape from prison; nor was any thing upon the subject ever intimated among themselves; nor had they, at any time, from any source, any notice or suspicion that said Dodd contemplated any such escape; and they thus declare their entire innocence, in thought, word or deed of his escape. And they ask this statement to go upon the record in this cause.   M. M. RAY,
                                            J. W. GORDON.

Sworn to before me, and subscribed in my presence, this 7th day of October, 1864.
                        H. L. BURNETT,
Judge Advocate Department of the Ohio and Northern Department.

The Commission then adjourned, to meet at 11 o'clock, A. M.

AFTERNOON SESSION.

Court Room, Indianapolis, Indiana,
October 7, 1864, 11 o'clock, A. M.

The Commission met pursuant to adjournment.

The same members present as at the morning session. Also, the Judge Advocate, and the counsel for the accused.

The Judge Advocate then addressed the Commission as follows:

The accused, Harrison H. Dodd, having made his escape, as I announced at the first session to-day, I had thought of asking the Commission to proceed on the evidence already before them to their finding and sentence; and though it may be the course I

The following extract from the report of Colonel A. J. Warner, Commander of the Post, Indianapolis, to Captain A. C. Kempor, A. A. G., gives all the particulars known of the escape of H. H. Dodd, on the morning of the 7th of October:

Mr. Harrison H. Dodd, who was on trial in this city before the Military Commission, on a charge of treason and conspiracy, made his escape from the room occupied by him, in the third story of the Post Office Building, a few minutes before 4 o'clock this morning. He escaped through the window, opening on Pennsylvania street, by means of a rope attached to an iron rod, which was held fast between his bed and the iron window shutter. A ball of twine had been conveyed to him by some of his friends who had been permitted to visit him, by means of which he had drawn up to his window a large rope, furnished by some persons outside, who assisted in his escape.

There was no guard on the outside of the building, and the attempt was not detected, until the prisoner had reached the ground and escaped. The street lamps near by had been previously darkened to conceal the movement.

When Mr. Dodd petitioned Brevet Major General Hovey, Commander of the District, to be allowed to occupy a room in the Post Office Building, instead of being closely confined in the Military Prison, he gave his parole of honor, that he would make no attempt to escape. His brother also pledged his word, and stated he would risk all he was worth that H. H. Dodd would not try to escape, if this privilege was granted.

Measures, therefore, that would have been taken to prevent escape, by placing guards on the outside as well as within the building, were not, under the circumstances, resorted to in this case.

shall finally ask the Commission to pursue, I think it best at present to recommend that the Commission adjourn till such time as they think best. In the mean time, I will prepare the papers against some other prisoners, with whose trial we may proceed, allowing the present case to remain for the time in its present condition.

The law, so far as I have been able to examine the decisions in the United States Reports, and the reports of the States of New York, Indiana, Alabama, Arkansas, and one of the Ohio Reports, all go to this extent: That where a prisoner, by his own default, is not present to receive the verdict of the jury and the sentence of the Court, waives, by his own act. the constitutional right which he had, that he could not again be put in jeopardy of life or limb; but having, by his own act, deprived himself of that privilege, he may again be put upon trial for the same offense. Or, as the law expresses it, there was from the beginning no jeopardy, or it can not be said there was a real jeopardy, because he may, from the beginning, have had an intent to escape before the sentence of the law could act upon him. The civil decisions say, further, that while he has deprived himself of that privilege, yet, as a general rule, the Court can not proceed to sentence, or the jury to give a verdict, because he may have the privilege of "polling the jury." It is one of the rights of the accused to make a claim or plea to the Court, and his presence is necessary to the rendition of the verdict and the passing of sentence. Later decisions, however, by the Supreme Court of this State, and also the Supreme Court of Ohio, go to the extent that if a person, of his own default, is not present to receive the verdict of the jury and the sentence of the Court, yet the Court may receive the verdict of the jury and give sentence. I apprehend, therefore, that this reasoning would hold with greater force before a court-martial or military commission, for the reason, that in a court-martial or military commission, the accused is never present when the Court proceed to their finding and sentence. The moment I say to the Commission, "The evidence on behalf of the Government is closed," the accused may introduce evidence to rebut that which has been introduced on the part of the prosecution, or he may waive that privilege, and present his defense in the shape of an address, called "the Address of the Accused," and given under oath, or otherwise, and which may be received by the Court in extenuation or mitigation of his sentence. But if, for any reason, the accused abandons his cause, and fails to rebut the evidence produced on the part of the Government, he waives his right of address; in other words, he says, "I have no defense." The Court then proceeds to close the doors to deliberate on the finding and sentence.

I do not see why such a course could not be pursued in strict accordance with reason and justice, and the due observance of military law.

I make these suggestions at this time, that the gentlemen engaged as counsel for the accused may be made aware of what may be claimed in the premises on the part of the Government.

I now ask the Commission to adjourn to such time as they may deem best.

The Commission, after deliberation, adjourned to meet on Thursday, October 13, 1864, at 2 o'clock, P. M.

COURT ROOM, INDIANAPOLIS, INDIANA,
October 13, 1864, 2 o'clock, P. M.

The Commission met pursuant to adjournment.

In consequence of the absence of a member, the Commission adjourned to meet on Saturday, October 15, 1864, at 9 o'clock, A. M.

COURT ROOM, INDIANAPOLIS, INDIANA,
October 15, 1864, 9 o'clock, A. M.

The Commission met pursuant to adjournment.

All the members present; also the Judge Advocate, and the counsel for the accused.

Absent, the accused, Harrison H. Dodd.

The proceedings were read and approved.

The Judge Advocate then addressed the Commission as follows:

As I intimated at the last session of the Commission preceding our late informal meeting, I propose now to submit the case of the accused, Harrison H. Dodd, on the evidence already introduced, and to ask the Commission to proceed to their finding in the case, and, in the event of finding against the accused, to sentence.

For authorities in support of such a course, I propose simply to cite certain late decisions in similar cases, by the Supreme Court of Ohio, and also by the Supreme Court of this State.

The first case is from the *Ohio Reports*, vol. VII, page 180. *Charles Fight* vs. *The State*. The plaintiff was arraigned at the August term of the Brown Common Pleas Court, plead not guilty, and, on his motion and giving security, the prosecution was continued to the November term. He was placed on trial before the jury on the fourth day of the succeeding term, and the testimony being partly heard, the Court adjourned until the next morning, at which time the Court met, and the plaintiff being called, made default. The Court then issued a bench-warrant for the plaintiff, and proceeded to charge the jury. On the next day the jury rendered a verdict of guilty, which was received by the Court in the absence of the plaintiff. At the succeeding March term, the plaintiff asked for a new trial, assigning, among other reasons, that the jury had heard only a part of the testimony, and that the verdict was brought in during his absence. This was overruled, when the plaintiff moved an arrest of judgment for substantially the same reasons. The case was argued before the Supreme Court, and the opinion delivered by Judge Wood was concurred in by all the Court.

The synopsis gives the point of the case in these words:

"Where, pending a trial upon a criminal prosecution, the accused, being on bail, absconds, it is legal to proceed with the case, and to receive a verdict of guilty in his absence."

The opinion of the Court is as follows:

"In England, in misdemeanors, where the defendant is on bail, a trial, a conviction and sentence may be had in his absence. He is present or not, at his option. In felonies, a different rule, it is true, prevails. The accused must be present when every principle of the law is discussed and determined in which he is concerned. The reason of this difference in the mode of proceeding in the two cases can not, perhaps, at this time, be satisfactorily ascertained; or, rather, no satisfactory reason can be given for it. A prisoner in close custody may be so easily oppressed and deprived of his rights, and it would be so extremely difficult for him to make known his injuries and obtain redress, that to prevent unnecessary restraint, and to afford the accused an opportunity of being fully and fairly heard, the rule in reference to *him* may be reasonable and salutary; but it would apply with force to all classes of offenders. But in felony, the accused is not necessarily confined within the four walls of the prison. Both before and after the conquest, all felonies were bailable by the common ancient law. The *Stat. Weston*, 1 and 3 *Ed.*, 1 c., 15; 23 *Hen.*, 9, c. 9; and 1 and 2 *Ph. and Mar.*, c. 13, except treason and murder, and certain other crimes from those for which the King's justices may bail. (*Bl. Com.*, 4 vol., 208.) But the Court of King's Bench, or any judge thereof, in vacation, may, at their discretion, admit persons to bail, *in all cases whatsoever.* (3 *East.*, 163, 5 *J. R.*, 169), but none can claim this benefit *de jure* (2 *Hale*, 129). If on bail, 1 apprehend, neither the courts of Great Britain nor the United States would proceed to impannel a jury, in a trial for felony, unless the accused were present to look to his challenges. If the trial, however, is once commenced, and the prisoner, in his own wrong, *leaves the Court, abandons his case to the management of counsel, and runs away,* I can find no adjudged case to sustain the position, that in England the proceedings would be stayed. Such a case must form an exception to the general rule, and the verdict may be legally received *in the absence of the accused.* The prisoner can not be deprived of his right to be present, at all stages of his trial; but that he *must* be, under all circumstances, or the proceedings will be erroneous, can not, we think, be sustained."

The next case I shall cite is from vol. 14, *Indiana Reports,* page 39. It is an opinion delivered by Judge Perkins, of this State, in the case of *McCorkle* vs. *The State.* I shall read only that portion of the opinion applicable to this point:

"The constitution and laws provide that a defendant in a criminal case shall be present at his trial. This is for a twofold object:

"1. That the defendant may have the opportunity of meeting the witnesses and jury face to face, and of directing the causes of his trial.

"2. That the State may be in possession of his person, so that judgment may be executed thereon.

"Now, the question is, are not these provisions, so far as they are in favor of the defendant, designed to confer a privilege which he may waive? He can waive a trial altogether, and plead guilty. He can waive the constitutional and legal privilege of trial by jury. He can waive the constitutional and legal privilege of being a second time put in jeopardy. And shall it be said that he can not waive his privilege of being present when his witnesses are examined, or any one of them? Then did he, as a question of fact, make such waiver in this case? If he had voluntarily arisen in Court, and asked to be absent in the custody of an officer, or otherwise, for a period of time, requesting that the trial should proceed in his absence, the waiver would be clear. But how does such a step differ, in substance, from a voluntary departure without asking that the trial shall stop? In one case the consent is vocally, in the other, tacitly, but equally clearly, expressed."

This was a case in which the prisoner absented himself during a portion of his trial. The next case in point is reported in the *Sixteenth Indiana Reports,* page 357. *The State* vs. *Wamire.* The opinion was delivered by Judge Perkins, and is the last case in point, on record, that I know of.

"3. The court is not bound to discharge the jury because of the voluntary absence of the defendant during the trial, he having been present at the commencement, [*McCorkle* vs. *The State, Fourteenth Indiana,* 39; *Fight* vs. *The State, Seventh Ohio (Ham.) Reports,* Part 1, page 181], but may proceed on to verdict, at all events, in his absence."

In all the cases I have cited, the authorities go further than I ask the Commission to proceed. I do not propose to introduce testimony in the absence of the accused, but simply to submit the case to the Commission upon the evidence already introduced, and upon this evidence I ask the Commission to proceed to its finding and sentence. The reason for such a course is stronger in a court of this kind, than it would be before a civil tribunal. The moment I am able to say to the Commission, "The evidence in the case is closed," the accused would have to withdraw by the rules of the court, and the court-room would be cleared, and the Commission would at once proceed to deliberate upon the evidence and to arrive at their finding and sentence. When that finding and sentence is arrived at, it is not made known to the accused by this Commission; it is not known as possessing vitality or even existence, until it has been submitted to the convening authority, and by him reviewed and approved. If approved, it is made known to the accused by the Commanding General, or, in technical phrase, it is "promulgated" in General Orders.

In this case the accused has waived—as is frequently done by prisoners—his right and privilege of introducing rebutting testimony, and also his right and privilege of submitting his final appeal or address to the Commission.

I therefore submit the case to the Commission, and ask them to proceed to their finding and sentence.

REPLY OF J. W. GORDON, ESQ., COUNSEL FOR THE ACCUSED.

May it please the Court:

I wish to say one word in relation to the position taken by the Judge Advocate upon the authorities he has just read. These authorities—more properly decisions—at least in the State of Indiana, have been gravely and severely questioned by learned members of the profession, and by the profession generally; and I doubt whether in the future they will not be overruled. They yet stand, however, as the opinion of our Supreme Court. If it be granted, therefore, that they are law—that they govern to a certain extent the proceedings of our State courts, in the trial of felons, is it quite certain that they are applicable to the case now before this Commission? Is it certain that they can be properly employed as authorities even analogically, in a military court, upon the trial of a military offense?

Precedent makes law. I apprehend, however, that no military man, or, indeed, any one else, will be able to find, after the most thorough examination of the military authorities, a single precedent, where a military prisoner, having been once before a military court, entered upon his trial, proceeded to some length therein, and then escaped, and has yet been proceeded against in that trial unto sentence. I apprehend that no precedent can be found to that effect. I am quite certain that the books which I have been able to consult, furnish no such precedent; and I think it is so for the best of all possible reasons—the reason that there does not exist such a precedent.

In all military proceedings of this character, the accused is arrested. If he be an officer, the order of arrest confines him to his quarters, or to the camp, or gives him such limits as the commanding officer may think proper to prescribe. If he be an enlisted man, he is generally confined, and especially if the offense be heinous, to the guard-house, a close prisoner. There is no bail in military cases; no such thing as allowing the accused to go at large; and, hence, when his trial begins he must be present. He is accordingly brought before the court, if he be an enlisted man, under guard; if an officer, by citation; but, in either case, he is always required to be present when the trial opens; present all the way along through the trial; and, as I said before, I have yet to find the first precedent in military law, where, in a military court, a prisoner has been proceeded against in his absence.

The case before the Commission is not unlike that of an enlisted man. The accused here, not being an officer, had the limits of no camp allowed him. He was confined to his prison, to his room, with a guard at his door, and subjected to pretty severe surveillance. I know it has been said that he was on his parole of honor; and no doubt he did give his word to the General, or to the party who enlarged him and placed him in more comfortable quarters in this building; but it was not a case of parole of honor, as that existing in the army with prisoners of war. It was not a case in which there was any provision made by the law of the land, or military law for paroling. On the contrary, it was a case in which the order of the President, the only law on the subject, provided that there should be no writ of *habeas corpus;* and, of course, no enlargement of the prisoner. He was, then, a prisoner under guard. He has escaped. These authorities, therefore, can not, as I conceive, be held applicable to this case, however fit to be followed in civil courts, where all felons, except traitors and murderers, may be at large during their trial, as in the case of McCorkle, and, I think, of the others whose cases have been cited.

If, therefore, the accused has escaped, the law must, in my opinion, be held to be different in his case in this court from that maintained in the civil courts of the State of Indiana upon the cases cited; and, I think so, not only for the protection of the accused, should he be again arrested, but also for the protection of the rights of the Government. True, the Government may waive its rights as against him; but, as I understand, there is yet more evidence to be adduced against him. Should the case, therefore, be now submitted to the Commission, upon the evidence already before them, and should that evidence turn out, in their opinion, not to be sufficient to sustain the charges and specifications against him, why, then, the Government, by this course—which, I admit, is not my affair, and I only make the suggestion by permission—will lose forever the opportunity of bringing him to condign punishment, even should he be really guilty of these offenses. If the cause is submitted now upon this evidence, and the constitutional provision shall be held to apply to this case, he will not be allowed to be put in jeopardy again for any one of these offenses. This is a consideration, however, which belongs entirely to the Government side of the case. The prosecutor may introduce further evidence if he think proper; or may stop at any stage of the proceedings.

But the accused is not here; and the nature of the punishment that may be inflicted, should he be found guilty, affords another reason why he should be present before proceeding to sentence him. These are all of a corporeal, physical nature, operating upon the person. The leading characteristic of them all is, that they operate upon the person; and there is, indeed, no means of enforcing a pecuniary punishment inflicted by such a court as this, except where the prisoner is in custody; and much less certainly of punishing him personally without having him first in custody.

In view of these considerations, then, the first question before you will be:

1. "Shall we proceed with the case now before us to final sentence?"

If this question should be determined in the affirmative, upon the authorities cited by the Judge Advocate, then the second question for your decision will be:

2. "Shall we proceed in pursuance of these authorities, and admit further evidence should it be offered, because these authorities go to that extent?"

If the prisoner had escaped during the trial in a civil court, that court would have allowed the trial to go on to verdict and judgment in his absence, just as it would have gone on in his presence. Evidence would have been adduced, and argument of counsel heard, just as if the prisoner had remained present. If we take civil precedents for our guides, and abandon the path generally followed by military tribunals, we should confer upon the absent defendant the right to go on to final judgment by the same stages, that he would have been allowed to proceed in, had he remained personally present. The cases cited go thus far.

I submit, then, that, in the first place, the court will not proceed to final sentence in this case; and, in the second, that, if they do, they will proceed by the same stages indicated by these authorities, allowing evidence to be adduced in behalf of the defense, and the case to be closed just as it would have been, had the accused remained present.

The Judge Advocate, in reply, said:

With respect to going forward with testimony on the part of the accused in his absence, the Commission will find, on an examination of the cases cited—especially the *Seventh Ohio* and *Fourteenth Indiana Reports*—that a prisoner's counsel has no authority, the prisoner having abandoned his cause, to introduce evidence and make a defense. He certainly can not do it in a military court. But the authorities go further, and say that the Government shall not be prejudiced by the action of the prisoner. Now, I apprehend that if the prisoner was not present at the commencement of the trial, and proof was introduced in his absence, and the case begun while he was away, that the court, seeking for truth and justice, would decide that the defendant's counsel should have the privilege of coming in with evidence in his behalf; but the case supposed is not analagous to that now before this Commission. Here the prisoner sits on until the Government has proved its case, and if at that stage of the proceedings he abandons his case, he says, in fact, "I have no defense;" and, having thus waived his right of a further hearing, he can not come in *by counsel* and ask that he may be heard, when he is not present for the law to act upon him.

On the evidence already before the Commission, produced in the presence of the accused, and subjected to the cross-examination of his counsel, I submit the case, and ask the Commission to proceed to their finding and sentence.

The Commission may grant to the counsel for the accused, as a matter of courtesy, and not as a matter of right, the privilege of putting in their views on the evidence before the Commission.

The court-room was then cleared for deliberation. On being reopened, the Judge Advocate announced that the Commission would proceed to their finding on the evidence already introduced, and that no more evidence should be heard in the case; but that, as a matter of courtesy to the counsel for the accused, they would be permitted to put in their argument on the proof already submitted.

The Commission then adjourned, to meet on Monday, October 17, at 10 o'clock, A. M.

COURT ROOM, INDIANAPOLIS, INDIANA,
October 17, 1864, 10 o'clock, A. M.

The Commission met pursuant to adjournment.

All the members present; also the Judge Advocate, and the counsel for the accused.

The proceedings were read and approved. The counsel for the accused then submitted the following argument to the Commission:

Mr. President and Gentlemen of the Commission:

This cause has been brought to an abrupt conclusion by an unforeseen contingency, which otherwise might have been prevented. No men regret the fact more sincerely than we, the counsel for the defendant. We regret it both for public and private reasons; for we have no doubt that the cloud of suspicion which must have arisen from the testimony for the prosecution, as it now stands unimpeached, uncontradicted, and seemingly corroborated by the sudden disappearance of the defendant, might have been, in a good degree, if not indeed, altogether, dissipated by counter-proof and a thorough defense. Just as little do we doubt that a more thorough and complete investigation of the whole case, by an examination of all the witnesses, and a careful discussion of the great questions of law involved, would have limited the apprehension of danger to the peace of society and the stability of the Government, which may have arisen in the public mind from the testimony already before the country; and thus have restored confidence between man and man, as well as general tranquillity. The absence of the defendant, however, prevents the further development of the facts of the case; and the sudden determination of the trial puts an end to investigations of the law applicable thereto, which we had determined should be thorough and exhaustive. In both respects, therefore, we feel that we have reason for sincere and profound regret, for we are under the necessity of giving up to you for final judgment an imperfect cause—the broken fragment of what we had fondly hoped to make it; and upon this fragment you are expected to render complete justice to the whole of which it forms but a part. While this labor and the difficulty thereof are yours, we shall follow your action with a solicitude for the result far more painful and profound than we should have felt had our own labors been more thorough and complete.

Duly grateful for the privilege accorded to us by the Commission of addressing it upon the whole case, before it is finally submitted for adjudication, we shall proceed at once to the consideration of the questions arising in the 'record. These questions are of two kinds:

I. Questions of law;
II. Questions of fact.

I.—OF QUESTIONS OF LAW.

These again naturally divide themselves into classes. Thus, we have questions:

1. In relation to the jurisdiction of the Commission to try the defendant upon the charges and specifications preferred against him:

2. In relation to the liability of the defendant to be tried before any court for certain alleged offenses charged against him; and

1. *Of questions in relation to the jurisdiction of the Commission, etc.*

Of these questions we should not have spoken at this time had the determination of the Commission been final; for the question of jurisdiction has already been presented and decided. The whole case, however, we understand, will be reviewed before any sentence can be inflicted upon the defendant; and in order, therefore, that the reviewing officer may have all the lights we can furnish upon this important point, we recur to it in this place. And we feel that, whether this Commission shall deem itself authorized to review its decision in relation to its jurisdiction or not, its members will not take offense at our recurrence to that topic, nor deem it an abuse of the privilege accorded to us of submitting this final address.

If this Commission has jurisdiction to try the defendant upon the charges preferred against him, it must be because *martial law* had been proclaimed before these offenses were committed, and is still in force in the State of Indiana; for it will hardly be contended that, if *martial law* was not in force at the time of the alleged offenses, or has ceased to operate since that time, this Commission can have jurisdiction of this cause. The question then, which meets us at the threshold of this discussion, is this:

Is martial law in force in the State of Indiana at the present time?

Upon the right answer to this question must depend the right answer to the question:

Has this Commission jurisdiction of the cause now before it?

Before we can determine whether *martial law* is in force here or not, it is important for us to ascertain what *martial law* is. What then is *martial law*, the presence of which alone can authorize this trial, and give validity to its results?

We will answer this question by the authorities.

"*Martial law* is the law of war, and depends on the just but arbitrary power of the king, or his lieutenant; for though the king does not make any law but by common consent in Parliament, yet, in time of war, by reason of the necessity of it, to guard against dangers that often arise, he useth absolute power, so that his word is law."—*Smith on the English Republic*, Book 2, ch. 4.

"*Martial law* may be defined as the law, (whatever it may be,) which is imposed by military power."—*2 Steph. Comm. on the Laws of Eng.*, p. 561.

"*Martial law* is neither more nor less than the will of the general who commands the army."—Duke of Wellington in *Hansard's Debates in Parliament,* (3 series) vol. 115, p. 880.

" *Military law* " [employed here as synonymous with *martial law,*] " as applied to any persons, excepting the officers, soldiers, and followers of the army, for whose government there are particular provisions of law in all well regulated countries, is neither more nor less than the will of the general of the army."—*Dispatches of the Duke of Wellington,* vol. 6, p. 43.

"I am sure that I was not wrong in law, for I had the advice of Lord Cottenham, Lord Campbell, and the Attorney General, Sir J. Juves, and explained to my noble friend, that what is called proclaiming *martial law* is no law at all, but merely, for the sake of public safety, in circumstances of great emergency, setting aside all law, and acting under military power."—Earl Gray, as cited by Hough in *Precedents in Military Law,* p. 515.

When *martial law* is proclaimed, *courts-martial* are thereby vested with such a summary proceeding that neither time, place, nor person are considered. Necessity is the only rule of conduct; nor are the punishments which *courts-martial* may inflict under such authority, limited to "such as prescribed by law."—*Hough on Courts-martial,* p. 383.

" In truth and reality, it "—martial law—" is not a law, but something indulged rather than allowed as a law. The necessity of government, order, and discipline in an army, is that only which can give those laws a countenance; *quod enim necessitas cogit defendi.*"—1 *Hale His. Com. Law.* Sergeant Runnington's edition, London, 1794, p. —.

This, then, is *martial law*—"the will of the general;" "the arbitrary power of the king, or his lieutenant;" the means whereby "he useth absolute power, so that his word is law;" "the law which is imposed by military power;" "not a law at all;" the "setting aside all law and acting under military power;" a state in which "necessity is the only rule of conduct;" and "neither time, place, nor persons are considered;" and wherein "the punishments which courts-martial may inflict" are neither limited nor prescribed by law.

Does this law exist here, at this moment? Has it ever existed here? Is it, indeed, our law? Are the people of the State of Indiana thus stript of all their legal and constitutional rights; and reduced to this absolute bondage? Are the Constitution and laws of the United States suspended? Have the State Constitution and laws in like manner ceased to operate? If not, then, *martial law* does not exist here. If so, then, by what authority have they ceased to operate? By whom have they been suspended? Whence was the power derived that has suspended them? All power, the underived power of Almighty God, must have an origin. But from whom comes this power to put an end, for the time being, and, it may be, forever, to the Federal and State Governments of the United States; and to all the rights they were organized to protect and defend?

These questions must be answered before *martial law,* as insisted upon, can stand justified in the presence of the intelligence of the nineteenth century. But how shall we answer them?

It has been insisted by the Judge Advocate, that *martial law* is in force here for two reasons. These are as follows :

1. Because the President of the United States proclaimed *martial law* on the 24th of September, 1862, in the following terms :

" *First.* That during the existing insurrection, and as a necessary measure for suppressing the same, all rebels and insurgents, their aiders and abettors, within the United States, and all persons discouraging volunteer enlistments, resisting militia drafts, or guilty of any disloyal practice, affording aid and comfort to rebels against the authority of the United States, shall be subject to martial law, and liable to trial and punishment by courts-martial or military commission.

" *Second.* That the writ of *habeas corpus* is suspended in respect to all persons arrested, or who hereafter during the rebellion shall be imprisoned in any fort, camp, arsenal, military prison, or other place of confinement by any military authority, or by the sentence of any court-martial or military commission."

2. Because the enforcement of *martial law* is essential to the preservation of the life of the Republic.

It may be that we do not state these reasons in the order in which they were propounded, nor in the language employed. But the order of statement can not effect the questions they present; and the substance of the reasons are here given as presented. Let us, then, proceed to consider them.

1. Does the Proclamation of the President just cited, suspend the Constitution and laws of the United States, and of the several States? This question involves two others, namely :

a. Had the President authority to proclaim *martial law,* and suspend the *habeas corpus* as to the subjects thereof, at the time he issued this Proclamation?

b. If so, is this Proclamation still in force; or, if rescinded, has it been followed by a subsequent one of equivalent force?

a. It will be admitted that if the President had no authority to suspend the privilege of the writ of *habeas corpus* throughout the United States, at the date of the foregoing Proclamation, he could have had no authority to proclaim *martial law* to the same extent; for a proclamation of *martial law* involves not only the suspension of the writ of *habeas corpus*, but, also, the privileges and immunities of all other laws, whether State or Federal, common or statute, municipal or constitutional.

Had the President power, then, to suspend the privileges of the writ of *habeas corpus?* It would seem not, both on principal and authority. During the progress of our country, this question had been judicially considered and settled before the commencement of the present war, and the authorities stand thus on this point:

"Practically, as yet, Congress has never authorized the suspension of the writ. It is understood that as the unlimited power is vested in Congress, the right to judge of the expediency of its exercise is, also, absolute in that body."—*Sedgwick on Stat. and Const. Law*, p. 598; *Martin* vs. *Mott*, 12 *Wheat.*, p. 19.

"But it is at any rate certain, that Congress, which has authorized the courts and judges of the United States to issue writs of *habeas corpus*, in cases within their jurisdiction, can alone suspend their power, and that no State can prevent those judges from exercising their regular functions, which are, however, confined to imprisonment professed to be under the authority of the United States. But the State courts and judges possess the right of determining on the legality of imprisonment, under either authority."—*Rawle on the Const.*, pp. 114, 115.

"Hitherto, no suspension of the writ has ever been authorized by Congress since the establishment of the Constitution. It would seem as the power is given to Congress to suspend the writ of *habeas corpus* in cases of rebellion or invasion, that the right to judge whether the exigency had arisen, must exclusively belong to that body."—2 *Story on Const.*, § 1342.

The list of American authorities might be indefinitely extended; but these are deemed sufficient.

The only instance in the history of the United States since the adoption of the present Constitution, in which an effort was made, prior to the present insurrection, to procure a suspension of the *habeas corpus*, occurred during the Administration of Mr. Jefferson; and, in that instance, the authority was conceded by all departments of the Government to reside in Congress. The President submitted the question to that body; and they treated it as belonging without question to them."—See 3 *Benton's Abridg. Debates in Congress*, pp. 488–491; 504–515; and 520–542.

The English authorities are not less decisive of the point in controversy; for whenever the king in the recess of Parliament imprisons offenders, and denies them the privilege of the writ of *habeas corpus*, he is under the necessity of submitting his action to Parliament at its next session, and asking an act of indemnity for what he has done. Otherwise, his officers and agents engaged in such unauthorized imprisonments of his subjects, would be held liable for the arrests so made. Such had been the practice in England for near a century before our Declaration of Independence. A different course even in England, could not have been allowed without giving full sanction to the frequently assumed, but almost constantly denied, prerogative of dispensing with the laws of the land. The *habeas corpus* is the creature of law—originally of the old Common Law; but since the 31 *Car. II*, of the Statute Law of England; and hence to allow its suspension by proclamation, would be to permit the King to dispense with the laws of the land.

We can not better present the light in which these attempts on the part of the King to suspend this great writ are viewed by English statesmen, than by the following observations of Lord Brougham upon the subject:

"This is a far worse measure," he observes, "at all times than the restriction of public meetings; but the exercise of the power is, at least, under some check; for a bill of indemnity is always required to secure the government which has used such power of imprisonment; and, as the bill must be carried through after the alarm has passed away, possibly when a new ministry is in office, they who have occasion for it, are exposed to considerable risk, if they have at all abused the power temporarily bestowed. I have conversed with ministers who have been parties to such proceedings; and I have invariably found in them a very natural, may I add also, a very wholesome aversion to the whole plan."—*Brougham on the British Const.*, pp. 283 and 284.

In the language of Mr. Justice Woodbury, "it would be a little extraordinary if the spirit of our institutions, both State and National, was not much stronger than in England against the" exercise of such powers.—7 *How. U. S. I. C. Rep.*, 62.

It may be well questioned, we think, whether an American Congress possess authority to pass a valid act of indemnity in such case. Certain it is, it can not be done without a violation of the spirit of the Constitution, which prohibits the passage of *ex post facto* laws and bills of attainder. There is little difference between subjecting a man to punishment for an act, not criminal when committed; and depriving him of a remedy for a wrong done him, after his right to redress has accrued. An act of indemnity is, in such case, an act of injustice and oppression; and clearly within the spirit of the prohibition against *ex post facto* legislation.

But while this objection to such legislation lies in full force against it in this country, no such objection exists to it in England. There Parliament is omnipotent. No constitutional restraints are imposed upon it. It has, at all times, all the power that we could confer upon a constitutional convention. Hence, it is entirely competent for it to give legal validity to an act that was before entirely illegal and void. Congress has no such omnipotence, however. Such power does not exist in this country, except in the hands of the people.

We are, also, led to the same conclusion by the contemplation of the manner in which the executives of the two governments have originated. In theory yet, and undoubtedly original in practice also, they start from different and absolutely opposite principles.

The Government of Great Britain proceeds from the King. He is the *fons et origo* of power, justice, and honor. He is immortal—can do no wrong—stands above the law. Acts of Parliament are acceded to by him in language which still implies, that he but grants the petition of the two houses of Parliament. Originally acts of Parliament not unfrequently became laws by being first presented to the King in the form of humble petitions on the part of the two Houses, the prayers whereof he was graciously pleased to grant. Such was the justly celebrated Petition of Right. Another form, equally indicative of this claim of absolute power on the part of the King, is that of charters. In these the King speaks the law, thus: *Dedimus et concessimus*, etc.—we give and grant, etc. Such is the style of the *Magna Charta*, and many other ancient statutes of England, still extant. This power of the King to grant charters to corporations is still claimed as one of the royal prerogatives; and may, at any time, be exercised in the creation of new bodies politic. The great city of London derived its charter thus originally from the King; and it was said to have been sealed by William the Conqueror, who granted it with wax, which was

Bitten with his tooth
In token of sooth.

In order, however, more fully to grasp the whole vast extent of the power thus exercised by the King in the granting of charters of government, it must be remembered that under them legislative, judicial and executive powers have been exercised amounting almost to absolute sovereignty. This is illustrated in the charter governments of America, one of which, since its separation from the parent country, has declared *martial law*. But the power is far more grandly illustrated in the career of the East India Company—a corporation created by Queen Elizabeth, still existing, and ruling an Empire embracing vast territories in the fairest portions of the earth, and teeming with a population of more than a hundred million of souls.

Starting thus with a ruler, in theory at least, if not in fact, absolute, we can only arrive at a knowledge of his present powers and prerogatives by a careful study of what he has already granted to his Parliament or people in the way of charters, petitions and acts of Parliament *in propria forma*, and in the private charters of different corporations, which have from time to time been created by him, both in Great Britain and other parts of his dominions.

Whatever has been thus given away, he can not resume. It is in the hands of his subjects, and constitutes the body of their liberties. The perfect sphere of a power once absolute in his hands, has thus, as it were, undergone, through a succession of ages, a slow but constant disintegration, and the golden sands thereof have as constantly been gathered up and hoarded by his subjects, in whose hands they have become rights. Thus, according to the theory of the British Government, rights are the gifts of the crown to the people. Whatever has not been thus given, is still in the hands of the King—constitutes his prerogative.

The Government of the United States, on the other hand, presents exactly the reverse of this picture. It is the creature of the people, in whom all power is inherent. It can have no power which they have not conferred upon it, either by express grant, or by necessary implication. In order, therefore, to determine its powers, we have only to turn to the charter of its creation—the Constitution of the United States. A careful examination of that instrument will, we think, satisfy any candid mind that all the implied powers conferred upon the Government thereby must, in the first place, be ancillary to some substantive power expressly granted; and must, in the second place, whenever it is not a mere matter of form, become the subject of legislation before it can be constitutionally exerted by any department. This view is, in our opinion, sustained by the language of the Constitution, in which these implied powers are supposed to be embraced. Thus, it is declared that "Congress shall have power * * * to make all laws which shall be necessary and proper for carrying into execution the foregoing powers, and all other powers vested by this Constitution in the Government of the United States, or in any department thereof."

It is plain to our minds, from this language, that as often as the Executive may find his powers, as expressed in the Constitution, about to fail of their legitimate purposes for want of some ancillary power not expressly conferred, instead of seizing upon and exercising such necessary power without an act of Congress authorizing him to do so, that functionary must first ask Congress for the required power. Otherwise, he transgresses a plain provision of the Constitution. For, if the power belonged to the Executive prior to the passage of a law, why was it provided that Congress should have power to make all laws which shall be necessary and proper for carrying into execution the foregoing powers, and all other powers vested by this Constitution in the Government of the United States, or in any department thereof? If the President had a right to exercise the power in the first instance, why empower Congress to make the law necessary and proper to enable him to do so?

It was, therefore, plainly not the intention of the people that the President should exercise any implied powers.

If we are right in this conclusion, then how can any one concede a right in the President, as ancillary to his executive functions, to suspend the privilege of the writ of *habeas corpus?* If the King of England, all the vast residuum of power not embodied in charters, petitions granted, and acts of Parliament, must still look to an omnipotent Parliament—himself constituting one equal and independent branch thereof—for authority to enable him to suspend the *habeas corpus*, or indemnify his officers when, by mere power, they have already done so, shall we admit that a greater power over the priceless privilege of that writ, resides in the hands of the republican President of the United States? And more especially we do so, when no such power is expressly granted him in the Constitution; and when, by the fairest intendment, all implied powers are denied him, until conferred and made express by law?

But the privilege of the writ of *habeas corpus* is conferred by a law of the land. To allow the President to suspend it would, therefore, be to enable him to suspend a law of the land; in other words, to legislate. But, as Executive, he must see that the laws are faithfully executed; and it is not for him to select what laws shall, and what laws shall not, be thus executed. All laws must stand alike to him, until, by suspension of one or more, Congress enables him to neglect or disregard those that are suspended, in his execution of the rest.

The Act of Congress, of March 3, 1863, cited in our previous argument on this subject, and the President's subsequent proclamation in conformity therewith, are equivalent to a clear declaration that the power to suspend the *habeas corpus* does not originally reside with the Executive; and as the President approved that act, and issued that proclamation under it, we must hold that he now accepts the power from Congress, and does not claim it as properly pertaining to his function. If this were not the case, then his second proclamation was entirely unnecessary — a mere work of supereroga-

tion. If the proclamation of September 24, 1862, had already suspended the privilege of the writ of *habeas corpus*, what occasion was there for the proclamation of the 15th of September, 1863?—See 12 *Stat. at Large, App.* pp. 6 and 7.

Hence, we hold it established, that the President of the United States does not possess an original constitutional authority to issue such a proclamation as that of September 24, 1862, in so far as it relates to the suspension of the privilege of the writ of *habeas corpus;* because,

1. Precedents, both English and American, are against—precedents both legislative and judicial;

2. The King of England never exercises the power without going to Parliament for an act of indemnity, while it may be well questioned whether Congress has power to indemnify the President;

3. The authority is not conferred upon the President by express; and all implied powers are, by the terms of the Constitution, denied him;

4. The *habeas corpus* exists by law. To suspend it is a legislative function; and one plainly, therefore, not conferred upon the President; and

5. Congress by the act of March 3, 1863; and the President by his subsequent Proclamation, in pursuance thereof, in effect negatives the Proclamation of September 24, 1862; and the assumption of authority by which the same was originally issued.

But, arguing from the *less* to the *greater*—from *one* of a species to *all*—we conclude, that if the President has not authority to suspend the privilege of the writ of *habeas corpus*, until it is conferred upon him by Congress, he can not have power to declare *martial law*, which we have seen is, for the time being, the suspension of all law, both Federal and State—municipal and constitutional.

No lawyer will contend that the privilege of the writ of *habeas corpus* is placed upon higher ground by the Constitution, than any other constitutional privilege. On the contrary, it does not stand so high as *any* other; for it is provided that it may be suspended, "when in case of invasion or rebellion, the public safety may require it." It stands alone subject to this contingency of suspension. All other privileges of the Constitution stand high above it therefore; and yet we have seen it stands above the reach of Executive power until Congress intervenes. All other constitutional privileges stand above the reach even of Congress itself. Among these vital elements of popular freedom are placed the right of every citizen to be exempted from answering "for a capital or otherwise infamous crime, unless on presentment or indictment of a grand jury, except in cases arising in the land or naval forces," etc.; and that other great right parallel thereto, that "in all criminal prosecutions, the accused shall enjoy the right to a speedy and public trial by an impartial jury of the State and district wherein the crime shall have been committed," etc. There is no provision for a suspension, in any contingency, of these sacred rights. The power that suspends them may, without any further stretch, overthrow every other constitutional and legal right. It can be done by no power derived from the Constitution; for it strikes down and destroys its most sacred provisions. The people have never conferred any such power. Congress has never assumed to sanction it: but have, on the contrary, expressly provided a method by which the public safety may be secured, and the liberty of the people preserved. The Act of March 3, 1863, already so frequently cited, after providing for military arrests, and for the suspension of the privilege of the writ of *habeas corpus*, as to persons so arrested, provides also for their trial in a strictly constitutional manner; and, if they are not presented or indicted by the grand jury of the proper district within twenty days after they have been reported to the proper Circuit or District Court, or after they have been imprisoned, provided such grand jury shall, in the mean time, have closed its session, for their discharge from such military custody, either absolutely or conditionally, according to the circumstances of each case. Here is an express limit, then, to the suspension of the *habeas corpus* in case of such persons as the defendant; and an express provision for their trial wholly incompatible, as we conceive, with the jurisdiction of this honorable Commission.

It is, therefore, not within the constitutional authority of the President to declare *martial law*, and thereby deprive the defendant of his right to a constitutional trial by jury, upon an indictment duly presented by the proper grand jury. Congress has no power, under any known or conceivable state of affairs, to pass a valid act to deprive him of such a trial. Any such power, if it exist at all, as part of the resources of our Government, must result to it from a present military necessity—a necessity in the presence of which the functions of Congress are suspended, and all the powers of civil government at an end. Then, and then only, when the laws are silenced by the din of arms, can such a power be admitted upon the public theater; and it may be well questioned whether it is not to be regarded as rather the successor than the instrument of the Government whose constitutional organs have disappeared from the scene—whose constitutional functions have ceased.

And this naturally brings us to the second proposition we are controverting, namely:

2. *Martial law* is essential in the present emergency to the preservation of the national life.

In the discussion of this proposition, we were informed that "it is one of the innate principles of every existing thing, that it is endowed with the right to meet and overcome the force that seeks to destroy it." And this is true. But how endowed?

The right of self-defense may legitimately call into play all the forces of the *self* to be defended. Has it any claim upon any more? any right to extrinsic aid? "Every existing thing" must exercise its right of self-defense according to the principles of its constitution; and it can not find one thing to defend, or one capability of defense outside of its constitutional existence and power. The analogy to which the prosecution thus appeals, is against the position in support of which it has been invoked. If it shall be said that it is not an argument from analogy; but an argument from *all*, to *one* of the same kind—from "every existing thing" to the Government as one "existing thing," then it proves nothing at all; for the question recurs upon us: How is the "existing thing" known as the Government of the United States endowed with the right to meet and overcome the force that seeks to destroy it? Plainly by virtue of its Constitution; and only to the extent of its Constitution. Whenever this constitutional endowment ceases, there we are bound, according to the argument, to hold that its creator—the people—intended it should cease to live. If it is not constitutionally qualified to make good the battle for its life without an entire subversion and destruction of its Constitution, then it must die. It may be well questioned whether an emergency requiring a declaration of martial law in all parts of the United States at the same time, would not be equivalent to the death of the Republic. Indeed, we can not see how it could be otherwise.

While we hold these opinions, we concede, on the other hand, that there may be large sections and districts of the country in such condition as to require the exercise of *martial law*. Wherever lawless force has subverted all other law, there this "rude substitute," known as martial law, may properly enter, and control the relations of persons to each other and to the Government, until the reign of law and order returns. Again, wherever lawless force confronts lawful force in martial array, and the contest of the two puts an end to the civil administration, there *martial law* is called for and may properly be declared; or rather, it exists without any declaration at all. In the camp of an army in the field, or near the enemy, martial law may become necessary for the preservation of discipline, and thereby of the fidelity, and even of the existence of such army. But in all such cases, the "existing thing" to be preserved is more immediately the army involved in the case than the Government; and it must be remembered that an army is always a mere instrument of force—and to martial law as the sum of organized force—for that end. But, even then, it can only take such an extreme step, when compelled to do so, by necessity—a present controlling necessity.

Now upon this point, it seems to us, that the Judge Advocate has already conceded the question in dispute, for he says: " The Government stood on the brink of a precipice. The conspirators *were foiled by the military power of the Government.* * * * Self-preservation demanded that these men should be seized by the military power. *Foreseeing the danger, martial law had been declared by the President, and military courts given jurisdiction.*" Upon these sentences, which, we think, fairly represent the Judge Advocate, are we not entitled to say, that they do not imply a present necessity for *martial law?* He informs us that "the Government stood," *i. e.*, at some indefinite past time, "upon the brink of a precipice." There is no pretense that such is its present condition owing to the defendant and his associates, for he declares that "the conspirators *were foiled* by the military authorities." How had they been foiled? By being "seized by the military power." From all which it is plain that the necessity had passed, and that this defendant might safely have been delivered over for trial to the civil courts, which have never yet been closed in this district. But, if the necessity that led to the organized declaration of martial law did not exist at the commencement of this trial, or has since ceased to exist, the jurisdiction of this Commission has ceased with it. But it seems that the President's declaration of martial law was prospective—to meet a necessity foreseen, but at the time non-existent. Now, granting the President's power in proper circumstances—in the presence of an existing and controlling necessity—to declare martial law, it surely will not be contended that he may, without such present necessity, fulmine such a Proclamation in an anticipation of its future existence.

In this view, then, the Proclamation was premature—two years almost in advance of the necessity in which alone it can find a valid excuse for appearing at all. Of course, it was not valid at its date, on the hypothesis of a present necessity, and being invalid then, it can not be revived for the present occasion.

That the one sole ground upon which it is competent for a military commander to declare *martial law,* is the existence of a present and controlling military necessity, we beg leave to offer some authorities:

"The only principle which the law of England tolerates what is called *martial law,* is necessity; its introduction can be justified only by necessity; and its continuance requires precisely the same justification of necessity; and, if it survive the necessity in which alone it rests, for a single minute, it becomes instantly a mere exercise of lawless violence. When foreign invasion or civil war renders it impossible for courts of law to sit, or to enforce the execution of their judgments, it becomes necessary to find some rude substitute for them, and to employ for that purpose the military, which is the only remaining force in the community. While the laws are silenced by the noise of arms, the rulers of the armed force must punish, as equitably as they can, those crimes which threaten their own safety; but no longer—every moment beyond is usurpation. As soon as the laws can act, every other mode of punishing supposed crimes is itself an enormous crime. If argument be not enough on this subject—if, indeed, the mere statement be not evidence of its own truth—I appeal to the highest and most venerable authority known to our law. '*Martial law,*' says Sir Matthew Hale, 'is not a law, but something indulged rather than allowed as a law. The necessity of government, order, and discipline in an army, is that only which can give it countenance. *Necessitas enim, quod cogit, defendit.*'—*Sir James Mackintosh's Miscellaneous Essays and Speeches.* Cary and Hart's edition, p. 540.

"Suppose," says Lord Brougham, "I were ready to admit that on the pressure of a great emergency, such as invasion or rebellion, when there is no time for the slow and cumbrous proceedings of the civil law, a proclamation may justifiably be issued for excluding the ordinary tribunals, and directing that offenses should be tried by a military court—such proceedings might be justified by necessity; but it could rest on that alone. Created by necessity, necessity must limit its continuance. It would be the worst of all conceivable grievance—it would be a calamity unspeakable—if the whole law and Constitution of England were suspended one hour longer than the most imperious necessity demanded. * * * * * I know that the proclamation of *martial law* renders every man liable to be treated as a soldier. But the instant the necessity ceases, that instant the state of soldiership ceases, that instant the rights, with the relations of civil life, ought to be restored. * * Only mark the dilemma in which the Governor might have found himself placed by his own acts. The only justification of the *court-martial* was the Proclamation. Had that court sat at the moment of danger, there would have been less ground of complaint against it. But it did not assemble until the emergency had ceased; and it then sat for eight-and-twenty days. Suppose a necessity had existed at the commencement of the trial, but that, in the course of the eight-and-twenty days, it had ceased; suppose a necessity had existed in the first week, who could predict that it would not cease before the second? If it had ceased with the first week of the trial, what would have been the situation of the Governor? The sitting of the court-martial at all, could be justified only by the proclamation of martial law; yet it became the duty of the Governor to revoke that proclamation. Either, therefore, the court-martial must be continued without any warrant or color of law, or the proclamation of martial law must be continued only to legalize the prolonged existence of the court-martial. If, at any moment before its proceedings were brought to a close, the urgent pressure had ceased, which alone justified their being instituted, according to the assumption I am making in favor of the court, and for the Governor's sake; then *to continue martial law one hour longer would have been the most grievous oppression, the plainest violation of all law."—Speeches of Lord Brougham*, vol. I, pp. 390, 391.

It is distinctly said by the Supreme Court of the United States, in the case of *Luther* vs. *Borden, 7 How.*, pp. 46 and 47, that "no more force can be used than is necessary to accomplish the object," under a declaration of martial law. From this we infer that the same rule must apply to the adoption of force—*martial law*—in the first instance.

"In time of war, by reason of the necessity of it, he"—the King—"useth absolute power, so that his word is law;" and this is *martial law*—"the law of war."—*Smith on the English Republic, supra.* And Hale says it is "indulged" on account "of the necessity," etc. It was never, the same author assures us, "so much indulged as intended to be executed, or exercised upon others" than soldiers. "For others who were not enlisted under the army had no color or reason to be bound by military constitutions, applicable only to the army whereof they were not parts. But they were to be ordered and governed according to the laws to which they were subject, though it were a time of war. * * * The exercise of *martial law*, whereby any person should lose his life, or member, or liberty, may not be permitted in time of peace, when the King's courts are open for all persons to receive justice according to the laws of the land. This is in substance declared by the Petition of Right, 3 *Car. I*, whereby such commissions and *martial law* were repealed, and declared to be contrary to law."—*Hale's His. of the Common Law*, pp. 54 and 55.

Thus, it appears that a controlling military necessity alone can afford a just excuse for a declaration of *martial law*—a necessity that closes the civil courts of justice, or prevents the enforcement of their judgments by the ordinary process. Military necessity has been defined by the Government in General Orders, No. 100, 1863, to "consist in the necessity of those measures which are indispensable for securing the ends of the war," etc.

Has any such controlling necessity existed in the present instance? Does it still exist? Have the courts been closed and the laws silenced by the din of arms? Are they still closed? If not, then, we think, we are authorized to say that no necessity has existed, or still exists, for declaring *martial law*, for suspending the constitutions and laws, and proceeding against citizens charged with high crimes and misdemeanors in a manner never before resorted to in this country since the first settlement at Jamestown and Plymouth; and one wholly disused in England since the abdication of James II.

It is the fact of the civil courts being open, and justice having its ordinary course, that distinguishes a state of peace in any country from a state of war; and to this effect Lord Chief Justice Coke lays down the law. He says: "When the courts of justice are open, and the judges and ministers of the same may by law protect men from oppression and violence, and distribute justice to all, it is said to be a time of peace. So when by invasions, insurrections, rebellions, etc., the peaceable course of justice is *disturbed and stopped*, so as the courts of justice be, as it were, shut up, then it is said to be a time of war."—See *Coke upon Littleton*, 249, *b. n.* 1; and *Viner's Abridgment, tit. Prœrogative, (L. a.) War.*

In view of this great authority, is not this a time of peace in Indiana, at least in so far as the administration of justice is concerned? If it is a time of war, it can not be said, in that respect, to be made so by the rebellion—by any act of the common enemy. The courts are open, and "the peaceable course of justice is not disturbed and stopped." But if it be a time of peace, if "the courts are open for all persons to receive justice according to the laws of the land," then according to Lord Hale, *supra*, "the exercise of *martial law*, whereby any person should lose his life, or member, or liberty, may not be permitted;" and this is in substance declared by the Petition of Right, 3 *Car. I*, whereby such commissions of *martial law* were repealed, and declared to be contrary to law. And accordingly was that famous case of Edmond, Earl of Kent, who being taken at Pomfort, 15 *Edw. II*, the King and divers lords proceeded to give sentence of death against him, as in a kind of military court, by a summary proceeding, which judgment was afterward, in 1 *Edw. III*, reversed in Parliament."

* * "For *martial law*, which is rather indulged than allowed, and that only in cases of necessity, in open war, is not permitted in time of peace, when the ordinary courts of justice are open."

But even if this were a time of "open war," and "the ordinary courts" of law "were shut up," and the "peaceable course of justice disturbed and stopped," so that "the judges and ministers of the same may" not, "by law, protect men from oppression and violence, and distribute justice to all," has the Government of the United States taken the necessary steps to the enforcement of *martial law*, according to the usages of war? It will not be denied that the Duke of Wellington understood as well as any man of his times, the duties and rights of a military commander in this respect. His whole great life was devoted to the profession of arms; and the administering of governments according to the rules and usages of war. Speaking upon this subject, he says: "In fact *martial law* is no law at all. Therefore the general who declares *martial law*, and commands it to be carried into execution, is bound to lay down distinctly the *rules*, and *regulations* and *limits* according to which his will is to be carried out."—*Hansard, supra.*

Now, if *martial law* has been declared, and is in force in the whole United States, as claimed by the Judge Advocate, we have been able to find no order whereby the President, Lieutenant General, or others acting under either, have laid "down distinctly;" or, indeed, at all, "the *rules, regulations* and *limits* according to which his" or their "will is to be carried out." If this is not done, the declaration of *martial law* must become a snare to entrap the unwary; and, indeed, the wary also; for where the law resides in the breast of the ruler until it alights upon its subject in the form of a prosecution for a "capital or otherwise infamous crime," the good have no assurance of safety above the evil. All are alike insecure. Such a system would be worse than that of the Emperor Caligula who wrote his edicts in a small character, and hung them on high pillars the more effectually to ensnare his subjects.

b. But that it may not be said that we have overlooked the military character and power of the President, we beg leave to say, that this discussion has proceeded upon a consideration of his entire character; and if this method of considering his powers, is not so clear as one founded on the separation of his character and powers as a civil magistrate, from those belonging to him as the commander of the army and navy, we have been led into it by the method in which that functionary himself has proceeded in the exercise of those powers. Thus, the Proclamation relied upon in this prosecution as a declaration of *martial law*, was originally issued from the office of the Secretary of State; and is published with the acts of Congress, as an ordinary civil document of the kind. Had the President not given us evidence of the fact, that he is in the habit of distinguishing between his war powers and his civil functions, this course might not have led us to regard the Proclamation in the light of a purely civil act. But it is well known that he has issued several war orders purely as such. Hence, we had a right to look to the War office, and not to that of State, for so important an order as that which declares all the provisions of the Constitution and the laws suspended; and *martial law*—the President's mere will—substituted therefor. If the Proclamation is not a war order resulting from a paramount and controlling military necessity, then we submit, it is not, and can not, possibly be a declaration of *martial law;* and so we contend, *martial law* has not been in force, and can not be under it.

If it be regarded as a war order and in force at its date, has it not been since rescinded by act of Congress? We think it clearly has been, provided the legislative function of the Government has not been suspended by its operation; and it would seem from the President's recognition of Congress, as not suspended, by delivering to both Houses thereof sundry messages; by approving their acts; and, in some instances, by afterward acting upon laws passed by them, that he still regards the national legislature as still existing and in full life and power. If it is, then it may prescribe rules to govern the exercise of his power as Commander-in-Chief of the Army and Navy. It may say how far he shall declare *martial law;* and where his power, in that respect, shall cease. And this it has done.

The power to suspend the writ of *habeas corpus* Congress have already given him, if, indeed, they have power to delegate that discretion—a proposition not involved in this discussion; but one which we should otherwise controvert upon authority. That suspension, however, of the writ of *habeas corpus*, while it provides for military arrests and imprisonments, is not coupled with any power of military trials. On the contrary, it is expressly provided that a trial, in case of military imprisonments, shall not be postponed indefinitely; but shall be had at the next term of the proper Circuit or District Court, provided the grand jury of the district find an indictment; and if not, then that such court shall, upon proper application made, discharge persons so imprisoned, either absolutely or conditionally. Here, then, is a legal limit to the President's power even to imprison; and a clear denial of his right to punish, by military law, such offenders against the United States. He approved this limitation upon his power, as asserted in the Proclamation upon which alone it is contended this prosecution can proceed. It, is therefore, plainly rescinded, if it ever was valid. And we desire to observe that the law which does this, expressly refers to the same classes of persons declared subject to *martial law* by the Proclamation of September 24, 1862; and provides, as already said, for their trial, or discharge from custody, by the ordinary civil tribunals.—*Act of Congress of March* 3, 1863—12 *Stat. at large*, p. 766, §§ 2, 3 *et seq.*

We conclude, therefore, that *martial law* does not now exist in the State of Indiana; and, in fact, never has so existed; because,

1. It was not competent for the President to declare, or proclaim it;

2. If it ever were proclaimed, the Proclamation has been rescinded by act of Congress, with the full approval of the President.

And, as the existence of *martial law* is conceded to be necessary to the jurisdiction of this court, we conclude, therefore, that this court has no jurisdiction of the defendant upon the charges and specifications now pending against him.

[Of questions of the second and third classes, namely:

II. In relation of the liability of the defendant to be tried before any court for some of the offenses alleged against him;

III. In relation to the nature and sufficiency of the evidence adduced against him to support the charges.

These two classes of questions are here considered together.]

Mr. M. M. Ray continued the argument, as follows:

In approaching the evidence of the case, we are almost subdued and awed into silence, by considering the perilous precipice on which society, in the North-west, so lately hung, if the testimony, in the plenitude of its details, or even in its general scope, is to be believed. But, when we consider that much of that evidence is open to criticism from the perfidious relations which one or more of the witnesses bore to the defendant, and especially that the evidence is entirely *ex parte*, we are reassured that an exalted duty rests still upon us, as well as upon this Court, to analyze the testimony and apply it to the case according to the eternal and unchangeable rules of justice, of truth, and of good faith; even though the defendant may have fled from the perils of his situation. And just here we beg to enter our protest against the dangerous legal heresy that the escape of a defendant during trial and before judgment, carries with it any inference of either law or fact prejudicial to his innocence. The most that can be predicated of the fact is, that he has *waived* his constitutional right to be present, in person, for the remainder of the trial—leaving the whole question of his guilt or innocence, intact, before the Court to the same extent as if he had chosen to remain absent from Court in his prison. To this

extent, the cases cited from *Seventh Ohio, Fourteenth* and *Sixteenth Indiana* go, and no further. Such absence gives no additional weight to the Government's testimony. Such absence is no confession of guilt. Such absence, whether by escape from custody, or by voluntary absence in his *prison*, only waives his right to be present at *the* trial and at the rendition of judgment, in the civil tribunals, but it waives no legitimate matter of defense—no defects of law or evidence in the case which the Government has made. We will be pardoned, therefore, for dwelling with emphasis in denial of this most unwarrantable assumption. The most obvious and intelligible manner of treating the charges against the defendant and applying to them the evidence, is to consider, first, the charges and specifications based simply on the supposed character of the secret organization of which the defendant was a member, and the evidence applicable to the same—and, secondly, the charges and specifications based on the extraneous acts and declarations of defendant and the evidence in their support. To deny that the defendant was a member of a secret political society of the name charged, would be to ask the Court to discredit. the only corroborated testimony in the case. So it may be accepted as true, that there was such a society, and that the defendant was a member, and at the head of the organization in this State. But we deny that the organization was, by its framework, rituals, written and unwritten work, a *conspiracy*, as the specifications assume. We also deny, in the light of the evidence, that the order is intrinsically disloyal or treasonable, however vicious and unjustifiable it may be on general principles, in other respects, and however bad and ambitious men may pervert and use it to surprise a misguided society and betray into the great crime of conspiracy, insurrection and treason. If we can feel justified in assuming this position, in the light of the *ex parte* case made by the Government, how much more fortified we would feel, were we at liberty to draw on the supposed support which rebutting testimony might have furnished us? We feel warranted, from the evidence, in saying that the Order of the Sons of Liberty did not spring at once from chaos, nor from the plastic hands of one man or council of men, but, in its present framework and proportions, it is the symmetrical edifice of three years of experiment, change, failure, and elaborate reconstruction. Starting from the rude home-made order of self-protection, thence matured into the "Circle of Honor," "Knights of the Golden Circle," thence into the "American Knights," and finally into the "Sons of Liberty." Springing at first from real or fancied necessity, it was at first a crude, immature, stupid, and in many re spects a ridiculous imposture and a gross political fraud on the credulity of unsophisticated people. Still, in all, or any of these stages and changes, we look in vain for the criminal element, or conspiracy, or treason. The members glided from one name into another without any conscious change of purpose or character, and without assuming any new obligations, or realizing any shame or criminality by virtue of the change. Hence, the conclusion forces itself upon our minds that there was neither conspiracy or treason in the *written* work of the order, *per se*; nor was there any treason or conspiracy in the *unwritten* work of the order, for the mass of the members, without any new light, passed from one stage of the order to another, believing it only a political society. So, if we are right in this, the first, second, and third specifications of charge first, fall, as they are based on the theory that the organization is, *per se*, a conspiracy. In saying this much, we do not forget that the evidence shows much loose and unreliable *hearsay*, in regard to the purposes of the order in certain localities; but then we remember at the same time, and this Court will not fail to recollect, that all this testimony comes from the three witnesses, viz.: from Warren county, Illinois, Martin county, Indiana, and Randolph county, Indiana, and in the case of the latter two, from men who only knew the "Knights of the Golden Circle;" an organization without system, uniformity, community of creed, and without national, state or county head to the organization. The defendant can not be held responsible for any light, trivial, loose or wanton utterances of irresponsible, disconnected associations, whose names are not even mentioned in any of the charges. We do not feel called upon, as counsel for the defendant, to apologize for these or any other secret political organizations, and especially in revolutionary times like these. But we do feel called upon as a mark of respect to this Court, and in the interest of a common country, to place on record our unqualified reprobation of all secret political orders, by whatever name or party affiliation, as, at best, but pestilential hotbeds for the most incendiary political heresies, leading to the worst fruits of Jacobinism. It is in vain for the purest and wisest patriot to offer words of truth and patriotism to the people, if they conflict with the decrees of a secret, irresponsible, bloody tribunal. Through the machinery of secret organizations, the worthless and irresponsible place-hunters come to the top, get the popular ear, and have more weight and influence in directing the popular mind, than all the lessons of history, or the appeals of our most learned, independent, unselfish and trusted public men. Who, then, that has had the sagacity to detect the baleful influence of secret societies in the whole political atmosphere for two years past, can find any apology or palliation for them? We offer none. It would be too much labor to go into the evidence in detail, so we can but classify it, and be content with very general observations in its application. If we have not erred in the foregoing speculations in regard to the *character* of the order, then the specifications, Nos. 1, 2 and 3, of charge first, are in no wise proved. For we may observe that it is not competent to fix the character of the order as treasonable in Indiana, by producing an *obligation* of a highly objectionable character, through a member of a different order, in a particular locality, in the State of Illinois, when the printed ritual of the whole order in Indiana is in evidence containing no such obligations. This remark applies to Wm. Clayton, a witness from Warren county, Illinois, and it applies with equal force to the verbal testimony of the witnesses from Martin and Randolph counties, in this State, whose experience relates to irregular organizations anterior to the existence of the "Sons of Liberty," and revelations have no warrant in the ritual of that order, in this State. How can Dodd be held responsible for the insane ravings of persons with whom he had no connection? For it will be steadily borne in mind, that, before the defendant can be chargeable with the dictations and acts of others in this or any other order, the evidence must establish the essential preliminary fact that the order is, *per se*, a conspiracy, for it travels on the ground that they are co-conspirators. We leave the fourth specification of charge first, as falling within class of charges based on positive independent acts, and pass to charge second. The four specifications of charge second, charge treason, if any thing. The task of disposing of the whole of this charge is easy.

By article 3d, of section 3d, Constitution of United States, it is provided that "No person shall be convicted of treason unless on the testimony of two witnesses to the same overt act." We submit, with entire confidence, that no overt act has been proved by even one witness. It is true, the witness, Stidger, talks vaguely about the "order" having patronized the Greek fire machine, and about the burning of Government stores; all of which was mere *hearsay*, coming from Bowles, which is not admissible against defendant, except on the supposition that the order is a *conspiracy*—and even then it would only have the force of one witness, if that.

The same logic disposes of the same witness' testimony in regard to the starting of couriers into Kentucky to give notice of the culmination of the scheme; but the couriers were never started. All the specifications of charge third, we suppose, fail for want of proof. We do not remember any evidence on the subject of arming and inciting the people to insurrection, except what tends to support the fourth specification of charge first, involving a conspiracy to put on foot an insurrection. The evidence in regard to the arms bought in New York, and shipped to one Parsons, does not connect the defendant in any degree with that transaction. The evidence of all the witnesses touching the arming of the order is very unsatisfactory and inconclusive, even in the irregular local organizations. And as to supposed insurrectionary character of the defendant's official addresses and casual speeches, we have only to suggest that there is not now, never was, and in the nature of things never can be, any test or standard of legitimate debate. Where the press and speech are as free as they have been in this country in the past, more or less abuse and licentiousness must exist, and must be tolerated. And it is respectfully submitted as a sound maxim in statesmanship, and a safe guide for legislators and courts, that great errors and abuses in this respect may be safely tolerated, if reason is left free to combat them. Why shall the defendant be arraigned for insurrectionary appeals, while the carnival of licentious utterance goes on all around us? Power, in all ages, has been jealous of a free press. While on this subject, we conceive that we can do our client and country no better service than to commend to the attention of the Court an eloquent passage from the speech of the great English orator, Sheridan, on the liberty of the press.

Mr. Sheridan says: "Give me but the liberty of the press, and I will give the Minister a venal House of Peers—I will give him a corrupt and servile House of Commons—I will give him full swing of the patronage of office—I will give him the whole host of ministerial influence—I will give him all the power that place can confer upon him to purchase submission, and overawe resistance; and yet, armed with the liberty of the press, I will go forth to meet him undismayed; I will attack the mighty fabric he has reared with that mightier engine; I will shake down from its hight, corruption, and lay it beneath the ruins of the abuses it was meant to shelter."

There are five specifications under charge fourth, for "disloyal practices;" a charge suggestive of boundless elasticity, and an illimitable field of inquiry. What is a disloyal practice? When we say that no law has defined it, no court has expounded it, and no precedent has illustrated it, we have shown the dangerous character of a conviction under that charge.

As to the two specifications under charge fifth, for a violation of the laws of war, is it not enough for us to say, that the defendant was not in the military or naval service of the United States, and that if the rules and articles of war are meant, he owes *no duty* to them; and that if the international common law of war is meant, then it can only relate to the rights and duties of belligerent powers, and not to the rights and duties of government and citizen. We have now traversed over all the charges, and recur to the fourth specification of charge first. If the evidence establishes any specification, it is the one under consideration. This charge rests, not upon the supposed treasonable character of the order, but upon extrinsic testimony of particular facts, and those facts consisting of admissions and communications made by defendant to a Government Detective by the name of Stidger. If this witness' testimony is to be taken without any deduction, it would convict the defendant of a willingness to commit murder, as well as treason. The witness appears to be an intelligent and accomplished detective, and all the more dangerous on that account, unless strictly honest and impartial. A professional detective is quickened by the same instincts, and stimulated by the same motives, that influence even the better class of practicing lawyers in their zealous pursuit of the interest of a client. Such a detective starts out with hope, pride and professional ambition, all involved in his success in making a case against some one. His zeal leads him into every species of sham intrigue; his strategy leads into the confidence of the ambitious, the vain, the visionary, or the corrupt, and he sedulously cultivates the germ of every prurient weakness to folly, ambition or crime, so that in the end he has deliberately manufactured half the circumstances of guilt, and stands before God a joint criminal with the accused—standing with a guilt of twofold enormity—the guilt of treachery and dishonor in betraying the confidence of his dupe, and the guilt of an accomplice in the crime itself. Or, to say the least of it, in every case he stands dishonored in the eyes of those he has betrayed, and when honor is lost, truth holds precarious sway. Honor and truth are the Siamese Twins; if you sever the ligament that binds them, they sicken and die together.

The scheme of murder and insurrection developed in that evidence is most atrocious and revolting, and whatever visionary schemes of ambition and adventure may have entered into the calculations of the defendant, we can not believe that murder was one of them. And although it constitutes no part of the charges on which he is tried, and although a conspiracy in aid of the rebellion is a crime of sufficiently dark a hue, we would fain vindicate his character from the infamy of a foul murder—a deed so foreign and repulsive to every element of his nature. But the evidence to support this degrading accusation is supplied by the same detective, and by the abrupt termination of the trial, has denied us even the chance to disprove what is said to have taken place in open council in reference to the assassination of Coffin. And, indeed, the Court will be bound to receive all the evidence of the witness Stidger, with all that hesitation and doubt to which the treacherous relations which the witness bore to the defendant, expose it, and subject to the force of the fact of the abrupt and unexpected termination of the trial, operating with exclusive detriment to the defense. If the Court find the defendant guilty on this specification, it will be by giving full force and credit to the witness Stidger, and by taking a different view from us as to the true standard that measures the character of a professional detective, and weighs the credibility of his testimony. If we have not done injustice to the position of that class of witnesses, he stands not only dishonored, as taking all the obligations and vows of secrecy of the order, with the deliberate and premeditated purpose to violate these oaths, and to betray his comrades, but he stands, by virtue of his own machinations, progressing step by step to the clear and confessed relations of an accomplice, morally and legally. The rule of law upon the subject is, that while the testimony of an accomplice is to be received, yet it should be received with great caution, and when received, is entitled to less weight than the testimony of other witnesses.—See 2 *Ind.*, 652; 4 *Ind.*, 128; 7 *Ind.*, 326; 9 *Ind.*, 106.

With much solicitude and anxiety, we commit the cause of the defendant, in his absence, to the learning, to the patriotism, to the honor, and to the justice of this Court. To the learning, because the great legal question of jurisdiction, lying at the threshold of your inquiries, is still open; to your patriotism, because the highest interests of public liberty, and the victory of reason over passion, are in ,your hands; to your honor, because the graces of magnanimity and mercy should follow the weak, the unfortunate, and even the guilty, and plead against the calamities of conviction; to your justice, because she sits blind to the scenes of our national drama, unseduced by the blandishments of power, and deaf to the cries of resentment and passion.

M. M. RAY,
J. W. GORDON,
Counsel for H. H. Dodd.

REPLY OF THE JUDGE ADVOCATE.

Gentlemen of the Commission:

I do not propose to go into an extended argument upon the question of jurisdiction. The Commission having already passed upon that question, it would be a vain and useless labor for me to collate and review all the decisions and authorities that might be brought to bear upon that question. It is not necessary to occupy the time of the Commission in making an argument simply to meet what the gentlemen may say upon their side, for the arguments made by the counsel here, are not those of the accused, and are received by the Commission merely as a matter of courtesy, and, therefore, do not force me to take issue upon what they personally may place before you. I, however, desire to submit, very briefly, one or two points, and then leave the case with you.

On the question of jurisdiction, volumes might be written, and digests innumerable compiled. The question of martial law has, for centuries past, been a subject of thoughtful consideration by the ablest jurists; what it was, and what were the necessities that justified it. Martial law is born of necessity, and it is but a matter of opinion and judgment as to when that necessity exists. He who is to judge of that necessity, is the chief executive power of any government, or the subordinate military officers acting under the orders of that executive.

All the argument in the case resolves itself into one proposition, namely: that martial law can only exist, and does only exist, in times of great, controlling, overpowering necessity. Martial law, as has been well said, is a setting aside of the whole machinery;of the civil law. The civil law must go down before it, and nothing but a great and all-powerful necessity should be permitted to take from the people of any land the rights, privileges and immunities of the civil law. And who shall be the judge of that necessity? It can only be the Chief Executive who wields the military power of any government. Congress can not be the judge. Our legislative body, Congress, usually convenes but once a year, not oftener than twice a year, and, in times of foreign war, invasion or rebellion, shall we wait the expiration of that year for the declaration of martial law, to preserve the life of the Government? Such a course would be suicidal and destructive of the Government itself. The statement of the proposition shows its absurdity. If the necessity for action should arise between the sessions of the legislative body, where is the power that must step in to save the Government before that legislative body meets? The circumstances of the times necessitate martial law, and when this necessity exists, martial law must be proclaimed, and the civil law, for the time being, remains silent, to be revived in its native force when the necessity for proclaiming martial law shall have passed away. The civil law sleeps; it is not dead.

In this case the President has not said that martial law shall be proclaimed through the length and breadth of the land. On this point the counsel for the accused have gone astray. The President has not declared that the whole machinery of the civil law shall remain dormant, that there shall not be any punishment of civil offenses in our courts. But he has said, that when men step in and undertake to assist this great rebellion, by acting in concert with these armed rebels against the Government, thus threatening the life of the nation, that they then clothe themselves with a certain military garb that brings them within military law, and that the military law shall act upon them, and thus far martial law is proclaimed; no further. When men, for instance, here in the State of Indiana, undertake to bring about an insurrection, undertake to release and arm these hordes of rebel prisoners, here in our midst, they then become part and parcel of that rebel army, and make themselves subject to military law. They are as soldiers for the time being, and, like them, subject to military regulations. Take the case as it exists. We are engaged in a war; and the ways of war are not the ways of peace. That which may be lawful in times of war is unlawful in times of peace. Let me illustrate. Would it be lawful in times of peace for the military commander of this district to go out to the ground on which Camp Morton now stands, and take possession of five hundred acres of land on which to build structures, in which to confine these rebel soldiers? Would it, in times of peace, be lawful for him to seize and take possession of a house to occupy as his headquarters? Would it be lawful for him to go upon another man's land, and camp his troops, and seize his corn and provisions? Would not each single act be a trespass, for which he would be liable to prosecution? But it is no crime under the circumstances supposed, that is in times of war. And it is no higher assertion of military authority to take possession of the person, than it would be to seize that person's property for military service, if the safety of the Government demanded it. All these things come as a concomitant to a state of war. Again, in times of peace, do we recognize or know of any such officer as the Commanding General of a Department? Take, for instance, the Commanding General of this Department, General Hooker, who commands the States of Ohio, Illinois, Indiana, and Michigan—not one of which States is in rebellion; what are his powers and duties? Is he simply a man of straw? Is his position recognized by the civil law? And yet will any man claim that he can be prosecuted for any acts done in the exercise of his authority, not one of which is recognized by the civil law, and but for the condition of war, would be without legal sanction. The position of General Hovey is another illustration. At present he exercises in his military supervision as much power over the people of the State as the Governor himself, and yet in times of peace, his office has no existence. If peace were declared to-day, he would be as powerless as any private citizen in the land. It is because the foundations of society are broken up, that we are forced to recognize the necessities that grow out of this new order of things. The state of things now existing in this country, has never before been exactly paralleled in any age of the world. The whole country has been taken possession of by military force. Why? Because, and only because of its necessity. To preserve even the form of government, it was necessary that the whole force and energy of the nation should be employed against those who were arraying themselves against it. The whole nation, each man individually, and all collectively, constituted a physical power that might be used to preserve the nation against its enemies. The civil rights of the citizen became dead for the time being, if necessary to preserve the life of the nation.

The counsel for the accused, in quoting my arguments respecting the jurisdiction of this Commission, evidently misconstrued my remarks as to each existing thing exercising its rights of self-defense according to the law of its organization. I am, for instance, organized and created as a single, individual thing, without weapons or means of defense, save my hands, and if my life were threatened by an antagonist, I must not, according to the theory of the gentleman, take up a club or any weapon to defend that life, or call in the aid of my friend, but I must defend it according to the law of my organization, without any extrinsic aid. Is not the fallacy of the position apparent? Self-defense, self-preservation inevitably carries with it every means which that power can bring to assist in that self-defense and self-preservation. Just as defensive war may become offensive-defensive war. For the sake of saving yourself from invasion, you may invade the enemy, and yet it is but a defensive war. Each individual—every existing unity or community—is endowed, by the very laws of its creation, with the power and the right to defend its own existence. That right is not lessened when individuals join together and make communities. A man who has that right of self-protection does not, by joining himself to fifty or a hundred others, make his individual right less sacred; and when communities combine to form a government, the life of that government is at least as sacred as the life of an individual. In defending the life of the nation and its constitution, necessity becomes the sole law. Whatever is *necessary* to be done, the Government is not only authorized, but is in duty bound to do. I accept it as a maxim that the only criterion for the exercise of martial law is its necessity. Whenever an officer, or the Chief Executive of this Government, acts without that necessity, he commits an act unauthorized; but so long as he keeps within that necessity, the law and the people—the givers of all power—will indorse him.

It was not my intention to refer to the exigences that might necessitate martial law, or to the distinctions between martial law and military law—a distinction often disregarded—but I beg to submit the following from the *New American Cyclopedia* which very clearly states the distinction:

"Martial law has often been confounded with military law, but the two are very different. Military law, with us, consists of the 'Rules and Articles of War,' and other statutory provisions for the government of military persons, to which may be added the unwritten or common law of the 'usage and custom of military service.' It exists equally in peace and in war, and is as fixed and definite in its provisions as the admiralty, ecclesiastical, or any other branch of law, and is equally, with them, a part of the general law of the land. But in the words of Chancellor Kent, 'martial law is quite a distinct thing.' It exists only in the time of war, and originates in military necessity. It derives no authority from the civil law, (using the term in its more general sense,) nor assistance from the civil tribunals, for it overrules, suspends, and replaces both. It is, from its very nature, an arbitrary power, and extends to all the inhabitants (whether civil or military) of the district where it is in force. It has been used in all countries, and by all governments, and it is as necessary to the sovereignity of a State as the power to declare and make war. The right to declare, apply and enforce martial law, is one of the sovereign powers, and resides in the governing authority of the State, and it depends on the Constitution of the State whether restrictions and rules are to be adopted for its application, or whether it is to be exercised according to the exigences which called it into existence. But even when left unrestricted by constitutional or statutory law, like the power of a civil court to punish contempts, it must be exercised with due moderation and justice; and, as a permanent necessity alone can call it into existence, so must its exercise be limited to such times and places as this necessity may require; and, moreover, it must be governed by the rules of general public law, as applied to a state of war. It, therefore, can not be despotically or arbitrarily exercised any more than any other belligerent right can be so exercised." (*Cushing's Opinions of U. S. Attorney General*, vol. 8, p. 365; *Wolner's Jus Gentium*, sec. 865; *Grotius De Jus Bel.*, B. lib. 3, cap. 8; *Khuber Dicit des Gens*, sec. 255; *O'Brien's American Military Law*, p. 23; *Halleck's International Law and Laws of War*, p. 303.)

It is one of the concomitants of an army, as the counsel for the accused well remarked, that wherever that army goes, it carries with it martial law; and just to the extent that we here are under the rule of an army, just to that extent are we subject to the rules of martial law, without any proclamation of the President on the subject. And further, martial law, in my judgment, is not a thing to be authorized by Congress. The decision of our ablest legal authorities may be shown to that effect. It is an Executive power, only to be exercised under circumstances of all-controlling necessity, by the Commander-in-Chief, or the executive power of the Government. It is one of the prerogatives of the Executive, and it can only be used by him and his subordinates—his lieutenants.

If, for instance, the commanding officer of Kentucky, acting under the authority of the Chief Executive, the President, conceives there is a necessity for martial law to be declared in his district, he can declare it at his will; but his superior will hold him responsible that he did not declare martial law till there was a necessity for it. So with General Hovey and his orders while commanding in this District.

Martial law has, during the war, been declared by almost every commanding General in the field; and the power and the right to do so, have not, to my knowledge, ever been questioned in any department, and no prosecution has been known for the unlawful exercise of that power by any military commander.

When General Hovey convened this Commission within the limits of his jurisdiction, and committed the case of Harrison H. Dodd, the accused, to this Commission, with orders to try it, he, by virtue of his military power, acting under the authority that was given to him by the Commander-in-Chief of the army, namely, the President of the United States, he suspended the civil law, and put in operation the military or martial law. The officers of this Commission could not, under the oath that they have taken, refuse to obey the orders of the officer placed over them. They could not stop and go back of that order, and refuse to hear and determine this case.

Benét, who is our best authority upon military law, says, p. 13: "In the United States, martial law is a thing not mentioned by name, and scarcely as much as hinted at, in the Constitution and statutes. The former declares that 'the privilege of the writ of *habeas corpus* shall not be suspended unless, when, in cases of rebellion or invasion, the public safety may require it.'"

Upon that point much might be said, in connection with the condition of Indiana, as to whether the public safety did require the suspension of *habeas corpus*, and the declaration of martial law. I did not suppose there were two opinions on that question.

Benét continues: "The opinion is expressed by the commentators on the Constitution, that the right to suspend the writ of *habeas corpus*, and also that of judging when the exigency has arisen, belong exclusively to Congress. But the rebellion or invasion may demand such suspension during a recess of the national legislature, and, by the laws of war, the executive has then the right to assume the power for the public safety. The relation between the proclamation of martial law and the suspension of the writ of *habeas corpus*, is extremely intimate; although it is but one of its consequences, and by no means the largest or gravest, since, according to every definition of martial law, it suspends, for the time being, all the laws of the land, and substitutes in their place no law; that is, the mere will of the military commander." Here is another sentence in which much, very much, is included. I cite it, that it may be reflected upon:

"*It must be observed, however, that many offenses which in time of peace are civil offenses, become in time of war military offenses, and are to be tried by a military tribunal, even in places where civil tribunals exist.*" p. 16.

I will only add a word further in respect to the necessity that existed for martial law to step in at the time it did, here in the State of Indiana. It may be asked, did the necessity exist? The proof shows that there existed in this State an organization numbering from fifty to eighty thousand men, military in its character, and, about two-thirds armed, ready at any time to be called out to obey the orders of their superiors, regardless of the law and authorities of the United States. That organization was armed and drilled with the avowed purpose of assisting the enemy as against the Government. This organization was ready at any moment to be called into the field, to release in our midst large numbers of rebel prisoners, feebly guarded. Did not such a state of things warrant the interference of the military power to stop this insurrection, and the possible bloodshed and anarchy that might have ensued here at our very door?

I now pass for a moment to the fact of the absence of the prisoner. While I admit that his absence should not prejudice him in the consideration of the proof, nor should it be taken, perhaps, as any confession of guilt. When, however, the counsel attempt to argue on the force of the testimony that might have been introduced by the defense, they touch upon ground which they have no right to approach. This Commission does not know that any more proof could come before it. They must consider the evidence they have heard, and only that. The accused, by his absence, as I have before said, waves his right to any rebutting testimony, and says, in fact, "There is no further defense to be offered in this case." If nothing is confessed against him, nothing certainly can be said for him by his act of escape.

The counsel who last addressed the Commission, contends that the organization known as the Order of American Knights, or the Order of the Sons of Liberty, is not a conspiracy. Then what is a conspiracy? As defined by law writers, it is a combination or agreement between two or more persons to do an illegal act, or to do a legal act in an illegal manner. If we take this association and try it by this rule, what do we find? A body of men who were bound together by the most binding of oaths—the oath itself an unlawful thing, and the very organization of the society being unlawful in and of itself—recognizing military as well as civil officers unknown to, and in violation of, the Constitution and laws of the land. And for what purpose does the proof show this organization to have existed? For the express purpose of defeating and overthrowing the Government, while engaged in war against its enemies, for the purpose of aiding those enemies in their rebellion against the duly constituted authorities of the land. Other witnesses swear it was for the additional purpose of resisting the draft; but every witness testifies directly to the fact, that the express purpose of the organization was to resist the Government in its efforts to suppress the existing rebellion. Is this lawful, or unlawful? Is this conspiracy, or is it not? It seems to me that one moment's consideration of the principles upon which this society was organized, would determine the question beyond dispute. It needs no argument. I refer the Commission to the proof.

The counsel say further that while this organization was vicious, it was not treasonable. Why, my God, what is treason? What does a traitor do but try to destroy his Government? Is it treason to organize a society, the members of which take a solemn oath that when the enemies of their Government come over into their State, they will receive them as friends, shake hands with them, and, as opportunities offer, give them information from time to time of the movements of the Government forces? Is it treason to assist in turning loose upon us the tigers that we have imprisoned here in our very midst, to arm those very men who are our avowed enemies, and the enemies of our Government? Is it treason to endeavor to organize those rebel prisoners into a formidable military body to assist in the general rebellion against the Government? Is it treason to send messengers to the enemies of the Government, to tell them of the number of friends they have here in a loyal State, and assure them of sympathy and support? I can not conceive how a doubt for one moment can exist as to the treasonable nature of these designs.

I wish to say one word with respect to the testimony of the witness Stidger. No member of this Commission, and I think I may say that no person sat in this hall, who did not believe that the witness testified to the truth. If he had not testified to the truth, he was a witness who could more easily have been convicted of falsehood than any one brought upon the stand. There was not a fact to which he testified, for which he did not give the place, date and person. When a witness does that, every lawyer knows that you can trace up that man's history in his cross-examination. If Captain Jones did not send him on a certain day to a certain person, to have a certain conversation, nothing would be easier than for Captain Jones to be called upon the stand to testify to the fact. If the witness Stidger had not met Bowles at the time and place he mentions, and have the conversation narrated, it would be easy to show that Bowles was elsewhere at the time. If he did not meet Dodd, and talk with him, at the time and place he says he did, how easily it could be refuted! When Stidger came upon the stand, he expected that he was to be met by every possible proof that could be brought against him. This witness testified that when he entered into this organization, it was with the express intent and determination to develop its end and purposes. True, he was a Government detective; he states that he was so hired and employed. As a rule, I have no kind of fellowship or sympathy with this class of men. But I believe that such a work could be engaged in and accomplished with a good intent and purpose. It is a species of strategy fully justified by the circumstances of the case, and is not unlike that to which our commanding Generals in the field often resort in their efforts to deceive the enemy. They send false messages, .write and forward false missives, on purpose to mislead them. They employ every means in their power to induce them to believe in and rely upon a certain state of things, the opposite of that which really exists. Stidger engaged in the work of revealing the designs of this treasonable organization, with the express purpose of giving information to the Government and saving bloodshed, and possibly National

disaster. Such a man engaged in such a cause, and for such a purpose, can not be called an accomplice. Such a man can not be called a criminal, or a scoundrel. On the contrary, he perils his life to obtain facts which have proved of the greatest importance to the cause of justice, law and order. In such a cause, every man, loyal and true to his Government, will stand by him; and it ill becomes any man, especially in this State, to withhold that meed of praise which is his due for the services rendered to the Government.

The case is now submitted to this Commission on the evidence before it; and I am content to leave it in your hands, after simply quoting the opening remarks of the counsel who last addressed you: "In approaching the evidence in the case, we are almost subdued and awed into silence by considering the perilous precipice upon which society, especially in the South-west, so recently hung, if the testimony, in the plenitude of its details, or even in its general scope, is to be believed." Respecting that testimony, this Commission is abundantly able to judge. If this testimony is to be believed, this Government was on the brink of a precipice; and the evidence given upon this stand, under the solemnity of an oath, and with the eye of Almighty God resting on each witness, is of such a character that no argument of counsel, or finely drawn sophistries, can change the perilous and treasonable nature of the circumstances testified to.

The Commission then adjourned, to meet at 3 o'clock, P. M., to deliberate on the finding and sentence.

———•◆•———

It is not thought advisable to longer delay the publication of these Treason trials, for the final action of the President in the matter.

When the findings and sentences are approved, they will be promulgated in General Orders, and will then be generally made known by means of the daily press.

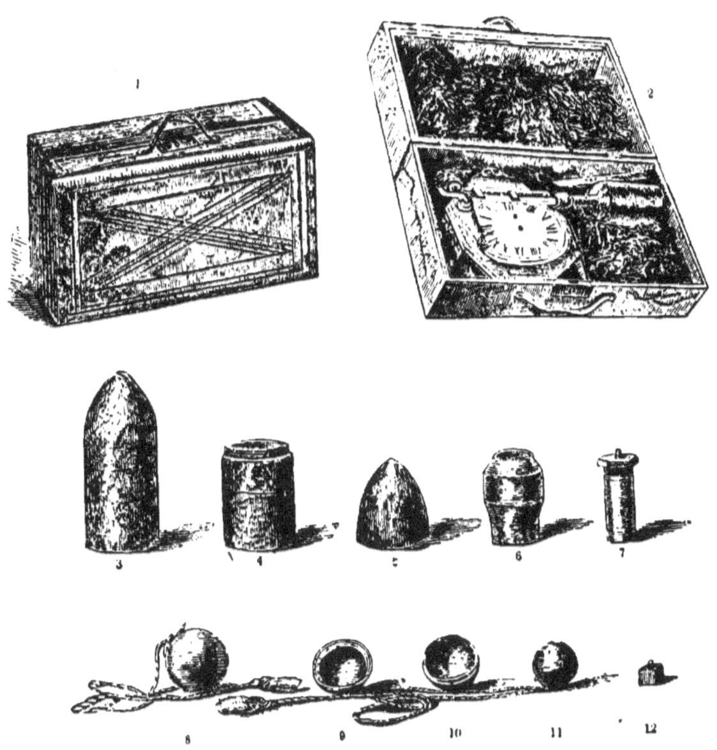

ᴣᴎ⅃ᴜ   ᕕƆƆ19-�.   10th ⅃ᴊ0-ᕐᕼᒪ-
                                ᴣᴘ14ᴜ ᴣᴉᵠƆᴣ1ᵴᴣƆ ᕕᴢᴢᕼᒪᴎ.

ᴜᴣᵠ ᴣᴉᵠƆᴣᴣᴣᵴ22Ɔ,

        ᴉᴎ ᴣ127 40 ᵱᴣᴣᴣᴣ70 ⅄ 100 ᵠᕐ0-ᕐᴣ0 ᴣ5ᵠ
ᴎᕐ2ᵠ -ᵴᴉᵴ40ᴣᵴᵠ   ᴣ- ᴣ0 ᴣᴦᕌᕌᴣ00ᴣᵠᴎ -ᴣᴉ- -ᴣᴣᴎ ᴉᵠᴣ
ᵠᵶᴉᴦᴦᴣ ᴣᴣ -ᴣᴣ ᴣᴉ4ᴣ0 ᴣᴣ ᴣ0ᵠ \ᵠᕐ-ᴣᴣᵠ0 ᕼᴣᴣᴣᴎᴣᕐᴉ-ᴣᴣᴎᴀ.
ᕼᴣᴣᵠᵠᴣ ᴎᕐ2ᵠ ᴣ5ᴣᵠ14ᴎ -ᴣᴉ- -ᴣᴣ 1930 1ᵴᴣᴣ \ᴣ ᵠᴣᴜᴎ
ᴉᴣᴣᵠᴣ0ᴣᴎ ᵴᴣᴣᴣ-.   ᴎᕕᴣᵠ0,   I.I.ᴣL.   ᴣ—ᴉ

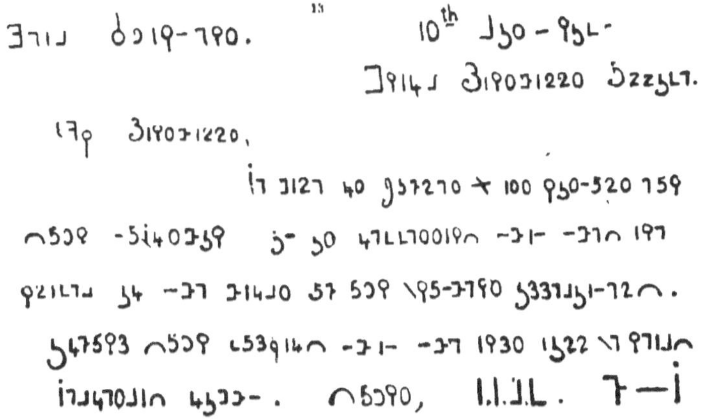

PROCEEDINGS

OF A

MILITARY COMMISSION,

Which convened at Indianapolis, Indiana, by virtue of the following Special Orders,
to wit:

HEADQUARTERS DISTRICT OF INDIANA,
Indianapolis, September 17, 1864.

Special Orders No. 129.

A Military Commission is constituted to meet at the United States Court Rooms in the city of Indianapolis, on the nineteenth (19th) day of September, 1864, at 10 o'clock, A. M., or as soon thereafter as practicable, for the trial of Harrison H. Dodd, and such other prisoners as may be brought before it.

DETAIL FOR THE COMMISSION.

1. Brevet Brigadier General Silas Colgrove, United States Volunteers.
2. Colonel William E. McLean, 43d Infantry, Indiana Volunteers.
3. Colonel John T. Wilder, 17th Infantry, Indiana Volunteers.
4. Colonel Thomas I. Lucas, 16th Infantry, Indiana Volunteers.
5. Colonel Charles D. Murray, 89th Infantry, Indiana Volunteers.
6. Colonel Benjamin Spooner, 83d Infantry, Indiana Volunteers.
7. Colonel Richard P. DeHart, 128th Infantry, Indiana Volunteers.

Major Henry L. Burnett, Judge Advocate Department of the Ohio and Northern Department, Judge Advocate.

The Commission will sit without regard to hours.

By order of Brevet Major General Alvin P. Hovey.   AND C. KEMPER,
Assistant Adjutant General.

Also Special Orders appointing as members of the Commission:

Colonel Ambrose A. Stevens, Veteran Reserve Corps.

Colonel Ansel D. Wass, 60th Infantry, Massachusetts Volunteers.

Colonel Thomas W. Bennett, 69th Infantry, Indiana Volunteers.

Colonel Reuben Williams, 12th Infantry, Indiana Volunteers.

Colonel Albert Heash, 100th Infantry, Indiana Volunteers.

Also a Special Order, authorizing the Judge Advocate to employ an additional phonographic reporter.

———

COURT ROOM, INDIANAPOLIS, INDIANA,
October 21,* 1864, 11 o'clock, A. M.

The Commission met in compliance with the foregoing Special Orders, and pursuant to adjournment.

All the members present;† also the Judge Advocate.

The Commission then proceeded to the trial of William A. Bowles, Andrew Humphreys, Horace Heffren, Lambdin P. Milligan and Stephen Horsey, who were present before the Commission, and who, having heard read the orders appointing the Commission, were severally asked by the Judge Advocate if they had any objection to any member named in the orders, to which William A. Bowles, Andrew Humphreys, Horace Heffner and Stephen Horsey severally replied: "I have none." Lambdin P. Milligan replied, "I have no objection to any member but Colonel Wass."

Colonel Wass having withdrawn from the court-room, the accused, Lambdin P. Milligan, stated his objection as follows:

"I object to Colonel Wass, because he is from a locality where there are extreme prejudices against Western men, and he is likely to be influenced by those prejudices."

The Court was then cleared for deliberation.‡ On being reopened, the Judge Advo-

---

* An informal meeting was held on the 19th, pursuant to adjournment, but the case not being ready for trial, the Commission adjourned over to the 21st.

† If a member of the Commission was absent from sickness, or other unavoidable cause, the case was proceeded with only on the consent of the accused being given in open Court, and such member was only allowed to again take his seat on the Commission with the consent of each and all the accused being given in open Court, and after reading the testimony taken during the absence of such member.

‡ During the trial of these treason cases, the Commission, instead of " clearing the Court," as is the custom in

cate announced to the accused, Lambdin P. Milligan, that his objection was overruled.

Colonel Ansel D. Wass then took his seat as a member of the Commission.

The members of the Commission and the Judge Advocate were then duly sworn in the presence of the accused.

Benn Pitman and W. S. Bush were duly sworn by the Judge Advocate, as recorders to the Commission, also in the presence of the accused.

The accused, William A. Bowles, requested permission to introduce M. M. Ray and J. W. Gordon, Esqrs., as his counsel.

The accused, Andrew Humphreys, requested permission to introduce M. M. Ray, E. A. Davis, Cyrus L. Dunham and J. W. Gordon, Esqrs., as his counsel.

The accused, Horace Heffren, requested permission to introduce Cyrus L. Dunham, E. A. Davis, M. M. Ray and J. W. Gordon, Esqrs., as his counsel.

The accused, Lambdin P. Milligan, requested permission to introduce John R. Coffroth, Esq., as his counsel.

The accused, Stephen Horsey, requested permission to introduce John Baker and C. L. Dunham, Esqrs., as his counsel.

The requests of the accused were granted, and their counsel appeared in Court.

The Judge Advocate stated that he had consented, by agreement with the counsel for the accused, that the question of the jurisdiction of the Commission should be considered at the close of the case, with its full force and effect upon the Commission, as though it were taken up and considered now. It was also agreed between the Judge Advocate and the counsel for the accused, that any substantial objection to the charges and specifications, as now presented, should be considered at the final summing up of the case.

The accused, William A. Bowles, Andrew Humphreys, Horace Heffren, Lambdin P. Milligan and Stephen Horsey were then arraigned on the following charges and specifications:

CHARGES AND SPECIFICATIONS

PREFERRED AGAINST

WILLIAM A. BOWLES, ANDREW HUMPHREYS, HORACE HEFFREN, LAMBDIN P. MILLIGAN, AND STEPHEN HORSEY,

Citizens of the State of Indiana, United States of America.

CHARGE FIRST.—Conspiracy against the Government of the United States.

SPECIFICATION FIRST.—In this, that the said Wm. A. Bowles, Andrew Humphreys,

Horace Heffren, Lambdin P. Milligan, and Stephen Horsey, did, among themselves, and with Harrison H. Dodd, of Indiana, Joshua F. Bullitt, of Kentucky, J. A. Barrett, of Missouri, and others, conspire against the Government and duly constituted authorities of the United States, and did join themselves to, and secretly organize and disseminate, a secret, unlawful society or order, known as the Order of American Knights, or Order of the Sons of Liberty, having both a civil and military organization and jurisdiction, for the purpose of overthrowing the Government and duly constituted authorities of the United States. This, at a period of war and armed rebellion against the authority of the United States, at or near Indianapolis, Indiana, a State within the military lines of the Army of the United States, and the theater of military operations, and which had been, and was constantly threatened to be, invaded by the enemy. This, on or about the 16th day of May, 1864.

SPECIFICATION SECOND.—In this, that the said Wm. A. Bowles, Andrew Humphreys, Horace Heffren, Lambdin P. Milligan, and Stephen Horsey, during an existing rebellion against the Government and authorities of the United States—said rebellion claiming to be in the name of, and on behalf of certain States, being a part of and owing allegiance to the United States—did combine and agree with one Harrison H. Dodd, of Indiana, Joshua F. Bullitt, of Kentucky, J. A. Barrett, of Missouri, and others, to adopt and impart to others the creed or ritual of a secret, unlawful society or order, known as the Order of American Knights, or Order of the Sons of Liberty, denying the authority of the United States to coerce to submission certain rebellious citizens of said United States, designing thereby to lessen the power and prevent the increase of the armies of the United States, and thereby did recognize and sustain the right of the citizens and States, then in rebellion, to disregard and resist the authority of the United States. This, at a period of war and armed rebellion against the authority of the United States, at or near the city of Indianapolis, Indiana, a State within the military lines of the Army of the United States, and the theater of military operations, which had been, and was threatened to be, invaded by the enemy. This, on or about the 22d day of February, 1864.

SPECIFICATION THIRD.—In this, that the said Wm. A. Bowles, Andrew Humphreys, Horace Heffren, Lambdin P. Milligan, and Stephen Horsey, citizens of the State of Indiana, owing true faith and allegiance to the Government of the United States, and while pretending to be peaceable, loyal citizens of the Government, did secretly and covertly combine, agree, and conspire,

---

military courts, retired to an adjoining room for deliberation, to avoid the inconvenience of dismissing the audience assembled to listen to the proceedings.

among themselves, and with one Harrison H. Dodd, of Indiana, Joshua F. Bullitt, of Kentucky, J. A. Barrett, of Missouri, and others, to overthrow and render powerless the Government of the United States, and did, in pursuance of said combination, agreement and conspiracy, form and organize a certain unlawful, secret society or order, and did extend, and assist in extending, said unlawful secret society or order, known as the Order of American Knights, or Order of Sons of Liberty, whose intent and purpose was to cripple and render powerless the efforts of the Government of the United States, in suppressing a then existing formidable rebellion against said Government. This, on or about the 1st day of October, 1863, at a period of war and armed rebellion, at or near the city of Indianapolis, Indiana, a State within the military lines of the Army of the United States, and the theater of military operations, which had been, and was constantly threatened to be, invaded by the enemy.

SPECIFICATION FOURTH.—In this, that the said Wm. A. Bowles, Andrew Humphreys, Horace Heffren, Lambdin P. Milligan, and Stephen Horsey, did conspire and agree with Harrison H. Dodd, David T. Yeagle, John C. Walker, and Joshua F. Bullitt, and others, these men at that time holding military positions and rank in a certain secret, unlawful society or organization, known as the Order of American Knights, or Order of the Sons of Liberty, to seize by force the United States and State Arsenals at Indianapolis, Indiana, Columbus, Ohio, and Springfield, Illinois, to release by force the rebel prisoners held by the authorities of the United States, at Camp Douglas, Illinois, Camp Morton, Indiana, and Camp Chase, Ohio, and the Depot of Prisoners of War on Johnson's Island; and arm those prisoners with the arms thus seized, and that then said conspirators, with all the forces they were able to raise in the secret order above-named, were, in conjunction with the rebel prisoners thus released and armed, to march into Kentucky and Missouri, and co-operate with the rebel forces to be sent to those States by the rebel authorities, against the Government and authorities of the United States. This, on or about the 20th day of July, 1864, at a period of war and rebellion against the authority of the United States, at or near the city of Chicago, Illinois, a State within the lines of the Army of the United States, and the theater of military operations, and threatened by invasion of the enemy.

Charge Second.—Affording aid and comfort to Rebels against the authority of the United States.

SPECIFICATION FIRST.—In this, that the said Wm. A. Bowles, Andrew Humphreys,

Horace Heffren, Lambdin P. Milligan, and Stephen Horsey, being then members of a certain secret, unlawful society, or order, known as the Order of American Knights, or Order of the Sons of Liberty—the United States being then in arms to suppress a rebellion in certain States against the authority of the United States—said Wm. A. Bowles, Andrew Humphreys, Horace Heffren, Lambdin P. Milligan, Stephen Horsey, and others, then and there acting as members and officers of said secret, unlawful society or order, did design and plot to communicate with the enemies of the United States, and did communicate with the enemies of the United States, with the intent that they should, in large force, invade the territory of the United States, to-wit: the States of Kentucky, Indiana, and Illinois; with the further intent, that the so-called secret, unlawful society, or order, aforesaid, should then and there co-operate with the said armed forces of the said rebellion against the authority of the United States, and did communicate to said armed forces the intent and purposes of said secret, unlawful society or order. This, at a period of war and armed rebellion against the authority of the United States, at or near the city of Indianapolis, Indiana, a State within the military lines of the Army of the United States, and the theater of military operations, which had been, and was constantly threatened to be, invaded by the enemies of the United States. This, on or about the 16th day of May, 1864.

SPECIFICATION SECOND.—In this, that the said Wm. A. Bowles, Andrew Humphreys, Horace Heffren, Lambdin P. Milligan, and Stephen Horsey, while the Government was attempting by force of arms to suppress an existing rebellion, while guerrillas, and other armed supporters of the rebellion, were in the State of Kentucky, did send a messenger, and brother member with them of a secret, unlawful society or order, known as the Order of American Knights, or Order of the Sons of Liberty, into said State of Kentucky, with instructions for Joshua F. Bullitt, Grand Commander of said secret, unlawful society or order, in said State, and other members of said secret society or order in said State, to select good couriers or runners, to go upon short notice, and for the purpose of assisting those in rebellion against the United States, to call to arms the members of said secret society or order, and other sympathizers with the existing rebellion, whenever a signal should be given by the authorities of said secret society or order. This, on or about the 20th day of July, 1864, at a period of war and armed rebellion against the authority of the United States, at or near Indianapolis, Indiana, a State within the military lines of the Army of the United States, and the theater of military operations, and which had been, and was constantly threatened to be, invaded by the enemy.

SPECIFICATION THIRD.—In this, that the said Wm. A. Bowles, Andrew Humphreys, Horace Heffren, Lambdin P. Milligan, and Stephen Horsey, being citizens of the State of Indiana, United States of America, and owing true allegiance to the said United States, did join themselves to a certain unlawful, secret society or order, known as the Order of American Knights, or Order of Sons of Liberty, designed for the overthrow of the Government of the United States, and to compel terms with the citizens or authorities of the so-called Confederate States, the same being portions of the United States, and in rebellion against the authority of the United States, and did communicate the designs and intent of said order to those in rebellion against the Government of the United States. This, on or about the 20th day of July, 1864, at a period of war and armed rebellion against the authority of the United States, at or near Indianapolis, Indiana, a State within the military lines of the Army of the United States, and the theater of military operations, and which had been, and was constantly threatened to be, invaded by the enemy.

CHARGE THIRD.—Inciting Insurrection.

SPECIFICATION FIRST.—In this, that the said Wm. A. Bowles, Andrew Humphreys, Horace Heffren, Lambdin P. Milligan, and Stephen Horsey, did, during a time of war between the United States and armed enemies of the United States, and of rebellion against its Government, organize and attempt to arm, and did arm, a portion of the citizens of the United States through an unlawful, secret society or order, known as the Order of American Knights, or Order of the Sons of Liberty, with the intent to induce them, with themselves, to throw off the authority of the United States, and co-operate with said armed enemies of the United States, against the legally constituted authorities of the United States. This, on or about the 20th day of July, 1864, at or near Indianapolis, Indiana, a State within the military lines of the army of the United States, and the theater of military operations, and which had been, and was constantly threatened to be, invaded by the enemy.

SPECIFICATION SECOND.—In this, that the said William A. Bowles, Andrew Humphreys, Horace Heffren, Lambdin P. Milligan, and Stephen Horsey, did, by public addresses, by secret circulars and communications, and by other means, endeavor to, and did arouse sentiments of hostility to the Government of the United States, and did attempt to induce the people to revolt against said Government, and secretly organize and arm themselves for the purpose of resisting the laws of the United States, and the orders of the duly elected

President thereof. This, on or about the 16th day of February, 1864, at a period of war and armed rebellion against the authority of the United States, at or near Indianapolis, Indiana, a State within the military lines of the army of the United States, and the theater of military operations, and which had been, and was constantly threatened to be, invaded by the enemy.

CHARGE FOURTH.—Disloyal Practices.

SPECIFICATION FIRST.—In this, that the said Wm. A. Bowles, Andrew Humphreys, Horace Heffren, Lambdin P. Milligan, and Stephen Horsey, at a time of war, and during an armed rebellion against the legally constituted authorities and Government of the United States, did counsel and advise citizens of, and owing allegiance and military service to the United States, to disregard the authority of the United States, and to resist a call or draft, designed to increase the army of the United States, and did make preparation, and attempt to arm, and did arm, certain citizens of the United States, belonging to a certain unlawful, secret society or order, known as the Order of American Knights, or Order of the Sons of Liberty, for the purpose and with the intent of resisting said call or draft. This, on or about the 1st day of July, 1864, at or near Shoal's Station, Martin county, Indiana, a State within the military lines of the army of the United States, and the theater of military operations, and which had been, and was constantly threatened to be, invaded by the enemy.

SPECIFICATION SECOND.—In this, that the said Wm. A. Bowles, Andrew Humphreys, Horace Heffren, Lambdin P. Milligan, and Stephen Horsey, at a time of war, and during an armed rebellion against the legally constituted authorities and Government of the United States, did counsel and advise citizens of, and owing allegiance and military service to the United States, to disregard the authority of the United States, and to resist a call or draft, designed to increase the army of the United States, and did make preparation, and attempt to arm, and did arm, certain citizens of the United States, belonging to a certain unlawful, secret society or order, known as the Order of American Knights, or Order of the Sons of Liberty, for the purpose and with the intent of resisting said call or draft. This, on or about the 1st day of November, 1863, at or near Green Fork township, Randolph county, Indiana, a State within the military lines of the army of the United States, and the theater of military operations, and which had been, and was constantly threatened to be, invaded by the enemy.

SPECIFICATION THIRD.—In this, that the said Wm. A. Bowles, Andrew Humphreys, Horace Heffren, Lambdin P. Milligan and

Stephen Horsey, at a time of war, and during an armed rebellion against the legally constituted authorities and Government of the United States, did counsel and advise citizens of, and owing allegiance and military service to, the United States, to disregard the authority of the United States, and to resist a call or draft, designed to increase the army of the United States, and did make preparation, and did attempt to arm, and did arm, certain citizens of the United States, belonging to a certain unlawful secret society or order, known as the Order of American Knights, or Order of Sons of Liberty, for the purpose and with the intent of resisting said call or draft. This, on or about the 16th day of May, 1864, at or near Indianapolis, Indiana, a State within the military lines of the army of the United States, and the theater of military operations, and which had been, and was constantly threatened to be, invaded by the enemy.

SPECIFICATION FOURTH.—In this, that the said Wm. A. Bowles, Andrew Humphreys, Horace Heffren, Lambdin P. Milligan, and Stephen Horsey, at a time of war, and during an armed rebellion against the legally constituted authorities and Government of the United States, did counsel and advise citizens of, and owing allegiance and military service to, the United States, to disregard the authority of the United States, and to resist a call or draft, designed to increase the army of the United States, and did make preparation and attempt to arm, and did arm, certain citizens of the United States, belonging to a certain unlawful secret society or order, known as the Order of American Knights, or Order of the Sons of Liberty, for the purpose and with the intent of resisting said call or draft. This, on or about the first day of August, 1864, at or near Salem, Washington county, Indiana, a State within the military lines of the army of the United States, and the theater of military operations, and which had been, and was constantly threatened to be, invaded by the enemy.

SPECIFICATION FIFTH.—In this, that the said Wm. A. Bowles, Andrew Humphreys, Horace Heffren, Lambdin P. Milligan, and Stephen Horsey, did accept and hold offices of the military forces for the State of Indiana, in a certain unlawful secret society, or order, known as the Order of American Knights, or Order of the Sons of Liberty, which said offices and military forces were unknown to the Constitution and laws of the United States, or of the State of Indiana, and were not in aid of, but opposed to, the legally constituted authorities thereof. This, on or about the 16th day of February, 1864, at a time of war and armed rebellion against the authority of the United States, at or near Indianapolis, Indiana, a State within the military lines of the army of the United States, and the theater of military operations, and which had been, and was constantly threatened to be, invaded by the enemy.

CHARGE FIFTH.—*Violation of the Laws of War.*

SPECIFICATION FIRST.—In this, that the said Wm. A. Bowles, Andrew Humphreys, Horace Heffren, Lambdin P. Milligan, and Stephen Horsey, did, while the Government of the United States was carrying on war with the enemies of the United States, engaged in rebellion against their authority, while pretending to be peaceable, loyal citizens of the United States, violate their allegiance, and did, as citizens of said Government, attempt to introduce said enemies of the United States into the loyal States of said United States, thereby to overthrow and destroy the authority of the United States. This, on or about the 16th day of May, 1864, at or near the city of Indianapolis, Indiana, a State within the military lines of the army of the United States, and the theater of military operations, which had been, and was constantly threatened to be, invaded by the enemy.

SPECIFICATION SECOND.—In this, that the said Wm. A. Bowles, Andrew Humphreys, Horace Heffren, Lambdin P. Milligan, and Stephen Horsey, did, during a war between the United States and the said enemies of the United States, engaged in rebellion against their authority, and while pretending to be peaceable, loyal citizens of the United States, organize and extend a certain unlawful, secret society or order, known as the Order of American Knights, or Order of the Sons of Liberty, having for its purpose the same general object and design as the said enemies of the United States, and with the intent to aid and insure the success of said enemies in their resistance to the legally constituted authorities of the United States. This, at or near the city of Indianapolis, Indiana, on or about the 16th day of May, 1864.

HENRY L. BURNETT,
Judge Advocate Department of the Ohio and Northern Department.

To which charges and specifications the accused, all and severally, to each and all the charges and specifications, pleaded NOT GUILTY.

The Judge Advocate then asked the accused if they were ready for trial.

J. W. Gordon, counsel for the accused, William A. Bowles, Horace Heffren, and Andrew Humphreys, moved for a separate trial in their behalf, and submitted the following reasons:

Mr. President and Gentlemen of the Commission:

Recognizing the law which governs this Commission—as the common law, the old English common law, which has been adopted by every State in the Union—as the law which shall influence this Commission in determining how these defendants shall be tried, I ask you to favor them each with a separate trial. All the States, I believe, have enacted statutes on this subject. Our own State has enacted a statute providing for separate trials of defendants jointly charged with criminal offenses. The civil courts of the United States generally accord to the defendant, or person charged with an offense, the same rule of practice which they enjoy as a right in their State courts. But we do not ask a separate trial on that ground. We put the plea on the discretion of this Court, as governed by the common law, believing that these defendants have interests that can not be subserved by trying them together, and as a matter of justice I ask the Court for their severance on trial. In behalf of Horace Heffren, Andrew Humphreys and William A. Bowles, for whom I appear, I move the Court for a separate trial for them.

I may also state to the Court a fact which will be apparent on the trial of these causes. Each will have separate witnesses, and will pursue a different line of defense. Each has his own character to defend. The trial going on as one trial during the prosecution, will assume in the defense the attitude of separate trials, and the defendants and their counsel will labor under great inconveniences and difficulties in their behalf.

Another point I make is, that as these men are all charged as citizens of Indiana, they are entitled as such to separate trials, as there are no rules laid down for the regulation of these trials, and one might put in a plea on that ground. We trust the motion for a separate trial for the defendants to the discretion of the Commission, as a matter of justice to the accused.

Cyrus L. Dunham, counsel for Stephen Horsey, one of the accused, moved for a separate trial for the accused, for the following reasons:

It is, in my opinion, entirely without precedent in Military Courts, to put two prisoners on trial at the same time. Defendants, jointly charged, are entitled to all the benefits they can derive from separate trials. In a joint trial, the evidence introduced against one defendant might militate against another, and bear more strongly against him than if he was tried separately. The prosecution, he presumed, would, in its evidence, follow the line pursued in the Dodd trial, proving one act of one party by one witness, and separate acts of other parties by other witnesses. The defense would branch out into separate lines, according to the side issues presented. The evidence might not bear as strongly against one defendant as against the other, and this might confuse the Commission when it comes to a final decision.

Lambdin P. Milligan, one of the accused, moved in his own behalf, for a separate trial, for the following reasons:

"It is exceedingly inconvenient for me to be present at the trial, on account of sickness. I wish as short a trial as possible, and the evidence introduced against others may protract the trial to great length. It is impossible, I am advised by my physicians, to be in any position but a recumbent one, without permanent injury to my limb. If granted a separate trial, I will waive all technical objections in the progress of the case. For these reasons, I ask the Commission to grant me a separate trial."

The Judge Advocate replied:

Gentlemen of the Commission:

An application has been presented to the Commission, from each of the accused, for a separate trial. I do not propose personally to object to those applications. I only desire to put before the minds of the Court the reasons and facts that present themselves to my mind against the grant of the application.

The offenses charged against these defendants are joint. They are in the nature of a conspiracy. Conspiracy is the gist of the charges, and the other offenses charged grew out of this. Once having established the conspiracy, the acts of any one of the conspirators are liable to be brought in proof as evidence against any other member of the conspiracy. About that principle of law there can be no question. Not only can the acts of any member of a common conspiracy be brought as proof against other co-conspirators, but also their admissions, their letters, their writings, and the records they leave behind them. In that case, the proof on the part of the Government will be no more complicated in the matter of proof against the accused in a joint trial than if separate trials were granted. The proof against one is proof against all the accused. That being the case, we may prove against Milligan the acts of Dodd, and the testimony introduced by Milligan that he did not do these acts himself, constitutes no defense for him. When he takes upon himself the responsibility of joining an unlawful body, he takes upon himself the responsibility for every unlawful act of that body. The law also holds that when men combine together for such purposes, having greater power for evil through such an organization, they shall be held to a greater accountability. There is also a greater latitude given in proof against conspirators than against any other class of criminals known to the law. That being the case, the argument for a separate defense has but little weight. Even if it is important that each man should put his character in issue and prove his good character, he can do that as well when on trial jointly as singly. You, gentlemen of the Commission, make up your verdict against each one of these defendants separately. If you find that any one of these men has been misled, you may take into consideration the absence of evil intent in joining this organization, as well in a joint trial as in separate trials. There is no argument the accused can advance against joint trials which will show that they are deprived of any rights and privileges which would accrue from separate trials. They can not, and do not claim that under the common law they may sever these prisoners and introduce them as witnesses, one in favor of the other. They know that they can not do that. No benefit in that respect would accrue to them from a separate trial.

The question submitted to the Court is a matter of policy simply, and in respect to that, there are two important considerations. There are the rights and privileges of the accused to be considered, and also the rights and privileges of the Government. One should be weighed and balanced against the other. I would say to the Commission, give to the defendants the greatest possible latitude consistent with the interests of the Government, where no rights will be waived. I will grant them every thing that involves mere form and courtesy. I will go further to issue processes to bring in witnesses for the accused than I would for the Government. But while granting all possible latitude to the accused, I can not forget that there comes up a strong plea from unnumbered thousands who have an interest in the results of this Commission.

There are, sitting around me officers, none under the rank of Colonel; one who presides over the Commission, with the rank of Brevet Brigadier General. Each of you is entitled to command a regiment of one thousand men; and some, if not all of you, were in command of brigades in the field, numbering from one to three thousand men. You are the representatives of fifteen thousand men at least, who, under your leadership, would do gallant service for your country. You, gentlemen of the Commission, are needed in the field, and whether you shall consume unnecessary time by protracting these trials, is a matter of importance to the Government, and to the untold millions who look forward with interest and hope to the future for the success of its armies.

There is also another consideration of some importance to the Government. You sit on this Commission at a great cost to the Government, for the pay of members, of witnesses, and other expenses. That is a point to be considered in determining the motion for separate trials. If no rights of the accused are to be prejudiced by a joint trial, the question in economy becomes an important argument in favor of proceeding with the trial of the prisoners as arraigned.

I would also add, that if any single right of any one of the accused would be prejudiced by a joint trial, I would not urge it. I have looked at this matter in all its lights, and can not see that, individually, they will be prejudicial in a single right which they would have if separate trials were accorded them.

As Judge Advocate of this Department, I have vast rights, duties and responsibilities. My detention here will result in holding hundreds of persons now in prison, charged with military offenses, who are waiting their trials. I have to organize Courts for their trials, to prefer the charges against them, and exercise a general supervision over the proceedings of these courts. There are other men besides the prisoners now in Court, who are asking of the Government a speedy hearing. They have rights at stake as well as the accused here. While, therefore, I ask of you no one thing which can do the accused any wrong, or which will limit them in bringing every fact, which will accrue to their benefit, before this Commission, while I would grant them every possible courtesy, I must ask the Commission to use its discretion so wisely, that it shall not wrong others, or the Government.

One of the counsel for the accused states that he has examined military books, and has not found a single case where prisoners have been jointly arraigned before a military court. I will state that in my military experience, and as Judge Advocate, I have not seen a single case that did not make precedents. This war has been constantly making precedents. The army of the United States has exceeded in magnitude, during this war, any thing conceived by the founders of this Government. The army has progressed in all respects further in two years than it would have done in two centuries at its former rate of existence. This fact has given rise to new conditions. We do not act entirely in accordance with the common law, as recognized two centuries ago, but settle its principles, as applied to military offenses, and make precedents, in every case which we try in military courts. We make precedents in the government of the army, and in the military courts. All that the accused have a right to ask here is, that this Commission violate no law, and do them exact justice. I, therefore, submit to you for decision the application for a severance of the defendants.

The court-room was then cleared for the purpose of deliberation on the application of the accused.

On the re-opening of the court-room, the Judge Advocate announced that the Commission proposed to hold the application of the accused under advisement until 2½ o'clock, P. M.

The Commission then adjourned, to meet at half past 2 o'clock P. M.

AFTERNOON SESSION.

COURT ROOM, INDIANAPOLIS, INDIANA,
October 21, 1864, 2½ o'clock, P. M.

The Commission met pursuant to adjournment.

All the members present. Also, the Judge Advocate, the accused and their counsel.

The court-room was then cleared for deliberation on the question of granting the accused a separate trial.

On the re-opening of the Court, the Judge Advocate announced to the accused that the Commission, after a full and careful deliberation of the question, had concluded that in view of the fact, that no right or rights of any of the accused, in any particular, would be prejudiced by a joint trial, it was their duty to proceed with the trial of the prisoners as they were arraigned.

William M. Harrison, a witness for the Government, was then introduced, and being duly sworn by the Judge Advocate, testified as follows:

Question by the Judge Advocate: Please give to the Court your name and residence?

Answer. William M. Harrison; I reside in this city.

Q. State your business for the last year or two?

A. I have been in no particular business for the last year. I was traveling and collecting for George W. Howes a portion of the time during last year.

Q. Have you had any other employ for which you received pay and compensation?

A. I was employed as Grand Secretary of the Grand Council of the Sons of Liberty in the State of Indiana, at a salary of $800 per annum. I became a member of the Grand Council, on or about the 27th of August, 1863, and became Grand Secretary of the Grand Council on or about the 10th of September, 1863.

Q. When and where did you first have any knowledge of the Order of American Knights, or Order of the Sons of Liberty, or Knights of the Golden Circle?

A. The first knowledge I ever had of the Order of American Knights was at Terre Haute, on or about the 27th of August, 1863. I received a letter from H. H. Dodd at Terre Haute, requesting me to go there; when there I was invited to attend a meeting that night. I did so; there were but twelve or fifteen present.

Q. Whom did you meet there?

A. Among those I recollect were P. C. Wright, and a person by the name of D. R Eckles, John E. Risley, Callum Bayley and John G. Davis. Most of them were strangers to me.

Q. What was done at that meeting?

A. Mr. Wright appeared to have charge of the meeting. He stated that it was called for the purpose of organizing a secret society. He proceeded to initiate members, and, after that, to organize the Grand Council of the State of Indiana. Those who were initiated, were initiated in the three degrees at the same time.

Q. Were you initiated in the three degrees at that time?

A. I was.

Q. Who were elected officers?

A. D. R. Eckles was elected Temporary Grand Commander; H. H. Dodd, Temporary Deputy Grand Commander; John E. Risley, Temporary Grand Secretary, and I was elected Temporary Assistant Secretary.

Q. Where was the next meeting held?

A. In this city, about the 10th of September following, at the Military Hall, over Talbot & Co.'s jewelry store. It was an adjourned meeting of the Grand Council that had met at Terre Haute. It convened about 9 or 10 in the morning of, I think, the 10th of September. They adjourned at noon, and met again at 2 o'clock.

Q. What business did they transact?

A. In the morning, those persons who were delegates from various counties, who had not been initiated into the Order, were initiated by Mr. Wright.

Q. Who was President?

A. Mr. Dodd, both in the forenoon and afternoon. Mr. Wright initiated members present who had never received degrees; after he got through initiating those, he initiated the members present in the Grand Council Degree, and declared the Council open for business. I was initiated in that degree.

Q. In what did it differ from others?

A. Simply in the sign of recognition and colloquy.

Q. Who were initiated that day?

A. David T. Yeakle and Dr. Bowles. The great majority of the members were initiated on that day.

Q. Were any other citizens, now present in this court room, initiated that day, that you remember?

A. No, sir.

Q. Was any other business done besides the initiation of members?

A. After the members had been initiated in the Grand Council Degree, Mr. Wright declared the Council ready for business, and proceeded to the election of officers, which resulted in the election of H. H. Dodd as Grand Commander, and David T. Yeakle, Deputy Grand Commander. I was elected Grand Secretary. We immediately proceeded to other business. A committee, under the name of a military committee, was appointed to draft a military bill. Mr. Dodd was a member, and Yeakle and Bowles. I think there were one or two others, but I do not remember their names.

Q. Was any military bill drafted by them?

A. It was the subject of discussion in the afternoon.

Q. What became of it?

A. It was in my possession, and I destroyed it.

Q. When?

A. I destroyed all the papers belonging to the organization after the exposition in the Indianapolis *Journal*.

Q. Give the Court the features of that bill, as near as you can recollect.

A. It provided for the division of the State into four districts; the National Road divided the north and south parts of the State. The names of the districts were the North-eastern, North-western, South-eastern and South-western. The counties in these districts were divided as nearly equal as could be. It also went into detail to provide for the organization of the whole military force, the number and size of the regiments to be raised, duties of officers, etc.

Q. What was to be the size of the regiments?

A. They were to consist of nine companies of infantry, one company of rifles, and one section of artillery. The bill provided for the election of major generals; and they spoke of providing that major generals should appoint brigadiers, the brigadiers appoint colonels, colonels appoint the captains, and captains the subordinate officers.

Q. Were any major generals appointed?

A. Yes, sir; David T. Yeakle and Andrew Humphreys were appointed under that bill; Mr. Milligan, and Mr. Conklin, living of this city. These four were all.

Q. Was Milligan appointed one of the major generals?

A. Yes, sir.

Q. Do you know him?

A. I see him there.

The witness here pointed to the accused, Lambdin P. Milligan.

Q. Is that the Milligan you have reference to?

A. Yes, sir.

Q. Do you see any others present in the court room who were appointed major generals?

A. Dr. Bowles I see present, and Mr. Humphreys.

The witness here pointed to the accused, Wm. A. Bowles and Andrew Humphreys.

Q. Is that the Dr. Bowles who was present at that meeting?

A. It is.

Q. Is that the Andrew Humphreys who was appointed major general?

A. Yes, sir.

Q. Were any other appointments made then?

A. No, sir.

Q. Were any of those appointments made outside of the membership of the order?

A. My understanding of the matter was, that appointments were made among members of the order only.

Q. Were any speeches made at that meeting?

A. Dr. Bowles spoke at considerable length, but I do not remember the matter of his remarks, except that they were on the features of the military bill. Dr. Yeakle spoke on the same subject.

Q. State whether or not, at that meeting, he urged the arming of the members of the order.

A. As far as I recollect, I can not say.

Q. To what time did it adjourn?

A. To meet during the month of November following.

Q. State if it met, and if so, who presided.

A. It did, at the former place of meeting. Harrison H. Dodd presided, and I acted as secretary.

Q. Who were present?

A. Mr. Milligan and J. J. Bingham, and delegates were present from some thirty counties.

Q. Were any others present at that meeting that you now see in this court room?

A. I do not think there were. Neither Stephen Horsey, Andrew Humphreys, nor Horace Heffren was present. Dr. Bowles was present.

Q. Was L. P. Milligan present?

A. Yes, sir.

Q. State what was done at that meeting.

A. There was not much business transacted. A committee was appointed to get up a prospectus of a newspaper, to advocate the distinctive principle of the order. That was discussed at considerable length. There was some discussion in regard to the extension of the Democratic party. The extension of the order in the various counties was particularly talked of. Discussion on education also took place at that meeting. No speeches were made at that meeting, as far as I can recollect; they did not go beyond an organization for political purposes.

Q. What was said at that meeting about the object of the military organization?

A. Nothing was said about it, except that it was necessary to organize in a military capacity, to protect the rights of the members against the encroachments of the Administration.

Q. Where was the next meeting?

A. It was held in this city, on the 16th or 17th of February, 1864.

Q. Were there present any of the persons now in the court room, as far as you remember?

A. Mr. Heffren, Mr. Milligan and Mr. Bowles were present. Mr. Humphreys and Mr. Horsey were not present. I can not say positively whether Mr. Milligan was present or not; he was absent from one meeting, and I think it was that one. Heffren and Bowles made speeches.

Q. What was the general object of this meeting of the 16th or 17th?

A. It was the regular annual meeting of the organization. It had been said that the anniversary of the order was the 22d of February. It was called in advance of the meeting of the Supreme Council to be held in New York on the 22d, to enable delegates to attend that meeting. At that meeting an election of officers took place.

Q. Who were elected?

A. H. H. Dodd, Grand Commander, Horace Heffren, Deputy Grand Commander, and myself Grand Secretary.

Q. Was there any voting in regard to major generals?

A. The election of major generals took place at the same meeting. Humphreys was elected in his district, Milligan in his district, and Bowles was elected in the south-west district. Walker was elected in the north-western district.

Q. Did Yeakle or others resign?

A. No, sir.

Q. How did they get out of office?

A. All officers were to be elected yearly. The first elections were made until the 22d day of February. As this was the annual meeting, a new election was held, that resulted as I have just stated.

Q. Who were the delegates to the New York meeting?

A. Several delegates were elected by the Grand Council at the New York meeting. I can not say positively who were elected in February.

Q. Can you state some of the delegates to the various meetings in September and November?

A. At the meeting in September, John G. Davis and D. R. Eckles were elected delegates to the Council in Chicago, in September, 1863, and I think Humphreys also.

Q. To what Council?

A. The Supreme Council. Milligan was elected delegate to the Supreme Council. Dodd was elected to the Supreme Council by virtue of his office.

How many attended?

A. I understood Dodd that Milligan was present at the meeting of the Supreme Council at Chicago or New York, and Humphreys was present either at the Chicago or New York meeting, I do not recollect which. Dr. Bowles was present at one or both places. The first meeting was held in Chicago, in the latter part of the month of September, 1863.

Q. Was Dodd at that meeting?

A. He left to attend it; I understood he was there himself. I understood also that Humphreys was present at that meeting, and Yeakle and Dr. Bowles. I got this information from Dodd.

Q. Have you no means of telling whether Milligan was present at that meeting?

A. None but the information I derived from Dodd. I have no means of saying positively.

Q. Was any written address read at the meeting of February 16th and 17th?

A. Yes, sir; an address was read by Mr. Dodd, which was subsequently printed and circulated among the members of the order.

Q. How?

A. An order was passed that the address of the Grand Commander and such portion of the proceedings of the State Council as was necessary should be printed.

Q. What was that?

A. That the address of the Grand Commander, the report of the Grand Secretary, and the report of the Finance Committee, should be printed. After the meeting adjourned, it was printed in pamphlet form; and I sent two copies to each branch Temple in the State.

Q. Did you send to any of the lodges where Mr. Milligan lives?

A. I sent them to Huntington county, directing them to Mr. Milligan.

Q. Did you send any to Mr. Humphreys' county?

A. Yes, sir; directing them to Mr. Humphreys?

Q. How many did you send?

A. Two of the addresses to each one.

Q. Did you send any to Dr. Bowles?

A. I think I did; I generally sent two to each county.

Q. Did you send any to Mr. Heffren?

A. I can not say positively whether I sent any to Heffren or not.

Q. Is that one of the pamphlets you have spoken of?

[A pamphlet entitled "Proceedings of the Grand Council of the State of Indiana," was here handed to the witness by the Judge Advocate.]

A. It is.

Q. What does that pamphlet contain?

A. It contains an address delivered by Dodd, and proceedings of the State Council, and the reports of committees.

Q. Was this pamphlet sent out to the counties in which the order existed?

A. Yes, sir.

[The pamphlet entitled "Proceedings of the Grand Council of the State of Indiana," was here put in evidence by the Judge Advocate. See Appendix.]

The Commission then adjourned, to meet on Saturday, October 22, 1864, at 10 o'clock, A. M.

COURT ROOM, INDIANAPOLIS, INDIANA,
October 22, 1864, 10 A. M. }

The Commission met pursuant to adjournment.

All the members present. Also, the Judge Advocate, the accused, and their counsel.

The proceedings were read and approved.

The accused, Andrew Humphreys, then made the following application to the Commission:

"I respectfully request that E. H. C. Cavins, Esq., and William Mack, Esq., may be admitted to act as counsel for me upon the trial of this cause.

[Signed.] ANDREW HUMPHREYS,
"For himself."

Which application was granted, and the counsel appeared for the accused.

The testimony of Wm. M. Harrison, a witness for the Government, was then continued as follows:

Question by the Judge Advocate:

State what the circular now handed you is?

Answer. This circular is one I sent out to the various County Temples, with a copy of the Constitution and By-Laws for the County and Branch Temples. The circular was read to the Court by the Judge Advocate. Said circular introduced in evidence.*

Q. Did you, or did you not, inclose one of these circulars with all the addresses you sent to the different County Temples?

A. With that circular I sent out a copy of the Constitution of the Grand Council, and one or two copies of the proceedings of the meeting held here on the 16th and 17th days of February.

Q. For what purpose was this assessment referred to made?

A. For defraying the expenses of the Grand Council.

Q. What was the nature of those expenses?

A. Payment for printing, the salary of the Secretary, and the payment of the assessment of the Supreme Council, as well as for the payment of rent and other expenses.

Q. Were any members of the different County Temples sent in pursuance of the last clause of this circular?

A. Members were sent with respect to the change in the Ritual of the organization. The obligations and the lessons and a portion of the passwords and colloquies had been changed.

Q. Was there any change in the name of order?

A. Yes, sir; the name of the order had been changed to the Order of the Sons of Liberty.

Q. When and by what authority was that change made?

A. It was made at the meeting of the Supreme Council. I was informed by Dodd that the change was made by the authority of the Supreme Council on the 22d day of February.

Q. Do your records show any change in the name of the order?

A. No, sir. I never made any record of the change in the proceedings of the meetings.

Q. From whom did you first receive information of the change?

A. From Dodd.

Q. What position did he occupy?

A. That of Grand Commander of the State of Indiana.

Q. How soon after the 22d day of February did you learn of this change?

A. Immediately after the arrival of Dodd here; but I can not state positively. It was within two or three weeks after the 22d of February.

Q. Was that change made known to the subordinate lodges throughout the State? If so, how?

A. It was made known by means of the circular just read, and through the agents sent out to give information.

Q. Did any messengers come up from Mr. Milligan's district?

A. I believe there were some from his Congressional District. I have no recollection of any messengers coming up from his county. There were a number of counties in that Congressional District that were organized in this society.

Q. Was any person sent up from Mr. Humphreys' district or county?

A. No, sir; but persons came up from Sullivan county to obtain instructions, and I believe persons also came up from Vigo county for instructions.

Q. You may state what these changes were.

A. A change was made in the name of the organization; a change was also made in the colloquies of the order, in the obligations, and also in the lessons.

A pamphlet was here handed to the witness.

---

*OFFICE GRAND SECRETARY, S. L.,
Indianapolis, ——, 1864.

Mr. ——— ———

DEAR SIR: Inclosed please find the Constitution for the government of *County and Branch Temples*, the Constitution for the government of the Grand Council, and a portion of the proceedings of the Grand Council at their meeting held on the 16th and 17th days of February, 1864.

You will find, on reference to the Report of the Finance Committee, that the Grand Council has assessed a tax of twenty cents on each member of the organization throughout the State, to be paid on or before the first Monday in May next. It is also required that each and every County Temple in the State send the Grand Secretary full reports of the number of their membership, names of their officers, and the number of branches organized on the first day of May and each three months thereafter. Prompt attention to the above is urgently requested.

The assessment of $20.00 on each county, in addition to the twenty cents for each member, is still in force, as far as those counties are concerned that have not paid that assessment.

You will please present the papers to your County Temple immediately, and see that the above requirements are promptly carried out.

By the authority of the Supreme Council of the United States, there have been some material changes made in the Ritual, etc. You will please send an accredited member of your Temple here, as soon as possible, for instruction; and with him you can send the amount due from your county, as the money is absolutely necessary, and must be forthcoming.

Q. Please to examine and state what that pamphlet is?

A. That was the ritual of the Order of American Knights; the vestibule lesson and the first degree of the Order of American Knights.

Q. Does this contain the obligation that was required to be taken by every member of the Order of American Knights?

A. I believe it does, sir. The obligation of the first degree also required in the vestibule.

A pamphlet entitled V. was here offered in evidence by the Judge Advocate.

The counsel for the accused objected to its introduction, and proposed to ask the witness some questions respecting the authenticity of the pamphlet, to which the Judge Advocate objected; the counsel for the accused replied:

May it please the Court: As I discover now that many of these documents are to be introduced, it is important that we should settle the course to be pursued as to their introduction, and, therefore, I desire to submit the question now.

It is not sufficient for the Judge Advocate, in my judgment, to offer such a document as this to the witness, and the witness, after glancing over it, to say that it is the ritual, without being asked how or where he knew it to be such, and by what authority it was promulgated. Before the document is introduced as evidence, the witness should be passed over to the other side, and we should be at liberty to cross-examine him with respect to this isolated fact, of where this document comes from, how he knows it, and how he knows it was promulgated by competent authority. How does he know that it was received and acted upon. In all courts of justice, before a document can be offered in evidence, all these distinct facts as to its identity are gone into and proved. And when a document has once gone into evidence, we can not object to it. If it goes in evidence on insufficient identity, how are we to remedy it?

It may be said, that if, after the document has once gone in evidence, we show, on cross-examination, that it is not properly authenticated, the Commission would reject it, or give no weight to it. That might be true with this Commission, but we ought to have the rules of law and cross-examination applied here. We all know that if we were trying a case of this kind before a jury, that the evidence, after once getting before the jurors, would have its influence, though it were testimony that ought not to have been introduced.

I submit, that before the document can be submitted to this Commission, we ought to have the privilege of cross-examination, confined strictly to the document, its authenticity, and the propriety of its admissibility to the Commission as evidence. I do not know that this is a matter of very much importance, but it is one which we may as well settle at once, that we may know how we are to be governed hereafter.

The Judge Advocate replied:

It has already been proved before this Commission, that the witness on the stand, Mr. Harrison, is Grand Secretary of a society or order, known at present as the Order of the Sons of Liberty. That that order was changed from the Order of American Knights. Mr. Harrison stated that he belonged to that order; that he assisted at the inauguration of the order, and was one of its first members in this city, and that he has been its Grand Secretary from that time to this. I hand him this paper, and ask him what it is. After a careful examination, he answers, that it is a ritual of the Vestibule and First Degree, and obligation of the First Degree of the Order of American Knights. I then propose to introduce this paper before the Commission as evidence; before that they know nothing of its contents.

I differ from the counsel. His right, under the common law, is to object that the paper has not been sufficiently proved. The question then arises, has it been so brought before this Commission as to make it material, and been sufficiently connected with the matters in issue to make it important that this Commission should call that paper before them for their examination? I do distinctly say that the counsel for the accused can not stop my examination, nor have the power to cross-examine the witness before I turn him over to them for that purpose. He can object that I have not sufficiently laid the foundation of any question, or for any paper which I propose to place before the Commission and they pass upon that objection; but he can not ask at my hands that I shall turn that witness over to him, until I am through with him, and I do not propose to do it until the Commission orders it.

The objection, as I take it, is to my mode of examination, and I insist on the introduction of the paper, because I consider the foundation has been sufficiently laid. If the objection is not insisted on, there is no question before the court.

The counsel for the accused replied:

I interpose the objection that the paper should not be received in evidence until we have the power at some time—I do not care whether it is now or after the Judge Advocate has closed his examination, as to the paper—to test by a cross-examination the authenticity of that document. The members of this Commission know, that at least in this State, when a note is introduced into court, before that note shall be offered in evidence, the counsel on the other side are permitted to examine the witness as to its identity and authenticity, but not as to its contents. And not until that identity and authenticity have been tested and proved, is the document introduced.

The court was then closed for deliberation upon the objection of the accused, as to whether the pamphlet should be received in evidence, before the counsel for the accused have an opportunity to cross-examine the witness upon it.

On the re-opening of the court, the Judge Advocate announced that the objection was overruled, and the pamphlet was received in evidence. [See Appendix.]

Q. State what that is, commencing on page 5?

A. That is the obligation of the Neophyte in the First Degree. The Neophyte lesson was the first in the Order of American Knights, and given in the Vestibule.

Q. Wherein do they differ, if at all?

A. A person elected to become a member of the Neophyte organization, received that lesson and no other; he never attended any of the meetings of the Order of American Knights; he was simply taken into the Vestibule, received the obligation, and was discharged.

Q. What was the status of a person taking the Neophyte degree?

A. All persons becoming members of the organization were obliged to take the Neophyte degree, as the preliminary; and those considered only worthy to take the first degree were taken, and the oath administered without their having any knowledge of any further degrees.

Q. State whether or not the change in this order released the members from the obligations they had taken in the American Knights?

A. My understanding was, that when the change was made, the members were released from the obligations of the American Knights, and took those of the Sons of Liberty.

Q. Were there any cases in which no changes were made in the order, or in the change of name?

A. We endeavored to make the changes as perfect as possible. Each of the counties was organized under the Order of American Knights, and I can not say positively that there were any counties in which the change was not made, though there may have been some that did not send up delegates.

Q. Did the Supreme Commander of the Sons of Liberty exercise control over the American Knights?

A. Yes, sir; it is my opinion that he did.

Q. Upon what do you base that opinion?

A. The difference between the Order of American Knights and Sons of Liberty was this, that when the ritual and obligations were changed, it was not necessary for the American Knights to take the obligations of the Sons of Liberty, but simply to assume them. It was the same organization with a different name, and different ritual and colloquies, as I understood it.

Q. Do you know of any thing being done by the Supreme Commander of the Sons of Liberty, as to exercising control over the American Knights?

A. I do not know that the present Supreme Commander was ever in the American Knights?

Q. Who is that?

A. Vallandigham. The Grand Commander of this State was Grand Commander of the Order of American Knights, and exercised the same powers over the Sons of Liberty.

Q. After the change, did he exercise the same control as before?

A. It was considered the same organization.

Q. I understood you to say that it was not necessary to take the obligation of the Sons of Liberty, but to *assume* it. What do you mean by that?

A. The persons taking the obligation of the Order of American Knights were not required to re-obligate themselves, and take the obligation of the Sons of Liberty; it was understood that they assumed the obligation, and no requirement was made or carried into force. None of those who took the obligation of the Order of American Knights took the obligation of the Sons of Liberty.

Q. I understood you that those who went into the Sons of Liberty were released from the obligation of the Order of American Knights—how do you explain it?

A. I understood that they were released so far as the change was concerned. The obligation had been changed, and it was understood that they assumed the new obligation.

Q. If they took any new obligation, were they or were they not released from the obligation?

A. I never perfectly understood whether they were or not.

Q. Were they held to the old obligation, supposing they took no new obligation?

A. They were supposed to be held to the obligation they had taken.

[Certain pamphlets were handed to the witness.]

Q. State if you know what those are? If so, state what they are?

A. This book (entitled "S. L.") I know to be the ritual of the first degree, containing the first lesson of the Order of Sons of Liberty. This (entitled "General Laws of the S. L.") is the Constitution of the County Temple of the State. This (entitled "Constitution of the Grand Council," etc.,) is the Constitution of the Grand Council of this

State for the Sons of Liberty. This (entitled "I") is the ritual of the First Conclave degree, or second degree of the Order of Sons of Liberty, and also the Second Conclave or third degree of the Order of Sons of Liberty.

Q. Who were required to take the obligations contained in these Rituals?

A. All persons who became members of those degrees. Those who had become members of the Order of American Knights (of the second and third degree) simply assumed the obligations of the new order.

The above-named Rituals were here put in evidence on the part of the Court. [See Appendix.]

Q. I understand you to say that this new order of things was brought about after the return of the Grand Commander from New York. Am I correct?

A. Yes, sir; it was after his return from New York, but I can not say positively how long after.

Q. When was the next meeting after that of the 16th and 17th of February? and where?

A. The next meeting of the Grand Council of this State was on the 14th of June, 1864, at the Hall of Marion Temple.

Q. How many counties of the State were represented at that meeting?

A. About thirty counties.

Q. How many delegates to a county?

A. Some counties had one, some two, and some more than two.

Q. How many delegates were present at the meeting?

A. I should judge about forty members.

Q. Who presided at that meeting?

A. The Grand Commander, Mr. Dodd.

Q. Who was Secretary?

A. I was.

Q. Who, if any of the accused, were present at that meeting?

A. Mr. Bowles, Mr. Humphreys, Mr. Milligan and Mr. Horsey were present at that meeting. A gentleman by the name of Stephen Horsey was present, but I do not know whether he (the accused) is the man or not; I do not recognize him; at all events he was a delegate from Martin county.

Q. Did any initiations take place at that time?

A. Those members who were present who had not received the Council Degree, received it at that meeting, but I do not recollect who took it.

Q. Do you remember whether a Mr. Lasalle was present at that meeting?

A. Yes, sir.

Q. Where is Lasalle from?

A. From Cass county. I do not know his name, but I think it is Charles.

Q. Do you remember any persons of this city who were initiated?

A. There were no persons from this city initiated.

Q. Commence at the convening of the Council and give to the Commission, as nearly as you can, what took place in detail; how and by whom it was opened, how you gained admittance, and what was done?

A. The Grand Council convened about 10 o'clock on the morning of the 14th of June, and was in session till 5 or 6 in the evening. I remember that I was very late at the meeting. It was delayed on account of my absence. It was convened by the Grand Commander, who delivered a short verbal address at the opening of the meeting. I have no recollection as to what was said in the address. The next business in order was conferring the Grand Council Degree upon those members that had not received them.

Q. Was the Grand Council Degree superior to the Third Degree?

A. Yes, sir.

Q. Who was entitled to receive that degree?

A. Those persons who were present who had not received it before.

Q. Did any member receive that degree?

A. No person was given that degree unless he was elected as a delegate to the State Council; every delegate to the State Council was bound to receive that degree before he could act as a member of the Council.

Q. What was done after the speech?

A. There was general business transacted, the most important, I think, was the appointment of a committee of thirteen, whose duty it was to act in the interim of the meeting of the State Council, and to exercise the same power that the State Council had.

Q. Who was appointed on that committee?

A. I can not say; it was a secret committee; the appointing power was placed in the hands of the Grand Commander, Dodd, who was supposed to be, *ex officio*, a member of that committee, and had the appointing of them. It was intended to be a secret committee, that should not be known, even to the members themselves, until they were called together.

Q. Do you know whether or not they were called together?

A. I do not.

Q. Do you know of any address being issued by them?

A. I have no knowledge of any, save a printed one, that I have seen since I have been in prison; but I knew nothing about it before.

Q. What was done after the appointment of the committee of thirteen?

A. After discussions on political matters, there was a resolution to appoint a committee of five to proceed to Hamilton, Ohio, on the next day, the 15th.* That resolution afterward was amended, by authorizing all

---

*The occasion of Mr. Vallandigham's return to Ohio.

the members to consider themselves members of that committee. A resolution was also brought up with respect to Government detectives becoming members of the organization. It was understood that some Government detectives had become initiated as members of the organization, and a discussion took place, to find whether it was the case or not.

Q. Was any one named?

A. A man by the name of Coffin was said to belong, and there was a general discussion in reference to the looseness of the manner in which the initiations were carried on, and an appeal made to the members to be more particular in future.

Q. Was any thing said as to what was to be done in the matter?

A. Nothing within my recollection or knowledge came before the meeting in a business capacity.

Q. Did any thing come before the meeting in an unofficial capacity? or did you learn what was to be done?

A. No, sir; I did not; but I heard Mr. Dodd remark that a person who came into the organization as a Government detective ought to be made away with; it was a remark made in private conversation, and was not brought before the meeting officially.

Q. Was that remark made during the meeting?

A. It was during the meeting that I heard it.

Q. What other business was done at that meeting?

A. I can not recollect any other particular business, save that there were resolutions passed in reference to the increase of the organization. I looked upon it at the time as an unimportant meeting. There was no important business transacted.

Q. Do you know whether or not any person did go to Hamilton?

A. Not of my own knowledge.

Q. Were any other officers or men appointed? or any other formal business done at the meeting?

A. No, sir; the officers for the present year had all been appointed at the meeting in February.

Q. How was that meeting adjourned?

A. *Sine die.*

Q. Was the June meeting a regular meeting of the Council?

A. It was a called meeting, called by the Grand Commander, through printed notices issued by me, and sent by mail. He requested me to issue notices to the various County Temples, calling a meeting on the 14th of June. That was the last meeting of the Grand Council held that I attended, and I believe there has been no other meeting of the Grand Council held since that time, either here, or in any portion of the State.

Q. Do you remember what the strength of the order was computed to be at the meeting in June?

A. At the meeting in February I received reports from seventeen counties, who reported the strength within their limits at something over five thousand members. There were some seventeen to twenty other counties that made no reports. I computed their number at twelve thousand. From the reports made in June, there was an increase in the organization of about twenty per cent., making it about fifteen thousand.

Q. What did you compute it to be in September, from the best data you had at that time?

A. Taking the ratio of increase from February to June, I should not have put the organization to exceed eighteen thousand members.

Q. In this number do you include the Order of American Knights, and Sons of Liberty, all who had taken any of the degrees?

A. I mean that it includes the members of first, second and third degree, members of the organization, but it would not include the members of the Vestibule, simply because there was no report made of those members, they were not considered members of the organization. As a general thing, the Vestibule members were very few.

Q. You may name the counties in which this organization existed as far as you can?

A. I can not name all of them. The organization. so far as I have received reports, existed in the counties of Marion, Marshall, Allen, Huntington, Laporte, Fulton, Cass, Harrison, Washington, Orange, Grant, Madison, Crawford, Posey, Vanderburg, and Warrick. The reports received were from forty-five counties in all.

Q. Did this order exist in Randolph county, to your knowledge?

A. I never received any report of the establishment of any County Temple. There may have been branch Temples; but the order existed to no extent in that county?

Q. How about Dearborn county?

A. So far as I can recollect, there was no organization in that county.

Q. Was Randolph county represented in any of these meetings by delegates?

A. I think not, sir; but I will not state positively.

Q. Was Cass county represented?

A. Yes, sir; by Mr. Lasalle.

Q. Was Howard county represented?

A. No, sir.

Q. Do you know any thing of the strength of the organization in adjoining States?

A. Nothing positive. I understood that the order was better organized in Illinois than in any other State in the Union. But I had no information that was official.

Q. State to the Commission whether any

steps were taken, to your knowledge, and if so how far, for the arming or drilling of the organization?

A. There was, to my knowledge, no resolution passed at the meeting of the State Council to arm this organization, or looking to the arming or purchase of arms, or to the drilling of the organization.

Q. I ask you what, to your knowledge, was done?

A. I have no knowledge of the arming or drilling of the members of the organization.

Q. Do you know of any attempt to arm the organization?

A. I do not know any thing at all about arms, except those that were seized here last August.

Q. What was done or said in an official way, looking to the drilling and arming of the organization, and any acts of the leaders.

A. I have no knowledge of the purchase of any arms, or any attempt to arm the organization, or of the organization or any portion of it being under drill.

Q. What do you know about the arms seized here?

A. I had no knowledge of the purchase or the shipment of these arms until about four or five days previous to their arrival. Mr. Walker came to my house one night, between 9 and 10 o'clock. He asked me if I knew whether Mr. Dodd had informed Parsons that there would be some boxes coming here addressed to him. I told him I did not. He then said that he should like me to say to Parsons that there would be some boxes arriving in a day or two, which he would like him to take in and take care of until he returned. I can not say whether Walker stated at that interview that these boxes contained arms or not. I went down the next morning and asked Parsons if Dodd had informed him that these boxes were coming. He said that he had, and that he had received the information. I left the city on that day, and was absent three or four days. The morning after my return to the city, I went down to Dodd's office, and I saw on the sidewalk five or six boxes addressed "J. J. Parsons, Indianapolis, Ind." Parsons was engaged in getting these boxes into the building. I asked him if these were the boxes spoken of, and he said they were. The boxes were taken up to the second floor, and put in a back room of the building. I went there as they had been placed there, and asked him if he knew what those boxes contained. He said he did. I asked him what they contained. He said pistols.

Q. Was Mr. Parsons a member of the Order of Sons of Liberty?

A. He was, sir. He gave me the information as to what the boxes contained.

Q. Did he say what they were for?

A. No, sir.

Q. Did Dodd say what they were for?

A. No, sir. Dodd never mentioned the boxes or pistols in any manner.

Q. How many boxes were received here at that time?

A. I understood ten boxes were received.

Q. Were any more received?

A. Yes, sir. Twenty-two boxes were received about two weeks after.

Q. Did you learn who had purchased or shipped these arms?

A. I never learned who purchased these arms until after I was arrested, when I saw the card published by Mr. Walker. I do not know of my own knowledge.

Q. What became of these arms?

A. I understood that they were seized by the authorities here.

Q. Did you have any conversation with Parsons about the dispositions of these arms?

A. No, sir. I think Mr. Parsons knew nothing about the matter until the arms had been shipped, and until a few days previous to their arrival. It is my impression he derived his information from Dodd.

The Judge Advocate here handed the witness a letter, and asked:

Q. Do you know by whom that letter was written?

A. That letter is in Mr. Walker's handwriting, I should judge, but I could not swear particularly to it.

Q. Did you ever see that letter before?

A. I never did, sir.

The letter dated "New York, May 11, 1864," addressed to "My Dear Dodd," and signed "Yours truly, W.," was here introduced in evidence by the Judge Advocate.

The Judge Advocate handed a letter to the accused, L. P. Milligan, and asked: "Is that your handwriting?"

A. The accused, L. P. Milligan, replied "that is my handwriting."

A letter, dated "Huntington, 9th May, 1864," addressed to "Gen. H. H. Dodd," and signed "L. P. Milligan," was here introduced in evidence by the Judge Advocate.*

---

*HUNTINGTON, IND., 9th May, 1864.

Gen. H. H. DODD—*Dear Sir;* Yours of the 2d inst. came when I was absent at Notre Dame, and I have now just read it, and am unable to make any definite reply. I will barely allude to what may afford a text for reply in future.

As to the Gubernatorial question, it may not have occurred to you the unenviable connection in which my name has been used. It was announced in consequence of the declination of the Hon. J. E. McDonald to be a candidate, conceding that if he was a candidate there was no desire to use my name; now I understand he is; hence I am not called upon by any public notice to be such. But waiving all this as the result of mere accident, and not proffered as an indignity to me, by placing me second in talents and patriotism to J. E. McDonald, there is a still more grave difficulty in the way. The announcement of my name for Governor, was made by McDonald's friends. Now it is due to them that I should decline, because I could not represent them; there is no similarity between us. And all this is not so discouraging as the fact that men of the stamp of Judge Hanna, whose pro-

Q. Do you know P. C. Wright?

A. The first time I met him was at Terre Haute, about the 27th of August, 1863. In a conversation I had with him, he informed me that he had originally resided at New Orleans. That he had been compelled to leave there on account of his Union sentiments, and removed to St. Louis, Missouri. At the time I saw him, he was staying in Chicago, and represented himself to be an Attorney at Law.

Q. Do you know where he is now?

A. I do not know positively, but I understood he was in Fort Lafayette.

The Commission then adjourned, to meet on Tuesday, October 25, at 2 o'clock, P. M.

Court Room, Indianapolis, Indiana,
October 25, 1864, 2 o'clock, P. M.

The Commission met pursuant to adjournment.

All the members present. Also, the Judge Advocate, the accused and their counsel.

The proceedings were read and approved.

Edwin A. Davis, one of the counsel for Andrew Humphreys and Horace Heffren, submitted to the Commission the following paper:

To the President and Members of the Military Commission:

At the commencement of this trial, two of the defendants asked and obtained leave of this Court for me to act as their counsel. I now, with their consent, desire to withdraw from the position I have since then occupied, in such a manner as not to prejudice their interest before this tribunal.

The determination of the Court that all the defendants should be tried jointly, insures them all able and experienced counsel.

I may also say, that when I was retained in behalf of the defendants, I had but little idea of the nature of the charges and evidence that would be produced against them; but from the nature of these prosecutions, and for other reasons growing out of my relation to the Government as United States Commissioner, which renders it improper that I should defend a class of cases frequently brought before me as an examining officer of the Government, I ask of this Court that my request be granted, and these reasons for my withdrawal be spread upon the records of the Court.

EDWIN A. DAVIS.

The request of Mr. Davis was granted by the Commission.

The testimony of William M. Harrison, a witness for the Government, was then resumed as follows:

Question by the Judge Advocate:

State whether a Military Committee was appointed at the meeting of the Grand Council, on the 14th of June? and if so, who were appointed?

A. I have no recollection of the appointment of such a committee at that meeting.

Q. Did you receive any reports from any of the accused, relative to the strength of the organization in their respective counties?

A. I received a report from Mr. Heffren, at the meetings of the 16th and 17th of February, of its strength in his county. I have no recollection of any report from others.

The Judge Advocate here handed the witness a letter addressed to "H. I. Stewart, Boundary, Indiana," and signed " H.," and asked:

Q. Do you recognize the handwriting of that paper, and know by whom it was written?

A. Yes, sir. It was written by me as Secretary of the order, on the day on which it is dated, in reply to a letter addressed to me as Secretary by H. I. Stewart.

Q. Was he a member of the order?

A. The letter was from a man I had never heard of before I had received it. The writer purported to be Secretary of a County Temple. He wrote on business connected with the order.

The Judge Advocate here proposed to introduce the letter in evidence. The counsel for the accused objected for the following reasons:

That the letter is a reply to a communication from a person not yet proven to be a member of the order. It is an immaterial letter, and proves nothing in issue before this Court.

The Judge Advocate replied:

There are several issues presented in this case, which I view differently from the counsel for the accused. Mr. Harrison says this letter was written by him in his official capacity as Grand Secretary, to a man whom he supposed was a member of the order. Any instructions the witness gave,

---

fession of principles I could represent, prefer McDonald on account of his supposed availability, it detracts much from my confidence in our ultimate success. When men of so much seeming patriotism are willing for mere temporary purposes to abandon the great principles of civil liberty, what will those of less pretensions do, when the real contest comes, when life and property all depend on the issue, when bullets instead of ballots are cast, and when the *halter* is a preamble to our platform? For unless Federal encroachments are arrested in the States by the effort as well of the legislators as the executive, then will our *lives* and *fortunes* follow where our honors will have gone before.

I am willing to do whatever the cause of the North-west may require, or its true friends may think proper, but I am as well convinced that upon mature reflection they will not ask me to obtrude myself upon the public, nor will they ask me to be McDonald's contingent.

I have great confidence in your good hard man *sense*, and cool judgment, hence I find it difficult to disregard your advice in the matter, and before giving to the world my position on the question I wish to see you personally. Yours truly, L. P. MILLIGAN.

N. B. My last was confidential; this is more so, because I have given vent to feelings that are purely private. L. P. MILLIGAN.

whether written or verbal, in reference to the order, are competent as evidence, and are competent as showing how the order worked, and whether its affairs were conducted in an open or secret manner. Instructions given to any temple, are also competent evidence.

The counsel for the accused wished the objection to go on record, that the letter might go in as evidence, under protest.

The Judge Advocate replied:

There can be no protest in this Court. If objections are made by the counsel for the accused, they come before the Court to be sustained or overruled.

The court room was then cleared for deliberation.

On the re-opening of the court room, the Judge Advocate announced to the accused that the objection had been overruled by the Commission, and the letter was received in evidence.*

The letter was here read by the Judge Advocate.

Question by the Judge Advocate: I understood you to say this letter was never sent; how was that?

A. I wrote the letter the same day I received the letter from Stewart. I had in a measure become dissatisfied with the order, and had resolved to abandon it. I hesitated about answering any letters, but wrote this on the spur of the moment and placed it in my pocket, without determining whether I should send it. I was arrested, and this letter was found upon me and taken from me.

Q. When were you arrested?

A. On Saturday, the day the letter was written.

Question by the Court:

Q. Did an answer to the letter from H. I. Stewart come within the general scope of your duties as Grand Secretary?

A. I answered every letter that came directed to me as Grand Secretary, without any special directions from the Council.

Question by the Judge Advocate:

State to the Court if there ever came to your knowledge any plan for the intended uprising of this order? If so, state from whom you obtained that knowledge, where the uprising was to be, and all the circumstances connected with it.

A. I received my information from Harrison H. Dodd, that there was a design in progress, or in contemplation for the release of the prisoners of war confined at this point, at Chicago, and at Rock Island, Illi-

nois. That plan had not been fully decided on; but if decided on, he was to have charge of the release of the prisoners at this point. He desired to have a Democratic mass meeting called about the 16th of August, and used his influence to induce the Democratic State Central Committee to call that meeting. If they did so, he intended to send out circulars to the members of the order in the various counties, authorizing the members to come up to that meeting armed. If the meeting had been held at that time, there would have been an uprising.

Q. When and where did he state this to you?

A. At his residence, on the evening of the 29th of July I think. It was on Friday evening, the same evening that the bulletin board of the *Journal* office announced that there would be a full exposition of the Order of the Sons of Liberty in the *Journal* of the next morning.

Q. Was that prior or subsequent to the meeting at Chicago, to which you have al luded?

A. It was after the Chicago meeting.

Q. Did Dodd at that time state to you when and where this plan for revolution had been agreed upon?

A. He stated to me that he had been to Niagara Falls, and from there to New York City; that he returned again to Niagara Falls, and from there he went to Chicago. I understood him that this whole plot had been arranged at Chicago.

Q. Did he give the names of the persons whom he consulted in reference to this plan?

A. He mentioned no names.

Q. Did he mention whom he had met at Niagara Falls?

A. He stated that he met there the parties representing themselves as Peace Commissioners.

Q. At what date and to whom did he refer?

A. It was about the time of the meeting of the Peace Commissioners at Niagara Falls. I suppose he referred to the Peace Commissioners on the part of the rebel States.

Q. Did he state what the rebel prisoners were to do after the uprising on the 16th?

A. He stated, in an informal way, that they were to aid and assist in the uprising here.

Q. What were they to do after the uprising?

A. If successful in the uprising, they were to be taken South.

Q. What was that success to consist in?

A. In revolution.

Q. What was to be revolutionized?

A. The Government, as far as the State was concerned.

---

* INDIANAPOLIS, August 20, 1864.

MR. H. I. STEWART, Boundary, Indiana—*Dear Sir:* Yours under date of the 17th instant is at hand. Any information that you may desire can be had by sending an accredited person here. Written communications are *played out*, as all letters are opened and read by Lincoln spies and hirelings during their transmission through the mails. The Reader can be had at $1 20 per dozen.

Truly yours,　　　　H.

Q. Did he have reference to the General Government?

A. He said nothing about the General Government. It was a revolution which was to take place in this State.

Q. How was this uprising to take place, and at whom was it aimed?

A. By the aid of the rebel prisoners, who were to be released through his instrumentality, and that of the persons who came in to the meeting to be held here on the 16th, they were to have an uprising and overturn the State Government.

Q. Who was to be Governor after that revolution?

A. He did not state.

Q. Did he state particularly his plan for the release of the rebel prisoners, and how the guards were to be overpowered?

A. He said if the thing was decided on, he was to release the prisoners here. He was to surprise the camp, and seize the artillery here, and in the confusion and excitement of the moment effect the success of the plan. He thought he could do this with about one hundred and fifty men. That was his idea which he communicated to me?

Q. You may state whether there is an unwritten work of the order?

A. There is.

Q. You may now give to the Court an exposition of what that is, giving the colloquies, signs, grips and passwords.

A. The unwritten work of the order consists in the signs, grips, passwords and colloquies of the order. That portion of the work of the organization was never written, but communicated verbally.

Q. You may now give the unwritten part of the Vestibule degree?

A. The Vestibule lesson is that in which all persons who design to become members of the order are first instructed. It was so arranged that a person who took the Vestibule degree, knew nothing beyond that. In a large city they could have societies of the Sons of Liberty, composed of members who had gone no further than the Vestibule lesson, and meet as general political clubs. They would be bound by the obligations of the Sons of Liberty, but know nothing further of the organization than that lesson.

The sign of recognition was made by standing erect on both feet, placing the heel of the right foot in the hollow of the left, with the arms folded in the ordinary manner. A member of the order noticing me in this posture, would suppose he was challenged. He would place himself in the same position and challenge me. He would extend his right foot to meet mine and use the following colloquy: I would say "nu," he would answer "oh," I would reply "lac," he would say "S.," I would answer "L.," he would say, "Give me liberty"—I would answer "or give me death." There is also a signal of distress. You place the left hand on the right breast, and raise the right hand directly in front to its full hight once. This is given in the day-time. If at night, you give the cry of distress "oak-houn," repeated three times. You wait a moment, and then repeat it three times, and continue this until assistance comes. The members of this degree were also instructed that it was the duty of each member of the order to repair immediately to the spot and assist the member giving the signal. They were also instructed that the acorn was the universal emblem of the society. If the person was not deemed worthy to take any further degrees he was dismissed. The members of that degree never knew any thing officially of the further organization of the order.

In the first degree the sign of recognition is the same as in the Vestibule degree, except that the index finger of the left hand was placed on the right arm, when the arms were folded. We were instructed that this meant State rights and State sovereignty. If a member gave that sign, it was the duty of another seeing it, to advance and recognize him. The grip of the first degree is an ordinary grip, in which the index finger is placed upon the wrist, extending upward. That is entitled the grip of the acorn. The colloquy is repeated thus: "If I go to the East"—"I will go to the West." "Let there be no strife"—"between mine and thine"— "for we"—"be brethren." "O"—"S"—"L"— "Resistance to tyrants"—"is obedience to God." [The colloquies are pronounced alternately, as indicated by the dashes.] This is the colloquy of the first degree. In this degree members were instructed in the mode of entering a temple. The password of that degree was changed monthly in each County Temple, which adopted its own password. The members were instructed that the acorn was the universal emblem of the order, representing strength, growth, and durability. Those initiated into this degree were welcomed as full members of the Order of Sons of Liberty.

The sign of recognition of the second degree is given with the body in the same position as in the first degree, the hands being crossed on the abdomen, the right hand on the left and the thumbs pointing upward to a point, which is said to represent the star Arcturus. The colloquy is: "What—a star— Arc—turus. What of the night?—Morning cometh—Will ye inquire?—inquire ye—return—come." Members were instructed that a five-pointed star of any metal could be used as an emblem of that degree. The password was "Orion," pronounced as a test, by giving the long sound to "i" in the second syllable. This is the unwritten portion of the second degree, except the manner of entering the temple.

The third degree is similar to the second in the position of the body. The sign of recognition is made by crossing the arms on the chest, the right arm upon the left, and the fingers pointing to the shoulders. The colloquy is: "Whence—scir? How—by the ford? Name it—Jaback—Your password —Washington." The response is "Bayard." The distinct pronunciation of the last syllable, "yard," being a test of membership.

The sign of the Grand Council degree is given by clasping the right hand, and taking hold of the elbow of the right arm with the left hand; then give a simple shake of the hand; turn one quarter to the left, with the arms folded, and repeat the colloquy: "Whence—America—North—South." The password of the Grand Council degree is "America."

A member who wishes to enter a Temple of the first degree, makes some alarm at the outer door   If he is known to be a Son of Liberty, he would be admitted on giving the password, without any further trouble.   If not known, he gives the password and is admitted into the ante-room, and sends in his name and that of the County Temple to which he belongs, and states that he is a visiting brother. His name is reported to the presiding officer. When the name is announced to the members present, if any know him they vouch for him; if not vouched for, a committee of two is appointed to test him in the degree in which the Council is working.   If found perfect, he is admitted; if he fails, he is rejected. The manner of entering Temples working in other degrees, is the same, with the exception of the password used.

Close of the direct examination.

CROSS-EXAMINATION.

There were no other lessons or teachings pertaining to the unwritten work of the other degrees, than those I have given. The military features of the Order of the American Knights and the Sons of Liberty were the same. From what Dodd communicated to me, I was impressed that the revolutionary scheme included Illinois as well as Indiana, and that himself mainly, and certain others who knew of the intended scheme, as far as it was decided upon, were to participate in carrying it out, and in the event of circumstances favoring, the whole organization was to be drawn into it. The intended revolution was not discussed in Council; Dodd seemed to look rather to the action of individual members of the order in this State. He was to take charge of the liberation of the prisoners at Camp Morton, near this city. Dodd remarked to me that he wanted to influence the State Central Committee to call a Democratic mass meeting here about the 16th of August. If it had been called he was to issue secret circulars to members of the order, and have them come armed and prepared for an uprising. I do not believe that the majority of the first and sec-

ond degree members ever knew or thought that revolution in Indiana was contemplated. Dodd, I know, contemplated holding a meeting here, of the leading men of the organization, for the discussion of his plans, and the meeting, I understood, took place on the Tuesday following the Friday on which I had the conversation referred to. The meeting was convened by circular sent by Mr. Dodd. The military bill adopted in the Council, referred to in my direct examination, was introduced in pursuance of injunctions received from Mr. Wright, the originator of the organization in this State. His instructions were that the order must have a certain number of major generals, brigadiers, colonels, etc. Mr. Wright was Supreme Commander at the time. The military bill was in Dodd's handwriting. The military appointments were made by the delegates present from various military districts, who selected a person for major general for their district; that person was announced to the Council, and the nomination confirmed in Council. I can not state positively whether Mr. Milligan was present or not when the military bill was discussed. Neither Mr. Heffren nor Mr. Humphreys was present. These appointments were made at the first meeting held about the 10th of September, 1863. Heffren was present at the meeting of the 16th and 17th of February, and that was the only meeting I ever saw him at. Bowles in the February meeting declined becoming a major general unless certain changes were made in the length of the term of service. The change I understood was made, and I did not hear him object after that. I have no knowledge as to Humphreys accepting his nomination. He was not present at either the February or September meetings; but was present here at the June, 1864, meeting; though I did not see him in the room till the evening, and then only for half or three-quarters of an hour. I did not see him at the Terre Haute meeting. I know that Mr. Humphreys was a member of the order from the fact that I saw him at the meeting on the 14th of June, but have no knowledge of his initiation, nor of that of a majority of the members of that Council. No person who was not a member, ever, to my knowledge, entered the Grand Council. It convened in the Marion County Temple, in the fourth story of Dodd's building, and was in session from 10 in the morning until 9 in the evening, adjourning for dinner and supper. Mr. Humphreys was there at night. I saw him there, and also saw him at my office after the meeting adjourned. Mr. Dodd told me he saw the Peace Commissioners at Niagara Falls, and had conversations with several of them, but did not say any thing about meeting them in a secret manner; I do not know whether he was conspiring with them, or was simply introduced to them. I know that

Mr. Heffren was Deputy Grand Commander, but never heard from him in reference to the organization after the 17th of February; he was not present at any meeting after that.

RE-EXAMINATION.

Question by the Judge Advocate:

Who were the parties that were sent for to be present at the Tuesday meeting?

A. Mr. Dodd informed me that he intended sending for Mr. Milligan, for Dr. Bowles, Mr. Humphreys, and Dr. Yeakle; those are all that I recollect his mentioning to me.

Q. Did you learn whether he sent for those persons?

A. I did not; from him.

Q. Did you learn it from any other member of the order?

A. Dodd told me he had sent his boy for one of those parties, and he sent me for another of the parties. He said he sent his boy to Dr. Bowles; I went to Mr. Milligan.

Q. Did you see him?

A. I did.

Q. Did you tell him your message?

A. I did.

Q. What did he say?

A. He said that he did not know whether he could be present, but would try to be. I was instructed by Mr. Dodd to say that there would be a very important meeting, and he ought to be present. I do not know whether they were present or not.

Q. How do you recollect the presence of Mr. Humphreys on the 14th of June?

A. He had never been present at any meeting before.

Q. Was your mind specially directed to him?

A. No, sir.

Q. Did you see him enter the room?

A. I do not recollect seeing him enter it. I saw him in the room just previous to the adjournment.

Q. Were any persons admitted to the Grand Council who were not members before?

A. No, sir; not to my knowledge.

Q. Could any person have obtained admittance except through the regular process of working into the meeting?

A. No person who was not a member could gain admittance. Those delegates who were not members of the Grand Council degree, were initiated. They had to be delegates to be initiated in the degree, and become members of the Grand Council.

Q. In case that uprising was to have taken place, who was the proper officer to lead the uprising?

A. I should judge Mr. Dodd was the officer.

Q. Had he the power, in an official capacity, to order that here?

A. It was vested entirely in Mr. Dodd.

Q. Had he the power to order members of the order at will?

A. He had.

Q. Did he have the power to call all meetings?

A. Yes, sir.

Question by the Court:

Was the circular sent which said he would send to the different temples, directing the members to appear here at the Democratic Convention armed?

A. He did not send any to my knowledge. He did not say he had sent them.

Q. Was the convention called?

A. It was not.

The Commission then adjourned, to meet on Thursday, the 27th of October, 1864, at 10 o'clock, A. M.

COURT ROOM, INDIANAPOLIS, INDIANA,
October 27, 1864, 10 o'clock, A. M.

The Commission met pursuant to adjournment.

All the members present. Also, the Judge Advocate, the accused, and their counsel.

The proceedings were read and approved.

The whole of the session being occupied in reading the testimony, the Commission adjourned, to meet at 2 o'clock, P. M.

COURT ROOM, INDIANAPOLIS, INDIANA,
October 27, 1864, 2 o'clock, P. M.

The Commission met pursuant to adjournment.

All the members present. Also, the Judge Advocate, the accused, and their counsel.

WESLEY TRANTER, a witness for the Government, was then introduced, and being duly sworn by the Judge Advocate, testified as follows:

Question by the Judge Advocate:

State your name and place of residence.

Answer. Wesley Tranter; Shoals Station, Martin county, Indiana, has been my home for four years.

Q. What has been your business for the last year?

A. I have been running a saw-mill and building bridges down South. My occupation before was that of a miller.

Q. State whether or not you ever joined a society called the Knights of the Golden Circle, American Knights, or Sons of Liberty?

A. Yes, sir; I joined an order in May, 1863, called the Circle of Honor; the last I joined was called the Knights of the Golden Circle.

Q. Where was that?

A. It was close to the Shoals.

Q. How long did you belong to that organization?

A. Up to January, 1864, when it was turned into the Knights of the Golden Circle, the second degree.

Q. State the circumstances of your joining the Circle of Honor.

A. I saw Mr. Horsey, the man sitting there (the witness here pointed to the accused, Stephen Horsey), at the Shoals, in May, 1863. He came to me and said they were getting up a concern; he did not state what it was, but it was something in defense of the country—but he did not exactly tell me what it was at first, nor the name of it. I joined it, and they called it the Circle of Honor. Horsey said they wanted to find out what was the strength of the Democratic party at that time.

Q. Where were you initiated?

A. In an old house belonging to a man by the name of Gaddis, about a mile and a half from the Shoals. It was a vacant house at the time.

Q. How many were there?

A. I could not say, exactly; I reckon about ten.

Q. Who initiated you?

A. Mr. Horsey and Clayton initiated me.

Q. Who presided at that meeting?

A. Mr. Horsey.

Q. Did you take any obligation at that time? If so, state what it was.

A. Yes, sir; but I do not recollect what the oath was; it was pretty long. There was something about being torn into four parts before we would reveal the proceedings; one part was to be cast out at the east gate, one at the north gate, one at the south gate, and one at the west gate.

Q. Did you learn what the gates meant?

A. No, sir.

Q. Was any business transacted at the meeting besides the initiation?

A. None at all.

Q. When was the next meeting you attended, and where?

A. I think the next meeting was across the river, at the Pinnacle, at a little vacant house. About the same persons were present as at the other meeting. Mr. Horsey presided at that meeting.

Q. What was done at that meeting?

A. They took in two others.

Q. When and where was the next meeting?

A. In the latter part of the summer of 1863, somewhere in the woods, about a couple of miles from the Shoals; it was back and east of Horsey's place. About eight or ten were at that meeting.

Q. Were any steps taken, by the order, toward arming or drilling?

A. Something was said about it; they wanted to give me an office, but I would not accept it. They said we were to drill, and be ready; that we were to have our guns fixed in case any thing should happen or the soldiers should ever molest us, or any thing of that kind.

Q. What was the purpose of this organization.

A. Its purpose came out toward the last, that we were to support Jeff Davis; that we were to have our guns fixed; that we did not know what hour we should be called on to have a general turn-out to support Jeff Davis, either North or South. That is what they said in the Knights of the Golden Circle; but in the Circle of Honor they did not go so far.

Q. You say this meeting in the woods was in the latter part of the summer; when was the next?

A. About the 27th or 28th of January, 1864, when the order was changed to the Knights of the Golden Circle.

Q. Who were the officers of that organization?

A. The head man was John W. Stone.

Q. Where did you meet?

A. At Gaddis' house.

Q. How many were present?

A. Somewhere about thirty.

Q. How did you happen to go to that meeting?

A. I was asked to go by Anderson Scarlett.

Q. Whom do you remember seeing at that meeting?

A. John W. Stone, John Teney, William Teney, Ike Teney, Stephen Horsey, the accused, Golden Green, and some few others.

Q. State, as nearly as you can, what was said and done at that meeting.

A. I went there from the Shoals, and got into the meeting by giving the sign. It was a grip. After we were in, Horsey made a little speech, and said we were to have something different from the other order. He had a book, and said something about the K. G. C.'s and Knights of the Golden Circle. He said that before any man was taken in, two persons were to stand good for him, that he should not divulge any of the secrets. William Teney and Hiram Apples rose and stood for all. Some ten or fifteen were sworn in. The oath differed from the former oath, but I can not recollect it; there was something about supporting Jeff Davis, North or South. In a speech that John W. Stone made, there was something said about putting Governor Morton out of the way.

Q. Was Horsey present during this speech?

A. Yes, sir.

Q. Did he make any speech?

A. Not that I recollect.

Q. Was any thing said at this meeting as to how these purposes were to be carried out?

A. Yes, sir; they stated they were first to put Morton out of the way. A man who signed himself M. D. was to pay Governor Morton a visit, and he was to live but a short time afterward; this visit was to be made about the 26th or 27th of March. There was to be a raid made on this place about five days from the 1st of April.

Q. Who were to make this raid?

A. The men of the lodge, and we were to arm ourselves to be ready. We were to take this place, wear out the soldiers, and release the prisoners.

Q. What was to be done with the rebel prisoners?

A. Nothing that I recollect; only that we were to go at the blue coats.

Q. Was any thing said about the invasion of Ohio or Indiana by the rebels?

A. They said that when we made the raid on this place, the members of the order in Illinois were to make a raid on Springfield, and those in Missouri on St. Louis. Washington was to be attacked, and Forrest was to make a dash into Kentucky. He did make a raid a few days from the 5th of April.

Q. Who developed these plans?

A. John W. Stone.

Q. State, as far as you can, the signs, grips, and passwords of the Knights of the Golden Circle.

A. If you wished to know if a man belonged to the order, you gave him a challenge, by placing the right foot in the hollow of the left, then you folded your arms; if he is a member and notices you, he does the same thing. Then each advance his right foot and touch toes and shake hands, running the fore-finger up the wrist, and giving a single shake. After you had shaken hands you were to say O, he says A, and you answer K, and he pronounces Oak. He was then known as a brother.

Q. What were the signs of the Circle of Honor?

A. To know if a man was a member of the order, you draw your hand across the upper lip; he answers by doing the same thing with the left hand. You then step forward and give one single shake of the hand. If you doubt the fellow, you ask him if he saw that star; if he was a member, he would reply by saying he saw that star in the East. You would ask what it represented, he would answer, "five points." That proved to you that he was a full member. To recognize and test a person at a distance, the hands were clasped and raised above the head. He would answer by placing his hands upon his shoulders.

Q. When was the last meeting you attended of the Knights of the Golden Circle?

A. On the 26th or 27th of January.

Q. Have they met since?

A. Not to my knowledge.

Q. Why did you not continue with them?

A. Because I thought they were getting along a little too far for me, when they talked about helping the rebels; and as I had been in the army, and as what they avowed was against my principles, I came here in March, 1864, and reported to the Lieutenant Governor?

Q. What, if any thing, was said in reference to acting with Morgan?

A. Something was said about Morgan's making a raid, but I do not recollect what.

Q. Was any thing said about offering him assistance in case the State was invaded?

A. We were to go to his assistance, as I understood it.

Q. Who advocated going to the assistance of Morgan in case he invaded the State?

A. John W. Stone.

Q. What has become of Stone?

A. I don't know. He had some difficulty with the men of the 17th Indiana, and some of the boys went after him when he made off, and the boys fired, and I understand he has since been seen, minus a finger.

Q. Who were the most active members of the organization?

A. John W. Stone and William Clayton.

Q. Was the order armed?

A. Not to my knowledge. Something was said about a box of pistols. Shirkliff and a man named Coffin got off at a station five miles from the Shoals, and Shirkliff had a box that was rather heavy. Coffin asked him what the box contained, and he said jewelry; but Horsey and Shirkliff told me afterward, the box contained pistols, and laughed at Coffin for the way Shirkliff had fooled him.

Q. Did he say what became of them?

A. No, sir.

Q. Or who they were for?

A. No, sir. He said there would be pistols taken round the country, and any one could have them at cost and carriage.

Q. Did he say whom you could get them from?

A. No, sir; but I suppose he meant from himself.

Q. Have you been in any lodge since that meeting?

A. No, sir. I have had no connection with the order since January.

Q. Who did you first reveal this order to?

A. To my father, who was vexed at my having joined it. I then went to my uncle at Washington, and told him. I then came and had a talk with Captain Henly, of the 17th Indiana, and got him to write out an affidavit. And the statement he made out was, I understood, sent to the Lieutenant Governor.

Q. In case Governor Morton was assassinated, who was to succeed him?

A. H. H. Dodd was, according to what was said at the meeting.

CROSS-EXAMINATION.

I forgot to mention in my direct examination that the signs of raising the hands above the head and the answer, were called the Morgan signs. If we joined the army and were captured, we were to give these signs, and then we should be better treated. This was told us by Horsey or Clayton at the time of giving us these signs. I did not understand that because they were given us, we were to join Morgan, but I understood they were for self-protection. We were not sworn in the Circle of Honor to help the South, nor were we pledged to do so. It was changed to the Knights of the Golden Circle in June, 1864, by John W. Stone. A man named Baker asked why the order did not come out at first as the Knights of the Golden Circle, and Horsey and Clayton said they wanted to find out how far the Democratic party was in favor of such an order, and if they came into it well, then they would change it into the Knights of the Golden Circle. By the two men standing good for us at the initiation into the Knights of the Golden Circle, I mean that they were to kill us and report us dead to the lodge, or bring us up for trial, in case we divulged the secrets. In the obligation that we took there was something said about having Jeff Davis for the next President, and voting for him; I can not remember how it was worded; we were sworn into the service of Jeff Davis, and were to support him whenever called upon. They said that all Jeff Davis asked, was that the three States of Indiana, Illinois, and Missouri should join him, and he would soon thrash out all the blue-coats, and then they would go eastward, and clean out all the rest like a hurricane. I took the oath voluntarily; I thought I would see what they did, and if it did not suit me I would report the order. The first time I divulged the order was to my father the next day, and to my uncle William Tranter, at Washington, soon after. About the last of February I mentioned the matter to Captain Henley, here at Indianapolis. I came here on purpose, and found him at the Bates House, and got him to write out my statement for me. John W. Stone said there were 100,000 members in the Circle of Honor in Indiana, and about 60,000 in the Knights of the Golden Circle. When they changed to the Knights of the Golden Circle they dropped off a little. I took one degree in this order. John W. Stone said publicly that if we took the oath of the order, and were caught, we should not be hung, but treated as prisoners of war. I had a conversation with Horsey near the railroad, within two or three days after the last meeting I attended. We were talking about Stone getting me into a difficulty, and I said some of the soldiers would come and take us. Horsey said he did not think the soldiers could do it. He also said that Stone had stated what was false, and that there was no truth about paying Gov. Morton a visit. I said that a man who would preach such doctrine

ought to be rallied, and I wanted Horsey to go with me and tell him of it, but he would not. Horsey might have said that Stone's doctrines were too secesh, but I do not recollect his saying so. If Mr. Horsey had gone over there with me, there would have been no Mr. Stone.

RE-EXAMINATION.

Question by the Judge Advocate:

Q. When was it that you had this conversation with Horsey?

Answer. It was a few days after the meeting.

Q. Who first induced you to join the order?

A. Horsey was the first man; he initiated me.

Q. Did he make any objection to your taking the Morgan sign?

A. No, sir.

Q. Did he make any objection to your taking the oath?

A. No, sir; he took me into the organization and administered the oath to me.

STEPHEN TENEY, a witness for the Government, was then introduced, and being duly sworn by the Judge Advocate, testified as follows:

Question by the Judge Advocate:

State to the Court your name and residence.

Answer. Stephen Teney; I live at Washington, Daviess county, Indiana, where I have resided about a year. Previous to that I lived for seven years at Pleasant Valley, Martin county.

Q. What is your business?

A. I am a cooper by trade

Q. Did you ever know Stephen Horsey?

A. Yes, sir.

Q. When and where did you make his acquaintance?

A. At the Shoals. It is about five years since I first knew him.

Q. Did you ever join any secret order called the Circle of Honor, Order of American Knights, or Sons of Liberty?

A. Yes, sir; I joined the Circle of Honor.

Q. Where, and when?

A. In Columbia township, Martin county, near Connell School House, in the fall of 1863, at Mr. Horsey's solicitation.

Q. Is Mr. Horsey present in this room? If so, point him out.

[The witness here pointed to the accused, Stephen Horsey.]

Q. What, if any thing was done at that meeting?

A. Fourteen members were taken in that night?

Q. How many were present at that meeting?

A. About twenty-five.

Q. Who presided?

A. Mr. Horsey and a Mr. William Clayton were the presiding officers at that meeting.

Q. Were you sworn in that night?

A. Yes, sir.

Q. Do you remember what obligation you took?

A. We were to be cut into four pieces if we told any thing. One part was to be cast out at the east gate, one at the north gate, one at the south gate, and one at the west gate, if we told any of the secrets?

Q. What were the secrets?

A. We were not to tell who belonged to the order, nor any thing that was done at the meetings.

Q. What did you learn to be the objects and purposes of the order?

A. From what I saw and learned, we were to assist the South, if called on.

Q. Were any of the ways by which you could assist the South talked of?

A. Yes, sir. If we were called on we were to rally, each in his township.

Q. Under whom?

A. I do not recollect, but we were to rally in each township to assist the rebels if they came through.

Q. With arms or how?

A. They did not say. They also said if we did not rally, and stick up one for another, that the Democratic party would be torn down.

Q. What had that to do with giving assistance to the rebels?

A. I do not know; that is the way Horsey and Clayton talked to us that night. Horsey told us about it first, and then Clayton.

Q. Did Horsey say any thing about opposing the Government?

A. He told us we were to hold ourselves in readiness at any time to be called out.

Q. State whether or not there was any arming or drilling in this order?

A. We drilled a few times in the township; we just marched.

Q. Do you know any thing about an attempt to arm the order?

A. I was told by one of my brothers, William Teney, who was a member of the order, that they were getting arms all the time. This was after I removed, and went back, that he told me this. The order was then called the Knights of the Golden Circle.

Q. Who was the chief of that order?

A. I do not know. I went there once, and they told me the oath, but I would not take it.

Q. What did your brother tell you about arms?

A. He said that they had three hundred pistols in that county; and that Baker, of Dover Hill, went to Cincinnati and got some, and some he got from Philadelphia.

Q. Had you any talk with Horsey?

A. Not about the arms.

7

Q. When was the last talk you had with Horsey?

A. It must have been some four or five months since. He told me they were getting along finely with their order.

Q. What order did he refer to?

A. I suppose he meant the Golden Circle.

Q. Did you ever hear Horsey make any other speeches?

A. No, sir.

I am in the army now, and have been since the draft. No inducements have been held out to me to testify in this case, but McDonald, who is a Government detective, told me if I told all I knew, he would do what he could for me, and relieve me from the draft. Nothing was said in the obligation about supporting the Constitution of the United States, or the Constitution of the State of Indiana. Mr. Horsey said we were to support the South; he swore us to support Jeff' Davis, North or South. That was a part of the oath, and we were to suffer ourselves to be torn into four pieces if we did not support Jeff' Davis North or South. My brother told me this last summer that he was a member of the Knights of the Golden Circle. During the summer, when I visited my brother, I went with him to the Knights of the Golden Circle, and they wanted me to take the oath, but I would not.

RE-EXAMINATION.

Question by the Judge Advocate:

Has any officer of the Government held out any inducement to you that you should receive any benefit for testifying in this case?

A. No, sir; only what that detective said; he promised to do all he could for me.

Q. Have you ever asked any officer of the Government to relieve you?

A. No, sir.

Q. Do you expect to be relieved from the draft?

A. No, sir.

Q. Do you testify from any such inducement?

A. No, sir; I think more of my oath than that.

The Commission then adjourned, to meet on Friday, October 28, 1864, at 9 o'clock, A. M.

———

COURT ROOM, INDIANAPOLIS, INDIANA, }
October 28, 1864, 9 o'clock, A. M. }

The Commission met pursuant to adjournment.

All the members present. Also, the Judge Advocate, the accused, and their counsel.

The proceedings were read and approved.

J. J. BINGHAM, a witness for Government, was then introduced, and being duly sworn by the Judge Advocate, testified as follows:

Question by the Judge Advocate:

State your name, place of residence, and business?

Answer. Joseph J. Bingham; I reside in the city of Indianapolis, and am editor of the *Daily and Weekly Indiana State Sentinel.*

Q. How long have you resided in Indianapolis?

A. Since August, 1856.

Q. Where did you reside previous to that?

A. At Lafayette, in this State.

Q. How long have you published the *Indiana State Sentinel?*

A. Since the 26th of August, 1856.

Q. Did you ever join an order called the American Knights, or Sons of Liberty?

A. I joined an order which was called the American Knights, in the latter part of October or the beginning of November, 1863.

Q. Where?

A. In this city, in the Military Hall, on Washington street, between Meridian and Pennsylvania.

Q. Who was in possession of the Hall?

A. It was leased by the Democratic Club of this city.

Q. Was it under their control?

A. It is my impression that it was under their control at the time.

Q. What was the first meeting of the American Knights that you attended?

A. The first meeting, if you can call it such, was my initiation; there were very few present.

Q. Who were present?

A. Mr. Dodd, Mr. Harrison, a man by the name of Jacobs, Dr. Johnson, and I think a person of the name of Vandegriff.

Q. Was Mr. Ristine or Hord there?

A. Not at that time.

Q. What took place at that meeting?

A. It was only an informal initiation; we did not go through all the ceremonies, the greater part was omitted.

Q. State to the Court how you came to join the order, and at whose solicitation you joined?

A. In the latter part of August, or the first of September, I was introduced by Mr. Dodd to a man by the name of P. C. Wright. He brought him to my office and left him there; said he wanted to have a talk with me. Mr. Wright went on to state his business; gave me a little history of himself; he stated that he was a lawyer in business in New Orleans, at the breaking out of this rebellion; that he was forced to leave on account of his Union sentiments; that he went to St. Louis, and practiced alternately between St. Louis and New Orleans—in St. Louis in the summer, and New Orleans in the winter; he said he was a lawyer in the celebrated Gaines case, and that in examining the papers of General Gaines, he came across what purported to be a secret organization that existed during the Revolutionary War. He told me that General Lee was President of the Association, as appeared from the papers; that Madison, Jefferson, and I believe Washington, had belonged to it; that it had exerted a very powerful agency in maintaining the contest during the war, and establishing our present form of government; that he thought he would establish a similar order. He told me that the principles of the order were the same as existed during the Revolution; that the ritual and obligation were nearly the same; that the papers were not perfect, but the omissions were supplied; and that he came to this State for the purpose of extending the order here. He said it existed in Missouri, Illinois, and even in the Central American States; it was not confined to the United States, but was to extend over all the world, not limited by any geographical divisions. He urged me to join, and take part in it, and be one of the persons to establish the order here. I said I was opposed to all secret political organizations—that I never saw any good come from them—and declined. He visited the prominent Democrats of the city, and used the same arguments, but most of them declined. I do not know whether Mr. Dodd was a member of the order at that time; I understood he intended to be. Mr. Dodd is a gentleman very fond of excitement; he has a natural taste for secret associations. He was a prominent and one of the most active members of the Know Nothing order; and he was head and front of the Sons of Malta, in this city; his taste runs that way. I have known Mr. Dodd for many years; for three or four years I have had business relations with him that threw him constantly in contact with me. After Wright left, Dodd urged me to join the association. I declined at first. Finally he told me what its objects were; that it was to be a permanent organization; political, but not partisan; that it was to sympathize with the principles of the Democratic party. He said that the object was to educate the people in the old fashioned republican doctrines, the same as those entertained by Madison and Jefferson; that it was designed to establish a paper here, to be the organ and advocate of its principles, and that it was intended to have a large university near the city, to educate young men in what he termed correct political doctrines; and that the organization was to be permanent, like the Odd Fellows or Masons.

When the proposition of the paper was started, he said he wanted to advise with me about many matters which he could not unless I was a member of the organization, and that he could not even tell me the names of the members of the order; that was one of the obligations of secrecy; but if I would join, he would not put me through the regular ceremonies, but would initiate me informally, and if I did not like it, as I joined voluntarily, so I could leave it whenever I pleased. I thought I saw in this the seeds of discord, so far as the Democratic party was concerned. Being a party man, I thought the only way to secure success was by the uniting of the different elements in opposition to the Administration. With that view of the case I joined at the time I named. Dodd informed me that he had appointed me a delegate to the State Council, which met in November, 1863. I attended; took what they called a Council degree; but what it is I can not now tell, I paid so little attention to it. The meeting was held in the Military Hall. Dodd presided at the meeting, and Mr. Harrison was Secretary. I do not recollect what other officers were there. I saw Mr. Vandegriff at the meeting; and I think Dr. Athon, Mr. Ristine, and Mr. Milligan, the accused, were present. A gentleman named Cushman, from the northern part of the State, was present.

Q. Were any others of the accused present?

A. No, sir.

Q. What business was done at that meeting?

A. The Council was opened in due form; those that had not taken the Council degree were initiated, and then various committees were appointed. I found myself placed as Chairman of the Committee on Literature.

Q. What other committees were appointed?

A. I do not recollect.

Q. Was a military committee appointed?

A. I do not recollect.

Q. Were any appointments made by Dodd?

A. Not in my hearing.

Q. At what time of day was the meeting held?

A. It convened at 10 o'clock in the morning.

Q. How long did it last?

A. I was there about an hour, but I understood it lasted till evening.

Q. Why did you not remain?

A. I withdrew to write my report. I wrote a brief report, advising, as far as a paper was concerned, that nothing be done until means were raised to support it a year; and I recommended the indefinite postponement of the university scheme until the next meeting of the Council. I returned then, and some other business was going on, but I do not recollect what. I handed my report to the committee, in which was a Dr. Bryant. I told Cushman that my engagements were such that I could not remain, and he would oblige me if, when the report was called, he would read it.

Q. Did you learn from any members present about the appointment of major generals?

A. No, sir.

Q. Did you ever hear of any military appointments being made?

A. No, sir. I did not know that the organization embraced any thing of a military nature till the exposure of the Sons of Liberty.

Q. You will please proceed with your narration?

A. I never attended what is called the meeting of the temple. On the 16th of February another State Council was held. Mr. Dodd informed me that by virtue of my appointment, I had a right to attend. I went in on the morning of the 16th. I had been to the post office, and stopped on my way to my own office, for a few minutes. I had nothing to do with the meeting, and did not feel much interest in the matter. I was in again for a little while in the afternoon, when I went to the post office a second time. When I went in there was a gentleman of this city making a speech, Major Conklin, and this was the first time I recollect hearing about any military appointments. I suppose he had been called on for a report of what he had done, for the drift of his speech—what I heard of it—was, that he had not drilled any body, and had not any body to drill. That is all my recollection of that meeting.

Q. How did he come to report that fact?

A. I suppose he had been called upon for a report; that was what I gathered from the nature of his speech; and that was the first idea I had of its being a military organization. I never read the ritual, or the constitution, or by-laws. I think Mr. Heffren was present at that meeting. Mr. Heffren is an old friend of mine, and came to my office to see me several times. At one of those interviews we exchanged our opinions as to this association. I told him that I thought no good would come of it. Mr. Heffren coincided with my views, and said he believed it was a humbug. These are the only meetings I attended. I did not wish to belong to the organization. I paid my fees, and asked Mr. Dodd if any formal withdrawal was necessary; he said that my joining was voluntary, and I might withdraw when I liked. I did not consider myself a member of the organization since that time, and have not been a member, though my having been in the order gives me the confidence of the members, and I have learned many things that I otherwise should not have known.

Q. Did you hear the address of Dodd at the meeting of the 16th or 17th of February?

A. No, sir.

Q. How long were you present?

A. I was not there over twenty or thirty minutes. I heard afterward that he had delivered an address, but I never read it till I saw it in the *Journal* of the 30th of July.

Q. Who was present at that meeting?

A. Colonel Bowles, the accused, Dr. Bryant, Mr. Blake, of Terre Haute, Mr. Cushman and 'Squire McBride, of Evansville. There must have been some thirty or forty there, but few that I was acquainted with.

Q. Was Mr. Milligan or Mr. Humphreys present?

A. Not to my knowledge. I did not see them there. Mr. Heffren was present.

Q. Did you learn what business was transacted at that meeting?

A. I asked the question after the adjournment of the meeting, and was told nothing particular had been done.

Q. Did you learn who had been appointed to the Supreme Council?

A. No, sir.

Q. Do you know who composed the Committee of Thirteen?

A. No, sir. The Committee of Thirteen, in my opinion, was a myth. The next thing that came up, in connection with the order, was this: Dr. Bowles, Mr. Dodd, Judge Bullitt, and Barrett were at my business office. I met them on the platform as I was going down from my room; I was introduced to them, and supposed they were all members of the order, though nothing was said about it; I supposed so from their association. Judge Bullitt I had known previously, I think fifteen years ago; he had done me a great kindness; we renewed our acquaintance, and he asked me to call and see him at the Palmer House; said he had some fine Kentucky whisky, and invited me to take a drink. About half past 11 I thought I would go to my dinner early and stop in and see him. I knew where the room was, it was No. 28; I went right up stairs and knocked at the door. He said, "Come in," and I opened the door. The first man I saw was a person of the name of Coffin. I did not know then what his occupation was, but from his associations I thought he was a Republican, and I thought it was queer company for Democrats. I walked up and shook hands with him; he whispered to me, "I've have caught you at last." I thought that was very strange, very singular; I walked around the room, and mentioned to one of the gentlemen that it was a singular company. We passed the salutations of the day, and I then said to Bullitt, "If you have any good whisky, bring it out." He brought it out, and we had a drink. I asked Coffin if he was going to dinner; he said he was, and we walked together. As we walked out, I asked an explanation of the remark he had made to me, "I've caught you at last." He told me a story not necessary to be repeated here, and applied it to me; said that was all he meant. A few days afterward I met Joseph E. McDonald, on Wash-

ington street. I told him the circumstance, and he remarked to me, "Don't you know who this Coffin is?" "He is a United States Detective; he is in the employ of the Government, and has been for two years." I remarked to him that it was a singular secret society, the members of which should sit in council with a United States Detective.

Q. Did you at that time unfold to Mr. McDonald your association with that order?

A. No, sir; I do not think I told him till sometime subsequent.

Q. What was done by these gentlemen?

A. They never told me their business; and to this day I do not know what they met together for.

Q. You say that you met McDonald, and that you remarked to him that it was a singular secret association that should have a United States Detective in it; how did you come to tell him that, if you did not make known to him that you were a member of the order?

A. We had talked upon the subject frequently; I do not know if he knew whether I was a member or not.

Q. Did you ever give him to understand that you were a member?

A. No, sir.

Q. From your conversation do you know whether he was aware that you were a member of the order?

A. No, sir.

Q. When was this conversation with Mr. McDonald?

A. The interview occurred about the middle of May, and it was, I think, within a week afterward, that I had this conversation with McDonald.

Q. Where were you first introduced to Mr. Stidger—in your office?

A. I first saw him there. Every Sunday morning, about 9 o'clock, a number of political friends met in my office to hear the telegrams read. One Sunday morning, about the 1st of June, I was coming down to my office, and I met Dodd and Stidger. Dodd introduced him to me, and I recollected the man, though not his name; he said he was the Private Secretary of Judge Bullitt; and either at that interview or within a short time, a day or two, Dodd or Stidger made this remark, that this man Coffin had compromised Judge Bullitt, or that Judge Bullitt thought he had, I don't recollect which. The next meeting of the order here was held in June, but I know nothing of its proceedings, as I was not present. That brings us along to about the first of August. In the mean time I had seen Colonel Bowles once; he came to my office one evening; said he wanted to talk with me about matters generally; and he asked me if I thought this man Coffin was a detective; he had his doubts about it. I told him there was no doubt about it.

Q. From whom did you have it?

A. Mr. McDonald. Another circumstance it may be well to relate; it shows the perfect system of espionage here.

[The Judge Advocate remarked that it was unnecessary to state that here.]

I do not recollect any thing special occurring until the 2d or 3d of August. About that time, one morning Mr. Dodd came into my room and said, "I want to have a talk with you." He said he wanted to tell me something; "but," said he, "you must give me your word of honor that what I say to you, you will not reveal to any living being." Not knowing what it was, I said, "Certainly." He went on to say it had been determined at a meeting, or Council, I do not recollect which, I think he said at a Council of Sixteen; I believe he said something about its being composed of four from Indiana, four from Illinois, four from Kentucky, and four from Missouri; I do not think any names were mentioned but Judge Bullitt and Mr. Bowles; he said that at the Council, a resolution had been determined upon, and he went on to explain it. He said that arrangements had been made to release the prisoners on Johnson's Island; at Camp Chase, near Columbus, Ohio; at Camp Morton, and also at Camp Douglas, and that the prisoners at Camp Douglas, after their release, were to go over and release those at Rock Island. At the same time there was to be an uprising at Louisville, at which the Government stores, etc., were to be seized.

Q. An uprising of what and who?

A. He did not state what or who; he said an "uprising." I looked at the man in astonishment. I thought it was a wild dream; I could not believe it possible. I studied a moment, and said, "Mr. Dodd, do you know what you are going to undertake? Do you know the position of military affairs here at this post? Do you think you can accomplish this scheme with any number of unarmed and undisciplined men you can bring here?" Another thing he remarked to me was that this revolution was going to take place at several points on the 16th of August, and that I was the only person he communicated this to in the city. I asked "how is this revolution to take place, and nobody know any thing about it?" As to the way in which it was to be done here, and at Louisville, he made a suggestion to me, as I was Chairman of the Democratic State Central Committee, which was that I should call a mass meeting of the Democracy on the 16th of August. I said we had had experience enough of Democratic mass meetings, and there would be no excuse or apology for calling such a meeting here. I asked him what excuse he could give for calling the meeting. He said to take some expression against the draft, and to give some instructions to the delegates who attended the Chicago Convention, which was to be held on the 29th of August. I told him I could consent to nothing of the kind, and would be a party to no such scheme. W. H. Talbot, Chairman of the Democratic Central Congressional District, had gone to New York, and he left me to act in his absence. Dodd knew this, and on my declining to call a meeting, as chairman of the Democratic State Central Committee, he wanted me to call a District mass meeting to nominate a candidate for this Congressional District. I told him I would not. Dodd then made application to others, also to McDonald to urge him to induce me to call a mass meeting, but I declined to do it. I then began to think seriously about the matter, and to reflect what was best to be done. I had been intrusted with an important secret, and it was of such a nature that I thought I ought not to keep it. I then determined to investigate the matter. I first called on Mr. Ristine, and I put leading questions to him to find out whether or not he knew of any such project, as that which had been communicated to me by Mr. Dodd, and I felt satisfied that he did not. I then called upon Mr. Athon, and in the same way I asked him leading questions to find out what he knew about the matter, and I felt satisfied he knew nothing about it. I spoke to others, to Mr. Hord among the rest. I went to bed and slept over it.

In the morning I went to see Mr. J. E. McDonald. I told him I had secret information that I wished to consult him about; that it was a matter involving us all, and that some action had to be taken immediately. He said he was willing to listen to all I had to say. This was on the night of the 4th of August. I told Mr. McDonald all that Dodd had told me, and the circumstances under which he had told it, and that I had come to advise with him as to what was my duty in the matter. We talked the matter over sometime, and finally came to the conclusion that we would sleep over it, but that the thing must be stopped at all hazards. I left him at 9 o'clock, and went to my office. As I walked down Washington street I saw a gentleman coming up rapidly, and I stopped him: "Halloo! Kerr, what has brought you here?" I said. He seemed very much excited. "Do you know any thing?" he said; and I said, "Do you know any thing?" "Yes," he replied. "What is it?" said I. He then said, "The devil's to pay in our section of the State; the people of Washington, Harrison and Floyd counties, and that neighborhood, had got the idea that a revolution was impending; the farmers were frightened, and were selling their hay in the fields and their wheat in the stacks, and all the property that could be was being converted into greenbacks."

Q. What Kerr was that?

A. Michael C. Kerr. "Is that all you know?" I said. "No," said he. Then he went on and represented to me just what Dodd had before told me. He went over the whole scheme, just as Dodd had revealed it. As we walked along, he turned around once or twice to see if any detectives were following us. I didn't let him know that I knew anything about the matter. I said, "This is a most important matter, and I insist that you go up to Mr. McDonald's with me, and tell him what you have told me." We got him up, and I said to him, "Kerr has got some important information, and I want him to tell you the same story that he has told me."

Q. Did you, previous to that time, or at that time, as a matter of safety to yourself, state to McDonald your whole connection with the matter?

A. I think he understood that I was a member of the order.

Q. Did you give him the whole history of the matter?

A. He understood I was a member of the order. In this conversation with Mr. Kerr, he involved Dr. Athon in the scheme. I think, also, he told me that Governor Morton was to be captured or taken prisoner, and that Dr. Athon was to be Provisional Governor, and that was to be part of the scheme. McDonald said we would all meet in the morning, as had been agreed upon. Coming out, I said that I could not rest under the suspicion that Dr. Athon knew any thing of the scheme. I did not think that he did; and I said that although it was after 12 o'clock, I would go to his house. We went and called him up. He came down, and I told him, that although it was such a late hour, yet as Mr. Kerr had come with such important information he ought to know it that night. He agreed to meet with us the next morning at McDonald's office. Coming out, I asked what he thought of Dr. Athon? He said, "He is an innocent man. He knows nothing about this scheme." Athon would scarcely believe that such a scheme was entertained. I think he said: "It's all gas; such a scheme can not be entertained by sensible men."

The next day we went about 8 or 9 o'clock to McDonald's office. I had invited in all the prominent Democrats I could see. Judge Rhoads was present; McDonald was present; William Henderson, of this city; Mr. Hord, Aquilla Jones, Samuel H. Buskirk, Mr. Ristine, I think, Dr. Yeakle, and Colonel Caldwell, of Lafayette, and there may have been others. Mr. Kerr then told the story to those present. Then we had a consultation about the matter, and came to the conclusion that the matter must be stopped right then. After awhile Dodd and John C. Walker came in.

Q. Was Dodd sent for, or did he come of his own volition?

A. I think he was told that a meeting was to be held there that morning for consultation. Walker had arrived from New York that morning. This meeting occurred on Friday, the 5th of August. Mr. Kerr made a speech. He spoke about this excitement—this revolutionary scheme—and that he came up on purpose to put a stop to the thing. I think he said that it was our duty to stop it, and I coincided; and if it could not be stopped in any other way, it was our duty to inform the authorities. Coloner Walker and Dodd did not acknowledge at that interview that any such scheme was entertained. They both spoke, and very earnestly, about the state of public affairs, and they used about these arguments: That the Government could not be restored again under the old state of things without a forcible revolution. That an appeal to the ballot-box was all folly; that the people were prepared for revolution; that they would not submit to the draft; and that it was better to direct the revolution than to have revolution direct us. That was about what they said. Before we left there, these gentlemen agreed that this whole matter should be stopped, and we were satisfied from the pledges they gave us, that the thing would be stopped. But how they intended to do it, I do not know; I understood they would send messengers to those various points, and state that that was their determination. They assured us that we need have no further apprehensions about the matter, and we rested content with that.

I was satisfied at that time—and the question was asked me the other day why I did not inform the authorities, but I was satisfied that the authorities knew as much as I did, and from this one circumstance among others. The signal of the uprising at Louisville, was to be the notice of a barbecue to take place in the neighborhood of Louisville. It was understood that the uprising was to take place on the day announced for that barbecue. Mr. Kerr informed us that night, in our interview with McDonald, that Judge Bullitt had that day or the day previous been arrested. Also that many of the prominent members of the order and others, had fled the State, and the reason was the publication of that barbecue. A good many of them had come up on the same train with him, and others had left the day before. They had gone to New York and Canada. I was satisfied from that fact that the authorities knew as much about the matter as I did. And this was confirmed a day or two afterward by a remark that fell from General Carrington. He spoke of this thing to Mr. McDonald, and

Mr. McDonald and myself were both satisfied that the authorities were fully informed, and the circumstances seem to have shown that they were. They were informed of it before I was. Stidger was informed of it on the 29th of July, three or four days before it was communicated to me, so that General Carrington and the authorities must have known of it on the night of the 29th of July. We had then called the Democratic State Central Committee to meet on the 17th of August, to fill vacancies on the State ticket, and to report, etc. I regarded this matter as most important in its effects upon the Democratic party, and that was another reason why I did not wish to say any thing about it, for if this thing had been made public, it would injure us in the coming election; the charge would be made that the Democratic party was a revolutionary party, and we would have been saddled with the sins of these men. Another thing, it was a matter of personal honor. I received this information from those gentlemen under peculiar circumstances, and after I found the thing was stopped, I did not feel it incumbent on me to inform the authorities. I advised the gentlemen to leave before they should be arrested. Dodd was here two weeks after, and Walker was here from the 5th to the 15th of August without being arrested. My conversation at the time the authorities knew about it—for I had every reason to believe it—made me come to this conclusion. I told them as a friend, that if they remained here they would be arrested. They thought so and left.

Q. At this meeting, at which Mr. McDonald and others were present, did Mr. Dodd confess that his scheme was true?

A. No, sir; but rather denied it. He neither confessed nor denied it, but said that revolution was necessary.

Q. Was it charged upon him by Mr. Kerr that it was true?

A. Yes, sir.

Q. And did he refuse to acknowledge the fact?

A. He refused to deny or acknowledge it.

Q. Why did you not make known to those persons who did not know it, that it was true?

A. We did, sir. All present understood it thoroughly. We conversed an hour or two before these gentlemen came in.

We had a meeting of the Central Committee on the 12th of August. I stated in the notice sent out on the 6th of August, that matters of grave importance demanded a large attendance, and it was hoped that all the Committee would attend, and we invited other prominent men in the State. We had quite a large meeting. We filled up the vacancies on the State ticket, and then this matter came up for discussion. Mr. Kerr was present, and at my request he laid this whole affair before the members of the Committee, and the same resolution came up there we had in our previous consultation, that, if the thing had not been stopped, it must be now. We had to be satisfied on that point.

Colonel Walker came to that meeting. We had a two-days meeting—the 12th and the 13th. And he assured the Committee that it was stopped, that nothing of the kind should take place.

Q. Was it previous to, or after this meeting of the Council of Sixteen at Chicago, that you met Mr. Walker here, and had a conversation with him, in reference to any rebel officers going to Illinois, to take charge of the rebel prisoners?

A. I saw Mr. Walker previously, once or twice, while he was here. I met him on the street, and he complained that I had not seen him. He was sleeping at Colonel Rose's room, in this building, at the time. Colonel Rose was absent at the time. He is a brother-in-law of Colonel Rose. This was on the morning of the 11th. He went to the Bates House, and said he regretted to have to go to the Bates House, it was a bad place to stop at. I asked him why he was going. He said he had to meet these gentlemen by appointment. I understood him to say they were rebel officers. They would be there that day, and unless he was there, they would not know where to find him. He said they were on their way to Chicago to take charge of the rebel prisoners when they were released from Camp Douglas. It was necessary that he should see them, to tell them that the whole scheme was stopped. He met me afterward, and said he had seen them, and they had gone on and stopped all operations at that time, for the release of the prisoners.

CROSS-EXAMINATION.

Question by the accused:

To what extent was this scheme of revolution known and entertained in this order, and out of it, as far as you know?

A. All that I know is that it was communicated to me under those circumstances, and I know nothing further than those to whom I communicated it in this city and those who came from a distance.

Q. To what extent did Dodd state that he had communicated the matter?

A. He stated to me that I was the only person to whom he had communicated it. That was about the 2d or 3d of August.

Q. Did Mr. Kerr get his information from the same source?

A. No, sir. I do not know where he got it.

Q. Do you say this Council of Sixteen had resolved upon this revolutionary scheme when it convened at Chicago?

A. Yes, sir.

Q. How long before that?

A. I don't think he told me, when I saw

him here from Chicago or New York; he got back about the 29th of July.

Q. Did you not know, from other sources, and through other medium, that, so far from Mr. Dodd's statement being true, the proposition had actually been voted down in that Council?

A. Yes, sir. I heard that.

Q. Did you hear it from the members of the order?

A. I heard it, but it did not come directly from a member of the order.

Q. Did you learn from Dodd, that Bowles was a member of that Council?

A. That is what I understood.

Q. Did you understand from Bowles, as a member of the Council, that the proposition for revolution had been voted down?

A. Not directly.

Q. Who were the members of that Council? Was either of the accused—Heffren, Horsey, Milligan, or Humphreys a member?

A. I did not understand that either of them was.

Q. You say that it was not until a very late period of your connection with the order, that you got any knowledge of its military feature. Did it, either with or without its military feature, contemplate in its teachings, as you got them in the order, or in the ritual, or any of its written or unwritten works, any such revolutionary scheme as the purpose and object of the order?

A. I did not so understand it; I never read the Constitution or Ritual until long after I joined; not until the 30th of July.

Q. What was the purpose of the organization as you understood it?

A. Purely political. That was my understanding of it at the time I joined it.

Q. This conflict of the Government, then, that was concocted by these men, you say was not within the scope or contemplation of the order?

A. Nothing was ever mentioned in the order, or by any member of the order, until it was communicated by Dodd to me.

Q. Do you know any thing about the Committee of Thirteen?

A. I think it was some time in August. On the Saturday that these arms were discovered, a young man came to my house after supper, and brought me a communication from Dodd and Walker. I think they were in Chicago. They inclosed an address from what was called a Committee of Thirteen, and requested me to publish it in the *Sentinel*; and if I did not publish it, they wanted to have it printed in Dodd's office. I told him I had not time to look at it, but if he would come in on Sunday morning, I would let him know. I declined to publish it, and I told him that as I had an interest in Dodd's establishment, it could not be published there. I inclosed the communication back to Mr. Walker.

Q. You say, do you not, that Walker said he wrote the address, and was authorized to use Dodd's name as chairman of the Committee of Thirteen?

A. I understand there was no such committee.

Q. Had you any evidence that Walker signed the communication?

A. Yes, sir. It was in his handwriting. Dodd also wrote to the same effect from Chicago.

Q. Had you any more than one conversation with Heffren?

A. Yes, sir. Heffren came to my office several times; the night before and the night after the meeting on the 16th and 17th of February.

Q. Was it on that occasion you said you would have nothing to do with the order?

A. Yes, sir; and Heffren said he considered it a humbug.

Q. Did he express any opinion about abandoning it?

A. Yes, sir. I so understood him. He coincided with my opinion and would do as I had done.

Q. Did you have any information of Mr. Heffren's meeting with the organization after that?

A. No, sir.

Q. You stated, did you not, that Mr. Milligan was present at the State Council in November?

A. Yes, sir.

Q. Was that the only time you met him at the State Council?

A. I met him only that time, and that was the only knowledge I had of his connection with the order.

Q. Have you not stated that nothing was discussed in the order but pure politics, education and literature?

A. That was all that was discussed in my hearing. There may have been other matters that I did not hear.

Q. What was the date of the time when you expressed your determination not to have any more to do with the institution?

A. It was after the February meeting.

Q. Did you not after that time maintain your previous intimacy with members or persons belonging to the organization?

A. Yes, sir.

Q. From October until the 15th of August, when Dodd revealed to you the purpose to inaugurate a revolution, did you hear, in or out of the order, of any purpose to inaugurate a revolution by the order itself?

A. Nothing of the kind.

Q. Then what was the organization? Was it not purely political?

A. That was my understanding.

Q. Then I will ask you to state whether this conspiracy that Dodd revealed to you was not a conspiracy of Dodd, Walker and one or two others, and not a conspiracy by the order?

A. That was my understanding, sir.

Question by the Judge Advocate:

Do you say that was your understanding?

A. Yes, sir.

Q. Was it not your understanding that the leaders of the order were to use the order to accomplish this revolution? What position did Dodd hold in the command of the order?

A. He was Grand Commander.

Q. Had he not, according to the Constitution and Ritual, the power to call it together?

A. Yes, sir.

Q. Were they not sworn to obey implicitly his order?

A. Yes, sir.

Q. Then could he, or could he not, order them to come here armed, as he chose, Was that not in accordance with the obligations of the order?

A. It was not so far as I understood it.

Q. I ask you the plain, simple question, whether or not, according to the Constitution of that order, you were not to obey him implicitly over and above all other commands? Did you ever see the constitution and laws of the order?

A. I saw them as they were published in the Indianapolis *Journal.* I saw the book containing them, but never read it?

Q. Would you recognize them if you saw the books?

A. Yes, sir; I think I should.

Q. The Judge Advocate here handed the witness a copy of the Constitution of the Supreme Council of the order, and asked, is this one of the books you saw?

A. It looks something like it.

Q. Will you read section 17 of the General Laws?

A. The witness read the following:

"Sec. 17. The Grand Commanders shall be the presiding officers of the Grand Councils of the States, execute all laws passed by such Councils, and shall be commanders-in-chief of the military forces of their respective States."

What I saw was the ritual and the oath; I never saw this before.

The Judge Advocate here handed the witness a pamphlet containing the Ritual of the third degree, and asked:

Q. Is that not the Ritual of the third degree?

A. That is what it purports to be.

The Judge Advocate then read the following portion of the obligation:

"I do further swear, that I will, at all times and in all places, yield prompt and implicit obedience to the utmost of my ability without remonstrance, hesitation or delay, to any and every mandate, order or request, of my immediate M. E. G. C.,* in all things touching the purposes of the O. S. L., and to defend the principles thereof, when assailed in my own State or country, in whatsoever capacity may be assigned to me by authority of our order."

Q. Is that one of the obligations taken by the order?

A. Yes, sir.

Q. I will ask you again, whether the Grand Commander had power to call this order together, and to give them such orders as he saw proper?

A. Yes, sir. That matter came up for discussion, I think. I asked the Grand Commander the question, when I went into the order, whether there was any obligation that would violate my duties or my obligations as a citizen, and he said there was not. I think that was the construction placed upon this obligation: that there would be nothing violating our obligation as citizens.

Q. You have spoken of this uprising on the 16th. By whom was it contemplated?

A. Dodd gave me no information but this, that he desired me to call a mass meeting of the Democracy, and under cover of that he could accomplish his ends.

Q. How?

A. By revolution.

Q. Who were to inaugurate that revolution?

A. He expected the men that came here to do it.

Q. Who were to come here?

A. That he never explained to me.

Q. Who, did you gather from what he said, would do it?

A. I should infer from what he said that he expected the assistance of the members of the order.

Q. Were any promises or pledges, or threats made, on behalf of the Government, to induce you to give this testimony?

A. None whatever.

I think it is due to this Court and to the Judge Advocate, to state that this statement is made voluntarily. That I intended to have made it in writing and publish it for my own vindication.

The Commission then adjourned, to meet at 2 o'clock, P. M.

———

COURT ROOM, INDIANAPOLIS, INDIANA, October 28, 1864, 2 o'clock, P. M.

The Commission met pursuant to adjournment.

All the members present; also, the Judge Advocate, the accused and their counsel.

———

* Most Excellent Grand Commander.

Felix G. Stidger, a witness for the Government, was then introduced, and being duly sworn by the Judge Advocate, testified as follows:

Question by the Judge Advocate:

State your name, place of residence, and business for the last two or three years?

Answer. Felix G. Stidger; I live in Mattoon, Illinois. For the last two or three years I have been in the dry goods business, and I have been a carpenter, and served in the army.

Q. Where did you reside immediately preceding your living at Mattoon, Illinois?

A. At Louisville, Kentucky. I came there on the 15th of April, 1864.

Q. Where previous to that?

A. At Taylorsville, Kentucky.

Q. How long did you reside there?

A. Two months after leaving the army.

Q. When did you leave the army?

A. On the morning of the 14th of February I received my discharge.

Q. From what regiment were you discharged?

A. From the 15th Regiment Kentucky Volunteer Infantry. I was discharged for physical disability.

Q. Were you with your regiment?

A. No, sir; not a day. I served as clerk in the Adjutant General's office, 1st Division, 14th Army Corps.

Q. Who was the Adjutant General?

A. Major McDowell, Captain Taylor, now Colonel 15th Kentucky Volunteers, Captain Nevin, Lieutenant Colonel Lyme Starling, formerly chief of General Crittenden's staff, and when I left Captain Wells was Assistant Adjutant General.

Q. Who commanded the corps?

A. General Thomas, and part of the time General Palmer.

Q. What particular duties did you perform as clerk?

A. Applications for resignations, leave of absence, furloughs, sometimes reports of the troops, and special and general orders.

Q. Please state to the Court how your attention was first called to the Order of the Sons of Liberty; and when, if ever, you joined them?

A. I was in Captain Jones' office on the morning of the 5th of May, 1864, and he showed me a letter from General Carrington, stating something in reference to Dr. Bowles being a dangerous man, and requesting him to send a Kentuckian to him; on the receipt of that letter, Captain Jones sent me to Dr. Bowles. I received instructions in the Vestibule, or Neophyte Degree, on that morning; Mr. Prentice instructed me before I went to see Dr. Bowles. That was on the 5th of May, 1864. I started to see Dr. Bowles on the morning of the 6th, and arrived at his house on the 8th. He resides at French Lick Springs, Orange county, Indiana.

Q. Did you go directly to his house?

A. No, sir; I stopped at Salem, thinking that was the nearest railroad point, but I found it was twenty odd miles to French Lick Springs, and no regular conveyance. By going further up the railroad to Orleans, it was not so far; there was a regular conveyance all the time. I stepped off the train at Salem about 11 in the morning of the 6th of May, and remained there until the night train came along, which was probably 10 o'clock; I then went to Orleans and staid there till 12 o'clock the next day, Saturday the 7th, when I took the regular conveyance out to Paoli. On the 8th I went to Dr. Bowles' house. On the way to Mr. Bowles', I saw Mr. Heffren at Salem.

Q. State how you happened to meet him, and your conversation with him.

A. I fell in with a man by the name of Drom. I think he stated his name was John, but I am not sure whether it was John or S. He is a clothing merchant, and keeps a store. He saw Mr. Heffren walking across the square, and remarked that there was one of the Democratic leaders of that part of the country. He said something about Heffren wearing a butternut pin, and that there had been something said about taking it off him, and that if it had been done there would have been one thousand or fifteen hundred men ready to revenge the insult. Drom told Heffren that I was from Kentucky; Heffren came up and asked if I wished to see him. He then went on to tell me that he was expecting a commissioner from Kentucky, from the rebel forces there; and I told him about three of Forrest's regiments being disbanded there—in the State of Kentucky.

Q. Did he explain what he meant by the word "commissioner?"

A. Not at that time; afterward he did. I told him of the three regiments of Forrest's men having been disbanded, and he told me that there were four more to be disbanded. This was what he was expecting to hear of, and was expecting a commissioner from the forces in Kentucky to see him that day or the next, and he did not know but I was probably the man, as I came from Kentucky. I knew nothing more about these three Kentucky regiments being disbanded than what I had seen in the newspapers. I understood they were furloughed soldiers who were to remain at home a certain time, and at a certain signal they were to concentrate whenever ordered. Mr. Heffren told me during the evening that he could call together, within twenty-four hours, from one thousand to fifteen hundred armed men in that section, in connection with that secret organization. He did not say particularly for what purpose he could call them. He asked me if I knew any thing about the

Democratic organization; I said I was a member of the first degree of it. He did not mention the name of the order.

Q. What further conversation had you with Heffren?

A. I had no particular conversation with him that evening; he promised to see me after supper; but his wife being ill, he did not come.

Q. Did you state your name and business to him?

A. I believe I told him my name was Grundy, but I did not state my business at all.

Q. What time did you leave him?

A. I suppose it was about sundown when he left me to go home. He warned me of some two or three gentlemen whom he pointed out; one was Joe Faulkner; that I must be particular about what I said; for he told me he was a United States Detective. He also referred me to the Persise House as being of a different stripe to the one I was stopping at, which was known as a Union House. He remarked to a gentleman that evening, or a gentleman asked him why a certain lady was sent from Kentucky; he said he didn't know why it was, except that they expected trouble in Kentucky, and that this would be a safer place. He also said, that if Lee succeeded in permanently holding Pennsylvania, and some one else some other point, as he understood it—"things would be different."

Q. What "things" did he refer to?

A. I suppose he meant the workings of the Government. I left him that night and went to Orleans?

Q. When did you see Dr. Bowles?

A. I went there Sunday morning; got there about 10 or 11 o'clock. He was from home, and did not return till 6 or 7 in the evening. His wife gave me an introduction to him. My name was given as J. J. Grundy. I gave this name to Mr. Banning, the keeper of the house, and he so registered it. My first conversation with Bowles was on Monday evening. He asked me if I knew any thing about the Democratic organization. I told him I was a member of the first degree of it. He did not test me as to whether I was a member. He told me I was surrounded by members of that order. He told me that he was a military chief of the order, and that a man by the name of Wright, of St. Louis, was the civil chief, and that the order was numerous. He gave me the name of Mr. Halloway, and said he was the only man in Illinois that he could put his finger on with reliability. He said the forces of Indiana would concentrate in Kentucky, and make Kentucky their battle ground; that the forces in Illinois would concentrate in St. Louis, and co-operate with the forces in Missouri; that Illinois would furnish 50,000, Missouri 30,000, and Price was to invade the State with 20,000

men; with that 100,000 men they were to hold and permanently occupy that State, and the troops of Indiana and Ohio concentrate at Louisville. I also heard him speak of a man by the name of Stone; who said he had organized a regiment of men in six weeks in this State, (Indiana,) and that he expected him to raise another regiment. He spoke of another man named Dickerson, who went to Richmond at his pleasure. He lived in Baltimore. He wanted to know how many men Kentucky could furnish, and stated that a rebel force under Buckner would come into the eastern part of the State, and with these forces they intended to hold Kentucky. At that time no time had been set for the movement.

Q. Did you learn from him, or not, that this organization, or secret order, was to act in conjunction with the rebel forces?

A. They were. He told me that this order was made out of the Knights of the Golden Circle, of which he had been a member, and that he resurrected this order out of it. He appeared to claim a great deal of credit.

Q. Was any thing else said at that meeting between you and Bowles?

A. These were the important parts.

Q. Where did you go afterward?

A. I went back to Kentucky. He was anxious I should use all my exertions in extending the order as much as possible. Bowles told me there was to be a meeting in Indianapolis in about two weeks from then; and said he would get other reports from Kentucky, but he wanted me to go to Kentucky and see what could be done; he was anxious to know what he could report at that meeting.

I arrived at Dr. Bowles' on the 8th of May, 1864; stayed at his house four days, and returned to Kentucky about the 12th or 13th of May.

Q. Who did you see upon your return that was connected with this order?

A. Dr. Kalfus was the only one I knew to be connected with it. I had some talk with him, and he further initiated me into the order.

Q. What degrees did you receive from him?

A. He gave me the first degree. I had previously taken only the Vestibule degree.

Q. Did you meet Judge Bullitt, of Kentucky?

A. Not until after the second interview with Bowles. I started from Louisville about two weeks after my return from Bowles', probably on the 24th or 25th of May. I did not go direct to Dr. Bowles, but stopped at Salem to see Heffren. I saw him and had some talk with him. He told me he had been to Indianapolis, and had seen Mr. H. H. Dodd, and that they had concluded to call a meeting of the organization some day between the 13th and 16th of June. He said they were the only two men in the State who had the power to call that meeting; that was himself (Heffren) and Dodd; and that the organization of the State was now about complete; that it would number between 75,000 and 80,000 men.

Q. Did you register your name at Salem?

A. If I did, it was as J. J. Grundy.

Q. Where did you have this talk with Heffren?

A. It was in the sitting-room of the Persise House, on or about the 25th of May.

Q. How are you enabled to fix that date?

A. By its being on Wednesday, near two weeks after my return from seeing Dr. Bowles the first time.

Q. Did you make any report of your visit at that time?

A. I made my report to Captain Jones, and I understand he sent it to General Burbridge.

Q. State the particulars of your second visit to Dr. Bowles?

A. I left Salem about 11 o'clock in the morning, and arrived at Dr. Bowles' that evening. He was not at home. That was on Wednesday. He returned Saturday, at noon. At his home no one appeared to know where he had gone. He told me himself, that he had been to Indianapolis; had seen Mr. Dodd, Mr. Barrett, of Missouri, Judge Bullitt, and some other gentlemen; and that there would be a meeting of the Grand Council on the 14th of June. He told me that Barrett pledged from Missouri 30,000 men, and that Illinois pledged 50,000. The leaders of those States pledged that number of men. The forces of Illinois and Missouri were to co-operate with Price. He said that 20,000 men or more, if Jeff Davis could spare them, were to be sent into Missouri. He told me, also, that Indiana pledged 40,000, which were to co-operate with those from Ohio, concentrate near Louisville, and co-operate with whatever troops Jeff Davis could send into Kentucky under Buckner or Breckinridge; or, if he thought it advisable, he would send Longstreet with them. They had no regular communication with Ohio, but had made arrangements to open up regular communication with their friends there. He also told me of the change in the Supreme Commander to Vallandigham, and that he had been appointed a commissioner to visit Vallandigham in Canada.

Q. What further conversation had you with Dr. Bowles, at that time?

A. He told me that on the Sunday which was the 22d of May, that himself, Mr. Dodd, and a Dutch chemist, whom he had known for years, and a number of other men, while people thought they were at church, were in a basement, experimenting with Greek fire, which they had now brought to perfection, through this Dutch chemist; that they intended to use it for the destruction of Government property; that the Jeff Davis Government was to pay them ten per cent. for all the property destroyed, taking the estimate, as given in the Northern papers, of the amount destroyed. He also told me that the two boats burned at the Louisville wharf last spring, and boats belonging to the Government that had been destroyed on the Mississippi river, and elsewhere, had been burned by this Greek fire.

Q. Did he then, or at any other time, show you an instrument that would be used for that purpose?

A. Yes, sir, he did.

A conical shell was here handed to the witness. [See Illustrations.]

Q. Have you ever seen this or a similar instrument?

A. I saw a shell similar to this, at Mr. Bocking's room, at the Louisville Hotel, Louisville.

Q. Who were present?

A. Dr. Bowles, Bocking, Kalfus, Boyd, Winchester, Miller, and a number of others.

Q. Were they members of the order?

A. Yes, sir.

Q. You may explain how the shell works.

A. The space between the innermost cast and the inner shell was to be filled with liquid Greek fire. The space between the inner and outer shell is designed to give room for the inner shell to easily move so as to strike the percussion cap, when projected from a gun, at the moment of striking an object, igniting the powder and bursting the shell. At the same time the Greek fire is ignited.

A spherical shell was here handed to the witness. [See Illustrations.]

Q. Was there a weapon similar to this shown you by Bocking?

A. Bocking had none of them at that time, but he drew a diagram of them, and explained the principle of their action to them.

Q. You may describe its mode of action?

A. The glass vial inside of the inner shell contains Greek fire, and after it is placed in the inner shell, is surrounded with powder. The inner shell is capped with percussion caps placed on the nipples, which are so arranged that at the moment it strikes, the three caps will be exploded, no matter how it falls. It could be thrown by the hand, and on striking any thing the caps would burst, igniting the powder and bursting the shell.

Bocking, who had some of the Greek fire and experimented with it, also said that the liquid fire if thrown in a vial would burn any thing against which it was thrown. He also explained a kind of clock machine, which, being wound up, would run a certain length of time, and at that point would in some way ignite the Greek fire, and a conflagration would be the result. He did not have one of these machines, but said he could make them for the benefit of the Order of Sons of Liberty. He also showed the muster roll of a battery, which he said he had been authorized to raise, and this muster roll exhibited nothing but a list of the rebel prisoners confined in one of the prisons of the United States, and he said that every one of those enlisted in his battery, were enlisted with the understanding that at the first opportunity they were to desert to the enemy, and that one section had deserted and taken over two of the guns. This was said in the presence of Dr. Bowles.

Q. When was this meeting held?

A. On the 28th of June, at Louisville, in Bocking's room.

Q. State what took place in the interview with Dr. Bowles on the 26th of May. What did he say in that interview about Greek fire?

A. He said they had been experimenting, and had got it about perfect; that Bullitt knew how it was made; that he wished me to go home and get the order organized and spread over the State, and he wanted me to impress upon the people the idea of this Greek fire, that they would thereby come more readily into the order. He was anxious I should make Judge Bullitt's acquaintance, and assist him all I could. From Dr. Bowles I went back to Louisville, and carried a message to Judge Bullitt. He told me to make Bullitt's acquaintance, and say to him that he had seen Mr. Andrew Humphreys since their meeting in Indianapolis, and Mr. Humphreys had agreed to take the position of a brigadier general and charge of the forces in the rear in case of an uprising of the order.

Q. Did you not speak of Heffren as the person you saw at Salem?

A. Yes, sir.

Q. Can you identify him as one of the accused?

A. Yes, sir.

[The witness here pointed to the accused, Horace Heffren.]

Q. Is that the same man with whom you had the conversation at Salem?

A. It is, sir.

Q. You stated, did you not, that Humphreys would take charge of the forces in the rear?

A. Yes, sir. But Bowles did not say what they were to do. We were talking of the order, and I suppose he meant the forces comprised all the members of the order.

Q. Did you see Judge Bullitt?

A. I did.

Q. Was he a member of the order?

A. Yes, sir, he was.

Q. You may state what was done and said in your interview with Judge Bullitt.

A. I made his acquaintance, and told him what Bowles had told me to tell him. He said it suited him exactly, that Humphreys was willing to take that position.

Q. What position did he refer to?

A. It seems that Humphreys had been known as a Major General in the order. Bullitt said: "I have spent a good deal of money in this affair, and I am willing to spend every cent I have; for I hope soon to be able to steal a good living from these damned sons of bitches."

Q. What official position did Bullitt hold at that time?

A. He was one of the Judges of the Supreme Court of Appeals of the State of Kentucky.

Q. Had you any further conversation?

A. Not until a day or two afterward. There were Judge Bullitt, Dr. Chambers, of Gallatin county, Mr. Kalfus, D. C. Whips, Mr. Piper, of Springfield, Illinois, and myself, in Kalfus' office—in his private room. Chambers had just come down from Gallatin county, for the purpose of getting instruction in the work of organizing his county; there was something said about a man by the name of Coffin having been in the room with Dr. Bowles and others in this city. Chambers said he knew Coffin, that he was a United States Detective, and called him a good many hard names; he knew he was a United States Detective, he had been a stanch Union man—and that was the only evidence he had of his being a United States Detective. After talking the matter over, they decided he should be murdered. Dr. Bowles had been instrumental in getting him into the order, and they thought that Bowles ought to be instrumental in getting him out. They determined to put him out of the way; he was a United States Detective, and he should be murdered at all hazards. They sent me with these instructions to Bowles, and I was to go to Indianapolis and get some constitutions of the order, and I was to inform Dodd, and whoever I might see, to be on their guard, and do all they could to get shut of him.

Q. Who sent you?

A. It was with the unanimous consent of all parties that I was sent.

Q. Who were they?

A. Judge Bullitt, Mr. Piper, Dr. Chambers, Dr. Kalfus, and D. C. Whips; they gave me that message to Dr. Bowles; I started on the next day, which was about the first day of June, and took the message to Dr. Bowles. I saw him that same evening.

Q. What did you say to him?

A. I told him what was the decision of Judge Bullitt and others in Louisville; that Coffin was unquestionably a United States Detective; and that as he had been instrumental in getting him into the order, he ought to be instrumental in getting him out. He said he knew that two men at the Shoals had initiated Mr. Coffin, and he knew he had been in the United States employ, but he could explain that to their satisfaction. "But," he said, "I will put two men on his track." He gave me their surnames, but I do not remember them. He told me to say that he would put two men on his track. He did not seem to think Coffin was a dangerous man at all.

Q. Where did you go after that interview?

A. To Indianapolis.

Q. Had you any further conversation with Bowles?

A. I revealed to him my true name, and explained to him why I had come to him under an assumed name. I told him that when I came to Louisville, I had been watched on the streets by a United States Detective—which was true—and to avoid being troubled by that man I had to go somewhere else, and that I had come to his house to escape him, and that was the reason why I had come to his house under an assumed name.

Q. At that time did you hold any office? If so, what?

A. Not until the first of June. From Dr. Bowles' I went to Indianapolis and saw Mr. Dodd and Mr. Harrison. I also received an introduction to Mr. Bingham and Dr. Gatling. The first man I saw to whom I made myself known was Mr. Dodd. I stopped at the Palmer House and registered under my real name, Felix G. Stidger. It was on the first Saturday in June that I arrived here.

Q. Where did you see Dodd?

A. Judge Bullitt directed me how to go from that house to Dodd's building that I might be able to find it without inquiring of any one, and creating suspicion. I went there, but did not find him. I inquired where he lived, and went out to his house. I was told there he had gone down town, and that I would probably find him at Bingham's office. I went to Mr. Bingham's office and found him there. I gave him the letter of introduction from Judge Bullitt; and Mr. Dodd then called out to Mr. Bingham and Dr. Gatling and gave my introduction to them. Mr. Dodd invited me and Dr. Gatling to go up to his office.

Q. What passed between you and Dodd at his office?

A. I told him that he had neglected to put up the constitutions in the books Bullitt had brought. I also spoke about Coffin, and said that Bowles would put two men on his track, but I had forgotten their names. Gatling came up in the office during the time I was there, but I do not remember whether he was present at the time or not.

Q. What else occurred?

A. Dodd went with me to Harrison's house, and he inquired of some persons in the building if they knew where Mr. Harrison lived. Some one told him where he lived, and we went out to Harrison's house. He showed him my letter of introduction

from Bullitt, and said that I would like to see him at his office in the evening. I saw him at his office in the evening, and had some conversation with him. He gave me the rituals and constitution of the order, and the address of the Grand Commander of the State of Indiana, delivered on the 16th or 17th of February, and also instructed me in the third degree of the order; I never took the obligation, but he instructed me in it.

Q. Did you receive any money from members of the order?

A. Judge Bullitt gave me a check on the Bank of Kentucky for $25.

Q. Did you have any conversation with Dr. Gatling in Dodd's office?

A. There was something said about his coffee-mill gun, and he remarked that he was glad the Government did not take it, as he wanted it for the South; that he had sent a man to Europe, or had made arrangements to send him, to have it patented for the use of the South.

Q. Was Dodd present?

A. Yes, sir; he was.

The Judge Advocate here handed the witness a pamphlet containing Dodd's address. [See Appendix.]

Q. Is that the address you referred to?

A. Yes, sir; Harrison gave me a copy of that for Judge Bullitt.

Q. Did you take them to Judge Bullitt?

A. Yes, sir. I saw many copies of them in Harrison's office. This is the book they used for their secret cypher in this city. By it they sent all important communications through the mail. Harrison told me that was the book they used for their secret cypher. Bullitt and Bowles also told me about the secret cypher, and that a person might get hold of that secret cypher, but if he had not the key, he could not read it.

Q. You may explain how the book is used for the secret cypher.

A. We counted from the left, and used figures entirely to spell words. If I wanted to spell the word "the," I would put the figure "3" at the top of the page to indicate the page of the book I used. I would put the figure 6 in brackets, as indicating the line of that page, and then 1, 2 and 3, to denote that they were the first, second, and third letters of that line.

Q. Did any thing take place at Dodd's office that day?

A. No, sir; not that I recollect.

Q. Did you see Dodd again at that time?

A. I came here on Saturday evening, and went home on Monday morning. I did not see Dodd again, and had no further consultation with him. I saw General Carrington and Governor Morton while here, and I made known to them what I had done. General Carrington copied the works

I had with me. I went back to Louisville from here, and took some books.

Q. What were those books?

A. The constitutions of the county temples, of the Grand Council of the State, and of the Supreme Council of the United States, and one or two rituals of the order, also an address of the Grand Commander of the State of Indiana. I delivered them first to Dr. Kalfus, and when Dr. Kalfus returned them I gave them to Judge Bullitt. I arrived at Louisville on Monday, about the 4th of June. It was immediately after my appointment as Grand Secretary of the State of Kentucky by Judge Bullitt. The date of that appointment was about the 4th or 5th of June.

Q. Was that appointment verbal or written?

A. We did nothing in writing that we could avoid. I was to receive a salary, but there was nothing stipulated; we were to go according to the Constitution of the Grand Council of the State of Indiana. I was to receive, as I understood, about $800 per annum.

Q. Did you ever receive pay for the position you held?

A. I received pay from the members of the order, and I collected the initiation fee, and was told by Kalfus and Bullitt to keep it for my pay. I received about $200.

Q. What office did Judge Bullitt hold?

A. He was elected Grand Commander of the State. At that time he was the only Grand Councilman in the State. He was elected at the meeting of the Grand Council by members of the different counties of the State of Kentucky. I was not at that meeting. I was at the meeting of the Grand Council in Kentucky on the night of the 27th of June, 1864.

Q. Who was present at that meeting?

A. Judge Bullitt, Mr. W. K. Thomas, a Mr. John J. Felix, of Lawrenceburg, Kentucky, two gentlemen from Paris, and Mr. T. J. Bosley; D. C. Wipps, who was treasurer of the Grand Council, was there; also Judge G. Williams, of Hancock county, and some others I do not now remember. There was also a Mr. Tirrell, of Owen county, or Boone county; he had formerly been in the Federal army. There were about sixteen or seventeen persons present.

Q. Was any business transacted?

A. Delegates were elected to attend the Supreme Council in Chicago on the first day of July. Judge Bullitt, by virtue of his office as Grand Commander, was a member. Prior, Winchester and Wipps were all three elected.

Q. Was any other business of importance transacted at that meeting? Any talk there with reference to the sentiments of the order?

A. Mr. Bosley made a short speech about the operations in his part of the country;

he is from Shelby county; and Judge Williams also made a short speech, I believe, about the operations and organization of his county, and of its action in connection with the uprising to resist the Government. This received the general sanction of all present.

Q. Did you attend any meeting in this State before that?

A. Yes, sir; on the 14th of June. I was told by Dr. Bowles when the meeting would be held, and also by Mr. Dodd. They both said they would like me to be here if I could come, and I did come.

Q. Who was present at that meeting?

A. The meeting was held in the building occupied by Dodd as a printing establishment. Dodd was present and presided over the meeting. Mr. Harrison was there as Secretary. Mr. Heffren's name was called as Deputy Grand Commander, but he was not present. Mr. Bowles, Mr. Milligan and Mr. Humphreys were there. Mr. Dodd told me it was Andrew Humphreys. I think I know Mr. Humphreys, but I could not swear to him positively. Mr. Milligan, whom I see present in this room, (the witness here pointed to the accused, L. P. Milligan,) is the same that was present; also Dr. Bowles, one of the accused. There was a Judge Borton, or Borden, also present. A Mr. Otey, an old gentleman, was there; also, Mr. Gatling, and Dr Athon, Secretary of State; Mr. McBride, from Evansville, and a Mr. Everett, from Evansville, also a Mr. Thompson. I remember his being appointed on a committee. Thompson and, I think, Dr. Athon and McBride were the three gentlemen appointed on that committee to examine an invention that had been invented by a member of the order, and the committee reported that the invention was a good one, and ought to be adopted by the order; they recommended that it be turned over to the Committee of Thirteen, who should distribute it to those members of the order that in their judgment might be intrusted with it. I know he was on two committees during the day. There was also a committee on military affairs, and one on the subject of education. Milligan, Bowles, McBride and Dr. Gatling were four of the military committee, the other I do not remember.

Q. Was any thing reported by the Military Committee?

A. Yes, sir; they reported a bill setting forth their views, that the order ought to be organized as a military organization at once, and armed.

Q. When was this?

A. This was on the 14th of June. Dodd, at the opening of the meeting, read an address to consider if the order had any politics, and if so, what they were. The subject of education was considered, and also if the time for action was not at hand. These were the main points of his address.

Q. Were any military appointments made at that meeting?

Yes, sir; one Mr. Walker was elected a Major General. There were elections of delegates to the Supreme Council, which was a meeting of delegates from the different State Councils, to be held at Chicago on the first day of July.

Q. Who was elected?

A. Mr. Dodd, by virtue of his rank as Grand Commander, was one; J. G. Davis and Mr. Lasselle were elected; and the Major Generals, by virtue of their rank, were *ex officio* members.

Q. Do you know who were the Major Generals of the order at that time?

A. Mr. Milligan, Mr. Bowles, Mr. Humphreys and Mr. Walker, who was elected *vice* Mr. Yeakle, who, it seems, had been a Major General, but was now thrown out. Walker was said to be a man who had some military experience.

Q. Was there any protest on the part of Milligan on his accepting this appointment?

A. Not a word. They were not elected that day; they had been elected before. Mr. Dodd called over their names as Major Generals. Walker was the only Major General elected that day.

Q. Did any thing else take place at that meeting?

A. The subject of Mr. Coffin was discussed at considerable length. McBride, of Evansville, had a great deal to say about it. He knew Coffin about Evansville as a Government Detective; that he had been engaged in sending contraband goods South, they were taken, and it got the people into trouble; he believed that he was still in that kind of business. McBride also said he had a report of the order known as the Loyal League; that he had men in the order who reported to him every thing that occurred; he said a good deal about the Government damning secret organizations, when here was one they supported themselves. He also said that the men of Vanderburg and Posey counties were members of this order, and also several of the Home Guard companies of the Legion, and he said that two or three companies there who had Government arms, were under his control. He said something about an election there, when the members of this order went to the polls armed; the members of the Home Guards were there, also armed, he said, but they knew the members of the order were armed, and did not attempt to do any thing. He did not say how he knew those other men were armed, but McBride said the members of the order were armed.

Q. What else was done at this meeting?

A. The meeting, generally, was appointed a committee to attend a meeting at Hamilton, Ohio. Coffin was expected to be there.

He had not been seen for several days, and was supposed to be there. Dodd volunteered his services to go to Hamilton, and if Coffin was there, pick a quarrel with him and shoot him. He wanted to know who would go with him. McBride said he knew Coffin, but he was sorry, he said, that his business was such that he could not go. Bowles, Dodd, Milligan and myself, went to Hamilton the next day.

Q. Did you see Dodd or Bowles at Hamilton?

A. Yes, sir. I went up to Dodd and Bowles after Vallandigham had got through speaking, to bid them good-by, as I was starting for Cincinnati; and Bowles leaned down and asked me if I had seen Coffin. I said, "I don't know the man." They then remembered that I had previously told them that I did not know him. They said they did not think Coffin was there, as they could not find him.

Q. What did Dodd say at the meeting?

A. I do not remember any thing, save that he said that Government detectives ought to be murdered; he might have said killed. He said if Coffin was at Hamilton, he would pick a quarrel with him and shoot him.

Q. Where did you go then?

A. To Cincinnati, and thence to Louisville.

Q. When were you here next?

A. I got to Louisville on Thursday night, and came up here about the first of the next week—some time during the week. I then saw Dodd and Harrison, and Mr. Joseph Ristine, Auditor of State.

Q. Was any thing said or done?

A. I was sent by Judge Bullitt to see about the dispatch which he had received?

Q. What was that?

A. The dispatch was something about Aunt Lucy being sick, and he wanted to know if such a dispatch had been received. Dodd knew nothing about the dispatch. He asked me if I knew what Aunt Lucy meant. I said I did, and told him it had reference to the Southern Confederacy; and he seemed to be satisfied. Bullitt also said something about a letter that Mr. Dodd had gotten. It was a letter to Dodd, Bowles and Ristine, and signed "Dick." He warned them against a man named Coffin. Dodd showed me the letter; he then took me down to the office of Ristine, and they said they supposed the letter was written by Dick Bright. Dodd gave me an introduction to Ristine's son, and requested me to stay pretty much all day, and see if Coffin passed by—if so, have Ristine's son point him out to me. They succeeded in pointing him out to me, about sundown. I staid there pretty near half a day. I had some talk with Ristine about this letter, but I don't remember whether any thing was said about the order or not.

Q. Did any thing further take place at Indianapolis during that visit?

A. Not that I recollect.

Q. Where did you go next?

A. From here I went back to Louisville. There I saw Thomas, Bullitt, Kalfus and others, in Kalfus' office. I was initiated into the order at Louisville.

Q. When were you here next after that?

A. I was here the next time about the last of July. I then saw Dodd, Dr. Athon and Mr. Harrison.

Q. Did you learn any thing of importance?

A. Yes, sir; Judge Bullitt had started to Chicago on the evening of the 19th of July. He said that Dodd and a number of the other leaders of the order from this State and Illinois were to be at Chicago to have a conference there. Bullitt started to Chicago on the 19th of July. We expected him back in four or five days, and as he did not come on Thursday night, July 28, I came up here, and on Friday morning I saw Dodd coming up from toward the depot. I went down to his office about 10 o'clock, and he told me he had just come into the city on a train. He said Judge Bullitt would be at home on that day or Saturday: He thought likely he might go through here, but he was not sure. He therefore wished me to go home and get twenty or thirty good runners, so that as soon as Judge Bullitt returned they might be sent off. He said the programme was arranged, and every thing ready. I went to see Dr. Athon, and had some talk with him. Dodd went around without me, and said, "You can come around after a bit." He didn't want both of us seen going there together, as he thought it would look suspicious.

Q. What did Dodd tell him?

A. He did not tell him that the time was set, but I told Dr. Athon afterward what Dodd had said.

Q. When did you tell him that?

A. I told Dr. Athon of it the same day. Athon did not seem to think that the time had come yet for revolution, but that it would come. He said it would not be successful now.

Q. Did he discourage you in any way?

A. No, sir. He said the time had not come, but that the time would come when it would be successful.

Q. Did Dodd open to you this scheme, in any way?

A. No, sir. He told me there was to be a meeting of some of the heads of the order here on the Tuesday following, and he would like Judge Bullitt to be here; and he wished me to tell him to come, or send some reliable man that he could depend upon to learn what their conclusion was.

Q. What were those couriers to do?

A. They were to notify our men where and when to concentrate.

8

Q. What was decided at Chicago?

A. There was a difference of opinion there as to the day when the programme was to be carried out, and the time was to be settled here at the meeting on Tuesday.

Q. When did you see Bullitt next?

A. When I was on the cars the next day I saw Bullitt. He was dusty, as though he had been traveling. He said he had come in on the Bellefontaine train, and that he had left a note for Dodd, but had left it at the house of some one else. He asked me to go on into the front car. He said he had been registering his name as Charles Smith. We went into a car where there were but a few people, and he told me the programme was all arranged for this uprising, how it was to be conducted, and all about it. When we got to Jeffersonville, he got him a buggy. On Saturday he wished to have A. O. Brannan and Dr. Bayless sent out to him, and on Sunday Kalfus and Thomas, and to those four he would communicate the uprising of the order. He said he expected to be arrested, but if he saw all these men, he didn't care if he was arrested.

When we got to Louisville, as soon as the ferry boat landed, a young man came on board for his arrest. Young Hewitt did it.

On Monday night I was sent back here to Dodd by Kalfus and Thomas, to get the final arrangements as soon as they were concluded on, and I was to go back and report to them. I came on Monday night. On Friday night, when we were at Dodd's house, he said he would send his son for Bowles to be here, and that he sent Mr. Harrison to go after some other gentlemen. Mr. Harrison was to go to Lafayette for one person, and he pulled out his money, and gave him sufficient to pay his expenses.

I went to see Dodd after I came back. He seemed very much excited, gritted his teeth, and said that he hoped they had acted the gentlemen, and had not searched Bullitt, as he had drafts on Montreal. He then went to work and gave me the programme. I think this was about the 2d of August. He showed and read me letters from two or three gentlemen. They were not signed by any name, but they were fully concurring in the matter. He had sent them word, and they didn't come here. Then he told me what the programme was, and impressed upon me the importance of secrecy. He said if Bullitt had not been arrested, I could not have got the programme at all.

He said they had abandoned the idea of holding the secret meetings, but would hold them hereafter as Democratic mass meetings, and that one was to be held at Peoria, Ill., on the 3d of August, I think. Another here on the 15th or 16th of August, and that his men would be instructed to come here armed: that they were going to work to release the prisoners here, and seize the arsenal here, at Springfield and Chicago, Ill., and Columbus, Ohio, on the same day, and to re'ease the prisoners at Johnson's Island and Camp Chase, Ohio, and at Camp Douglas and Rock Island, Ill., and then proceed to Louisville, and take possession of the arsenal there and at Frankfort, Ky., and with the rebel prisoners armed they would go to work. Their difference at Chicago was whether they should wait until the rebel forces should be sent into Eastern Kentucky to co-operate with them, or to make their uprising now, and co-operate with the rebel forces when Davis could send them.

Q. What was Dodd's opinion?

A. His idea was to go ahead on the 15th or 16th of August, and these letters from these men agreed with him. Mr. Walker was to be here from New York on the Thursday after I saw Mr. Dodd, which was on Tuesday.

Q. Do you know why this insurrection was put off?

A. I do not. I never saw Dodd afterward until I saw him here.

The Commission then adjourned, to meet on Tuesday, November 2, at 9 o'clock, A.M.

COURT ROOM, INDIANAPOLIS, INDIANA,
November 2, 1864, 9 o'clock, A. M.

The Commission met pursuant to adjournment.

All the members present. Also, the Judge Advocate, the accused, and their counsel.

The proceedings were read and approved.

The accused, Stephen Horsey, presented the following:

To the President and Members of the Military Commission, now in Session:

The undersigned, Stephen Horsey, one of the defendants now on trial, being without counsel, respectfully requests that the Hon. Thomas R. Cobb be admitted as counsel for him on this trial.

[Signed]   STEPHEN HORSEY.
November 2, 1864.

The examination of Felix G. Stidger, a witness for the Government, was then resumed as follows:

Question by the Judge Advocate:

State whether in any of those conversations with either Heffren or Bowles, they stated to you what this order numbered in the States of Indiana, Illinois, Missouri, and Ohio.

Answer. Heffren told me that the organization of the order was about complete in Indiana, and the number was between seventy-five and eighty thousand men. I never understood any definite number in Illinois or Missouri, but I understood that the heads of the order from those States pledged from Illinois fifty thousand to go to the field, and thirty thousand from Missouri. Ohio never stipulated any definite number, but would furnish men.

Q. What, if any thing, was said to you by Heffren or Bowles, as to the extent of the arming of the organization, and with what kind of arms?

A. Bowles made a statement in the Council of the 14th of June, that the organization in his county numbered about six hundred men, but that there was a military organization amounting to nine hundred men, armed and equipped.

Q. Was this military organization outside of the order?

A. I do not know. He said the Order of the Sons of Liberty numbered six hundred men in his county, and nine hundred men armed and equipped; but he did not say with what arms. He also stated that he had an arrangement with a man to furnish any number or kind of arms. He made this statement in the Grand Council of the 14th of June, in the way of a speech.

Q. Who was present at the time he was making that speech?

A. Mr. Dodd was present; Mr. Harrison and Mr. Milligan were there, and Mr. Horsey was there at one time. Mr. Bowles made a remark two or three times during the day.

Q. Was Mr. Bingham present at that meeting?

A. No, sir; not on the 14th of June that I saw.

Q. Was it stated what State should be made the battle-ground?

A. Kentucky and Missouri; that was what Bowles and Dodd told me.

Q. What was said, if any thing, in reference to any understanding with the Confederate forces?

A. Bowles said they would go to Kentucky and have a regular understanding with the Confederates, and act in concert with them; and that they had sent a man named Dickerson to Richmond to have the Confederate authorities send an invading force to act in concert with their order.

Q. Was there any concert with the rebel forces in Kentucky or elsewhere?

A. There was communication between this order and the guerrillas in Kentucky. Bullitt instructed a man to try and get a place appointed for him to meet Colonel Jesse, said to be a rebel Colonel in command of the rebel forces in Kentucky; and he instructed this man to go to Colonel Syphert, a rebel Colonel, said to be in command of a rebel squad, and have a conference with him about the capture of Louisville.

Q. Had you any conversation with Bowles in reference to communication with the rebels?

A. I had. Bowles at first objected to this uprising, until the rebels should invade the eastern part of the State, as he said they would. This man Dickerson was sent South to communicate with the rebel forces.

Bowles said he would consent to the uprising on the 15th or 16th of August, as Dodd had said, provided Colonel Syphert, Colonel Jesse, and Walker Taylor would assist in the capture of Louisville until the forces of this State could get there.

Q. What forces of this State were referred to?

A. The uprising of the Sons of Liberty.

Q. Have you any knowledge of attempts or efforts on the part of any members of this order to procure arms? If so, what kind?

A. Not directly. The question of arming was discussed on the 14th of June. Some said, tax the members of the order; others contended that each district should arm itself; while others contended that each individual should arm himself, to resist the Government, and that to do so, they would dispense with the luxuries of life, to procure money to get arms with which to resist the Government.

Q. Had you any talk, individually, with Bowles, or any other member of the order, in reference to procuring arms?

A. Bowles wanted to know, the last time I saw him, if I knew Peters, of Cincinnati; he wanted to get arms of him; and also B. C. Kent, of New Albany, Indiana; he wanted to communicate through him with Dr. Gordon, of New Albany, that he might have arms shipped to Gordon, and wagoned out into the country.

Q. Have you any knowledge of any efforts to procure lances?

A. Dr. Bowles asked me if I could have three or four thousand lances made; he wanted that number, and thought they could be made in Kentucky without suspicion. He wanted three or four thousand men armed with lances and revolvers; he said he could make them of great service.

Q. I think you stated, did you not, that Bowles was present at the meeting in New York?

A. He told me he was.

Q. Did he tell what was done at the meeting in New York, on the 22d of February?

A. He said that Vallandigham was elected Supreme Commander that day; that there was a change in the name of the order, that the ritual was changed, and a slight change in the colloquy, though I do not remember what it was. There was a committee appointed to make a change in the ritual, and after it was made, the manuscript was sent to Vallandigham for his revision. He revised it and made one or two additions. He made the addition, "Resistance to tyrants is obedience to God." This was said by Mr. Piper, by Mr. Bowles and other members of the order to have been made by Vallandigham. And there was an invocation at the end of the first degree said to have been added by Vallandigham, and a reference to a passage of Scripture, which occurs in the first or third degree, was also said to have been added by Vallandigham.

Q. Have you any knowledge of money being raised or expended, to procure arms and organize the society?

A. I was told by Mr. Kern, a member of the order, that Judge Williams, of Kentucky, had given $100, and other members $200 for organizing the order, and that he had expended that money in the purchase of arms, and that they had sent the men with the arms South.

Q. Where did Kern live?

A. In Louisville.

Q. How do you know him to be a member of the order?

A. By having met him in Council, and having conversations frequently with him. Kalfus also told me that Booking was furnished with money for the purpose of getting this Greek fire.

Q. Have you known Bowles to spend money?

A. He told me he had spent $2,000, for the benefit of the order, and would spend all he had, were it necessary. He did not say in what way he had spent the money.

Q. Have you ever had any talk with Bowles with respect to the uprising, and when he favored its taking place?

A. He told me he cared nothing about the election; he was satisfied Lincoln would be elected; he wanted the time spent in perfecting the organization and getting ready for the uprising. He said he would agree to the uprising on that day, provided the rebel Colonels could be got to act in concert with the order.

Q. What do you know about this Committee of Thirteen?

A. The question of a Committee of Thirteen was discussed in the Grand Council of the 14th of June. They were desirous to have this Committee of Thirteen to carry on the concerns of the Grand Council during its recess; and it was a question whether they should be appointed by the Grand Council or by the Grand Commander, and known only to him. There was a Committee of Thirteen so called, in Kentucky, but I understood from Kalfus it was composed only of seven; they were to carry on the business of the order during the recess.

Q. State whether or not this organization appointed any men to act as spies upon the Government.

A. McBride said on the 14th of June that he had men acting as spies in the Loyal League, who reported to him everything that was done. Mr. Harrison also said they had men from outside the order, so that they should not act both ways, employed as spies and acting for the benefit of the order. Dodd wanted me to act in that capacity.

Q. Have you ever met, or had consultation with a man by the name of Hines?

A. No, sir. Piper told me that Hines was appointed on Vallandigham's staff, and that he was then waiting in Canada to take charge of the releasing of the prisoners on Johnson's Island, or Rock Island, and Bowles of the other. Hines was formerly a Captain in the rebel army, and made his escape from the Ohio State Penitentiary with John Morgan.

Q. Have you any knowledge of members of the rebel army being initiated into this order? If so, when and where?

A. There was a rebel Colonel Anderson, of the 3d rebel Kentucky regiment of Infantry, initiated into the order, about the last of June, 1864.

Q. Who initiated him?

A. Kalfus told me that he gave him the first degree, and directed me to give him the second and third. There was also a Captain Van Morgan who was initiated into the order, and had the full confidence of the members of the order in Kentucky; also Dick Pratt and Jim McCracklin. There was also another who said he was a Captain of a squad of guerrillas. I saw him initiated in Kalfus' office.

Q. Who initiated him?

A. Either Kalfus or myself, I do not recollect which. Kalfus I know gave me an introduction to him. Kalfus I know initiated those other men.

Q. Where?

A. He told me that he did it in his office. I conversed with one of them afterward, and satisfied myself that he was a member of the order.

Q. You may now give to the Court some of the signs, grips, passwords, and colloquies of the different degrees of the order.

[The witness here replied substantially and in detail as on page 51.]

[A pamphlet was here handed to the witness by the Judge Advocate.]

Q. What is that?

A. It is the Constitution of the Supreme Council. I recognize it by having seen it frequently before, and from having been instructed by Dodd, Bullitt, and Harrison, that it was that work.

Q. Have you ever used it in instructing others?

A. No, sir. I do not know that I have. We only had one or two copies in our State. I have frequently told persons of such a book.

A pamphlet entitled Constitution and Laws of the S. C. was then introduced in evidence by the Judge Advocate. [See Appendix.]

Also, a letter bearing date October 8, 1863.

Also, a letter bearing date June 28, 1864.

Q. Are there any private marks of the order on the letter of June 28th?

A. Yes, sir. There are. The letters O. S. L. are written under the date, in small characters, and would be calculated to mis-

lead a person who did not particularly notice them. S. C. means Supreme Commander; or it may mean Supreme Council. These letters make it an official letter.

I was initiated in the Vestibule degree of the Order of the Sons of Liberty on the 5th of May, 1864. I took the first degree about the 25th or 26th of May, 1864. I entered the order as a regular member, and as a United States Detective, and I took the several degrees for the purpose of disclosing its secrets to the officers of the Government. I kept the authorities posted by reporting sometimes as often as twice a week. While a member of the order, I was engaged part of the time in Nelson and Bullitt, Kentucky, in extending the organization. I organized some county temples, and initiated probably forty or fifty members. The authorities knew that I was engaged in this work.

Q. Then your private and ostensible purposes were different. Your private purpose was to commit as many as possible to the treasonable schemes of the order, and to keep the Government officials advised of it, and to bring them to justice at the proper time?

Question objected to by the Judge Advocate.

The counsel for the accused said it was always competent to show the character of the witness, his feelings, and the connection he has had with the transaction he details.

The Judge Advocate replied that the counsel for the accused were at liberty to show what were the feelings and purposes of the witness, by inquiring as to his acts, but they could not inquire as to his purposes and feelings.

The Court was cleared for deliberation. On being reopened, the Judge Advocate announced to the accused that the objection was sustained.

Before the Court was cleared, the counsel for the accused, W. A. Bowles, Andrew Humphreys, Horace Heffren and Stephen Horsey, desired to withdraw the question. It was insisted on, on behalf of L. P. Milligan.

The only instructions I gave to members were those I received from Judge Bullitt, Dr. Kalfus, Dr. Bowles, Mr. Dodd, Mr. Piper and other members. Piper represented himself as from Springfield, Illinois, and as having an appointment on Vallandigham's staff. He said he had orders from Vallandigham to Judge Bullitt and Dr. Bowles, respecting the time set for the uprising of the order. Judge Bullitt was Grand Commander of Kentucky. I carried messages from Bullitt to Kalfus and Bowles about the murder of Coffin. At a meeting in Dr. Kalfus' office, at which Bullitt, Kalfus, Piper, and Dr. Chambers, of Warsaw, Gallatin county, Kentucky were present; Bullitt and Chambers were the strongest in their expressions that Coffin should be killed, and no one disagreed.

[A lengthy cross-examination on the witness' interviews with Horace Heffren here took place, but no additional facts were elucidated.]

I understood from Dr. Bowles that Bocking was a member of the order. Bocking is a foreigner. Dr. Bowles, Dr. Kalfus, Charley Miller, Boyd Winchester and others, were present when Bocking explained, in his room at the Louisville Hotel, Louisville, his different applications of Greek fire. He exhibited his shell, and drew a diagram of his hand-grenade, and explained it, together with his clock invention. I never heard of these things being brought to the notice and offered to the United States Government. Dr. Bowles said that the rebel Government would pay ten per cent. for all Government property destroyed, taking the estimated amount from Northern papers. He wished me to impress it upon the people of Kentucky that this was a fact, and the inventions of Bocking and the Greek fire were to be spoken of to give the people confidence in the order as to what it was to accomplish. Bocking, I know, had been to Canada with his inventions. Bowles, in referring to this, said, "We sent him to Canada to see if he was willing to spend his money for the benefit of the Order of the Sons of Liberty."

Bowles, in making his speech before the Grand Council on the 14th of June, when the Council was getting an estimate of the number of men in the order that they could depend on, said they numbered six hundred in his county, and that he had an organization of nine hundred men armed and equipped. He did not state what they were to do, or what they were armed for. Dodd, in the course of that meeting, said it was for the purpose of forming a military organization, and to see if the time of action was not near at hand. I do not know that there had been any military organization up to that time, but the object stated then was, to perfect a military organization; and to this end a Committee on Military Affairs was appointed to report on a plan for its complete military organization.

At the June meeting of the Council there was a Mr. Andrew Humphreys, or Dr. Humphreys. He was called by both names. The Mr. Humphreys I refer to, resembles that gentleman (the witness here pointed to the accused), but I could not swear positively that he is the man. Mr. Heffren's name was called as Deputy Grand Commander, but he was not present. I could not say, positively, that Humphreys was ever initiated into the order, unless he was the same that was present that day. I heard it said that he was a Major General.

There were three sessions that day, the first from 10 to 1, another in the afternoon, and another after supper. Dr. or Andrew Humphreys was present at the morning and afternoon session. I do not remember whether he was present at the evening session or not. This Humphreys sat just back of me, and was referred to once or twice.

I met Bowles in the Council of the 14th of June, and at the meeting of members of the order at Bocking's room at the Louisville Hotel. Horsey was at the Council of the 14th of June, but he came in late. He was asked why he was so careless as to initiate such men as Coffin into the order, which he had done.

The murder of Coffin was discussed in open Council. Dr. Bowles participated in that discussion. There was not a dissenting voice with respect to the murder of Coffin at that or any other time. I did not know that Coffin contemplated being at the meeting, though I expected that he would be, and I started a Mr. Prentice, a Government Detective, to Hamilton that evening, the 14th, to inform Coffin of his intended murder. I told him to tell Coffin if he was at Hamilton, to be on his guard, as there would probably be an attempt to assassinate him. Coffin did not go to Hamilton.

I do not know with respect to this State, but in Kentucky, members of the order who were initated, were instructed in the military character of the order. Judge Bullitt, Dr. Kalfus, myself, or whoever initiated members, always instructed them that the order was for the purpose of resisting the Government by force of arms, and for assisting the South. More or less of these instructions were given, according as the members were deemed reliable or otherwise. The order had a means of ascertaining the number of arms possessed by the members, by having returns made by the County Temples, in or under the guise of a subscription list for certain Democratic newspapers. For instance, a person pretending to subscribe for the Cincinnati *Enquirer*, meant that he had a revolver; if for the Chicago *Times*, that he had a shot gun; if for the Louisville *Democrat*, that he had a rifle; and under the head of Miscellaneous, would be indicated the amount of ammunition he had on hand. This method of obtaining returns was resorted to, that it might be kept a secret from those who were not acquainted with the plan.

The Commission then adjourned, to meet on Thursday, November 3, at 9 o'clock, A. M.

COURT ROOM, INDIANAPOLIS, INDIANA,
November 3, 1864, 9 o'clock, A. M.

The Commission met pursuant to adjournment.

All the members present; also the Judge Advocate, the counsel, and the accused.

The proceedings were read and approved.

The cross-examination of Felix G. Stidger was then resumed as follows:

As a detective, I was in the habit of communicating the progress the order was making to General Carrington, Captain Jones, Provost Marshal, and afterward to Colonel Thomas B. Farley, when he occupied that post. Governor Morton I probably met two or three times, and communicated to him what I knew. My reports to General Carrington were sometimes written and sometimes given in person. I was entirely free and confidential in my communications with the General, and as a general thing he left me entirely to my own discretion, as to the course I should adopt in my investigations. The man named Dickerson, referred to in my direct examination, Bowles told me, lived in Baltimore, and that he went to Richmond at his pleasure. Bowles also told me, that he had received a letter from Dickerson, who was just home from Richmond. He wanted to know how many men Kentucky would give. I told him probably forty, fifty, or sixty thousand men; as it was a revolutionary State, I thought she would furnish that number to assist in the design he was speaking of, namely, revolution in the North and assisting the South,

The last conversation I had with Dr. Bowles was about the 6th or 7th of August, when I was at his house with the programme which I got from Dodd. He remarked that Dodd had no right to change the programme; that they should have awaited the action of the rebel forces; but finally he determined that they would act without the co-operation of the rebels, if they could not get it. Bowles told me he had received notice of the change. That was the time I met Dodd's son returning from Bowles' house, and Bowles told me he had been there.

When Milligan's name was called as a Major General, he made no particular response, and he made no objection that I heard; the list was called by the Grand Commander. The Council at Chicago, at which Dr. Bowles was present, was about the 20th of July. I do not know whether Mr. Milligan was present or not. The meeting at Hamilton, at which Mr. Milligan was present, was a Democratic mass meeting to nominate delegates to the Chicago Convention. Bowles, Dodd, Milligan and myself went on the same train to Hamilton, but I had no conversation at all with him.

RE-EXAMINATION.

At the meeting of Bowles, Kalfus and others at Bocking's room, at the Louisville Hotel, Louisville, Bocking explained, but did not exhibit, some kind of clock machinery that could be wound up and set to run any specified length of time; it had a Greek fire attachment. This machine could be put into a box or trunk, and without exciting any suspicion, be left on board a steamer, or in a building, which would be set on fire at any time at which the clock might be set.

The nine hundred armed men, of whom I have spoken, that were in Dr. Bowles' county, were all amenable to the officers of the order; and though some of them had only been initiated into the Order of American Knights, they were amenable to the officers of the Order of the Sons of Liberty. Those members of the Order of American Knights who had only taken the first or vestibule degree, and were armed, were counted on in case of necessity. I was requested by Judge Bullitt, Dr. Kalfus, Mr. Thomas and other members of the order, to organize the order as fast as possible; they furnished me with money to pay my traveling expenses. They also sent me down the Nashville Railroad to learn the position of the Federal troops, and the number of guns on that Railroad at different points. I went down as far as Bowling Green.

Colonel WARNER, a witness for the Government, was then introduced, and being duly sworn by the Judge Advocate, testified as follows:

Question by the Judge Advocate:

State your name and the position you hold?

Answer. A. J. Warner, Colonel of the 17th V. R. C., and Commander of the Post at Indianapolis.

Q. State to the Court where you met with that letter?

[The Judge Advocate here handed to the witness a letter marked Government Exhibit "N."]

A. This letter was taken by me among other papers from the office of Mr. H. H. Dodd, at the time the arms were seized. This letter was found either in the safe or desk, I am not certain which. I recognize it especially by the signature, and some words which I could not make out.

Q. In what capacity were you acting, and under what orders, when you seized those papers?

A. On Saturday evening, I believe about the 20th of August, I received information that a lot of arms had been shipped secretly to this place, and had come to the Bellefontaine Depot. I immediately, in the absence of the District Commander, ordered the Provost Marshal of the Post to seize the arms, and arrest all parties known to be connected with the transaction. From the time I first heard of the shipment of those arms to the time the Provost Marshal reached the depot with wagons, etc., they had been removed to the old *Sentinel* building. That night, I think, twenty-six boxes of arms and ammunition were taken.

Q. State what those boxes contained, and how they were marked?

A. The boxes were shipped to J. J. Parsons. On the way-bill they were marked "Stationery," I think. On some of them there were marks indicating that they were Sunday School books, or tracts. Twenty-four or twenty-six boxes contained fixed ammunition for large sized revolvers; the balance contained large sized revolvers. They were self-cocking; and were the largest sized revolvers I have ever seen.

Q. What was done with those arms?

A. They were taken possession of by me, and are now deposited, with the ammunition, in the United States arsenal.

Q. How many arms were there?

A. Between three hundred and fifty and four hundred revolvers. The boxes contained mostly ammunition.

Q. Did you find any others?

A. On Sunday morning I went down myself to make a thorough search of the building, and found secreted in the office or room occupied by II. H. Dodd, under books and stationery, six more boxes, making in all thirty-two boxes.

Q. What did those six boxes contain?

A. Part of them contained arms, and part ammunition; of the same description as those taken on Saturday night. Upon finding those arms there, I concluded to look further and see what papers I could find relating to them, to see what parties were implicated; consequently a search was made in the desk and safe in the room occupied by Dodd. A search was made in other rooms in the building also.

Q. State whether this instrument was found there?

[A stamping press was here handed to the witness.]

A. This was found in the room said to have been occupied by the Grand Secretary of the Order of the Sons of Liberty, together with about two bushels, or more, of rituals, constitutions, etc., of the order. Also, a roll of the members of the order in this city, and papers relating to the order. There were also blanks, note books and orders, some of them printed, and others stamped.

Q. You may state to the Court whether you recognize that letter.

[A letter bearing date May 12, 1864, was here handed to the witness.]

A. This letter was also taken from the office of II. H. Dodd; but I do not remember whether from his safe or desk. Part of the letters were found in his desk rolled up in bundles, and part were taken from a little drawer in the safe.

[The letter was here offered in evidence by the Judge Advocate.*]

ELLIOTT ROBERTSON, a witness for the Government, was then introduced, and being duly sworn by the Judge Advocate, testified as follows:

I am a farmer, and live in Randolph county, Indiana. I became a member of the organization called the Golden Circle, in the spring of 1863, in Greenfork township, Randolph county; our place of meeting was in the woods; we met at night, and about fifteen or twenty persons were present. John D. Burkebile initiated me. There were between sixty and seventy-five members in our township; among them I remember Nathan Brown, John D. Burkebile, Henry Robbins, Augustus Bunch, John Fudge, Abraham Platt, Henry Wooden, Amos Cren, Francis Durvidge. Burkebile was Captain, Amos Cren Lieutenant, Henry Wooden Sergeant, and Eli Thomas Inspector. The Captain and Lieutenant were appointed by the members of the order; the Sergeant was appointed by the Captain. A week after I was initiated, I appointed a meeting of the order in Washington township; a part of the members of Greenfork township were present; Daniel Barnes presided, and some four or five additional members were initiated. From the time I was initiated, to September or October, I mostly met with them once a week. The members of the order were ordered to drill; but I did not. One Sunday I met the Captain, who asked me why I did not attend drill; he said I should have gone, for they had had some good sport. About one-half the members were armed; revolvers were the principal arms. I heard from the members of the order that they drilled every week or two. So far as I learned, the object of the order was to oppose the Administration in putting down the rebellion, and in making arbitrary arrests; this was to be done by force of arms; but exactly how it was to be done, had not been decided. The information I got from the Captain, was that the members of the township were to compose the company; we were to act in squads, under the direction of the Captain, in case the guerrilla mode of warfare was adopted. We were to take up arms and resist the enforcement of the draft. This, I understood, had been decided by the authorities here in Indianapolis. The Captain and Nathan Brown spoke of the State being divided into four military districts; and that a man by the name of Milligan com-

---

manded our district. I know of members of the order having assembled to resist arrests. Burkebile, our Captain, expected to be arrested, and he called a meeting of the members. I had notice to go to his house, with other members, to prevent his arrest, in case it was attempted. I was at his house two nights; four or five others were there; among them Burkebile's two boys, Henry Robbins, Henry Wooden, John Fudge, and John L. Mack. Some were armed with revolvers, and two of them with shot-guns. Our instructions were to resist the authorities, and not to let them take our Captain. John D. Burkebile induced me to join the order; he said it was an organization for self-protection among the Democrats. He did not at first give me the name of the order. A meeting was appointed to take place on the next Thursday, and I went and was initiated. The last meeting I attended was in September or October, 1863. About that time they changed their name, and were called the Order of American Knights. They did not change their plans or principles, that I know of; I did not take any new obligation, but was instructed in the change by the Captain. I attended one meeting of the American Knights in Preble county, Ohio, about August, 1864; the password by which we entered, was "Liberty." I learned of the change of name to the Order of American Knights from the Captain. Nathan Brown was sent to Indianapolis in September, 1863, to represent our township, and when he came back the change was made. He called a meeting, and the Captain wished me to go into the new order; I told him I would have a few days to study over it; he insisted, and told me it was a nice thing, but I would not go into it.

The signs by which members recognized each other, are these: You pass the right hand down over the mouth and beard, with the fore-finger of the right hand down the right side of the nose. If the man you are testing is a member, he will reply by taking the lobe of the left ear with the left hand between the thumb and finger, and draw it down. You then take a grip, and give one shake of the hand, with the fore-finger running up the wrist as far as possible. They had some military signs, which, we were told, would protect us in case of battle, or being taken prisoner. The hands were clasped in front, and raised over the head, in which position you stood a few minutes, or till the sign was recognized; the answer to this sign being made by placing the hands, with the tips of the fingers resting on the shoulders. There was another sign, which consisted in writing the number thirty-three on a piece of paper, which, being handed to a member, signified that he who used it was in danger.

I understood that the arms were procured from the authorities at Indianapolis. It was stated that Beck & Bros. had agreed to furnish arms. Nathan Brown and Burkebile were sent as representatives to a convention at Indianapolis, in the latter part of July, 1863. The Captain, on his return, stated, as I understood, that most of the States, including the rebel States, were represented; and he also said that they had not concluded what was to be done in case of a draft. I entered the order in good faith, but I left it because I thought it was disloyal. I first reported the order to 'Squire Hough, I think, in October, 1863.

HENRY L. ZUMRO, a witness for the Government, was then introduced, and being duly sworn by the Judge Advocate, testified as follows:

I reside at Markle, Huntington county, Indiana, and am a practicing physician; have resided there ten years. I became a member of the Order of the Sons of Liberty on the 20th of July last, at the solicitation of Dr. Horton, directly through Mr. Hantz. Dr. Horton was said to be a member. I was initiated in the first degree in Isaac Decker's barn; at the same time there were initiated John Hantz, Isaac Decker, Edward Decker, William Decker, Daniel Highland, Adam Young, Edward Johnson, Joseph Johnson, William Lever, Nathan Johnson, William Hantz, and William Cashman; fourteen were initiated by Dr. Horton. The society numbered in that township between forty and fifty. John Hantz was Grand Seignior; Isaac Decker, Treasurer; Joseph Johnson, O. G.; Nathan Johnson, G. D.; Daniel Highland, G. M.; William Decker, G. S.; Henry Johnson, A. D.; I was Secretary. [The witness was unable to explain the initials.] The obligation I took was that of the first degree of the Order of American Knights. Dr. Horton told me that there were from eighty to one hundred thousand members of the order in this State. I understood there was a military organization connected with the order. We got up a constitution and organized a company of about forty members. David Lash was Captain; Joseph Johnson, First Lieutenant; Henry Johnson, Second Lieutenant; Isaac Miller, Orderly; there were none but members of the order in this company; it did not comprise all the members of the order in that township; some were aged, and these we did not consider good fighting material; but all that were considered able were in that company. I did not know of our company drilling. At Bluffton, Wells county, they drilled; I went to see them drill; that was in the early part of September, in this year; some forty to sixty were drilling on the commons back of Bluffton. Some of the members of our company were members of the Bluffton company: that is how I come to know that the Bluffton company belonged to the order.

After Dr. Horton initiated us, he told us that the object of the order was to subdue the Abolitionists, resist the draft, and to assist the Southern Confederacy. I heard of the contemplated uprising of the order, but learned nothing definite with regard to it. I attended, perhaps, ten or twelve meetings of the order. After Huntington county was drafted, a meeting of the order was held, and a committee sent to Bluffton, and one to Huntington, to ascertain if there was a concert of action in regard to resisting the draft; Jacob Farling was the committee to Bluffton, and I was appointed the committee to Huntington. At Huntington I saw Mr. Cummings; he could not tell me any thing about it, and the Sheriff referred me to Mr. Milligan, whom I saw about the 16th of September last. I was instructed to ascertain if there was a concert of action, and if so, what arrangements were to be made to resist the draft. I asked Mr. Milligan his opinion as to whether we had better resist or not; he said it was as good a time now as any to resist. I did not know that Mr. Milligan held any military position in the order; the Sheriff referred me to him because he was the leading man there, and he would know. His message I brought back to the order, but as there was no concert of action, the members felt somewhat disappointed, and took the papers of the order into Decker's barn yard and burnt them. The order was disbanded about the 17th of September, when we found the thing was a failure; and we agreed not to meet any more. On the same day that I saw Mr. Milligan, I also saw Mr. Winters, the editor of the *Huntington Democrat*, who, I believe, was a member of the order. I asked him the question that I had put to Mr. Milligan, and he advised resistance.

The Commission then adjourned, to meet on Friday, November 4, at 10 o'clock, A. M.

COURT ROOM, INDIANAPOLIS, INDIANA,
November 4, 1864, 10 o'clock, A. M.

The Commission met pursuant to adjournment.

All the members present. Also, the Judge Advocate, the accused and their counsel.

The proceedings were read and approved.

H. L. ZUMRO, a witness for the Government, proceeded with his testimony as follows:

In my conversation with Mr. Milligan, on my visit to him, as a committee sent to Huntington, after advising resistance, he said, that if he was well, and in the woods, he could kill twenty men himself before he would be taken. When I asked him in what way we should resist, he concluded that we should form in companies or squads, just as we could; that ten men

would be sufficient to start with in resisting the draft, and in resistance to the Administration. Shortly after I was arrested. I had a conversation with Mr. Milligan in reference to my own arrest; he thought it was a bad thing to be arrested as I had been, and he said if a man were to arrest him, he would kill him, even if he had to go forty miles to do it. Something was said in the conversation as to whether we should need horses in this resistance, when Mr. Milligan said that we should; that we might find it necessary sometimes to assist a squad ten, fifteen, or twenty miles distant, and should need horses to do it.

I came to join the order from a conversation I had in the early part of March, with Colonel James R. Slack, of the 47th Indiana, in his office; he resides in Huntington. He asked me if there was not a secret organization in our neighborhood; I told him there was. He then wanted to know if I could not get the secrets of it; and said they were not Democrats, but a set of traitors who would undermine the Government. He wished to know if I would not go into the matter to find out their purposes, and to aid in keeping down this strife. I told him that I could, but I did not think it would be prudent to do it, from the fact that my practice was here; and if at any time it should be found out that I had been operating in favor of the Government, in all probability they would endeavor to injure me. He said there was no danger at all, from the fact that the loyal portion of the Democratic party would only think the better of me; and that the traitors to this Government would go down so that there would not be enough left to make a boot black; that was just his language. He afterward had a conversation with Colonel Schuler and Governor Morton, and Colonel Schuler came up and induced me to operate in that way. My purpose in joining the order was to endeavor to keep down any treasonable uprising. My subsequent operations I reported from time to time to General Carrington.

CROSS-EXAMINATION.

No inducements have been held out to me to testify in this case. I was arrested by order of General Carrington, and placed under bonds; but this was simply a pretense on the part of the authorities. After I was placed under arrest; and before I reported at Indianapolis, I went to Mr. Milligan to consult him in reference to my arrest, and I stated to Mr. Coffroth, a counsel, when I met him at Peru, that I might employ Mr. Milligan to assist in my defense. I made application to be admitted a member of the order at Huntington at different times. I joined the order at Rockcreek township. I was solicited by Mr. Milligan's student to go into the temple.

At the time I called to see Mr. Milligan on the 16th of September, Mr. Joseph Johnson went with me. Mr. Johnson was present during the whole of the conversation I had with Mr. Milligan. Mr. Johnson lives in Rockcreek township. He is the Joseph Johnson, O. G., I referred to as being initiated at the time I was. Mr. Milligan was sick in bed, and I understood he had been for a considerable time under the influence of opium and mercury, and he wished me to see if any effect was being produced by the opium and mercury. After my conversation with Milligan, I said I thought it worried him; he told me that it did; and I replied that I would then say nothing further. I do not think Mr. Milligan was at the time under the influence of narcotics, or opium. I next visited Mr. Day, to whom I was referred by Mr. Milligan. I told Mr. Day that Milligan had advised resistance, but said that he was so sick I did not like to say a great deal to him. Mr. Day said it would be foolish to resist. I asked him as I had Mr. Milligan, if there was to be any concert of action, and if so, that we were ready to resist in our township. Mr. Samuel Winters and Mr. Reinbarger were present during my conversation with Mr. Day. I remember Milligan saying, when I asked him if they were going to resist, that they had no fighting men there; that there were only five or six fighting men in Huntington. I might have spoken also, but Mr. Ibach and I also called at Mr. Coffroth's office. I called at Mr. Coffroth's office at the instance of Mr. Johnson, who wanted to know what was his opinion about resistance. Mr. Coffroth said he was not a member of the order, and would not advise resistance in any way. I did not go to Mr. Coffroth to act as a spy upon him, but simply because Mr. Johnson said he was an influential Democrat, and he would like to know his opinion.

When Dr. Harden stated that the objects of the order were to oppose the Administration, resist the draft, and assist the Southern Confederacy, there were present John Hantz, Isaac Decker, Edward Decker, William Decker, Daniel Highland, Adam Young, Henry Johnson, Joseph Johnson, Nathan Johnson, Wm. Hantz, Wm. Cushman, and myself. The memorandum to which I refer for these names, I made at the time.

The date of the meeting at which I was appointed as a committee to go to Huntington, and Jacob Farling to go to Bluffton, was on the 14th of September. Among those who were present at the meeting of the 14th of September, were Mr. Farling, Joseph Johnson, Mr. Eders and others. Mr. Johnson was present at my appointment, and agreed to go with me. David Lash, who was the Captain of our company, is the brother of the merchant of that name, and is a carpenter. Though Mr. Winters and Mr. Reinbarger advised resistance, and

Mr. Milligan said it was as good a time as any to resist, I reported that there would be no concert of action; and the consequence was that the papers of the order were burned. When it came to the test, the order failed.

My purpose in going into the order was not to betray its members, but to keep the Government posted as to their designs. There appeared to be a great danger of an outbreak and rebellion at home, and I thought if I could do any thing to prevent it, I was doing the community a kindness, and not injury.

I consulted with Esq. Bratton, but he knew my position with reference to the order; it was he who arrested me and brought me from Markle.

I never told any one that Mr. Milligan could be got clear or convicted for money; but a person who, I understood, was a friend of Mr. Milligan, wanted to know of me, if he could be got away from the guards. The idea that I held out was, that I thought he could be. My impression was that they wanted to bribe the guards, but I do not know from whom I got the idea. But I never stated to any one, that if I was furnished with money, I could or would use it secretly for the benefit of Mr. Milligan, either upon officers or members of the guard.

The statement of Mr. Milligan, that if he was well and in the woods, he could kill twenty men before he was taken, and also the statement that ten men would be sufficient to start with, were made in the presence of Joseph Johnson.

The military company connected with this order was organized perhaps three or four weeks before we abandoned the order, which was about the middle or latter end of August, and after the organization had been exposed in the papers at Indianapolis. The organization in our township was not understood to be an independent order, but was connected with the order generally, and we were to co-operate with them in any outbreak or resistance to the Government. When I called on Mr. Milligan, I did know him to be a member of the order. I represented to Milligan that I had been arrested at the instigation of Dr. Scott, who, I represented, had been actuated by motives of rivalry, so as to get me out of the way as a practicing physician, and it was in this connection that Mr. Milligan said, if he had been arrested at the instigation of any one governed by such motives, that he would go forty miles to kill the man.

The Commission then adjourned, to meet at 2 o'clock, P. M.

COURT ROOM, INDIANAPOLIS, INDIANA, November 4, 1864, 2 o'clock, P. M. }

The Commission met pursuant to adjournment.

All the members present. Also, the

Judge Advocate, the accused, and their counsel.

The Judge Advocate here stated that all proceedings against Colonel Horace Heffren were withdrawn on the part of the Government; that he was released from arrest by the proper authorities, and that he would now appear on the stand as a witness for the Government.

HORACE HEFFREN, a witness for the Government, was then called to the stand, and duly sworn by the Judge Advocate.

The counsel for the accused said that when the accused were jointly indicted, as in this instance, it was not competent for an accused to testify either for the defense or prosecution, till a verdict of "not guilty" has been entered.

The Judge Advocate, in reply, said:

The Government can at any time, or at any stage of the proceedings, quash any set of charges and specifications against the accused, when the interests of the service may seem to demand it, and with that is an end of the case. When the Judge Advocate says to the accused, the Government withdraws its charges and specifications against you, the man is then free, without any proceeding pending against him. As to this Commission giving a verdict of acquittal, or proceeding to a finding before this witness can be used, let me say that no such rule can obtain. It makes the finding, and passes its sentence in any given case; the proceedings are then forwarded to the Commanding General convening the Court, for his approval and confirmation, or disapproval. If it is a case in which he has the power to execute the sentence, it is then promulgated in general orders and made known to the accused and to the world. If it is a case which the Commanding General has not the power to execute, he adds his approval or disapproval, as the case may be, and forwards it to the proper authority for approval, and after being acted upon by that authority, it is made known. In this case, for instance, the proceedings would probably have to go to the President of the United States, and be delayed perhaps for months.

The very nature and constitution of a military court, precludes the possibility of the existence of any such a rule in this Court.

The witness, Horace Heffren, then testified as follows:

Question by the Judge Advocate:

Please state your name, place of residence, and business.

Answer. My name is Horace Heffren: residence, Salem, Washington county, Indiana; my profession, that of an attorney; my office is at Salem.

Q. How long have you resided there?

A. Since March, 1857.

Q. Please state to the Court whether you ever joined an order called American Knights, or Order of Sons of Liberty; if so, when and where?

A. I joined an order called American Knights, somewhere in the latter part of the year 1863, probably in November or December. I have no means of telling the precise time. I have not my diary of last year with me; if I had, I could tell the precise day.

Q. Did you belong to any similar order, or one with similar intents and purposes, of a different name, previous to that?

A. I did not.

Q. Did you ever belong to the Golden Circle?

A. No, sir. I belong to the Freemasons, but to no other secret order.

Q. At whose solicitation did you join the order?

A. I do not know that I can say it was at the solicitation of any person. Mr. Bailey, of Terre Haute, came to Salem; I knew his face and recognized him, but could not call his name; he told me what his business was, and I got twelve more men beside myself, and we were taken into the Order of American Knights in my office.

Q. Who initiated you?

A. Mr. Bailey.

Q. Where does he reside now?

A. I understand he is dead; I have made inquiries since I have been in prison, and that is what I am told.

Q. Who else were initiated at that time?

A. James B. Wilson, William C. McCoskey, Townsend Cutshaw, Deloss Heffren, Eli Bouser, William P. Green, and John B. Pitts, I think—I am not certain about him; these are as far as I recollect now.

Q. What was the first lodge or county temple you attended after your initiation?

A. In order to make my story connected, I must explain. After we had taken the three degrees, I was elected Grand Seignior of the County Temple, James B. Wilson Ancient Brother, W. C. McCoskey as Secretary, and Townsend Cutshaw as Treasurer. The lodge was in my office, in the town of Salem.

Q. When did you take the first, second and third degrees?

A. I took the three degrees that very night.

Q. When did you next attend a county temple?

A. There never was but one county temple after that, in our county, to my knowledge: and that was for the election after my time was up, and that was not far from the 22d of February, 1864. I was instructed that there was to be a meeting on the 16th and 17th of February, and that, as Grand Seignior, I was the delegate from the county temple. I came here and attended the meetings of the 16th and 17th; when there, I was instructed that there was to be a new election of officers for the ensuing year, and we elected officers, probably, a week from that time, when Garrett W. Logan was elected Grand Seignior in my place.

Q. Had you attended any meeting previous to the 16th and 17th of February?

A. That was the first and only one of the Grand Council.

Q. How did you come to that meeting?

A. As delegate from the county temple.

Q. Who presided?

A. H. H. Dodd.

Q. Who was Secretary?

A. Mr. Harrison, who was a witness here.

Q. Did you meet any of the accused at that meeting?

A. I met Dr. Bowles there, and Mr. Milligan, I think, the second day; I did not see Mr. Humphreys; never met that gentleman any-where as a member of the Order of American Knights; I never met him except as a Freemason. I never saw Mr. Horsey till I came into Court, and he was required to plead the same time as I was.

Q. At that meeting on the 16th and 17th of February, you say you met Dr. Bowles and Mr. Milligan?

A. Yes, sir; Mr. Milligan on the second day, I believe.

Q. Give to the Court the business transacted, and what you learned was transacted at those meetings on the 16th and 17th of February.

A. The Grand Master read an address; certain committees were appointed—one, I think, upon a newspaper to disseminate the views of the organization, and educate the Democratic mind up to what was thought it ought to be; a Committee upon Literature was appointed; and a committee to see whether a person by the name of Michael Malott had been divulging the secrets of the organization.

Q. Who constituted those committees?

A. I could not tell.

Q. Were you on any committee?

A. I was, sir.

Q. On what?

A. To ferret out whether Mr. Malott had been revealing the secrets of the order.

Q. What did you do in pursuance of that?

A. We called the committee together; brought Malott before us, and a person whose name I do not remember. We investigated all we could. Mr. McBride, of Evansville, was one of the committee; the others I do not remember. It was mere rumor and hearsay; and I told the committee that I professed to know something in regard to law, and I did not think that the evidence was such that we could report to the Grand Council that the man was guilty, and I recommended that we report that the man was not guilty of revealing the secrets.

Q. What was the penalty in case he

did reveal them? What did the rules of the order enjoin as to the obligation?

A. I took some obligations, but do not know what they were?

Q. Do you not know what the penalties are for revealing the secrets of the order?

A. I understand the penalty from what I have read, and what I knew at the time and have learned since, to be death, figuratively speaking.

Q. What do you mean by that?

A. The same as in other organizations.

Q. Was it a figure of speech, or was it to be carried out as fact?

A. That I can not answer.

Q. Did you hear any consultation at that meeting, in reference to a man by the name of Coffin?

A. I do not think that I did; I do not recollect any person mentioning his name.

Q. Were you at the meeting of the 14th of June?

A. I was not.

Q. Were not the Military Committee appointed on the 16th and 17th of February?

A. No, sir: they were not appointed in Council as I understood.

Q. Were any military appointments or elections made?

A. Yes, sir.

Q. What were they?

A. Grand Commander, Deputy Grand Commander, and Major Generals for the four divisions of the State of Indiana, a Secretary, and I think Treasurer. Mr Dodd was elected Grand Commander; I was elected Deputy Grand Commander; Mr. Milligan was elected Major General of his district.

Q. Was Mr. Milligan present at his election?

A. I can not say that he was present till the second day, and the election of Major Generals took place on the first day I believe. Mr. Humphreys was elected in his district. He was not present either day. Major McGrane, of Harrison county, was elected in my district as Major General, and Colonel John C. Walker was elected for the North-west district. The State was divided into four divisions. I do not know exactly how the lines run; but it was divided by counties. Dr. Bowles lived in Orange county, and the line ran between Washington and Orange counties. Major McGrane lived immediately south of Washington. He and I roomed together, and we had a great deal of talk, and he told me he would have nothing to do with it. The next morning Orange county was added to the southeastern division, in which Dr. Bowles was. Major McGrane declined, and Dr. Bowles was unanimously elected in the place of McGrane.

Q. What other business of importance took place at either of these meetings?

A. The next thing I recollect was reports from some committees about literature, and I think a university; but I did not pay any attention to it. My impression is that we laid the matter on the table. I was on the committee with respect to the newspaper; and I think Mr. Bingham was on that committee with me; and we decided that it was all a humbug, and we would have nothing to do with it, but recommended an indefinite postponement with regard to the newspaper. Matters in regard to the progress of the order were also talked of, and reports were called for.

Q. What was said to be the strength of the order at that time?

A. I do not know what the strength of the order was.

Q. Was any thing said about the aggregate number of the order at that time?

A. I think the Secretary reported that he had not received returns from several counties, so that the correct number could not be ascertained.

Q. Of what political faith were the majority of the men comprising that organization?

A. They were all Democrats.

Q. State whether any other class of men were admitted, or was it a *sine qua non* that a man must be a Democrat?

A. I do not think any one would have got in unless he professed to be a Democrat.

Q. State to the Court what were the general purposes and objects of that order, so far as you learned.

A. In the first place, I understood there were two organizations, one within the other; the civil organization, to which the mass of the members belong, and which, as far as I ever knew, was purely political, to bring out the Democratic vote to the polls, and to insure the success of the principles of the Democratic party, by every means in our power to get every voter out to cast his vote; and as we had been told by those who instructed us, that it was the deliberate design and arrangement of the Abolition party to prevent voting, we determined to have a free fight or a fair election. I have been told by members of the order that the other portion of the organization had for its object the separating of the States of Ohio, Indiana, Illinois, Missouri, and Kentucky, from the Eastern States, to make a North-western Confederacy; and failing in that, join our fortunes with the South. That was the military part of it, which was not communicated or known to the members of the civil organization; and I presume I never would have known it, had it not been for the position I held as Deputy Grand Commander.

Q. What proportion of the members belonged to the military portion of the organization?

A. Only the leaders; they were to control the matter through a Committee of Thirteen, who were to be known only to the Grand Commander and themselves. They were to so control us as to bring us into their trap. That was why I said it was a humbug, and said I would have nothing to do with it.

Q. Have any of the schemes of the order come to your knowledge since then?

A. Yes, sir. The schemes of a few of the leaders of this military part of the order, and the schemes of these were unknown to the great mass of the order.

Q. Do you say that it was to these military leaders alone this was confined?

A. Yes, sir; I think so.

Q. Was Dodd considered a military leader?

A. He was; but there was a man over him.

Q. Who was that?

A. It was Dr. Bowles.

Q. Please to explain that?

A. The State was divided off into Military Departments, and there was an officer of the Military Department, who was Supreme Commander to the Grand Commander of the Civil Department, who had his Adjutant, Staff, etc. He controlled the Military Department, and saw to the arming, ammunition, and the procuring of funds.

Q. Then the civil was subservient to the military?

A. Yes, sir; and knew nothing except the few who were in the confidence of the military.

Q. Did you learn who was on the staff of this military leader, Dr. Bowles?

A. Yes, sir; it is James B. Wilson; he told me so himself.

Q. What is the position he held?

A. He told me he was Adjutant General on Dr. Bowles' Staff. In fact, nearly all the information I ever received, except what I received on the 16th and 17th of February, I received from Mr. Wilson, after his return from Dr. Bowles' at French Lick Springs, Orange county.

Q. What did you learn in reference to the arming of this order?

A. I never understood that the men of the rank and file of the civil organization were to be armed, that is, at the expense of the order.

Q. How were they to arm?

A. They were to do it among themselves?

Q. Who was it that was to be armed by the order?

A. These men who were to be under the control of the Commanding General, that is the Military Commander.

Q. How did they make the division as to who were to be armed by the order, and who were to arm themselves?

A. There were certain men they selected to whom to communicate that which it would not do to communicate to every body.

Q. Did they go into a township, for instance, and pick out the men that were to be armed by the order?

A. I think not, sir.

Q. Then how could they tell whom they were to arm, and whom they could rely upon to arm themselves?

A. I do not know. They had a way of ascertaining the number of arms of different kinds that the members of the order had; they would take a sheet of paper and rule it in columns, as for keeping a tally, heading each column with apples, corn, beans, or any thing you please, so that you could understand what these things were intended for. Apples might stand for rifles; corn for shot-guns; beans for pistols, and potatoes for ammunition, and any thing else for lead. This sheet would be a report of the number of arms found by those making the return.

Q. Was there any agreement between the members of the order, as to how it should be understood by those to whom the report was made?

A. My instructions were to report by the secret cypher how many there were. Each township temple reported to the Secretary of the mother temple how many arms and how much ammunition they had, and then that Secretary reported to the Grand Secretary of the State Council.

Q. Do you know of any attempts on the part of the members of this order to arm the order?

A. I only know that from hearsay, from members of the order. I only know what Mr. Wilson told me.

Q. Was Mr. Wilson a member of the order?

A. Yes, sir; he was initiated when I was.

Q. What did he state to you?

A. He had been to French Lick Springs, to Dr. Bowles. When he came back from there, myself, and I think Townsend Cutshaw, a man by the name of Purlee, and my impression is that Mr. C. McCoskey also, were sitting or standing at the Clerk's office door. The people in that country were at fever heat, anxious and unquiet, with rumors of this, that and the other; and the matter came up in that conversation in regard to resisting the draft, when Mr. Wilson pulled a roll out of his pocket, wrapped up like a banker's parcel, and said there was one thousand dollars he had just got from Dr. Bowles, to procure arms and ammunition for our county, and there was plenty more where that came from.

Q. Did he state any thing else?

A. Not at that time, but he did afterward.

Q. What was that?

A. That there was a half a million of dollars sent to Indiana, Illinois and Kentucky, I think, by rebel agents in Canada, for the purpose of procuring arms and ammunition for these North-western States, to arm themselves with.

Q. Who received this money in this State?

A. Mr. Dodd, I was told, and Mr. John C. Walker.

Q. By whom were you told?

A. By Dr. Wilson. I never got a word from Mr. Bowles, Mr. Humphreys, Mr. Milligan or Mr. Horsey, in my life as to the money.

Q. What amount did they receive?

A. A hundred thousand dollars each.

Q. How was it to be expended?

A. A portion of it was to go to Dr. Bowles, to be spent in his part of the State in purchasing arms and ammunition.

Q. For whom?

A. For the military order that had its connection with the Order of American Knights.

Q. When did you have this conversation with Dr. Wilson?

A. It could not have been far from the middle of June, 1864. I think so from the fact that I was told a Grand Council was to be held here about that time, and it was shortly after that, that he and I had this conversation. It must have been in June.

Q. Did he get that information at that meeting?

A. I am not certain that he came to Indianapolis, but it was shortly after that meeting that he told me. Whether he went to the meeting, or got it from Dr. Bowles, I can not say.

Q. Did you learn from him, or other members of the order, for what purpose those arms were to be used after they were purchased and distributed to the members of the Order of American Knights?

A. I never heard how they were to be distributed, neither do I know to whom they were to be distributed; but I supposed, as a matter of course, they were to be distributed to members of the order, and were to be used either to defend themselves from oppression and wrong, or to fight any thing that came to fight them.

Q. Were, or were not these arms to be used in carrying out the purposes of the order that you have detailed?

A. I understood they were to be used for the purpose of carrying out the military part of the organization of the American Knights.

Q. Do you know when the order was changed?

A. I presume it was changed before June.

Q. Before you had this conversation with Dr. Wilson?

A. I think it was.

Q. Do I understand you to say that the

object of the military part of this order was to establish a North-western Confederacy in conjunction with the Southern Confederacy?

A. I understood the object to be to separate themselves from the Eastern States, and form a Confederacy of themselves; or else, failing to do that, join their fortunes to the Southern Confederacy.

Q. Then were, or were not those arms to be used in carrying out these objects of the military organization?

A. That was my understanding.

Q. Did you ever see more than this one thousand dollars that you saw with Mr. Wilson?

A. I never did.

Q. Did you learn of any arms being bought by him?

A. He and I had very little talk for three months past; but I never heard of his offering to buy an arm or ammunition. I never learned from any body that he did. I was asked what he did with the money, but I did not know.

Q. Were these military objects of the order discussed either individually or publicly, at the meetings of the 16th and 17th of February?

A. The matter was talked of by some of us, perhaps a few of us in a corner, or off to one side.

Q. Did you at that time ever talk with Mr. Milligan or Mr. Bowles upon that subject?

A. Mr. Bowles was probably there one morning when we were talking about it. I remember there was something about his papers, about his being a major general, that did not suit him; and I know we had talks among ourselves, probably five or six of us at a time.

Q. Did there ever come to your knowledge, at any time, any intention on the part of this order to take possession of the State Government?

A. Yes, sir.

Q. Detail to the Court what you learned in reference to that.

A. This I also received from the same source—Dr. Wilson. He told me that upon a certain day, the 16th, but whether of August or July I am not certain, of this year, there was to have been an uprising; the prisoners were to be released at the camp near Chicago—I think Camp Douglas—at Camp Morton, and a camp near Columbus, Ohio, Camp Chase it is called, I believe. The arsenals of the United States were to be seized, and the prisoners armed with the arms and equipments contained therein.

Q. What then was to be done?

A. Governor Morton was to be taken care of.

Q. What do you mean by being taken care of?

A. He was to be held as a hostage for those who might be taken prisoners, and engaged in the uprising. Dr. Athon was to be Governor, under the law of the State of Indiana, passed a few sessions since; in case of the Governor failing to serve, he would be Governor; we should call out the militia, and have every thing our own way.

Q. In case you failed to capture Governor Morton, what then?

A. In case he was not captured and made hostage, he was to be made away with in some way, but I never was told how.

Q. After the arsenals were seized, the rebel prisoners armed, and the members of the order armed, what then was to be done by the members of the order?

A. I did not understand that all the members of the order were to take part; it was the military part, and as many as could be induced by excitement or any means, or be drawn into it through the influence of the military leaders. Then the State Government was to go ahead, with the law and Constitution as we had it, except that Dr. Athon was to replace Governor Morton.

Q. Was this scheme known or imparted to any but members of the order?

A. Not that I ever knew of.

Q. State whether or not leading Democrats of the State were given this scheme?

A. It was given only to members of the order; I never knew of its being communicated to any Democrat unless he was a member of the order, and I think it was not.

Q. Did a man by the name of John Bow-.man, of Washington county, belong to this order?

A. I never met him, but I understood he was a member. There were very few Democrats in our county (Washington) but what were members. I think Mr. Bowman knew nothing about the military part; at least not to my knowledge.

Q. Did you learn what was done at the meeting in New York on the 22d of February?

A. Nothing except that the ritual was changed. I am not certain whether that was in New York or Chicago.

Q. Do you know who this Council of Sixteen were?

A. I do not know of such a Council; never heard of it till I was arrested. I have some indirect knowledge of a Council of Thirteen.

Q. Was Dr. Wilson at that meeting in Chicago?

A. I can not state.

Q. Did he tell you whether he was or not?

A. I am not positive; I do not think he did.

Q. You say you did have some indirect knowledge of the Committee of Thirteen? What was it?

A. I understood there was such a Committee; that it was appointed by the Grand

Commander, and known only to him and the members themselves.

Q. Did you ever hear of the appointment of a Committee of Ten?

A. The Committee of Ten that I think you refer to was not a Committee. They were individuals selected, as my understanding was, to take care of Governor Morton.

Q. Did you learn who they were?

A. I did not.

Q. What do you mean by taking care of Governor Morton?

A. To hold him as a hostage, or in case he could not be held, whether he was to be killed or not, I did not hear; but he was to be put out of the way by some means.

Q. They were to dispose of him and get him out of the way; how?

A. I can not say; but they were to get rid of him in some way if he was not held as a hostage?

Cyrus L. Dunham, one of the counsel for the accused, here said:

There are peculiar circumstances attending what has taken place this afternoon, and I regard it as my duty to make a statement which I ask to be put upon the records of this Court. My relations to all parties here are well known to this Commission. I have not only been counsel for Mr. Heffren, but as the records show, I am counsel for other defendants. It places me in rather a queer position before them, and perhaps before this Court; and I desire to make this statement, which I have put in writing, and which I ask to have put upon the records:

INDIANAPOLIS, November 4, 1864.

May it please the Court:

Being counsel for Mr. Heffren, and also for other defendants on this trial, I deem it due to those other defendants, and to my own professional and personal honor, most solemnly to state to this Commission, and in the presence of those other defendants, that I had no knowledge or intimation that the prosecution against said Heffren was to be abandoned, and that he was to be put on the stand as a witness, until, in open Court, he was called to the stand by the Judge Advocate; that I was in no wise, or by any person, consulted in regard to it; that I never, directly or indirectly, sought, or even entertained the idea of the bringing about of such a result.

[Signed]   CYRUS L. DUNHAM.

The Commission then adjourned, to meet on Thursday, November 10, at 2 o'clock, P. M.

———

COURT ROOM, INDIANAPOLIS, INDIANA,
November 10, 1864, 2 o'clock, P. M.

The Commission met pursuant to adjournment.

All the members present, except Colonel Reuben Williams and Colonel Benjamin Spooner. Also, the Judge Advocate, the accused, and their counsel.

The proceedings of Friday, November 4, were read and approved.

Reuben Dailey was then sworn by the Judge Advocate, as Assistant Recorder, in presence of the accused.

The examination of Horace Heffren, a witness for the Government, was then proceeded with as follows:

Question by the Judge Advocate:

Did you not state that Dr. James B. Wilson was Adjutant General on Dr. Bowles' staff?

Answer. Yes, sir.

Q. Do you know of any other staff officer?

A. Yes, sir; Garrett W. Logan was Quartermaster.

Q. Where did he reside?

A. In Salem, Monroe township, Washington county, Indiana.

Q. How do you know that?

A. David D. Hamilton and Garrett W. Logan went to see Colonel Bowles sometime during the past summer or spring. Hamilton was a member of the organization, so was Logan, who is now the Grand Seignior of Washington county; he was elected sometime in February. Mr. Hamilton told me what Logan was going for; but I had no confidence in him, and I wrote a letter to Dr. Bowles telling him not to trust him, that he would betray him. When Hamilton came back he said that Dr. Bowles had offered him a Brigadier Generalship, and he would not accept of it, and Bowles said their business was at an end, and Logan was appointed Quartermaster; Logan told me so himself; and the reason was, that he had a sore leg, and would have the advantage of riding on horseback instead of going afoot. To my positive knowledge he has had a sore leg for seven or eight years.

Q. Were there any other staff officers except Dr. Wilson and Mr. Logan?

A. Not that I know of.

Q. State whether you have any knowledge of a regiment of lancers being organized, or of any provision being made to furnish the members of the order with lances.

A. I have not of a regiment, but of companies composing a regiment. The first I knew of it was from Dr. Wilson telling me that Bowles had made an arrangement to have nine companies of infantry, one of lancers, and one section of artillery, to comprise each regiment in this order. The lancers were to be armed with lances, of what length I do not know, but there was to be a hook, somewhat after the fashion of a sickle; the lance to punch with, and a sickle to cut the horse's bridle; there was to be a thrust and a cut, a thrust for the man and a cut for the horses' bridles; he thought the enemy would become confused and distracted, and if a charge was made upon them when they had no means of controlling the horses, they would be easily mashed up.

Q. Were any steps taken toward procuring those lances?

A. I do not know that ever a lance was made, or contracted to be made; I only know that Dr. Wilson told me that arrangements were on foot to get them, but he did not say where, or by whom, or when they were to be furnished. He said they would be a terrible weapon in a fight. I thought he did not know as much about it as I did, or he would not try it.

Q. Give to the Court the secret cypher used by the order, as far as you have knowledge of it.

A. If I wanted to write to the Judge Advocate, he and I would understand what book we would have to write from; it might be Dellart's Military Law, the Bible, or a hymn book, it would not matter what, so that we understood what book was referred to. I would make my date, and place under it in parenthesis the figures denoting the page, and the figure at the left end of the line would designate the line on which I commenced; for instance, if it was the figure fifteen, it would indicate the fifteenth line from the top. The page of the book would be placed on the right hand side, in parenthesis; and the number of the line on the left. When I could not find the letter I wanted on any line in that page, then I left a line in blank and put another number, which was to designate the page to which I wanted to refer in parenthesis in that blank line, and then proceeded as before. If I wished to write, "I do not want them," I would count the letters in the designated line, counting from the left, and put down for "1" the number three ("3"), if that is the third letter, and "13" for "d," if that is the thirteenth letter in line, etc.

Q. You were appointed as delegate to Chicago, were you not?

A. I was told by Mr. Dodd, that, by virtue of my office as Deputy Grand Commander, I was a delegate to Chicago; but I did not go. William P. Green, of Salem, Indiana, was started in my place. This must have been about the 17th or 18th of June, 1864; it might have been a few days before or after.

Q. Then it was not the July meeting he attended, was it?

A. I can not state positively.

Q. Did you learn from him whether he had been there?

A. He went there; he had my proxy; and I saw him after his return.

Q. Did he state to you what was done?

A. He told me, and others in my presence, that he had been there, and made a report of what was done; but I was afraid that he was not telling the truth, and so were some others, Mr. Cutshaw, Dr. Wilson, Mr. McCoskey, and also Mr. Bowser. I sent my brother to Mr. Dodd, at Indianapolis, to see whether what he stated was true, and we found that he had fallen in the hands of the detectives, that they had got my proxy, and that he did not get into the Grand Council at all; he made a bad failure of it.

Q. Did you learn the names of the men comprising this Committee of Ten, who were to take care of Governor Morton?

A. No, sir; I never did; they were to be selected by the Committee of Thirteen, and were only known to the Grand Council, and to the members of this Committee of Thirteen. Mr. Harris told me he knew more about the order than I did.

Q. Did I understand you to say the Committee of Thirteen selected the Committee of Ten?

A. Yes, sir; they were to hold Governor Morton as a hostage for those that were taken prisoners, or to make away with him some way, but they never told me how.

Q. State whether or not there was any arrangement, or instructions given, by which the property of members of this order was to be saved in case of invasion by the rebels?

A. There was, sir; there was a flag that was to be the emblem; it was to be a white flag placed upon a flag staff, with a red ribbon running along the flag where it was tacked on to the staff, down each side of the staff, and three or four inches below, making red, white, and red; the flag was to be hung out at the house or stable, or any-where else, and that property would be saved or protected.

Q. When was this to be used?

A. Whenever there was a rebel invasion or raid.

Q. Was this knowledge imparted to any but members of the order?

A. No, sir, I told it to no one except to my father.

Q. When did you expect this raid?

A. About the 16th of August. Dr. Bowles had sent a man to see General Price, but he had not returned.

Q. Do you know whether Mr. Michael C. Kerr is a member of this order or not?

A. He was; I initiated him in New Albany, Indiana, at a harness shop on the right hand side of Main street, as you go east, I believe at Mr. Graff's.

Q. How many degrees did he take?

A. I was only there two nights, but I took him through; I recollect that I gave him all three the same night.

Q. Do you know the cause of the failure of the insurrection contemplated here on the 16th of August last? If so, give it to the Court.

A. I know one reason of it, I presume; Mr. Kerr, I am told by members of the order, received word what was to be done, and he came to Indianapolis and reported to the authorities here, Mr. Athon, Mr. Ristine, McDonald and others, and did what he could to prevent it.

Q. Do you know any other reason?

A. Yes, sir; because the army of the Confederacy did not come up through Cumberland Gap as they had agreed to do, or as it was reported they had agreed to do.

Q. Was there, or was there not, any communication with General Price, in Missouri?

A. There was, sir.

Q. Who told you they had communication with General Price?

A. Dr. Wilson said Dr. Bowles' man had gone to see Price, and another had gone to Richmond to arrange for troops to come through Cumberland Gap, and when they returned, they thought it would be before the 16th of August 1864, about which time the rumpus would take place.

Q. Did they fail to communicate with the Confederate forces, and if so, did that have any thing to do with the failure of the insurrection?

A. I understood these men failed to get back in time.

Q. Did that have any thing to do with the failure?

A. I do not know; I was not in their secrets at that time.

Q. Did you learn from any members of the order whether they had any communication?

A. I believe I did, sir; from Mr. Harris.

Q. What did he say?

A. He said that the Richmond man got on his way, but we never heard from the messenger.

Q. What do you mean by the Richmond man?

A. The man that went to communicate with the rebels at Richmond.

Q. Did you hear any thing with respect to the man that went to communicate with Price?

A. No, sir; I never learned his name, and do not know whether he communicated with Price or not; there was a man who had been communicating with rebel officials, but I do not know what or who they were, for about March or April some of the members said I would not do to tie to.

Q. Do you know of any tax being levied upon the members of the order? and for what purpose?

A. Yes, sir; it was to be twenty cents per month; one dollar for the first degree, one dollar and a half for the second degree, and two and a half for the third degree, which was to go into the treasury.

Q. How was that money to be expended?

A. I do not know that?

Q. Do you know of any direct tax being levied upon members of the order, and do you know how it was expended?

A. It was spent for arms and ammunition for the military part of the order; I presume that the large mass of them did not know how it was to be expended, or what they were paying taxes for; it was said to be for establishing a university and starting a newspaper, but the real purpose was for the purchase of arms and ammunition.

Mr. Kerr received some information from a gentleman at Salem, and set himself to work to find out in regard to the whole thing, and by some means, I know not how, obtained, I am told, the information that a meeting was held here by the Republican party, and that the arrangement was made to fix up things to secure the election, and that I had sold out Washington county to the Republicans, and was to receive therefor the sum of ten thousand dollars; and Mr. Kerr, as I am told, sent a runner with a letter to Dr. Wilson for the committee to come at once to New Albany, Indiana. The committee consisted of James B. Wilson, John L. Menaugh, and Dr. Painter; they went there, and had their consultation; what it was I do not know, for since returning home, I have not staid at home a night, for I have been threatened to be hung since testifying.

Q. Do you know by whom these threats were made?

A. I do not wish to state that at present, unless you desire it particularly.

Q. For what reason?

A. For my own safety. I have not staid at home a night since I last testified on Friday last.

Q. Do you know either by report, or from any members of the order, where any arms or ammunition of this order are stored?

A. As a man of a little honor left, at least, I do not think that question should be asked, for I do not think I ought to state what was said to me when I was in prison with other men.

Objection waived on the part of all the accused.

I know what Mr. Horsey told me and Mr. Humphreys; he told where he hid his buckshot, caps and powder; some of it was hid in a manger under the horses' feed, and in a barrel the caps were hid; other portions were hid in a stable and upon the plates in the corncrib; Shirkliffe carried off much of it; and the powder was hid in barrels in his house.

Q. When did he tell you this?

A. When I was in prison with him; four hundred pounds of lead are hid in different places, some of it left with a man by the name of Baker, and a man he called Miller helped to pack some of the powder across the river. Shirkliffe has since been drafted, and is now in the army; he told where the money came from that they got it with; from Dr. Bowles.

Q. Did you learn what quantity of ammunition was hid?

A. There were four hundred pounds of lead and several thousand musket caps; I think some six or seven kegs of powder. Both Mr. Humphreys and myself wanted Mr. Horsey taken from our cell; we did not wish to be associated with him, and we had even written a letter to Colonel Warner, which Mr. Humphreys and myself signed, requesting a change.

CROSS-EXAMINATION.

Question by the accused:

When do you say you joined this order?

Answer. I find I was mistaken in my answer in the examination-in-chief. It must have been in September I joined the order; because I let a gentleman read the obligation and ritual instead of swearing him to it.

Q. What is his name?

A. His name is Joseph V. Cutshaw. He is now Clerk of the Court. He was then a candidate for that office. I gave him the ritual to read with the understanding that he would take the obligation.

Q. At what time did you attend the first Grand Council?

A. On the 16th and 17th of February.

Q. Were you not at the Council in the fall?

A. I was not at the November session. I was entitled to go as delegate, by virtue of my office, but I could not attend, and got Mr. Wilson to go in my place.

Q. What do you know about the military bill?

A. I do not know any thing about its adoption. That bill, I understood, was confided to the Committee of Thirteen, who had exclusive control of it.

Q. Who did you learn this from?

A. I understood from Dr. Wilson that this was the case.

Q. Was Dr. Wilson at the November meeting?

A. I think he was.

Q. Did he tell you this after his return?

A. Yes, sir.

Q. When did you first hear of the military organization of the order?

A. I can not state the date. If I could be positive about Dr. Wilson's attendance at the November meeting of the Grand Council, I could tell you how long it was before or after it.

Q. At what time did you first learn of the military feature of the order?

A. It was some time in the latter part of 1863, or in the first part of 1864.

Q. From whom did you learn it?

A. From Dr. Wilson, and I believe also from Mr. Harris. It was at the time they told me about the arsenals.

Q. Did you learn it prior to the meeting in February?

A. Yes, sir.

Q. Did Dr. Wilson tell you prior to that meeting that he was on Dr. Bowles' staff?

A. No, sir. He never told me so but once.

Q. How often did you see Dr. Bowles?

A. I never saw him except once at his own house, once in attending Court at Paoli, and once at a meeting of the State Council.

Q. When was that meeting held?

A. On the 16th and 17th of February.

Q. Do you know that Dr. Bowles was elected major general?

A. I was present at the election, and arranged the counties, attaching Orange county to the District, so that when Major McGrane refused to serve, Dr. Bowles could take his place. Major McGrane declined, and Dr. Bowles was elected.

Q. Was not Dr. Bowles the junior major general?

A. No, sir.

Q. How does that come?

A. The military and civil organizations were not regulated alike in regard to rank of junior or senior.

Q. Did not the military organization of the order adopt the same rules in regard to grades and rank as are in force in the army of the United States, ranking according to the date of their commissions?

A. Not that I know of.

Q. As Dr. Bowles was elected after the other major generals, because Major McGrane had declined, how do you know he was not the junior officer?

A. Dr. Wilson said he was the ranking major general, through his military experience in the Mexican war, and had control of the military part of the organization.

Q. Did not Major McGrane hold the same position and the same rank as that to which Dr. Bowles was afterward elected?

A. I think not.

Q. Why not?

A. Because I never knew that he was in the confidence of the order, and had control of it, as I knew Dr. Bowles was, from what I heard Dr. Wilson, Mr. Hamilton, and Mr. Logan say.

Q. Did Dr. Bowles' election differ from any other?

A. It did not.

Q. Are you acquainted with any act which led you to the conclusion that Dr. Bowles was at the head of the military organization?

A. Yes, sir.

Q. What was it?

A. What Dodd stated, at the February meeting, that Dr. Bowles was boss of the whole machine of the military part of the order.

Q. Who were the other Major Generals?

A. Major Conklin was one. Dr. Yeakle was also appointed as a Major General, and Mr. Humphreys was appointed for another district.

Q. Who was intrusted with the arming of the order?

A. I understood the Commander-in-chief of the military part of the order, Dr. Bowles, had charge of it.

Q. Who received the money for that purpose?

A. Colonel John C. Walker and Dodd, each, received $1,000, and Dr. Bowles received his share.

Q. How much was that?

A. I do not know.

Q. From whom did he receive it?

A. I never heard. Probably from Walker and Dodd.

Q. Did he have to depend on his juniors for funds?

A. I do not know whether you would call them his juniors or seniors.

Q. But seniors do not have to depend on their juniors in the army, do they?

A. If they did not, they would never get into any battle.

Q. Did Dr. Bowles have to rely entirely upon his Grand Commander for funds?

A. I can not state whether he relied entirely on him or not.

Q. Did you ever hear of Dr. Bowles getting money from other sources?

A. I did not.

Q. When did you determine to have nothing more to do with this order?

A. On the 16th of February, after the case of Mr. Malott had been investigated. I had been on the Committee of Investigation on the charge against Mr. Malott, of having divulged the secrets of the order. After the report was made, Mr. Moss, of Greene county, and Mr. Malott, left the room with me to take a drink. We came down to the foot of the stairs; there Mr. Moss and Mr. Malott asked me what I thought of the investigation; I said I thought it did not amount to much, and that the whole concern was a humbug, and not worth a damn. One of them said, "Let's go and take a drink on that." We came down to Hezekiah's and took a drink, and then agreed to have nothing more to do with the order.

Q. Did you inform the rest of the order of that intention?

A. I did not; I did not propose to make a blowing-horn of myself at that time.

Q. When were you elected?

A. I was elected Deputy Grand Commander on the 16th or 17th of February.

Q. Before you resolved to quit it?

A. Yes, sir.

Q. Did you communicate your intention to have nothing more to do with it to anybody else?

A. I informed nobody but Mr. Moss, Mr. Malott, and Mr. Bingham, with whom I had talked frequently, and we thought we would let it alone, and let it grind out itself.

Q. At what time did you leave Indianapolis after coming to this resolution?

A. That evening, or the next day.

Q. What members of the order do you remember went home with you?

A. Nobody; I went by myself; I was the only member from Washington county here, that I recollect.

Q. Did you keep that resolution to have nothing more to do with it?

A. I did, sir; except so far as was necessary to inform my particular friends of any insurrection that might take place.

Q. Were you a civil member?

A. Yes, sir; and a military one, too.

Q. How far were you military?

A. As far as a Grand Commander.

Q. What were your powers?

A. The same as the Grand Commander, when he was deposed, or out of the way.

Q. How was it when you acted for or under him?

A. I never acted under him; I had nothing to do except when he was out of the way.

Q. Had he any right to act through you as his deputy?

A. No, sir.

Q. Then you only acted in the absence or death of the Grand Commander?

A. Then I would be Grand Commander de facto.

Q. From what part of the organization or order did you come to the conclusion that when you acted as Grand Commander, Dr. Bowles would have a right to command you?

A. Dr. Wilson said Bowles had said so himself. That is all I did know.

Q. Do you know whether that was any part of the order, military or civil?

A. I suppose it was; I was so instructed; and I presume that the officer who had seen service would rank those who had not been in the service; Colonel Bowles had been in the Mexican war.

Q. How long, after you went home, did you elect the officers of your county temple?

A. Within a week or so of the 22d of February, which was said to be the anniversary of the order, when Logan was elected Grand Seignior.

Q. How many members had been taken into the order up to that time?

A. I have no means of knowing.

Q. Had there been a temple established in each township at that time?

A. I think not.

Q. Did you ever participate in the establishing of temples after that?

A. No, sir.

Q. Did you ever meet with temples after that?

A. Yes, sir; when we wanted to elect a couple of Justices of the Peace, sometime in March, I think, I went once to a meeting.

Q. Who presided at that meeting?

A. I believe I did, as Deputy Grand Commander.

Q. Did you correspond with members of the order at that time?

A. I can not say that I did; except that about the time of Dodd's arrest, I wrote a letter to each of the major generals in the order, one to Mr. Humphreys, one to Mr. Milligan, who, I remember, was sick in bed as the answer informed me, and one I wrote to Dr. Bowles, which was to be taken by a man by the name of Rainbow, but it was never sent.

Q. What was the substance of those letters?

A. It was that Dr. Wilson had come to me and said he had not talked with me for two or three months; that he now considered it his duty to do so; that as I was Deputy Grand Commander, and Dodd was arrested, I must write to Vallandigham and to each of the major generals; I did not want to do so, but he insisted, and I did write to Mr. Humphreys, Mr. Milligan, John C. Walker, and Mr. Vallandigham; I wrote to Mr. Bowles, but as I understood he was arrested for harboring deserters, I did not send the letter.

Q. How did you write to Vallandigham?

A. As Supreme Grand Commander of the Supreme Council of the United States.

Q. How did you sign your name to this letter?

A. Horace Heffren.

Q. Did you sign it officially or unofficially?

A. I do not recollect; I might have signed it officially. Dr. Wilson said that as Mr. Dodd was arrested, he thought it best to do something. Thomas G. Wilson, of Campbellsburg, Washington county, had been to Illinois, and pretended to have seen the Grand Commander of the State of Illinois, and reported to me that Illinois was ready to raise, and was only waiting for Indiana, I told him I did not know about such a movement, but thought it was best to go slow and not get themselves into trouble. Wilson wanted me to write to the Supreme Grand Commander, and also to the major generals in the State; I talked with him some time, and said it was best not to write, but he insisted, and I wrote. He said Dodd was arrested, and asked what shall we do—submit or fight? that was the substance of my letter.

Q. What do you mean by we?

A. I mean the members of the Order of American Knights.

Q. You forgot your resolution to have nothing more to do with the order, did you not?

A. I acceded to Dr. Wilson's earnest solicitations and wrote, although I considered myself out of the order?

Q. Did these gentlemen write back?

A. None but Mr. Milligan and Mr. Humphreys. Mr. Milligan's letter was signed by some gentleman as "student," as he was sick, and it said that it would not do at the present time, but we must abide our time.

Q. What did he say about the salvation of God?

A. He did not say any thing about the salvation of God, for I did not think it was near any of us at that time.

Q. What did Mr. Humphreys say?

A. Last spring, coming to Indianapolis, we met at the Green Castle Junction, had a talk about the order and its organization, and Mr. Humphreys said it would not do. We had got to depend on Chicago; he said he was for his country, right or wrong, and would have nothing to do with it. He advised me to quit the order, and I said I had quit it, and would have nothing more to do with the order; and I told him about Mr. Moss and Malott on the 17th of February; Humphreys said he was glad of it.

The Judge Advocate here objected to this class of testimony.

Q. In regard to resisting the draft, did not Mr. Humphreys say that it would not do to resist the law?

A. He did; he said so in the letter and in the conversation I have referred to.

Q. What did he say about the men having, or not having, authority to use his name at the February meeting?

A. He said it was without his knowledge or consent, and they had no right to it; he said he was for his country right or wrong, and for the Constitution as it was.

Q. What did Mr. Milligan say?

A. I received that letter signed "student;" I suppose written by a student in his office.

Q. Did Vallandigham write to you?

A. No, sir. I did not have the honor of receiving a letter from him; I was too small fry I expect.

Q. What was the date of your letter to this gentleman?

A. I should judge it must have been two months ago; it was just after Mr. Dodd was arrested.

Q. How many members were at that time enrolled in your county?

A. From what I understood, there must have been one thousand or eleven hundred.

Q. Who organized the county?

A. I did; together with Dr. Wilson and Mr. Logan.

Q. When did you initiate the Hon. M. C. Kerr?

A. At Mr. Graff's saddlery; it must have been near Tuesday night, the 8th of March, 1864.

Q. How often did you meet with the temple in New Albany?

A. Only those two nights; I do not think Mr. Kerr was there the first night, but he was there the second.

Q. When did you organize them?

A. It could not have been far from the

28th of March; it might have been about the 25th of February that we organized that temple.

Q. How many members did you take in?

A. About twenty or thirty.

Q. Did you take in some each time you met?

A. Yes, sir; of course that was my business.

Q. Were you allowed any thing for the organization of this temple?

A. Yes, sir. I suppose I was; but I never got any thing, with the exception of what Mr. Jones, of New Albany, paid me, which was about three dollars, which paid my expenses to New Albany and back.

Q. Had you any correspondence with other members?

A. I never wrote any letters in regard to the order save to Messrs. Vallandigham, Humphreys and Milligan, and one letter I wrote to Dr. Bowles, but did not send.

Q. About what time did you appoint William P. Green to act as your proxy?

A. I think it was in June.

Q. At what time did Dr. Wilson show you the thousand dollars?

A. It could not have been far from the middle of June, 1864, or when he came back from seeing Dr. Bowles at French Lick Springs.

Q. How long was that before he told you to write to these men, in regard to what you should do?

A. The money was shown to me some tim ein June; the writing was some time in September. I know it was near the time of Dodd's arrest. Mr. Dodd had not been arrested when he showed me the money. I do not know whether he had been to Chicago, or to Dr. Bowles'. I should state in regard to Mr. Milligan, I think that he was present at the second day of the Grand Council in February. I have not a distinct and positive recollection of his being there; what makes me think he was there is because Harry Vandegrift was very anxious that Mr. Milligan should be nominated for Governor.

Q. When was the ritual changed, if ever?

A. Mr. Dodd, at the February meeting, reported a constitution, by-laws, etc., oaths and obligations, but when they were changed I do not know; those published are not the same as those read; I am certain of that. I do not know who changed them, or any thing about it.

Q. How were the ordinary expenses of the order kept up?

A. By the initiation fee; $1 for the first degree, $1 50 for the second, $2 50 for the third degree, and twenty cents per month; and they had a right to tax if they saw fit.

Q. How were the expenses of the Supreme Grand Council of the United States to be kept up?

A. I do not know, except by contributions from grand and branch temples

Q. Do you know what the expenses of the Grand Council of the State of Indiana were estimated at?

A. I do not.

Q. What was the salary of the Secretary?

A. My impression was that it was to be eight hundred dollars per year.

Q. Do you know any thing else about the expenses of the order?

A. No, sir.

Q. Mr. Green, then, lied to you when he returned, or pretended to return from the Grand Council, did he not?

A. Either he, or Mr. Dodd, or my brother; Mr. Dodd said that Mr. Green did not get in.

Q. How did you sign that proxy?

A. I signed it "Horace Heffren," and I gave him a letter of introduction to Dodd beside; I do not know whether I signed it officially or not, but I presume it would be signed officially to Dodd.

Q. At what time did you say the rebel raid was to be made in Indiana?

A. I did not say that a rebel raid was to be made in Indiana.

Q. The raid in which you were to participate?

A. I did not state that either.

Q. What was to take place on the 16th of August?

A. An uprising in the States of Indiana, Kentucky, Ohio and Missouri; the Confederates were to come up through Cumberland Gap; but we did not rise, and the rebels did not come.

Q. What was the name of that man who was sent to Missouri?

A. I do not know; nor whether he got there, or had any communication with Price.

Q. Do you know whether he had correspondence with General Price?

A. Yes, sir; I understood so from Dr Wilson, George R. Harris and Harry Vandegriff, of Salem.

Q. Who was sent to Richmond?

A. I do not know that.

Q. Did you ever inquire?

A. I did, of Mr. Wilson and Harris; but I did not find out from them; they did not say they knew.

Q. Who told you about this emblem to save property?

A. It was to save the property of those belonging to the order. I only told it to two men, my father and father-in-law.

Q. Did they avail themselves of it?

A. I do not know.

Q. Did you ever make one?

A. I told my wife to make one; but she did not.

Q. Did you ever see one?

A. No, sir; nor did I see any person making one.

Q. What banner were you to march under when you rallied?

A. The banner they carried in the army.

Q. In what army?

A. The Confederate army, of course. If we could not gain a North-western Confederacy, we were to join our fortunes with the South.

Q. How would you know when you could not get a North-western Confederacy?

A. As any fool would know when he got whipped.

Q. Do you know that the Committee of Thirteen was appointed?

A. I do not know, except that Mr. Harris said he knew more about that Committee of Thirteen than I did.

Q. When was it that Mr. Harris told you this?

A. It was after I came back from Terre Haute. He laughed at me, and said he knew better than I did what was going on in Terre Haute.

Q. Did he mention the Committee of Thirteen?

A. He and I have talked about it perhaps fifty times; he spoke of it and its arrangement, and thought the thing was played out, and said that the thing might go to the devil, for all he cared. I think Mr. Harris has had nothing to do with it since, probably, last winter. He never formally withdrew, that I knew of.

Q. When did you first know of this Committee of Thirteen, connected with the order?

A. When Mr. Bailey initiated us; twelve beside myself, which was emblematical of the thirteen original States, and also of the thirteen stars on the flag; that was before the election of 1863.

Q. Was not that committee appointed to save the expense of calling the Grand Council together?

A. I never was present but at one meeting of the Grand Council, and it was not spoken of then.

Q. Did you hear any thing said about the Committee of Thirteen at that meeting?

A. I might, but if so, I have forgotten it.

Q. Did you ever hear any thing about this Committee of Thirteen before last June?

A. I did, sir; I never heard any thing since June, that I recollect; I heard of it when Mr. Bailey initiated us, sometime in September, 1863; the Committee of Thirteen belongs exclusively to the Grand Council of the State.

Q. Were the county temples instructed in relation to it?

A. I can not state, except that I was so instructed, and so were the gentlemen that were initiated with me.

Q. This committee, you say, had power to appoint ten murderers, or men who had the dark work of taking care of Governor Morton?

A. I did not say they appointed ten murderers; I said they were a committee to select ten men to take care of Governor Morton, and hold him as a hostage; or failing in that, to take care of him.

Q. What do you understand the words "take care of him," to mean?

A. Just what any sensible man would; that if they could not use him for their own purposes, they might take him out and kill him.

Q. When did you first understand that?

A. I think it must have been about June, 1864; and I packed up my carpet-sack to go and tell Governor Morton in regard to it, but my wife was taken sick, and I did not go. I tried to communicate with him when I was in prison, but I could not do it.

Q. When did Wilson tell you this?

A. I think he must have been to Chicago or New York, or French Lick Springs; I am not certain; he told me when he came from one of those places. I knew there was a Grand Council somewhere about June that I did not attend; and there was a Supreme Grand Council held in Chicago, to which I gave Green my proxy.

Q. Were you told this before or after you gave Green your proxy to go to Chicago?

A. I can not say for certain, but I presume it would be after.

Q. Then you had heard this statement of Wilson in regard to the appointment of ten men to do this dirty work?

A. My impression is that I had, but I am not positive.

Q. Could you not have let Governor Morton know that it would be best for him to be careful?

A. I suppose I could, sir.

Q. Did you believe that those ten men would do this to Governor Morton?

A. I did, sir; I had good reasons for believing it.

Q. Did Kerr come to see you when this alarm was got up?

A. No, sir.

Q. And you did not meet him when he was on his way to Washington county, did you?

A. No, sir; or if I did, he did not inform me as to his business. I never knew of Mr. Kerr doing any thing but what, in my judgment, was right and proper.

Q. Did you ever talk with Dr. Bowles on this matter?

A. Never, in my life.

Q. How far did you live from Dr. Bowles?

A. About thirty to thirty-five miles.

Q. Why was this flag to be put on the property of members of the order and their friends?

A. To save our property. It was understood that property that was not so designated would be destroyed when a rebel raid should take place; but if that flag was displayed the destroying angel would pass over it, and it would not be disturbed.

Q. You were very anxious to save Governor Morton, but did care about your neighbors, did you?

A. I had nothing to do with them. My feelings were that I did not care after Morgan came through, and they treated me as they did; I mean the soldiers under Hobson.

[Objected to by the Judge Advocate.]

Q. When did you meet Felix G. Stidger first?

A. I do not know that I ever saw him till I saw him on the stand here. I do not recollect any conversation with him in Salem.

Q. Did you meet a gentleman like Stidger, from Kentucky, to whom you said you were expecting an envoy or commissioner from Kentucky to bring you word about the disbanding of some of Forrest's regiments?

[Question objected to by the Judge Advocate.]

The counsel for the accused remarked as follows:

The witness, Stidger, has fixed the time and place when he had two several conversations with this man Heffren, and he has given the substance of these conversations: I now propose to show by this witness that no such conversation ever took place at either of the times mentioned by Stidger. I make him my witness for that purpose in order to save time; if this is not admitted, I shall introduce him as a witness for the defense afterward.

To which the Judge Advocate replied:

This is the rule of law: that the accused have a right to cross-examine this witness as to any matter on which I have examined him in chief; only by courtesy and consent of the opposite party, can they step outside and enter upon new ground. If that consent is yielded, then I may cross-examine him upon that new matter; but under my objection they can not introduce new matter. They may recall him, and place him upon the stand as their witness.

Question withdrawn.

Q. In the month of May last, from the 4th to the 8th, in the town of Salem, and at the Persise House, did you, or did you not have a conversation about the order, and your relations with it, with Felix G. Stidger?

A. I have no recollection of any conversation with him.

Q. At that time and place, and in conversation with Felix G. Stidger, did you not inform him that you wished to see him?

A. I could not ask him that if I did not see him, and I do not recollect seeing him.

Q. Did you not further tell him that you were expecting a commissioner from certain disbanded rebel regiments in Kentucky, and that you had mistaken him for that commissioner?

A. I do not recollect any conversation with such a man, or of such an import.

Q. If you had had such a conversation, would you not remember it?

A. I do not know whether I should remember it or not. It is possible some man played himself off on Stidger that time for me. A great many men about Salem, at that time, were expecting a man from Cumberland Gap to report rebel movements. My diary shows that I was not in town then.

Q. What days do you refer to?

A. The 6th and 7th, and 27th of May. On the 6th of May I was making a speech in Franklin township; on the 7th I was at Little York township; and on the 26th of May, I was at——school house, in Madison township.

Q. How far is that from Salem?

A. Ten or twelve miles. I drove my ponies, I recollect.

Q. Did you see any man who resembled Stidger?

A. I do not recollect any one of his personal appearance. There was a tall, stoop-shouldered, black-whiskered man, called on me some time in the spring—Coffin I suppose it was. He did not look like Stidger who testified here. He had a large Roman nose.

Q. Did you have any such conversation with Coffin as that testified to by Stidger?

A. I do not think I did. I thought he was a spy or a detective. I believe I got rid of him by writing a letter of introduction to Judge Carlton. There was a way of writing a letter to have it mean the opposite of its purport. For instance, I wrote he was an exceedingly loyal man, and then put in the left hand corner the letters O. A. K., with a dash before and after "O. A. K.," the first letters of the signal of distress, which gave the opposite meaning to the letter.

Q. Did you not act while in prison as legal adviser to Stephen Horsey?

A. I did not. I acted as a legal adviser to no one. You and others were my legal advisers, and I could not get you up to my room as often as I wanted you.

Q. Did not Horsey rely on your advice as a lawyer?

A. I can not say that he did.

Q. Are not you and Mr. James B. Wilson on bad terms?

A. We are not.

Q. When he came into Court the other day, did you not say angrily, that you would like to know whether he heard the story of Haman and Mordecai, of his being hung on the gallows he had built for others?

A I do not think I made such a remark, but thought it pretty strong.

RE-EXAMINATION.

Question by the Judge Advocate:

I understand you to say that you have no recollection of having any conversation with Felix G. Stidger. Is that correct?

A. I do not recollect any such conversation. He might have had such a conversation with some one.

Q. Is it not possible that he might have had such a conversation with you?

A. It is, but I do not recollect it.

Q. In regard to the incidents of that day, you say you have an absence of recollection?

A. I do.

Q. What is the personal appearance of this Mr. Bailey, of Terre Haute, you have referred to?

A. He is a man about twenty-five years of age. I understand he is dead.

Q. I understood you to state that Mr. Humphreys had abandoned this order. Were you not informed by a letter from Humphreys and others, of his having charge of and being concerned in a general drill at a meeting of about one thousand men connected with this order, on or about the lines of Green, Clay, or Sullivan counties, during the month of September last?

A. I did not hear of it.

Q. Did you not hear of his drilling members of the order in his county?

A. Not before his arrest, or since.

Q. Did you hear of his assisting to arm members of the order, or giving instructions as to resisting the draft?

A. No, sir. He said a great many men had come to him to know whether he would fight, and he told them to go home and behave themselves.

Q. Did you ever hear of his advising resistance to the draft?

A. I never did, sir.

Q. Did you ever meet him at any meeting of the order?

A. I did not, sir.

Q. How did you first know that he was a member of the order?

A. I think it was probably the letter he wrote to me last fall.

Q. Did you learn that he was a member of the order from that letter?

A. I am not positive.

Q. If he had told you about the time of the June meeting here, and previous to that, that the thing was a humbug, and he had abandoned it, why did you wr.'e to him as a major general, to hear whether you were to come to arms on the arrest of Dodd?

A. At the request of Dr. Wilson, ne insisted that I should write to all the major generals; that I was the only one to write, and I, as Deputy Grand Commander, , rote to him as major general. That was after he told me that he had abandoned it, as it was a humbug. I wrote to him in the same manner that I wrote to Mr. Milligan, but I wrote a little more to Mr. Vallandigham; and the purport of it was to see whether we should back out or fight, and if to fight, to bring the heads together at once. It was only to accommodate Dr. Wilson that I did it.

The Commission then adjourned, to meet on Friday, November 11, 1864, at 10 o'clock, A. M.

———

COURT ROOM, INDIANAPOLIS, INDIANA,
November 11, 1864, 10 o'clock, A. M.

The Commission met pursuant to adjournment.

All the members present. Also, the Judge Advocate, the accused, and their counsel.

The proceedings of yesterday were read and approved.

The following Special Field Order was then read by the Judge Advocate:

HEADQUARTERS DEPARTMENT OF THE CUMBERLAND,
Atlanta, Ga., October 15, 1864.

Special Field Orders, No. 275.

EXTRACT.

* * * * 1. The resignations of the following named officers are accepted, to take effect from this date:

Colonel J. T. Wilder. 17th Indiana Mounted Infantry. Disability.

By command of Major General Thomas.

SOUTHARD HOFFMAN,
Assistant Adjutant General.

Some of the members of the Commission having expressed a desire to ask Mr. Heffren some questions, he was called to the stand, and the following questions were submitted:

Question by the Court:

Do you know from your own knowledge, or from any member of the order, how many States were represented in the Grand Council of the Order of the Sons of Liberty, at any of their meetings?

Answer. I was told by Dr. Wilson, when he returned from Chicago, that they were all represented but five; all the States both North and South.

Q. Do you recollect what five were not represented?

A. Florida and South Carolina I remember being mentioned, but the other three I am not sure about.

Q. Do you recollect any thing about a session of this order about the time of the Democratic Convention at Chicago?

A. I know nothing of it except what Dr. Wilson said at a meeting we had called to raise money to buy substitutes for the poor men drafted in our county. He there stated that the object was to concentrate all the votes against McClellan, and prevent his nomination at Chicago.

Q. Do you know the names of any who were there?

A. I do not know whether he gave any. At the called meeting there were present Colonel Menaugh, Mr. Kerr, General Cravens, I think, Mr. Trotter, Mr. Hamilton, Mr. Logan, I think, Mr. Spears, Isaac Baker, George Beck, R. G. Weir, a Doctor, whose name I forgot, he used to live in Little York; Dr. Newland was present, and Mr. Joseph Denny; there must have been fifty; the Sheriff of Washington county, B. F. Nicholson, was in the room.

Q. Were these persons members of the order?

A. Some were; I do not think Dr. Newland ever was a member of it.

Q. Do you know of this order having any connection with or interest in blockade running, with reference to arms?

A. I was so told by members of the order; I was told by Mr. Dodd and by Dr. Wilson that Vice President Stephens had gone to Nassau; that a good many arms and ammunition had been shipped there for the Southern States from England, but could not get through the blockade, and he went to make arrangements with Commissioners from the North to have them shipped to Canada, and thence distributed through the North, for the use of the military part of this organization. They were to come to Chicago, through Canada.

Q. Do you say General Cravens was present at that meeting?

A. Yes, sir. I think he was; but may be mistaken. I was Chairman of the meeting; and it was held in Salem, in the Grand Jury room, in the Court house, on the Monday after General Harlan, of Kentucky, spoke at Salem. At that meeting a great deal was said conversationally, as to what was to be done, and several persons asked me to make an announcement, which I did, requesting that each McClellan Club in the county would meet at 2 o'clock the next day, (Sunday,) as the business was urgent, to send five delegates from each township to meet at Salem on the next day.

Q. Was General Cravens a member of the order?

A. Not that I know of. Dr. Wilson initiated persons that I knew nothing of; but I do not think he was a member.

Q. You have seen those shells exhibited here, have you not?

A. Yes, sir.

Q. Have you seen them before?

A. Not those, but some similar to them.

Q. State when, where, and under what circumstances?

A. I can not state the exact time, but it was sometime last summer. Mr. Persise, who keeps a hotel in Salem, called me, and introduced me to a gentleman who was stopping there; he requested me to go to his room, and I went—to the stranger's room. He had a box something like a conductor's box, but much deeper. He asked me if I had ever seen these things; I said I had not. Mr. Persise told me he requested him to register his name, but he did not. He also had a hand grenade. As soon as I saw the one in Court, I saw it was on the same principle. He said what it was to be used for, but I did not exactly understand him, and did not talk much to him. He had a ritual of the first degree, and asked me if it was true. He was a shortish man, about five feet eight, or ten, wore specs, had dark hair and whiskers. He represented himself as coming from back of Louisville. I concluded he was a Detective, and did not have as much to say as I otherwise might, for I had been threatened with arrest. I did not learn his name; neither do I know if he was in the habit of wearing spectacles, or not.

Q. Do you know if he was a member of the order?

A. He said he was; but I did not try him. He unscrewed the hand-grenade, and showed me the nipples on the inner shell, and that is how I recognized it as soon as the Judge Advocate brought it up in Court.

Q. For what purpose did he say it was to be used?

A. For the purpose of destroying Government property. The Greek fire, he said, had been improved, and was much better than that used before. It was to be so arranged that a person could take it in a viol and walk along a building, and throw it down, and it could be so prepared in regard to its strength, as to take fire after three or four, or more hours; and neither vinegar, water nor molasses would put it out. I was told by Bocking, when in prison, how it was made; he said it was bi-sulphate of carbon and phosphorus.

Q. Was the man you saw at Salem, Mr. Bocking?

A. I can not say positively; he is a man who fits his description as near as possible, but I can not positively swear to his identity. Mr. Humphreys said, from my description, after Bocking's arrest, that he was the same man. I am not certain he is.

Q. You may describe his personal appearance.

A. He had on pretty much the same clothes as Bocking had; he wore glasses, and talked very much like Bocking.

Q. Why was he exhibiting this Greek fire and the hand-grenades?

A. I can not tell why.

Q. What was his professed object?

A. He wanted to know whether I had seen these inventions, and asked whether I had not heard that Government stores and boats had been burned at St. Louis and Louisville. He then said, in reference to the Greek fire, "That is what did it." I answered that I had heard of these shells, but had not seen them.

Q. Was he a member of the order?

A. He claimed to be such. Mr. Persise ought to know better than I do. He asked me if I recollected him about the time I was arrested; and when he told me of these circumstances, I remembered them.

Q. Did Bocking make this communication to you as a member of the order?

A. That is what I understood, sir. I did not know whether he professed to be a member of the order for the purpose of finding out something, and reporting it, or whether he was a *bona fide* member. I mistrusted him as a *bona fide* member; but subsequent events proved that he was. I was confirmed in my judgment that he was a member from what he told me after I was put in prison with him. I reported to Colonel Warner what I knew of the gentleman. He was released on parole on the same day Humphreys was put in with me.

Q. Why did you report him?

A. I reported to Colonel Warner that he took a letter out for a prisoner in the next cell. I did so, because I did not want to be accused of being with a man who was trying to get out and injure me afterward.

Q. Is Mr. Bocking a member of the order?

A. I understand he is; he told me so himself.

Q. In this same conversation, did he tell you that he exhibited these machines to any body else; and if so, to whom?

A. I can not say positively whether he did or did not; it seems to me he said something about exhibiting it in Louisville.

Q. Do I understand you that Mr. Bocking told you this while he was in prison with you?

A. Yes, sir; and the same conversation took place with him in Salem, if he is the same man.

Q. Will you describe the man you saw at Salem?

A. He was a man, I should judge, about five feet nine inches high, darkish hair; he wore glasses, and, from his accent, I should judge him to be a foreigner; he is between thirty-five and forty years of age.

Q. Please describe Mr. Bocking.

A. I will have to give the same description for him.

Q. Will you describe Mr. Bocking as you saw him in prison?

A. He was about five feet nine inches, wore dark clothes and glasses; a foreigner, I judge, and I believe he told me so; he is from thirty-five to forty years of age, and used to stay at Ryan & Elliot's store, he said, in this city, and does yet, if he is released.

Q. Have you seen or conversed with him since you saw him in prison?

A. Yes, sir.

Q. What did he say, at any time, of his being a member of the order?

A. He did not deny it. When he was in the same cell with me he wanted to see Mr. Gordon, and to know why he was in prison, and said that they had got suspicious of him because he would not tell what he knew, and that was the reason he was put in prison.

Q. He always maintained that he was a member of the order, did he not?

A. Yes, sir, in all the conversation I had with him. He told me, also, of a man that was put in with him for horse-stealing. Colonel Warner, I believe, said this man was a spy, for he had my name on his books.

Q. Was this man, who exhibited the Greek fire at Salem, a fleshy or a lean man?

A. I do not think he was either.

Q. How is Bocking, fleshy or lean?

A. He was just about the same in that respect. The very instant I set my eyes on Bocking, after I was arrested, I took him to be the same man I saw at Salem.

Q. Did you notice the color of his eyes?

A. When at Salem he wore glasses, and I never saw the color of his eyes.

Q. Were both these persons foreigners?

A. They were. I called him at first a German; but he said that he was a Belgian.

RE-CROSS-EXAMINATION.

The counsel for the accused requested, as a courtesy, the privilege of cross-examination of the witness on the new points brought out by the examination by the Court, to which the Judge Advocate waived all objection.

Question by the accused:

At what time was this man, who exhibited the Greek fire, at the Persise House, in Salem?

Answer. Sometime last summer.

Q. You will please fix the time as near as you can?

A. I can not fix it with certainty, except that it was sometime in June, I judge. I have no memorandum to fix it by. It was in May or June.

Q. Did he give you his name?

A. He did not.

Q. Why did he refuse to give it?

A. I did not ask him for it.

Q. How did he register his name?

A. Mr. Persise said he refused to register his name.

Q. Is Mr. Persise a member of the order?

A. He is.

Q. Do you know that this man you saw at Salem is a member of the order, from any thing except from what he said?

A. No, sir.

Q. Did you test him?

A. No, sir.

Q. You stated, did you not, that after you saw Booking conceal this letter for a prisoner, you told Colonel Warner of the matter?

A. I told Colonel Warner of his taking a letter out for a prisoner in the next cell, which was passed to him through a crack. Colonel Warner told me that this man had my name on his book. There was a secret back pocket in the lining of his coat, between the shoulders, in which he put the letter. I saw him put it there, and take it out with him when he was released, on parole.

Q. At what time was this?

A. I think it was when they called for him and he was released on parole. Mr Humphreys was put in the same cell with me after his release. I think I told Colonel Warner I thought it very strange he should be released, and we should be kept in?

Q. How did you come to make this statement to Colonel Warner?

A. From the fact that I did not want any body in the cell next to me, who had concealed a saw, and was trying to cut his way out, and have the suspicion of assisting in his escape rest on me, and suffer punishment for it. I thought we were in a bad enough scrape, without getting into a worse one. I told Colonel Warner to search his carpet sack, and it was searched, so the sergeant said.

Q. Did you not, at that time, commence making arrangements with Colonel Warner to become a witness?

A. No, sir; and I made no arrangements with the Judge Advocate. When he spoke to me to take the stand, I thought he spoke to Dr. Wilson who sat behind me, and supposed he was going to put him on the stand, until he spoke to me the second time. Instead of making any arrangement to be put on the stand, on the contrary I told the Judge Advocate I would not be put on the stand under any pledge or promise, and only on the condition of making a full and true statement, for if sworn I would tell the truth.

Q. I will ask you, with the permission of the Judge Advocate, whether that morning, before dinner, you did not have a conversation with Governor Morton or General Hovey, either with one or both of them?

A. I did. The conversation was confidential.

Q. Did you not let them know that you were willing to become a witness?

A. I think General Hovey asked me if I would be a witness; I said that if I was put upon the stand, I would have to tell the truth as any other man would.

Q. Do you know how long this conversation was before you were put upon the stand?

A. It could not have been long before, because the Court was waiting when I came in.

Q. Was it in this room or out of it?

A. If it had been in this room, I would not have come in and found the Court waiting. I had endeavored to obtain an interview with General Hovey, and wrote to him requesting one, but received no answer.

Q. Why did you seek an interview?

A. Because I wanted to get out of the scrape.

Q. How did you propose to get out of the scrape?

A. I made no proposition.

Q. Did you tell them you would reveal what you knew?

A. No, sir; I told them I would have to testify as any other man would who was sworn.

Q. Did you not know that they could not make you a witness without discharging you?

[Objected to by the Judge Advocate, and withdrawn.]

RE-EXAMINATION.

Question by the Judge Advocate:

Please state whether you ever had from any Government official any pledge or promise, if you would come upon the stand as a witness?

A. I did not; I had not received or expected any pledge.

Q. Did I ever hint to you that you were to be a witness?

A. You did not, sir; and I asked Colonel Dunham, just before I was called on the stand, to ask the Judge Advocate if I should have my witnesses subpenaed or not. The next thing I was on the stand.

Q. Your interview with me was without any pledge or promise, and by your own inclination, was it not?

A. Yes, sir.

The witness here requested the privilege of making a correction in his previous testimony, in regard to Mr. Kerr's taking three degrees. The first night I organized the Council at New Albany, Indiana, they all took three degrees, for it could not be organized unless they had taken the three degrees. Mr. Kerr was not there the first night, and I think he took only the first degree the second night.

Q. Do you mean the first degree proper?

Yes, sir.

The Commission then adjourned, to meet on Saturday morning, November 12, 1864, at 9 o'clock, A. M.

———

The Commission met pursuant to adjournment.

All the members present. Also, the

Judge Advocate, the accused, and their counsel.

The proceedings were read and approved.

James L. Mason, a witness for the Government, was then introduced, and, being duly sworn, testified as follows:

I have resided in Greenfield, Hancock county, Indiana, for the past eight years. I am Senator from that district. I do not know that I have ever joined any secret society except the Freemasons. I never took the obligation of either the Order of Sons of Liberty, or the American Knights; and I never read the obligations of these orders until I saw them in the newspapers. A gentleman, a Mr. Hall, who reported himself as from Rush county, came to my office in 1862, and told me about a secret order, and read a ritual to me, but I did not consider that I took it, and I really do not remember what was the name of the order about which he spoke; it certainly was not the American Knights, or Sons of Liberty, but it might have been the Circle of Honor. I do not know the purpose of his visit to our place, nor do I remember that he said it was for the purpose of establishing a lodge. I never saw that gentleman before or after. He stated what the order was, and certain facts about it, but I do not think he stated the obligation, nor do I remember repeating any thing after him. My present recollection is, that I did not; nor did he authorize me to form lodges, that I remember. Our interview did not last more than fifteen or twenty minutes. I believe he came with a letter of introduction from his brother. I do not remember that he had any further business with me than talking about this order. Possibly his object might have been to induce me to form a lodge. I did not take any steps to establish the order; nor did I assist in organizing any lodge in the State.

Harrison Connell, a witness for the Government, was then introduced, and, being duly sworn by the Judge Advocate, testified as follows:

I reside in Martin county, Indiana. I joined a secret society in our county, about two years ago. I believe it was called the "American Knights." I joined at the solicitation of Stephen Horsey. We met in the evening at a school-house in Columbia township. Mr. Horsey lives in the adjoining township. I do not remember how many meetings I attended; I never drilled with the order. Some ammunition was brought to that neighborhood; by whom I do not know, nor do I know for what purpose. Stephen Horsey, the accused, told me to meet him about a mile and a half from the Shoals, on a certain evening, and we went some distance down the railroad, where we found some ammunition lying near the road. We put it in a sack, and carried it home. There was a keg of powder, a package of lead and a package of caps. I do not know where the ammunition was concealed; it was Mr. Horsey who took me to it. When I started, he did not tell me where he wanted me to go with him. He wished me to take care of the ammunition, and I put it in my barn, in the granary, and it was covered over with thrashed oats. When I was arrested, I gave it up to the Detectives. I do not know where the money came from with which the ammunition was purchased. It was in August, or the latter part of July, 1864, that I went with Horsey to fetch the ammunition.

CROSS-EXAMINATION.

I should have stated that William Clayton initiated me. I attended a meeting of the order last winter at the Gaddis House, at which a Mr. Stone spoke, and the man who spoke led us to think that we were sworn into the service of Jeff Davis. I remember the men were very much dissatisfied with his speech.

The Commission then adjourned, to meet on Monday the 14th, at 2 o'clock, P. M.

Court Room, Indianapolis, Indiana,
November 14. 1864, 2 o'clock, P. M.

The Commission met pursuant to adjournment.

All the members present. Also, the Judge Advocate, and the accused, (except W. A. Bowles,) and their counsel.

The proceedings were read and approved.

The following communication from W. A. Bowles, one of the accused, was then read to the Commission, by the Judge Advocate:

To the President and Members of the Commission:

My health being such that I can not attend the sittings of your body, I hereby waive my right to attend the same, and authorize you to proceed in my absence with my trial, as if I were present.

[Signed]   W. A. BOWLES.
November 14, 1864.

A member of the Commission objected to proceeding with the trial during the absence of one of the accused.

The Court was then cleared for deliberation.

On being re-opened, the Judge Advocate announced that the objection was overruled.

Elisha Cowgill, a witness for the Government, was then introduced, and, being duly sworn, testified as follows:

I reside at Greencastle, Putnam county, Indiana. In 1863, I was Provost Marshal in the Seventh District. While in the performance of my duties there, I was brought in contact with Mr. Andrew Humphreys. It was about the 4th of June, 1863, when I saw Mr. Humphreys at the head of about four hundred men. When I first came up, Mr. Humphreys was speaking to the crowd. When I rode up toward him, he came toward me, and was introduced to me by Edward Price, of Sullivan county.

I asked a number of persons who were there, what they were assembled for, and they answered to protect themselves. All that I saw were armed, except perhaps one or two. Mr. Humphreys had command of them. They did not profess to be called out as militia, by the United States, or by the State authorities. I had a conversation with Mr. Humphreys of about an hour. Mr. Humphreys talked a great deal about the President of the United States, calling him an old tyrant before the crowd, who was usurping a great deal of power, and wasting the treasure of the United States, and the lives of the citizens. He also stated that he was killing off about forty thousand men per day. He also spoke of Vicksburg, and asked what I knew about it. Threats were made against me, by men in the crowd, and some of them swore they would kill any man who attempted to enroll Cass township. They called me a "damned abolition rascal," a "Lincoln pup," and a "Lincoln dog," that deserved to be killed. Some said they ought to kill me before I got out of the crowd. They wanted me to tell them who the enrolling officer of that township would be. I told them he would be known to them in due time. His name was Fletcher Freeman. I had given him the enrolling papers the night before. He was afterward shot and killed. Mr. Humphreys made a second speech to the people, and advised them to go home and mind their own business; he asked me if I did not indorse this; I answered that I did. He also told them, "Do not sleep too soundly." I then went off, and a man named Ursey came into Sullivan with me. I regarded Andy Humphreys as a leader of the rabble.

CROSS-EXAMINATION.

This took place about the 4th of June, 1863, in Sullivan county, and I understood it was in Cass township; just beyond there is a little town called Caledonia. Mr. Humphreys did advise the crowd to go home and mind their own business. They manifested no violence toward me except in their talk, and Mr. Humphreys remarked that there was no danger unless they got to drinking. I do not remember that Humphreys said in my hearing, that the people had got excited because some soldiers had shot at a man. A small portion of the crowd were on horseback. I thought Mr. Humphreys' remarks were intended to stop them from committing any violence until he told them "not to sleep too soundly." When he spoke about the President as a tyrant, he was standing on a log, and the crowd were close around him. He dealt in about such epithets, as the Democratic speakers used at that time. Mr. Humphreys was armed with a revolver. I did not say that I could indorse Mr. Humpheys' speech, except that part where he advised them to go home. I think Mr. Humphreys asked the crowd to hear me; it was when Mr. Price introduced me to Mr. Humphreys, and then he (Humphreys) told the crowd that I was the son of Judge Cowgill, and that he was a mighty good Democrat. I said I did not want any credit on that account, as I differed with my father on political topics. I may have tried to make a speech to them, for I asked them to select a subject if they wanted to hear me. They selected the Conscription Bill. I then told them that the first thing to be done was to have an enrollment. They all swore that they would not have one. At this point Mr. Humphreys came up and made them keep quiet.

In coming out from Sullivan, I met some soldiers that day. They were marching back toward Sullivan. There was probably fifty or sixty of them. When I saw them they were stopping, and were not marching either way. The men in the crowd were armed, some with squirrel rifles, some with shot guns, and others with pistols and bowie knives.

The meeting was in the woods, near the little town of Caledonia. The country about there is sparsely settled. I do not know why the crowd assembled beyond what they stated, that they were there to protect themselves, and vindicate their rights.

Mr. Ursey came to Sullivan and tried to get me drunk. When I got him drunk, he became very communicative, and told me that Mr. Humphreys commanded the cavalry and he the infantry. I do not know that the crowd did any violence to anybody that day. While I was there, Mr. Humphreys was evidently trying to keep the crowd quiet, and he succeeded to a certain extent. I left before they dispersed. I saw Mr. Humphreys' revolver, for he happened to be in his shirt sleeves, and was sitting down by a tree talking to me; his revolver was buckled on behind. He did not say why he wore it, but remarked that he was expecting to be arrested.

I remarked his asking me about the news from Vicksburg, as to whether the Government troops would take it; he also asked me what General Grant's daily losses were. I said I could not tell. He then commenced talking about himself, and asked me whether I knew of any arrangements being made to have him arrested. I said I did not. He did not say what he expected to be arrested for; but I think while we were in conversation, he remarked that if I would go there by myself, he would take care of me over night at his house, and would go over the next morn ing to Indianapolis with me, as he did not want any parade about it, if he was to be arrested.

There were no flags in the crowd that I saw, and each man wore his own citizen's suit.

In answer to interrogatories put by the Commission, the witness testified as follows:

I do not know that the enrolling officer was shot and killed while in the performance of his duty. My knowledge of his death came from Colonel Thompson. He had two townships to enroll, and was killed while working on the road, after having nearly completed the first township. I got his papers, and went down and finished it myself; and got a man to attend to the other.

RE-CROSS-EXAMINATION.

I have no personal knowledge of the manner of his death; I speak from hearsay. His death occurred about ten days after the meeting referred to.

Dr. JAMES B. WILSON, a witness for the Government, was called to the stand, and, being duly sworn by the Judge Advocate, testified as follows:

Question by the Judge Advocate:

Please state your name, and where you reside.

Answer. James B. Wilson, Salem, Washington county, Indiana.

Q. What is your profession, or business?

A. I am a farmer at this time.

Q. How long have you resided in Salem, Indiana?

A. About fourteen years next February.

Q. State whether you ever joined any secret order or society known as the American Knights, or Sons of Liberty.

A. Yes, sir; I joined an order known as the American Knights; I think it was in September or October, sometime in the fall of 1863.

Q. Where?

A. At Salem, at the office of Colonel Heffren.

Q. By whom were you initiated?

A. By Mr. Bailey.

Q. Who else were initiated at that time?

A. I do not think I can give the names of all, but I can of some: Mr. Heffren, Mr. Harris, Mr. McCoskey, Mr. Cutshaw, Mr. Garris, Mr. Green, Mr. Fultz and Mr. Beck.

Q. What was the next meeting that you attended after your initiation?

A. A meeting at this place. It was said to be a meeting of the members of the order in the State, and was composed of delegates sent from the different county temples.

Q. Who presided at that meeting?

A. Mr. Dodd; I do not remember who was in the chair at first.

Q. About what time in the day, and at what date, did this meeting occur?

A. I think about the 6th of November.

Q. Were any of the accused present?

A. Dr. Bowles was present.

Q. What business was transacted at that meeting?

A. There were some committees appointed; a Military Committee, a Committee on Education, and one committee in reference to establishing a newspaper to be considered the organ of the organization.

Q. Who composed the Military Committee?

A. I can not tell; I thought, from the actions of Dr. Bowles, that he must be the Chairman of that committee, as he made a verbal report.

Q. Did Mr. Dodd make a speech?

A. Yes, sir.

Q. Do you remember what that speech was?

A. I remember something of it; he spoke about talking treason for awhile; it was toward the close of the meeting.

Q. State about how he said that, and what he was talking about at that time.

A. I can not give his language, because it is so long ago, and I did not refer to it very often. I can only give you the impression it left upon my mind. He said that he would "kick down the walls of common decency," or some such expression, "and talk treason for awhile." He said, "if the purposes of this organization could not be carried out, as explained by Mr. Wright, there were others that could be resorted to; they could very easily, if their organization was fully completed, take possession of the railroads, cut the telegraph wires, and throw in at one time troops enough at the capital to take the State Government and have things our own way."

Q. About what time in the day did he make this speech?

A. In the afternoon.

Q. Was Mr. Bowles present at that meeting?

A. I think he was.

Q. Was Mr. Humphreys present?

A. I did not know Mr. Humphreys then.

Q. Do you know if Mr. Bingham was present at that time?

A. I did not know Mr. Bingham at that time.

Q. What else was said, if any thing?

A. There was a great deal said.

Q. Was there any thing done or said in reference to any member who might have revealed any thing in regard to the order?

A. Not that I can call to my recollection. I think there was something said on that subject, but I can not now recollect it.

Q. Did you ever attend any other Grand Council of the State?

A. No, sir; I never did.

Q. Did you not attend a meeting of the Council at Chicago, or of a committee?

A. I did, sir; I understood from a gentleman who was present in the meeting, that it was to be composed of the military part of the organization; and he had called it at his own instance.

. Q. From whom did you learn this?

A. Mr. Barrett said that it was to be composed of the military men of the order.

Q. Did you ever establish any lodges, or take any active part in the propagation of this society?

A. Yes, sir, I did.

Q. To what extent?

A. I established lodges in three different townships in Washington county.

Q. How extensive were these lodges in the townships of your county?

A. There were lodges in all townships in our county except two.

Q. Did you visit all these lodges?

A. I think I did.

Q. When you visited these lodges, what did you go for?

A. For the purpose of giving them the work of the Neophyte or First Degree.

Q. Did you ever give them more than the Neophyte degree, or the First or Vestibule degree?

A. I think I assisted in giving the second and third degrees to a couple of gentlemen.

Q. To whom?

A. Captain Hamilton and B. F. Nicholson, of Washington county.

Q. Did you go for any thing else?

A. Yes, sir; for the purpose of giving them instructions in the object of the order, and give them information that I thought was reliable.

Q. What information did you give them at any time?

A. I gave them information about the preparation in Illinois, which I received from a gentleman named Wright, from the State, and formerly from Washington county.

Q. What did he tell you?

A. I learned from Mr. Wright that they were ready for any movement; that they had arms in their hands, generally, and were ready for any emergency that the order might contemplate, or wish to carry out.

Q. Did he report to you how extensively the organization was armed in Illinois?

A. Yes, sir; he said they were generally prepared.

Q. What were the preparations in Illinois?

A. In the county where he resided, he said almost the entire Democratic party.

Q. Did you learn the extent of the order in the State?

A. No, sir.

Q. State what you know in regard to the arming and drilling, or the attempt to arm and drill in your county, preceding your visit to Chicago, Illinois.

A. I am not aware of any special efforts made at arming, only as individual members of the order armed themselves. I know of a great many members of the order buying pistols.

Q. Do you know of any attempts to drill?

A. I understood that Mr. Hamilton had a company, and that they had drilled.

Q. Now please tell the Court about your visit to Chicago; and how you came to go there?

A. I think I went there mostly at my own suggestion; I was in bad health, and thought a trip up there might be of service to me, and suggested that if no one desired to go there, I would go myself; I spoke to Mr. Heffren, Mr. Harris, and a number of persons about it.

Q. Did any one accompany you?

A. Mr. Green did.

Q. Is he a member of the order?

A. Yes, sir.

Q. What time did you start to Chicago?

A. I think about the 19th of July, 1864, and arrived on the morning of the 20th, I think.

Q. Where did you stop in Chicago?

A. At the Tremont House.

Q. Whom did you see there from this State?

A. I believe only Mr. Dodd and Dr. Bowles.

Q. Give an account of where you went and what you did while in Chicago?

A. I think we got in early in the morning of the 20th; and after taking breakfast we went down to the Richmond House, where Dr. Bowles said he stopped, and inquired for his room; we were shown to it by a servant of the house, but he happened to be in an adjoining room. There seemed to be a promiscuous conversation going on; they talked about politics a little and on sundry matters. After having listened for some time, I think I asked if there was not going to be a meeting. Dr. Bowles remarked to me that there would be a meeting, but they were not ready for it, as the persons they expected had not arrived.

Q. Who were those persons?

A. Mr. Dodd, for one.

Q. Where did he say Dodd was?

A. He said that he was gone to Niagara Falls, or had started to go there; but expected to get back in time for the meeting. After remaining some time, we found there was not to be a meeting until the next day. The next morning we went back to Dr. Bowles' room, and learned that Judge Bullitt and Mr. Williams had arrived. When we had remained a little while in Dr. Bowles' room, these gentlemen came in, and I am not sure but we went into another room.

Q. Who was there?

A. Judge Bullitt, Mr. Piper, Mr. Williams, and Mr. Barrett, I remember.

Q. What was said there?

A. The conversation was again of a promiscuous character. After sitting a while, some one suggested that perhaps we had better hear why Mr. Barrett had called the meeting. He said that he had called for a military meeting, to be composed, as he had expected, of the military men of this organization, and that he had used his best efforts to get men of that character to the meeting, but that he believed he had failed. He did not name whom he expected.

He then stated that his object in calling the meeting was, that he thought the Government could be restored, and he was satisfied it could be if we could get the co-operation of the North with the South, or a portion of the North, Ohio, Indiana, Illinois, Missouri and Kentucky; he said if the members of the Sons of Liberty in the States would co-operate with the South, he had no doubt the entire Government would be saved through their action. He also said that it had been contemplated to have an uprising at some time soon, perhaps as early as the third of August, but that had failed from some cause; and he thought every thing could be got ready for an uprising, perhaps, by the 10th or 15th of the month, and that the South, in order to show her willingness to engage in some movement that would restore the Government, had authorized him to place at the disposal of members of the organization, a large sum of money, amounting to two millions of dollars.

Q. Did he say where the money came from?

A. He said that it had been captured from a United States Paymaster on Red river, and that the organization could have the use of that amount of money in preparing themselves to rise against the Lincoln administration; that it would be distributed to the several Grand Commanders of those States, and by them subdivided among such persons inside of the order as in their judgment was prudent, and to be expended by those who received it for arms and other appliances of war. And he further stated, that in calling this meeting it was done at his own suggestion; that this money was to be used for the benefit of the order, and that as he did not wish any of the delegates there to be at any expense, if we would make out our bills of expenses in coming and while there, he would pay us; and he did; at least I got mine, forty dollars.

Q. Where did he get this money from?

A. I do not know; but I think he said it was captured from a paymaster on Red river.

Q. And did he pay all their expenses?

10

A. I understood they would all receive their expenses if they desired it.

Q. What else was said at that meeting?

A. That was about the amount of what was said; I do not recollect that any one discussed the matter, or offered any particular opinion at that time.

Q. Was any thing said about the destruction of Government property?

A. Yes, sir; but not at that meeting; I think it was on the afternoon of that day or the next, I am not sure which, he stated, in speaking of the money, that it had been used for the purpose of paying for the destruction of United States property, arsenals, burning boats, etc.

Q. Did he say how this was to be paid?

A. He said they would pay ten per cent. on property so destroyed, and were willing to make an estimate upon the value assessed by Government officers, that would generally be announced through the Northern newspapers; that they would take the Government estimate as a basis for calculation.

Q. Did he give any instance where Government property had been destroyed?

A. Yes, sir; the burning of some Government stores in Louisville, on Eighth street, I believe; also the destruction of some Government boats on the Ohio river, and one, I believe, at St. Louis.

Q. And those persons were to receive ten per cent., you say?

A. Yes, sir.

Q. Did he say what means were used to destroy this property?

A. I afterward learned from Dr. Bowles that the means employed was Greek fire.

Q. What else took place at that meeting in Chicago?

A. There was an explanation made, I afterward learned from Dr. Bowles more particularly, in regard to a flag; that the members of the organization should be careful to have instructions sent to their friends that in case of an invasion by the guerrillas, the members should make use of a flag, made of white cloth, with a red ribbon running along the top and carried down the sides and hanging below, like streamers; this was to be tied to a stick.

The Commission then adjourned, to meet on Tuesday, November 15, 1864, at 9 o'clock, A. M.

———

COURT ROOM, INDIANAPOLIS, INDIANA, }
November 15, 1864, 9 o'clock, A. M. }

The Commission met pursuant to adjournment.

All the members present. Also, the Judge Advocate, the accused, (except W. A. Bowles,) and their counsel.

The proceedings were read and approved.

The examination of James B. Wilson, a

witness for the Government, was then resumed as follows:

Question by the Judge Advocate:

Did you meet any persons who purported to represent the Southern Confederacy at the Chicago meeting, or convention, to which you have referred?

Answer. Yes, sir. A man calling himself by the name of Majors; and Mr. Barrret, also, stated that he was authorized to represent the Southern Confederacy.

Q. You say that Mr. Barrett represented himself as a representative of the Southern Confederacy at that meeting?

A. Yes, sir.

Q. Did any of those gentlemen profess to represent any special States, or only the Southern Confederacy generally?

A. The Southern Confederacy generally.

Q. Did you learn who were the parties that were expected there, but did not come?

A. I do not think I did. I think that Mr. Amos Green, of Illinois, was mentioned as being expected, and it was also expected that Mr. Vallandigham would be there, but they had learned prior to the meeting that he would not be there, and had sent a messenger to him.

Q. Who was that messenger?

A. I think it was Mr. Green, or Mr. Holloway, or perhaps both.

Q. Did you learn whether they saw Mr. Vallandigham?

A. I do not think I did.

Q. Did you hear Mr. Dodd, or Mr. Holloway, or any other person say in reference to this meeting, that they had had any conversation with Mr. Vallandigham?

A. No, sir.

Q. Where did Mr. Dodd come from? where did he represent himself to have been?

A. At the Clifton House, near Niagara Falls.

Q. For what purpose?

A. To meet with the commissioners, or delegates, that were duly authorized by the Southern Confederacy to meet at that meeting.

Q. Who were they?

A. Holcomb, Clay, Saunders, and another, whom I supposed was this Majors, Captain Majors, as he was called. The way I remember this is, that something was said about a safe conveyance being asked for by Mr. Holcomb in his address to Mr. Greeley for himself, Mr. Clay, Mr. Saunders, and another; this other man, I understood, was Captain Majors.

Q. Is this Captain Majors the one you spoke of as being at Chicago?

A. Yes, sir.

Q. Did you learn of any part that was to be taken by the different leading men in this contemplated uprising? If so, what? Who, for instance, was to lead in this State, who in Ohio, and who in Illinois?

A. I do not think I heard that matter definitely spoken of, except with regard to our State, Indiana; I understood Dodd was to be the leader in Indiana.

Q. Did you hear who was to take care of Ohio?

A. I understood from some source that Ohio was to be taken care of by Vallandigham.

Q. In what event?

A. In the event of a general uprising. He had some forces at his disposal in Canada, and would bring those forces into Ohio to co-operate with other forces at Cincinnati and Louisville.

Q. From whom did you learn this?

A. I can not be positive; my impression is that I learned it from Dr. Bowles.

Q. At this meeting in Chicago you say, do you not, that the expenses of the delegates were paid by Barrett out of the two million dollars that he had received from the Southern Confederacy?

A. I understood it was so.

Q. He paid your expenses, do you say?

A. Yes, sir. I receipted him for mine and Mr. Green's, which I forgot to mention yesterday.

Q. Was that money to be returned or repaid in any way?

A. No, sir; not that I understood.

Q. On what day did you start back from Chicago?

A. I can not be positive as to the day; but I think we were there two days.

Q. Have you named to the Court all the persons that were at that meeting when Barrett made that proposition?

A. I can not say, but I will state now those that I can remember: Mr. Barrett, Dr. Bowles, Mr. Williams and Judge Bullitt, both from Kentucky; and Mr. Piper was there.

Q. Where was he from?

A. I can not say.

Q. Did he profess to hold any position in the order?

A. I understood from Dr. Bowles that he was a kind of general missionary.

Q. What does that mean?

A. A man that was going about diffusing a knowledge of the order.

Q. And carrying light into dark places?

A. Yes, sir.

Q. Who else was there?

A. Mr. Majors, Mr. Swem.

Q. Who is Mr. Swem?

A. A citizen of Chicago. Mr. Walsh, also a citizen of Chicago, was present, and Mr. Holloway, Mr. Dodd, Mr. Green and myself.

Q. You say that Mr. Barrett announced this as a meeting of the military heads of the order; will you state how you happened to be present?

A. I knew nothing of the character of the meeting, but Dr. Bowles afterward told me that he had reported me as one of his staff officers, and also Mr. Green.

Q. In what capacity?

A. He did not state.

Q. Then he reported you simply on his staff, and you gained access in that way?

A. Yes, sir.

Q. Was Dodd considered the military head of the order?

A. He was to be so considered in this State, I understood.

Q. What position did Bullitt and Barrett hold, militarily?

A. I did not learn.

Q. You did not learn the position of any of these men then, except that they were military chiefs?

A. I did not.

Q. You started back, did you, about July 23d, 1864?

A. I think I did.

Q. Was any thing resolved upon at that meeting?

A. Not that I know of; the discussion was not of a definite character in my presence.

Q. Did they hold any meetings when you were not present?

A. I suspect they did.

Q. What made you suspect that?

A. Because I saw other men that I did not know, and to whom I was not introduced, in another room, having close conversation.

Q. Did you learn if Vallandigham was expected?

A. Judge Bullitt said so.

Q. Did you understand that any one had come from Canada?

A. I understood that Mr. Green and Mr. Holloway had been to see Vallandigham, and that Mr. Dodd had been to Canada to see the Commissioners.

Q. Who came back with you?

A. Mr. Green, my lady and Dr. Bowles were on the same train.

Q. Did you have any conversation with Dr. Bowles after you returned?

A. Yes, sir.

Q. Did you learn of any thing that was to be done, or contemplated to be done?

A. I understood that Mr. Dodd had abandoned the project, and that he had sent his son to say that he would drop it.

Q. At what time did you learn that?

A. My best recollection is, that it was about two weeks after my return, near the 7th of August.

Q. Did you learn why the project had been abandoned?

A. Not definitely.

Q. Do you know whether any communication was attempted to be had, or was had, with any rebel forces, commissioners, or messengers?

A. No, sir, I do not; I heard it spoken of.

Q. By whom?

A. It was spoken of at the Chicago meet-ing; I think Dr. Bowles said messengers were sent to the rebels.

Q. Where were they sent?

A. I do not know, sir; I think they were sent into Kentucky and Missouri.

Q. Do you know with whom communication was attempted to be made?

A. I inferred it was to be with Price and Buckner, because they were to be the co-operating forces in case of an uprising.

Q. Will you give to this Court, to the best of your knowledge, how this uprising was to take place, where the rendezvous was to be, and under what circumstances?

A. It was to take place by the order of Mr. Dodd; he was to send out couriers to the different commanders of the several districts of the State, the major generals of the four districts into which the State was divided; and they were to send out couriers into the respective counties composing their several districts, who were to give notice of the uprising in their counties, and then it was expected that that information would be conveyed to certain persons in each county that had been prominent and leading men of the organization, who were to see that it was conveyed to the different townships in the county. The general signal for the uprising was to be the appearance of guerrillas or troops in the vicinity of St. Louis and Louisville. It might have been on the 16th August, or a few days later; or, if these couriers got through in time, and the Southern forces were to get the information, they might appear sooner than the 16th.

Q. To whom were the couriers to go?

A. To Generals Buckner and Price.

Q. Were these couriers to return, and then the uprising to take place?

A. There was nothing said about their returning; the appearance of the troops was to be the signal.

Q. Where were the troops to rendezvous?

A. The forces of Southern Indiana were to be rendezvoused at a place some eight or ten miles from New Albany.

Q. Under whom?

A. It was expected they would be under Dr. Bowles.

Q. Where were the forces in this part of the State to rendezvous?

A. I did not learn that.

Q. And the forces in Illinois?

A. At several points; in the neighborhood of Rock Island, Springfield, Chicago, and some other points, perhaps.

Q. Did you learn who was to be the leader in that State?

A. No, sir.

Q. Did you learn where the rendezvous was to take place in Missouri?

A. I understood that after they had completed the seizure of the arsenals in Illinois, they were to march to St. Louis, to co-operate with Price's forces in the taking of that place.

Q. Did you learn what they were to do after the rendezvousing at the different points in this State?

A. There was nothing said about it in Chicago, but I learned that what was to be done in Indiana, was to be under the supervision of Mr. Dodd.

Q. What was that?

A. I did not understand what persons were to lead them in particular, but they were to be concentrated at Indianapolis, and perhaps at Terre Haute, New Albany, and Jeffersonville; perhaps Evansville was named, I am not positive. The capture of the State Capitol at Indianapolis was left, as I understood, to the special supervision of Mr. Dodd, and he was to do it by getting up public meetings. There was to be an ordinary political meeting called at Indianapolis, as well as I could understand, east of the city, at some place of resort for Sabbath school picnics, where water was convenient; as I understood, at some fashionable place for public meetings. I do not know whether there is such a place or not. It seemed, as well as I could learn, that there were three places in an easterly direction, perhaps from Camp Morton; I may have misunderstood it, but I give my best recollections of it. The three points were east of Camp Morton. One meeting would, perhaps, be a Sabbath school meeting; another a political meeting; and the third, perhaps, a political meeting—or something of that kind; those of the order who assisted at the meeting, and those who were members of the organization, would come to these meetings in wagons, bringing their families; as a general thing, they would have arms, secreted in the wagons under straw or hay. After arriving at the different points, some one would propose, to be in the fashion, that they drill, and they were to come out and drill.

Q. Were they to drill with or without arms?

A. Without arms. The object of the drill was, that each individual who was to take part in the affairs of the day, would understand where his place was, what was his duty, and what was expected of him. At the time of day when the soldiers came on dress parade, at some place east of the camp ground, some one at the camp would throw up a signal, which would be seen from these meeting places; when the signal was seen, those who understood what they had met there for, would at once seize their arms and march immediately in the direction of Camp Morton. At the time they were thus marching, the fences and buildings of Camp Morton were to be fired. It was understood that the released rebel prisoners would participate in the affair, and that these rebel soldiers could come up in the rear, and that the Federal soldiers, finding themselves surrounded, would be easily overcome. The rebel prisoners would be armed with the soldiers' arms, and the soldiers would be held as prisoners of war. At the time this was going on—the work of freeing prisoners and the capturing these soldiers—a detail of persons was to be sent to take care of the Governor, and secure him; in some way take care of him; and then the arsenals at this place were to be seized, and a better quality of arms procured; those that went on with this expedition were to be as fully armed from the arsenal as was necessary. They were also to take such munitions of war as they thought proper with them. They were then to seize the railroad to Jeffersonville, and make use of the cars for the transportation of troops and the rebel prisoners; they were then to go on and complete the same work at Jeffersonville and New Albany, and also to cooperate in the capture of Louisville.

Q. That was the general scheme, was it?

A. Yes, sir; a great deal of the minutia I may have forgotten; that is my general impression.

Q. How extensively was this plan made known to the members of the order?

A. It was made known to all the members of the order in my county.

Q. Can you state how extensively in any other county?

A. No, sir.

Q. What county do you reside in?

A. In Washington county?

Q. Does Mr. Kerr live in your county?

A. No, sir.

Q. What prominent men was that scheme made known to in your county?

A. To all the members of the organization.

Q. How many does the order number in your county?

A. I can not say; I think above a thousand men.

Q. Was Mr. Heffren present at the November meeting of the Grand Council in Indianapolis, that you referred to yesterday?

A. No, sir.

Q. Was Mr. Milligan?

A. I did not know him at that time.

Q. Was Dr. Bowles present?

A. Yes, sir.

Q. Do you know Dr. Athon and Mr Ristine, of this city?

A. Yes, sir; I know Dr. Athon.

Q. Was either present at that meeting?

A. I do not think they were, sir.

Q. Were you ever furnished any money for the purchase of arms for this order? If so, by whom, and what amount?

A. I was furnished with a thousand dollars by Dr. Bowles, for the purchase of arms for those of the order who were un derstood to be unable to procure arms themselves.

Q. Were they to be distributed to any particular class, or only to members of the order?

A. It was understood that they were to be distributed to those who were unable to arm themselves.

Q. Did you make any attempt to purchase any arms with that thousand dollars?

A. I went to see Mr. Kent, at New Albany, about the purchase of the arms.

Q. What did you do with this money?

A. I gave it out to men to furnish substitutes with.

Q. You loaned it, did you not?

A. No, sir; I took no note of it: it was only an accommodation loan to personal friends, to men whom I could trust, and from whom I could get it any time I needed.

Q. Then this money was diverted from the channel for which it was originally intended, was it not?

A. Yes, sir.

CROSS-EXAMINATION.

Dr. Bowles told me that he obtained my admission to the meeting at Chicago, by representing me as a member of his staff; that is not true, however; I hold no position in the order. I did not see Milligan, Humphreys or Horsey at the Chicago meeting; nor did I get any information of the contemplated uprising from either of the accused, save Dr. Bowles. I never spoke to Mr. Horsey in my life; Mr. Humphreys I have seen but once, having passed the compliments of the day with him at the Chicago Convention; with Mr. Milligan I became acquainted at the State Convention here in July. From what I saw during the Chicago meeting, I was led to think that there was a meeting inside of the one I was permitted to witness. There were many schemes proposed for carrying out the uprising, the release of prisoners, etc., but the one I have given in my direct testimony was that which was deemed most plausible, and most likely to be adopted; but I do not know that it was resolved upon.

The thousand dollars I received from Dr. Bowles for the purchase of arms, he gave me to understand, was from his private funds; and what he said impressed me with that idea.

I have been under arrest; but no inducement or promise of favor has been held out to me by the authorities to induce me to testify against the defendants in this case; neither has promise of immunity from punishment been held out to me, as an inducement to testify; nor has any one visited me while in confinement to ascertain what I could testify to. Not until 12 o'clock yesterday, did I know that I should be required as a witness; the guard then informed me that I was required in the court room.

Q. Did you tell any one after you were arrested, and before you were called upon, what your testimony would be?

Question objected to by the Judge Advocate, and withdrawn.

RE-EXAMINATION.

It was distinctly stated to me before testifying, that the Government authorities would make me no pledges, nor did any Government official make any threats to me. The only position I held in the order was that of Ancient Brother in our County Temple. Dr. Bowles told me that he would appoint me to the position of Adjutant General on his staff, if I desired it; but I told him I did not wish it, as I had no knowledge of military matters. I and Mr. Heffren had some talk about it. The organization, which I afterward understood to be the Sons of Liberty, was in session in Chicago at the time of the Democratic Convention, when General McClellan was nominated. The meeting was at the Richmond House; Mr. Dodd was there. I was there, but not as a delegate; there were no persons there to represent the South, or from Canada, to my knowledge. Mr. Moss, from Missouri, was there, and distinguished himself in the meeting; Mr. Green, from Illinois, was there; and a Mr. Jackson, I believe—a large man—from Ohio; and also Mr. Vallandigham, who acted as Chairman of the meeting of the Sons of Liberty. I was present at only a portion of each meeting. When I first went, Mr. Moss was speaking. An introductory speech was made by Mr. Vallandigham, as Chairman. He spoke in reference to the divided condition of the Democratic party; he said that until very recently he had thought that the Chicago Convention would result very much as the Charleston Convention did; that is, that it would break up; but since he had come to Chicago, and had seen persons from all parts of the country, he had changed his opinion on that subject; he had found a wonderful unanimity of feeling, and oneness of idea, and he believed the party could be made more united and more efficient than it had been for years; and he did not doubt we would be able, through his and others' instrumentality, to secure a proper platform for the party to stand upon. Vallandigham acted as Chairman until the close of the meeting, and adjourned it to the next day, when he presided again. The meeting was held at the Richmond House; I think the rooms were Nos. 94, 96, 98, and 100, in the fifth story; there were folding-doors by which the rooms communicated; and probably from one hundred and fifty to two hundred were present. Dodd was there, and I think Mr. Barrett. I did not see Judge Bullitt, or Mr. Piper, or Captain Majors. I saw Mr. Swem in Chicago, but not at the meeting. Mr. Vallandigham presided at the meeting by a vote. I did not know but that the meetings were open, for no one was present at the doors, and no password was required that I know of, nor did I know that all present were members. Mr. Moss, in his remarks, gave a history of the condition of Missouri; how the citizens there were exposed to both rebel and Union troops; that some really good Union men, and others really rebels, were suffering great indignities at the hands of the troops. First the rebels would come along and rob them of their pork and crops; then the Union troops came and took the negroes; that if this organization was worth any thing, if it was intended to be efficient in the restoration of the Government under the Constitution, now was the time to strike; that these indignities were unbearable; and if they had true American blood in them they would not bear it any longer, but strike at once.

No practical remedy was proposed to meet the emergency. The first meeting was held on Sunday evening, the second on Monday. On the Monday evening going to the Richmond House, somewhat before the meeting, I met John Singleton and Mr. Barrett, of Missouri. They were endeavoring, so I understood, to arrange for the bursting up of the Convention, in case it disowned the order. In that event they would make a public demonstration of the order, and proposed to nominate some candidates other than that nominated by the Convention. John Singleton had a great many mottoes for transparencies made, some of which he read. They were patriotic, and not connected with any secret conspiracy; some of them were mottoes from the speeches and writings of Douglas, Jackson, Jefferson and Washington; but they were phrases which seemed to suit the circumstances of the times. At this second meeting Vallandigham presided, and made some remarks similar to those he made at the first meeting. He drew out of his pocket a platform, substantially the same as that adopted at the Chicago Convention, which, he said, he had presented to most of the delegates, and to members from each of the States, and that it had met with universal approval. If he could get that platform as the platform of the party, he should be willing to take McClellan as the Presidential candidate. He said he would be willing to take any man as a candidate if the platform was only right. He announced his conviction that, by the adoption of this platform, the organization would merge its action with that of the Democratic party. Singleton's proposition was not adopted, in conse-

quence of the Democratic party being united. This meeting of the organization in Chicago, at which Barrett made his proposition for an uprising, was on the 20th of July; the second meeting was on the 29th of August. Barrett, who was present at the meeting, at which Vallandigham presided, made no objection to the course of the proceedings on that occasion. Mr. Dodd was present at the July meeting. The speeches made at the meeting at which Vallandigham presided, I thought, were addressed to those who were members of the order. Mr. Green, of Illinois, made a speech at the meeting. I have no recollection that the strength of the order was mentioned by any present who seemed to know; but one person said it had about five hundred thousand members. The organization was referred to by Mr. Moss, and others, as a distinctive organization then existing. Mr. Vallandigham presided when these statements were made.

RE-CROSS-EXAMINATION.

I did not understand that this meeting was a mere caucus of the friends of Mr. Vallandigham, to consider matters that would probably come up at the Convention. The gentlemen who were present at Chicago, representing the Sons of Liberty, were unanimously opposed to the nomination of General McClellan. The Mr. Barrett, of whom I have spoken, is from Missouri. He stated to me that early in this war, Mr. Douglas had suggested to him the propriety of getting up a regiment, and going on the Plains to hold in check marauding bands which might congregate there, in the territory; that he had got up a regiment, and went down to the neighborhood of Pilot Knob, Missouri. Mr. Douglas had promised to get some order for him, but failing to do this he had resigned. Since then he had been engaged in sending persons across the lines to the Southern Confederacy. I think before the war, he was a resident of Illinois, and since raising the regiment he has made claim to Missouri as his State.

W. S. Bush, a witness for the Government, was then introduced, and duly sworn by the Judge Advocate.

The Judge Advocate proposed to introduce a speech, as reported by the witness, and printed in the Cincinnati *Gazette*, of August 16, 1864, which was made by the accused, L. P. Milligan. Some parts of the report were verbatim, and others a condensed report; and he proposed to examine the witness in reference to its correctness.

The accused objected to its introduction as incompetent, and claimed that a witness must first state his recollection of a speech, or conversation, and might refresh his memory by any memorandum made at the time; but that report could not be used as evidence. It was not competent to introduce a report which was only partially verbatim, in which the omissions might give a different construction to what was said, and to ask the witness to define what was verbatim, and what was not.

The Judge Advocate replied:

It seems to me that it is a well established rule that a printed report of a speech, published in a public journal at the time it was made, the reporter being present to state whether the report of the speech is or is not correct, can always be introduced in evidence. I recollect a somewhat similar question occurred in the trial of Captain Hurtt, at Cincinnati, which was strongly argued by his able counsel, T. D. Lincoln and Colonel Jackson. I had introduced, on the part of the Government, private letters which had been written by him, containing disloyal sentiments, or sentiments tending to injure the Government; and, to rebut the force of those letters, his counsel proposed to introduce articles written by him and printed in the *Ohio State Journal*, of which he was one of the editors, showing that he had labored, by his speeches and in the leading articles of his paper, to advocate the general cause of the Government. We were unable to keep that evidence out, although we contested it with as much force as we were able. During this trial we have introduced an address of H. H. Dodd, in printed form, which was delivered as a speech to the order at one of their meetings in February, and no objection was made by the accused or their counsel.

The counsel for the accused replied:

The address of Mr. Dodd was published as a correct official report of his speech, while the correctness of the report of Mr. Milligan's speech is not yet proven.

The Judge Advocate continued:

The gentlemen now make the issue on the correctness of the report, and not on the right to introduce the report of that speech. I allow the whole force of his argument to the effect that it is not competent to introduce it as a correct report. Now, then, I propose to show that the speech, as reported in that paper, is a correct report, and to prove its correctness by the man who reported it.

It may, perhaps, be said that it would be better to introduce the original itself. It is a rule that the highest grade of testimony shall be introduced which it is possible to obtain, or which the case in its nature is susceptible of; but when the original notes can not be produced, is it not better to go to the printed report of the speech than to trust to the uncertain memory of any witness?

The President of the Commission said the document referred to as the address of the Grand Commander to the Grand Council, came to us in the shape of an official document, in the minutes of the order. This report purports to be a speech made by one of the accused, and published in the newspapers of the country, and only when its identity is proven is it competent in evidence.

The Judge Advocate replied:

One is a speech made in an official capacity, and the other is simply an ordinary speech to the masses. We can introduce the admissions and speeches of a man, made upon any and all occasions as against himself, if necessary. I propose to introduce it, if for no other purpose than to show that while the accused was a member of this order, knowing its intents and purposes, and while this order was being agitated with plans for the release of rebel prisoners, marching upon Indianapolis, Louisville, New Albany and other places, and attempting to overturn the Government, the accused was abroad through the land addressing bodies of men, and making incendiary speeches certain to have the effect of arousing their passions, and inciting to insurrection.

The counsel for the accused said:

The address comes in the character of an official document, while the other is that of a reported speech. The character of these two seems very different.

The Judge Advocate replied:

I introduce the first document not as an official document, in and of itself. We first had the testimony of Mr. Harrison as to whether it was a correct copy of Mr. Dodd's speech, and whether Mr. Dodd delivered it at that time. It was only because it was a correct copy that we were entitled to introduce it.

I desire to introduce that paper itself, and to submit to the Commission the report of the speech, as a correct report of the speech, and the very words used by the accused.

The court room was then cleared for deliberating.

On the opening of the Court, the Judge Advocate announced to the accused that the Court had decided that the objection was premature at the present stage of the examination of the witness, and the objection was overruled.

The witness, in reply to the questions of the Judge Advocate, testified as follows:

You may state whether you were present at a convention at Fort Wayne, Indiana, on the 13th of August, and if so, whether or not you reported any speeches made at that time?

Answer. I was present at that meeting and made a full report of Mr. Milligan's speech, and partial reports of the speeches of A. M. Jackson, of Ohio, and C. W. Reeves, of Plymouth, Marshall county.

Q. What was your occupation at that time?

A. I was reporting for the Cincinnati *Gazette* the speeches made at political meetings of both parties in Indiana.

Q. Did you at that time make a report of Mr. Milligan's speech?

A. I did; Mr. Milligan's speech was made on Saturday. I wrote my report on Sunday in part or in whole, and returned to Cincinnati Monday morning.

Q. Did you take short hand notes of that speech at the time it was delivered?

A. I did, sir.

Q. How large an audience was present?

A. I estimated it at five thousand persons.

Q. Have you looked at your notes or at the report in the paper, to refresh your memory?

A. My notes were destroyed at the time the report was made. I have seen the report since, but have not carefully examined it to refresh my memory.

Q. Do you now recollect the main points of that speech?

A. I do, sir.

Q. State to the Court what was said by Mr. Milligan on the state of the country, whether it was prosperous or otherwise?

A. He referred to the country as desolated by this war, and the oppressions of the Administration. That was the general tenor of his remarks on that point.

Q. What did he state in reference to the freedom of the press and of speech?

A. He spoke of the freedom of speech allowed as simply that granted by a Lincoln mob—as a freedom in name rather than in fact.

Q. What did he say in reference to the draft or conscription?

A. Prior to Mr. Milligan's speech, a series of resolutions was adopted as the platform of the Democracy of that Congressional district and of adjoining districts. The audience were expecting to hear from him in reference to the draft. He stated, if the war was right, the draft was right, and if they considered the war right, and were good citizens, they would not grumble about the draft.

Q. What else did he say about the rightfulness of the war?

A. He denied that the war was right, and proceeded to argue, that under the Constitution the President had no power to coerce a State, and asked if those entered the army would look in the future for their laurels to such battles as Bull Run, Chicamauga, and Red river. He also appealed to them to consider the condition of their wives and children at home, destitute and dependent on the charity of their neighbors, if they entered the army, and asked whether they considered it a duty to make such a sacrifice.

Q. State to the Court what he said about the powers that be; whether they were existing by rightful authority or otherwise?

A. I do not recollect his exact words, but the tenor of his remarks were that the Administration had usurped power.

Q. What did he say about the President of the United States?

A. He spoke of him as a tyrant, and an usurper, I think.

Q. What did he say in reference to the arrests of disloyal persons by the Government?

A. I do not remember distinctly the words he used.

Q. Did he denounce arbitrary arrests?

A. I think he did.

Q. What did he say about this war being inaugurated for the restoration of the Union, and its power to act in that direction?

A. He held that the war itself was disunion, and that the Union could not be restored by war.

Q. How did he treat this Government, as a unit or otherwise?

A. He spoke of the Government as a confederation of the several States, rather than a unity.

Q. What effect did he state the war had produced?

A. That it had made the Government a despotism.

Q. How did you understand him to speak of the Government at that time, as a Government of all the States, or only of the States which were left in the Union?

A. I understood him to refer to what were left.

Q. What did he say as to whether the Government was still divided or existing as a unit?

A. He treated the war itself as a dissolution of the Government.

Q. Did he make that statement?

A. I think he did.

Q. Give to the Court his words as near as you can recollect.

A. I have not referred to the report lately for the purpose of refreshing my memory, and can not state positively what he said.

Q. What did he state as to the right of the Government of the United States to make war upon rebels, or those in rebellion against the General Government?

A. He denied the right.

Q. Did he state any thing to the audience in reference to the number of men who had been destroyed in this war, and the amount of treasure expended?

A. I think he stated that two millions of men had lost their lives during the war. I do not remember exactly what he said in reference to the amount of treasure expended, but I believe he referred to it.

Q. What did he state about the prospects of the war after that expenditure, as regards the two contending forces?

A. He spoke of the Confederate Government as successful, as holding its own; and that the future prosecution of the war would only tend to greater losses to the United States Government.

Q. I will ask you now this general question, whether his speech at that time was loyal, and in favor of the Government, or whether it was disloyal, and against it?

Question objected to by the counsel for the accused.

The Judge Advocate stated that he could produce ample authority in favor of the competency of the question.

The Commission then adjourned to Wednesday, November 16, at 10 o'clock, A. M.

Court Room, Indianapolis, Indiana,
November 16, 1864, 10 o'clock, A. M.

The Commission met pursuant to adjournment.

All the members present. Also, the Judge Advocate, the accused, (except W. A. Bowles,) and their counsel.

The proceedings were read and approved.

The Judge Advocate then submitted the following in favor of the competency of the question objected to yesterday, by the accused:

When the last witness was upon the stand, the accused objected that it was not competent evidence for the witness to state whether the general tenor of Mr. Milligan's speech was loyal, or disloyal.

My duties have given me but little time to search for authorities on the point at issue, and I have not been able to find a large number of decisions applicable to the issue made by the accused. I remember very distinctly, in the commencement of this trial, investigating the general principle of conspiracy, and found the proposition broadly stated, in so many words, that you could ask a witness who heard a speech made by a conspirator to an audience, of which the witness was part, whether the general purport and tenor of the speech was against the Government, or for it.

I read first a paragraph not so applicable as others to the question at issue, but for the purpose of bringing to the mind of the Court the class of evidence that may be introduced in trials of this character, I read from Roscoe's *Criminal Evidence*, page 87:

"Not only are the *acts*, and the written *letters* and *papers*, of one of several persons engaged in the same conspiracy, evidence against the others, if done or written in furtherance of the common purpose, but his verbal declarations are equally admissible under similar restrictions. Any declarations made by one of the party in pursuance of the common object of the conspiracy, are evidence against the rest of the party, who are as much responsible for all that has been said or done by their associates in carrying into effect the concerted plan, as if it had been pronounced by their own voice, or executed by their own hand. These declarations are of the nature of acts; they are in reality acts done by the party, and generally they are far more mischievous than acts which consist only in corporal agency. All consultations, therefore, carried on by one conspirator, relative to the general design, and all conversations in his presence, are evidence against another conspirator, though absent. 1 *Phill. Ev.*, 95, 7th ed. The effect of such evidence must depend on a variety of circumstances, such as whether the party was attending to the conversation, and whether he approved or disapproved; still such conversations are admissible in evidence. See *Eyre C. J.*, *Hardy's case*, 24 *How. St. Tr.*, 704. In Lord George Gordon's case, the cry of the mob, being part of the transaction, was held to be admissible against the prisoner. 21 *How. St. Tr.*, 535. And upon the same principle, the expressions of the mob in the Sacheverell riots, that they designed to pull down the meeting-houses, were admitted in evidence. *Damoree's case*, 15 *How. St. Tr.*, 552."

I read this to bring before the minds of the Court the general principle of conspiracy. On page 88, Roscoe's *Criminal Evidence*, I find the following:

"As in trials for conspiracies, whatever the prisoner may have done or said at any meeting alleged to be held in pursuance of the conspiracy, is admissible in evidence on the part of the prosecution against him; so, on the other hand, any other part of his conduct at the same meetings, will be allowed to be proved on his behalf. For the intention and design of a party at a particular time are best explained by a complete view of every part of his conduct at that time, and not merely from the proof of a single and insulated act or declaration. *Phill. Ev.*, 499, 8th ed. On the trial for an indictment to overthrow the Government, evidence was given to show that the conspiracy was brought into overt act at meetings, in the presence of the prisoner Walker. His counsel was allowed to ask, whether at those times, he had heard Walker utter any word inconsistent with the duty of a good subject. He was also allowed to inquire into the general declarations of the prisoner at the meetings, and whether the witness had heard him say any thing that had a tendency to disturb the peace. *Ibid.*, 23 *How. St. Tr.*, 1131; 31 *Id.*, 43."

I do not propose to go into any lengthy discussion of this subject, as I have drawn from the witness the main points of the speech. I am certain, however, that the law goes further than I have even claimed. That I have the right to ask whether Mr. Milligan, in talking to that crowd, spoke for or against the Government, is conceded by the authorities; and each loyal man of the land is perfectly cognizant of what is loyalty, and what is disloyalty. This is not a question of opinion, but one of fact. It is an old remark that every man is for his Government or against it. The dividing line is clear to the mind of every man who heard that speech. Now, I propose to ask the witness who reported that speech, whether it was for the Government, or against it. There on the 13th of August, when the uprising was to take place on the 16th, he was making an incendiary speech, at the very time when Dr. Wilson testifies that nearly every man in his county belonging to the order knew that the insurrection was to take place on the 16th of August.

The accused replied:

I have not had an opportunity to search the law upon this point, but it seems to me it does not support the point made by the Judge Advocate. He states that this speech was made a few days previous to the time when this uprising was to take place. The exposition of the order was made on the 29th of July, and the testimony given shows that the whole project was abandoned, and that messengers had been dispatched to the people making that announcement. Instead of that speech being made to goad on the minds of the people, it was made at the time when this uprising had been set at naught, abandoned, and the whole thing exposed in the public print. If Mr. Milligan had knowledge of this uprising, it is fair to presume that he had knowledge of its abandonment. It is said that this speech was made for the purpose of inflaming the minds of the populace; but that is a matter for the consideration of the Court in summing up the case. It is competent for the prosecution to ask the witness the general question, "Was that speech loyal, and in favor of the Government, or disloyal, and against the Government?"

You will notice that Walker had expressed no sentiments; and when the Government undertook to prove his sentiments, he had the right to object, that the Government could prove intents only by affirmative acts, and not by mere opinions. We may, on the contrary, introduce evidence to show that his sentiments were not disloyal, and propose to prove that he made no remark tending to such a conclusion as that. If they will ask the witness what was the substance of his remarks, in regard to obedience to the Constitution and the draft, or against enforcing the draft, I make no objection; but they can not ask the witness whether the whole speech was in favor of the Government, and loyal, or against the Government, and disloyal. Look at the fallacy of such a position. There is not a speech made, but what you can find an individual who will come up and swear that it is disloyal; and, on the other hand, you could find some Democrat who would swear that the tendency of the speech was loyal

and in favor of the Constitution. I take for granted the witness would say the speech was disloyal; and, I dare say, a Democrat would say it was calculated to maintain the Constitution. You, gentlemen of the Commission, are to decide what this tendency is. The prisoner is charged with disloyal practices, and the opinion of the witness as to the effect of his speech, whether disloyal or not, is not competent evidence. Most of the members of this Commission are lawyers; and they know that it is a question at one time mooted, how the damages were to be ascertained in a case of actual slander. The facts must be given to the jury, and they must fix the amount. So the facts in regard to this speech, the declarations must be given to the Court, and they must decide whether it is loyal or not. It is a matter of political controversy, whether the Administration is or is not the Government. Some would insist that every thing said against the Administration, is disloyalty to the Government. Other witnesses would say that the Administration is only one-third part of the Government. We would, therefore, have to inquire of the witness what his political views were, to understand what he meant by loyalty.

Mr. Greenleaf, in treating upon the subject of evidence in courts-martial, lays down the same general considerations by which courts of law are governed.

He says, in paragraph 476:

"It has already been intimated that courts-martial are bound, in general, to observe the rules of the law of evidence by which the courts of criminal jurisdiction are governed. The only exceptions which are permitted, are those which are of necessity created by the nature of the service, and by the constitution of the court and its course of proceeding."

Again, paragraph 478, he says:

"The opinions of witnesses are, perhaps, more frequently called for in military trials than in any others; but the rule which governs their admissibility, is the same here as elsewhere, and has already been stated in a preceding volume. But it is proper here to add, that where the manner of the act, or of the language with which the prisoner is charged, is essential to the offense, as whether the act was menacing or insulting, or cowardly, or unskillful, or not; or whether the language was abusive or sarcastic, or playful, the opinion which the witness formed at the time, or the impression it then made upon his mind, being cotemporaneous with the fact, and partaking of the *res gestæ*, is not only admissible, but is a fact in the case which he is bound to testify."

Just so here. The facts are before the Court. Is it fair to receive the opinion of the witness upon the general tenor of the speech as to its loyalty or disloyalty? You, gentlemen of the Commission, are thoroughly versed in the politics of the day, and quite as competent to decide whether these declarations are loyal or disloyal, as is the witness.

The court room was then cleared for deliberating on the objection of the accused.

On reopening the court room, the Judge Advocate announced that the objection had been sustained, and the question overruled.

Question by the Judge Advocate:

Please state to the Court whether at that time you had any conversation with Mr. Milligan.

Answer. I do not know that I had any conversation with him the day of the meeting, but I did the day after.

Q. Did Mr. Milligan know, at the time he made that speech, what was the action of the State Central Committee at their meeting on the 12th and 13th of August?

A. I learned from another gentleman what the action of the committee had been, and I asked Mr. Milligan if he had heard of their action. He answered that he had not. I then told him that General Manson had been nominated as Lieutenant Governor. He seemed surprised, and remarked that it looked as if it had been done to spite us.

Q. That was the next day after his speech was made, was it not?

A. It was on Sunday afternoon.

Q. When did Mr. Milligan make this speech?

A. On Saturday afternoon, August 13th, 1864.

Q. Do you mean the Saturday preceding your conversation with Mr. Milligan?

A. Yes, sir.

Q. What did Mr. Milligan say at that meeting in reference to the draft? Did he advise the people to submit and aid the Government in the enrollment, or did he advise them to oppose it?

A. Nothing was said about the enrollment.

Q. Was any thing said about the draft?

A. The draft was expected on the 5th of September, 1864. This meeting was on the 13th of August. He spoke in favor of the draft as the best mode of getting soldiers. He said if the war was right, the draft was right; but the war was wrong, and the draft was wrong; and he spoke of those who went into the army as making a sacrifice of life instead of a risk.

Q. Will you give the substance of his remarks and the manner in which he spoke about the war?

A. I think he spoke about the war as unjustifiable, and a dishonorable war. I am not positive about the word dishonorable.

Q. What did he say upon the subject of peace and of quitting fighting?

A. He was in favor of stopping hostilities, and allowing the South the terms she had always asked.

Q. What were those terms?

A. To be let alone.

CROSS-EXAMINATION.

The meeting referred to was a Democratic mass meeting, called by the Peace Democracy to take action in regard to the draft. I learned this first from Captain Bracken, who said that he learned it from Mr. Barry, who was acting as correspondent of the Chicago *Times*. I understood that on the morning of the meeting there had been a caucus there, composed of individuals who were opposed to adopting any resolution as their platform, as well as of those who were in favor of adopting it. After the radical peace men carried their point in regard to the adoption of resolutions, I understood that those withdrew. The convention numbered about five thousand. I went to that meeting as the reporter for the Cincinnati *Gazette*. I was not in the employment of the Government at the time. I sent a telegraphic dispatch of Mr. Milligan's speech to the Cincinnati *Gazette*, which was confined mainly to the resolutions adopted. The report of the meeting, as well as the telegraphic dispatch of the resolutions, was made by me. I called Mr. Milligan "Dr. Milligan," because I had thus heard him spoken of. In his speech he said the war was an unjustifiable and unconstitutional one. Then he spoke of the draft, and appealed to his hearers in regard to making a sacrifice of life, and of the comforts and happiness of their families, and then asked them if they thought it best to go into the army. In making this argument, he appealed to his audience for approval, and they indorsed what he said. He said if the war was right, the draft was right; and he said that the draft was the best method for raising men. I can not say that he advised submission to the draft. He said that those who believed the war was right ought to go, and not growl about the draft. He did not discuss party differences; but in his remarks he opposed the war and the Government; his remarks against the Government were loudly cheered. In speaking of the Administration, I do not remember his referring to the different departments of the Executive; I understood him to speak of the Government as a whole: and he did not single out any one or any department, except, perhaps, the President. He said nothing denunciatory of the Constitution, but the whole tenor of his speech was in favor of the Constitution as he construed it. His construction of it permitted States to secede at will, and denied to the Government the right of coercion. The resolutions adopted referred more to the draft, and were denunciatory of it and the war generally, rather than to its having influence upon the Chicago Convention. The name of the Chairman of the Committee on Resolutions was Mr. O'Rourke. I was not present at the convention that met in the morning. The resolutions were reported to the meeting before the speaking began; they were first in order. I understood Mr. Milligan to say that about two millions of men had fallen in this war. He spoke of two million seven hundred thousand men having gone into the army and made a sacrifice of life, while the rebels still held their own; and my deduction was that the great majority of them had lost their lives. He said that while the Government had called out two million seven hundred thousand men, we were not able to make any headway, while the rebels were holding their own. At the time of the meeting, I intended to give a full report of all the points of the speech in Mr. Milligan's own language, condensing his references to Colonial history, and his discussion of the constitutional right of coercion, and perhaps some minor points; otherwise, I think the report is correct, and many parts of it are verbatim. I consider the report more reliable than my recollection of the meeting. I wrote my report partly or wholly on Sunday, and it was printed in the *Gazette* on the Tuesday following. I glanced over the report when it appeared in the paper, and I recognized it as the one I had made. Mr. Milligan did not perhaps say, in so many words, that the President had not the power to coerce the rebels; he was speaking of the right of the Government to subdue sovereign States, and my conclusion was that those were rebellious States. I think he spoke of the right to coerce sovereign States, and the right to coerce people who had chosen to leave the Union, referring not only to the States, but to the people; and he may have been talking about the right of revolution. I think he denied not only the right to coerce States, but individuals also. The character of the paper for which I was reporting is that of a general newspaper; I do not regard it as a partisan newspaper, and do not think it claims to be the organ of any party. It may have been regarded as a Republican paper; it certainly is in favor of the Union. Since I have been acquainted with it, it has taken an independent course, and has supported the Union candidates whenever its editors saw fit to support them, and approved or criticised the Administration whenever they thought they had reason for so doing. I have no recollection of Mr. Milligan or any other speaker being cheered for speaking in favor of the Government. In addition to Mr. Humphreys, Mr. Jackson and Mr. Read spoke at that meeting, and were all cheered; and Mr. Humphreys was loudly cheered when he took the stand.

Mr. Milligan was cheered not only when he spoke against the policy of the Government, but also when he spoke against the war; I do not make any distinction between the Government and the Administration; Mr. Milligan's speech was an argumentative one, and contained many points calculated to draw out the approval of the audience. My present connection with the Government is only as one of the Recorders to this Commission. I have acted with both parties. I acted with the Democratic party in 1859. I voted for Mr. Lincoln.

Q. Was there any thing more denunciatory of the Administration in Mr. Milligan's remarks than in the remarks of the other gentlemen who spoke there on that day?

Question objected to by the Judge Advocate, and withdrawn.

There was, perhaps, nothing more offensive in Mr. Milligan's speech than there is in the average of Democratic speeches delivered during the present campaign. There might have been less abuse in Mr. Milligan's speech than in some other speeches that have been delivered, and more than in others.

RE-EXAMINATION.

Mr. Milligan in his speech that day used the term Government rather than Administration, and I do not recollect his making any distinction between the Government and the Adminstration. He said that if the war was right, the draft was right; but he denied that the war had been, or could be constitutional and right.

NICHOLAS COCHRANE, a witness for the Government, was then introduced, and, being duly sworn by the Judge Advocate, testified as follows:

I reside in Jackson township, Sullivan county, Indiana. I am acquainted with Mr Humphreys, one of the accused. I have seen him a few times. I reside nine or ten miles from him. I heard Mr. Humphreys on one occasion speak in Jackson township. The occasion was said to be a Democratic picnic. I think it was about the 15th of September, 1863, a year ago; at any rate, it was the day after Mr. Collins was shot in Terre Haute by Mr. Brown. Mr. Humphreys spoke of that in my hearing. There might have been three hundred people, more or less, present; the meeting was out of doors. Mr. Humphreys was standing in a wagon-bed. Besides Mr. Humphreys, there were Mr. Hammil, an attorney at law, Mr. Edward Price, and an attorney named Burton, besides another person whose name I do not know. This latter said he was a rebel from the State of Georgia, I believe. He said he did not know why he was required to speak to the audience there, composed as it was mostly of farmers, unless it was that they had heard a great deal about rebels and had never seen one, and that he was a rebel from Georgia. Mr. Humphreys was present when the rebel spoke. Mr. Humphreys made the first speech, and a short one again afterward. I remember that he criticised the Administration somewhat strongly. He seemed to be solicitous for peace, and to be opposed to the war; and he seemed to think that the Democratic party was imposed upon, and ought to stand up for their rights. He said that the time had come when Democrats should not appropriate their money, or be willing to spend their means in levity, but should be preparing for self-defense. The general run of his speech was in opposition to the present Administration. The rebel from the State of Georgia remarked that he was not concerned about our State policy, for he did not belong to our State; but he had a piece of advice that he would give to his friends, and that was, to resist the present abolition Administration at the sacrifice of their means, their families, and themselves, if necessary; and that for nothing short of that would he call them honorable. I can not say particularly whether these remarks called forth approbation or disapprobation. There were several cheers, and the people said that he was a good-looking fellow; he was considerably cheered at the close of his speech. I do not remember hearing any hissing or any marks of disapprobation at any thing he said. Mr. Hammil, Mr. Burton, Mr. Allen and Mr. Humphreys were in the wagon, but I am not positive they were in when the rebel spoke. He spoke about the death of Collins, and advised the crowd to go home. He said he had received a dispatch stating that he would probably be arrested that night; and I heard from another source that such a dispatch had been carried to him. The crowd then dispersed.

CROSS-EXAMINATION.

I staid during the whole of the speech. I have forgotten the name of the rebel from Georgia, but it seems to me they called him Captain Manderville. He did not say that he had taken the oath of allegiance to the United States Government, or that he had been in the Quartermaster's Department for several months. When Mr. Humphreys spoke of the death of this man and the dispatch that he had received, and that it was likely that he would be arrested, he spoke quite solemnly.

The Judge Advocate here announced to the Commission that he had closed the case on the part of the Government.

The Commission then adjourned, to meet on Thursday, November 17, 1864, at 9 o'clock, A. M.

———

COURT ROOM, INDIANAPOLIS, INDIANA,
November 17, 1864, 9 o'clock, A. M. }

The Commission met pursuant to adjournment.

All the members present, except Colonel Wass. Also, the Judge Advocate, the accused (except W. A. Bowles), and their counsel.

The proceedings were read and approved.

WILLIAM G. MOSS, a witness for the accused, was then introduced, and, being duly sworn by the Judge Advocate, testified as follows:

I reside in Green county, Indiana, and am a farmer. I was elected Sheriff of the county in 1856, and served until 1860, when I was elected as Representative, and served in two sessions of the Legislature. I was re-elected Sheriff last October. I am acquainted with Mr. Humphreys; have been a neighbor of his for about twenty-two years, and was in partnership with him in the mercantile business for nearly a year. I joined an order called the American Knights, in September, 1863. I took the first degree in our store, in Green county. This was before I entered into partnership with Mr. Humphreys. I believe he was at a meeting of the order in Indianapolis on the 16th or 17th of February, 1864. I did not know of the meeting at the time I came here to visit Indianapolis on business. When here I met Mr. Heffren and Mr. Malott, from Sullivan. They insisted on my going to the meeting. I was present when an election, or an appointment of officers, took place; major generals and deputy commanders, probably, but I am not certain, and other officers, were appointed. Mr. Milligan, Mr. Humphreys, Mr. Walker, and probably Mr. Bowles, were elected or appointed Major Generals. I took back to my own county the news of this meeting, and in a few days after the meeting I saw Mr. Humphreys, and I informed him of what had taken place—that he was appointed a Major General.

Q. What did he say about it?

Question objected to by the Judge Advocate, and withdrawn.

Q. Were you authorized to take the news of that election to Mr. Humphreys?

Question objected to by the Judge Advocate.

The counsel for the accused requested the Judge Advocate to state his grounds of objection.

The rule of law is clear, that while in the prosecution of cases of conspiracy, the Government may prove the admissions of the accused as against him, he can not, in his own defense, prove counter statements which were made at any different time than the specific time when the admissions are proven. In illustration of what I mean, suppose I prove that in a certain conversation Mr. Milligan made certain admissions to any party, they may call out that entire conversation, and any explanatory facts and statements he then made in his own behalf. But while I may prove any distinct admission as against him, they can not prove any distinct, separate statements in his favor. Such a rule of law as is contended for by the accused, would destroy the possibility of the conviction of any individual for crime. If an individual is indicted for murder, the act may be proven against him, and his admissions as against himself; but any counter statements after the deed, to the effect he did it in self-defense, or in defense of his property, can not be admitted in his favor. In conspiracy trials, the rule is: if a person is engaged in a common conspiracy, and addresses a meeting, or is at any of the meetings of the Council where the general purposes of the conspiracy were discussed, if the State proves against him any distinct statements or admissions, the defense may call out all the statements and surroundings under which it was made, as a part of the *res gestæ;* but they can not go into any separate statement made at a different time and place. These distinct statements stand alone, and not as part of the *res gestæ.* The accused can not exculpate himself from crime by his own assertions.

The accused replied:

The accused have come to the conclusion that they have no other resort to vindicate themselves from the inferences which the Judge Advocate seeks to raise against them, than to introduce testimony concerning their own relations to and declarations about the order. If we can not introduce our repudiation and rejection of the office which was attempted to be thrust upon us in our absence, and show that from the moment we knew of it until the dissolution of the order, we repudiated it, then we have no opportunity to vindicate ourselves from the charges sought to be proven against us. It has been shown by the prosecution that Humphreys was elected a Major General at the February meeting of the order, which he did not attend, and of which he could have no knowledge at the time, nor until he was informed of it, and that is as far as the evidence shows his connection with it. Another fact has been proven, namely, that the military branch of the order was intended for the subversion of the Union, detaching certain States, either to form a North-western Confederacy, or be attached to the Southern Confederacy; and from this fact will be argued the treasonable character of the military part of the order. Now, the accused is only connected with the military part of the order by the fact of his election as a Major General, which transpired in his absence, and of which there is no proof he had any knowledge. Now, we present the counter fact, that when he was informed of that election, he rejected and repudiated the office, and thereafter had nothing to do with that part of the order. That is what we propose to prove. The Judge Advocate objects to it,

because it is not a part of the conversation he has seen proper to introduce. The Commission can not determine what conversations he has introduced. It is impossible to determine when the conversation he has introduced transpired, and when he said certain things; as, for instance, they have proven, or assume to have proven, that he accepted a Brigadier Generalship, and agreed to command a certain portion of the forces in the order. There is no evidence of this fact. The whole history of Mr. Humphreys' connection with the order, from his initiation until the commencement of this trial, has been dragged before this Commission, without reference to time or place, or under what circumstances his admissions were made. To show his character and real connection with the order, we shall offer, and claim the right to offer, until it is denied us, evidence covering the whole period from his election to a Major Generalship, to the commencement of this trial, to show that he was guilty of no treasonable project, declaration, act, or conspiracy. That, on the contrary, he avowed himself ready to obey and support the laws and Constitution of his country, and even to death, and against every proposition inimical to the laws and Constitution of his country.

You see, gentlemen of this Commission, that unless this is permitted, we can not introduce any proof in fact, for written communications are not admissible. There is no evidence, but hearsay, that he accepted this Commission. There is no evidence that he is connected with any treasonable acts, or tending to show this fact. Now, we want to show his acts, his life, his confidential communications to his intimate friend, his partner. The law, I grant you, is not definite on that point. I read from Roscoe's *Criminal Evidence,* page 88:

"The acts and declarations of a prisoner, given in evidence in his favor, ought to be connected both in point of subject-matter and of time, with the acts or declarations proved against him. See *Phill. Ev.,* 500, *8th ed.* In the two following cases, however, great latitude was allowed on trials for high treason. When the overt act charged was, that the prisoner to compass the King's death, conspired with others to call a convention of the people, etc.; the prisoner's counsel was allowed to ask the witness whether, *before the time of the convention,* he had ever heard from the prisoner what his objects were, and whether he had at all mixed himself in the business. *Hardy's case,* 24 *How. St. Tr.,* 1097. So in *Horne Tooke's case,* 1 *East. P. C.,* 61; 25 *How. St. Tr.,* 545, evidence having been given, on the part of the crown, of several publications containing republican doctrines and opinions, which had been distributed by the prisoner during the period assigned in the indictment, (for high treason,) for the existence of the conspiracy, the prisoner offered to put in a book, written by him, expressive of his veneration for the King and the constitution; this was objected to as being antecedent to the period of the conspiracy, and not relating to the particular transaction. After argument, the book was admitted, on the ground that it had reference to the proof given in support of the charge, to rebut the idea, that a reform in Parliament was a pretense made by the prisoner, and that his real object was to overturn the Government."

Now, if the Judge Advocate is correct in his conclusions, there can be introduced against Mr. Humphreys the acts and declarations of others, and implicate him in their transactions, and make him liable for all that was done at that meeting, in his absence, unless he shows that he repudiated the whole thing. Roscoe, in another paragraph, says:

"On the trial of an indictment for a conspiracy to overthrow the government, evidence was given to show that the conspiracy was brought into overt act, at meetings, in the presence of the prisoner Walker. His counsel was allowed to ask, whether, at those times, he had heard Walker utter any word inconsistent with the duty of a good subject. He was also allowed to inquire into the general declarations of the prisoner at the meetings, and whether the witness had heard him say any thing that had a tendency to disturb the peace. *Ibid.*, 23 *How. St. Tr.*, 1131; 31 *Id.*, 43."

Now, the act of the election is proved against Mr. Humphreys. We propose, on the point of time and fact, to connect his declarations on receiving the first news of his appointment, to show that he repudiated it, and was in no way mixed up in the business. We, also, propose to show, that before the time of this illegitimate uprising, which was to have taken place in pursuance of this conspiracy, and immediately after his election to military office, he rejected and repudiated his election, and declared that he would have nothing more to do with the order, and would not be mixed up with this business by the action of others. The case quoted of Hardy, was a simple hearsay case. The prisoner's counsel was allowed to ask the witness whether, at any time before the convention, he had ever heard from the prisoner what his objects were, and whether he had at all mixed himself up in the business. So in Horne Tooke's case, the prisoner's counsel was permitted to introduce a book, written before the time of the alleged offense, to prove his fealty to the King, and that his design was not to overturn the Government. True, Lord Ellenborough doubts the soundness of this decision; but his is the opinion only of one judge, while the other judges concurred against him.

This decision stands in the light of as good authority as if it had not been questioned. It can not overturn the decision of the whole Court.

If, in the case of Horne Tooke, a book written before the time of the conspiracy, could be introduced to show the loyalty of the prisoner to his King, with how much stronger reason may we press our claim to be permitted to introduce evidence about the time of the election of Mr. Humphreys as Major General, to show that he then repudiated the whole scheme. The point seems to me to be too clear for argument, that justice requires that the accused be allowed to introduce counter-statements, occurring during the period of his alleged connection with the order, to rebut the hearsay evidence introduced against him by the Government. This necessity involves the introduction of conversations and acts, running through the whole period from September, 1863, to his arrest in 1864. This is necessary to show, in the light of all his declarations and acts, what his whole conduct has been. It is due to every man's individual acts, that they should be construed by all his surrounding acts which have reference to the same transactions. This is allowed to the defense. The general character of the accused for loyalty and devotion to his country is needed as a rebutter to the charge of conspiracy or treason, when the evidence on which that depends is doubtful. This rule we apply to the present case. It is evident that Mr. Humphreys had no connection with the order at the time this conspiracy was planned. We show that as soon as he was elected, he repudiated the office of Major General; and that in every step of his life since he joined the order, he has acted the part of a good citizen. We shall show that, in the case of the men pursuing the soldiers near Caledonia, he overtook them and called them back from their pursuit, and reminded them of their duties as good citizens. If, in some degree, he identified himself with the mob, and went half-way with them, or assumed to be of them, to get influence over them, it can not be an evidence of his guilt, but of that tact which is necessary to the performance of his duties as a citizen. We will go through his whole life, if need be, and show that he had been devoted to the laws, constitution, and peace of his country, and opposed to every thing which would tend to the subversion of the Government.

The charge in this case is that of conspiracy, and it extends as far back as the meeting at Terre Haute, in July or August, 1863, up to the time when these conspirators were arrested. I believe there is evidence tending to fix guilt on these conspirators, even after their arrest. It is charged that from July or August, 1863, until September or October, 1864, this conspiracy was maturing, and its members ripening treasonable schemes to overturn the Government. To prove these charges, the Judge Advocate introduces evidence to show what each one has done or intended to do, during this time, in the prosecution of this crime. The evidence consists of the declarations and acts of the several conspirators, what they have said and done, and that their design and purpose was to overturn the Government. All this forms a part of the *res gestæ* of the transaction, of the crime with which they are charged. In the case of any particular act of crime, we prove the act and the circumstances connected with it as the *res gestæ*, as confined to that particular time. But this is a continuous act, universal, and involving, in its meshes for ruin, all these men. If this order is, *per se*, a conspiracy, these acts are part of this constant act, and if they are arraigned before this Commission, their admissions, in justice, should be introduced in their own defense. I am willing that every fiber shall be woven, in the web of testimony, of the acts of each one as against them all, if the connection be established between these men, and I am willing that the men who are connected thus, shall go with that man who is connected with the treasonable effort. But let us not *attempt* to entangle, in this terrible drag-net, a man who is not guilty, who never concurred in their treason, but repudiated the act which would have brought him to ruin. Let him have the benefit of his acts from the first until now. It is not proven that he had any other connection with the order, than that he was elected Major General. There is no evidence that he had attached himself to the order until then, and that is only an inference. If he was not a member, it is due to him that he should explain that matter by his own declarations, made at the time he learned that he was elected. That if he knew nothing of the military part of the order, it is proper that he should prove his repudiation of it at that time.

What would Mr. Bingham have thought, who, having been told that there was nothing in the order incompatible with the duties of a good citizen, had he been elected a Major General and assigned to the command of a district of the State? And suppose, when they elected Humphreys, they had pointed out his duties and given him the ulterior purposes of the organization, namely, to establish a North-western Confederacy, or that failing, to attach themselves to the treasonable Confederacy of the South? Suppose all that had been explained to him, would he have no right to go forward and show why he eschewed the office, and any relations to such an organization as this? If he has no such right, he has no defense at all. The worst enemy he has in the world may bind him hand and foot, and deliver him over for trial, to be doomed to a dishonorable death. I can not think the laws justify such a construction, or that this Commission will determine this point in such a manner, and I submit the point for their decision.

The Judge Advocate, in reply, said:

I desire to direct the attention of the Court to a few points, not because I deem the question at issue of so much importance to the Government, but because it may settle the rule of examination to be pursued in this case. At the same time, I believe if it should be decided against the Government, it would work great injustice. The gentleman's own law is all I ask to decide the case against him. The authority from which he quoted, says:

"As in trials for conspiracies, whatever the prisoner may have done or said at any meeting alleged to be held in pursuance of the conspiracy, is admissible in evidence on the part of the prosecution against him; so, on the other hand, any other part of his conduct, at the *same meetings*, will be allowed to be proven on his behalf; for the intention and design of a party at a particular time, are best explained by a complete view of every part of his conduct at that time, and not merely from the proof of a single and insulated act or declaration." *Roscoe's Criminal Evidence, page* 88.

Had the counsel for the accused read a little further, he would have found the decision he quoted overruled. *Roscoe* adds: "The soundness of this decision has been doubted by Lord Ellenborough, who said, if the point should ever occur before him, it would become his duty seriously to consider whether such evidence should be admitted. *Lambert's case*, 2 *Comp.*, 409. In the following case, a stricter limit was placed to the investigation of the acts and declarations of a prisoner. On the trial of Lord George Gordon, a witness was asked by his counsel on cross-examination, as to a statement made by the prisoner on *the night before the meeting* in St. George's Fields, and with respect to which such evidence had been produced. The question was overruled, and Lord Mansfield said, that as the counsel for the crown had given evidence of what the prisoner said at the meeting on the 29th of May, the counsel for the prisoner might show the whole connection of what the prisoner said, besides, at that meeting, but that they could not go into evidence of what he said on an *antecedent day.* 21 *How. St. Tr.*, 542."

This decision was reaffirmed in a subsequent case to that of *Horne Tooke*, overruling the decision in that case, as will be seen from the closing sentence of the paragraph just quoted:

"So in *Hanson's case*, on the charge of promoting a riot, the prisoner's counsel was not allowed to prove what he said privately to a friend, previously to his going to the place of riot, respecting his motives in going thither. 31 *How. St. Tr.*, 1281."

That is the most recent decision. But, the rule, even as given by the gentleman, does not go to the extent he claims. On the other hand, I claim for the Government that if the alleged conspiracy had been inaugurated on the first day of August, I could, on the part of the Government, go back a few days or months, and introduce acts of the accused to show the intentions and purposes of the act, before the 1st of August. At the same time, the accused can go back, and show that the tenor of his life had been against his entering upon any such project; but they can not go back and prove distinct counter statements on the part of the defendant. If we examine the argument of the gentleman, its fallacy, I think, will be apparent. He asks, shall this defendant be bound by what transpired in his absence? He says that he should not. I say that he shall: and thus saith the law. When any man takes upon himself the obligations of the Order of American Knights, or Sons of Liberty, he takes upon himself the responsibility for the acts of that body, whether he be absent or present.

From the time a man takes the oaths of this conspiracy, he takes upon himself responsibility for the acts of the entire organization, he agrees to stand by the illegal and treasonable acts of every member of the organization. So says the law. I propose to connect these men not only with what was done in their presence, but in their absence, and hold them accountable. The law says that when there is a conspiracy formed, and men league themselves together, that they may have greater power to accomplish their evil purposes, they shall be held to a greater responsibility, and all those who perform any part, however minute, or however remote from the scene of action, but who are actually leagued in the general conspiracy, are to be considered as aiders and abettors in the same.

The accused argue that this association is not *per se* a conspiracy, and that the Judge Advocate has assumed this point; that as yet it is an open question before the Court, and until it is settled, the argument of the Judge Advocate is not pertinent, and that it can not be settled until the close of the case. All the evidence introduced would never have been permitted by the accused to come in, but on the ground that the Government had proven the organization a conspiracy *per se*. If not a conspiracy *per se*, then the declarations of other members as co-conspirators could not be introduced against any one of the accused. Almost every witness we have put on the stand on the part of the Government could have had his mouth closed by

the able counsel for the accused, on any other foundation than that the order was a conspiracy *per se*. They are not the able counsel that I take them to be if they permit their clients to be convicted on defective and irrelevant testimony. We have examined the witnesses on the hypothesis that it was a conspiracy in itself. Except on that hypothesis, we could not have proven a single act or statement of Dodd, or Walker, or Wright, or any member of the order, except the accused. The question has been put to nearly every witness, "Is this man a member of the order?" If so, there was no objection to the admission of any one of his statements or acts.

Is it a conspiracy within the meaning of the law, an agreement to do a legal thing in an illegal manner, or to do an illegal thing in a legal manner? Is this not a conspiracy where men bind themselves with oaths—the penalty for the violation of these oaths being death—oaths violative of all laws, and peace and order—bind themselves to execute without hesitation the commands of their officers in the order, and agree that the National Government is only a compact to be dissolved at pleasure? Is that order a conspiracy the members of which pledge themselves to form a Northwestern Confederacy, and failing in that to attach themselves to the Southern Confederacy; where they plot the release of the enemies of the Government, the seizure of arsenals, the capture of State officers, the subversion of State Governments, and the destruction of the lives and property of the citizens of the States where those men reside? Is not all this a combination and agreement to do an illegal act? The accused argue that they do not defend the acts referred to, but that the civil part of the order was purely political; and that the military purposes of the order were confined to the military part of it, and that those who belonged to that part of the organization are alone responsible for it. They can not separate the parts of the order, each belonged to the other, and all those in the civil portion were bound by their oaths to obey the military chiefs. It was only on the hypothesis that the order was illegal as a means and an end, that we could introduce proof of the acts and admissions of its members. Benét, page 291, says:

"The acts and declarations of other conspirators, in the absence of the prisoner, are admissible against him; and the prisoner may be affected by writings from other persons which come into his custody before his apprehension. In these cases the evidence is of a direct nature, applying to the acts in furtherance of a conspiracy, and not circumstantial, as proving only collateral circumstances from which these acts are to be inferred."

11

Let me explain this rule of law, which works no injustice to the accused. On the part of the Government, I may show that the order is a conspiracy, and that the accused is a member of it; and then prove the acts of the body or of any member of it, in pursuance of the general purposes of the order. The accused can not go into isolated facts to show that he is not connected with its purposes. For instance, if I prove that he was consulted at a certain meeting of the order about breaking up the Government, and made attempts to arm the members, they can not rebut it by showing that at other meetings of the order, or at other times and places, he said things in favor of the Government. They attempt to disprove a bad act by proving a good one. If I indict a man for horse-stealing, he can not rebut that crime by proving that he has restored to their owners horses stolen by others. The transactions of this order are made up of separate acts, which I prove as parts of a whole. The accused can rebut or explain what I have undertaken to prove took place at these meetings. They say that Humphreys repudiated this office. They must prove this by showing that he repudiated it to the source from which it came. What he said to this or that man, or to a hundred men, about repudiating that office, is not sufficient proof. The appointment came from the Grand Council, and the official notification would be given by the Grand Commander or Grand Secretary. If he wrote to them repudiating the office, the production of the letter would prove that fact. Or, if the letter could not be produced, if it was lost, he could prove the fact, and prove by the parties who received it what the contents of the letter were. But he can not prove his repudiation of the office by what he has said to other and outside parties. It has been proved that Humphreys was willing to accept a Brigadier Generalship and stay in the rear. They have the right to prove that his command was not of that character. That fact does not show that he was a Brigadier General; but shows that he was so connected with the order, that he had its confidence, and especially does it connect him with the military part of the order. If they prove that no such conversation took place, and no such thing was stated, or that there was no communication on that point, they destroy the evidence adduced on this point. The question is whether the order undertook to make him a Brigadier General.

We also prove that he was with a body of men at a certain time, who were engaged in an illegal act. Let the accused show why he was there. If they prove that he was at the meeting for legal purposes, they have the benefit of it. We prove that he was at a meeting addressed by an avowed rebel. Let them prove that he was not a rebel, and that he made no such speech as is attributed to him. His acts at these times and places show the character of the transaction. But he can not disprove bad acts and speeches, by proving good ones at other times and places.

The law of conspiracy is clear, that its members are bound by the acts of co-conspirators. Whatever Walker or Dodd did at Chicago, or here, in pursuance of the purposes of the order, binds Humphreys, just as though they were proven as acts of Humphreys. Because he is an arm, and Dodd the head in the conspiracy, it is no defense for him to say he is not the head.

The accused have attempted to make a distinction between the Administration and the Government. They can not do this. The Administration is the Government *de facto*. It exists in three branches—the executive, legislative and the judicial departments. They are co-ordinate parts of a whole, and he who arrays himself against any one of these departments contrary to law, commits treason. And when any body of men so far forget themselves as to do this, they must be taught that every part of this Government must be respected, and can only be set aside by legal means. If men plot treason, and array themselves with the enemies of the Government, when it is struggling for its very existence, they must feel the power of that Government, and meet the fate that conspirators and traitors so richly deserve.

The court room was then cleared for deliberation.

On reopening the court room, the Judge Advocate announced to the accused that the objection was sustained.

Mr. Humphreys, on receiving information of his appointment, rejected it.

I remember the time of the excitement at Caledonia, in Sullivan county. I overtook Mr. Humphreys on the road, as he was going there; he said that his purpose in going there was to put down the disturbance and quell the riot, and that he had sent on a couple of men to have the thing stopped; Mr. Snow was the name of one of these men, the name of the other I have forgotten. The men who had arms were stopped by Mr. Humphreys at Caledonia. Mr. Humphreys made a speech of considerable length, urging them to return home, and saying he did not think the soldiers intended to do any thing wrong—that he could not think for a moment that the Government had sent soldiers to trespass upon the rights of citizens. They had taken a horse or two from Mr. Wagner, and another from the widow McBride, and a bridle and saddle from Mr. Pigg; they took his son out through the pasture to make him hunt horses. The report was, that Mr. Pigg had been shot at, and from the appearance of his hat, I should judge he had been. Mr. Humphreys, in his speech, advised the people to go home and behave themselves; he knew that the Government would not send soldiers to harass them; he said the soldiers had made ample satisfaction, and restored the horses to Mr. Wagner; this was four and a half miles from Sullivan. The soldiers had gone toward Sullivan, and the disposition of the crowd was to go after the soldiers; but Mr. Humphreys said that satisfaction had been made as regarded the horses, and it was best to be peaceable and go home. He said if they went to Sullivan they would get to drinking, and get in a row with the soldiers. Mr. Humphreys said that Mr. Cowgill was a Government officer, and must be heard, and he made a speech, and told them to go home. Mr. Cowgill said he could indorse Mr. Humphreys' speech. I don't remember that politics were mentioned in Mr. Humphreys' speech, but the whole tendency of it was for the purpose of quieting the crowd. I have been personally acquainted with Mr. Freeman, the enrolling officer, for four or five years before his death; we lived in the same township. He lived in Sullivan county, Cass township, and Mr. Humphreys lived in Green county; I think they lived about ten or eleven miles from each other.

Q. State whether, at the time of the assassination of Mr. Freeman, and afterward, Mr. Humphreys did not denounce the killing of Mr. Freeman, as a cowardly and base act?

Question objected to, and withdrawn.

I have known Mr. Humphreys very intimately; we boarded and roomed together. I do not know that Mr. Humphreys ever drilled any body of men; I do not think he knows any thing about military tactics.

Q. Are you acquainted with the general character of Mr. Humphreys as a law-abiding, peaceable man, devoted to the maintenance of the laws and Constitution, and the union of his country?

Question objected to, and withdrawn.

Q. Are you acquainted with the general character of Mr. Humphreys?

A. His general character, I think, is good.

Q. Are you acquainted with his general character as a peaceable, law-abiding man, devoted to the conservation of the laws, the Constitution, and the union of the country?

Question objected to by the Judge Advocate, for the reason that it is a leading one, and it covers the very points which this Commission is to decide, whether or not the accused is a law-abiding, peaceful citizen, devoted to the laws of his country. He can introduce testimony as to his general moral character. In some cases, before military courts, the accused can prove his particular traits of character, as in a trial on a charge of cowardice, he can prove particular acts of personal bravery to rebut the charge. It is not permitted to prove by a witness what the Commission is sitting here to determine.

The accused replied:

The Judge Advocate admits that it is competent for us to prove general moral character. That if a witness questions the truth and veracity of the accused, we could prove his general character for truth and veracity. If he were charged with a crime involving a lack of chastity, it would be competent to introduce proof of his general character for chastity. If he were arraigned on a charge involving violence, brutal assault, or murder, it would be competent to introduce proof that his general character was that of a peaceable man, indisposed to quarrels or to participate in them. The charge against the accused is one involving his disposition to obey the laws of his country, and it is on that question that he seeks to introduce proof. He has the right to show his general character for obedience to the laws and the Constitution, and to have the benefit of that evidence on this trial.

Questions as to character are always leading ones. The witness is asked: "Do you know what his general moral character is?" If so, he states whether it is good or bad. General character and general reputation I consider synonymous. We, in like manner, put the question as to his general character as to obedience to the Constitution and laws of his country. The law denies us the privilege of putting other than a leading question. If the witness states that he knows what that character is, we ask him is it good or bad? Surely we ought not to be denied the right to put that question. That is conceded in principle by DeHart in his work on *Military Law*. I quote from page 344:

"The prisoner is allowed to call witnesses to prove his character, but then it must be understood that character unconnected with the charge can not be admitted as evidence to influence the finding of the Court. General character thus presented for the notice of the Court, may be of advantage by modifying the punishment to be decreed by the Court, or presenting the case to the reviewing authority as one in which mercy may be exercised, and thus procure pardon for the offender, of mitigation of the sentence."

The proof must be connected with the charge. One reason why general military character is allowed to be introduced is because it embraces all the specific details which make up that character. That is exactly in point to the present case.

I read still further:

"Courts-martial will always permit the prisoner to present evidence of character, and do not require that it should bear analogy, and have reference to the charge in issue, and such testimony, when the evidence against him is doubtful, may be sufficient to warrant an acquittal. It must be apparent, that wherever intention is a principal ingredient in the offense charged, depending too upon presumptive proof, evidence as to character which applies directly to the nature of the accusation may be exceedingly important."

In this case intention is an important ingredient, showing how and why as a loyal man he connected himself with the order. If he is a loyal man, always obedient to his Government, never in any manner interfering with its peace, nor attempting to break up the Union, this is testimony in his favor, which should be admitted in his favor to rebut the doubtful evidence against him.

The Judge Advocate replied:

It will save the time of the Court to settle these preliminary questions now. I admit most certainly, as the gentleman knows, that you can inquire as to the general character of a person accused of certain classes of offenses. In this case the character of the accused is made up of his acts, they have a right to prove that his acts alleged to be disloyal were not so, but they can not settle the question of character by putting the leading and affirmative question whether he is devoted to the Constitution, laws and Union of his country. They go too far when they attempt that. When they attempt to prove his devotion to the laws and Constitution, they go beyond the bounds allowed as to general character. If they wish to present it as a matter to secure mitigation of the sentence, I may allow its introduction.

I will, however, waive the objection for the present, and allow the question to be put to the witness.

I do know the general character of Mr. Humphreys as a peaceable, law-abiding man, devoted to the conservation of the laws and Constitution, and the Union of his country; and that general character is good.

Q. State whether or not the general character of Mr. Humphreys, during the period of time since the war broke out, has not been that of a peacemaker, and in favor of the enforcement of the laws.

Question objected to.

The accused stated that if the objection was insisted on he should be obliged to go into the detail of the times, and show by what sort of population Mr. Humphreys had been surrounded. He wished to prove his acts right along through this period referred to, by men who were always politically opposed to him.

The Judge Advocate replied:

Then it must be proved by acts and not by opinions—"What have been his acts as a general peacemaker, and what has been his uniform conduct in regard to keeping the country quiet."

The question was withdrawn.

Question. What have been his acts as a peacemaker from the inauguration of the present rebellion to the time he was arrested?

Question objected to, and withdrawn.

Q. What have been his acts from the commencement of the organization of the order at Terre Haute, until his arrest?

Question objected to by the Judge Advocate on the ground that the question must be confined to specific acts.

The question was withdrawn.

Q. Do you remember to have been at any meeting where Mr. Humphreys addressed the people, besides the one you have spoken of?

A. I attended some two or three a year ago. One was at Linton; and he made two or three speeches, at which I was present, from the start of the organization until the time of his arrest. He always advised obedience to the Government and the laws, or words to that effect, and every thing that had not the semblance of law about it, he would not advise obedience to, no matter what it was.

Q. Do you know any thing about his sentiments as to the action of his friends at the time of his arrest?

Question objected to, and withdrawn.

A. Before Mr. Humphreys was arrested, it was frequently talked about by us.

Q. When he received this report, what course of conduct did he advise his friends to take?

Question objected to, and withdrawn.

Q. State what you know, if any thing, about Mr. Humphreys having incurred the displeasure of his party friends, because he insisted on obedience to the laws and the draft?

Question objected to, and withdrawn.

Q. State what you know, if any thing, about Mr. Humphreys having repudiated Dodd and his schemes?

The Judge Advocate objected to the question because it was not confined to a particular time.

Q. State what you know of Mr. Humphreys' repudiation of Dodd and his schemes during last summer?

Question objected to, and withdrawn.

Q. State what you know on that point during his connection with the order?

Question objected to, and withdrawn.

Q. State whether, from the 16th of last February up to the time of his arrest, Mr. Humphreys did not repudiate any public and private scheme of Mr. Dodd?

Question objected to by the Judge Advocate.

The court room was then cleared for deliberation. On being reopened, the Judge Advocate announced to the accused that the objection was sustained.

After I returned home from Indianapolis, I went to Mr. Humphreys and talked with him about the order. He then went to the secretary of the temple, got the papers and destroyed them. He said he had not understood before that it was a military organization; and as soon as he learned what were the purposes of the military organization, he said he would have nothing more to do with it. That was shortly after his appointment as Major General. Mr. Gray, who had the papers, was the secretary of the township temple. I received my first degree at our township temple; the second degree I took in this city, in February, after which I returned home and informed Mr. Humphreys of his appointment as Major General. I never met with any temple after that, nor to my knowledge has Mr. Humphreys. I believe I saw Mr. Humphreys in about ten days after I returned home from this city; and the papers must have been destroyed by him in March; they were destroyed in our store; I saw him tear them up. I do not know what papers they were, for I did not read them; Mr. Humphreys, Gray and myself, were at that time partners. In reference to that meeting of armed citizens, Mr. Humphreys said they had sent for him; he went, and advised them to go home and be peaceable; that the soldiers did not mean to harm them. I have heard that the horse that was taken by the soldiers, was taken to carry a sick soldier a few miles, and that it was so stated, and would be returned. I believe the horses that were taken, were all returned. Mr. Humphreys might have been armed, as he generally carried a revolver. I did not hear any threats made against Mr. Cowgill at that meeting; the people listened to Mr. Cowgill while he was speaking, and heard all he had to say. The crowd said they came there to get their property from the soldiers. I did not hear any threats made against the soldiers or the Government; nor did I hear Mr. Lincoln's name mentioned. Nor did I hear Mr. Humphreys advise the people to go home, but not to sleep too soundly, though I was there all the time. I know Mr. Humphreys said that Mr. Cowgill had been appointed by the Government, and that he must be heard; and I think he was listened to as attentively as Mr. Humphreys was. I have heard Mr. Humphreys during the summer say, that he did not indorse Mr. Lincoln's policy respecting the war, and that he thought the policy of arming the negroes was bad; that the way to remedy it was to beat him at the next election. I have heard him say it was the duty of the people to obey the laws. I never heard any thing about arming members of the order, till I heard of Dodd's having arms here; and I never knew any thing of the military organization till the appointment of the Major Generals. I understood at the February meeting, that the State was divided into three or four districts, and a Major General was appointed for each district, and their commands, I supposed, were to consist of the members of the Order of American Knights; I knew nothing of the change of the name of the order to the Sons of Liberty. I do not know positively whether Mr. Humphreys was at home on the 14th of June; the books do not show any handwriting made by him on that day, though he is in the habit of making entries. I know he was at home on the 13th. I never saw any members of the organization drill with or without arms. No assessment on our lodge was made, that I know of, for the purchase of arms, or for any other purpose.

RE-EXAMINATION.

It was stated at the February meeting of the order. held in this city, that the object of the order was the more perfect organization of the Democratic party, the establishment of a newspaper, and the distribution of campaign documents, etc.; I am not aware that it had any other than a political object, except the appointment of these officers; and I did not know the purpose for which those appointments were made. I heard Mr. Humphreys say at Linton, that we ought to obey the laws as long as they were laws, no matter how oppressive they might be, and that good citizens would do so; that we must bear with them until we had a change in the Administration. The last entry but one made in our books on the 13th of June, for articles sold, is in the handwriting of Mr. Humphreys. It is sixteen miles from our place of business to Sullivan, the nearest point at which Mr. Humphreys could have taken the cars for this city; and had he left by the first train, he would not probably have been here till 7 o'clock on the evening of the 14th of June.

The Commission then adjourned, to meet on Friday, November 18, 1864, at 9 o'clock, A. M.

COURT ROOM, INDIANAPOLIS, INDIANA,
November 18, 1864, 9 o'clock, A. M.

The Commission met pursuant to adjournment.

All the members present. Also, the Judge Advocate, the accused (except W. A. Bowles), and their counsel.

The proceedings were read and approved.

D. O. DAILEY, a witness for the accused, was then introduced, and, being duly sworn by the Judge Advocate, testified as follows:

I reside in Huntington, Indiana. and am a lawyer. I have been intimately acquainted with Mr. Milligan eight years; and during the greater part of that time have practiced at the same bar; politically, I am not a sympathizer with Mr. Milligan.

Q. You may state what is Mr. Milligan's peculiar characteristic with regard to the concealment of his sentiments, or the expression of them openly and publicly, without concealment.

Question objected to by the Judge Advocate as immaterial and irrelevant.

The Court was cleared for deliberation. On being reopened, the Judge Advocate announced to the accused that the objection was sustained.

I am acquainted with Mr. Milligan's character in the neighborhood in which he lives, and it is good. His general character as a peaceable, law-abiding citizen, is good, as far as I understand it. During the last year he has not taken an active part in politics, and during the campaign he took no part at all. Mr. Milligan, as a citizen, has the reputation of being a straight-forward, law-abiding man; as a lawyer, I think him very able; as a politician, I do not think he amounts to any thing at all, for this reason, that he takes special occasion to publish the most ultra and obnoxious sentiments; and this he has always done, as far as my knowledge extends. Mr. Milligan, I know, was at home on the 22d of February; he was there when I went away; I returned on the night of the 23d, and went to Court next morning, and Mr. Milligan was there.

On the 20th of July, I know, by reference to my papers, that Mr. Milligan and myself were engaged in Huntington, in the case of *Ripley* vs. *Ripley*, before the Mayor.

RICHARD A. CURREN, a witness for the accused, was then introduced, and, being duly sworn by the Judge Advocate, testified as follows:

My residence is in Huntington; I am a Presbyterian minister, belonging to that part of the Presbyterian body generally denominated old school; my ecclesiastical connection, presbyterially, is with the presbytery of Fort Wayne, and synodically with the presbytery of Northern Indiana. I am acquainted with Mr. Milligan; I have known him intimately for the past six years. When Mr. Milligan attends ministerial services any-where, he generally attends mine. The general moral character of Mr. Milligan is good. I am acquainted with his general reputation as a peaceable, law-abiding citizen, devoted to the Constitution and the institutions of our country; and that reputation is generally good.

Q. Have you any means of knowing Mr. Milligan's private or particular views upon the subject of revolution in this State, in the North-west, or in the United States?

A. I have on several occasions had conversations with Mr. Milligan on that subject.

Q. You may state them.

The Judge Advocate objected to the question, stating his objection as follows:

It is perfectly apparent that what Mr. Milligan might have said in outside conversations, is immaterial to this Court. It is immaterial and illegitimate. I do not propose to argue that point. The Commission, I think, have already passed upon that question.

The counsel for the accused replied:

I propose to limit the time of this conversation to that covered by the alleged conspiracy. We claim the right to show that the purpose Mr. Milligan had in view in going into the order, was to control and direct it so that it should do no mischief. If his declarations, which are a part of the *res gestæ*, are not admitted in evidence, we can not show his real purposes, which may have been laudable. His declarations as to his purposes, are accompanying facts, and are, we contend, competent in evidence. The counsel here cited *De Hart, page* 354. Then, again, in the case cited in *Hanson*, of *The Queen* vs. *Lambert*, growing out of the Chartist case, Lambert was allowed to introduce testimony to show that he had made speeches in favor of law and order.

The same principle is admitted in the case of *Rex* vs. *Whitehead*, 11th *English Common Law Reports, page* 316. *Roscoe*, in his work on *Criminal Evidence*, remarks in this case: "On the trial of an indictment for conspiracy to defraud, the written correspondence of the defendant with another of the conspirators, relating to the transaction in question, was allowed to be read, in order to show that the defendant was deceived by his correspondent, and was not a participant in the fraud." Per Best, J., "I think them admissible, for what the parties say at the time, is evidence to show how they acted;" page 89. The same author, on page 22, says: "Where the inquiry is into the nature and character of a certain transaction, not only what was done, but also what was said by *both* parties, during the continuance of the transaction, is admissible; for to exclude this, would be to exclude the most important and unexceptionable evidence. In this case, it is not the relation of third persons unconnected with the fact, which is received, but the declarations of the parties to the facts themselves, or of others connected with them in the transactions, which are admitted for the purpose of illustrating its peculiar character and circumstances. Thus it has been held on a prosecution for high treason, that the cry of the mob who accompanied the prisoner, may be received in evidence as part of the conversation."

In a foot note, the author says:

"Where the state of mind, sentiment or disposition of a person at a given period become pertinent topics of inquiry, his declarations and conversations, being part of the *res gestæ*, may be resorted to. *Bartholomy* vs. *The People*, 2 *Hill*, 248."

These decisions apply to the present case. It has been claimed that this organization was both civil and military, each being distinct. It is proper to show the declarations of the accused, in order to show to which branch of the organization he belonged. If he expressed contempt for the office of Major General, and denounced the military organization, it becomes an important part of the *res gestæ*, to show that he had nothing to do with, nor any sympathy with, the ulterior purposes of this organization. It certainly will not be claimed that each one of the eighteen thousand men who have joined this organization is responsible for the acts of Dodd and company.

Page 24, the same author says:

"If it be material to inquire whether a certain person gave a particular order on a certain day what he has said or written, may be evidence of the order (see *Jenkins' case*, 1 *Lewin*, *C. C.*, 114); or where it is material to inquire whether a certain fact, be it true or false, has come to the knowledge of a third person, what he has said or written, may as clearly show his knowledge, as what he has done."

Russell on *Crime*, 2d vol., page 779, says on the same point:

"As other acts and declarations of the prisoner, besides those charged in the indictment, may be given in evidence on the part of the prosecution, so he himself in his defense may, in some cases, prove other acts and declarations of his own, as evidence of his innocence. Thus on a charge of murder, expressions of good will and acts of kindness, on the part of the prisoner toward the deceased, are always considered important evidence, as showing what was his general disposition toward the deceased, from which the jury may be led to conclude that his intention could not have been what the charge imputes." Also the case of *Rex* vs. *Lambert*, the cases of *Walker*, *Hardy*, *Horne Tooke*, and *Whitehead*, *Russell*, pp. 779, 780.

In the case reported in 29th *Georgia Reports*, page 430, *Freeman* vs. *The State*, on a charge of taking a slave from his master, the defendant was permitted to introduce his whole declarations while carrying off the negro, as giving character to the act itself.

As the transactions which, it is alleged, the prisoner was a party to, were each for the overthrow of the Government, it is proper to introduce the declarations of the prisoner as part of the *res gestæ*, and as showing his intent.

The Judge Advocate replied:

In proving a case against the accused, we prove his acts; and the only reason why his *words* are permitted to be proven in the case, is that they tend to prove what his acts have been. They are admissions of acts. You can prove admissions against himself, because the law says a man is not going to make admissions against his own interest.

That is the reason why his words, which are admissions, are permitted to be proved against him. But you can not prove his declarations which are in his own favor, because it is maintained to be constantly giving a favorable tinge to his own conduct. The only case, in which the declarations of the accused in his favor can be given, is when they constitute a part of the distinct act charged, and are a part of the *res gestæ*. The words which a man utters while doing an act can be proved, because they are in reality a part of the acts. The Government proves that Humphreys was at a certain illegal meeting. He proves what he said in going, as to his purposes and intentions in going, and what he did, and I do not object, because it is part of the act itself. The defense can not introduce any declarations except as they become a part of the *res gestæ*. We prove particular acts, at certain times and places, months intervening between them. The accused can not step in and prove, that between these times, at other places, he made assertions of loyalty. He can not thus purge himself of crime.

And further, I do distinctly assert, that these eighteen thousand members of the Order of American Knights, or Sons of Liberty, are all of them parties to this conspiracy, and held responsible for what Dodd and others did. I do maintain that when they joined that order with these oaths, they took upon themselves the responsibility for the acts of every member who took the same oaths. They can prove character, and the extent of their knowledge of the bad purpose of the order, only in mitigation of their sentence. When they joined an illegal body they became responsible for the acts of all. That is the rule of law; the *onus* is then upon them; and they can only meet the proof by showing a want of knowledge of the extreme criminal intents of the order, and that they took only the first or vestibule degree. That lack of criminal knowledge would go in mitigation of the sentence.

The court room was then cleared for deliberation on the objection of the Judge Advocate.

On reopening the Court, the Judge Advocate announced that the objection had been sustained and the question overruled.

I have heard public declarations made by Mr. Milligan about the Order of the Sons of Liberty, in the presence of a large crowd, and about his being made a Major General in the organization. That declaration was made on Jefferson street, in Huntington, and there may have been fifteen or twenty persons present.

Q. State what these declarations were.

Question objected to by the Judge Advocate.

The Court was then cleared for deliberation. On being reopened, the Judge Advocate announced to the accused that the objection was sustained.

This was some considerable length of time before Mr. Milligan's arrest, and was at the time I first heard of the office of Major General being conferred upon him. It was before Dodd's arrest, and was about the time of the exposure of the order in the public prints, though I had not at that time seen them myself.

I am acquainted with Dr. Zumro, and have for the past four years been quite intimately acquainted. He lives in Rock Creek, and I preach within four and half miles of the place, and a portion of my congregation reside in Dr. Zumro's visiting district. I am acquainted with his general reputation for truth and veracity in the neighborhood where he lives. That general reputation is bad: and from that reputation I would not believe him under oath.

CROSS-EXAMINATION.

His reputation is bad among the class of men that attend upon my ministry. I am a Democrat, but do not consider myself a Butternut.

I have heard Mr. Samuel D. Hays frequently say that Dr. Zumro was not to be trusted—that he would not place confidence in his word. Mr. Hays is a Democrat. I have also heard Mr. Samuel Brubaker say, during the past four or five years, that Zumro was not a man of truth. I heard him say this during last summer. I have heard Dr. Zumro thus spoken of within a month. Mr. Brubaker also spoke of Dr. Zumro as being a traitor to the Democratic party—professing to vote the Democratic ticket, when he held exactly the opposite sentiments.

I have heard Mr. John Brubaker frequently speak of him in the same way. I have heard him so speak within the last two months, when I was at his house. Dr. Zumro had complained to me that the Democrats had not patronized him—that after he had voted the Democratic ticket, his patronage had fallen off, and requested me to make use of my influence to get people to employ him. In the course of the conversation, Mr. Brubaker said that he had no confidence in the Doctor. Mr. Brubaker and his brother are Democrats. I have also heard James Bandwit represent him as a decidedly deceptive man; Mr. Bandwit is a Democrat. I have heard Mr. Peter Bandwit speak of him in the same way. I have known Mr. Peter Bandwit for six years, but I do not know whether he is a Democrat or not.

Soon after I became acquainted with Dr. Zumro, I was cautioned as to the amount of confidence I should place in him. I heard his character spoken of to great disadvantage fully four years ago. At one time I felt interested in him; I stayed at his house one night, and have called on him often, and he has called at our house, and we regarded him as a pleasant man; but he did his utmost to get me and others into this organization, and thus involve us in trouble. I have no particular animosity toward the Doctor on that ground. Since the sitting of this Commission, I have refused to hold any communication with him, as I do not consider it safe to talk with him. But I had the most kindly feeling toward him, up to the time I discovered his treachery toward me; still I have no ill feeling toward him. I could do him a kindness now as well as I ever did. It is not a fact that the church over which I preside is composed almost entirely of Democrats; nor is it true that Union men have refused to attend my preaching on account of my disloyal sentiments. I suppose that most of those who attend my preaching belong to the Democratic party, but others do attend. The Democrats would be but a small majority. I have not said to any person that the Republicans refused to attend my ministry.

I never excluded one of my own daughters from my house for marrying a Union man, nor did I threaten to whip her for that offense. I never laid a hand on her. My daughter visits my house now when she is inclined, and my wife visits her.

Q. Did you use any violence whatever toward her?

A. None whatever.

Q. Did you not call her an Abolitionist?

A. I never did.

Q. Have you not yourself, and have not members of your family, worn Butternut badges at public meetings?

A. No, sir; neither myself nor family; I do not approve of such things.

RE-EXAMINATION.

The trouble about my daughter grew out of the fact that I did not wish her to marry at that time, on account of her ill health; she was at that time suffering from the effects of a sun-stroke. After she had left my house I was so interested in her, that I went after her in company with Mr. Colfroth.

Some of the strongest Republicans in the town of Huntington have attended my preaching, among others Mr. Davis, who said the reason he attended, was because I abused no persons, but preached the gospel. I received a Christmas present of four or five hundred dollars; I was furnished with a list of the donors, and many of them were Republicans. Mr. Milligan's name was not on the list. The men whom I have mentioned as speaking of Dr. Zumro's character, are the most respectable farmers in the place, and there are others I have not mentioned, who speak of him in the same way; that reputation has been the same for some years past. Those who have thus spoken against Dr. Zumro are not, according to their own declarations, members of the Order of American Knights or Sons of Liberty.

The Commission then adjourned, to meet at 2 o'clock.

AFTERNOON SESSION.

COURT ROOM, INDIANAPOLIS, INDIANA, }
November 18, 1864, 2 o'clock, P. M. }

The Commission met pursuant to adjournment.

All the members present; also, the Judge Advocate, the accused (except W. A. Bowles), and their counsel.

JOHN G. SCOTTON, a witness for the accused, was then introduced, and, being duly sworn by the Judge Advocate, testified as follows:

I live in Huntington, and am a farmer; I am Justice of the Peace. I have lived in the neighborhood twenty-two years. I have known Dr. Zumro about seven years, and I am acquainted with his general reputation for truth and veracity in the neighborhood in which he lives. That reputation is bad; and from that general reputation I would not believe him under oath.

CROSS-EXAMINATION.

I have heard Albert Draper, who I believe is a Republican, say that Dr. Zumro was not an honest man; I do not know that he said any thing against his truth and veracity. I have heard Dr. Scott say, that he did not consider him a true man; he said he was a bad man. I have heard Thomas Smith speak of him; his opinion was, that he was a mean man. I have heard Jacob Rausch say that he was a damned mean man, and that he would not believe him under oath. Adam Smith spoke against his truth and veracity.

Q. Do you belong to the Union or the Democratic party?

Question objected to by the accused.

The Court was then cleared for deliberation; on being reopened, it was announced by the Judge Advocate that the objection was overruled.

A. I voted the Democratic ticket. I do not belong to any secret organization. I do not know but that I joined a secret order called the "Mighty Host." I took the oath, but never acted with them.

RE-EXAMINATION.

Dr. Scott, Adam Smith, and Mr. Draper, of whom I have spoken, are Republicans. For the last four years Dr. Zumro has been holding himself out as a Democrat, professing to act with the Democratic party. It was during this time that these Democrats thus spoke of him.

WILLIAM SATLER, a witness for the accused,

was then introduced, and being duly sworn by the Judge Advocate, testified as follows:

I reside in Markle, and am a house carpenter; I have lived there some twelve or thirteen years; I have known Dr. Zumro ever since I have lived in the place. I know his general reputation for truth and veracity; that reputation is bad; and I would not believe him under oath.

CROSS-EXAMINATION.

I am a Democrat; I belonged to a secret society called the Mighty Host I do not know that that society merged into the Sons of Liberty, though I saw it mentioned in the papers. Dr. Zumro and I have not been friends, but I have never to any person made threats against Dr. Zumro.

RE-EXAMINATION.

The society called the "Mighty Host," existed about three years ago, and I was only present at one meeting, and had nothing to do with it afterward.

GEORGE BAILEY, a witness for the accused, was then introduced, and, being duly sworn by the Judge Advocate, testified as follows:

I reside in Union township, Wells county, Indiana, and am a house carpenter; I have known Dr. Zumro seven or eight years. I am acquainted with his reputation for truth and veracity; it is bad, and I would not believe him under oath.

CROSS-EXAMINATION.

I have always voted the Democratic ticket. I belonged to the Order of the Sons of Liberty, but only attended two meetings. I also belonged to the society called the Mighty Host; that was before the Sons of Liberty.

RE-EXAMINATION.

I have heard conversations in regard to Dr. Zumro's want of truth and veracity, from both Republicans and Democrats.

WILLIAM ALLEN, a witness for the accused, was then introduced, and, being duly sworn by the Judge Advocate, testified as follows:

I live in Markle, Huntington county, Indiana, and am a blacksmith. I have been acquainted with Dr. Zumro seven or eight years. I am acquainted with his reputation for truth and veracity, and that reputation is bad; I would not believe him under oath.

CROSS-EXAMINATION.

I belong to the Democratic party I think Dr. Zumro's reputation in the neighborhood in which he lives may be as good as my own. I have never heard Mr. Coffroth say in the Common Pleas Court, of our county, that he would not believe him under oath. I am not a member of the Order of Sons of Liberty, nor of the Circle of the Mighty Host.

WILLIAM WOLF, a witness for the accused, was then introduced, and, being duly sworn by the Judge Advocate, testified as follows:

I live in Rock Creek township, and am a farmer. I am acquainted with the reputation of Dr. Zumro for truth and veracity in the neighborhood in which he lives. That reputation, from what I have learned, is bad, and I would not believe him under oath.

CROSS-EXAMINATION.

I belong to the Democratic party. I joined a secret society that, I think, was called the Circle of the Mighty Host, but I only attended one meeting. I never learned what was the purpose and object of the order, and I left it because I thought it did not amount to much. I understood it was a loyal organization.

W. M. SWASEY, a witness for the accused, was then introduced, and, being duly sworn by the Judge Advocate, testified as follows:

I reside in Huntington, and am a physician and surgeon. I have practiced medicine for twenty years. I have been Mr. Milligan's physician since I have been at Huntington—though Dr. Layman has attended Mrs. Milligan. Mr. Milligan was taken sick in August, and consulted me before he went to the Chicago Convention; he again consulted me after his return. My first charge I notice is for the 7th of September. About the 12th of September I first visited Mr. Milligan, when he was confined to his bed with bilious intermitting fever of the nervous character, which had assumed a typhoid form. I had to administer calomel, mercurials and opiates. He was consequently very nervous and irritable, and was scarcely rational any part of the time I was there during my daily visits. I continued to treat him up to the time he was arrested, and though much improved, he was then very feeble. On the 12th, when I commenced giving him opium and morphine with mercurials and quinine, and for ten days from the 12th, he was continually under the influence of anodynes. During this time he was what might be called flighty.

GEORGE BAILEY was then recalled as a witness for the Government, and testified as follows:

The witness was requested to look at the following obligation, and state if that was the obligation of the Mighty Host.

The following oath, purporting to be the obligation administered to the Knights of the Golden Circle in De Kalb and Allen counties, Indiana, was then read by the Judge Advocate:

"I, —— ——, do solemnly swear, in the presence of Almighty God, that I will go to the relief of all good and loyal Democrats, and will not suffer the confiscation of their property, either North or South; and I further promise that I will suffer my body to be severed in four parts, one part to be cast out at the east gate, one part out at the west gate, one part out at the north gate, and one part out at the south gate, before I will suffer the privileges bequeathed by our forefathers to be blotted out or trampled under foot forever. I further promise and swear, that I will go to the aid, from the first to the fourth signal, of all Democrats, North or South. I further promise and swear, that I will not reveal any of the secret signs, passwords, or grips, to any one not legally authorized by this order to receive the same, binding myself under no less a penalty than having my bowels torn out, and cast out to the four winds of heaven; so help me God. I further promise and swear, that I will do all in my power to bring all good Democrats into this Circle of Hosts. I further promise and swear, that I will do all in my power, by all honorable means, and all other means in reach, to subvert, or overthrow, the present damnable, Yankee, Abolition Administration; so help me God."

I do not think this is the obligation I took; nor do I ever remember hearing of such a one. The obligation I took agreed to sustain the Constitution of the United States, and the Constitution of Indiana. The penalty for revealing the secrets of the society, was, that we were to be torn into four parts.

The Commission then adjourned, to meet on Monday, the 21st of November, 1864, at 2 o'clock, P. M.

———

COURT ROOM, INDIANAPOLIS, INDIANA, }
November 21, 1864, 2 o'clock, P. M. }

The Commission met pursuant to adjournment.

All the members present. Also, the Judge Advocate, the accused (except W. A. Bowles), and their counsel.

The proceedings were read and approved.

The following dispatch was then read to the Court by the Judge Advocate:

"WASHINGTON, D. C., November 18, 1864.

"To Major H. L. Burnett, Judge Advocate:

"This is authority from the Secretary of War to retain Colonel Ansel D. Wass, 60th Massachusetts, as member of Court-martial, as requested in your telegram of yesterday, to Judge Advocate General.

[Signed]   "THOS. M. VINCENT,
                            "A. A. G."

The following was then submitted by the counsel for the accused, William A. Bowles:

"To the President and Members of the Military Commission:

"I hereby waive any objection to the absence of Colonel A. D. Wass, 60th Massachusetts, during the past few days; and do now consent to his taking his seat as a member of the Commission, and request that he may do so; and I hereby waive all objections that might otherwise be raised against his remaining on said Commission, until the close of my trial; and legalize and sanction the same as far as my request and full consent thereto can possibly do.

[Signed]   "W. A. BOWLES.
" November 21, 1864.
[Signed]   "J. W. GORDON,
"M. M. RAY."

Colonel Wass, being present in Court, by consent and expressed desire of all the accused, then took his seat as a member of the Commission.

WILLIAM HINES, a witness for the accused, was then introduced, and, being duly sworn by the Judge Advocate, testified as follows:

I live in Green county, in this State, and am a farmer. I am acquainted with the accused, Andrew Humphreys. I have known him from twelve to fourteen years. Politically, we do not agree. I know that Mr. Humphreys has abused the Administration since the war broke out. Since that time I have heard him deliver two political speeches. In the first speech I heard him make, he criticised the acts of the Government pretty severely. Speaking in relation to the draft, and obedience to the law, he used about this language: "I advise no man to resist the draft, nor evade any law passed by Congress, but I advise all to be good, law-abiding citizens." That speech was made during the summer of 1863, in Green county, on what is called the Five Mile Prairie. It was delivered to the citizens of Washington township; and there were, perhaps, one hundred or one hundred and fifty men and women there. In his remarks he paid a good deal of attention to the financial policy of Mr. Chase. He wound up by telling the people that they had better not resist the draft, or the law of the United States. There had been some talk about house-burning, and I remember Mr. Humphreys directed his remarks to me in his speech, and said that he would knock the chunk out of any man's hand that would attempt to set fire to my property, or to any Republican's property. I think I was the only Republican at the meeting. The next occasion on which I heard him, was about the middle of September last, a few days prior to his arrest. He was speaking to the citizens of Green and Sullivan counties. This speech was made in the town of Linton. I was only passing by, and heard but part of it. A good many people were present. I heard him say that resistance to the Government would not do at all, in any shape or form. That resistance was sure to bring disaster upon them. That they must remain at home, and quietly submit to the laws of the Government. I believe he proposed to receive money to pay for substitutes for drafted men, who could not afford to get them themselves. I may have heard him speak five minutes; I was sitting on my horse at the time; I did not hear any one else address the meeting. He exhorted them to obey the laws. There seemed to be some excitement among a part of those who were present, and I think it was in regard to the resistance of the draft. I so judged from what I heard them say. The reason why the people were "down" on him, as I understood, was for advising them to submit to the draft. Mr. Humphreys has for years been an active Democrat, and has usually taken an active part in all political matters in the county. He is a man of influence in the party. I believe Mr. Humphreys' reputation is that of a moral man; I do not know that he is a religious man, or that he makes any pretensions to religion. As to his political principles, some of my friends call him a "Butternut" and a "Copperhead," and even a "traitor," speaking of him politically. Outside of mere political controversies, I believe that the majority of his neighbors consider him a loyal man.

WILLIAM JOHNSON, a witness for the accused, was then introduced, and, being duly sworn by the Judge Advocate, testified as follows:

I reside in Green county, Indiana. I am a farmer. I am acquainted with Andrew Humphreys; I live about a mile and a half from where he does business, and about six miles from his residence. I have known him for ten years. I am acquainted with his general reputation and moral character, and as a law-abiding citizen, and it is good. Politically, I differ from Mr. Humphreys. His general reputation outside of what politicians say in our county, and so far as I know, he is respected by both parties. I heard him make a speech, I think, in August last, in Linton, Green county. It was delivered to the citizens of Green and Sullivan counties. It was a Democratic political meeting. Mr. Burton, of Sullivan, spoke. Mr. Humphreys, in his remarks, quoted from Jefferson's writings, and from Washington's farewell address; and he spoke of secession as the right of a State.

He uttered no sentiment or exhortation to the people to resist the laws, or to oppose the Government. Mr. Humphreys has always expressed himself personally to me in favor of obedience to the laws.

Q. State whether or not Andrew Humphreys in the localities of Green and Sullivan counties has, according to your observation, been engaged in exciting and inflaming, or allaying the passions of the people?

Question objected to by the Judge Advocate, and withdrawn.

CROSS-EXAMINATION.

In Mr. Humphreys' speech, I understood him to argue in favor of the right of a State to secede, and that secession, therefore, was right. I can not say that he endeavored to convince the people of this in his speech, but such seemed to be the inference from the extracts which he read. Among the people of our county, the character of Mr. Humphreys is not considered loyal.

RE-EXAMINATION.

When I speak of those who do not consider Mr. Humphreys loyal, I mean the Union party, and it embraces some Democrats. I only consider those loyal who are in favor of the prosecution of the war for the suppression of the rebellion. That is my only test of loyalty.

Q. Did he argue that while the Federal Government could enforce its laws against *individuals*, that yet there was no power to coerce *States* in their sovereign capacity?

Question objected to by the Judge Advocate, and withdrawn.

The Commission then adjourned, to meet on Tuesday, November 22, at 10 o'clock, A. M.

COURT ROOM, INDIANAPOLIS, INDIANA,
November 22, 1864, 10 o'clock, A. M.

The Commission met pursuant to adjournment.

All the members present. Also, the Judge Advocate, the accused (except W. A. Bowles), and their counsel.

The proceedings were read and approved.

WILLIAM C. KOCHER, a witness for the accused, was then introduced, and, being duly sworn by the Judge Advocate, testified as follows:

I reside in Huntington county, and practice law. I am Mayor of Huntington borough. I have known Mr. Milligan for ten years; and am acquainted with his general moral reputation, in the neighborhood in which he lives; that reputation is good. His reputation also as a peaceable, orderly, law-abiding citizen has been good in that community as far as I know. The relations existing between myself and Mr. Milligan since the summer of 1855, have not been friendly.

CROSS-EXAMINATION.

The reason why my relations have not been very friendly with Mr. Milligan are, that when I came to Indiana, a young man and a stranger, Mr. Milligan was one of the older members of the bar, and he took a strong position against me. I am not aware that he had any reason for so doing. He opposed other young attorneys in that place in like manner. His opposition took the form of brow-beating when I appeared as counsel on the opposite side. In politics I am a Democrat, though I do not belong to Mr. Milligan's party; I am a War Democrat. In saying that Mr. Milligan's general character is good, I do not refer to his reputation as a loyal man in the support of his Government.

JOSEPH JOHNSON, a witness for the accused, was then introduced, and, being duly sworn by the Judge Advocate, testified as follows:

I reside in Wells county; my occupation is farming. I am acquainted with Dr. Zumro, of Markle; I have known him some ten years. I am acquainted with his general reputation for truth and veracity in the neighborhood in which he lives, and know that that reputation is bad, and I could not believe him under oath. I became a member of the Sons of Liberty about June or July last, in Rockcreek township, Wells county. I was initiated in company with Dr. Zumro, John Hautz, Isaac Decker, Henry Johnson and Nathan Johnson; I joined at the solicitation of Dr. Zumro. Dr. Horton, who initiated us, told us it was an organization to support the Constitution of the United States, and the Constitution of the State of Indiana, and to protect the rights and liberties of the people at the ballot-box. He said nothing about the organization being intended to subdue the Abolitionists, resist the draft, or assist the Southern Confederacy. The military part of the organization was gotten up by Dr. Zumro, or, at any rate, the subject was introduced by him, but for what purposes I can not tell. I went with Dr. Zumro, at his request, in September, to see Mr. Milligan. Dr. Zumro asked him what we should do about the draft; Mr. Milligan's reply was, "We can not do any thing." Dr. Zumro asked what the boys were doing about Huntington; his reply was, "They are doing the best they can, they are hiring substitutes, and every man is taking care of himself in the best manner he can." The Doctor said, "I do not like to submit to the draft myself, but I think it would be a poor chance for a man to try to get away." Mr. Milligan replied, "If I were to make an attempt to get away, I would not be afraid of twenty men arresting me." Nothing was stated to the effect that if a revolt was started by ten men, others would flock in in large numbers; Mr. Milligan at the time was very sick on his bed. The Doctor spoke a few words to him, and he replied that he was very weak, and did not wish to converse. Dr. Zumro stated to me, after leaving Mr. Milligan, that if he was drafted he would take medicine and be sick all the time, and if I was drafted he would serve me in the same way. When Dr. Zumro asked Mr. Milligan what the order was going to do about the draft, to the best of my recollection Mr. Milligan said that the order was disbanded, and that he could not expect any thing from it.

CROSS-EXAMINATION.

On the morning of the day on which I saw Mr. Milligan, I called at Dr. Zumro's house, as we had arranged the night before at a meeting of the Sons of Liberty; some twenty-five or thirty members were present, and John Hautz, who was the Grand Seignior, presided. At that meeting Dr. Zumro was requested by some members to go to Huntington to see Mr. Milligan, and the Doctor invited me to accompany him. It is eleven miles from where I live, and we went on horseback. The meeting was held at Jacob Farling's, Rockcreek township, Wells county, and Dr. Zumro was the only member present from Huntington county. I never attended any meeting at Huntington township. I think that Mr. Milligan had said that the order was disbanded; it was not at that time in our township; I did not, however, so state to Mr. Milligan. Dr. Zumro was appointed by the meeting in general, as a committee to visit Huntington; at the same time Jacob Farling was sent to Bluffton to see what they were going to do about the draft, I suppose. Nothing was said in the meeting, to my knowledge, as to what they were to be sent for, or who they were to see; and it was only as we were going along, that Dr. Zumro said that he thought Mr. Milligan was about as good a man to see as we could go to. The military article which Dr. Zumro introduced to the order, he said, was written by Mr. Milligan; at the next meeting he pretended Mr. Ibach wrote it; I do not remember how many members signed it; I did; but I never drilled. There was no rule requiring us to drill. I have no arms, except a rifle and a revolver, which I have had for some years. The draft was frequently spoken of by members, but no decision was come to. Some talked of hiring substitutes, and others proposed running off. Something might have been said about resisting the draft, but not by the leaders of the organization. Some said, "I will resist;" some, "I will fight or run off." On our return from Huntington we met Mr. Samuel Day; but I did not say to him or to Mr. Coffroth, or Mr. Winters, whom we saw afterward, that Mr. Milligan had advised resistance to the draft, nor did I hear it said by any body. Mr. Coffroth, I remember, advised us to go home and rest easy about the draft, or something like that.*

Sᴀᴍᴜᴇʟ Wɪɴᴛᴇʀs, a witness for the accused, was then introduced, and, being duly sworn by the Judge Advocate, testified as follows:

* In giving the testimony of unimportant witnesses, it has been the aim of the Editor to omit all irrelevant matter, or matter that did not elicit, or confirm, some fact inquired for. The record of the examination of this witness—an exceedingly ignorant one—fills thirty-nine pages of legal cap, averaging two hundred words to a page, but the brief synopsis here given contains all the facts to which he testified.

I reside in Huntington, Indiana, where I publish the Huntington *Democrat*, a Democratic newspaper. I became a member of the American Knights—but not of the Sons of Liberty—in Huntington, sometime in October, 1863. Mr. Milligan was a member of that association, but held no office. He used his influence to prevent any but responsible and respectable men from becoming members; I never knew of any efforts on his part to extend the organization or establish branch temples. The order was disbanded sometime in April, and we ceased to meet as an organization. It never was merged into the Sons of Liberty. I was a delegate from the Huntington temple to the Council held here in February; Mr. Milligan was not present; I know it from the fact that I asked him to attend with me, and he declined on account of being too unwell. I attended the meeting of the Council on the afternoon of the 17th; I know nothing of Mr. Milligan's appointment as Major General.

I am only slightly acquainted with Dr. Zumro; I know him when I see him. In September last he called at my office in company with another man, and asked me what the order was going to do about the draft; I asked "What order?" He then asked, "What are the boys going to do about the draft?" I said, "I do not know." I inquired, "What do you propose to do?" His reply was, "to resist it;" to which I rejoined, "If you think so, why the devil don't you resist it?" I had no knowledge at the time of the part he was playing, but I did not trust him, and did not want to have any thing to do with him.

I understood the object of the Order of American Knights was to disseminate correct political principles in relation to the theory of our Government; and also as an offset to the Union League in our county. I understood it to be a purely political organization, and it had no avowed purpose of resisting the draft or any law of the Government.

I was present at the Fort Wayne meeting, and heard the whole of Mr. Milligan's speech. It was in his usual style, elaborate argument, and, as I thought, not suited to the occasion, and was not calculated to create any enthusiasm among the masses. Nothing was said denunciatory of the Government. Mr. Milligan always separated the Administration from the Government; whether he did in that speech or not, I can not distinctly remember. I believe he stated that opposition would occur under any Administration, and that if there were any present who expected him to arraign the Administration, they would be disappointed, as he would leave that to persons who delighted to arraign it. He spoke of coercion; he denied the power of the Government to coerce States, but admitted its power to coerce individuals. Nothing to my recollection was said calculated to excite insurrection, or resistance to the draft; if any thing had been said, I should probably remember it. I made a report of that speech at the time, but have not consulted it recently. I have been intimately acquainted with Mr. Milligan since the fall of 1858, and I know his general reputation as to moral character in that community; it is good; and also his reputation as a peaceable, law-abiding citizen, which is also good.

Q. Are you acquainted with his general character as a loyal man, well disposed to the preservation of the Government?

A. I do not know what you mean by the word "loyal." I am acquainted with his general reputation for attachment to the general principles of our Government, and its preservation; it is good.

CROSS-EXAMINATION.

I understand Mr. Milligan to be in favor of the Union of the States, but I do not know that he is favor of the prosecution of the war for the suppression of the rebellion. In conversations which I have had with him, he has always maintained that a war waged against foreign States was an absurdity, and I have heard him say that he was against the present war, because it was an unconstitutional one. He is, therefore, opposed to the prosecution of the present war, and I have heard him say so. He said at the Fort Wayne meeting, that the existing war was an absurdity. He said that if the war was right, the draft was right; but he did not say that if the war was wrong, the draft was wrong. I never saw any thing of the military part of the order until I saw it in the public prints. The purpose of the order was the inculcation of correct opinions or principles of Government, among which were the Kentucky Resolutions of 1798. These resolutions I understand give the States the right to judge of their own grievances, that they are on an equality with the General Government, and are co-equal with it, and may be so construed as to give them the right to dissolve the contract. I was initiated in the three degrees of the order by Dodd, who took us through the three degrees the first evening. I took the obligation and assented to its principles. The expression, "the Supreme Commander shall be Commander-in-chief of all military forces belonging to the order, in the various States when called into active service," I considered a figurative expression. I remember this part of the obligation which I subscribed to:

"I do further promise, that I will, at all times, if needs be, take up arms in the cause of the oppressed—*in my country first of all*—against any monarch, prince, potentate,

power, or government usurped, which may be found in arms, and waging war against a people or peoples, who are endeavoring to establish, or have inaugurated, a government for themselves, of their own free choice, in accordance with, and founded upon, the *eternal principles of truth*, which I have sworn in the V——, and now in this presence do swear, to maintain inviolate and defend with my life. This I do promise, without reservation or evasion of mind; without regard to the name, station, condition or designation of the invading or coercing power, whether it shall arise within or come from without."

I do not know that it had any reference to an attempt to establish a government within this Government. I did not understand that the order was to assist in the establishing of the Southern Confederacy; I did not understand it so, nor do I believe that they have established a separate Government; they have established a sort of a Government, but I do not understand that it is their intention to absolve themselves from their allegiance to the old Union of the States. I believe if the Constitution was construed as the Supreme Bench construed it in the Dred Scott case, they would come back to the Union. I do believe that they are waging war to establish a separate Government, but that they intend to come back to the Union. I do not think that the President of the Southern Confederacy, when he said that they were trying to establish a separate Government, represented the people of the South. I could not say that any prominent man in the South has said other than that they were fighting to establish a separate Government, but I have read something from Alexander H. Stephens in which he does not say they will not come back; and though he may not have said a word in favor of it, he has said nothing against it. There is not, to my recollection, any thing he has said in favor of any peace, save on the terms of equality. I do not believe that the Southerners are fighting for a separate Government, but for the Constitution as interpreted by the Dred Scott decision. That decision is in relation to their slave property—they want guarantees to protect it in transit through the States, and the right to take it into the Territories. This is my own judgment. I have also seen it advocated in public prints, more especially the New York *Day Book*. I recollect reading copious extracts from Southern speeches, avowing that they were not fighting for a separate Government. I assert that the South has been fighting for their rights as defined in the Dred Scott decision, and I regard the reason of their flying to arms to obtain that which they already had a right to, by the decision of the Courts of the land, with the whole executive power of the Government pledged to enforce it; that they supposed their rights would not be sufficiently respected to suit them; and I do not think the decision in that case was enforced to suit them.

Q. Can you tell when and where that decision was not enforced?

Question objected to by the accused, for the reason that it was not pertinent to the question in issue in this trial.

The Judge Advocate said:

This witness has undertaken to state that Mr. Milligan was loyal in his sentiments, reputation and character, and devoted to the maintenance of the laws and Constitution of his country; and he further said, that the order had nothing in it but a simple exposition of the theories of the Government, as held by certain persons. I deem it material to show this Court that Mr. Milligan's principles were opposed to the Constitution, and to the very life of the Government itself; that the theories promulgated in this order were false, disloyal, and destructive of the foundations of good order and of society. That the foundations of the order were lies, and that it was treasonable in its very inception and organization. This goes to the very foundation of the issue. It becomes material to show what these principles were. It is important, further, in this view: they call members of the order as witnesses, who swear that this order is loyal; that there is no harm in it, so far as they knew. We must get at the foundation of their belief, to judge of the credibility and force of their testimony. Without doing this, the Commission can not judge what principles, theories, or acts, they believe to be loyal, and what disloyal.

The court room was then cleared for deliberation.

On reopening the Court, the Judge Advocate announced that the objection had been overruled.

The Commission then adjourned, to meet on Wednesday, November 23, 1864, at 9 o'clock, A. M.

COURT ROOM, INDIANAPOLIS, INDIANA,
November 23, 1864, 9 o'clock, A. M.

The Commission met pursuant to adjournment.

All the members present. Also, the Judge Advocate, the accused (except Wm. A. Bowles), and their counsel.

The proceedings were read and approved.

The examination of Samuel F. Winters, a witness for the accused, was then resumed, as follows:

I can not state when and where the Government has failed to execute the decision of the Dred Scott case, but there are personal liberty bills or statutes in most of the free States, which are a nullification of that decision, at least in Wisconsin, New York, Vermont, New Hampshire, Massachusetts, and I think in Pennsylvania and Maine; and it is my impression that these States punish any person who assists in the capture of an escaped slave.

Q. Do not these bills expressly state, and are they not expressly for the punishment of kidnapping in violation of the laws of the State?

Question objected to by the accused, and withdrawn.

I took notes of the speech of Mr. Milligan at Fort Wayne. I am not a short hand reporter, but I am a rapid writer, and I wrote down as much of the speech as I could in long hand, giving the substance of it as I could recollect.

Q. Do you recollect whether this portion of Mr. Milligan's speech is as he gave it: "They (the States) were thirteen nations, and finally formed a Constitution, adopted separately by the several States, Virginia reserving to herself at any time to withdraw from the Union, and what Virginia reserved all the States had a right to reserve. Their action was based entirely on State rights. The Declaration of Independence states who is to be the judge when the Government shall be subverted. It guarantees to the people the right of revolution when they can no longer tolerate the invasion of their rights. I do not mean that Governor Morton, or the Legislature, or any machinery of office, getting its authority from the people through elections, is the State. But I mean the free range of all its people is the State. The officers are the mere servants of the people, the mere agents of the Government. Where does sovereignty rest? It is time to settle this question. If you are wrong in your theories, you should change your principles. I know no sovereignty in the Federal Government, or in the State Government, as contra-distinguished from the people of the State. I believe in the doctrine of popular sovereignty, instead of sovereignty in the machinery of the Government."

I think that is the substance of what Mr. Milligan said on that subject.

Q. Do you recollect this portion of Mr. Milligan's speech, and whether it is correct?

"If we have no power to make war upon a State that secedes, was it right to take up arms against a people who were doing what they contracted to do, and what your fathers and our fathers did eighty years ago? Was it right? How many believe it was right? If it was right, shoulder your guns, and go forward, and don't growl about the draft."

In speaking of the draft, I think he said something like that; that if the war was right, the draft was right; that the burdens of the Government should rest equally upon all; and that you might as well leave it to the voluntary act of citizens to raise the revenues of the country, as to raise an army by volunteering, or something like that; the deductions that I made from his speech were that the war was unconstitutional.

Q. Did he use these words: "Was it right because you were more peaceable than your neighboring States, and unwilling to rebel, to compel them by force of arms to remain your partners? When you have answered that question, I am ready to talk about the draft." Is that correct?

A. I do not think that corresponds with my report, and I do not think he said it. I have not a copy of the paper, in which the speech was reported, with me, nor do I know that I have a copy on file at my office. Mr. Milligan has occasionally written communications for my paper, but he has never written any of its leaders; they were letters referring to local matters. He wrote several communications last winter, but perhaps not more than a dozen altogether. I was present at the Grand Council that met here on the 17th. I went to see Mr. Milligan before I came here; I wanted him to go with me, but he felt too sick. I brought a series of resolutions; they were given me by Colonel Milligan, but I did not see them, nor did I read them; certain resolutions were read at the meeting of the Sons of Liberty. I do not know in whose handwriting they were.

[A paper containing certain resolutions was here handed to the witness by the Judge Advocate.]

These resolutions were adopted at Fort Wayne, but whether or not these are the ones I brought I can not say. These, to the best of my recollection, are the resolutions which were read at the meeting of the Order of American Knights.

Government exhibit "A" was here handed to the witness by the Judge Advocate.

Q. Are the resolutions in this book the same that you heard read at the February meeting of the Sons of Liberty?

A. I believe they are the same, but I could not state positively whether they are or not.

Re-examination.

The resolutions to which reference has been made, that were read at the Fort Wayne meeting, I think, are nearly like the resolutions of the 11th Democratic Congressional Convention assembled at Huntington. I only know that certain resolutions were contained in the envelope which Mr. Milligan handed me, and I know that in the pamphlet referred to, certain resolutions are printed that were read before the Grand Council, but I can not say positively that they are the same.

G. R. CORLEW, a witness for the accused, was then introduced, and, being duly sworn by the Judge Advocate, testified as follows:

I reside in Huntington county, Indiana, and am Deputy Sheriff in that county. I have been in the hardware business. I moved to Huntington in the spring of 1843, and have lived there since. I have been acquainted with Mr. Milligan for the past sixteen years, and know his general moral character in the neighborhood in which he lives; I should call it good. I am acquainted with his general reputation as a peaceable, orderly, law-abiding citizen, and it is good. I joined an order called the American Knights, in October or November, of 1863, at Huntington. Mr. Milligan was connected with the organization. I attended most of its meetings, till sometime in April, 1864, when we quit meeting. I think about twenty or twenty-five belonged to it. I never knew of Mr. Milligan making any efforts to increase the number of members, nor was he in favor of organizing branch temples throughout the country; the only members that he seemed willing to admit were good, reliable and responsible men. As far as I understood the organization, it was entirely political, and was to be an offset to the Union League. The object of the organization was to influence elections, and to get Democrats to stick together, so as to carry elections, and not by force of arms or any thing of that kind. I never knew any thing as to its military organization.

Cross-examination.

I know nothing of the purposes of the order, save what I have mentioned; I never heard any thing about arms or ammunition, nor of any attempt to establish a Northwestern Confederacy. I joined in October or November, 1863, and continued a member till it was broken up, in March or April, 1864. I think I took three degrees in the order, but I never attended any meetings, save those of our own assembly. For a part of the time I acted as treasurer, and received probably fifty or sixty dollars, with which I bought wood, and the rest had to be expended in the rent of the hall, lights, etc.; none of the money collected was, as far as I know, sent to the Grand Council. I know of no assessments having been made on our members for money. I know nothing of members of the order pledging themselves to each other that they would resist the draft. I have heard other individuals talking about it, and I told them it was nonsense to resist. I never recollect taking an obligation of which the following is a part:

"I do further promise that I will, at all times, if needs be, take up arms in the cause of the oppressed—*in my country first of all*—against any monarch, prince, potentate, power, or government usurped, which may be found in arms, and waging war against a people or peoples who are endeavoring to establish, or have inaugurated, a government for themselves of their own free choice, in accordance with, and founded upon, *the eternal principles of truth*, which I have sworn in the V——."

I will not swear that I did not subscribe to that obligation, but I do not remember. If it was read to me, I swore to it.

SAMUEL F. DAY, a witness for the accused, was then introduced, and, being duly sworn by the Judge Advocate, testified as follows:

I reside at Huntington, Indiana, where I have lived for four years. I am engaged in the livery business. I am acquainted with the general moral character of Mr. Milligan in that county, and it is good as far as I know. I am acquainted with his general reputation as a peaceable, orderly, law-abiding citizen, and that reputation is good.

I joined a secret organization last September, at Huntington, about the time Mr. Dodd made a speech there; I think it was called the Order of American Knights. We had meetings about once in two weeks up to the time we sent a delegate to Indianapolis; from that time our meetings were irregular until March or April; and about the last of April the organization was abandoned from want of interest in it by the members. Between twenty and thirty belonged to it. It was a County Temple. I learned from Mr. Dodd that the organization was a political one. All the degrees I ever took, I took the first night. I suppose there were three degrees. The purpose of the organization, it was stated, was to consolidate the Democracy, and to get influential men into its ranks, so that we might influence the election, and carry the Democratic ticket. It was also supposed that the organization would counteract the effect and purposes of the Loyal League in that county. I never learned any thing of the order being a military organization. I do not know of any attempts of Mr. Milligan to extend the order; I have known him to blackball members to keep them out, and I have known of his objecting to organizing branch temples; I never knew of his assenting to but one, namely, at Rockcreek township, Huntington county; they were organized there, and had forty-five or fifty members.

I am acquainted with Dr. Zumro, of Markle. I remember a conversation I had with him about the 16th of September, at Huntington. He and Mr. Johnson came to my stable door. Mr. Zumro stepped into my office, and stated that he had just come from Mr. Milligan's; he said that he and Mr. Johnson were appointed to come over to Huntington, to see what was to be done about the draft. Zumro said that Mr. Milligan did not give him much encouragement as he was sick, and told him to go to me. Zumro said, "We are bound to resist the draft, and we want to know if you can give assistance." I said it was foolishness and

nonsense to resist the draft; that fellows were already making preparations to get substitutes. We talked a few minutes, and when he went away, he said, "I suppose we will have to give it up, as we can get no encouragement here." I do not remember positively whether he said "we" or "they" are bound to resist.

CROSS-EXAMINATION.

I was elected Grand Seignior of the organization, and served for two or three months. The man who preceded me was named John Jones, but no one was elected to succeed me. The books and papers of the order were in the care of the Secretary, Mr. Cummings; Mr. Corlew was Treasurer; I do not know what became of the papers. I think there was a meeting in May, but I was not there. Mr. Milligan never gave any reason, that I remember, for not wishing to extend the order. He would often say when asked about establishing a branch lodge, "there is no use," or "do not be in a hurry," and the probability was that it would not be done.

I never heard of Mr. Milligan being appointed a Major General in the order, until I heard it on the street. I heard nothing of the military organization of the order, or of its army; Dodd said not a word about it, nor was any thing said about organizing a North-western Confederacy. I have heard Mr. Milligan speak in the lodge, or out of it, of the manner of conducting the war; and he approved of it, if it was conducted on a right policy, namely, for the Union. He objected to it, so I understood, because it was prosecuted for the abolition of slavery, and he believes that the Union could be restored by better means than by war.

When Dr. Zumro said "they" or "we" are going to resist the draft, Mr. Johnson said nothing to contradict it, that I remember. I think Zumro also stated that Mr. Milligan had said "we must do the best we can," or something to the effect that each one would have to take care of himself, and do the best he could; but he did not say that Mr. Milligan advised him to resist.

OCHMIG BIRD, a witness for the accused, was then introduced, and, being duly sworn by the Judge Advocate, testified as follows:

I reside in Allen county, Indiana, and am a farmer. I am a member of the Legislature. I was present at Fort Wayne, at the Democratic Convention, on the 13th of August last, at which Mr. Milligan spoke, but I was not by Mr. Milligan all the time he was speaking. It was called a mass meeting for the people of the county. Mr. Milligan was one of the invited speakers. Mr. Milligan's was an argumentative speech on the subject of States rights, and the rights of the Constitution. It did not elicit much enthusiasm from the audience. I judge it had an adverse tendency. Mr. Milligan did not denounce the Government, but he did speak against the Administration, and the manner in which the war was conducted; and I understood him to discriminate between the policy of the Administration and the Government.

I took one degree in the organization called the Sons of Liberty. Its purposes, as I understood then, were to rally the strength of the Democratic party. The entire strength of the order might have numbered about fifty or sixty persons. There was an impression in our place that the Loyal Leagues were armed. We found some papers that they had dropped around requiring a very strict organization; it was also reported that they intended to usurp unreasonable authority at the polls; and one of the objects of this organization was to stand by and see that the people had a fair chance at the election, and that no inroads were made on our party in delivering their votes.

CROSS-EXAMINATION.

In Mr. Milligan's argument at Fort Wayne, as I understood it, he did not justify the States in the right to secede. His argument went to prove that there was a certain way to settle these things peaceably between the States and the Government. My impression is that he did not consider this a constitutional war, from the manner in which it was conducted, and he may have said that the war itself was wrong—that fighting for the coercion of seceded States was unconstitutional, but I am not positive. I am under the impression that he treated the States as already out of the Union, and the Union dissolved; but I did not understand him to say that there was no power in the Government to bring them back.

I do not know that I have, in conversation, expressed the view that a State had the right to secede, and that there is no power in the Government to coerce it back after having seceded; those are not my views. I think it possible that a State may be coerced, though I do not entirely believe in the prosecution of the present war for the suppression of the rebellion; but I am in favor of it if prosecuted under constitutional principles.

Q. What would be a constitutional prosecution of this war?

Objected to by the accused, for the reason that the politics of the witness are not a subject of inquiry before this Court.

The Judge Advocate replied:

The question seems to me to be relevant, and most material; and I insist upon its being put. The accused bring witnesses here to prove a good character for loyalty, and the law-abiding nature and conduct of the accused, Mr. Milligan. If they saw proper to bring upon the stand a member of the rebel army, and ask him whether Mr. Milligan was a law-abiding, loyal man, his test of loyalty would be the fact that any man living in this Government would permit those States to secede, and establish a Government for themselves, and not interfere with them.

In speaking of the speech at Fort Wayne, this witness states that Mr. Milligan's speech had no tendency to create insurrection, that it separated the Government from the Administration, etc. The only way to get at the foundation of these speeches and acts, is to find the basis, or premises, from which the witnesses drew their conclusions. It is, therefore, important, when they bring witnesses upon the stand to prove the loyalty of any speech or act, to get at the standpoint from which the witness himself judges of loyalty.

This question goes to show the principles of the witness, and his theories of Government, and enables the Commission to find out what he believes to be constitutional, and what, in his judgment, is loyal, and what disloyal.

The court room was then cleared for deliberation.

On reopening the Court, the Judge Advocate announced that the objection was overruled.

The Commission then adjourned to 2 o'clock, P. M.

AFTERNOON SESSION.

Court Room, Indianapolis, Indiana,
November 23, 1864, 2 o'clock, P. M.

The Commission met pursuant to adjournment.

All the members present. Also, the Judge Advocate, the accused (except W. A. Bowles), and their counsel.

The testimony of Ochmig Bird, a witness for the accused, was resumed, as follows:

As a Democrat, I think the President of the United States has exceeded his power in requiring the abolition of slavery, as the right to hold slaves is guaranteed by the Constitution to every person who holds slaves. I think, therefore, the Emancipation Proclamation is unconstitutional; outside of this proclamation I am in favor of the suppression of the rebellion, though I am by no means strenuously in favor of the war, for I believe in settling the difficulty by conciliation and compromise. I am not in favor of letting the rebel States go, but I am in favor of the union of all the States; I am in favor of prosecuting the war, if that is the only alternative, and I am in favor of coercion, if that be necessary for the preservation of the Union.

We had a Democratic majority of twenty-seven hundred at the last election in our county. We organized this society to protect ourselves against the Loyal Leagues. Some of the leading members who belong to the organization, are Mr. France, who is the principal officer, Mr. Dills, Secretary, Mr. Walkie, Mr. William Jones, Mr. John Murray, Mr. Marshall Noll, Mr. Hogan and Mr. James W. Borden.

B. F. IBACH, a witness for the accused, was then introduced, and, being duly sworn by the Judge Advocate, testified as follows:

I reside in Huntington, Indiana, and have lately been admitted to the bar in our county. I joined a secret political organization in September, 1863. I was initiated on the day that Mr. Dodd addressed the Democratic Convention at Huntington. The objects of the organization were set forth in certain declarations of principles which were read to us, and which I understood to be to advance Democratic principles, as we understood them, and also to counteract the influence of a society called the Loyal League. It was a purely political organization. I continued to attend its meetings till May; at that time it had died out entirely. In connection with the society of American Knights, we had lectures every two weeks, and no one was permitted to lecture unless he indorsed the declaration of principles taught in the order. I was a delegate from that county temple to the Grand Council which met here in June. Mr. Milligan and myself came together, but he did not accompany me to the Council. I reached the city a little before noon on the first day of the meeting. We had a meeting on that and the next day. I remember at this meeting a young man from the northern part of the State was very uneasy about the draft, and thought the order should do something. This is the first I learned that there was any idea among the members that there was a military part connected with the order; he seemed to be very uneasy about the draft, and thought that we ought to combine. A resolution was offered by some member of the Council, which was voted down; the resolution was to the effect that the different temples in the counties should organize for the purpose of resisting the Government. It created quite a turbulent time there; some thought that the order was purely political, and others that there was a military branch in it. The majority of the members did not want any military action, but preferred to wait for a change through the election. The resolution, I remember, was voted down. They thought the ballot-box was the remedy for our troubles. I do not remember that Mr. Milligan took any part in the discussion. It was at this meeting that Dodd, or the Deputy Grand Commander, I forget which, said that they had taken into consideration the appointment of military officers, and that some of those appointed had not accepted their offices, and others had not been heard from. There was then a discussion whether their action should be secret, and confined to the Grand Commander and themselves, or whether it should be known to the members generally. Mr. Dodd said there were some things about the order which all the members need not know. Others said that the whole Council should know what was done, and should not be confined to single individuals. Mr. Dodd said that the appointment of major generals would have to remain as reported until the 4th of July, if they did not report then, others would have to be appointed. Mr. Dodd did not press the matter then, because he saw it did not suit the Council, and that they would have voted the military part of it down.

CROSS-EXAMINATION.

I took the three degrees of the order all at one time. Part of the degrees were not read; only the obligations. The means by which Mr. Milligan and myself received notice of the meeting of the Council here in June was this: a notice was sent to the order in Huntington, addressed to its secretary, that we were to appoint delegates to that meeting of the Council. This was received in May, and we came up here to the State Council on the 14th of June. We had a meeting of the order in May, and I was appointed a delegate, and though our order died out in Huntington, I was here on the 14th representing it. Mr. Milligan was present at the first day's meeting. Mr. Humphreys I did not see here either day. I do not remember Mr. Dodd making use of any such expression as this: "I will now kick down the thin walls of patriotism and talk treason for a while." I remember they had quite a discussion on the subject of the grievances which the Government had inflicted, but could not come to an understanding about the matter.

The ascendency in the meeting seemed to be of those who concluded that we should rely on the ballot-box as a remedy for the evils we suffered. There was also some expression of opinion in favor of McClellan as candidate for the Presidency; they were in favor of the nomination of a man who favored the prosecution of the war.

Dodd and the Deputy Grand Commander were not in favor of the prosecution of the war, and I think were hostile to the Administration. I think from what Dodd said, that the appointment of the military officers was within his province. None of our organizations drilled as far as I know. I had a preamble for organizing a company; the list had fifteen or twenty names upon it, some of whom were members of the order; we intended getting seventy-five members, and then organizing under the State law, and drawing our arms from the State, in accordance with an act of the Legislature; my name, I believe, was at the head of the company. It was first commenced some eighteen months back, a long time before I belonged to any secret organization. We intended to drill; our object was to protect ourselves against the soldiers that were coming home. Some citizens, also, had made threats against our printing office, and we thought it best to take the arms in our own hands. Quite a number of our friends had received letters from soldiers in the army, saying that when they came home, they were going to take care of what they were pleased to term the Copperheads. Another reason why we contemplated protecting ourselves was that the Home Guards had been furnished with arms, and we thought that we had the same right to the State arms as they had. Had we been furnished with arms, our company would have been a Home Guard, to guard ourselves against what we called encroachments on our rights.

CAPTAIN SAMUEL PLACE, jr., a witness for the accused, was then introduced, and, being duly sworn by the Judge Advocate, testified as follows:

I am Captain in the 5th Veteran Reserve Corps, stationed at Burnside Barracks, Indianapolis. I was in command of the squad of men who arrested Mr. Milligan at his house in Huntington county, Indiana. I made the arrest on the authority of a written order from Major General Alvin P. Hovey, which was as follows:

HEADQUARTERS DISTRICT OF INDIANA,
Indianapolis, October 5, 1864.

Special Order No. 142.

6. Captain Samuel Place, jr., 5th Regt. V. R. C., with the force under his command, will proceed to Huntington, Huntington county, and arrest L. P. Milligan, and bring him to these Headquarters without fail.

By order of Brevet Major General Alvin P. Hovey. AND. C. KEMPER,
Assistant Adjutant General.

The above was then offered in evidence by the accused.

G. R. Corlew, a witness for the accused, was then recalled, and testified as follows:

I have heard Mr. Milligan say that he was born in 1812; he is therefore fifty-two years old. I have known Mr. Milligan for sixteen years, and I never knew of his being in the military or naval service of the United States.

MOSES W. MILLIGAN, a witness for the accused, was then introduced, and, being duly sworn by the Judge Advocate, testified as follows:

I reside in Huntington, Indiana, and am a son of L. P. Milligan. On the evening of Tuesday, the 16th of February, my father started to come here to Indianapolis; he went to the train, but it was crowded, and he returned home. My mother asked him the reason he did not go, and he said he was sick. On the next day, the 17th, he was at Court at Huntington. My father was not from home during the month of February, to my knowledge. The Common Pleas Court was first held, and the Circuit Court immediately afterward; and my father was in attendance during both terms, as far as I recollect. I was present at both Courts as acting bailiff.

CROSS-EXAMINATION.

I do not think my father was away from Huntington more than one day during the month of February; he was sick more or less the whole month of February. I can not state what he was doing on particular days. I am enabled to fix the date of the 16th of February, by knowing that a meeting of the Sons of Liberty was to be held here on that day, and that my father intended to be present, and he went to the cars on that day. I remember Mr. Winters went.

The Commission then adjourned, to meet Friday, November 25, at 2 o'clock, P. M.

———

COURT ROOM, INDIANAPOLIS, INDIANA,
November 25, 1864, 2 o'clock, P. M.

The Commission met pursuant to adjournment.

All the members present. Also, the Judge Advocate, the accused, and their counsel.

The proceedings were read and approved.

EDWARD PRICE, a witness for the accused, was then introduced, and, being duly sworn by the Judge Advocate, testified as follows:

I reside at Sullivan, Sullivan county, Indiana; I am Clerk of the Court at that place. I am acquainted with the accused, Andrew Humphreys; I have known him about twelve years. I was present at a meeting at a place called Caledonia, in June, 1863. I went there with Mr. Cowgill. On the morning of that day, two or three citizens of that township came to Sullivan and requested some of us to come down and see if we could not quell a disturbance that was going on there; they said, "Let some Democrats and Republicans go out and talk to the crowd, and see if they can not allay the disturbance." That was the purpose for which I went. I understood the excitement was occasioned by some soldiers, who, getting off the cars, went to the house of a Mr. Wagner, and asked for his horse. Mr. Wagner was not at home, and his wife told them they could not have it, but they went into the stable and took it. They also shot at a man by the name of Pigg. When I received this notice, I got my horse and carriage to go out there. Mr. Cowgill, who was introduced to me by Mr. Wolf, the old clerk of the county, went with me. There were two or three carriage loads that went, but we were ahead of all the rest. About a mile and a half from Sullivan we met the soldiers coming back. Mr. Cowgill stopped some of them and talked for a few minutes. He asked something about the excitement. I think he told them the best thing they could do was to go on to Sullivan, get on the cars and go home. I think he also told them that they had done wrong in taking away property without the consent of the owners.

We went on to Caledonia; when we got there, Mr. Humphreys was speaking to the crowd; they seemed to be very much excited when we drove up. I don't know how many there were present; perhaps about two or three hundred. I got out of the buggy and handed the lines to Mr. Cowgill. I went up to Mr. Humphreys and told him that the Deputy Provost Marshal was there, and asked him to come out, and I would give him an introduction. He stopped speaking for a few minutes, and I went out with him and introduced him to Mr. Cowgill; they walked into the crowd while I was hitching the horse. Mr. Humphreys spoke a little while to the crowd after that, and then introduced Mr. Cowgill; Mr. Cowgill got up and made a few remarks, advising the crowd to go home and disperse, that they had done wrong in taking the property, and told them the best thing they could do was to take Mr. Humphreys' advice and go home, and not be the cause of making any disturbance. Mr. Humphreys said that, as the soldiers were gone, there was no use of any excitement, and that the best thing they could do was to go home. I was walking around in the outskirts of the crowd, and was not paying a great deal of attention to what he did say. I think some of the crowd said they would follow the soldiers; that was the thing Mr. Humphreys advised them not to do. My opportunities for knowing what was going on, were good, as I was in the crowd all the time until we got into the carriage to go back. I do not remember Mr. Humphreys saying any thing about the Administration or the Government. He did not speak more than ten or fifteen minutes after I got there.

I was at the meeting in Jackson township in the September of 1863. Mr. Humphreys, Mr. Hammill, Captain Mandrell, S. G. Burton and myself, spoke. Captain Mandrell, it was said, was a rebel that had been captured at Fort Donelson, and had taken the oath of allegiance at Indianapolis. It was reported that he had been engaged here as clerk in the Quartermaster's office. He was in the Recorder's office, at Terre Haute, when I got acquainted with him; and he was the agent for some Illinois company for awhile. This was a political meeting—a Democratic picnic.

I am acquainted with the moral character of Mr. Humphreys, and it is good. I am also acquainted with his general character, as a law-abiding man, and it is good.

I reside twelve or fifteen miles from Mr. Humphreys, and I have often been at his house. I was a candidate on the Democratic ticket in the fall of 1863. In politics I am of the same principles as Mr. Humphreys, and my speeches, I presume, would be of the same class as his. Captain Mandrell, I do not think, spoke more than five minutes at the meeting I have alluded to. I do not remember what he said. Mr. Humphreys' speech was about like Democrats usually make. As I was a candidate at the time, I did not pay much attention to what was being said; I was more interested in myself than any body else. I joined an order called the American Knights, in August, 1863. I was initiated by P. C. Wright, at Terre Haute. I remained in the order until I was elected, in October, when I had nothing more to do with it. I took three degrees. I joined the order for fear they would defeat me. I have always been opposed to secret political organizations, not thinking that they were right, and I might have done what I believed to be wrong, for the sake of being elected.

S. G. Burton, a witness for the accused, was then introduced, and, being duly sworn by the Judge Advocate, testified as follows:

I reside at Sullivan, Sullivan county, Indiana, and practice law in that town. I am intimately acquainted with Andrew Humphreys, and have been for the last five years. I made a speech at Linton, in August last. It was at a large mass meeting; Mr. Humphreys followed me.

Q. You may state the substance of his speech, if you recollect it?

Question objected to by the Judge Advocate, and withdrawn.

Q. In the course of that speech, what did Mr. Humphreys say in relation to the Government and the right of secession?

Question objected to by the Judge Advocate.

The counsel for the accused said:

This witness is brought on the stand to testify in behalf of the accused, Andrew Humphreys, and we have a right to interrogate him as to Mr. Humphreys' speeches. That course of examination has not been objected to, up to this time. We introduced three gentlemen from Mr. Humphreys' neighborhood. One of them testified to the speech made in August last. We proved that speech as indicative of the sentiments which he offered to the people for their guidance. We have a right to prove what the accused has said, urged and enforced upon the people as their path of duty; the Court may determine whether his sentiments were loyal, or disloyal. We propose to prove by this witness that he pursued a particular line of argument. That he read from Washington's *Farewell Address*, and from Jefferson's writings, to enforce the same views. One witness stated that he understood Mr. Humphreys endeavored to support his argument for secession by the authority of Washington and Jefferson. No principle of law is better settled, than the right, as declared in the Statutes of Indiana, that a party may always, in the event of a witness being mistaken in his deductions, of having his errors corrected by other witnesses. If one witness is mistaken in a particular point, the defendants have the right to prove the whole facts in the case by another witness, that the Court may determine what is right and what is wrong. We had the right, first, to fortify one witness by corroborating testimony as to what Mr. Humphreys said, and show that all he uttered was manifestly in favor of preserving the integrity of the Government. Secondly, we had the right to prove what actually took place, to rectify what the other witness said about the speech.

One of the charges against the accused is that of making inflammatory speeches. We have a right to meet and to disprove this, and the law fixes no limit to the number of the witnesses that we may call.

The Judge Advocate replied: I understand the rule to be, that when they prove any particular statement to have been made by the accused, they are entitled to call out the entire statement. The Court has further ruled, that any acts or speeches made by the accused, at any meetings of the order, to show whether such acts were for a good or bad purpose, would be received as evidence; but I do not understand the Court to go so far as to say that because we proved that in the fall of 1863, certain treasonable speeches were delivered by the accused, that they can introduce, as rebutting testimony, loyal speeches made in 1864. We have introduced no witnesses as to speeches made in 1864. We certainly did obtain from one witness of the accused, in his cross-examination, that Mr. Humphreys, in 1864, spoke on secession, saying that a State had a right to secede; that in affirmation of his views he read from Washington's *Farewell Address*, and from Jefferson's writings. They are attempting to put a witness on the stand to testify to that which we have not introduced on the part of the Government. They can not disprove the disloyal utterances of 1863, by proving loyal speeches in 1864.

As to when one witness may be brought in to contradict another, Roscoe, in *Criminal Evidence*, page 178, says:

"Whether the party calling a witness, who gives evidence contrary to what is expected from him, may prove contradictory statements previously made by the witness, is a question on which there has been some difference of opinion."

The court room was then cleared for deliberation.

On reopening the Court, the Judge Advocate announced to the accused that the objection had been sustained.

Question by the accused:

What did Mr. Humphreys say in that speech about secession?

Question objected to by the Judge Advocate as illegitimate, and as already passed upon.

The counsel for the accused replied:

On the discussion of the right of secession, a man may speak of that right and not be in favor of it. In this country, it is a matter of opinion whether a man is for his Government or against it. It is not treason to maintain one side or the other of this question of secession; for in 1825 a very distinguished lawyer, who was long a servant of the Government, wrote a treatise on the Constitution of the United States, in which he justified and maintained the right of States to secede, under the Constitution, and denied the right of coercion. I always thought, and I think so still, that this gentleman, Mr. Rowle, of Pennsylvania, was greatly mistaken. But no man doubted the loyalty of his heart or his life, until the days when treason was inaugurated in this country.

De Tocqueville, in his *Democracy in America*, maintains it as an original proposition, that there can be no contest for the enforcement of the Union; that it is not a contest between the Government on the one side and the seceding State or States on the other; but that States seceding have the same interest to maintain secession, that the adhering States have to resist it, because it is a question of self-interest to each party. The General Government is dissolved.

We claim that we have the right to introduce testimony to show the loyalty of Mr. Humphreys, from the present time back to the organization of the order, at Terre Haute, as the testimony on the part of the Government goes back to this time.

The case of Horne Tooke is to the point. He was on trial for treason. He goes far back of the commencement of the prosecution, and finds a book that he had written in favor of the sovereign. In that book his loyalty is fully established, and he introduces it to show that he could not have had the intent, as alleged, of destroying the life of the King. It was admitted as evidence in his favor, and though Lord Ellenborough afterward questioned the correctness of the decision, it has not been reversed. It followed and reversed the decision in the case of Lord George Gordon, the decision in Lord George Gordon's case being decided in 1780, and the trial of

Horne Tooke following fully fourteen years after, during the turbulent scenes of the French Revolution.

The following is from Russell on *Crimes*, vol. 2, pp. 780–781:

"And, as in trials for conspiracies, whatever the prisoner may have done or said, at any meeting alleged to be held in pursuance of the conspiracy, is admissible in evidence against him, on the part of the prosecution; so, on the other hand, any other part of his conduct at the same meetings will be allowed to be proved on his behalf; for the intention and design of a party, at a particular time, are best explained by a complete view of every part of his conduct at that time, and not merely from the proof of a single and insulated act or declaration. In the case of Walker and others, who were tried for a conspiracy to overthrow the Government, evidence was produced on the part of the prosecution to show that the conspiracy existed, and was brought into overt acts at meetings in the presence of Walker, the counsel for the prisoners was allowed to ask a witness, whether, at any of these times, he had ever heard Walker utter any word inconsistent with the duty of a good subject? The question was opposed, but held by Mr. J. Heath to be admissible. The prisoner's counsel were also allowed, in the same case, to inquire into the general declarations of the prisoner at these meetings, whether the witness had heard him say any thing that had a tendency to disturb the peace of the kingdom; and questions to the same effect were put to many other witnesses in succession.

"On the trial of Hardy for high treason, where the overt act charged was that the prisoner, for the purpose of accomplishing the treason of compassing the King's death, did conspire with others to call a convention of the people, in order that the convention might depose the King, the counsel for the prisoner were allowed to ask a witness, whether, before the time of the convention, he had ever heard from him what his objects were, and whether he had at all mixed himself in that business. But the better opinion seems to be, that in order to make such other acts or declarations of the prisoner applicable to his defense, it must be shown that they are in some way connected with the facts that are proved against him. In the case of Horne Tooke and others, however, for high treason, several publications having been given in evidence on the part of the crown, containing republican doctrines and opinions, the distribution of which had been promoted by the prisoners, during the period assigned in the indictment for the existence of the conspiracy, the prisoner was allowed to read, in his defense, various extracts from works which he had published at a former period of his life; and these the jury were permitted to carry along with them, when they retired to consider their verdict. But the propriety of allowing such a defense has been questioned by very high authority."

The first question we present to the Court is, whether we have a right to prove by this witness that facts were different from what the other witness said they were. On that question I wish to cite authority. We called Mr. Johnson's attention to the meeting and the sentiments expressed by Mr. Humphreys about the Government. The witness stated that Mr. Humphreys made a speech. The Judge Advocate asked if he spoke in favor of the right of secession? He answered, he did. We now introduce a witness who made a speech at the same time and place, and who heard what Mr. Humphreys said. We introduce him not to contradict what other witnesses have said, but to show the real facts of the case.

Roscoe says, page 178:

"But where a witness is called and makes statements contrary to those which are expected from him, the party calling him may prove the facts in question by other witnesses." But it is stated that this decision applies only to the direct examination. It is not limited to that. In examinations as to character, we are confined to two questions. In cross-examination we are not so limited. Suppose on re-examination, a witness clings to a mistake made in his direct examination, and we could produce a hundred witnesses to prove a contrary state of facts, should we be bound by his statements, and cut off from correcting his mistake? If so, no man would be safe in introducing witnesses as to character.

Eminent authorities say on this point:

"Where a witness gives evidence against the party calling him, and is an unwilling witness, or in the interest of the opposite party, he may be asked by the party calling him, at the discretion of the Court, whether he has not on a former occasion given different testimony as to a particular fact. *Bank Northern Liberties* vs. *Davis*, 6 *Watts & Serg.*, 285.

"A party may prove the fact to be different from what one of his own witnesses has stated it to be. That is not discrediting his witness. *Spencer* vs. *White*, 1 *Iredell's N. C. Rep.*, 236.

"A party can not discredit his own witness or show his incompetency, though he may call other witnesses to contradict him as to a fact material to the issue, in order to show how the fact really is. *Franklin Bank* vs. *Steam Nav. Co.*, 11 *Gill & Johns.*, 28."

The same principle was decided in the case of *Wright* vs. *Beckett*, 1 *Moore & R.*, 416, in which Lord Denman held that a party calling a witness, who, on cross-examination, has given testimony unfavorable to him, may, on re-examination, ask the witness questions to show inducements to betray him. * * * An opinion adverse to the right of a party calling a witness to contradict him, by his own previous statement, has been expressed by a writer of great authority. *Phill. Ev.*, 309, *7th ed.* And this, the opinion, seems to have been followed by other text-writers. Mr. Phillips, however, in the last editions of his work appears to have changed his opinion, and observes that in the administration of criminal justice more especially, the exclusion of the proof of contrary statements might be attended with the worst consequences. *Phill. on Ev.*, pp. 451, *9th ed.*

I know that the Indiana Statutes are not authority in this Court, but its practice is supposed to be in harmony with the common law on these questions, and in conformity with the principles of humanity on which our Statutes are based.

Section 244, of Part 1, page 172, reads:

"The party producing a witness shall not be allowed to impeach his credit by evidence of bad character, unless it was indispensable that the party should produce him, or in case of manifest surprise when the party shall have this right; but he may, in all cases, contradict him by other evidence, and by showing that he has made statements different from his present testimony."

The foot-notes to that section contain the following decisions:

"The rule of common law is thus stated in *Thompson* vs. *Blanchard*, 4 *Comstock*, 303. A party calling a witness can not impeach his character or assail his credibility by general evidence; but he may prove by other evidence the truth of any particular fact in direct contradiction to the testimony of the witness."

"The right of a party to contradict his own witness, by showing that he has made statements different from his present testimony (*Civil Code, Sec.* 660,) does not depend on the ability of the party to prove, in addition, that the testimony of the witness is untrue; but he may contradict him, *first*, by other evidence; and, *secondly*, by showing that he has made statements different from his present testimony. Either or both of these modes may be adopted. *Champ.* vs. *Commonwealth*, 2 *Metcalf*, (*Ky*). 17."

We were surprised by the testimony of this witness on the point of secession.

In reviewing the whole case, it seems that the public life of Mr. Humphreys, for the time covered by the examination on the part of the Government, is on trial before this Court, and that whatever has been done or said at public meetings by him during that period is part of the *res gestæ* in this offense. Therefore, we think we are right in attempting to introduce evidence to show what he said in Linton, about the Union and Government. The Government has admitted evidence in reference to that meeting without objection, and, therefore, the whole of the facts in reference to it should come before the Court. It is necessary that we be permitted to introduce other witnesses to show what Mr. Humphreys said in that speech. If we can do this, it will enable us to correct any wrong impression which may have arisen from the answer, "Yes, sir," to the question, "Did he say secession was right?" Now, in the present state of the country, such a declaration would not be expected to come from a loyal source, but would be considered disloyal, and showing a disposition to enter into such an association as this secret order has been claimed to be.

The Judge Advocate replied:

I desire to correct a misapprehension, frequently entertained, and which appears to exist here, that the Judge Advocate is counsel for the accused as well as for the Government. His position is exactly defined by the Articles of War, which say that he "shall so far consider himself as counsel for the prisoner, after the said prisoner shall have made his plea, as to object to any leading question to any of the witnesses, or any question to the prisoner, the answer to which may tend to criminate himself." When the accused came into Court ably represented by counsel, I feel that the defense of the accused rests upon their shoulders, rather than on mine. I do not act as counsel for the accused in this case. On all questions of law, I put them on an equal footing with the Government, but in questions of fact, I act only for the Government, and leave the accused in the hands of their counsel.

I had supposed that the point at issue was already disposed of by the decision of this Court. Its ruling I understood to be, that what a man says, any statement he makes outside of the particular times and places proved by the Government, whether said to one person, or a hundred, is immaterial, and every sentence of law, read by the accused, goes to this, and only this extent, that all the prisoner said at the particular time proven by the Government, or while he was engaged in those particular proven acts, is competent. He can not go outside of that.

Permit me to say one word on the doctrine of the right of a State to secede, which is spoken of as only a political heresy. It is the heresy that has made a part of our land desolate. It is the phantom that has swept over one-half of the surface of our beloved country, leaving ruin in its wake. It has caused moaning and mourning throughout the whole land. Whether it is treason or not, it has caused the treason against which the nation is now struggling This heresy contains the doctrine and prin ciples, which, once acted on, constitute treason. You may advocate the right of secession as a principle, and the moment you convince enough people of the truth of that principle, it ripens into action, and you produce secession and disrupt the Government. When you convince a sufficient number of the people of Indiana that secession is right, and that there is no power in the Government to coerce them, and prove to them that a North-western Confederacy is to their advantage, you lead them to actual treason, and pave the way for a division of the Government, to any extent that interest or caprice may dictate. From this heresy have culminated the wrongs under which the nation is now groaning. Hence, I dislike to hear counsel argue that a man has the right to talk in favor of secession, and claim that it is not wrong, or treason. He argued that Mr. Rawle had advocated the right of secession, and no man doubted his loyalty. But he did not believe this was treason, and did not know that it would be against Mr. Humphreys, that he argued in favor of this doctrine. If so, why does he try to rebut the remark of the witness that Mr. Humphreys said secession was right? This doctrine is the foundation-stone on which treason is built. The question is, whether he joined a treasonable society which had avowed its intention to disrupt the Government; which conspired for the establishment of a North-western Confederacy, and proposed to seize the arsenals in the North-western States, release the rebel prisoners, and arm them to aid in this conspiracy; whether he had any knowledge of these purposes, and whether he was, by his membership and position, bound to assist in carrying out what this organization contemplated. They can not disprove this fact, or rebut its force, by proving that at another time, outside of the order, he made loyal speeches.

CROSS-EXAMINATION.

I joined a society called the Sons of Liberty, at Terre Haute, in August, 1863, and took three degrees. I have not met with the order for about six months. I was called Ancient Brother in the order; the principal duty of which office was to administer the obligations.

RE-EXAMINATION.

I regarded this organization as having only a political object. I thought I understood all about it, but since these trials commenced, matters have been developed of which I knew nothing before. Although I have conversed with members of the order outside of my own county, I never was able to ascertain that its designs were any other than to secure a better organization of the Democratic party; and I never knew of any thing more being revealed to third than to first degree members; I understood that the objects of the order were to be secured through the means of the ballot-box.

RE-CROSS-EXAMINATION.

I had in my possession the ritual of the order. The ritual of the first degree I have read.

The attention of the witness was called by the Judge Advocate to the following passage, which he was asked to explain:

"10. Whenever the officials, to whom the people have intrusted the powers of the Government, shall refuse to administer it in strict accordance with its Constitution, and shall assume and exercise power not delegated, it is the inherent right and imperative duty of the people to resist such officials, and, if need be, expel them by force of arms. Such resistance is not revolution, but solely the assertion of right."

That has reference to counter revolution. When the political party in power begins to trample on the rights of other citizens, these can take their rights in their own hands, and defend them by force of arms. My idea is, that it is right for every American citizen to defend his rights by force when they are trampled upon, and it was one of the purposes of the order, that in case of such encroachments, it should resist by force of arms. They had apprehensions that the ballot-box would be interfered with, and, in case they were driven from the ballot-box, it was their right to secure a free election by force of arms. If one class was driven from the polls to obtain the triumph of the other party, it was right for the party driven away to take up arms, and I suppose the passage quoted has reference to that, if such a state of things should arise. The passage has reference to the exercise of powers not delegated; and I claim that the Government has assumed powers not delegated, and I suppose the order claims the same. I believe it was one of its principles that the Government had assumed too much power.

WILLIS G. NEFF, a witness for the accused, was then introduced, and, being duly sworn by the Judge Advocate, testified as follows:

I reside at Sullivan, Indiana, and am engaged in the practice of law. I know Captain Mandrell, who has been spoken of in this case. I met him at Terre Haute, in the spring, in the Clerk's office, after the battle of Fort Donelson, and had some conversation with him. He then told me he was released on taking the oath of allegiance.

The Commission then adjourned, to meet Monday, November 28, at 2 o'clock, P. M.

In consequence of the absence of some of the members, the Commission adjourned over the 28th and 29th, to meet on Weanesday, November 30, at 2 o'clock, P. M.

Court Room, Indianapolis, Indiana,
November 30, 1864, 2 o'clock, P. M.

The Commission met pursuant to adjournment.

All the members present. Also, the Judge Advocate, the accused (except W. A. Bowles), and their counsel.

The proceedings were read and approved.

John Roach, a witness for the accused, was then introduced, and, being duly sworn by the Judge Advocate, testified as follows:

I live at Huntington, where I have lived for thirty years; I am a farmer. I am well acquainted with the people living near Huntington. I have known Mr. Milligan since 1847 or 1848. He has been my attorney for several years. I am acquainted with his moral character in the community in which he lives, and it is good. His general reputation as an orderly, peaceable, law-abiding citizen, is good. I never joined any secret organization.

CROSS-EXAMINATION.

Since 1854 or 1856 I have acted with the Democratic party, though not actively. I have never acted with the Republican party. I have heard Mr. Milligan make remarks, in which he held that some of the officers of the Government were exceeding their authority, and he complained that they were not acting according to law. I never heard him speak of the executive officers of the Government as usurpers. I have never heard people of our community speak of him as a disloyal man. I do not think they regard him as more disloyal than other Democrats. Some of our citizens believed that every one who did not vote the Republican ticket was disloyal. I believe Mr. Milligan has been regarded as a leader of the peace wing of the Democratic party. I have heard him spoken of as a "Butternut," but I have not heard of him working against the Government in her efforts to suppress this rebellion. Mr. Milligan, I believe, has a worse reputation, perhaps, than other Democrats, because he has worked with more earnestness than others of the peace party.

RE-EXAMINATION.

Though I have voted with the Democratic party, I have assisted the Government in aiding in the enlistment of soldiers, and I have helped soldiers' families. As one of the largest tax payers of the county, I have gone before the board of County Commissioners and asked them to make appropriations to encourage enlistments, and for the support of soldiers' families.

Wilson B. Lockridge, a witness for the accused, was then introduced, and, being duly sworn by the Judge Advocate, testified as follows:

I reside in Peru, Miami county, Indiana, and am now and have been, for the last two years, a lawyer. I am now the editor of the Miami County *Sentinel*—a Democratic paper. I have acted as Judge of the Court of Common Pleas for two terms. I have been intimately acquainted with Mr. Milligan since 1847 or 1848. I was two years a partner of his. I am acquainted with his general moral character in the community in which he lives, and it is good. I am also acquainted with his general reputation as a peaceable, orderly, law-abiding citizen, and it is good. I was, for a short time, a member of the Sons of Liberty. I was informally initiated, and only attended one or two meetings.

I attended a Council of the organization in this city in February last. I understood that the intention of the organization was altogether political; that it was intended to protect the members of the Democratic party against violence, which, it was thought, had been used against them in particular quarters; in short, to protect the Democratic party and see that their rights were not trampled upon. Mr. Milligan was not present at the Council in February while I was there, which was the first day. I looked for him in the meeting, and heard one of the prominent members inquire for "Milligan;" the reply was that he was not there. There was nothing said about the appointment of Major Generals while I was there. I had not a great deal of faith in the matter. I did not know it to be what it purported to be, and I came to Indianapolis more for the purpose of seeing into it than for any thing else, and from those I saw in attendance that day, I concluded that it would not be productive of much good After returning home, I had nothing more to do with it.

Dodd and Heffren were the principal leaders, and I did not think they were fit persons to take part in such a thing.

CROSS-EXAMINATION.

I understood that we were to protect the rights of the Democratic party, in the event of their being kept away from the polls, with such means as were necessary to afford us protection. We were first to exhaust all peaceable means, and if these failed, to resort to the right of self-defense. I do not know that any precise means were determined upon. Each member of the order had to judge of his own rights and the best means to maintain them, and when any member's rights were infringed upon, it was regarded as the duty of other members of the order to protect him—peaceably at first, forcibly if necessary. But there was to be nothing beyond acting in self-defense. I had learned of persons being attacked on account of their political principles, and being beaten and bruised; and if such a thing occurred again, I conceived it to be the duty of the order to protect such persons as were assailed.

The civil law might have been sufficient to protect them, but there were many instances where it had not afforded protection; I think if a man was attacked, he had the right to self-protection; and it was upon this principle that the order was to act. When I attended the Grand Council I gave no password; I was vouched for by some person at the door; I did not know that it was a rule that no person was admitted to that body who had not taken three degrees.

The following was then quoted by the Judge Advocate: "Whenever the officials, to whom the people have intrusted the powers of the Government, shall refuse to administer it in strict accordance with its Constitution, and shall assume and exercise power not delegated, it is the inherent right and imperative duty of the people to resist such officials, and, if need be, expel them by force of arms; such resistance is not revolution, but is solely the assertion of right."

I can not say whether I have heard that before or not. I probably did at Indianapolis. There was something to that effect among the cardinal principles of the order, and I do not know that I have heard members of the organization dissent from it. I have expressed the same opinion in my paper, but I can not say that the order generally held to it as a principle, though it is my opinion it did. I have said that the President had exercised power that the Constitution had not given him, and used authority not delegated to him.

I do not know that I have ever expressed myself to the effect that usurpation might reach a point where revolution would be necessary.

SAMUEL McGAUGHEY, a witness for the accused, was then introduced, and, being duly sworn by the Judge Advocate, testified as follows:

For fourteen years I have resided at Huntington, Indiana; am a farmer. For two years I served as Treasurer of the county. I became acquainted with Mr. Milligan soon after settling in Huntington. I am acquainted with his moral character; it is good; also with his reputation as a peaceable, orderly, and law-abiding citizen; it is also good. I became a member of a secret political society, in Huntington, about a year ago, but paid very little attention to the matter. I understood it to be purely a political association, and I remember the idea was suggested by some of the members that it was to counteract the influence of the Loyal League.

CUTTER S. DOBBINS, a witness for the accused, was then introduced, and, being duly sworn, testified as follows:

I reside at Dover Hill, Martin county, Indiana, and practice law. I have been acquainted with Stephen Horsey for nine or ten years. I am acquainted with his character as a quiet, peaceable, law-abiding citizen, and it is good.

Q. You may state whether Stephen Horsey is a man of influence in the neighborhood where he lives.

Question objected to by the Judge Advocate, and withdrawn.

HARRISON CONNELL, being recalled as a witness for the accused, testified as follows:

I am acquainted with the character of Stephen Horsey as a peaceable, quiet, law-abiding citizen; it is good.

CROSS-EXAMINATION.

It was not extensively known in his neighborhood that Mr. Horsey got the powder and shot, about which I testified; and I do not know that such a fact would conduce to his reputation as a peaceable, law-abiding citizen. I assisted in carrying the powder and lead from where it was concealed, but no one else knew of it, that I know. I do not know of his buying any more ammunition, or lead, or shot; nor do I know of any attempts made by him to arm the order. I do not know that I ever heard any one say that he was disloyal to the Government.

WILLIAM M. RANNEY, a witness for the accused, was then introduced, and, being duly sworn by the Judge Advocate, testified as follows:

I reside near Shoals, Martin county, Indiana; am a farmer. I am acquainted with the character of Stephen Horsey as a peaceable, quiet, law-abiding citizen, and it is good. I have known Mr. Horsey since 1833. I joined a secret organization that was formed in April, 1863; Mr. Shirkliff, I think, initiated me. Mr. Horsey and several others were there. I do not know whether Wesley Tranter, or Stephen Teney, was there; we met in a vacant house. The obligation we took, as I understood it, was to support the Constitution of the United States, and the State of Indiana. There was some other obligation, but I do not recollect what it was. I did not meet with the organization after that night.

CROSS-EXAMINATION.

The name of the order I joined was the Circle of Honor. At the time of Mr. Horsey's arrest, some people talked pretty hard about him, as they have done since.

RE-EXAMINATION.

Those who talked hard about Mr. Horsey at the time of his arrest, were political opponents, who thought him guilty of what he was charged with. Up to the time of his arrest, his character for peace and quietness was good.

The Commission adjourned, to meet on Thursday, December I, at 10 o'clock, A. M.

COURT ROOM, INDIANAPOLIS, INDIANA,
December 1, 1864, 10 o'clock, A. M.

The Commission met pursuant to adjournment.

All the members present. Also, the Judge Advocate, the accused, and their counsel.

The proceedings were read and approved.

General ALVIN P. HOVEY, a witness for the accused, was then introduced, and, being duly sworn by the Judge Advocate, testified as follows:

Question by the accused:

State your name and official position?

Answer. My name is Alvin P. Hovey. I am Commander of the District of Indiana.

Q. State whether or not it was by your order that Mr. Milligan was arrested?

A. It was.

Q. State upon what that order was based, whether upon affidavit made to you, or upon what it was based?

A. It was based upon my general knowledge of affairs in Indiana, the condition of the country, and Mr. Milligan's action in regard to it, together with the dangers that surrounded us at that time.

Q. What actions have you reference to?

A. To the conspiracies against the authority of the United States.

Q. What particular actions of Mr. Milligan in the matter?

A. Mr. Milligan, I understood from reliable authority, was a Major General of the organization, and had taken steps to aid it, and carry on revolution.

Q. Please state to us the source of that information?

A. The information generally came from Detectives.

Q. State who they were?

Question objected to by the Judge Advocate, and withdrawn.

Q. Am I right in understanding you as saying that the order was not based upon an affidavit?

A. It was not, sir.

Q. State whether you have not made the observation that Mr. Milligan was a dangerous man; if so, upon what information you made the remark?

Question objected to by the Judge Advocate, and withdrawn.

Q. Was this information from persons residing in Mr. Milligan's neighborhood, or elsewhere?

Question objected to by the Judge Advocate, and withdrawn.

CROSS-EXAMINATION.

Question by the Judge Advocate:

I suppose, General, the sum of the matter was this: that in your judgment it was necessary for the public welfare to arrest this man, and upon that you moved?

Question objected to by the accused, and withdrawn.

The witness:

I would like to make this further explanation. The first person arrested by me, was Dodd; that arrest was made without consulting the authorities any-where. Subsequently I made the others. In the first arrest, I took the responsibility on myself; I was authorized by the War Department to make the subsequent arrests, and to take what action I might deem advisable in regard to it, and I did so. The testimony which I have given with regard to these prisoners, applies to each and all of the others.

M. 3. BRANT, a witness for the accused, was then introduced, and, being duly sworn by the Judge Advocate, testified as follows:

I live in Huntington county, Indiana. Since the fall of 1844, I have been Auditor of the county. I became acquainted with Mr. Milligan in 1844, and since 1851 I have known him intimately. In politics I am now a Republican and a Union man. In years past, I was an Old Line Whig. The first vote I ever gave was for Andrew Jackson. I next voted for Martin Van Buren, next for Harrison, and since then I have been connected with the Democratic party. I am acquainted with Mr. Milligan's moral character in the community in which he lives, and it is good. I am acquainted with his general reputation as a law-abiding citizen; that reputation is good.

CROSS-EXAMINATION.

Mr. Milligan's character is that of a man who, till lately, has advised entire obedience to the law. The Democratic party still regard him as a law-abiding citizen, while Republicans speak of him as operating, of late, against the laws of our country. Republicans regard him as connected with a secret organization that is in favor of further secession among the States, and in favor of the establishment of a North-western Confederacy.

RE-EXAMINATION.

I think that that reputation is confined exclusively to the more rabid and bitter portion of the Republican party, and most of this reputation has grown up since about the time of Dodd's arrest, and since the exposure of the members of the Sons of Liberty in the public prints; though a year ago last fall Mr. Milligan made speeches, and some persons in the Republican party regarded him as a man opposed to the Government, and as seeking the establishment of a North-western Confederacy. By opposition to the Government, I mean opposition to Mr. Lincoln's Administration.

W. J. SMITH, a witness for the accused,

was then introduced, and, being duly sworn by the Judge Advocate, testified as follows:

I am Clerk in the United States District Court, and have held that position since May, 1863. The business of the Court has in no way been interfered with. We have had our special and regular terms, and processes have been issued and returned regularly. There have been one or two suits instituted for obstructing the processes of the Court, but the regular business of the Court has not been interfered with.

SAMUEL CHANDLER, a witness for the accused, was then introduced, and, being duly sworn by the Judge Advocate, testified as follows:

I am Deputy Clerk of the United States Circuit Court, and have held that position since the 4th of February, 1863. The Court has been exercising jurisdiction in this State; since that time it has been open, and holding its regular sessions, and there has been no disturbance or civil commotion to interfere with the business of the Court, that I know of.

D. GARLAND ROSE, a witness for the accused, was then introduced, and, being duly sworn by the Judge Advocate, testified as follows:

I am United States Marshal for this District, and have held that office since April, 1861. I do not know of any obstructions to the serving of processes during the past year; I do not know of any suits now pending in the Federal Courts for obstructing the service of process, though the District Attorney could answer that question better than I could.

I know threats were made, and resistance was apprehended, but none was offered that caused any arrests to be made, that I know of.

EDWARD HARRISON, a witness for the Government, was then introduced, and, being duly sworn by the Judge Advocate, testified as follows:

I live in Wells county, Union township, Indiana; I am a farmer, and at present substitute in the army. I have known Dr. Zumro for five years; I live about three-quarters of a mile from him. I know his general reputation in the neighborhood in which he lives, and that reputation is good, and from that reputation I would believe him under oath.

CROSS-EXAMINATION.

I am a Union man. Among those I have heard speak of Dr. Zumro, are Mr. Ratliff and Mr. Cagger, both of whom are Union men. Ratliff said that he respected Zumro; that he was a man of principle, and could be depended upon. No inducements have been held out to me to testify as to Zumro's character. I have been pretty intimately acquainted with him; he has been my family physician.

JOHN NAVE, a witness for the accused, was then introduced, and, being duly sworn by the Judge Advocate, testified as follows:

Dr. Zumro has been my family physician for seven or eight years. I know his reputation for truth and veracity in the neighborhood where he lives, and it is good; I would believe him under oath. The class of men that have usually spoken against Dr. Zumro, belong to the Democratic party. I have not heard any body else say any thing against him. I, myself, belong to the Democratic party.

CROSS-EXAMINATION.

I know that Dr. Zumro has had enemies in the medical profession; I have heard men say that he was a great liar; but it was by a Dr. Joseph Scott and others, who differ from him professionally, and it did not affect his character for truth and veracity. Before this controversy came up, I have heard Dr. Stockwell and Mr. Daniel Haeflee speak of him as a man of truth; they always spoke well of him.

RE-EXAMINATION.

Before these trials came up, I did not hear any one speak against Dr. Zumro, except for some special reason, or because he was a personal enemy.

W. C. SMOCK, a witness for the accused, was then introduced, and, being duly sworn by the Judge Advocate, testified as follows:

I am Deputy Clerk of the Markle Circuit Court, and *ex-officio* of the Common Pleas Court. The courts of this county have been unobstructed in the exercise of their jurisdiction.

DAVID STOCKMAN, a witness for the Government, was then introduced, and, being duly sworn by the Judge Advocate, testified as follows:

I live in Rock Creek township, Wells county, Indiana; I have been somewhat intimately acquainted with Dr. Zumro for about three years. I live about a quarter of a mile from him. I know his reputation for truth and veracity to be good, and would certainly believe him under oath. Politically I belong to the Democratic party.

CROSS-EXAMINATION.

I have heard people speak against Dr. Zumro, and say that he was not a very good Doctor. I have not mixed much with the people of the neighborhood, but as far as I have heard, no one has spoken against him as a man of truth.

JACOB FARLING, a witness for the Government, was then introduced, and, being duly sworn by the Judge Advocate, testified as follows:

I live in Rock Creek township, Wells county, Indiana. I am trustee of that township; I belong to the Democratic party, and joined the Sons of Liberty. I live about five miles from Dr. Zumro; have known him four or five years; he has been my Doctor; his reputation for truth and veracity in our neighborhood, where he doctors most of the people, is good as far as I have learned; the people of that neighborhood are mostly Pennsylvania Dutch. I did not hear any thing against his reputation before these treason cases came up; and I would believe him under oath.

CROSS-EXAMINATION.

I have not heard Dr. Zumro's character much discussed; it did not come up; I have not heard people speak against him until of late; since these cases came up, I have heard people speak ill of him.

RE-EXAMINATION.

I never heard any thing said against Dr. Zumro, till he came on the stand and testified about these Sons of Liberty.

WILLIAM R. TAYLOR, a witness for the Government, was then introduced, and, being duly sworn by the Judge Advocate, testified as follows:

I live in Rock Creek township, Wells county, in this State, and run a saw mill. I have acted as Justice of the Peace for two terms. Politically I am a Republican, and voted for the Union party. I have been drafted, and am now a soldier. Have known Dr. Zumro ten years, during which time he has been my family physician. I am acquainted with his general reputation for truth and veracity; that reputation is good, and I would believe him under oath.

R. C. BOCKING, a witness for the accused, was then introduced, and, being duly sworn by the Judge Advocate, testified as follows:

I am the inventor of certain Greek fire shells, and missiles of various kinds. I made a shell and applied for a patent, and had a caveat filed for it as well as for the Greek fire, which I invented, and which I claim to be the same as that used by the Greeks, and which burns under water. I have been traveling for the purpose of presenting my claims to the public, since the spring of 1863. Have been at Cincinnati, Louisville, Detroit and here. Being short of means, I was trying to find some person to assist me in getting my invention through. It was open to the public; and I came here to try it by order of General Burnside. I brought it before Adjutant General Noble, Colonel Freybarger, Major McClure, General Wilcox and his staff, Mr. Holloway, editor of the Indianapolis *Journal*, and I showed it everywhere to the public. General Wilcox was Commander of this State at that time. I am not a member of the secret organization known as the Order of American Knights or Sons of Liberty, and never was. My Greek fire had no connection with the order, nor did I receive any assistance from it in any way. I know Dr. Bowles. He asked me, when in Louisville, if I would show him and his friends some of the shells and the Greek fire; I told him yes. In the afternoon he came to my room at the Louisville Hotel, with several gentlemen, and I showed it and explained it to them. I told them it was a pity I could not get along with my inventions for want of means, and Dr. Bowles said he would see some of his friends and ascertain if something could not be done, so that I could get along with the shell. In the evening, when I was at the hotel, a young man came to me, and asked me to go up to Dr. Kalfus' office; when I went up, some person, I did not know who, said to me, that some of the gentlemen to whom I had shown my inventions had agreed to help me, and they gave me a little paper with money in it, which I did not count until I got back to the hotel, when I found that it was in the neighborhood of two hundred dollars.

This gift had no connection that I know of with the Order of American Knights, or Sons of Liberty, and not a word was said about any thing of the kind. Nothing was said that I know of, at the hotel, about using my invention for improper, disloyal or treasonable purposes; when the gentlemen talked together, they were quite far off from me, and they spoke very low. I was never in Salem, Indiana; though I may have passed through the place on the train; nor did I ever exhibit my shells, or experiment with my Greek fire to Mr. Horace Heffren, at Salem. I never saw him until I met him in the cell where I am now confined. I never received from Dr. Bowles any money, or aid in any way; nor did I have any contract with him to furnish my missiles to him or to the Order of Sons of Liberty.

CROSS-EXAMINATION.

Dr. Bowles was present when the money was given to me, but I do not know who it was that furnished it, and never heard any one say. I think it was some gentleman to whom I showed the shell. I did not know the name of any one present, except Dr. Bowles and Mr. Stidger. My object in going to the Louisville Hotel was to try to get help. I knew Dr. Bowles before going there, having seen him at his place, he keeps a watering place; I went there to board at one time when I was sick. When I went to Dr. Bowles' place, he was not there; I waited perhaps an hour; when he came back, he asked me what my business was, and I told him that I had an invention. In the conversation it came out that I was out of means, and I thought I would board there, as it was cheaper than here. He said if I would go to Louisville, he would meet me there with some friends, and try to help me. I staid at his house until after dinner, when I left.

Q. Do you pretend to say that you told them you were hard up, and they gave you two hundred dollars without making any agreement, or exacting any promise?

A. Yes, sir; they just presented me with two hundred dollars.

From Louisville I think I came here, and staid about a week; I then went to Detroit, and staid about another week; from Detroit I went to Cincinnati; from there to Adams county, Ohio; then back to Cincinnati, and from Cincinnati here, where I have staid until now.

Q. When was it you were in Windsor, Canada?

A. I think it was in April or May. I was there a couple of weeks, but doing nothing, I boarded with a Mr. Steele; I think they called him Colonel Steele, but I do not know why. Possibly he was a Colonel in the rebel army, though he never told me, and I never asked him. There were a couple of young men boarding with Colonel Steele; one was a nephew of his, the other I did not know. One of them, I believe, had been in the rebel army. I think I went from Kentucky to Canada. I knew Colonel Steele in Kentucky, when I was Major in Metcalf's Cavalry. It was when I was in Detroit that I went over to the Canada side, and saw Colonel Steele in a billiard saloon. I told him how I was situated; that I wanted a partner to go in with me to get that shell through; Mayor Barker, in Detroit, became my partner. I slept at Colonel Steele's, and went over to Detroit every day. I saw Mr. Vallandigham there two or three times, but never spoke to him.

WILLIAM H. CHAPMAN, a witness for the Government, was then introduced, and, being duly sworn by the Judge Advocate, testified as follows:

I reside at Markle, Huntington county, Indiana, where I have lived about eight years. I am acquainted with Dr. Zumro, and know his general reputation for truth and veracity, and, from that reputation, I certainly should believe him under oath.

CROSS-EXAMINATION.

I am a Union man, and have voted with that party for several years.

WILLIAM JOHNSON, a witness for the Government, was then introduced, and, being duly sworn by the Judge Advocate, testified as follows:

I reside at Markle, Huntington county, Indiana. I am Captain of a home guard company; I belong to the Union party. I have been acquainted with Dr. Zumro eight or ten years, and know his reputation for truth and veracity; that reputation is good, and I would believe him under oath.

CROSS-EXAMINATION.

I have heard some people speak against Dr. Zumro, but I believe they have been his personal enemies; and I do not know that Dr. Zumro has a larger share of men who speak ill of him, than other people who live in a town like Markle. There are between two and three hundred people in Markle.

SAMUEL D. PRICE, a witness for the Government, was then introduced, and, being duly sworn by the Judge Advocate, testified as follows:

I reside in Rockcreek township, Wells county, Indiana. I am a carpenter; at present a soldier in the army, which I entered about three weeks ago. I have known Dr. Zumro, intimately, for three or four years; he is our family physician. I know his general reputation for truth and veracity; it is good: and I would believe him under oath.

CROSS-EXAMINATION.

Dr. Zumro never made any promises, or told me that I should be assigned to easy duties, if I testified in this case. I am not much acquainted about Markle, nor in Huntington county. I never heard any one say any thing against Dr. Zumro, but I have heard several speak in favor of him before these treason cases came up. Among them I have heard Mr. Dresser, Mr. Ritting and Mr. Taylor. In politics I am a Republican.

THURSTON W. RITTING, a witness for the Government, was then introduced, and, being duly sworn by the Judge Advocate, testified as follows:

I reside in Rockcreek township, Wells county, Indiana, and am a farmer. I live four or five miles from Markle. I have been somewhat acquainted with Dr. Zumro about four years. His reputation is generally good, and I would believe him under oath.

CROSS-EXAMINATION.

I am a Union man. I have heard several people speak of Dr. Zumro, and they have said that he was a fine man, and that he was thought a good deal of.

BORZILLAI MESSLER, a witness for the Government, was then introduced, and, being duly sworn by the Judge Advocate, testified as follows:

I reside in Rockcreek township, Wells county, and live about two miles from Dr. Zumro, whom I have known eight or ten years; his reputation for truth and veracity is good, and I should believe him under oath.

CROSS-EXAMINATION.

I used to vote the Democratic ticket, but I voted for Fremont for President, and have voted the Republican ticket since.

THOMAS G. SMITH, a witness for the Government, was then introduced, and, being duly sworn by the Judge Advocate, testified as follows:

I reside in Markle, Huntington county, Indiana; have lived there since 1860; I have known Dr. Zumro since that time. My private relations with him have not been good. His reputation for truth and veracity in the neighborhood where he lives is generally good, and I would believe him under oath.

CROSS-EXAMINATION.

I have said, in times past, that Dr. Zumro was a scoundrel; that was before this controversy came up, and it arose out of a personal difficulty, which made me feel unkindly toward him at the time. I have heard Dr. Zumro spoken against, but I thought medical matters caused it. I have heard Dr. Zumro censured by some in connection with the church which he left; I believe the circumstances were these: In Pennsylvania there is a denomination which has a large fund for the education of ministers; Dr. Zumro was one of their students, and was educated for the ministry at their expense. He afterward changed his course, and instead of preaching, practiced medicine. Politically I am a friend of the Administration; I did not, however, vote for Mr. Lincoln the first time he was elected; in 1859 I voted with the Democratic party.

Mrs. ELIZABETH T. SIMONS, a witness for the Government, was then introduced, and, being duly sworn by the Judge Advocate, testified as follows:

I reside at Lagro, Indiana; formerly I resided at Huntington, Indiana. My father's name is Rev. Richard A. Curran.

Q. Did you have any difficulty with your father about the time of your marriage?

Question objected to by the accused, as it is incompetent to impeach a witness who is called as an impeaching witness. Mr. Curran having been called to testify to Mr. Milligan's good character, and to Dr. Zumro's bad character.

If it were permitted to call witnesses to impeach witnesses for character, they might call rebutting witnesses, and there would be no end to such testimony. A witness whose character is impeached, can not call rebutting witnesses to testify to his good character, but that ends it. You might inquire whether an impeaching witness has a good character, or whether he has not. It is also a rule of law, that, on all material matters, a witness can not be impeached by calling other witnesses as to a matter of fact.

The Judge Advocate replied:

The reverend gentleman who testified in this Court, was called for the purpose of certifying to the moral character of Mr. Milligan, as well as to his loyalty and law-abiding disposition. He testified at length upon that question. To ascertain from what stand-point he testified as to Mr. Milligan's character, in those respects, I asked about his own sentiments, also as to whether he had a difficulty with his daughter on this question, and whether he had not laid violent hands upon her.

I asked these questions to ascertain his sentiments toward the Government. When asked whether he had any difficulty with his daughter about her marriage with a Union man, and whether he had laid violent hands upon her, he flatly denied the charges. It is, therefore, perfectly legitimate to disprove his assertions. I propose to ask the character of the man by whom the accused undertook to establish his character.

The accused replied:

I do not remember that the foundation for the impeachment was laid by calling the attention of the witness to the time and place when he made the declarations, or committed the act upon which he is to be impeached. Unless this was done, the witness can not be impeached. I quote from Greenleaf *On Evidence*, vol. 1, page 602:

"The credit of a witness may also be impeached by proof that he has made *statements out of Court contrary to what he has testified at the trial.* But it is only in such matters as are relevant to the issue, that the witness can be contradicted."

I may here ask whether it was relevant to the issue to know whether the witness choked his daughter or not, or did not want her to marry a Union man?

The author adds:

"And before this can be done, it is generally held necessary, in the case of verbal statements, first to ask him as to the time, place, and person involved in the supposed contradiction. It is not enough to ask him the general question, whether he has ever said so and so, nor whether he has always told the same story; because it may frequently happen, that upon the general question, he may not remember whether he has so said; whereas, when his attention is directed to particular circumstances and occasions, he may recollect and explain what he has formerly said. This course of proceeding is considered indispensable, from a sense of justice to the witness; for as the direct tendency of the evidence is to impeach his veracity, common justice requires that, by first calling his attention to the subject, he should have an opportunity to recollect the facts, and, if necessary, to correct the statement already given; as well as by a re-examination to explain the nature, circumstances, meaning, and design of what he is proved elsewhere to have said."

The present case is one where an attempt is not only made to contradict the witness in regard to verbal statements, but also as to facts not relevant to the issue, and the rule of law just quoted is against the competency of the mode of examination proposed by the Judge Advocate.

The Judge Advocate replied:

If the testimony of the witness was not relevant to the issue, he should not have been put on the stand. It is relevant to the issue to find out whether he told the truth or not.

The court room was then cleared for deliberation.

On being reopened, the Judge Advocate announced that the objection had been overruled, and the question sustained.

The witness continued: I had a difficulty with my father at the time of my marriage, but he always said that he did not oppose my marriage on account of the politics of my husband, though my impression has been otherwise. I think his words were, that he would as soon I would marry a negro as an abolitionist. He did use violence toward me during that difficulty; he laid hands on me, and caught me by the throat, and made threats against my life.

Q. Did he choke you?

Question objected to, and withdrawn.

He ordered me to leave the house, and forbade me to return. He threatened to knock my brains out if he met me anywhere with Mr. Simons.

Cross-examination by John R. Coffroth, Esq.

My father drove me from his house in the morning, and, by the advice of my mother, I went to Dr. Blount's. In the afternoon of the same day, he came with Mr. Coffroth to the house where I was staying. I remember my father saying to me, in an under tone, that he was perfectly willing that I should return home. I had had a conversation with Mr. Coffroth prior to that. When I got to Dr. Blount's, I wrote a letter to Mr. Simons, stating the difficulty that had occurred. From there I went to his brother's. It was through Mrs. Blount's influence I sent for Mr. Coffroth.

Q. What motive did you have in sending for me?

Question objected to by the Judge Advocate.

The counsel replied:

I press the question, because the witness was laboring under strong mental excitement, and to show that her father went there with myself, and that the whole matter was talked over and reconciled, and

13

harmony restored between them. I propose, further, to show that she was laboring under hallucination, and misunderstood her father. There are many reasons why this question should be allowed. It is an act of simple justice to the accused, and to the witness, whose character is called in question, that this course of examination should be permitted.

The Judge Advocate replied:

The present question is: "What was your motive in sending for me?" It is perfectly immaterial to the Court what the motives of the witness were; that the counsel can investigate privately, if he desires. The simple question before the Court is, did Mr. Curran tell the truth when he said that he had never laid violent hands on his daughter, and never drove her from his house? The examination-in-chief was confined to that, and the cross-examination must be confined to the same point. If the accused can ask the witness what occurred after her father drove her from his house, he can ask her about every transaction in her life from that time to this.

The Court was cleared for deliberation. On the Court being reopened, the Judge Advocate announced that the objection had been sustained.

Question by the accused:

You may state whether on the day of the difficulty, your father did not visit you, and whether you did not become entirely reconciled with each other?

Objected to by the Judge Advocate, as involving the same legal question just passed on. Question withdrawn.

Question by the accused:

When your father came to see you, at that time, you may state, if in the conversation between yourself and your father, in talking over the difficulty, was it not admitted by you to him, that the difficulty grew out of your calling your father a liar, and putting his hand on your shoulder he stated to you that you must not speak to him in that manner?

A. I did not state any such thing.

Q. Were not Mrs. Young, Mrs. Dr. Blount, and Mrs. Wm. Blount present at that interview?

A. Mrs. Dr. Blount was present; I am not positive about Mrs. Young being there. They were in the room when you came in, but I think left, except Mrs. Dr. Blount.

Q. Was not Mrs. Dr. Blount present?

A. Yes, sir.

Q. Is it not true, that this matter of choking you was nothing more than the fact that your father laid his hand on your shoulder?

A. He did choke me.

Q. Where did he choke you?

A. He caught me by the throat.

Q. Have you not, for the last four or five

years, been laboring under strong mental excitement, induced by sun-stroke?

Question objected to by the Judge Advocate.

Such a question can only be put for one purpose: To prove the incompetency of the witness to testify. It is too late to make that point. It should have been made before going into such a cross-examination as has been had.

The counsel for the accused replied:

The objection of the Judge Advocate is not well taken as to the proper time of showing the mental condition of the witness. I may show that the witness is entirely incompetent to testify as to that particular occurrence, because she was laboring under such strong mental excitement that it rendered her statements entirely incredible. We may show that the witness was laboring under a partial hallucination. It may be shown that during this excitement, and partial derangement, the witness may have conceived ideas not founded on fact, and I do not confine my question to the particular time of this difficulty. It is well known that the witness had a sun-stroke several years ago, which affected her brain, and caused periods of strong mental excitement, and that they existed before the time of this difficulty, at the time, and since then.

I withdraw the question as to that particular time.

My father has accused me of insanity, but I never understood that his reason for so thinking, was the cause of his objection to my marriage.

Q. You may state whether, from that time to this, your father has not been the same kind father you have always known him to be?

Objected to by the Judge Advocate, as immaterial.

The counsel for the accused replied:

I propose to show that for a long series of years, and indeed up to this time, her father has been one of the kindest and most indulgent of parents. I think I can show that he did not do what she complained of, and that she may be mistaken in her impressions about this matter.

The Judge Advocate withdrew the objection.

The witness continued:

I can not say that my father was kind in his treatment of me. He is naturally a very passionate man.

RE-EXAMINATION.

When I was suffering from this mental excitement, I was always prepared for these attacks of delirium, by a severe pain in my head several hours before the delirium set in. Sometimes the attacks would last a day and a night. At the time of my father's making that attack upon me, I had not suffered from any paroxysm of delirium for more than a year, nor have I had any attack since that difficulty occurred, except immediately afterward. Within three or four days after this difficulty I was taken quite ill, and was delirious for twenty-four hours afterward, during which I ruptured a blood vessel. Though my father is a passionate and excitable man, he did not use any violence toward me before the difficulty of which I have spoken. He used threatening language to me in the fall, I think, previous to this difficulty, which was in the spring of 1863. His threat, I think, was that he would shoot me, and he made this threat several times. I never had any words with my father about political matters until the morning of my difficulty, and I do not recall any other instances of unkindness except the threats in connection with my contemplated marriage with Mr. Simons.

I never heard my father make use of any expressions against the Government.

The Judge Advocate then announced that the accused and the Government having no more witnesses to introduce, the testimony was closed.

The counsel for the accused desired the Commission to adjourn till Tuesday next, to allow time for the preparation of their final argument.

The Commission then adjourned, to meet on Tuesday, December 6, 1864, at 10 o'clock, A. M.

ARGUMENT

ON THE

JURISDICTION OF A MILITARY COMMISSION,

BY

JONATHAN W. GORDON.

Mr. President and Gentlemen of the Commission:

I appear for Colonel Bowles and Mr. Humphreys, who have directed me to discuss the question of your jurisdiction to try them. Before proceeding to this discussion, however, I may be pardoned for briefly referring to some preliminary considerations.

I will not deny that I am oppressed with the greatness and weight of the labor assigned me. Many circumstances conspire to make this day's work a burden, while but few sources of external encouragement and support are to be found.

I meet at the threshold of the solemn duty of this hour, the settled hostility of the Administration, the fierce and relentless spirit of the dominant party, and a strong tide of prejudice and passion created by a partisan press, which, during this trial, has continually prejudged the questions to be discussed and decided here to-day. Nor, indeed, has this uncharitable work been confined to the press. Public speakers have caught up the testimony of witnesses even before their cross-examination; and, with such one-sided, partial, broken fragments of the whole truth, have rushed eagerly into the popular arena, and proclaimed the guilt of the accused in every part of the State.

It is impossible that these facts should not have met your observation; and almost as impossible that you should not (although you are all unconscious of their influence) be more or less affected by them. They can not, indeed, have passed unobserved by you who have been at liberty, and circulating freely among the people; for they have found their way even into the lonely cells of the prisoners, and made themselves manifest by the dim and dismal twilight of their dungeons. They are, indeed, every-where. They have polluted the atmosphere, and infected the minds of the people. They are like the air around and within us; and pass unheeded and unthought of, while they give color, direction and tone to all our thoughts and actions.

Nor, in regard to one of the accused, has it been sufficient for the purposes of those who have joined in this hue and cry, to confine their assaults upon him to the present time, or to the offenses with which he now stands charged. They have gone back to the days of other years, and have dragged up and scattered over the land, old, and stale, and groundless imputations of delinquency originating in the time of the Mexican War. A record, made by interested men, for selfish and ambitious purposes, has been referred to, and old passions and prejudices invoked, upon a point whereon the people of Indiana are justly more sensitive than upon any other—the point of honor. But even that record does not assail his courage, his gallantry, or his patriotism; and, if it did, he might still proudly appeal from it to the testimony of his illustrious commander, Major General Zachary Taylor, under whose eye he fought on the glorious field of Buena Vista. To the report of that chieftain he appeals against the slanders born of subsequent and interested accounts of that contest; and prays that they may not be allowed to give a false and injurious coloring to the present accusation, and to the sentence which you are now about to pronounce.

I confess, however, that a still graver source of embarrassment to me, in the performance of my present duty, springs from the nature of the subject to be discussed—the importance of the principles to be defended. In view of these, the lives and fortunes of the accused—and, indeed, of us all—are as nothing. They and we are but mortal men. The worst that can possibly befall them at your hands, can, therefore, but anticipate, by a very few years, the common doom which time, or disease, or both together, will bring to them and to us all; for

"To every man upon this earth, death cometh soon or late."

It is not, then, merely because the lives and fortunes of the accused are suspended upon the result of this trial, that I confess myself embarrassed—overwhelmed at this moment, in the presence of the duty to which it calls me. That the lives, and fortunes, and good fame of the defendants are all involved in this cause, is, indeed, of itself, a fact of sufficient importance to touch very nearly any one whose heart is not dead to the gentle pleadings of pity and mercy; and weigh heavily upon him who in any, even the least degree, may divide the responsibility of an unfortunate result to either. I am not insensible to the weight of responsibility due, in that respect, to my relation to their cause. I am sure, however, that I should but ill represent their sentiments and wishes, if I allowed myself, in this defense of their individual interests, wholly to lose sight of the consequences which must follow to the cause of constitutional liberty in our country, by subjecting them to a military jurisdiction, to which, by the Constitution and laws of the land, they are, in my judgment, clearly not amenable. The general consequences which must flow from such a precedent, give this trial an importance far above any private interests involved in it; and make my sense of responsibility painful in the extreme, for fear that "*the good old cause*" may suffer detriment through some default of mine.

But amid all these sources of discouragement and embarrassment—and there are others which time will not permit me to notice—I acknowledge with due thankfulness that there are not wanting some great encouragements and supports. Among these is the fact of publicity. These things are not done in a corner, nor under a bushel. They will be proclaimed from the house-top; and read and known of all men. They will be reconsidered and rejudged long after they shall have lost all their importance to us who are now engaged in them. What is right in them will be retained and appropriated by mankind to aid the great cause of civil liberty, and advancing civilization. What is wrong will just as certainly be condemned and rejected, as useless or hurtful to the same cause, by the same judgment. The record which we this day make up and complete, will go to the tribunal of history—a tribunal where prejudice can not wound, nor slander kill. To all who earnestly strive to follow the path of truth and justice this day, the decisions of this tribunal can bring neither harm nor shame; for truth and justice are its eternal foundations.

Nor am I less encouraged and upheld by the voice of history. The labor assigned me will rest upon facts and precedents, handed down to us by the liberty-loving race to which we belong. If these shall be regarded as of any authority in this forum, then my labors shall not be in vain. Success shall crown them. The character of the members of this Commission, their habitual love of constitutional liberty, and of order maintained by law, do not permit me to doubt that they will carefully consider the great question of jurisdiction; and, indeed, all other questions properly before them, and render an honest finding and sentence according to the Constitution and laws of the land. That Constitution and those laws are but the organization of the facts and precedents transmitted to us with our blood, by our British ancestors. They are mingled with our very being; and permeate all the channels of our social and political life. To abandon them, is to give up our social and political life—is to die. And, indeed, in this time of national sickness, when the public mind is suffering under a melancholy and morbid excitement, amounting almost to frenzy, it would be madness to give up the sure foundations of the Constitution and laws, and the history and customs of a thousand years upon which they rest, for any new-fangled notion born of these evil times. It would be like a man, amid the delirium of a fever, abandoning the business and habits of a whole lifetime, for a new business and new habits with which he had no acquaintance whatever. His friends would confine him in a straight jacket, and send him to a lunatic asylum.

No, therefore, it must not be. The past is the only basis upon which to reconstruct the present—the Constitution, on which it is possible to reunite the belligerent members of this once glorious, but now broken Union. But we, who are devoted to this great work of reconstruction, must not exhibit to all the world our utter disregard of its plainest provisions, and most sacred principles. We must not throw down and destroy the fences, which it has built about the primordial rights of mankind; and then expect our enemies, or even our friends to believe us sincere in our professions of love for the Constitution, or desire to restore the Union; for, by such a course, we shall become scarcely less guilty of treason to our country, than rebels in arms against it. Indeed, the only distinction, in such case, would be that which separates *force* from *fraud;* and as between two such means to such an end, I am sure you will agree with me that force is by far the more noble and manly. But we stand opposed to both—we who stand for our country; and I am comforted to believe that you who have each offered your lives for its salvation from the dangers that assail it by force, will not hesitate to interpose your justice to save it from overthrow which may threaten it under the forms of law.

It is left for others to discuss the questions of guilt or innocence arising from the testimony in its application to the charges. I have nothing to do with it. Only so much of the evidence as tends to throw light on the question of jurisdiction falls to me; and I shall refer to the charges and specifications in so far only as they may aid in the same general purpose. The argument I am to make would be just as valid if the guilt of the accused stood admitted, as if their innocence were established by the proof, beyond all question.

There are rights which belong to the guilty as well as to the guiltless; and among them is that of a fair constitutional and legal trial, and all the legitimate consequences thereof This right, among the ignorant and unthinking, is often lost sight of, and sometimes disregarded. It is, nevertheless, as important as any other. Its denial is, therefore, a crime, not only against the individual, but also against society at large. To destroy a murderer or a traitor by any other process than that prescribed by law, is as much murder as to kill the best man in the country. Dr. Francis Lieber has well presented this subject in his treatise on *Political Ethics.* He says:

"The State never ceases to protect; even the blackest criminal, the moment before his head falls, is protected. It was a most fallacious argument that, *frustra legis auxilium invocat qui legem committit*, from the *lex talionis*, or as St. John said before the Lords, when he brought in the bill of attainder against the Earl of Stafford (April 29, 1641), 'He that would not have others have a law, why should he have any himself?' 'Why should not that be done to him, that he himself would have done to others?' Even modern writers have endeavored to derive the punitory power of the State, from the fact that the offender, by doing wrong, declares himself out of the jural society. Nothing can be more untenable in all its bearings. On the contrary, the State being especially a jural society, can not possibly act except by law, and upon jural relations, and as far as the right of an individual is the condition of his union with other rational individuals, punishment is the right of the offender, however paradoxical this may sound at first, because we are accustomed to imagine under right, some specific privileges. State punishment is likewise the protection of the offender, who, without it, would be exposed to all, even the most extravagant modes of private redress. No offender would hesitate to acknowledge and claim State punishment as his right, if the choice were left him, between State punishment, which, because it is State punishment, requires a formal trial on the one hand; and, on the other, those summary proceedings against criminals caught *flagrante delicto*, which we find, perhaps, in all early codes, and sometimes acknowledged to a very late period (*Blackstone*, 4, 308), or to which an excited people sometimes return, when the regular trial appears too slow for their inflamed passions, as has been the case in those riotous and illegal inflictions of death or other punishment, so unfortunately called lynch law in our country. I say unfortunately called lynch law, for it is ever to be deplored, if any illegal procedure receives a regular and separate name of its own. By this very application of a technical term, it assumes an air of systematized authority, which has an astonishing effect upon the multitude, and, in fact, upon most men." Book 2, § 345.

It is this simple principle that makes it murder for any one to kill even a man condemned to death by a competent court, in a different manner, or at a different time or place, than may have been fixed by the judgment. The law in this respect makes no difference between the lives of the guilty and the guiltless. Hence, when men seek to bring their enemies to justice and punishment by short and easy methods unknown to the law, and, therefore, in violation thereof, they but dig a pit into which themselves may, at any moment, fall and be lost. He who kills even a traitor in violation of law, kills at the same time the law itself.

Whatever may be your opinions, therefore, of the guilt or innocence of the accused, it can not effect the question of jurisdiction.

The next topic to which I desire to call your attention, arises from the language of the several specifications, and is particularly important for the purposes of this discussion, in so far as it may apply to those embraced under the last charge, namely, "VIOLATION OF THE LAWS OF WAR." It is this: that the alleged offenses were committed "within the military lines of the army of the United States, and the theater of military operations."

Whatever may have been the purpose of the Judge Advocate in inserting this clause, it is clear to any lawyer that no jurisdiction can arise from it, when taken in connection with the fact that the accused are citizens of the State of Indiana, and of the United States; and that Indiana has always sustained a relation of loyalty to the Union and its Government. But even if there was no proof of citizenship of the accused, it has not been proven that the State of Indiana is either "within the military lines of the armies of the United States," or "the theater of military operations." Had the averment been that it was within the theater of war, it would have been well; for the whole country is the theater of war. But that can not be said of the lines of the army, or of the theater of military operations. There is no definition of "the lines of the army" that extends so far as is here claimed by the Judge Advocate; and all military writers which I have been able to examine, define "the theater of operations" as follows, contradistinguishing it from the theater of war:

"*The theater of war* embraces not only the territory of the two belligerent powers, but also that of their allies, and of such secondary powers as, through fear or interest, may be drawn into the contest." * * *

"*The theater of operations*, however, is of a more limited character, and should not be confounded with the theater of war. In general, it includes only the territory which an army seeks, on the one hand, to defend, and on the other to invade." *Halleck's Elements of Military Art and Science*, p. 44; *Jomini's Art of War*, 74, 75.

I conclude, therefore, that "the theater of military operations," of a given army, must be in front of the base of operations of that army. Thus, the base of operations of General Buell's army, during the winter of 1861 and the succeeding spring, was the Ohio river; and his theater of operations, the whole country south of that base. And so of other armies. The base of our operations has generally been some line separating friendly from hostile territory; and hence, "the theater of operations," during this war, has generally been upon the enemy's soil. The sea-coast, I know, has frequently, during the present war, become the base of our operations; but, then, the enemy's country was still, in every instance, the theater of those operations. It is useless, however, to discuss these public and notorious facts; for the citizenship of the accused renders the attempt to make them responsible for a violation of the laws of war, wholly futile. Public enemies, only, are subject to the laws of war. The citizen, on the other hand, must answer for such acts as would, if committed by an enemy, be a transgression of the laws and usages of war, to his own Government, according to its own laws. I will offer a single example, which I quote from the autobiography of Lieutenant General Scott. It is as follows:

"In time of war all persons, *not* citizens of or owing allegiance to the United States of America, who shall be found *lurking*, as *spies*, in or about fortifications or encampments of the armies of the United States, or any of them, shall suffer death according to the law and usage of nations, by sentence of a general court-martial."

"'Not citizens;' because, if citizens, and found 'lurking,' the crime would be that of treason—'adhering to [our] enemies, giving them aid and comfort;' and is so defined by the Constitution." Vol. 1, pp. 290, 291.

But what are "the laws of war?" To whom do they apply? The answer to these questions must forever put an end to all attempts to invoke the aid of those laws, and of the tribunals in which they are administered for the trial and punishment of one of our own citizens; for it must be remembered that "the laws of war" constitute that branch of international law which regulates the intercourse and conduct of belligerent persons—public enemies—with each other. It is this code that condemns spies, when taken, to an infamous punishment at the hands of their enemy. It is for cruel breaches of this code, that we are sometimes compelled, as a measure of self-defense, to resort to the cruel practice of retaliation. It is to this code we refer for authority to punish guerrillas. And so I might go on until I had enumerated all its provisions; but I should not find one for the punishment of one of our own citizens among them all, unless it was established that he had first joined himself to, and become part of our acknowledged public adversaries. These laws of war are international—wholly international; and do not apply to the internal regulation of either one of two or more belligerent powers engaged in the same contest.

If, however, it shall be said that all persons, or the great body of them, engaged in the present contest, on either side, are citizens of the United States; and, therefore, that a difficulty results in the application of this public code to the parties, and that what character any citizen may sustain to either, may not always be clear, I grant it; but what follows? Can we give a man a hostile character before he has openly espoused it? Can we strip him of the rights of citizenship, before he has acquired that relation to the enemy which will entitle him to the protection of this code, as well as subject him to its penalties, in case he violates it? There must be some general rule on the subject; and there can be no other or better one than to hold all persons resident in the States which have seceded and still remain out of the Union, as *prima facie* public enemies; and all those who have adhered, and still adhere, to the Constitution and Union, as *prima facie* citizens of, and subject to the laws and authority of the United States.

I know, indeed, that there are at least two States which have hitherto sustained an ambiguous relation to the struggle. I allude to Kentucky and Missouri. They have never seceded by solemn act; and still maintain their Constitutional relation to the Federal Government. But, then, they are also repre-

sented in the Confederate Congress and army. The character of a citizen of either, must, therefore, depend upon his conduct; and he must be treated accordingly. If he has not joined the public enemy openly, but commits a crime against the Government, he is entitled to be tried therefor by the ordinary courts of the Union, in pursuance of the Constitution and laws. If he has joined the public enemy and been taken in arms, or "*lurking* as a *spy*," he is entitled to be treated according to "the laws of war:" in the former case to be exchanged as a prisoner of war; in the latter, to be hung for violating the laws of war. And this is just what our Government has been doing during this rebellion.

The form of these charges places the Government, then, in the following attitude toward the accused, namely: As claiming them as citizens on the one hand, but denying them the rights of citizenship on the other: as fixing upon them, for the purposes of this trial, and the punishment and infamy that may follow it, the character of public enemies, on the one hand; but denying them any of the advantages resulting from that character, on the other. Such a course, I submit, is unheard of in the judicial proceedings of our country; and with all deference to my friend, the Judge Advocate, is, in my opinion, wholly inadmissible. I have little apprehension, therefore, that you will claim jurisdiction of the accused on the ground that they are guilty of a violation of the laws of war; and, by consequence, public enemies. If you sustain your jurisdiction at all, it must, therefore, be upon the basis of *martial law*.

I beg leave to call your attention to a fact, in evidence, which must exercise an important influence upon your judgment on the question: Whether *martial law* is, or has been, in force in the State of Indiana, or not? and, of course, upon that of your jurisdiction. I allude, of course, to the fact that the courts, both of the State and of the United States, within the State of Indiana, have never, at any time, during the present rebellion, been thereby shut up, and the course of justice therein disturbed and stopped; but that those tribunals have all along remained open, and engaged in the administration of justice; and capable of enforcing their judgments, orders, and decrees, according to the established laws of the land. This fact was not proven in *Mr. Dodd's* case. His escape cut off all evidence in his defense; and, of course, this fact among others. Upon this fact, however, and a more thorough argument, I build my hopes of an ultimate decision against the jurisdiction. In pressing the argument and giving utterance to these hopes, I beg leave to say for myself, and for those whom I represent, that our objection to the jurisdiction does not spring from any objection to the individual members of the Court as fair-minded and honorable gentlemen, and worthy to sit in judgment upon any man in the land, subject, under the Constitution and laws, to their authority. It is, on the other hand, simply because as citizens, in no wise connected with the military or naval service of the United States, the accused are not within any military jurisdiction whatever. They claim the right to be tried by one of the constitutional courts of their country, and by a jury thereof. They ask justice at the hands of their peers of the District of the State of Indiana. For justice is properly justice only when legal, constitutional, and just means are employed in the attainment of legal, constitutional, and just ends. Your findings may correspond precisely with what would be those of a jury of the country; but if you lack jurisdiction—the right to find at all in the premises—it would be a mockery to call them, or any subsequent proceedings thereon, justice. Justice must have a right origin, or it can not exist. If what is called justice proceed from a tribunal without authority, it is injustice, outrage, crime; and, if it reach the life of him who is made its subject, *it is murder*. 3 *Co. Inst.*, p. 52; 1 *Hale's His. C. P.*, p. 6, 499–501; 4 *Bl. Com.*, 178; and 4 *State Trials*, p. 129.

A good citizen will not accept even a favorable judgment at the hands of an unauthorized tribunal, much less an adverse one; because it involves the overthrow of the laws and government of his country, on which all rights, whether of person or property, depend. A good State, alive to a proper sense of its duty and dignity, will never allow him to accept the one, nor to be made the victim of the other.

Has this Commission, then, jurisdiction of this cause? May it rightfully, lawfully, constitutionally try the accused upon the charges and specifications exhibited against them? If it may, whence does it derive its authority for that purpose?

I am here, to-day, to endeavor to answer these questions. You are here, to-day, to judge whether I give the true response, or not. That you may "the better judge," I ask your attention, your candor, and your patience.

I do not believe that you will hold, as was maintained before you on a former occasion, that you are precluded from going into the question of jurisdiction by the mere order of the General convening this Commission, and that sending the accused before you "for trial." That I may not misrepresent the position taken by the learned Judge Advocate, upon this point, I beg leave to quote the entire paragraph. It is as follows:

"When General Hovey convened this Commission within the limits of his jurisdiction, and committed the case of Harrison H. Dodd, the accused, to this Commission to try it, by virtue of his military power, acting under the authority that was given to him by the Commander-in-chief of the Army, namely, the President of the United States, he suspended the civil law, and put in operation the military, or *martial law*. The officers of this Commission could not, under the oath that they have taken, refuse to obey the orders of the officers placed over them. They could not stop and go back of that order, and refuse to hear and determine this case."

Now, whatever may have been your decision in that case upon the question of jurisdiction, I am very certain that you did not adopt the doctrine of this paragraph. I know you do not, and can not hold to the slavish and shameful notion, that you sit here to do whatever the commanding General may order. Obedience of the inferior to the superior is for the field, the march, the camp, the desk; and even there it has its limits. The law does not require obedience any-where in contravention of its own provisions. You are sworn to obey the "lawful" commands of your superiors; and there your obligation ceases. The employment of the word "lawful" (*Art. War*, Sec. 9), clearly excludes the idea of obedience to all but such commands. The unlawful order of a superior, even the highest, can not be given in evidence in justification of a trespass—much less of a felony. Can obedience, then, extend to the duties of the court room, and subordinate the justice which, in your judicial capacity, your are to administer there? If it does, what a mockery is all military justice! Who would, or could consent to sit as a member of a military court, and pass judgment upon the lives and fortunes of his fellow-men, when his own convictions of the law and the facts, in the case, were to have no control over his decisions!

"I had sooner be a dog and bay at the moon."

Held on such terms, your commissions would be but badges of the most odious and wicked servitude. Every free mind that has not quite escaped the direction of conscience, must reject such a position with indignation and horror! I think I hear you exclaiming at such a proposal: "No; let the General go directly to his purposes, and punish whom he will, and as he will, without the deceitful and wicked pretense of a trial. I will brave all consequences sooner than thus surrender my manhood. He shall never employ me in a mockery so foul, and so cruel!" Every honorable mind would so feel and so speak; and none, I am sure, more promptly and warmly than my distinguished friend, the General, who now commands this district; and under whose authority you sit. For, if it is all a matter of command and obedience, then let the command and its execution stand together, without the intervention of this hollow form of justice. Do not mock the predestined victims with the delusive hopes arising from the forms of a trial, that, from first to last, on this theory, can not rise higher than a miserable trick to deceive the looker-on; and divide the responsibility of acts not capable of justification, when placed before the world in their true light. Indeed, on such a theory, you do not constitute a court at all, in any received sense of the term; for "a court is a place where justice is judicially administered."

With these observations, I shall deliver this topic to your consideration and judgment.

I am thus brought at last to the discussion of *martial law*, as the basis, and, indeed, the only basis on which your jurisdiction of the present cause can possibly be sustained. If *martial law* does, in fact, exist in the State of Indiana, you may have jurisdiction. If it does not, you do not, and can not possibly possess such jurisdiction. The question, therefore, recurs upon us:

Has *martial law* an actual existence in the State of Indiana to-day? If so, how has it received such existence? Does it exist by proclamation, by law, or by necessity? If by proclamation, or law, when was the proclamation made, or the law passed? If by necessity, when did that necessity arise; and wherein does it consist?

As the first step toward a satisfactory answer to these questions, let us determine what *martial law* really is; for this is still a question. This question I propose to answer from the books. Smith says:

"*Martial law* is the law of war, that depends on the just, but arbitrary power of the King or his lieutenant; for, though the King doth not make any law but by common consent in Parliament, yet in time of war, by reason of the necessity of it, to guard against dangers that often arise, he useth absolute power, so that his word is law." *Smith on the English Republic*, book 2, chap. 4.

Sir Matthew Hale, in his *History of the Common Law*, says:

"*Martial law* is not, in truth and reality, a law, but something indulged rather than allowed as a law; the necessity of government, order, and discipline in an army is that only which gives these laws any countenance." 1 *His. C. L.*, p. 54.

I make this quotation, not because, in the present state of opinion and law, either in England or America, it gives us a very precise and accurate notion of *martial law;* but in order to bring it into relation to a criticism which, when taken in connection with the state of British military law at the time the venerable Hale wrote, is, in my opinion, entirely unjust; and, to show that, at that time, this definition was as accurate and complete as could be given. The criticism to which I refer is that of the late Attorney General Cushing. He says:

"This proposition is a mere composite blunder—a total misapprehension of the matter. It confounds *martial law* and *military law;* it ascribes to the former the uses of the latter; it erroneously assumes that the government of a body of troops is a *necessity*, more than that of a body of civilians, or citizens. It confounds and confuses all the relations of the subject, and is an apt illustration of the incompleteness of the notions of the common-law jurists of England in regard to matters not comprehended in that limited branch of legal science." 8 *Opinions of the Att'ys Gen.*, 365, *et seq.*

Now, I beg leave to say, that Sir Matthew Hale was not a mere common-law lawyer. His writings show him to have been familiar with the civil law; and to have read extensively the Continental writers on public law. Nor is it true that his observations on the nature and uses of *martial law* constitute a mere "composite blunder"—"a total misapprehension of the question." The "blunder," on the contrary, is on the part of the learned Attorney General; and not on that of the venerable Chief Justice. It will be apparent that

I am right, if we refer to the state of England and English military law at the time the *History of the Common Law* was written. Its author died in 1676. Up to that time England had properly no military code. Her armies were really subject to such laws as the King might impose, where a limit upon his will, in this respect, had not been fixed by Parliament. It was not until after Hale wrote, and had been gathered to his fathers, that the first military bill was passed, and military law thereby placed upon a different footing from that of *martial law.* The will of the King, until then, was the law of the army—a will regulated, indeed, by the principles of the civil law; but, even, in that respect, controlled no further than he chose; and this will is the same, whether applied to soldiers or civilians. "It is not, in truth and reality, a law." It was, nevertheless, pretty much all the law known to the British army in the time of Hale. 1 *Bl. Com.*, chap. 13; 2 *Sullivan's Lectures*, p. 257. In this view of the facts of history, and the state of military law when Hale wrote, the learned Attorney General seems to be guilty of the blunder which he attributes to the Chief Justice.

The first member of Mr. Stephens' definitions of *martial law* is sufficiently accurate. He says:

"*Martial law* may be defined as the law (whatever it may be), which is imposed by military power." 2 *Com. Laws of England*, p. 561.

The Duke of Wellington was also right when he defined it thus:

"*Martial law* is neither more nor less than the will of the General who commands the army." *Hansard's Debates*, (3d series), vol. 115, p. 880.

And again when he wrote as follows:

"Military law" [i. e., *martial law*], "as applied to any persons excepting officers, soldiers, and followers of the army, for whose government there are particular provisions of law, in all well regulated countries, is neither more nor less than *the will of the General of the army.*" *Dispatches*, vol. 6, p. 43.

The distinction between *martial* and *military* law is, in this last definition, made plain, the latter being confined to provisions of law for the regulation of the army; and the former to such as the will of the General may impose upon those—not soldiers—under *martial law.*

Earl Grey, in discussing the questions growing out of a declaration of *martial law* in Ceylon, again expresses the idea with sufficient accuracy. He says:

"What is called proclaiming *martial law*, is no law at all; but merely for the sake of public safety, in circumstances of great emergency, *setting aside all law and acting under military power;* a proceeding which requires to be followed up by an act of indemnity when the disturbances are at an end." *Hough's Prec. in Mil. Law*, p. 515.

Judge-Advocate-General Dundas, in writing upon the subject, says:

"*Martial law* is not a written law; it arises on a necessity to be judged of by the *Executive*, and ceases the instant it can possibly be allowed to cease. *Military law* has to do only with the land forces of the Crown, mentioned in the second section of the Mutiny Act. *Martial law comprises all persons, all are under it,* whether they be civil or military." *Second Rep. on Ceylon, Hough, supra,* p. 535.

"When *martial law* is proclaimed," says Hough, "courts-martial are thereby vested with such a summary proceeding, that neither time, place nor persons are considered. Necessity is the only rule of conduct; nor are the punishments which courts-martial may inflict under such authority limited to" such as are prescribed by law. *Hough on Courts-Martial,* p. 383.

Captain Benet, in his treatise on *Military Law and Courts-Martial,* in speaking of *martial law,* says:

"*Martial law,* then, is that military rule and authority which exists in time of war, and is conferred by the laws of war, in relation to persons and things, under and *within the scope of active military operations in carrying on the war, and which extinguishes or suspends civil rights, and the remedies founded upon them for the time being,* so far as it may appear to be necessary, in order to the full accomplishment of the purpose of the war, the party exercising it being liable in an action for any abuse of the authority thus conferred. It is the application of military government—the government of force—to persons and property within the scope of it, according to the laws and usages of war, to the exclusion of municipal government, in all respects where the latter would impair the efficiency of military law, or military action." *Benet on Mil. Law and Courts-Martial,* p. 14.

The late Commander-in-chief of the Army of the United States, Major General Halleck, observes:

"We remark, in conclusion, that the right to declare, apply and exercise *martial law,* is one of the rights of sovereignty, and is as essential to the existence of a State, as is the right to declare or carry on war. It is one of the incidents of war, and, like the power to take human life in battle, results directly and immediately from the fact that war legally exists. It is a power inherent in every government, and must be regarded and recognized by all other governments, but the question of the authority of any particular functionary to exercise this power, is a matter to be determined by local, and not by international law. Like a declaration of siege, or blockade, the power of the officer who makes it, is to be presumed until disavowed; and neutrals who attempt, in derogation of that authority, do so at their peril." *International Law and Laws of War,* p. 380.

Again, he says:

"The English common law authorities generally confound *martial* with *military* law; and, consequently, throw very little light upon the subject, considered as a domestic fact; and in parliamentary debates it has usually been discussed as a *fact,* rather than as forming any part of their system of jurisprudence. Nevertheless. there are numerous instances in which *martial law* has been declared and enforced, in time of rebellion or insurrection, not only in India, and British Colonial Possessions, but also in England and Ireland. It seems that no act of Parliament is required to precede such declaration, although it is usually followed by an act of indemnity, when the disturbances which called it forth are at an end, *in order to give constitutional existence to the fact of martial law." Id.,* 374.

I desire to remark, in passing, that a careful study of the English authorities alluded to, will, perhaps, explain them, and show that their confusion is only apparent, in relation to this subject. In the first place, as already shown, the English had no distinct system of *military law* until after the revolution of 1688; and before that time, their armies were subject, in a great degree, to simple *martial law.* It is true, the King's *will* was, in some measure, restrained by statute. In the second, as the only ground upon which that *will—martial law—*can apply to others than soldiers *within* the kingdom, is that of *necessity,* it was both natural and philosophical for them to regard it as simply a fact. Indeed, it is nothing else but a fact both in its origin and its application. It originates in necessity, which is a fact. It is the will of the commanding general, who always determines its extent and the mode of its application. It will thus assume a different form—will be more or less sweeping—cruel or merciful, according to the exigency of each particular instance of its exercise, as well as the character and temper of him who administers it. A thing thus variant and uncertain can not be allowed as a law; for a law must be a rule prescribed, must be uniform in its application, which can never be said of any thing resulting from mere necessity, and subject for its measure and duration to mere human will. The only element common to such a state of administration and law, is that both are applied to the affairs of men. It will, therefore, be subject, of course, to the judgment of public opinion as all other facts are, in which moral agents and relations are involved; but whatever restraint that imposes, can not change the fact into a law. Nor, it would seem, does the right of a belligerent depend upon the legality of the war, as remarked by General Halleck. On the contrary, we might naturally suppose that he who entered upon an illegal and unjust war, would be most likely to avail himself first of the advantages of *martial law,* which, in the language of Mr. Adams, would "sweep the laws of his adversary by the board," and substitute his discretion therefor. Hence, upon the whole, I see no reason why the learned general should criticise the English. The last two authors cited, seemingly without perceiving it, confine the operation of *martial law* to the territory of public enemies, or to the immediate theater of military operations. In either view, their remarks are inapplicable to our condition here; for we may admit the most unbounded authority to exercise *martial law* in our generals, in carrying on a foreign war in an enemy's country; or in a domestic war "*within the scope of active military operations,*" and it will not follow that any such authority can exist in a State devoted to the Government, and in no sense the theater of "*active military operations*." In the foreign country, the citizen will be subject to international law; and our public enemy can not look beyond that to see whether, in the exercise of *martial law*, we disregard our own Constitution. At home, the fact of war and the immediate presence of hostile armies puts an end to all other laws; and *martial law*, for the time being, exists by necessity. Military power is rather, in such case, a law to itself. They leave us, therefore, in quite as much doubt and confusion, so far as the case in hand is concerned, as they found us.

I beg your pardon for introducing here, a little out of place, the observations upon martial law of some of our own leading politicians. I say politicians advisedly; for I do not think that they were generally actuated in the utterance of these opinions by the motives that should govern statesmen; and I do not think so, because the whole spirit of the debates in which they were delivered, was of a most decided and even bitter partisan tone. I allude to the debates on remitting the fine imposed by Judge Hall upon General Jackson, at New Orleans, in 1815, for contempt of court in refusing obedience to a writ of *habeas corpus*. Democrats in Congress were in favor of the measure; while most, if not all the Whigs, were opposed to it. Mr. John Q. Adams, then in the House of Representatives, made it an occasion for striking at both the Democratic party and slavery. He maintained that the measure was a hobby, on which leading Democrats were seeking to elevate themselves to the Presidency upon General Jackson's popularity; and then turned upon the slaveholders of the South, and reminded them how easy it would be, in some fit emergency, to employ *martial law* for the abolition of slavery. And such generally was the spirit of the debate; a spirit, one would think, little calculated to render opinions remarkable for their legal accuracy. It was in this debate that Mr. Adams said:

"The power of Congress"—the power to declare martial law—"has, perhaps, never been called into exercise under the present Constitution. But when the laws of war are in force, what, I ask, is one of those laws? It is this: *that when a country is invaded, and two hostile armies are met in martial array*, the commanders of both armies have power to emancipate all the slaves in the invaded territory.

"And here I recur again to the example of General Jackson. What are you about in Congress? You are about passing a law to refund to General Jackson, the amount of a certain fine imposed upon him by a judge under the laws of Louisiana. You are going to refund him the money with interest, and this you are going to do, because the imposition of the fine was unjust. And why was it unjust? Because General Jackson was acting under the laws of war; and because the moment you place a military commander in a district that is the theater of war, the laws of war apply to that place.

"I might furnish a thousand proofs to show that the pretensions of the gentlemen to the sanctity of their municipal institutions, under a state of actual invasion, and actual war, whether servile, civil, or foreign, is wholly unfounded, and that the laws of war do, in all such cases, take precedence. I lay this down as the law of nations. I say, the military authority takes, for the time, the place of all municipal institutions, and of slavery among the rest; and that, under that state of things, so far from its being true, that the States where slavery exists have the exclusive management of the subject, not only the President of the United States, but the commander of the army, has power to order the universal emancipation of the slaves. I have given here more in detail a principle which I have asserted on this floor before now; and of which I have no more doubt than that you, sir, occupy that chair."

In the course of the same debates, Mr. Buchanan, taking it for granted that General Jackson had done no more than his duty in declaring *martial law* in New Orleans, in 1814 and 1815, said:

"If General Jackson did no more than his duty in declaring *martial law*, the moment that declaration was made, the official functions of Judge Hall ceased, with regard to his power of issuing writs of *habeas corpus*, which might interfere with the defense of the city. As soon as *martial law* was in force, every citizen of New Orleans, whether sustaining an official character or not, was bound to submit to it. * * * For it was quite a plain case, that, if *martial law* did not supersede and put in abeyance the civil power, it would be wholly insufficient in attaining the only objects for which alone it could be tolerated or justified."

Mr. Douglas, in the House of Representatives, maintained the same principles; bu', from his statement of the case, confined their operation to the defense of the city; in other words, to a state of siege. Among other things, he said:

"I maintain that, in the exercise of the power of proclaiming *martial law*, General Jackson did not violate the Constitution, nor assume to himself any authority not fully authorized and legalized by his position, his duty and the necessity of the case. General Jackson was the agent of the Government, legally and constitutionally authorized to defend the city of New Orleans. It was his duty to do this at all hazards. It was then conceded, and is now conceded, that nothing but *martial law* would enable him to perform that duty. His power was commensurate with his duty, and he was authorized to use the means essential to its performance. This principle has been recognized and acted upon by all civilized nations, and is familiar to all who are conversant with military history. *It does not imply the right to suspend the laws and civil tribunals at pleasure. The right grows out of the necessity.* The principle is that the commanding General may go as far, and no further than is absolutely necessary to the defense of the place committed to his protection. There are exigences in the history of nations, when necessity becomes the paramount law, to which all other considerations must yield. If it becomes necessary to blow up a fort, it is right to do it. If it is necessary to sink a ship, it is right to sink it. If it is necessary to burn a city, it is right to burn it." *Life and Speeches of Senator Douglas*, pp. 25, 26.

And so I might go on, adding opinions and definitions of *martial law* to endless extent. I will quote but one more; and that is the opinion of Attorney General Cushing, already referred to. He says:

"*Martial law*, as exercised in any country by the commander of a foreign army, is an element of the *jus belli*. It is incidental to a state of solemn war, and appertains to the law of nations. The commander of the invading, occupying, or conquering army, rules the invaded, occupied, or conquered foreign country, with supreme power, limited only by international law, and the orders of the sovereign or government he serves or represents. For by the law of nations, the *occupatio bellica*, in a just war, transfers the sovereign power of the enemy's country to the conqueror." *Wolff's Jus Gentium*, ¿ 255; *Grotius De Jure et Pacis, ed. Cocceii*, lib. iii, cap. 8.

Such occupation by right of war is, *so long as it is military only*, that is, *flagrante bello*, will be the case put by the Duke of Wellington, of all the powers of the government resumed in the hands of the commander-in-chief. If any local authority continue to exist, it will be with his permission only, and with the power to do nothing, except what in his plenary discretion, or his own sovereign, through him, shall see fit to authorize. The law of the land will have ceased to possess any proper vigor.

Thus, while the armies of the United States occupied different provinces of the Mexican Republic, the respective commanders were not limited in authority by any local law. They allowed, or rather required, the magistrates of the country, municipal or judicial, to continue to administer the laws of the country among their own countrymen, but in subjection always to the military power, which acted summarily and according to discretion, when the belligerent interests of the conqueror required it, and which exercised jurisdiction, either summarily or by means of military commissions, *for the protection or punishment of citizens of the United States in Mexico.*

That, it would seem, was one of the forms of *martial law*. A violent state of things, to cease, of course, when hostilities should cease, and military occupation be changed into political occupation. *Elphinstone* v. *Bedruchund*, 1 *Knapp's Rep.*, p. 388; *Cross* v. *Harrison*, 16 *How.*, p. 164.

If we now return, and endeavor to glean from all these authorities and opinions an idea of *martial law*, as applicable to the internal affairs of a State, we shall find ourselves scarcely nearer to it than we were at the start. The *laws of war* regulate a state of war, and define the rights of parties to it, with respect to each other; and can only afford, therefore, a remote analogy for our guidance in the internal concerns of a State in which riots or rebellions call into requisition the military power. True,

when a civil war assumes the magnitude of our present contest, and the parties thereto—rebels on the one side and Government on the other—from the necessity of the case, as well as from considerations of humanity, are compelled to adopt the public law of war, and to regulate their conduct according to its principles, the laws of war become, to that extent, a sufficient guide. But all this does not, in the least, help us, in regard to those States which have never been engaged against the Government. Whether any, and if any, what assertion of military power, incompatible with civil institutions and civil rights, is admissible in those States, does not appear from the books that treat of *martial law*. Earl Grey seems to approach the point more nearly than the rest; for in such case *martial law* would "*in truth and fact be no law at all; but the setting aside of all law and acting under military power.*" *Supra.* And this, he says, can only be done "in circumstances of great emergency," and must be followed "by an act of indemnity." It is, therefore, the substitution of military force for, and to the exclusion of, the laws; and can be justified no further than is absolutely necessary. And all the authorities and opinions cited go to this extent, and no further.

Has this substitution, then, of military power for civil law, and civil tribunals and institutions, taken place in Indiana? And if so, upon what necessity? When was it done? Who determined the necessity, and made the substitution? Where is the act of Congress, the proclamation of the President, or the order of the military commander of the department, or the district? Have these, or has any of them, acted upon this subject; and, if so, to what extent? And above, and before all, where is the grant of authority to any, or all of them combined, or, indeed, to the whole Government, thus to "set aside all law," and substitute "military power" therefor? To assume that any such authority can exist in a limited government, is a self-contradiction.

Let us examine, briefly, the nature of the Anglican system of civil liberty—institutional government—a system which, in a very large measure, we have inherited or adopted; and see whether such a system as *martial law* is at all compatible therewith. Can the two exist together?

I shall endeavor to answer this question by a brief review of English history and law; for if this power "to set aside all law," and to "act under military power," be at all consistent with such a system of law and government, we shall thus be able to determine in what emergencies and to what extent.

I enter the more cheerfully upon this review, because it will enable me to correct my friend, the Judge Advocate, in an assertion which he has frequently made during the progress of these trials, namely: "*We are making new precedents daily.*" Now, I think, I shall be able to show him that we are following old and bad precedents—the work of wicked and lawless princes in evil times—which were condemned, disallowed, and reversed by better princes immediately upon the return of better times; and which are only not known to him, because they have so long remained dead and buried among the rubbish of barbarous ages, that he has not been able, or, at least, has not chosen to dig them up for his own and your guidance on this occasion. I shall aid him in this respect; and, while I do so, must beg his pardon, and that of the Government he represents, for dispelling the illusion that either is entitled to patent a new precedent. In this regard they will find, after all, and, indeed, they should have known from the first, that the further back they go in the history of the past, the more precedents they will find for the easy but ruinous substitution of *force* for *law*. Wherever a free people have lost their liberties, there will be found a precedent in point. The history of Greece and Rome is fruitful of such precedents. Solomon had wiser conceptions of the methods by which history continually repeats itself, than to speak of new precedents; and the sum of wisdom on this point, as in his day, still remains happily expressed in these words: "There is no new thing under the sun."

I will not go back in the history of English law beyond *Magna Charta;* for that "solemn instrument" has been justly regarded as laying the imperishable foundations of the great political institutions of that country. *Creasy on the English Constitution*, 3. Ours, in America, rest on the same foundations—are referable to the same origin.

The 29th chapter of that instrument, as given by Henry III, contains these provisions, which have found a place in all our American Constitutions:

"*Nullus liber homo capiatur, vel imprisonetur, aut disseisietur de libero tenemento suo, vel libertatibus, vel liberis consuetudinibus suis, aut utlagatur, aut exuletur, aut aliquo modo distruatur, nec super cum ibimus, nec super eum mittimus, nisi per legale judicium parium suorum, vel per legem terræ.*" 2 *Coke's Inst.*, p. 45. Which has been rendered as follows:

"No freeman shall be taken, or imprisoned, or disseized, or outlawed, or exiled or banished, or in any ways destroyed; nor will we pass upon him, nor will we send upon him, unless by the lawful judgment of his peers, or by the law of the land." *Creasy, supra,* p. 134.

"These are," as Mr. Creasy observes, "all words that should be carefully read over, and over, and again; for, as Lord Coke quaintly observes, in his comments on them, 'as the gold-finer will not, out of the dust, threds, or shreds of gold, let passe the least crum,' in respect of the excellency of the metal; so ought not the learned reader to passe any syllable of this law, in respect of the excellency of the matter.'" *Id.*, 135; and 2 *Inst.*, 57.

Lord Coke in commenting upon the words: "No man destroyed," etc., gives the following commentary and illustration:

"That is, forejudged of life, or limb, disherited, or put to torture or death." * * *

"Thomas, Earl of Lancaster, was destroyed, that is, adjudged to die as a traitor, and put to death, in 14 *E.* 2, and a record thereof made; and Henry, Earl of Lancaster, his brother and heir, was restored for two principal errors against the same Thomas, Earl: 1. *Quod non fuit araniatus, et ad responsionem positus tempore pacis, eo quod cancellariu et aliæ curiæ Regis fuer, apertæ, in quibus lex fiebat unicuique prout fieri consuevit:* that is to say: Because he was not arraigned, and because in time of peace, he was put to trial while the Chancery and other courts of the King were open, in each of which the law was regularly administered: 2. *Quod contra cartam de libertatibus, cum dictus Thomas fuit unus parium et magnatum regni, in qua continetur*—and reciteth this chapter of *Magna Charta,* and specially *quod Dominus Lex non super eum ibit; nec mittet; nisi per legale judicium parium suorum, contra legem, et contra tenorum Magna Charta;* that is, because it was against the charter of liberties, since the said Thomas was one of the peers and magnates of the realm in which it is preserved; and reciteth this chapter of *Magna Charta*, and specially 'because the Lord the King will not proceed against any one, nor send upon him, unless by the legal judgment of his peers. Nevertheless, by the aforesaid proceeding, in time of peace, without arraignment, or pleading, or the legal judgment of his peers, against law, and the terms of *Magna Charta*, he was put to death. More examples of this kind might be found." *Id., supra.*

This case, when the mode of trial is shown, is the reversal of a precedent which the Judge Advocate would, perhaps, style "a new precedent;" for the historian tells us that Thomas of Lancaster was adjudged to death by a kind of military court, extemporized by the King, and consisting of himself and a few Earls and Barons. 2 *Lingard His. Eng.*, p. 248, and note; 2 *Hume His. of Eng.*, pp. 159, 160.

The learned Coke adds, immediately after citing this case, and its reversal:

"Every oppression against law, by color of any usurped authority, is a kind of destruction; for *Quando aliquid prohibitur, prohibiter et omne, per quod devenitur ad illud;* and it is the most grievous oppression that is done by color of justice." *Id., sup.*

The reversal of a second precedent that might be regarded as new, is recited by Sir Matthew Hale in his *History of the Common Law;* and is thus given:

"The exercise of *martial law*, whereby any person should lose his life, or member, or liberty, may not be permitted in time of peace, when the King's Courts are open for all persons to receive justice according to the laws of the land. This is, in substance, declared by the *Petition of Right*, 3 *Car.* 1, whereby such commissions and *martial law* were repealed and declared contrary to law. And accordingly was that famous case of Edmund, Earl of Kent, who being taken at Pomfret, 15 *Edw.* 2, the King and divers lords proceeded to give sentence of death against him, as in a kind of military court, by a summary proceeding, which judgment was afterward, in 1 *Edw.* 3, reversed in Parliament. And the reason of that reversal serving to the purpose in hand, I shall here insert it as entered in the record, viz.: '*Quod cum quicunq; homo ligeus domini regis pro seditionibus, etc., tempore pacis captus et in quacunque curia domini regis ductus fuerit de ejusmodi seditionibus et aliis feloniis sibi impositis per legem et consuetudine regni arrectari debet et responsionem adduci, et inde per communem legem antequam fuerit morti adjudicand' (triari) etc. Unde cum notorium sit et manifestum quod totum tempus quo impositum fuit eidem comiti propter mala et facinora fecisse, ad tempus in quo captus fuit et in quo morti adjudicatus fuit, fuit tempus pacis maximæ, cum per totum tempus prædictum et cancellaria et aliæ plac. curiæ domini regis apertæ fuer. in quibus cuilibet lex fiebatur sicut fieri consuevit, nec idem dominis rex unquam tempore illo cum vexillis explicatis equitabat, etc."* Which record may be rendered thus:

"Whenever the subject of the Lord the King, shall be arrested for sedition in time of peace, before he can be adjudged to death, according to the common law, he must be taken into some court of the King, and held to answer for such seditions and other felonies; whence it follows, that when it is made known and manifest, that all the time during which it is alleged that the crimes were done, on account of which he was arrested, to the time in which he was taken and adjudged to death, was a time of profound peace, and during all the time aforesaid, the Chancery and other courts of the King were open, in which any law could be executed, as it was the custom to have done, the same Lord the King had no power, during that time, to exercise military control.

"And, accordingly, the judgment was reversed; for *martial law,* which is rather indulged than allowed, and *that only in case of necessity,* in time of open war, *is not permitted in time of peace when the ordinary courts of justice are open.*" 1 *His. C. L.,* pp. 55, 56.

In order that these precedents may have their due weight in this case, I beg leave to give a legal definition of what is, in this respect, held to be a time of peace in England, according to the common law. I will quote the precise language of Lord Coke, who says:

"*When the courts of Justice are open,* and the judges and ministers of the same may by law protect men from oppression and violence, and distribute justice to all, *it is said to be a time of peace.* So, when by invasion, insurrection, or rebellion, etc., *the peaceable course of justice is stopped, so as the courts of justice be as it were shut up,* then it is said to be time of war." *Coke upon Littleton,* 249, b. n. 1.

In further commenting upon the great chapter of *Magna Charta,* already quoted, Lord Coke says:

"'By the judgment of his peers' are to be understood of the King's suit"—in other words, of a State prosecution. "And it extendeth to the King's suit in case of treason or felony, or misprision of treason or felony, or being accessory to a felony before or after, and not to any other inferior offense. Also, it extendeth to the trial where he is to be convicted." 2 *Inst.,* 49.

And upon the word "*legale,*" he says:

"By the word *legale,* amongst others, three things are implied: 1st. That the manner of trial was by law before this statute. 2d. That their verdict must be legally given, wherein

principally it is to be observed, 1st. That the lords ought to hear no evidence but in the presence and hearing of the prisoner; 2d. After the lords have gone together to consider of the evidence, they can not send to the High Steward to ask the judges any question of law, but in the hearing of the prisoner, etc.; 3d. When all the evidence is given, etc., the High Steward can not collect the evidence against the prisoner, or in any sort confer with the lords, touching their evidence, in the absence of the prisoner," etc. 2 *Inst.,* 49.

And again, upon the word, "by the law of the land," while, perhaps, going to the extent of permitting a party suspected of treason to be arrested without writ, upon suspicion and common fame, he totally excludes the notion of his continued imprisonment without some warrant; and leaves out of the question all other forms of trial, but that by the legal judgment of his peers. *Id.,* pp. 50, 55.

After the close of the long and glorious reign of Edward the Third, his unworthy grandson, Richard the Second, came to the throne, which he finally lost, by attempting to return to such precedents as those just cited of his great grandfather. His efforts to get rid of *Magna Charta* and the Common Law, and to substitute the Roman Civil Law for them, may be learned from the records of his reign. An outline sufficient for our purpose will be found in *Sullivan's Lectures on the Laws and Constitution of England.* (See vol. 1, p. 318, *et seq.;* and vol. 2, 257.) In the former place will be seen what great efforts he made to introduce the Civil Law, and in the latter, that this law became the law of the Marshal's Court; no doubt on account of the fondness of the kings therefor, and, also, that the jurisdiction of that court embraced the administration of *martial law* over soldiers and camp followers.

In subsequent reigns, the kings of England struggled almost constantly to extend this jurisdiction to others than soldiers; but it was a struggle against the free spirit of the nation. In the reign of Henry the Eighth, an instrument was placed in the hands of that monarch, by the Parliament, which seemed to go far toward making the king absolute; and which was subsequently used by him and his successors in such a way as almost to insure that end. This was done by the passage of a statute "which," as Lord Coke observes, "gives more power to the king than he had before;" and yet even there it is declared that he can not "alter the law, statutes or customs of the realm, or impeach any in his inheritance, goods, body, life, etc." The father of that King had gone so far, prior to this act, as to claim the right to control the subject's right of doing all things not unlawful (*Hallam's Constitutional History,* p. 15); and his daughter, Queen Elizabeth, carried the power under this act to such an extent as to set all law at defiance. "One Peter Burchill, a fanatical Puritan, and, perhaps, insane, conceiving that Sir Christopher Hatton was an enemy to the true religion, determined to assassinate him: but, by mistake, he wounded instead a famous seaman, Captain Hawkins. For this ordinary crime, the Queen could hardly be prevented from directing him to be tried instantly by *martial law*. Her council, however, (and this it is important to observe), resisted this illegal proposition with spirit and success." (*Hallam Cons. His.*, 143.) "The Queen had been told, it seems, of what had been done in Wyatt's business—a case not at all parallel; though there was no sufficient necessity, even in that instance, to justify the proceeding by *martial law*. But bad precedents always beget *progenium vitiosiorem*." (*Id.*, in note). But the same learned authority gives the following instances of the exercise by Queen Elizabeth of a power almost absolute, through proclamations. I quote:

"We have, indeed, a proclamation some years afterward, declaring that such as brought into the kingdom, dispersed papal bulls, or traitorous libels against the Queen, should, with all severity, be proceeded against by Her Majesty's lieutenants, or their deputies, by *martial law*, and suffer such pains and penalties as they should inflict; and that none of her said lieutenants, or their deputies, be in any wise impeached in body, lands, or goods, at any time hereafter, for any thing to be done or executed in the punishment of any such offender, according to the said *martial law* and the tenor of this proclamation, any law or statute to the contrary, notwithstanding." This Mr. Hallam regards as "by no means constitutional;" but apologises for it, because it was done "when, within a few days, the vast armament of Spain"—known in history as the Spanish Armada—"might effect a landing on the coast." "But," he remarks further, "it is an unhappy consequence of all deviations from the even course of law, that the forced acts of overruling necessity come to be distorted into precedents, to serve the purposes of arbitrary power." *Id.*, 143; *Hume's His. Eng.*, p. 344.

I quote the same author for the following instance of a still greater stretch of this arbitrary and unconstitutional power, which occurred during the same reign:

"No measure of Elizabeth's reign can be compared, in point of illegality, to a commission in July, 1595, directed to Sir Thomas Wilford, whereby, upon no other allegation than that there had been of late sundry great unlawful assemblies of a riotous sort, both in the city of London and the suburbs, for the suppression whereof (for the insolency of many desperate offenders is such that they care not for any ordinary punishment) it was found necessary to have some such notable rebellious persons to be speedily suppressed by execution to death, according to the justice of *martial law;* he is appointed provost marshal with authority by the magistrates, to attack and seize such notable, rebellious and incorrigible offenders, and in the presence of the magistrate to execute them openly, on the gallows." * * *

"This peremptory style of suspending the Common Law was a stretch of prerogative without an adequate parallel, so far as I know, in any former period." *Id.*, 143, 144; 4 *Hume's His. Eng.*, p. 344.

It must be remembered that these high-handed measures took place in the sixteenth century, a period when both religious and political revolutions were rife in Europe; that the life of Elizabeth was more than once the object of conspiracies, both foreign and domestic; that the ablest men in Europe were parties to and prompters in these perfidious and bloody schemes (*Motley's Dutch Republic*, vol. 2, part 3, p. 333; and *D'Israeli's Curiosities of Literature*, 1st. ser., p. 166); that the very persons at whom these proclamations were aimed, had, in the preceding reign of her sister, employed the same agencies for the overthrow of her religion in the kingdom, and the destruction of her friends; that the constable's and marshal's court, "whose jurisdiction was considered as of a military nature," and whose proceedings were not according to the course of the common law, had "sometimes tried offenders "—not soldiers—by what was called *martial law*, "either during or not long after a serious rebellion;" and, above all, that, at the time of the last-mentioned proclamation, the queen was a very old woman, and, it may be, somewhat subject to fits of ill temper. All these things must be reckoned in her favor, to mitigate the judgment of history against these arbitrary measures; but still can not save the acts themselves from the indignant condemnation of mankind. Accordingly, we find Lord Coke, in the next reign, condemning utterly the doctrine that the king's proclamation can either alter, repeal, or suspend the law, or make that criminal which before was not. He says:

"The King can not create any offense by his prohibition or proclamation, which was not an offense before; for that was to change the law, and to make an offense which was not; for *ubi non est lex, ibi non est transgressio:* therefore that which can not be punished without proclamation, can not be punished with it." "But," he further remarks, "we do find divers precedents of proclamations which are utterly against law and reason, and for that void; *quæ contra rationem juris introducta sunt, non debent trahi in consequentiam "—i. e.*, measures introduced contrary to the reason of the law, ought not to be drawn into consequence, or precedent. Again, he says that it had been held that the king, by his proclamation, can not create any offense which was not an offense before, "for then he may alter the law of the land by his proclamation, in a high point; for, if he may create an offense where none is, upon that ensues fine and imprisonment. Also, the law of England is divided into three parts—common law, statute law, and custom; but the King's proclamation is none of them. Also, *malum aut est malum in se, aut prohibitum*, that which is against common law is *malum in se, malum prohibitum* is such an offense as is prohibited by act of Parliament, and not by proclamation." 12 *Rep.*, pp. 74, 75, 76.

Yet, notwithstanding the law was thus cogently laid down in the time of James the First, we, nevertheless, find Charles the First, in the first year of his reign, endeavoring to return to the bad and unlawful measures of his predecessors. He accordingly addressed a commission to Lord Wimbleton, 28th December, 1625, empowering "him to proceed against soldiers, or dissolute persons joining with them, who should commit any robberies, etc., which, by *martial law*, ought to be punished with death, by such summary course as is agreeable to *martial law*." He, also, issued another commission of the same kind, in 1626. See *Hallam's Const. His.*, p. 223, and note.

These unlawful proclamations, among other grievances, subsequently moved Parliament to demand of His Majesty the justly celebrated Petition of Right, which forever put an end to all colorable pretenses of their legality. Let it be observed, too, that this great act is but declaratory of the common law. No measure was ever supported on the side of the Parliament with greater force of talents and learning; or opposed by the King with worse show of reason, or more barefaced attempts to deceive the public, and to prevent its final passage. Among the managers of the Commons, on that occasion, may be reckoned the great names of Coke and Selden—two names that may, perhaps, be equaled, but certainly not surpassed, for learning and ability, in English history. Under their management, the measure was finally perfected and passed; and became a new guaranty of Anglican liberty. I shall make no apology for reading here such parts of it as I deem pertinent to the subject under consideration. They are as follows:

"And whereas, also, by the statute called the Great Charter of the Liberties of England, it is declared and enacted, that no freeman may be taken or imprisoned, or be disseized of his freehold or liberties, or his free customs, or be outlawed, or exiled, or in any manner destroyed, but by the lawful judgment of his peers, or by the law of the land.

"And in the eight and twentieth year of the reign of King Edward III, it was declared and enacted by authority of Parliament, that no man, of what estate or condition that he be, should be put out of his lands or tenements, nor taken, nor imprisoned, nor disherited, nor put to death, without being brought to answer by due process of law. * * *

"And whereas, also, by authority of Parliament in the five and twentieth year of the reign of King Edward III, it was declared and enacted, that no man should be forejudged of life or limb against the form of the Great Charter and the law of the land; and by the said Great Charter, and other, the laws and statutes of this your realm, no man ought to be adjudged to death but by the laws established in this your realm, either by the customs of the same realm, or by acts of Parliament: and whereas, no offender of what kind soever, is exempted from the proceedings to be used, and punishments to be inflicted by the laws and statutes of this your realm: nevertheless, of late time, divers commissions under your Majesty's great seal have issued forth, by which certain persons have been assigned, and appointed commissioners with power and authority to proceed within the land according to the justice of *martial law* against such soldiers, or mariners, or other dissolute persons joining with them, as should commit any murder, robbery, felony, mutiny,

or other outrage or misdemeanor whatsoever; and by such summary course and order as is agreeable to *martial law*, and as is used in armies in time of war, to proceed to the trial and condemnation of such offenders, and them to cause to be executed and put to death according to the law martial.

"By pretext whereof some of your Majesty's subjects have been by some of said commissioners put to death, when and where, if by the laws and statutes of the land they had deserved death, by the same laws and statutes also, they might, and by no other ought, to have been judged and executed.

"They do, therefore, humbly pray your Most Excellent Majesty * * * that the aforesaid commissions for proceeding by *martial law*, may be revoked and annulled; and that hereafter no commissions of the like nature may issue forth to any person or persons whatsoever to be executed as aforesaid, lest by colour of them any of your Majesty's subjects be destroyed, or put to death contrary to the laws and franchises of the land."

And to this prayer the King was finally compelled to answer, "*Soit fait comme est desire*—be it as it is desired." *2 Parl. His.*, p. 374, *et seq.*; and *Creasy on the Eng. Const.*, pp. 260-264.

But this act was no sooner passed than the perfidious King set about violating its provisions; whereby he finally drove his Parliament and the people into open rebellion against him. In the contest which ensued they beat him, took him, and beheaded him, by the judgment of a tribunal not better in point of constitutionality than those by which he had doomed many of his subjects to death. The engineer was thus literally "hoist with his own petard." "The curse," which he had more than once sent abroad over his kingdom, thus, at last, "came home to roost."

It is necessary for our purpose to notice in detail the measures of the next two reigns. Let it suffice for the present to say that in the 31 *Car.* 2, the justly celebrated *habeas corpus* act was passed, and the personal liberty of the subject thereby more effectually guaranteed than ever before; and that for attempting to procure its repeal, dispense with acts of Parliament, by commissions or otherwise, and other similar illegal measures, his brother, James the Second, was obliged to abdicate, and fly the kingdom, and William and Mary were called to the throne. 1 *Macaulay's His. Eng.*, p. 186; 2 *Id.*, 8; *Id.*, 62, 64.

Upon the accession of William and Mary, the great principles of Anglican liberty were again distinctly asserted in the Bill of Rights; and all the guarantees thereof reaffirmed. *Creasy on the English Constitution*, p. 284, *et seq* Since that event there has been no trial of any citizen by *martial law* in Great Britain. The writ of *habeas corpus* has been suspended often; and in two instances, arising from both rebellion and invasion, *martial law* has been proclaimed; but it has never been carried further than to the arrest and imprisonment of suspected persons, until trial by the ordinary tribunals could be had. One would think, too, from a perusal of the State Trials which followed these invasions and rebellions, that the punishments inflicted were both certain and sanguinary enough to satisfy all the ends of State justice. It will be understood, of course, that I speak of the invasions of the Pretender in 1715, and again in 1745. But that I am not mistaken in regard to the fact, that *martial law* was not, in either instance, enforced to the trial and punishment of any citizen, and has not been in any other instance since or before, subsequent to the abdication of James the Second, I beg leave to show by reference to the case of *Grant* v. *Gould,* 2 *Hy. Bl. Rep.* 30; and the following passage from DeLolme's excellent treatise on the *Constitution:*

"At the time of the invasions of the Pretender, assisted by the forces of hostile nations, the *habeas corpus* act was, indeed, suspended (which, by the by, may serve as one proof, that in proportion as a government is in danger, it becomes necessary to abridge the liberty of the subject), but *the Executive power did not thus of itself stretch its own authority.* The precaution was deliberated upon and taken by the representatives of the people; and the detaining of individuals in consequence of the suspension of the act, was limited to a certain fixed time. Notwithstanding the just fears of internal and hidden enemies, which the circumstances of the times might raise, the deviation from the former course of law was carried no further than the single point we have mentioned. Persons detained by order of the Government were to be dealt with in the same manner as those arrested at the suit of private individuals; the proceedings against them were to be carried on no otherwise than in a public place; they were to be tried by their peers; and have all the usual legal means of defense allowed them—such as the calling of witnesses, peremptory challenges of jurors," etc. *DeLolme on the Const., by Macgregor.* p. 274.

It has been supposed by many that *martial law* was proclaimed in England, in 1780, during the great Protestant riot, headed in its incipiency by the celebrated Lord George Gordon. It is a mistake, however, due, perhaps, to the discussions in Parliament soon after that event, in relation to the King's ordering the military to suppress the riot, and which was done by direct military force. It was supposed, then, by many members of Parliament, that this could not be done without a declaration of *martial law;* and in that view the proceeding was condemned by them, and especially by those in the opposition. Two speeches, however, in the House of Lords, may be regarded as triumphantly maintaining the contrary opinion. I allude to the speeches of Lord Chief Justice Mansfield and Lord Chancellor Thurlow. In order that the Commission may see the ground on which the action of the military was placed by these great men and by Parliament—for that body adopted their views—I shall submit a brief quotation from that of the former, which has ever since been regarded by the English bar as an authority. It is as follows:

"I presume it is known to His Majesty's confidential servants, that every individual in his private capacity, may lawfully interfere to suppress a riot, much more to prevent acts of felony, treason and rebellion. Not only is he authorized to interfere for such purpose, but it is his duty to do so; and, if called upon by a magistrate, he is punishable in case of refusal. What any single individual may lawfully do for the prevention of crime, and preservation of public peace, may be done by any number assembled to perform their duty as good citizens. It is the peculiar business of all constables to apprehend rioters, to endeavor to disperse all unlawful assemblies, and, in case of resistance, to attack, wound, nay, kill those who continue to resist: taking care not to commit unnecessary violence, or to abuse the power legally vested in them. Every one is justified in doing what is necessary for the faithful discharge of the duties annexed to his office, although he is doubly culpable if he wantonly commits an illegal act, under the color or pretext of law. The persons who assisted in the suppression of these tumults, are to be considered mere private individuals, acting as duty required.

"My Lords, we have not been living under *martial law,* but under that law which it has long been my sacred function to administer. For any violation of that law, the offenders are amenable to our ordinary courts of justice, and may be tried before a jury of their countrymen.

"Supposing a soldier, or any other military person, who acted in the course of the late riots, had exceeded the powers with which he was invested. I have not a single doubt that he may be punished not by a *court-martial,* but upon an indictment to be found by the grand inquest of the city of London, or the county of Middlesex, and disposed of before the ermined Judges sitting in Justice Hall, at the Old Bailey. Consequently, *the idea is false that we are living under a military government, or that since the commencement of the riots any part of the laws, or of the Constitution, has been suspended, or dispensed with.* I believe that much mischief has arisen from a misconception of the Riot Act, which enacts that, after proclamation made, persons present at a riotous assembly shall depart to their homes, and that those who remain there above an hour afterward, shall be guilty of felony, and liable to suffer death. From this it has been imagined that the military can not act, whatever crimes may be committed in their sight, till an hour after such a proclamation has been made, or as it is termed, the 'Riot Act' is read. But the riot act only introduces a new offense—remaining an hour after the proclamation—without qualifying any pre-existing law, or abridging the means which before existed for preventing or punishing crimes." 2 *Campbell's Lives of the Chief Justices,* pp. 401, 402.

The same can not be said, however, of the dependencies of the British crown. Indeed, Ireland, the Indias, and other provinces have been frequently subjected to the rigors of *martial law*—the will of the king's lieutenants, or of the commanding general. But then, it must be remembered that *martial law* has not been the only hardship or outrage inflicted upon them. Any one who will but read the trial of Warren Hastings, must be satisfied, notwithstanding his acquittal, that in her colonies and dependencies, Great Britain inflicts, permits, or can not prevent great crimes against the people. Who does not remember to have read of the terrible punishments inflicted during the Sepoy rebellion? A man of sensibility can see, "in the mind's eye," the quivering fragments of the victims of *martial law* flying through the air, as they are blown from the mouths of cannon; and yet even the holy horror which our English cousins manifest at our cruelty in the present war, has not won our favor for their mild and Christian warfare as practiced in India. May we never be won to approve or practice such lessons of humanity! They really seem to regard their provinces as subject to the absolute will of the domestic government, very much as our law books treat our territories. The Constitution and laws do not exist for them. It was to rid themselves of such a relation, and from the oppressions incident to it, that the people of America rebelled against the parent country; and, after eight years of war, established their independence and freedom.

But before I quit this subject, I beg leave to notice two cases occurring in remote possessions of Great Britain, and which have become marked in history, from the fact that they were brought within the reach, and subjected to the public opinion and laws of that island.

The first of these, is the case of Colonel Wall, Governor of Goree. It seems that this officer, upon some apprehension of mutiny in the forces at his post—an apprehension which may or may not have been well founded, so far as I have been able to learn from the very meager report of the evidence found in the *Annual Register* for 1802, p. 560—convened a drum-head court-martial one evening upon dress-parade, and ordered a sergeant before it for immediate trial. The Court adjudged him guilty, and sentenced him to receive eight hundred lashes, which were thereupon inflicted on the spot, by the servants of the Governor, who stood by and urged them to lay on, employing language indicative of great passion. The sergeant died of the flogging. The Governor returned to England, where, after some two or three years had elapsed, he was arrested on a charge of murder. He escaped, and remained absent for seventeen or eighteen years, when he returned to England, was rearrested, indicted, tried at the Old Bailey, convicted, and hung for murder, in 1802. This case strongly marks the light in which *martial law* is regarded when enforced against Englishmen; and the writer of the report of the trial in the *Register*, employs the whole case as an illustration, on the one hand, of the harshness of *martial law*; and, on the other, of the impartial justice of English courts and juries.

The second case is that of missionary Smith, in Demarara. He was a missionary to the negroes of that colony. Among these, in 1823 or 1824, an insurrection broke out; *martial law* was proclaimed; and the rebellion almost immediately suppressed. Having already incurred

the ill-will of the planters, as the reward of his kindness to their slaves, he was arrested on a charge of having had knowledge of the insurrection before the fact, and failing to communicate it to the authorities; and was brought to trial upon this charge before a court-martial, and convicted and sentenced to be hung. Before the time for his execution arrived, however, he had died of consumption. This fact alone, it would seem, from what subsequently transpired in Parliament, saved the parties to this trial—the Governor and members of the court—from being proceeded against criminally. Sir James Mackintosh, in a speech of great power, delivered before the House of Commons in regard to this case, said that "the acts of this court were nullities, and their meeting a conspiracy: that their sentence was a direction to commit a crime; that if they had been obeyed, it would not have been an execution, but a murder: and that they, and all other parties engaged in it, must have answered for it with their lives." *Miscellaneous Essays*, etc., p. 542. Lord Brougham, in a masterly speech delivered on the same occasion, maintained and demonstrated the nullity of the sentence, and the criminality of the court. 1 *Speeches*, p. 890-891. One of Parliament, the *Edinburg Review* took up the case, in an unanswerable and scathing article of more than forty pages, and condemned the whole proceeding to everlasting infamy. 40 vol., p. 226 (Old Series).

I have been able to find but two instances in which the British Government declared *martial law* in this country during the Revolutionary War. The first of these occurred at Boston, Massachusetts, June 12, 1775, at which time General Gage issued his proclamation of *martial law*, resting it expressly upon the ground that, owing to the rebellion of the people, the ordinary courts of justice were closed, and the course of justice therein stopped; and the consequent necessity of proclaiming *martial law* as a substitute for the common law. Let it be remembered, that this was nearly two months after the battles of Concord and Lexington, and but five days before that of Bunker Hill, and that Boston was, at the time, almost in a state of siege, and it will scarcely be thought, by any one living in our country to-day, that this procedure was premature. Nevertheless, in the opinion of Americans of that day, it was an outrage well worthy to crown all the rest for which they were then every-where rushing to arms. It was spoken of in the old Congress as an attempt "to supersede the course of the common law, and instead thereof, to publish and order the use of *martial law*." *Journal of the Old Congress*, 147; *Ann. Reg.* 1775, p. 261.

Governor Dunmore adopted a similar measure in Virginia, November 7th, 1775, which the Virginia Assembly met and denounced as "an assumed power which the King himself can not exercise; because it annuls the laws of the land, and introduces the most execrable of all systems—*martial law*." 4 *Am. Archives*, 87; *Ann. Reg.* 1775, p. 28.

Sometime after the close of the war of Independence, and about the time of the adop-

14

tion of our present Constitution, I believe in the year 1787, a rebellion occurred in the State of Massachusetts. It is known in history as Shay's Rebellion. When it became too strong for the civil arm of the State government, and the *militia* were finally called out, it was not to supersede the civil authority, but was strictly employed in aid thereof. The writ of *habeas corpus* was, indeed, suspended for a brief period; but no *martial law* was proclaimed or enforced against the insurgents. On the contrary, Governor Bowdoin directed General Lincoln to "consider himself, in all his military offensive operations, constantly as under the direction of the civil officer, saying when any armed force shall appear and oppose his marching to execute these orders." In this way, the rebellion, though formidable both for its numbers, and the extensive sympathy it received among the people of the State who did not yet openly engage in it, was put down almost without bloodshed; and peace, order and good feeling were restored.

I am now brought to the era of the Federal Constitution; and we can form some notion of what was, most likely, the opinions and sentiments of its authors in relation to *martial law*, as an incident of the Government they were about to establish for themselves. They had received their notions of law from a country in which *martial law* had not been exercised for more than one hundred years; they had suffered, in two instances, during the late war, the outrage of *martial law;* and had repelled and denounced it as wholly incompatible with the limitations imposed by law upon the King's prerogative. They had claimed the great acts of English liberty as their rightful inheritance. (4 *Franklin's Works,* 274). They had asserted their independence; because, among other reasons, the King "had affected to render the military independent of, and superior to, the civil power," which was simply an attempt to establish *martial law.* And, finally, they had just seen a formidable domestic rebellion in one of the States, go down before the local authorities thereof, without a declaration of *martial law.* and almost without the shedding of blood. Now, may I not ask, Is there a single fact in all the experience of these men, that could possibly have given rise to a wish on their part for a Government capable upon every occasion, offered by invasion or rebellion, of suspending all its ordinary functions, and calling into play "the odious system of *martial law?*" On the contrary, we are led to conclude, that, with the ordinary feelings of men, they must have been utterly and intensely hostile to any such power in their Government. This would be our conclusion, if they had left us no record on the subject. But they have left us their solemn testimony in the Constitution, and it completely sustains the conclusion to which we are led by reasoning from the history of the past, and their experience; for, if ever any Constitution did entirely shut out the idea of any power being vested in any department of the Government to declare *martial law,* it is that of the United States of America. From its very nature, no less than by its express terms,

any such power is rendered totally impossible. while a vestige of the Constitution remains. Let us examine it, and see.

In the first place, it is a Government created by a written constitution, which limits it to the exercise of specified powers. The first section of the instrument stamps its entire character. Thus: "All legislative power *herein granted,* shall be vested," etc. But this is not all. After granting the powers intended for the Government, it limits them by express denials of others, which would otherwise have been embraced in those granted. The ninth section of the first article, is thus wholly devoted to these denials of powers. Among these negative provisions are some utterly incompatible with the notion that the framers of the Constitution could have entertained the thought, even for a moment, of conferring the power upon any department of the Government, to declare *martial law* over the whole United States, or any part of it, where the presence of embattled hostile armies had not already suspended all civil authority. Take a single instance: "The privilege of the writ of *habeas corpus shall not be suspended,* unless when, in cases of rebellion or invasion, the public safety may require it." Now, we have already seen that *martial law* is the suspension of the civil law, and of all the functions of the civil government—not only of the writ of *habeas corpus,* but of all other process and laws whatever. Why should the Constitution limit the power of suspending privileges to the writ of *habeas corpus* alone, and strictly to cases of rebellion and invasion, "*when the public safety may require it,*" if its authors had understood, or intended that, in every such case, all other provisions of the Constitution and laws, designed to protect the citizen against the encroachments of arbitrary power, might be suspended at pleasure, by the President, all over the country; or by any General, all over his department? The specific limitation of this power of suspension, to this one writ, in any extreme public necessity, the public safety, "in cases of rebellion or invasion," forever explodes the notion that they intended to confer, in such cases, the power to suspend all other writs and rights arising under the Constitution and laws of the land. The expression of one excludes the rest.

Let us, however, briefly consider this pretended power to proclaim *martial law* with special relation to a Government like ours—a Government with a written and limited Constitution. The power in question, provided it exists, must reside in some one, or in some two, or in all three of the departments of the Government. The categories are exhaustive. It will not be pretended that it resides in the Judiciary alone; nor, indeed, that any portion of it is vested therein. All writers who have supported the power, are silent as to any portion of it residing in the Judiciary. But not only so, the Supreme Court itself, when called to discuss the subject, seem to regard it as vested elsewhere by the Constitution, provided it exist at all. This is as it should be; for that department is, by its charter, confined to the exercise of judicial functions; and it will not be claimed that the entire suspension of such functions, and the laws upon which they depend, is a judicial function. Such a suspension of the Judiciary must come from without that department. It has to do with the laws, and with rights and wrongs under them; and as long as a case is presented to the courts under existing laws, they must, from their nature, needs act upon it. But this constitutional necessity under which the Judiciary is placed, is directly at war with the nature and existence of *martial law*, which puts an end, for the time being, to the courts. In other words, *martial law* can only exist when the courts have ceased to exist. As long as they remain open, *martial law* remains impossible. Hence, the courts can not possess any power to declare, or aid others in declaring *martial law*. The power in question must, therefore, reside in the Legislative or Executive departments separately; or in both together, provided it exist at all.

Is the power in question vested in Congress alone? If so, then what follows upon its exercise? Have you ever thought of that? If you have not, let me show you what must be the result. It is this: A declaration of *martial law* would, for the time being, put an end to the functions of Congress; and it would do so, by placing an absolutely unlimited power in the hands of the President, or of his Generals. Now, if Congress had this absolute power to bestow, does not all history tell us that once gone from their hands, it would be gone forever? But you know that Congress has no such power to confer. A single limitation upon the powers of Congress gives the lie to any such assumption of power as is implied in a proclamation of *martial law*. And yet the whole charter of Congress is hedged in by limitations—nothing but limitations; limitations as to the subjects of their jurisdiction; limitations as to their mode of proceeding in the attainment of specified objects; and limitations by the express reservation of all powers not granted to the Federal Government, to the people or the States. All the powers denied to Congress in the Constitution, leave that body so much less power than is necessary to a proclamation of *martial law*. All the powers reserved to the people and States by the Constitution, is a further limitation of the power requisite to a proclamation of *martial law*. All the power legitimately in the hands of the Judiciary, is still a further limitation of the power requisite to enable Congress to establish *martial law*. And the same may be said of the rightful powers of the Executive. Hence, it is plain that Congress has no power to proclaim or authorize the proclamation of *martial law*, which, according to the definition thereof, given by all writers on the subject, makes *the will of the Commander-in-chief the supreme and only law of the land;* or, to use the language of Mr. Webster, empowers the "officer clothed with it, to judge of the degree of force that the necessity of the case may demand; and," he adds, "there is no limit to this, except such as is to be found in the nature and character of the exigency." *Webster's Works*, 6 vol., pp. 240, 241.

But grant for the argument, that Congress has this power, what would be the inevitable result of its exercise? All history tells us that such an act would be the suicide of the National Legislature. All liberty, all laws designed to secure liberty, all free institutions would perish by the rash act; for what would laws, liberties, institutions, or life itself be worth, when all were placed at the will of an absolute master? The exigency in which such power passed from the representatives of the people, would be readily continued by him on whom it was conferred. The Government would be changed by the act from the freest to the most simple and absolute despotism on earth. Congress, therefore, has no such power to confer: 1. Because it is incompatible with the limitations imposed upon the powers of that body, both by denial and reservation. 2. Because it would be a power of self-destruction; and we can not justly hold that it was intended by the framers of the Constitution, that any Congress should, in its discretion in a given emergency, put an end, not only to its own existence, but to the possible existence of any future Congress.

If the power in question belongs to the President alone, then, in times of invasion or rebellion—times like these—the Constitution of the country affords no better guaranty for the security of the lives, liberty, and property of the people, than his will. And is that the end of the labors and solicitude of Washington and his compatriots, for the establishment of a free people upon the American continent? What signifies a limitation on the power of the Judiciary and on that of Congress, if the President has, in any event, an unlimited power over both, and all else in the land? The power, then, does not belong to the President alone.

The same result is attained, if the power to proclaim *martial law* is conceded to reside in the Congress and President jointly; or, indeed, in all the departments of the Government together; for its exercise involves the transformation of the entire Government from one limited and free, at least in form, to one unlimited and despotic, both in form and in fact. So that, in any view we can possibly take of this power, it can not exist in a limited government created by a written constitution. It is, indeed, an absurdity too gross to be admitted, until all pretense of liberties and rights on the part of the people is utterly abandoned.

But let us now glance at the war power conferred by the Constitution upon the Government, and ascertain where it is vested. Is any part of it bestowed upon the President by original constitutional grant? If not, upon what basis are we to rest the stupendous powers claimed for him, as the foundation of your jurisdiction? Let us examine, and see how he stands.

He is, I grant, appointed Commander-in-chief by the Constitution; but where is his command? It is in the discretion of Congress. If that body determine to have no army, why, then, the President can have none to command. If Congress takes the same view in regard to a navy, the President, again, will be in pre-cisely the same situation as a naval officer. Without an act of Congress, he can not, there-fore, raise a single soldier, or seaman, or build a ship, or fort, or do any other military act whatever. If Congress do not raise an army, he can have no military power to repel inva-sion, or suppress insurrection. But, if Con-gress authorize him to raise an army and navy, and provide him with the means neces-sary to the end, they may still provide just such rules and regulations for the government thereof as they please, and may thus leave him little or no power over either. The same is true of the militia of the several States. They are to be organized, armed, and discip-lined according to the will of Congress; and Congress alone has power to provide for call-ing them forth to execute the laws of the Union, suppress insurrection, and repel inva-sion. The President is powerless on all these subjects until Congress invigorate him. The very terms which designate him as Command-er-in-chief of the army and navy, and of the militia of the several States, limit his power over the last, until they are "called into the actual service of the United States." Is it not preposterous, then, to say of such an officer—one so entirely dependent upon Congress for every element of military power, and bound to accept it, subject to just such rules and regulations as they impose—that he is, never-theless, authorized, upon a given emergency, "to sweep the Constitution and laws of the country by the board," as Mr. Adams expressed it; to annihilate, for the time being, all the powers and functions of Congress and the Judiciary, by virtue of this same power, thus dependent upon Congress; and, going still further, to create a new political society, by equalizing all the people of the several States, by abolishing their several governments and institutions, and consolidating them into one social and political state, subject to one law only—his own mere will; for this is *martial law*. The power contended for by the Judge Advocate, as the basis of your jurisdiction, leads to this monstrous result; and some of the opinions cited in support of it, may even go to this extent.

It is, therefore, plain to my mind that the several departments of the Government do not possess the power in question, either jointly or severally; for, if given, it would be a power to subvert the Constitution and overthrow the Government.

But the nature and objects of the political society over which the Government of the United States was organized to preside, pre-cludes the idea that any such power, as that of declaring *martial law*, can exist therein. That society is confined and limited in its objects and purposes by the Constitution; and, in fact, has no existence beyond the terms of that instrument. The relations that in all consolidated nations most deeply and nearly interest mankind, and most strongly bind them together, are not embraced in the pur-poses and scope of the Federal Union at all. It is in the States that the great elements and relations of political society are principally found. The Government of the Union can not, therefore, assert the power in question, for two reasons, namely:

1. Because the people of the several States of the Union have formed no society—no com-munity—beyond that which results from the terms of the Constitution.

2. Because the exercise of such a power by the Federal Government would destroy the several distinct societies now represented by the several State governments; and to such destruction neither the people nor the govern-ments of the States have ever consented.

But from such destruction of the States fol-lows inevitably the destruction of the Federal Government; for the States are in many and essential regards constituents of that Gov-ernment, which can not exist without them.

That the Federal Government is thus limited by its Constitution, and from the special char-acter of the political society upon which it rests, is proven by its whole history. It can not, like a government of general powers, with no limitations upon them which it may not by its own legitimate act remove, exercise any power not conferred upon it by the char-ter of its creation. If its officers should do so, their acts are not the acts of the Govern-ment; but simply the acts of the individuals who do them; and are in no wise binding upon the people who have never consented to them. *Whitaker* v. *English*, 1 *Bay's Rep.*, 15; *Thayer* v. *Hedges et al.*, 22 *Ind. Rep.*, 282; *Wil-cox* v. *Griffin*, 21 *Id.*, 370; and *Little et al.* v. *Barreme et al.*, 2 *Cranch's Rep.*, p. 170.

In this-respect the British Government has greatly the advantage over ours; for there are no written limitations upon its powers, which Parliament—being omnipotent—may not ex-pand or remove altogether. A declaration of *martial law* by an act of Parliament; or under an authority granted thereby; or with the assurance that an act of indemnity will fol-low it, is in no wise inconsistent with the British Constitution. The highest written ele-ment in that constitution does not rise above an act of Parliament. Parliament, at all times, rep-resents the entire sum of all the politico-social capability, or possibility of the whole country. It may, therefore, properly take any step it may deem necessary for the conservation of the society over which it presides. As Parlia-ment itself is but a means to an end—the preservation and well-being of that society—it may, in a great emergency, without viola-ting any fundamental principle, surrender its own existence. And yet, a declaration of *martial law* is said to be unconstitutional there, by a high legal and military functionary of that country. *Hough's Precedents in Military Law*, p. 543.

In view of all this, it seems passing strange that the Government of the United States should ever have been compared with that of Great Britain in relation to the establishment of this transcendent fact; and still more strange that the President should have been set up as the equal in this respect of the King—nay, as his superior. The entire pro-ceedings of the convention that framed the Constitution, go to discountenance any such position. They intended to create an executive with altogether less authority than the King of Great Britain; and they succeeded in doing so, if it is possible to impose limitations by means of a written Constitution. How they regarded this part of their work, after its accomplishment, may be learned from the *Federalist.* (No. 69 *Hallowell's ed.,* 1831, p. 347). It is not contended that the king can rightfully suspend the writ of *habeas corpus;* but in times of great emergency, he is permitted to do so until the next meeting of Parliament, when an act of indemnity must be passed for the protection of those who were, in anywise, engaged in such suspension, against civil prosecutions on account thereof. Now, this act of indemnity is an admission of the original illegality of the previous suspension; for it is passed for the purpose of curing it, and giving it the sanction of law. But Dr. Francis Lieber maintains that there can be passed no valid act of indemnity by a government created by, and acting under a written Constitution like ours; and this opinion he cites in a second treatise published many years after his work on *Legal and Political Hermeneutics* was given to the public. (*Hermeneutics,* pp. 79, 80; and *Civil Liberty and Self-Government,* vol. 1, p. 134). If argument were wanting to support this authority, it arises from the very nature of our Constitution. But I leave it to stand upon the authority of a great name, adorned not only by great learning devoted to the noblest purposes of science; but, also, to the support of the cause of his adopted country in the existing struggle for the integrity of its territory and the supremacy of its Constitution. And yet, I know, there are not wanting men, native to the manor born, who claim that the President has the power, under the Constitution, to suspend the writ of *habeas corpus*. But do they forget that no such opinion was ever expressed by any one who had a hand in framing the Constitution, or who lived and acted with them? Mr. Jefferson did not think so. (2 *Jefferson's Corresp.,* pp. 274, 291; *Id.,* 344). On the contrary, he went to Congress and asked for a suspension of the writ at the time of Burr's conspiracy; and, while they refused to suspend it, not a member of that body was found to question the fact that the power to pass such an act, under proper circumstances, was vested in them. 3 *Benton's Debates in Congress,* p. 504 *et seq.*

About the same time, in the case of two men imprisoned by order of the President for complicity in that conspiracy, Chief-Justice Marshall, in speaking upon the writ of *habeas corpus,* and the act of Congress which authorizes judges and courts of the United States to grant it, said:

"It may be worthy of remark that this act was passed by the first Congress of the United States, sitting under a Constitution which had declared 'that the privilege of the writ of *habeas corpus* should not be suspended, unless when, in cases of rebellion or invasion, the public safety may require it.' Acting under the immediate influence of this injunction, they must have felt with peculiar force the obligation of providing efficient means by which this great constitutional privilege should receive life and activity; for if the means be not in existence, the privilege itself would be lost, although no law for its suspension should be enacted. Under the impression of this obligation, they gave all the courts the power of awarding writs of *habeas corpus.* * * *

"If, at any time, the public safety should require the suspension of the powers vested by this act in the courts of the United States, *it is for the Legislature to say so.* That question depends on political considerations, *on which the Legislature is to decide. Until the legislative will be expressed, the court can only see its duty, and must obey the laws."* 4 *Cranch's Reports,* pp. 75, 137.

In this opinion concur all respectable authorities that I have been able to consult. Among them are Rawle, Sedgewick, Story, and the late Chief-Justice Taney. *Rawle on the Const.,* pp. 114, 115; 2 *Story on the Const.,* §1342; *Sedgewick on the Const. and Statute Law,* p. 598; and 9 *Am. Law Reg.,* p. 524.

But if the President has no power to suspend the writ of *habeas corpus,* and Congress no power to indemnify him, and those acting under his orders, for forcibly denying it, then it follows that he can not have the far greater power of proclaiming *martial law*—a power which embraces the suspension not only of the writ of *habeas corpus,* but of all other writs and laws, even the Constitution itself.

And hence, I conclude, that there is not, and can not possibly be, any power in a government like ours to declare *martial law,* unless it be upon the theater of active military operations; and that every such declaration of *martial law,* in any State or place, not subject to such operations, is mere naked unauthorized force, and altogether unjustifiable; that the true test of the presence, in any State or place, of such military operations as justifies a proclamation of *martial law,* is found in the fact that the courts of justice therein are closed, and the administration of justice stopped by the presence of hostile armies; that, whenever that is not the case in any part of the United States, *martial law,* in no possible view, can rightfully exist; and, finally, as the courts of justice in this State are proven, in this case, to be open at this time, and to have been so all the time, both before and since the arrest of the accused, any attempt to enforce *martial law* against them is a grievous wrong, not only to them, but to the whole country; and, indeed, to the general cause of freedom and free government throughout the world.

While upon this branch of the subject—the power to declare *martial law*—I beg leave to repeat a few propositions urged in a former trial. I am now prepared to support them by high military authority, which was not then at hand. They are as follows:

"The charges in this cause involve capital and infamous crimes; and the Constitution of the United States expressly provides that

"'No person shall be held to answer for a capital or otherwise infamous crime, unless on a presentment or indictment by a grand jury; except in cases arising in the land or naval forces, or in the militia when in actual service in time of war or public danger.' (*Amend. Const. U. S., Art.* 5). And, again, 'in all criminal cases, the prisoner shall enjoy the right to a speedy and public trial, by an impartial jury of the State and district where the crime shall have been committed,' etc. *Amend. Const., Art.* 6.

"These provisions were adopted after the organization of the Government of the United States under the present Constitution, and for the purpose of placing the trial by jury entirely beyond the power of Congress, and of all other branches of the Government. The Constitution, as originally adopted, contained the following provision on the subject: 'The trial of all crimes, except in cases of impeachment, shall be by jury; and such trial shall be held in the State where such crime shall have been committed.' (Art. 4, § 2). So jealous were the people of the right in question that they required the amendments I have already quoted, notwithstanding this original provision.

"The accused are citizens of the United States, and of the State of Indiana, not in the land or naval forces, or in the militia in actual service. They are, therefore, not within the exception of the fifth article of amendments just cited. The exception does not affect their right any more than if it did not exist. [On the contrary, it makes it altogether more clear and undeniable]. These several provisions are absolute as to them; and if any constitutional provisions can protect a right, it would seem they ought to be protected from a trial not in conformity with them. Indeed, it would seem, they can not, in fairness, be tried without being first presented or indicted by a grand jury, nor without a petit jury of the district wherein their alleged offenses were committed."

Lieutenant General Scott, in his *Autobiography*, republishes an article published by him in the *National Intelligencer*, in 1842. From this article I extract the following paragraphs, which immediately follow the amendments of the Constitution already quoted:

"If these amendments do not expressly secure the citizen, not belonging to the army, from the possibility of being dragged before a *council of war, or court-martial,* for any crime, or on any pretense whatsoever, *then there can be no security for any human right, under any human institutions!*

"Congress and the President could not, if they were unanimous, proclaim *martial law,* in any portion of the United States, without first throwing these amendments into the fire. If Mr. Madison (begging pardon of his memory for the violent supposition) had sent an order to General Jackson to establish the odious code over the citizens of New Orleans, during, before, or after the siege of that capital, it would have been the duty of the General, under his oath, to obey the Constitution, and to have withheld obedience; for, by the Ninth Article of War (the only one *on orders*), officers are not required to obey any but 'lawful commands.'" Vol. 1, p. 292.

Again, he says:

"When Pompey played the petty tyrant at Sicily, as the lieutenant of that master despot Sylla, he summoned before him the Mammertines. That people refused to appear, alleging that they stood excused by an ancient privilege granted them by the Romans. 'What,' said Sylla's lieutenant, 'will you never have done with citing laws and privileges to men who wear swords.' Roman liberty had already been lost in the distemperature of the times. * * * If Pompey had gained the battle of Pharsalia, would his odious reply to the Mammertines have been forgiven by the lovers of human liberty? *With such maxims of Government,* it was of little consequence to the Roman world that Cæsar won the day. A Verres would have been as good as either." *Id.,* p. 294.

He also gives the following fact in our own history, which, although a little out of its place, I yet beg leave to insert as indicative of the spirit in which the struggle of 1776 was conducted by the founders of our Government:

"In South Carolina, during the Revolutionary War, at the moment when Sir Henry Clinton was investing the devoted city of Charleston, and the tories in arms everywhere, the Legislature empowered her excellent Governor, John Rutledge, after consulting with such of his council as he conveniently could, 'to do every thing necessary for the public good, *except the taking away of the life of a citizen without legal trial.*' Under that exception, at a time when there was no Constitution of the United States, there was no *Louallier* deprived of the one, and put in jeopardy of the other, by *martial law.*" *Id.,* pp. 297, 289.

But the same distinguished General has consistently, throughout his whole life, maintained the same opinions on this subject. In the month of October, 1846, he submitted to Secretary Marcy a *projet* for the purpose of enabling generals of our armies, then in the field in Mexico, to enforce *martial law* for the protection of our armies against lawlessness on the part of the people of that country, and the people against lawlessness on the part of our soldiers, in cases not provided for in our Articles of War. In this communication, among many other things, he says:

"It will be seen that I have endeavored to place all necessary limitations on *martial law.* 1. By restricting it to a foreign hostile country. 2. To offenses enumerated with some accuracy. 3. By assimilating *councils of war* to *courts-martial.* 4. By restricting punishments to the known laws of some one of the States." etc.

And, having shown the course usually pursued by British commanders, under like circumstances, he proceeds to say:

"This law"—he was asking for an act of Congress—"can have no *constitutional, legal,* or *necessary* existence *within* the United States. At home, even the suspension of the writ of *habeas corpus* by Congress, could only lead to indefinite incarceration of an individual, or individuals, *who, if further punished at all, could only be so through* the ordinary or common law of the land." 5 *Exec. Doc.,* 30 *Congress,* 1st *session, Doc.* 59, pp. 50, 52.

This *projet*, apparently so reasonable and so necessary, was, however, never adopted by the administration of Mr. Polk; and we accordingly find the Secretary of War, about the same time, directing General Taylor to release from confinement, and send out of his lines, a notorious murderer, because the Articles of War did not then authorize his trial by a court-martial, although he was a soldier. And so the Articles of War remained until the present rebellion, notwithstanding the international laws and usages of war clearly clothed our generals, in the enemy's country, with the power requisite to punish such offenses by *martial law. Grotius, De Jure Belli ac Pacis, lib. 3, cap. 8; Vattel's Law of Nations, lib. 3, cap. 8; and Wheaton's Elements of International Law, part 4, cap. 2.*

Since the present rebellion began, Congress have enlarged the jurisdiction of courts-martial over soldiers, so as to embrace such cases. In the same act, too, they have made the punishments affixed to such crimes by the laws of the State where they may be committed, the measure, in one respect at least, of the punishments to be inflicted by such courts. The act, however, is limited in its operations to soldiers. Hence, I infer that it was not intended to extend to citizens; and this upon the long established principle, " *that affirmatives in statutes that introduce new laws do imply a negative of all that is not in the purview.*" *Hobart's Rep.*, p. 298.

It might readily be shown that, upon all the principles of construction and interpretation applicable to constitutional provisions in regard to the right of trial by jury, that they occupy a favored relation to the other provisions of that instrument. In the first place, it stands among the reserved rights of the people. It is, as it were, placed in a Bill of Rights: and is thus entitled to a favorable, or liberal construction, as in favor of liberty, and against the powers granted, which, simply because they are encroachments upon liberty, must be strictly construed. There are no rules better established in our constitutional jurisprudence than these. Besides, amendments must always prevail as against provisions conflicting with them; and the right of trial by jury is secured by amendments to the Constitution. If they had not been so named, the mere fact that they were adopted after the Constitution, and by equal authority to that by which it was adopted, entitles them to prevail against any provision conflicting with them; for as it is not possible for one Parliament, or Congress, to bind the hands of a subsequent one, so one generation of the people can not bind the next, or even itself, at a subsequent time.

I disagree with the opinion expressed by Mr. Attorney General Cushing, in an opinion which I have already quoted, in which he seems to hold that these provisions in respect to the right of trial by jury, are of but little value, on account of the very general terms in which they are expressed. He should have remembered, however, that they were adopted by the framers of the Constitution from ancient English laws, and had received a fixed and practical signification and application for ages. Mr. Justice Story was not inclined to regard them as mere "glittering generalities;" for he thus descants upon the rights they secure:

"It seems hardly necessary, in this place, to expatiate on the antiquity or importance of the trial by jury in criminal cases. It was from very early times insisted on by our ancestors, in the parent country, as the great bulwark of their civil and political liberties; and watched with an unceasing jealousy and solicitude. The right constitutes one of the fundamental articles of *Magna Charta*, in which it is declared: '*Nullus homo capiatur, nec imprisonetur, aut exulit, aut aliquo modo distruatur,* etc.; nisi per legale judicium parium suorum, vel per legem terræ*; no man shall be arrested, nor imprisoned, nor banished, nor deprived of life, etc., but by the judgment of his peers, or by the law of the land.' The judgment of his peers here alluded to, and commonly called, in the quaint language of former times, a trial *per pais*, or trial by the country, is the trial by a jury, who are called the peers of the party accused, being of the like condition and equality in the State. When our more immediate ancestors removed to America, they brought this great privilege with them, as their birthright and inheritance, as a part of that admirable common law which had fenced round and interposed barriers on every side against the approaches of arbitrary power. It is now incorporated into all our State Constitutions *as a fundamental right, and the Constitution of the United States would have been justly obnoxious to the most conclusive objection, if it had not recognized and confirmed it in the most solemn terms.*

"The great object of a trial by jury in criminal cases is to guard against a spirit of oppression and tyranny on the part of rulers; and against a spirit of violence and vindictiveness on the part of the people. Indeed, it is often more important to guard against the latter than the former. The sympathies of all mankind are enlisted against the revenge and fury of a single despot, and every attempt will be made to screen his victims. But how difficult is it to escape from the vengeance of an indignant people, roused to hatred by unfounded calumnies, or stimulated to cruelty by bitter political enmities, or unmeasured jealousies! The appeal for safety can, under such circumstances, scarcely be made by innocence in any other manner than by the severe control of courts of justice, and by the firm and impartial verdict of a jury sworn to do right; and guided solely by legal evidence, and a sense of duty. In such a course there is a double security against the prejudices of judges who may partake of the wishes and opinions of the Government, and against the passions of the multitude, who may demand their victim with a clamorous precipitation. So long, indeed, as this palladium remains sacred and inviolable, the liberties of a free government can not wholly fall. But to give it real efficiency, it must be preserved in its purity and dignity, and not with a view to slight inconveniences, or imaginary burdens, be put into the hands of those who are incapable of estimating its worth, or are too inert, or too ignorant, or too imbecile to wield its potent armor. Mr. Justice Blackstone, with the warmth and pride becoming an Englishman, living under its blessed protection, has said: 'A celebrated French writer, who concludes, that because Rome, Sparta, and Carthage have lost their liberties, therefore those of England, in time, must perish, should have recollected that Rome, Sparta, and Carthage, at the time their liberties were lost, were strangers to the trial by jury.'

"It is observable that the trial of all crimes is not only to be by jury, but to be held in the State where they are committed. The object of this clause is to secure the party accused from being dragged to a trial in some distant State, away from his friends, and witnesses, and neighborhood, and thus to be subjected to the verdict of mere strangers, who may feel no common sympathy, or who may even cherish animosities or prejudices against him. Besides this, a trial in a distant State or Territory might subject the party to the most oppressive expenses, or, perhaps, even to the inability of procuring the proper witnesses to establish his innocence. There is little danger, indeed, that Congress would ever exert their power in such an oppressive and unjustifiable a manner. But, upon a subject so vital to the security of the citizen, it was fit to leave as little as possible to mere discretion. By the common law, the trial of all crimes is required to be in the county where they are committed. Nay, it originally carried its jealousy still further, and required that the jury itself should come from the vicinage of the place where the crime was alleged to be committed. This was certainly a precaution, which, however justifiable in an early and barbarous state of society, is little commendable in its more advanced stages. It has been justly remarked that, in such cases, to summon a jury, laboring under local prejudices, is laying a snare for their consciences, and though they should have virtue and vigor of mind sufficient to keep them upright, the parties will grow suspicious, and indulge other doubts of the impartiality of the trial. It was doubtless by analogy to this rule of the common law, that all criminal trials are required to be in the State where committed. But as crimes may be committed on the high seas, and elsewhere, out of the territorial jurisdiction of a State, it was indispensable that, in such cases, Congress should be enabled to provide a place of trial." *Story on the Const.*, §§ 1778, 1779, 1780, *et seq.*

M. De Tocqueville, in discussing the institution of the jury, gives very great weight to its character as a political institution. In times like these, we may, perhaps, learn something of the value of what we now seem about to lose, even from the words of a foreigner. He says:

"The true sanction of political laws is to be found in penal legislation, and, if that sanction be wanting, the law will sooner or later lose its cogency. *He who punishes infractions of the law, is, therefore, the real master of society.* Now, the institution of the jury raises the people itself, or, at least, a class of citizens, to the bench of judicial authority. The constitution of the jury consequently invests the people, or a class of citizens, with the direction of society." 1 *Democracy in America*, p. 309.

Again, he says:

"The jury is pre-eminently a political institution. It must be regarded as one form of the sovereignty of the people. When that sovereignty is repudiated, it must be rejected; or it must be adapted to the laws by which that sovereignty is established. The jury is that portion of the nation to which the execution of the laws is intrusted, as the House of Parliament constitute that part of the nation which makes the laws; and in order that society may be governed with consistency and uniformity, the list of citizens qualified to serve on juries must increase and diminish with the list of electors." *Id.*, 310.

He further says:

"The system of the jury, as it is understood in America, appears to me to be as direct, and as extreme a consequence of the sovereignty of the people as universal suffrage. The institutions are two instruments of equal power, which contribute to the supremacy of the majority. *All the sovereigns who have chosen to govern by their own authority, and to direct society instead of obeying its direction, have destroyed or enfeebled the institution of the jury.* The monarchs of the house of Tudor sent to prison jurors who refused to convict, and Napoleon caused them to be returned by his agents." *Id.*, p. 310.

How much it is to be regretted that any American citizen, and especially one in high position, should allow himself to be driven by the terrible condition of the country, or any other consideration, to disparage the trial by jury in criminal cases; and, in the very teeth of the Constitution of his country, publicly express his regret that the jury stands in the way of a system of penal administration, which may be more certain to conform to his own private views of justice; and to hold men to answer "charges of crimes" not "well defined by law." That any cause should have led an American citizen to such conclusions, is, I humbly conceive, one of the very worst signs of these evil times. If our country is to be successful in its present struggle, and if its liberties are destined to survive, the jury, venerable for its antiquity and sacred for its uses, must go with us, in all its vigor, through the Red sea, in the midst of which we are now journeying. To abandon it now, is to give up the contest for free government in which we are engaged. We must not, therefore, abandon it in these dark days, and it will follow us again into the light, and long continue to protect and bless us in the possession of a manly freedom, in the happy years to come.

I think it has already been sufficiently shown, that there is, in fact, no power in the General Government, nor behind that, in the society which it represents, to proclaim *martial law* throughout the whole country. It may, perhaps, have a local operation, as a mere fact, resulting from the presence of hostile armies; but, in that case, it will exist without a proclamation as well as with it. Dr. Leiber, whom I have already quoted, and whose works are of the highest possible value on all subjects which he touches, in General Orders, No. 100, 1863, of our War Department, fully sustains this view. He says, or rather the Commander-in-chief, speaking his words, says: "The presence of a hostile army proclaims its *martial law.*" If, therefore, there be no rightful power in the Government to proclaim *martial law* over any part of its own territories, where the fact is not already established by events, then Indiana is certainly not under *martial law* to-day, and has never yet been.

If, however, in the consideration of this branch of the subject, you should still hold that the Government, or any department thereof, may declare *martial law* without the presence of the fact, then other questions naturally present themselves. Among these I may be permitted to ask the following:

Has the Government of the United States, or any department thereof, declared *martial law* in the State of Indiana?

Who has done it?—the President, or some of his generals?

Has Congress authorized it? Let us examine and see how the fact stands. Has that body taken that great, and, for themselves, as a department of the Government, it may be, final step? Surely Congress has not turned *felo de se.* On the contrary, they have showed great prudence and discretion, as well as regard for the Constitution, and our free institutions existing under it; while, at the same time, *they have taken due care that the Republic may suffer no detriment.*

I can not more pointedly and briefly present the action of Congress on this subject than was done in the case of Mr. Dodd; and, therefore, adopt what was then urged upon your consideration:

"By an act approved July 31, 1864, (12 *Stat. at Large,* p. 284), conspiracies are defined and the mode of punishment prescribed, namely: by trial in the circuit or district courts of the United States, of the proper circuit or district. Can these parties be tried before any other tribunal? The defendants hold not.

"By the President's proclamation of September 24, 1862, suspending the privilege of the writ of *habeas corpus,* it was ordered, 'that during the existing insurrection, and as a necessary measure for suppressing the same, all rebels and insurgents, their aiders and abettors within the United States, shall be subject to *martial law,* and liable to trial and punishment by court-martial or military commission.' Without stopping to inquire whether this proclamation was authorized; and, if so, whether it embraced persons charged with committing a substantive offense, within a State not in insurrection, and where the United States courts were in full exercise of their powers, the defendants claim that it has been superseded by the act of Congress of the 3d of March, 1863, [12 *Stat. at Large,* 775], relating to the writ of *habeas corpus;* and by the President's proclamation based thereon, of September 15, 1863.

"The first section of this act of 1863, au-thorizes the President to suspend the writ of *habeas corpus.*

"The second requires the Secretaries of State and War to report to the judges of the United States circuit and district courts the names of all persons held in military custody by order of the President, in their respective districts; and, if the grand juries of the proper districts fail to find bills, it is made the duty of the judges to have all such persons discharged, on taking the oath of allegiance, and giving bond, if required.

"The third section provides that all persons so held, and not reported, shall be entitled to a discharge in the same manner as is provided in the second section, after a failure, on the part of the proper grand jury, to indict them.

"Here are all the sections of this act which bear on the question; and, it will be seen, that while they contemplate and sanction military arrests, they do not countenance or authorize military trials. On the contrary, they fairly discountenance them.

"The President's proclamation, based on this act, limits the suspension of the *habeas corpus* to persons amenable to military law, or to the Rules and Articles of War. No order is contained in the proclamation in regard to trial, and the inference is irresistible, that the proper courts are left to act under the rules of law upon that subject; and these are too well defined to require comment. Civil courts try offenses against the law, committed by citizens—military courts try such as are subject to the Rules and Articles of War; and the defendants claim that they do not fall within that class."

I have been able to find no other act of Congress, passed since the 3d of March, 1863, which authorizes or countenances in any manner whatever the notion that it has, at any time, been the intention of that body to establish *martial law,* or to authorize any one else to do so, or even to permit it. This act does, indeed, authorize the suspension of the writ of *habeas corpus,* if Congress can transfer the discretion conferred upon them by the Constitution, to determine at what time, in the progress of an invasion, or rebellion, the emergency required has arisen, when the public safety requires its suspension. That Congress can do any such thing, I deny; but do not choose to stop here to discuss the point, as it is not involved in this cause.

If we admit, for the sake of argument, that Congress have invested the President with the power both to judge and to act in the proper emergency; and that he has well availed himself of this power by publishing his proclamation of September 15, 1863, what follows? Certainly not, that Congress have proclaimed, or authorized him to proclaim *martial law;* but have, on the other hand, by a controlling implication, provided that *martial law,* so far as the trial of a citizen is concerned, shall not be tolerated; but that such citizen shall, in all cases, when under military arrest, be turned over to the proper civil tribunals—the circuit or district courts, of the proper district—for trial according to law; or discharged either absolutely or conditionally, if no bill of indictment be found against him. And this harmonizes well with what Colonel Scott, in his *Military Dictionary*, lays down as the consequence of a declaration or proclamation of *martial law* within the United States. He says:

"Within the United States, therefore, the effect of a declaration of *martial law* would not be to subject citizens to trial by courts-martial; but it would involve simply the suspension of the writ of *habeas corpus*, under the authority given in the second clause of section nine of the Constitution, viz.: 'The privilege of the writ of *habeas corpus* shall not be suspended, unless when, in case of rebellion or invasion, the public safety may require it.' * * *

"The suspension of this privilege would enable the commander to incarcerate all dangerous citizens; but, when brought to trial, the citizen would necessarily come before the ordinary civil courts of the land." *Military Dictionary, tit. Martial Law.*

And such would seem to be the opinion of Mr. Attorney General Cushing, who says:

"I say we are without law on the subject.

"The Constitution, it is true, empowers Congress to declare war, to raise and support armies, to provide and maintain a navy, to make rules for the government of the land and naval forces, to provide for calling forth the militia to execute the laws of the Union, suppress insurrections and repel invasions, and to provide for organizing, arming and disciplining the militia, and for governing such part of them as may be employed in the service of the United States. But none of these powers has been exerted in the solution of the present question.

"In the amendments of the Constitution, among the provisions of general right which they contain, are some, the observance of which seems incompatible with the existence of *martial law*, or, indeed, any other of the supposable, if not necessary incidents of invasion or insurrection. But these provisions are not sufficiently definite to be of practical application to the subject-matter.

"In the Constitution there is one clause of more apparent relevancy, namely, the declaration that 'the privilege of the writ of *habeas corpus* shall not be suspended, unless when, in case of rebellion or invasion, the public safety may require it.' This negation of power follows the enumeration of the powers of Congress, but it is general in its terms; it is in the section of things denied, not only to Congress, but to the Federal Government as a government, and to the States. I think it must be considered as a negation reaching all the functionaries, legislative or executive, civil or military, supreme or subordinate, of the Federal Government: that is to say, that there can be no valid suspension of the writ of *habeas corpus* under the jurisdiction of the United States, unless when the public safety may require it, in cases of rebellion or invasion. And the opinion is expressed by the commentators on the Constitution, that the right to suspend the writ of *habeas corpus*, and also that of judging when the exigency has arisen, be-

long exclusively to Congress." *Story's Comm.*, § 1342; 1 *Tucker's Blackstone*, p. 292.

"In this particular, as in many others, the Constitution has provided for a secondary incident, or a single fact, without providing for the substance, or for the general fact; just as when it gives power to establish post-roads, but says nothing of the transportation of the mails. It does not say that *martial law* shall not exist, unless when the public safety may require it, in case of insurrection or invasion; but only that the writ of *habeas corpus* shall not be suspended, except in such circumstances. But, if the emergency of insurrection or invasion, involving the public safety, be requisite to justify the suspension of the writ of *habeas corpus*, surely that emergency must be not the less an essential prerequisite of the proclamation of *martial law*, and of its constitutional existence.

"We have in Great Britain several recent examples of acts to give constitutional existence to the fact of *martial law*. One is the act of Parliament of the 3 and 4 *Geo.* 4, ch. 4, designed for the more effectual suppression of local disturbances in Ireland. Another act of that same nature, that of 57 *Geo.* 3, ch. 3, was for the case of apprehended insurrection 'in the metropolis, and in many other parts of Great Britain,' which act was followed the next year by the indemnifying act of 58 *Geo.* 3, ch. 6. These examples show, that, in the opinion of the statesmen of that country, the general fact of the existence of *martial law*, and its incident, the suspension of the writ of *habeas corpus*, alike require the exercise of the power of the supreme legislative authority. (1 *Blacks. Comm.*, p. 136, Coleridge's note; *Bowyer's Const. Law*, p. 424).

"That idea pervades the constitutional organization of the several States of the Union. Thus, in Massachusetts, it is provided that the writ of *habeas corpus* 'shall not be suspended by the Legislature, except upon the most urgent necessity, and pressing occasions, and for a limited time.' In other States, while the exigency for the suspension of the writ is defined, as in New York, the suspending authority is not specified. In others, there is express general provision, as to the suspension of laws, without specifying this writ—the general power of suspension being confided to the legislature, as in Maryland, Virginia and Tennessee. The State of Pennsylvania has both provisions in its constitution. And it may be assumed, as a general doctrine of constitutional jurisprudence in all the United States, that *the power to suspend laws, whether those granting the writ of habeas corpus, or any other, is vested exclusively in the legislature of the particular State.*

"How intimate the relation is, or may be, between the proclamation of *martial law* and the suspension of the writ of *habeas corpus*, is evinced by the particular facts of the case before me—it appearing, as well by the report of the Governor as by that of Chief Justice Lander, that the very object for which *martial law* was proclaimed was to prevent the use of the writ in behalf of certain persons held in confinement by the military authority, on the charge of treasonable intercourse with hostile Indians. That, however, is but one of the consequences of *martial law*, and by no means the largest or gravest of those consequences, since, according to every definition of *martial law*, it suspends, for the time being, all the laws of the land, and substitutes in their place no law, that is, the mere will of the military commander.

"There may undoubtedly be, and have been, emergencies of necessity, capable of themselves to produce, and, therefore, to justify such suspension of law; and involving, for the time, the omnipotence of military power. But such a necessity is not in the range of mere legal questions. When *martial law* is proclaimed, under circumstances of assumed necessity, *the proclamation must be regarded as the statement of an existing fact, rather than the legal creation of that fact*. In a beleaguered city, for instance, the state of siege lawfully exists, because the city is beleaguered; and the proclamation of *martial law*, in such case, is but notice, and authentication of a fact, that civil authority has become suspended, of itself, by force of circumstances; and that, by the same force of circumstances, the military power has had devolved upon it, without having authoritatively assumed, the supreme control of affairs, in the care of the public safety and conservation. Such, it would seem, is the true explanation of the proclamation of *martial law* at New Orleans by General Jackson." 8 *Opinions Atty's Gens. of U. S., supra.*

Now, this whole opinion establishes, I think, beyond successful controversy, three points, namely:

1. That an act of Congress is necessary to a suspension of the writ of *habeas corpus;*

2. That the suspension of that writ is embraced in a proclamation of *martial law* as one of the incidents thereof; and,

3. That, *a fortiori*, an act of Congress is necessary to authorize a proclamation of *martial law*.

We are thus, again, on solid footing; for, in all cases where a proclamation of *martial law* is necessary, Congress must act—must authorize it before it can properly issue. Hence, *martial law* can only be declared by act of Congress directly; or by act of Congress conferring authority on some other department or officer of the Government to make such proclamation. The measure, in either case, must proceed from Congress.

But a brief examination of the acts of Congress, passed since the commencement of the current rebellion, will satisfy you that Congress has not interfered in this matter either by direct or indirect means, except as already noticed, to deny any such power to the President, or those under him. If, therefore, *martial law* must, in any case, be brought in by an authoritative declaration, proclamation or other public act, before it can properly exist, then no such declaration or proclamation has yet been made, or act done; and for the best of all possible reasons, namely: Congress has not authorized any such declaration or proclamation to be made, or act to be done, and it can not, on our present hypothesis, be done without such authority.

I believe the Judge Advocate will find it exceedingly difficult to turn to any act of Congress conferring any such authority. The act of the 3d of March, 1863, is at war with any such authority; for why should Congress authorize the suspension of the writ of *habeas corpus*, if they intended to confer the greater power to declare *martial law?* Above all, why should they prescribe terms upon which military prisoners, *not of war*, should have a trial in the ordinary courts of the land, and, in case of a failure to indict them, should be allowed *habeas corpus* for their discharge? All this is quite opposed to any disposition, on the part of Congress, to confer any such authority; and, indeed, is quite at war with any act done by the President, before the passage of that act, either for the suspension of the writ of *habeas corpus*, or the establishment of *martial law*.

But, suppose that, although you should hold, as I conceive you must, that the President can not suspend the writ of *habeas corpus* without an act of Congress authorizing him to do so, you should yet maintain that he can, without any act of Congress, exercise the all-embracing power of establishing *martial law* all over the country, then the question arises:

Has he established *martial law?*

We have been told that the President established *martial law* by his proclamation of September 24, 1862, which has been held up here as the solid basis of your authority to sit in judgment on the lives of the citizens of Indiana, who are not in the military or naval service of the United States, and have not been, if ever, for many years. But this proclamation is co-extensive with the territories of the United States; and, if in force any-where, it must be every-where throughout the country. In this view, it is here, and suspends the civil laws and institutions of this State; and of all other States of the Union. Is such a supposition consistent with facts? Can it be reconciled with the subsequent action of the President himself? It is, on the contrary, directly contradicted by the acts both of Congress and the President. Thus, the act of Congress of March 3, 1863, six months subsequent to the proclamation, authorizes the President to suspend the writ of *habeas corpus*, but provides for a report of his military prisoners, not of war, to the proper courts at every term, and for their trial therein if indicted; but, if not indicted, then for their discharge, provided they have been imprisoned twenty days. These provisions are wholly incompatible with the force and effect of every part of the proclamation of September 24, 1862; and no less with the notion that *martial law* had actually been proclaimed and was in force, than with the notion that it should, in the future, be proclaimed, or exist in future in any place where the fact of war had not suspended the civil law, and closed the civil courts.

Yet what do we find? The President approved this act, and subsequently acted under it as the law of the land; and, of course, as the true exposition of the Constitution in respect to his power over the subjects it embraced. It is a plain expression, on the part of Congress and of the President, that the writ of *habeas corpus* can only be suspended by law; and that imprisonment of citizens by order of the President, or his inferiors, shall hereafter have a limit entirely independent of his will. Every circuit and district court, within its jurisdiction, is to be, under this act, a *jail delivery* to the military prisons of all persons, like the defendants, either by trial, or discharge without trial. I may repeat here the rule of interpretation applicable to statutes which bring in new remedies, namely: What is affirmed in such acts of one thing, is denied of all others. [*Hobart, supra*]. Then, as the civil courts are, by this act, expressly given jurisdiction of these cases, either to try, or, if no indictment be found, to discharge the prisoners, it follows that the jurisdiction of them is denied to military courts or commissions.

The President accepted the act of March 3d, 1863, as the negative of his proclamation of September 24th, 1862. Otherwise, why did he afterward issue another proclamation to suspend the writ of *habeas corpus?* If the former proclamation was valid, that writ was already suspended; and his second could add nothing to the force of the first. But the first proclamation contained a declaration of *martial law.* Now, if this was valid, it carried along with it, as its inseparable incident, the suspension of the writ of *habeas corpus;* and, if it is still in force, then the act of Congress authorizing a subsequent suspension thereof, and the proclamation to carry the same into effect, issued on the 15th of September, 1863, both proceed on a false basis; for it is taken for granted in both these measures, that the writ of *habeas corpus* was not, at the date of either of them, suspended, which could not have been the case, had either Congress or the President regarded *martial law* as then in force; for *martial law*, as already defined, always carries with it the suspension of the writ of *habeas corpus.* In his proclamation of September 15th, 1863, the President makes no allusion to *martial law*, manifestly intending to leave it just where the act of Congress had left it. This silence on the subject in the last proclamation clearly shows that the President, at its date, regarded himself as restrained by the act of Congress to the suspension of the writ of *habeas corpus;* and did not design to transcend the authority thereof, by a declaration of *martial law.*

But there is a still later act of the President's, that, in my opinion, utterly overthrows all pretense that *martial law* is now in force in the State of Indiana. The act to which I refer is the following proclamation:

"WHEREAS, By a proclamation which was issued on the 15th day of April, 1861, the President of the United States announced and declared that the laws of the United States had been for some time past, and then were, opposed, and the execution thereof obstructed, in certain States therein mentioned, by combinations too powerful to be suppressed by the ordinary course of judicial proceedings, or by the powers vested in the marshals by law;

"AND WHEREAS, Immediately after the issuing of the said proclamation, the land and naval forces of the United States were put into activity to suppress the said insurrection and rebellion;

"AND WHEREAS, The Congress of the United States, by an act approved on the third day of March, 1863, did enact that during said rebellion the President of the United States, whenever in his judgment the public safety may require it, is authorized to suspend the privilege of the writ of *habeas corpus* in any case throughout the United States, or any part thereof;

"AND WHEREAS, The said insurrection and rebellion still continue, endangering the existence of the Constitution and Government of the United States;

"AND WHEREAS, The military forces of the United States are now actively engaged in suppressing the said insurrection and rebellion in various parts of the States where the said rebellion has been successful in obstructing the laws and public authorities, especially in the States of Virginia and Georgia;

"AND WHEREAS, On the 15th day of September last, the President of the United States duly issued his proclamation, wherein he declared that the privilege of the writ of *habeas corpus* should be suspended throughout the United States in the cases where, by the authority of the President of the United States, military, naval and civil officers of the United States, or any of them, hold persons under their command or in their custody, either as prisoners of war, spies, or aiders and abettors of the enemy, or officers, soldiers, or seamen, enrolled, or drafted, or mustered, or enlisted in, or belonging to, the land or naval forces of the United States, or as deserters therefrom, or otherwise amenable to military law, or the rules and articles of war, or the rules or regulations prescribed for the military or naval services by authority of the President of the United States, or for resisting a draft, or for any other offense against the military or naval service;

"AND WHEREAS, Many citizens of the State of Kentucky have joined the forces of the insurgents, and such insurgents have, on several occasions, entered the said State of Kentucky in large force, and not without aid and comfort furnished by disaffected and disloyal citizens of the United States residing therein, have not only greatly disturbed the public peace, but have overborne the civil authorities and made flagrant civil war, destroying property and life in various parts of that State;

"AND WHEREAS, It has been made known to the President of the United States by the officers commanding the national armies, that combinations have been formed in the State of Kentucky with a purpose of inciting rebel forces to renew the said operations of civil war within the said State, and thereby to embarrass the United States armies now operating in the said States of Virginia and Georgia, and even to endanger their safety;

"Now, therefore, I, ABRAHAM LINCOLN, President of the United States, by virtue of the authority vested in me by the Constitution and laws, do hereby declare that, in my judgment, the public safety especially requires that the suspension of the writ of *habeas corpus*, so proclaimed in the said proclamation of the 15th of September, 1863, be made effectual and be duly enforced in and throughout the said State of Kentucky, *and that martial law be for the present established therein.* I do, therefore, hereby require of the military officers in the said State that the privileges of the writ of *habeas corpus* be effectually suspended within the said State, according to the aforesaid proclamation, and *that martial law be established therein, to take effect from the date of this proclamation, the said suspension and establishment of martial law to continue until this proclamation shall be revoked or modified,* but not beyond the period when the said rebellion shall have been suppressed or come to an end. And I do hereby require and command, as well all military officers as all civil officers and authorities existing or found within the said State of Kentucky, to take notice of this proclamation, and to give full effect to the same.

"The *martial law* herein proclaimed, and the things in that respect herein ordered, will not be deemed or taken to interfere with the holding of lawful elections, or with the proceedings of the constitutional Legislature of Kentucky, or with the administration of justice in the courts of law existing therein, between citizens of the United States in suits or proceedings which do not affect the military operations or the constituted authorities of the Government of the United States.

"In testimony whereof, I have hereunto set my hand, and caused the seal of the United States to be affixed.

"Done in the City of Washington, this fifth day of July, in the year of our
[L. s.] Lord one thousand eight hundred and sixty-four, and of the Independence of the United States the eighty-ninth.　　ABRAHAM LINCOLN.

"By the President:

"WILLIAM H. SEWARD, *Secretary of State.*"

Now, I respectfully submit: Why should the President deem it necessary to proclaim *martial law* in Kentucky, if *martial law* was already in force by a standing valid proclamation, not only in that State, but all over the Union? The question crushes the supposition. But the recitals of the last proclamation are equally destructive of it; and the special terms of the declaratory portion of the instrument go to the same end. Thus, it is declared that "*martial law* be, for the present, established therein "—that is, in the State of Kentucky. But, according to the theory of the Judge Advocate, *martial law* had already been established therein two years almost, prior to this proclamation; and in every other State of the Union. The President goes still further to overthrow the theory on which alone you can entertain jurisdiction of this cause; for he says, that the *martial law* "established" in Kentucky, by that proclamation, shall "take effect from the date" thereof, namely : the 5th of July, 1864. What nonsense is this proclamation if the Judge Advocate is right in his assumption, that the proclamation of September 24th, 1862, had already established *martial*

law throughout the Union? If the President, on the other hand, is right, what nonsense is the assumption, that *martial law* is in force in this State? The President had reasons for his discrimination against Kentucky; for he recites them. But it is quite unnecessary to go into them. That he did discriminate against her, is enough to answer my purpose; and to place Indiana before you in a different condition from that which she occupies in relation to *martial law.* Indiana is not yet touched with the curse 'of *martial law.* Kentucky is. I recur to the old rule of construction, and ask you to apply it to this proclamation. *The expression of one excludes the rest*—of Kentucky, Indiana.

Then, there is no existence of *martial law* in Indiana ; for I will not enter again upon the question, whether the order convening this Commission, and the other ordering the accused before it for trial, establish *martial law.* It was not convened until these men were imprisoned for the offenses for which they are now on trial. These offenses must, of course, have been committed, if ever, before they were arrested. Then, on this hypothesis, you are convened to try them for offenses against *martial law,* which had not been proclaimed, and did not exist until after their arrest!

Suppose, however, that there has, at any time, existed an intention, on the part of the President, or of the General commanding this district, to declare *martial law,* what have they, or either of them, done, to give vitality to such intention, or to establish it as a practical measure of public administration? What rules have they laid down to govern your action in its application? What crimes have they said shall be punished by it? And how shall they be punished?

No general in the world in the present age, or, indeed, in any age, since the dawn of civilization, has ever yet thought of establishing a *martial law,* the penalties whereof should be confined to his own breast, and that of his judges, until the moment they should fall with ruin and destruction upon its miserable subjects. God forbid that we should live to see such a system put into operation here! All writers on the subject agree that there must always be some notification of what the commanding general intends may be done, and what not done, by the people under his sway, when he proclaims *martial law.* But has any such notification gone before these proceedings? Truly, I should like to know where we are, and what we are about. Who has defined the offenses you are to punish? What is to be the rule and measure of your punishments? You are to select, I suppose, definitions and penalties at pleasure, from the boundless range of unlimited power; for, if *martial law* has been proclaimed, and is in force, all the laws of the land are suspended as to the accused, and to you, and to all. You are under no obligation to go to them, either for definitions or penalties, unless they have been adopted by the military power. But that power has adopted nothing, ordained nothing, defined nothing; in a word, has given us no definitions of offenses, and no measures of punishment.

It was not thus that Wellington administered *martial law;* for he declares that the commanding general is—mark the words—"bound to lay down distinctly the *rules,* and *regulations,* and *limits,* according to which his will"—which is *martial law*—"is to be carried out." *Hough's Precedents in Mil. Law,* p. 514.

And so our own illustrious military chieftain, Lieutenant General Scott, when he proclaimed *martial law* in Mexico, and enforced it, prescribed rules for its administration. Let me show you how *he* proceeded in the matter. He did not surprise the people of Mexico, though they were aliens and enemies, by announcing the advent of *martial law,* in the first instance, by arrests and trials. On the contrary, he published a general order, in which, among other things, he said:

"1. It is still to be apprehended that many grave offenses not provided for in the act of Congress 'establishing rules and articles for the government of the armies of the United States,' approved April 10, 1806, may be again committed—by, or upon, individuals of those armies, in Mexico, pending the existing war between the two republics. Allusion is here made to offenses, any one of which, if committed within the United States or their organized Territories, would, of course, be tried and severely punished by the ordinary civil courts of the land.

"2. Assassination, murder, poisoning, rape, or the attempt to commit either; malicious stabbing or maiming; malicious assault and battery; robbery; theft; the wanton desecration of churches, cemeteries, or other religious edifices and fixtures; the interruption of religious ceremonies; and the destruction, except by order of a superior officer, of public or private property, are such offenses."

Then, after going on and reciting the absence of any provision for the government of an army and people situated, as were the army of the United States and the people of Mexico, to each other, in our military code; and the necessity of such provision, and that it was found in *martial law* as a matter of necessity, he proceeded to order:

"8. From the same supreme necessity *martial law* is hereby declared as a supplementary code, in and about all cities, towns, camps, posts, hospitals, and other places, which may be occupied by any part of the forces of the United States in Mexico, and in and about all columns, escorts, convoys, guards and detachments of the said forces, while engaged in prosecuting the existing war in and against the said republic, and while remaining within the same.

"9. Accordingly, every crime enumerated in paragraph No. 2 above, whether committed—1. By an inhabitant of Mexico, sojourner or traveler therein, upon the person or property of any individual of the United States forces, retainer, or follower of the same. 2. By any individual of the said forces, retainer or follower of the same, upon the person or property of any inhabitant of Mexico, sojourner or traveler therein; or, 3. By any individual of the said forces, retainer or follower of the same, upon the person or prop-

erty of any other individual of the said forces, retainer or follower of the same, shall be duly tried and punished under the said supplementary code.

"10. For this purpose, it is ordered that all offenders in the matters aforesaid shall be promptly seized, confined, and reported for trial, before *military commissions,* to be duly appointed, as follows:

"11. Every military commission, under this order, will be appointed, governed and limited, as nearly as practicable, as prescribed by the 65th, 66th, 67th and 97th of the said Rules and Articles of War, and the proceedings of such commissions will be duly recorded in writing, reviewed, revised, disapproved or approved, and the sentences executed; all, as near as may be, as in the cases of the proceedings and sentences of courts-martial; *provided,* that no military commission shall try any case clearly cognizable by any courts-martial; and *provided,* also, that no sentence of a military commission shall be put in execution against any individual belonging to this army, which may not be, according to the nature and degree of the offense, as established by evidence, in conformity with known punishments, in like cases, in some one of the States of the United States of America."

The order covers many more topics, and presents a concise but masterly system for the administration of *martial law,* well worthy of the consideration of those who may be placed under a similar necessity to that which called it forth. It is manifestly the same which, nearly a year before its date, had been presented to the Secretary of War, and which, for some reason or other, that functionary had rejected, as I have already shown. The whole order will be found in *Scott's Mil. Dic., art. Martial Law,* p. 382.

Now, this order made all plain both for the army and the people; and, indeed, for the commissions sitting under it. There was certainty as to the crimes punishable; and, as far as practicable, as to the penalties to be inflicted. There could be no great surprises in either. But how is it here, to-day? Are we not left quite out at sea? And are we not thus left without compass, or chart, or guiding star? If such things be permitted, where will they end? I will not pause to picture the wreck that surely awaits us, if we allow ourselves thus to drift on, over the pathless ocean that lies before us. I have no heart to think of it.

You will not, therefore, entertain jurisdiction of this cause. I am sure you will not; for I can not see where such jurisdiction can begin, on what principles it can rest, or how it can be justified. You *will not,* I beg leave to repeat, entertain jurisdiction, because—

1. Such a jurisdiction is at war with the principles of constitutional liberty as derived by us from Great Britain, and embodied in the Federal Constitution;

2. Such a jurisdiction is at war with all the liberal principles of the good old laws of Father-land, which our ancestors brought over with them, as their best birthright, to the wilds of America;

3. Such a jurisdiction is at war with all the

inspiring facts of our early history; and renders worse than useless the noble examples of the men of 1776;

4. Such a jurisdiction is at war with the very nature of a limited constitutional government; and strikes it dead as soon as we permit it to cross our national threshold;

5. Such a jurisdiction nullifies the acts of Congress as well as the Constitution;

6. Such a jurisdiction, in Indiana, is at war with the proclamations of the President; and would make him the author of the most absurd and monstrous folly, as well as of the grossest injustice;

7. Such a jurisdiction outrages the facts of our condition—our courts, both Federal and State, being open—and the laws of the land having therein free course and full power.

In order to sustain such a jurisdiction, *you* must take the responsibility; for the General commanding has issued no order taking it upon himself; and the President is still more distant and disinclined to assume it. Why should you volunteer to do this thing? And why should you now take a step that may, in the future, be referred to as a precedent for the abolition of our liberties?

Under the administration of good honest men, almost any thing evil, in the way of precedent, may remain harmless. They will not use it; or, if they do, suffer it to die with the evil exigency that called it forth. But if you now go on with this business, may there not come a time when the land shall mourn for its lost freedom—lost through the evil example of this hour? Then shall our children curse the evil day in which the bad precedent—a fatal departure from law and right—was left by us for their ruin.

Mr. President and gentlemen, I have done. I know you have each defended our common country in the field; and, had it been your lot, would have cheerfully and nobly died to preserve its Liberty and Constitution from overthrow or harm. To-day, you have a greater duty to perform—a far more difficult one also. Perform it according to the Constitution and laws—according to justice and good conscience, as I trust you will, and posterity, more indebted to this day's work than to all the military achievements of the war in which we are now engaged, will rise up and call you blessed.

ARGUMENT OF M. M. RAY, ESQ.

Mr. President and Gentlemen of the Commission :

In discharging this last delicate and responsible duty to clients, I avail myself of the occasion to tender my acknowledgment to the Court and the Judge Advocate for the courtesy and kindness toward myself and clients, which we have uniformly enjoyed at your hands, during these long and otherwise painful trials. From day to day I have met the Court with increased pleasure, and have only to regret that our mutual duties may end with the crisis in the fate of each defendant, which will precipitate him into woe and misery, or send him forth to the world again, "redeemed, regenerated, and disinthralled." It is proper, too, that I should say to the Court, to my associate counsel, and to our clients, that the exhaustive discussion of the question of jurisdiction committed to the hands of our Brother Gordon, leaves nothing for me to say upon that subject. Learning and labor in his hands have achieved a splendid triumph. It is also due that I should say to Brother Coffroth, that I am indebted to him for the very forcible and learned argument with which he has favored us on certain points which, for that reason, I fail to notice, and I here apprise him and the Court, that I appropriate his learning and his logic, on these points, to the benefit of Mr. Humphreys and Colonel Bowles, when they are applicable. The question of jurisdiction is of common interest to all the accused. The question whether the secret order is, *per se*, a conspiracy, is likewise of common interest, but of greater interest to some than to others. I will consider it at some length. The charges and specifications are of common interest also, and I will briefly consider them. The evidence being individual, in the main, I shall only consider it in its relations to Mr. Humphreys and Colonel Bowles. But in all that I may say upon the charges and specifications, it must be understood, that only two of the charges are embraced in the terms of the President's Proclamation, declaring martial law—upon which alone the Judge Advocate predicates the jurisdiction of this Court. If, then, this Court only has jurisdiction to try civilians by virtue of the existence of martial law, established by that proclamation, and that proclamation enumerates only two offenses, subject to trial by military commission, I might, it seems to me, safely leave the other three charges, with all the evidence touching them, to the candor of the Judge Advocate, for dismissal. The two offenses covered by the proclamation, are—1st. Inciting insurrection. 2d. Giving aid and comfort to rebels. These, according to the proclamation. may be tried by military commission, and none others.

Whatever may be the fate of the two unfortunate gentlemen, for whom I shall speak, I shall utter no word whose literal meaning, even, on the one hand, would tend to subvert the fabric of Government, nor on the other to sanction the slavish abandonment of the privileges of free, legal controversy. Every word that I shall utter, shall commend the Constitution and Laws of my country to the reverence and obedience, not only of this tribunal, but of all my misguided countrymen, whose credulity, fears and passions have placed them in a false position toward that Government, whose existence has been so causelessly imperiled by the conspiracies of traitors, and the storms of civil war. A gigantic civil war rages in our once proud and happy land— great armies are raised, organized, fight, and perish, to maintain the great political necessity of one flag and one nationality—and whoever strikes an open blow for the rebellion in the South, or a secret one in the North, is an enemy of his country, in whom patriotism is dead, and is liable to be crushed by the iron hand of that Government, whose cause he has betrayed, and whose allegiance he has forsworn. The Northern people have risen to a sublime elevation of patriotism, and have declared that this Government, in its whole territorial jurisdiction and integrity, shall stand, and have pledged and dedicated the resources of the nation to the sacred work— all secret organizations have crumbled, and all factious opposition has fallen, and a united North will spring from the field of the late political conflict. All political rancor—all partisan clamor—all jealous intolerance of opinion—all governmental proscription for past differences, should cease.

While it may be true, in a very general sense, as has often been said, that, in reference to the struggle between the Government and the Rebellion, the people are all patriots or all traitors—yet in an exact, literal, and definite sense, it is wholly deceptive, delusive and false—an *ad captandum* proposition, adapted to the loose purposes of politics, but dangerous and inadmissible for all judicial purposes. Honest differences of opinion, based on high and unselfish considerations of the public weal, furnish no grounds for such a classification of our citizens. Whoever assumes to himself, or to his class, all the patriotism and loyalty of the country on no better grounds than some abstract theories of politics, is a sad victim of self-delusion ; and whoever pronounces the guilt of a political opponent on such grounds, wanders in the maze and twilight of lost principles and forsaken landmarks.

In addressing myself, therefore, to gentlemen who are not only jealous of their personal honor and judicial rectitude, but the sworn champions of the National cause, and zealous for the perpetuity of the Government, I feel all the more confident in urging certain great principles of English and American jurisprudence, not only essential to the safety of our clients, but absolutely necessary to the establishment and existence of that Government whose integrity they are accused of having conspired against.

Before attempting to analyze the testimony, I beg permission to offer some observations on the character and essential nature of this secret organization, called the "American Knights," or "Sons of Liberty." I am persuaded that most of the points that I shall see proper to make have not escaped, in the progress of the cause, the scrutiny of any member of this Court. What is the original, true character of the order, as fixed by the printed work of the order, and as understood by the honest masses of its members, when divested of all extraneous and local absurdities with which ignorance and passion have invested it on the one hand, and of the meditated crimes with which ambition and disloyalty in a few military leaders have blasted it on the other? After the question of jurisdiction, there is no other of such special gravity, because upon its solution may depend the guilt or innocence of several defendants. Although the first charge of the accusation against all the defendants is based on the assumption that the order is, *per se*, a conspiracy, yet if there were nothing but the written work of the order, which is fully before the Court, and the understanding of the purposes and objects of the order by its members—I hazard nothing in saying to this Court, that the charges would fall. Or to put the question in a more striking shape, permit me to ask, whether an order, innocent at first blush, and into which a half million of men have innocently gone, and from whom all knowledge of an evil purpose is studiously withheld, and confined to the breasts of the few, can be a treasonable conspiracy as to any but the guilty few? The intelligence of the whole world will answer no! So must this Court, in justice to itself. I do not speak of the mummery of its inductions, the blasphemy of its invocations, nor the solemn mockery of its charges, but of the obligations assumed by its initiates, and the lessons in the three Temple Degrees. It is with unwavering confidence that I invite the scrutiny of each member of this Court to the obligations and the lessons of the order in Indiana, as found in the printed works adduced by the Government and now before the Court. I appeal from that premature judgment of a partisan press, fulminated in the blindness and fury of a political campaign, to the calm, unimpassioned judgment of honorable, discriminating and critical minds—nay, I might even appeal to the ignorance and prejudice of zealots and fanatics for a triumphant vindication of the printed obligations and lessons of this order, from all charges of conspiracy, disloyalty, or treason—and as I challenge English and American judicial history, civil and mili-

15

tary, barbarous and civilized, for a precedent to justify such a forced, unnatural interpretation, to make constructive conspiracy and treason from a printed work which inculcates nothing worse than bad politics—as I challenge the liberal and enlightened spirit of this age of toleration in politics and religion, to find cause of treasonable accusation against these defendants, in the rituals and printed work of the order, without a shameless abandonment of the cause of free thought, speech, and press, and a return to a gloomy and ferocious period, when to hate was to accuse, and to accuse was to convict—so I challenge the judicial records of our own wise and beneficent Government, whose tribunals administer her laws according to established rules and forms, and in the spirit of magnanimity, mercy, and justice, to furnish an example of such obligations, such lessons, and such a secret association being held, *per se*, a treasonable conspiracy. The Vestibule, or Neophyte lessons and obligations avow nothing but the most common-place platitudes, in morals and politics, while the obligations and lessons of the Temple Degrees are but an embodiment and amplification of the Virginia and Kentucky Resolutions of 1798-9, to which the Democratic statesmen and masses have been committed by periodical conventions, from the days of Jefferson and Madison to the present hour—all parties, in fact, have at times subscribed to the orthodoxy of these Resolutions, with qualifications of interpretation. What is the true interpretation of these Resolutions can not be gathered from the repositories of angry debate, but is now undergoing a bloody and final solution by the arbitrament of the sword. I have no hesitation in saying that the construction of these Resolutions, which is apparently maintained by the order, is erroneous and mischievous, and that it has been in the baleful light of a less equivocal construction, that Southern aristocracy and Southern ambition have traveled, by a few short steps, from the base of a mere logical abstraction to a practical assertion of peaceable State secession, and finally to an armed struggle for Confederate independence and the overthrow of Federal authority, and possibly the overthrow of Republican liberty itself. With these fruits before me, I can not ask this Court to indorse State sovereignty in the sense of this mischievous interpretation—but I do for myself entreat, and for my clients demand of the Court, that they shall not be adjudged conspirators and traitors for holding an admitted abstract heresy in religion, politics, or constitutional law, because the precedent would be more pernicious and dangerous than the heresy—for the standard of orthodoxy and the oracles of death, which revolution throws into the places of power to-day, may tremble and quiver as the reed, and be washed away along with their red calendar of doomed victims, by the revolutionary move of to-morrow. What I ask, in a word, is, that these defendants shall not be hunted as felons for pledging their faith to abstract doctrines, which, for seventy-five years, have furnished the press, the legislative halls, the court, the colleges, the pulpits, with a profound theme of legitimate debate. It never has been, and never can be, the subject of governmental interference this side of the point where absolutism begins and liberty ends. This Court will not forget that the National Democratic Convention that convened in Cincinnati, in 1856, indorsed as a cardinal article of their creed the Resolutions of 1798-9—but in that undefined sense which committed the party to no given construction—still I never heard that the party was thereby committed to the cause of treason and rebellion. Some years ago, the advocates of State rights, in the worst sense of these Resolutions, held State rights conventions at Nashville and Charleston—the country was generally shocked at the sentiments they uttered, but they were not met by indictment, but by argument and rebuke. Startling utterances came from the Buffalo, Cleveland, and Boston convocations of anti-slavery Radicals—they were not answered by arrest, nor punished by bastiles. Societies were formed to promote the growth and dissemination of what conservatism pronounced rank heresy, fraught with discord and death; yet these agitators were never supposed to be amenable to the law of conspiracy and treason. But one political revolution after another has sanctified their doctrines, and their advocates now hold the power, dispense the honors, and move the armies of this great, but distracted country. Once their principles were condemned, but not contraband—they were proscribed, but not prosecuted. Give these defendants the benefit of the inherent, inalienable Anglo-American privilege of entertaining and promulgating odious doctrines at war with the supposed highest interests of the Church and State—let them entertain in secret, or proclaim in public, the Resolutions of 1798-9, and they will not be guilty of any crime, however you may differ with them on the doctrinal question, as I freely confess that I do.

This brings me to propound this question: whether, if the revelations published by General Carrington in a newspaper, last summer, constituted the sum of knowledge of this order, and none of the aims, plots, schemes and conspiracies with which the evidence connects Dodd and others, had been divulged—whether, I say, there is a member of this Court—whether the Judge Advocate would have supposed any conspiracy or treason lurked in the printed work of the order? The spontaneous answer to this question that rises to every tongue, sweeps away every vestige of accusation based on the theory that this order is, *per se*, a conspiracy. There are several legal consequences hinging on the solution of this question. If the order is a conspiracy *per se*, then not only the defendants, but all the members, from Mr. Vallandigham down, are conspirators, and each is affected by, and responsible for, every act and declaration of the other done in furtherance of the common design—for this is the law of conspiracy. Now, what is the "common design" of the order? Whether we go to the written work of the or-

der, or to the teachings and understanding of its members, we find the "common design" to be principally the success of the Democratic party, or at least the overthrow of the party in power, through the instrumentality of the ballot-box, and contingently to defend that ballot-box, and public and personal liberty from assault. No other purpose than to make a doctrinal issue with the party in power, is patent upon the face of the written work of the order; and no other purpose than to defend the ballot-box, and to shield and protect personal and public liberty, can be deduced from the reliable evidence in this case, and that, too, as a measure of defense against the supposed designs of another secret order, known as the "Loyal League," which was supposed to entertain views and purposes inimical to the general freedom of speech, press, and ballot. I can not conceive of any legitimate line of defense of either of these orders. Without approving or apologizing for either of them, I can readily see, and frankly admit, how a fanatical credulity, lightened by ignorant agitators and cunning imposters, can believe foul schemes of each other, and rush into these dens of political leprosy for mutual protection, and arm themselves against the phantoms of their own deluded imaginations. Yet the masses of both of these orders are law-abiding and patriotic, but open to the designs of wicked and ambitious men. If you will go to the rebel districts, you will find Free Masons and Odd Fellows among the chief conspirators that put this rebellion on foot, yet you can not arraign those orders in the North as disloyal and treasonable, because a large number of them raised the arm of rebellion against the Government. I regard it as one of the most melancholy marks of the disease of the times, that so many, otherwise estimable and sensible men, should voluntarily seek so miserable a refuge as the "Sons of Liberty," as a fortress for offensive or defensive purposes—since, born of delusion, it could only end in defeat, ignominy and shame; and whilst its ruin is hailed with general satisfaction, neither the bitterest sneers that can be uttered against its blackened memory, nor the most obsequious homage that adulation can pay to power, can convert its faults and its follies into crimes. It seems to me if the Judge Advocate had any confidence in the order being treasonable *per se*, he would not have procured the additional evidence of extrinsic facts, at the price of the liberation of Harrison, Bingham, Heffren and Wilson. The truth is, the common intelligence of the country revolt at the assumption that the members of this order are all traitors. The traitors in this order were embraced in a very small compass, and it is a noteworthy fact, that the villainous scheme of the few was first challenged, denounced and crushed by third degree members of the order; whilst the Stidgers, under the auspices of the Government officials, were extending the order, and urging treason to its culmination. The fact that a half dozen, or a dozen, restless and corrupt leaders of this order, conceived a wicked and treasonable plot, no more implicates the order than if such leaders had robbed a bank or burnt a church. All who participate in the robbery or arson are guilty, and if perpetrated in pursuance of a common design, the acts and declarations of each are good against the others, if charged with conspiracy, but to charge the whole order with what one or more said and did, in regard to the robbery or arson, would be a monstrous perversion of, and a lasting reproach to, the law, and the shadow of a military commission would become a frightful specter at every fireside in the land. By this illustration, I aim to demonstrate the obvious distinction and difference between conspiracy and treason by relation and construction, and that which is brought home to a party by proof of guilty knowledge, and actual participation. I shall not nicely discriminate the various shades of guilt or innocence, which might attach to membership in each degree of this order, for in the abstract theory of a conspiracy *per se*, the mystified, unsophisticated neophyte is, by construction, as guilty as the chief culprit, who bought arms to levy war; who received the gold of the enemy, to lavish in the work of hostility to the Government; or who entered into schemes with wicked, malignant and rapacious men, to plot against the Government, and to deliver up to the devouring flames of civil war the peace, the property, the liberties, and the lives of a betrayed people. No one with his moral and natural sense not wholly blunted by long indulgence in the gluttonous demands of a partisan appetite, can accept the doctrine. I confess that I hear the proposition advanced with horror, and I tremble for my clients in the presence of an imminent danger, which threatens to confound all distinctions, and expose those who should only be branded with absurdity and folly, to the penalties of wicked, atrocious, flagitious treason.

I presume it has not escaped the Court, that the formal *accusation* against the defendants embraces five *charges*, with as many *specifications* under each charge. The *first* charge is *conspiracy* against the Government of the United States—the *second* is a charge of *treason*, in affording aid and comfort to rebels against the authority of the United States—the *third* charge is for "inciting insurrection"—the *fourth* charge is for "disloyal practices"—and the *fifth* charge is for "violation of the laws of war." I am at a great loss to divine under which of these charges a conviction will be claimed by the learned Judge Advocate. If I were not already under many obligations for his numerous acts of courtesy and kindness during these protracted trials, I should have so far presumed upon his frankness and fairness, as to ask that information in advance, but I am left to conjecture. Is the defendant Humphreys guilty of conspiracy under the first charge and first three specifications? If so, it is solely by force of membership in an order, which is a conspiracy *per se*, for the first three specifications proceed upon that theory. I have elsewhere argued that the written work of the order may contain bad politics, but certainly violates no law—human or divine—civil or military. If a mere connection with

the order does not make him a conspirator, then where is the affirmative, positive, extrinsic evidence of conspiracy against him under the fourth specification of charge first? I answer, there is none. Is he guilty under charge *second*, of treason, by affording aid and comfort to rebels? Pretermitting all discussion and opinion, whether the giving of aid and comfort to domestic enemies or rebels can, in any event, constitute treason, I submit, without further debate, and in a spirit of exultation, that there is not a shadow of evidence to sustain the specifications under this charge, except on the very complicated, strained and visionary hypothesis, that the order is a treasonable conspiracy, and that Humphreys is chargeable, by a fiction of law, with all that every member has said or done, within two years past, however foreign to the avowed purposes of the order. The ghost of Jeffreys, in his star chamber, surrounded by the shades of his murdered victims, might hail, with delight, the revival in America of the long lost legal fiction, if constructive treason— if this ingenious, refined, cruel and fearful legal, military sophism is to obtain. Let the shades of the wronged and ruined men of the past come forth from their sepulchers, and protest against its revival in this land and age! Again, is Mr. Humphreys amenable to charge third, for "inciting insurrection?" The first specification lays the offense to consist in arming a portion of the citizens of the United States, through the Order of the Sons of Liberty, against the authority of the United States. Where is the evidence to sustain this against Humphreys? All attempts to prove, by credible witnesses, that the order, as such, armed itself against the United States, signally failed. As citizens of the United States they were invested, as by charter, of the indefeasible right to be armed, for purposes of defense. Mr. Erskine, on the trial of Thomas Hardy for treason, remarks, that the preamble to the English Bill of Rights enumerated the offenses of King James the Second; amongst the chief of which was, his causing his subjects to be disarmed; and then our ancestors claim this violated right as their indefeasible inheritance. "Let us, therefore, be cautious how we rush to the conclusion, that men are plotting treason against the King, because they are asserting a right, the violation of which has been adjudged against a King, to be treason against the people; and let us not suppose that English subjects are a banditti, for preparing to defend their liberties."

The second specification of the same charge is based on supposed incendiary speeches and seditious writings. And how much of this is Humphreys guilty of? It is in evidence, that he made two or three public speeches, always exhorting the people to loyalty, obedience and law; and generally at the expense of his popularity and influence among his ultra friends. Some say that he also criticised, with freedom, the policy of the Administration. Let the minions and parasites of power, and the sycophants of titled authority in other countries, swallow their speech and stifle their opinions, but I would not have this Court think so meanly of Mr. Humphreys, as to suppose he could so divest himself of all manhood as to do it—or that the standard of free thought and speech had fallen so low, as to call from me an apology to this Court, for the audacity of Mr. Humphreys. On the question of free thought and speech, the Court will allow me to borrow the following eloquent extract from the great Webster:

"Important as I deem it to discuss, on all proper occasions, the policy of the measures at present pursued, it is still more important to maintain the right of such discussion, in its full and just extent. Sentiments lately sprung up, and now growing fashionable, make it necessary to be explicit on this point. The more I perceive a disposition to check the freedom of inquiry, by extravagant and unconstitutional pretenses, the firmer shall be the tone in which I shall assert, and the freer the manner in which I shall exercise it. It is the ancient and undoubted prerogative of this people to canvass public measures, and the merits of public men. It is a 'home-bred' right, a fireside privilege. It hath ever been enjoyed in every house, cottage, and cabin in the nation. It is not to be drawn into controversy. It is as undoubted as the right of breathing the air, or walking on the earth. Belonging to private life as a right, it belongs to public life as a duty; and it is the last duty which those whose representative I am, shall find me to abandon. Aiming at all times to be courteous and temperate in its use, except when the right itself shall be questioned, I shall place myself on the extreme boundary of my right, and bid defiance to any arm that would move me from my ground. This high constitutional privilege I shall defend and exercise within this House, and without this House, and in all places; in time of peace, and at all times. Living, I shall assert it, and should I leave no other inheritance to my children, by the blessing of God, I will leave them the inheritance of free principles, and the example of a manly, independent and constitutional defense of them."

In weighing the seditious and insurrectionary character of speech in this country, regard must be had to the habits of our people, and the untrammeled indulgence of the right, at all times and places, and upon all subjects, by all parties, sects and associations. Who shall say, that one who has not only indulged the right, in the temperate support of his own opinions, but when he has heard the boisterous waves of popular excitement dashing against the side of the ship of State, at the hazard of alienation from friends, has allayed their strife and hushed their murmurs, should be dragged to the bar of public shame, and public justice, and punished for the enormous crime of inciting insurrection, against a Government whose excellence he was taught to lisp in his cradle, to love in his youth, and to defend in his manhood? What, in point of law, gives a seditious and insurrectionary character to speech? Such speech is always composed of two elements, viz.: 1. Of words of *seditious import*, addressed to the evil passions of disaffected men. 2. An insurrectionary intent, to foment civil commotion, and precipitate revolt against the Government. Who can escape prosecution, after the conviction of Humphreys, except the slavish echoes of a shifting partisan orthodoxy? It were better that the stroke of pestilence, the wail of famine, and the earthquake of revolution, should all visit the country, than to be stricken with a paralysis of such abject, sottish slavery.

The fourth charge accuses him and others of "disloyal practices," in six specifications, in this, viz.: 1. In advising others to resist the draft. 2. Arming the secret order to resist the draft. 3 and 4. The same specifications laid at different dates. 5. In holding military offices in the order of the "Sons of Liberty." I respectfully submit, to the recollection of this Court, that there is not a scintilla of evidence to countenance any of these specifications. On all occasions, he is shown to have exhorted submission to the draft, and obedience to law.

Under charge fifth, for a "violation of the laws of war," I am at a loss to know what to say. The very sound of the charge is strange, and the proposition itself is unfathomable, by the citizens of a State that has remained firm in her integrity to the cause of the Union—lavish in her sacrifices of life, labor, and money, for the National cause—but, perhaps, it is possible, in the anomalous condition of our National affairs, for a citizen adhering to the cause of the Federal Government—engaged in the peaceful avocations of life—in no way connected with the army, nor amenable to military or martial law—to subject himself to the laws of war, which only prevail inside of military lines, in the enemy's country, and in the presence of belligerent armies. But I confess that I do not believe that the laws of war prevail in Indiana. The first specification under this charge, lays the guilt of Humphreys, with others, in attempting to introduce into the loyal States the enemies of the United States. Will it not be a sufficient answer to this specification to ask, what witness connects Mr. Humphreys with any such attempt, actually or constructively? Whatever force it may have as against others, it is certainly gratuitous and without warrant in the evidence against Humphreys. The second specification under this charge lays the offense to consist of organizing and extending a certain unlawful secret order, known as the "Sons of Liberty," or "American Knights." It is not in evidence that Mr. Humphreys ever organized, or extended, this order, but it is in evidence, that he burnt the records, and disbanded the Temple to which he belonged, as early as last March. But, while there is no evidence connecting Humphreys with this enterprise, there is ample evidence that General Carrington, through his confidential agent, Mr. Stidger, engaged extensively in the work in Kentucky. This ought to be accepted as conclusive, that there was nothing wrong in the order *per se*. To fix responsibility on Humphreys, under this, as well as most of the other charges, you must first find that this order was a treasonable conspiracy, and that its boasted half million of members were all conspirators and traitors—and secondly, that the organization and extension of the order was in pursuance of the "common design" of the conspirators and traitors—and thirdly, that every thing that might be said or done, at any time, or under any circumstances, in any part of the United States, by any one of the half million of members, affects, with guilty knowledge and plenary responsibility, every other member. Logic is a mighty engine, and the human brain fertile in resources, but to compass the demonstration of these propositions, must be the work, not of dialectics, but of the sword that cut the Gordian knot. I have now gone through the charges and specifications, as they relate to Mr. Humphreys, with such observations as they necessarily suggested, to one anxious for the fate of his client. These observations having an equal application to the charges as they relate to the case of Colonel Bowles, I shall not recur to them again.

This brings me to a consideration of the measure of guilt, as indicated by the evidence, first, of Andrew Humphreys, and, secondly, of William A. Bowles.

The term, "common design," applied to this order, is suggestive of all that is absurd, incongruous, ridiculous, inconsistent, contradictory, and stupid. "Multifarious design" is the only term that adequately expresses the inherent quality of the order. If it had any "common design," it has not been made manifest, either by the written work of the order, or the testimony of its members, or both together. The written work binds the order in abstract faith to the Resolutions of 1798–9, as the embodiment of the doctrine of State rights—the educated, intelligent members of the order swear that it was simply a political organization, to advance the interests of a party, as they understood it—while others understood it to look to defense at the polls against violence—while the ignorant and superstitious witnesses, from the unenlightened localities, who left the order in a fit of *delirium tremens*, and came upon the witness stand under a subdued terror of nightmare, swear that they were actually sworn into the service of Jefferson Davis—though they did not, I believe, see either his claws or his horns. They also swear to what the Peter Noodles of the order said about things in general, at the meetings of the township temples—whilst the detectives and spies have a medley of all these, which they offer for our credence. The Court must see that this chameleon character of the order grows partly out of the difference in point of intelligence and opportunity of the members, and partly out of the confusion of the old orders of the Circle of Honor, Knights of the Golden Circle, the Circle of the Mighty Host, and the like—and partly out of the locality, people, and the teachers, in the order. Harrison, Bingham and Heffron, for example, understood it to be purely political as to the masses, and also military, as to a few, as they finally learned. I shall not stultify myself by denying this military feature in the order, nor that a few desperate men of that branch,

in and out of this State, sought to precipitate the order into revolution; but I do deny the complicity of Humphreys, and a great many others, who had been improvidently named to some military office. If Humphreys was guilty of complicity in the schemes of Dodd, Bullitt, and other military chiefs, why is it that he was not running up and down the country, attending Grand and Supreme Councils? Why was he not at Chicago at some of their meetings? Why was he not at the meeting of the Supreme Council, in New York, last February? Why was he not dangling at the heels of Vallandigham at Hamilton? Why did he not respond to Dodd's summons to attend the military consultation in this city? And how did he escape, and why did not he attract the attention of spies and detectives? For who does not know that the system of espionage in this State, would have marked him for the snares of duplicity and treachery? And yet he escaped. His innocence was his protection, and his character his shield.

Andrew Humphreys, when called on to answer these charges, was taken from the body of a loyal, but, in some respects, misguided people. He occupied a proud eminence, not in place and authority, but in the confidence and hearts of all who knew him. Impulsive in his nature, free in his thoughts, sincere in his attachments, confiding in his intercourse, firm in his convictions, and brave and generous in all his relations, imbued with hereditary jealousy of arbitrary power, he was the favorite companion of his political friends; and whoever sought his counsels in the interest of peace and law, ever found him faithful to the highest obligations of citizenship. The honest people with whom he lived, and who knew his worst faults, of partisan zeal, and who knew all of criminality that this trial has developed against him, and no one supposed him guilty of any one of the gross and enormous crimes with which he stands accused on the records of this Court. Clothed with conscious innocence, and with the kind wishes and blessings of those people, of all parties, he stands to-day before this Court without shame and without fear—without shame, because he has neither said nor done any thing at war with the true principles of religion, of liberty, of loyalty, or law—without fear, because he believes his fate is in the hands of those whose abilities and dispositions are equal to the task of his vindication—that the goodness of your justice is equal to the power of your trust. That Mr. Humphreys is free from fault, is more than I shall urge, but this Court was not clothed with power and authority to punish the social or political faults of men; and even if it were, the temporary reproach which this trial has conferred upon him, is penalty enough for his brief connection with an order whose claims upon his fealty and allegiance he indignantly shook off in March, 1864, and as a testimony against it, deliberately burned its records and washed his hands of all responsibility for its existence; and if others had done as well—if detectives had not given it Government aid—the whole fabric of the order would have tumbled into ruins long before it did. It is one thing, if it pleases the Court, for a party man, in a sanguine, warm, and even impassioned manner, without concealment and without apology, to plead against the measures of Administration and the abuses of power, looking all the while to the public good—this may be a partisan fault, but no crime; and quite another thing for a party man, when our Government is in the throes of a life and death struggle, to play the agitator, and, in the name of patriotism, to utter accents of despair; appeal to the selfish, bad passions of men; sow the seeds, by unworthy speech, of demoralization in our armies; thwart and paralyze the honest efforts of Government to maintain its authority, by calumny and denunciation—this would be a grievous abuse of the liberty of speech, but no crime of treason—and still another and a wickeder thing, to go howling about the country, and in flaming speech and mock patriotism, arraigning the public authorities as usurpers, tyrants and despots, poisoning the public heart against those in authority, clamoring for peace in the face of embattled armies, fanning the embers of discord and revolt, kindling, by incendiary appeal, the fires of insurrection and revolution, and finally identifying himself with the cause of rebels and traitors, and lending himself, in thought and deed, by night and by day, in secret and in public, giving aid and comfort to the public enemy against his own Government—*this* is *conspiracy* and *treason*—it has all the disloyal lincaments of treasonable deformity, and neither eloquence nor art, neither painting nor poetry, can change it—its office is discord, war and misery. The fault first mentioned is common to all Americans, and I consign Mr. Humphreys to the company of that class of men, whose whole fault is in ministering conscientiously and innocently, but perhaps too lavishly, to the partisan zeal of his friends, but this is more than compensated in the ready promptitude with which he has always responded to the demands of law, order, and authority, in those frank, earnest exhortations to the people, which never failed to allay the temper of excited men, and restore the supremacy of reason and law. If it please this honorable Court to assign him to the second category of offenders, then, I say, a bright life, of resolute devotion to the public good, is to that extent tarnished and obscured, but not stamped with the dark hues of *crime*, known to any established law, civil or military, common or martial. Censure, calumniate, revile him, if you please, for his mistakes, errors, and vicious sentiments, and I shall only find less in him to commend, and more to deplore, for the less happy position you have assigned; but, gentlemen, in the name of law and justice—in the name of that legitimate authority of better days, which, I trust, will return to us again, when the snowy banner of peace shall herald a restored Union, and a fraternal people—in the name of that shadow of compunction and retribution which follows the havoc of those who rule by passion, and persecute by faith—in the name of those sorrows and griefs which a harsh imprisonment has

added to the wounds of a sensitive and proud spirit—in the name of that liberty of opinion and speech which, in every country, has been the last which the subject has wrested from power, as it has always been the first which power has wrested from the subject—in the name of that little family circle whose memories and affections clustered around him in his happier days—in the name of that deep public interest which the magnitude of these trials has evoked, and that scrutiny of history which your record will invite—in the name, I say, of all these interests, I entreat you to make this, your judicial record, as illustrious for its probity, learning, impartiality and justice, as your military record can be, under the highest gallantry, and the most auspicious fortunes of war.

It would be a useless consumption of time to discuss the elements of the third category, in which I concede disloyalty, conspiracy, and treason all abide; and if you can, gentlemen, in your consciences, bound by the highest obligations of oath and honor, assign him to this category of shame, of guilt, of punishment, I could only say that the startling conviction would be more productive of horror, than the turpitude of the crime of which he is convicted. Is it an example that is wanted? Our people are practically a unit in their allegiance and devotion to the Constitution and the Government, and as long as I have a voice I will labor to keep them so; but no Government can rule long, by torture and terror, a people accustomed to be governed through their affections, and while one such example might be potent, to weaken the bonds of loyalty, for this latitude and generation, while the guiltiest of the accused have made their atonement on the witness stand; the liberality, the generosity, and the humanity of all parties, sexes, and ages, would embalm it in their sorrows, as a melancholy act of vindictive justice, such as history records only of crumbling and expiring dynasties. For this rebellion and its horrible consequences to the nation, I have but one language and one sentiment, in Court and out, from its commencement to the present day—and for those of the North who withdraw their sympathy and allegiance from the Government, in the hour of its trial, in this crisis of its fate, and conspire for its overthrow and the success of the rebel cause, no matter who administers the Government, or what the policy, I have but one sentence—for I feel too much interest in the cause as a citizen, to prove false as a lawyer—and if the law and the evidence demand their blood to fertilize the land they betrayed and dishonored, I will not murmur. But in the name of this National cause, I claim the right to protest against the useless sacrifice of any man, however humble, or however heretical in his partisan politics, either for the idle purposes of an example, for the atonement of political offenses, or for the propitiation of power.

Now, what is the evidence against Andrew Humphreys, that he should be forced through the solemn forms of trial? Mr. William M. Harrison, a witness for the Government, swears that Humphreys was appointed a Major General in the order, at a Council meeting at Indianapolis, 10th of September, 1863, and was also re-appointed at the February Council, 1864, but was not present at either meeting, and was never notified of his appointment by him, as the Secretary. That Humphreys never attended more than one State Council, and that was the night session of the meeting at Indianapolis, in June, 1864. The Judge Advocate asked one question in such form, as apparently made him say, that Humphreys was present at the September meeting, 1863, but he corrected it fully on cross-examination. He was not present when the military bill was discussed, or adopted. There is no legitimate evidence that he either knew of, or ever accepted this appointment. Stidger swears that Bowles had something to say about Humphreys accepting a brigadier's commission to stay in the *rear*. Stidger also pretends that he saw Humphreys at the Council in the day-time, in June, 1864; that he sat behind him on a seat in the hall, and was referred to by one or more speakers—this statement was wholly untrue. Heffron swears that Humphreys was not present when elected Major General. He also swears that he had an interview with Humphreys last spring, at the Greencastle Junction, when coming to this city—they talked about the order—and Humphreys said "it would not do. We must depend on Chicago"—and he said "he was for his country, right or wrong"—and "would have nothing further to do with the order, and advised me to quit it." Thus, the Government's own witness bears faithful testimony to Mr. Humphreys' steadfast loyalty. This is all the evidence that bears, in any way, on his connection with the order—an order on which he had set the seal of his condemnation, long before Dodd and his wild schemes had awakened suspicion any-where. I now invite the attention of the Court, while I follow Mr. Humphreys to the counties of Sullivan and Green, where he has lived for so many years, enjoying the confidence, respect, and official honors that are always held in reserve, by the people, for their *true* men. It is a source of no little pride and gratulation to Mr. Humphreys to see that the Government could bring not one of his neighbors, not even a personal enemy, to swear against him—that lived nearer than nine miles—Mr. Elisha Cowgill, the timid Provost Marshal, living thirty miles, and Mr. Nicholas Cochrane, nine or ten miles, from the home of Humphreys. This satisfaction is the reward of a well-spent life, in the midst of an honest, gallant, high-toned people. All parties and classes shrink from pursuing him, and stand appalled at the supposed perils of his situation. From this proud eminence of moral worth, he this day surveys his accusers with no narrow sentiments of hate or revenge, but with those calm and serene reflections which only spring from that honor and magnanimity, which make large allowance for errors and misunderstandings among men. From that same eminence he surveys the array of his judges, and while he thinks he can read his acquittal in the sympathetic expression of

the Court, he still leans upon you with the same anxious confidence which he reposed at the beginning of this trial, and will so continue, until your final verdict shall wipe away all reproach from his character. Mr. Cowgill, who lives thirty miles from the accused, comes before this Court to say that "about the fourth day of June, 1863, I saw Mr. Humphreys in Sullivan county, at the head of an army of four hundred men." What do the Court think of the witness? Do you think him a fair witness, in view of the sequel disclosed by other witnesses? He says some of the crowd called him a "damned Abolition rascal." I think, myself, that an army of four hundred men had very little to do in uttering such personal insinuations against so good a man, and I assure him, if Humphreys had had the training of that army, the offensive charge would never have been uttered. The Judge Advocate asks him, "What was Humphreys' share in the transactions of that day? Did he undertake to subdue the mob, or to lead it?" To which this meek and exemplary gentleman is compelled to answer—"Humphreys spoke a second time, and did advise them to go home, and mind their own business, and asked me if I did not indorse his speech—I said I did." I confess, I have had my suspicions of Humphreys' speech ever since this witness swore that he indorsed it—my confidence in the speech has been very much shaken. In the next breath this witness swears that "Humphreys did not try to stop the excited crowd, in my presence." How is this to be reconciled? Here was a crowd of two hundred excited men, which he put down at four hundred—here was Humphreys, who, having been sent for to quell the threatened disturbance, had come twelve miles—addressed the crowd twice, exhorting them to go home, and keep the peace, with the repeated assurance that the Government would do them no harm; that the soldiers had returned the horses, and the crowd must disperse—yet, he says, Humphreys did nothing in his presence to stop them, although the speeches that Humphreys made to the men he fully indorsed himself. But the coolest piece of imposture, that these fraudulent times have witnessed, was the request that he made on Humphreys, to tell the crowd that "he (the witness) was a *gentleman*, and the crowd must hear him speak"—and which was only equaled by the violent presumption and false charity with which Humphreys gave the unconscionable assurance to the crowd. He swore that a man by the name of Ussery tried to get him drunk, but that he got Ussery drunk—this matchless piece of generalship consisted in his capacity to drink more strychnine whisky than Ussery. He says Humphreys had a pistol to his side—and, I venture, the witness had two or three of them. The Government, then, makes nothing out of this meeting, but credit and honor for Humphreys. The witnesses for the defense explain the origin and character of this meeting, and if they show an undue excitement of the people, without adequate cause, they, at the same time, show a most commendable discharge of duty on the part of Humphreys. The Government next introduced a modest and fair-minded man, by the name of Nicholas Cochrane, living nine miles away. He heard Mr. Humphreys make a speech in Jackson township, Sullivan county, on the 5th of September, 1863, at a Democratic picnic. His description of the speech is in these words: "He criticised the Administration tolerably strong—he seemed solicitous for peace—to be out of the war—and he seemed to think that the Democratic party was imposed upon, and ought to stand up to their rights—the general run of his speech was in opposition to the present Administration." Is there any sedition or treason in this? But there were other speeches by other gentlemen, and among the rest one by some Georgia man, who called himself a rebel. I suppose he was not a very dangerous rebel, as another witness testifies that he had taken the oath of allegiance from the military authorities, and had been long employed in the quartermaster's department, in this State—so that if any one is responsible for a "rebel" being at large, it was not Humphreys—nor was Humphreys responsible for all who might attend a public meeting. This man, other witnesses say, was not an invited speaker, but was called on at the close of the meeting to get up that the crowd might see him—and then talked to them about five minutes. The Judge Advocate was imposed upon when he was led to give any consequence to this circumstance. He would scorn to throw such trash into the scale against the innocence of any man. Mr. Humphreys, witness says, advised this meeting to disperse, and go home in peace. Is there treason, or disloyal practice in all this? Shall the guileless simplicity of his character be tortured into hypocrisy, and from hypocrisy into crime? This is all the evidence of the Government touching seditious speeches by the accused. A number of witnesses were called for Mr. Humphreys, as to character and conduct at home, as a citizen, but much of their testimony is unimportant. They all sustain his unblemished reputation for morality, honesty, honor, patriotism and loyalty. Two Republican neighbors, among others, indorse him in these respects. Mr. Wines had heard him make two or more speeches on politics, the draft, and the duty of all his neighbors. He reports him as saying: "I advise no man to resist the draft, nor indeed any law of Congress, but I advise all to be good, law-abiding citizens." At another meeting, he heard him say to the people, in a speech, that "Resistance to the Government would not do, at all, in any shape or form— disaster would be sure to overtake them. They must remain at home, and submit quietly to the laws of the Government." I ask again, is this inciting insurrection? This witness says that Humphreys then made an effort to raise money to procure substitutes for poor men. Was this a disloyal practice? Again, this same witness says that Mr. Humphreys at another time "exhorted the people to obey the laws."

Mr. Johnson is another witness who gave Mr. Humphreys an excellent character for loyalty and patriotism in general, but thought, on one occasion, he read Washington's Farewell Address, and Jefferson's writings, in support of the doctrines of secession; but as we were not allowed to prove that he was mistaken, and as the Judge Advocate claims no affirmative force for the evidence, we will give it no further attention. Mr. Johnson was a Republican gentleman, of moderate literary accomplishments, and was prone to construe every argument against sectional agitation and in favor of State rights into a secession argument— in this he is, by no means, singular or eccentric, for it is a prevailing weakness of the times. But in view of all that Humphreys has said, under every change of circumstance, and under the strongest temptations to waver—if it were not indelicate—I would like to ask each member of the Court, whether he can show an escutcheon of loyalty as bright with the repeated utterances of fidelity to the Government, devotion to the Union, obedience to law, as Humphreys has registered upon the memories of these witnesses, and upon the hearts of his neighbors.

There is one other important fact, with which I will refresh the recollection of the Court, in favor of Mr. Humphreys. On page 35 of the Record, of November 17, after some discussion, Mr. Wm. Moss, a witness for Humphreys, and who was a delegate in attendance at the Grand Council, in February, when Humphreys was appointed Major General, swears that he was authorized to convey to Mr. Humphreys notice of his appointment— in answer to a question, whether Humphreys, on being informed of his appointment, rejected or accepted it? His answer was—"I know he rejected it." This would seem to be conclusive on the question, and ought to withdraw that point from all controversy. Mr. Moss also heard Humphreys' speech to the people when Mr. Cowgill was present—heard him exhort the people to disperse, and go home and keep the peace—that the Government had not, and would not, send soldiers out to harass them—and they did disperse. Mr. Price testifies to the same thing, at the same meeting. If Humphreys was a bad man, his neighbors would know it—but none appeared against him. From Moss' testimony, it appears impossible, from entries in their partnership books, late in the evening before, that he should have been at the Council in June last.

Bear with me, gentlemen, while I sum up the testimony for and against Colonel Bowles. I am betraying no trust, when I admit that I am oppressed with the weight of the circumstances which throw their dismal shadows across his pathway, and shut out some of that mellow sunlight which is so essential to quicken with gladness the feeble pulse of age. An old man, who comes down to us from a past generation of heroes and giants, is before you, struggling in the toils that accident, misplaced confidence, or foul intrigue has spread for his destruction. Such a sight has not been witnessed before in this country, and the pen of history is waiting to record the momentous issue made up between him and his Government. The moral sinews of a noble nature sustain him with dignity in the presence of any peril, and if only tears of mercy can win him deliverance, they would refuse to flow. The unsuspecting simplicity of the old man, has proved a snare to his feet, and marked him an easy prey for the kites and vultures of society, who, under the deceitful guise of curing abuses, and in the misapplication of doctrines and maxims, that underlie all free States, win, traffic and trade in confidence as a merchandise of the market. It is only to be regretted, that Colonel Bowles has not an abler and more learned counsel to give force to those circumstances, that tell but too plainly the extent of his wrongs, and to erect around him a bulwark of innocence, justice and law. I am not about to urge any new theory of human responsibility—all that the evidence proves. or fairly implies, he accepts, and it is with that evidence that I now propose to deal. But in this connection, I will ask this question, and I ask the Court to dwell upon it—it is suggestive of more than it expresses—does it not stagger human faith, that an old man, near seventy years of age—dead to all the motives of young ambition—with the whole field of human enterprise, by the advance of years, contracted around him, soon to be narrowed to the compass of the grave—no dream of ambition, of wealth, of fame, of love, of romance, of chivalry, to quicken his limbs, or fire his heart—should voluntarily become the leader, and chief conspirator, in these alleged crimes? Was it glory that he sought amid the din of arms?—there was no glory in the debasing plots of murder, rapine, insurrection, conflagration, and plunder. Was it wealth that he desired?—he needed not wealth, for he was surrounded by broad acres, and the refinements and elegancies of life. Was it a morbid political delusion in favor of the rebel cause?—if so, he could have enlisted in that cause four years ago, and secured its doubtful honors, while he could have saved himself an immense estate in the South from confiscation. Was it a mean, low, political popularity at home that he sought? No, for he had courted no political favor for near twenty years. But why dwell in the regions of fancy and speculation, when every thread, and every fiber. of the network that is woven around him, proclaim, in characters of living light, that his hospitality has been abused—that his open hand, open heart, and open house exposed him to the arts and wiles of reckless and unscrupulous men ?

Without attempting to deal with the evidence in detail, it will suffice for me to say, that the Government's evidence tends to bring Colonel Bowles within the charges: 1. Of conspiracy; 2. Of treason; 3. Of disloyal practices; and 4. Of violation of the laws of war. The acts and aims that implicate him in the one or the other of these charges are proved, in the main, by the statements and declarations of persons more or less connected with the "Sons of Liberty," but who do not admit that they were themselves implicated in any actual or contemplated scheme of disloyalty—and whose declarations and statements, therefore, can implicate no one but themselves—because, not being actual conspirators themselves, their declarations are inadmissible against others; for I maintain that unless the Government can bring declarations from actual conspirators engaged in a "common design" with the accused, they are inadmissible.

The whole question of the admissibility of these declarations of members of the order, simply because they are members, is held in abeyance by the Court, and is still an open one, to abide the antecedent decision of the question whether the order is a treasonable conspiracy? And unless you hold that it is, all these statements affecting Colonel Bowles fall to the ground.

The acts and aims which the evidence tends to establish against Colonel Bowles, consist, as will be claimed: 1. In his membership in an unlawful secret society; 2. The arming of men to resist the authority of the Government; 3. Conspiring to put on foot an insurrection in aid of the rebellion, by seizing the arsenals in several of the States, liberating rebel prisoners, deposing the Governor of this State, and striking for a North-western Confederacy, or an alliance with the Southern; 4. Accepting and acting under a commission of Major-General from the "Sons of Liberty;" 5. Attending the conclaves at Chicago, and mingling in the councils of traitors, and dividing large sums of rebel money with the military heads of the order; 6. By complicity with Bocking and others in his Greek-fire preparations to destroy Government property; 7. Having intercourse and correspondence with rebels, through one Dickerson, of Baltimore; 8. The distribution of money to the order to buy arms to resist the Government. This is a huge array of atrocities, and if the half has been proved by legitimate testimony, I should have more pity for his fate than hope for his deliverance. It would not be an improbable nor an improbable thing for a man like Colonel Bowles to follow a great way, blindly, the artful leaders in such a scheme, without comprehending or suspecting its bearings, because all was being done in the name of the order, whose legitimate objects he knew were lawful. This, I claim, is true of Colonel Bowles. It was somewhat different with Mr. Humphreys in this respect. He suspected the order as early as March, 1864, and when Mr. Moss conveyed to him the intelligence of his appointment as Major-General, together with information of the action of the Council at Indianapolis on the military bill, he at once denounced and renounced the order, and rejected the commission, and gave us a reason that he was not aware before that there was any such military feature connected with the order. He then sent for the records and papers of the temple in his township. burnt them in the stove, and washed his hands of the order. See testimony of Wm. Moss. November 17, 1864.

Was he a member of the order? Perhaps he was; and yet the evidence shows that he either did not know, or did not care for the obligations of secrecy, as he seems to have talked to every body with great freedom upon the subject. But even that membership, I have shown, amounts to neither of the offenses charged.

To constitute conspiracy, there must be concert, concurrence, agreement, assent, by all the parties, with a knowledge and approval of the common design. Where there is no common design, there can be no conspiracy, and where there is a common design, its object must be unlawful. After the escape of Dodd, the absence of Walker, the arrest of Bullitt and Barrett, and the discharge of Harrison, Bingham, Heffren and Wilson, the banishment of Kalfus and others, and the imprisonment of Yeakle and Bocking, Bowles becomes the most prominent, as he is the worst seduced, betrayed and injured figure in the foreground. It will, no doubt, be, argued by the learned Judge Advocate, that Bowles was a prime instigator of treason. All the testimony that makes him a traitor, tends to show that he was seduced and betrayed into a false position by the wily intrigues of designing men. Bowles was looking at one object, and his betrayers at another. They meant treason and revolution. He was dazzled by the glittering bauble of compromise, which he hoped to inaugurate by some kind of associated action. Is this not a more rational explanation of his conduct, than the harsh and incredible one offered by the Government? He was always as simple about it as a child, and is to this day, for he can see no crime in a compromise, nor in the means to accomplish it; and this was all the use he had for the order. Mr. Harrison knew Bowles simply as a member of the Council, and Major-General by appointment. Bingham only knew him as such. Dodd insisted on making him a Major-General. He refused and protested until the law was modified to suit his views. He was a man of considerable fortune. The Bullitts, the Dodds and the Barretts were poor and needy. It seems to have been a matter of indifference with them, and their tools, whether they lined their pockets with rebel money, or money from the coffers of Bowles. Stidger was sent, time and again, by Bullit to Bowles, to mislead and betray him. Bowles always received him without asking or caring whether he was a member of the order or not. What motive had Bullitt and Stidger, but to mislead him into complicity with treason? Bowles was passive—they were active. They even sought to commit the old man to a sanction of the assassination of Coffin. Bowles knew Coffin, and would not credit the imputation upon his fidelity, but finally promised to put men on his track, to watch him.

Behold this simple old man, beset by Coffin and Stidger, two Government spies, and also by Dodd, Bullitt and others, of the revolutionary type! Men less credulous and infirm than Bowles would have fallen before such a combined assault. Dodd and his Kentucky revolutionary schemers could not rest until they forced a major-general's commission on Bowles; and to do which, Dodd caused the county of Orange to be thrown into another district, to make him eligible. And now, that one set of them have got him on trial for his life, another set—Heffren and Wilson—who purchased their safety at the price of dishonor, broken faith and violated pledges, by exchanging the dock for the confessional—the soldier's home for the witness stand—and swearing Bowles into deep trouble, and themselves out; now scuttle the ship, and leave old age, blighted hope and ruined fortune to buffet the waves alone. Heffren's testimony was like the mountain avalanche of snow—small in the beginning, but gathering size and momentum as it rolls, until it sweeps down in its course every obstruction in its path. Heffren's testimony swept down, not only Bowles, but Dodd, Wilson and Walker, and buried himself, finally, in the common ruin. Wilson, not to be outdone by Heffren, comes upon the witness stand, redolent with the savory odors of the Chicago conclave, with forty dollars of rebel money in his pocket, obtained from Barrett as mileage, and a thousand dollars, obtained from Bowles, to buy arms, and strikes Bowles and Heffren "lick about." For history not to know and record the transcendent virtues of these two defunct witnesses, were to rob posterity of half of its inheritance. History has *already* appropriated them.

I can understand and appreciate how an honest man may join a treasonable order unwittingly, and on discovering its true character, abandon and expose it, in the interest of law and public liberty—I can understand also the reasoning and casuistry by which a detective reconciles his deceptions and bad faith with his paramount duty to society and stable Government—but I confess nothing but loathing and detestation for one who is *particeps criminis*, and so continues, until the trial proves his guilt, and then virtuously concludes to save himself, and ruin his accomplices.

It is proper that I should say, in behalf of all the accused, that there is an inconvenient redundancy of *testimony*, given on this trial, which is not *evidence*, for the reason that it does not support any issue—that it is mere political scandal. I allude to it simply that the Court may detect it, and dismiss it from consideration. There is another item of testimony affecting Colonel Bowles that I will allude to. Heffren swears that he understood from Wilson, that Dodd and Walker received one hundred thousand dollars, each, of rebel money, and that Bowles got his share. This is a great wrong to Colonel Bowles, if false, yet the Government did not ask Wilson whether it was true or not. Heffren left the impression that the thousand dollars handed to Wilson by Bowles, was part of this corruption fund—but Wilson virtually denies the whole story, by declaring that it was of Bowles' private funds—thus these witnesses contradict themselves—but when dishonored by apostasy, who can believe them, even when they corroborate each other? Heffren swears that Wilson told him thus and so—Wilson swears that Bowles told him thus and so. According to Stidger, there were two other gentlemen in this plot against Colonel Bowles—General Carrington and Captain S. E. Jones, of Louisville—they first sent Stidger as a spy to Bowles. Stidger also played the spy on Heffren, at Salem, as he swears—all of which is denied by Heffren. So Bowles has been, and is, confronted by the military power, the detective police of the country, and all the apostates of the State's evidence department.

Stidger swears to two interviews with Heffren at Salem—Heffren denies having ever seen Stidger at Salem. Heffren, in turn, undertakes to swear to an interview with Bocking, the Greek fire man, at Salem—Bocking, this Court will remember, denies having ever been in Salem—thus, when the Government witnesses are at variance on the most vital points in the case, Bowles may well exclaim, " When rogues fall out, honest men get their dues." Stidger's accomplishments as a detective are only equaled by his accomplishments as a witness—he is both artistic and esthetical in each character, and, I am inclined to think, without an amateur. My opinion is, if Bowles were liberated to-day, and at home, that these corrupt and belligerent witnesses could, by their blandishments, ingratiate themselves again into his confidence. My amateur witness, Mr. Stidger, has a marvelous story about Bowles, Bocking and Greek fire. He astonishes us all by detailing a meeting at the Louisville Hotel, when Dr. Kalfus, Colonel Bowles and others met Bocking and others, and heard an explanation of the infernal mysteries of shells and Greek fire. The effect of all this was greatly hightened by an exhibition, before this Court, of shells, grenades, etc., as if the globe itself could, and would be exploded by this infernal machine. This engine of universal destruction, says Stidger, was under the supervision and patronage of this order. Bowles profaned the Sabbath with Bocking, in a basement in this city, experimenting with Greek fire, says Stidger. Bocking swears, the Court will recollect, that he never met Bowles in this city, on any such business—that he did exhibit his invention at the Louisville Hotel, when Bowles and others were present—but that neither Bowles nor any one else ever furnished money to send him to Canada—that two hundred dollars were handed him in Louisville by a young man to meet his pressing wants—that his invention was, in no sense, at any time, under the direction, interest, patronage, or favor of this order—thus flatly contradicting Stidger *in toto*, and Heffren in part. Bocking swears that the invention claimed by him, was as open and public as the sunlight. He had filed a *caveat* at Washington, and under General Burnside's order, he came to Indianapolis, and brought it to the notice of the Governor, General Wilcox, and others, as he had done in other States. Thus, this specter, which seemed so fearful and ghostly, at one time, vanishes into thin air, and Colonel Bowles is relieved of another incubus which amateur swearing had placed on his vitals. Stidger attempts to damage Colonel Bowles still further, by swearing that Bowles said he had communication with rebels South. This, I venture, is all moonshine, like the rest. But after all Stidger's bold fancies, and his equivocal truths, he has not the effrontery to say that Bowles ever concurred in, assented to, or acted upon Dodd's scheme of insurrection; but, on the contrary, he refused to have

any thing to do with it, except on conditions which never happened, and could not happen, and this refusal of Colonel Bowles proves that no such scheme was agreed on at Chicago, and that he refused to agree upon any with Dodd at Indianapolis. No other witness attempts to connect Bowles with any actual conspiracy, and he falls short in the very essential point of consent and agreement. If Bowles had his own method and plan of bringing about the compromise between the two sections, and Dodd and Bullitt dissented, that was their fault, and not the fault of Colonel Bowles. Then if Colonel Bowles is not guilty of any of the charges, by reason of the Greek fire phantom—by holding correspondence with the public enemy—by arming the people for resistance to public authority—by contributing money to Bocking—by joining Dodd in his wild schemes—nor by receiving a part of the rebel funds—nor by agreeing at Chicago, or elsewhere, to an uprising—then he must be acquitted on every charge, unless, indeed, his membership in the order convicts him—but this latter proposition is without either authority or reason to support it. So if Colonel Bowles be convicted, it must be either, first, by force of the guilty character of the order, which would be monstrous—or secondly, by force of the statements and declarations of members of the order, vague and distorted by bad memory, and made veracity—or thirdly, by force of the testimony of spies and detectives, equally supported and contradicted, by professedly guilty accomplices, who purchase immunity from punishment by turning State's evidence. Will the Court be satisfied with a conviction on such testimony ? According to the law books, it is a very dangerous character of testimony. And when it is considered that you must find the defendants guilty beyond a reasonable doubt—and guilty of every essential element of the offense, without a reasonable doubt—Colonel Bowles feels strong in the law and the evidence—though feeble with disease, and infirm with age.

The Court will not fail to take notice, that the Government, the better to secure the conviction of these defendants, has not only pressed into the service accomplices, who prove themselves to be more guilty than most of those remaining on trial, but avails itself also of the labor and testimony of detectives, spies, and informers. He must be an innocent man indeed, or a prodigy of skill and management, or a miracle of luck, under a special Providence, who can escape from the meshes and machinations of such a formidable horde of accomplices, informers, detectives and spies. By the indulgence of the Court, I avail myself of the opinion of an eminent English historian, who described a late period of English history, in order to fix the moral and legal *status* of such witnesses, on the present trial, and in addition to which, I shall not offer any observations of my own—further than to say, that the law of evidence holds spies, detectives, informers, accomplices, and those who turn State's evidence, in very great detestation; and while such witnesses are competent, very little credit is given their testimony. I quote from *May's Constitutional History of England:*

"Next in importance to personal freedom, is immunity from suspicious and jealous observations. Men may be without any restraint upon their liberty; they may pass to and fro at pleasure; but if their steps are tracked by spies and informers, their words noted down for crimination, their associates watched as conspirators—who shall say that they are free? Nothing is more revolting to Englishmen than the espionage which forms part of the administration system of continental despotisms. It haunts men like an evil genius, chills their gayety, restrains their wit, casts a shadow over their friendships, and blights their domestic hearth. The freedom of a country may be measured by its immunity from this baleful agency. Rulers who distrust their own people, must govern in a spirit of absolutism; and suspected subjects will ever be sensible of their own wrongs.

"Our own countrymen have been comparatively free from this hateful interference with their moral freedom. Yet we may find many traces of a system repugnant to the liberal policy of our laws. In 1764 we see spies following Wilkes every-where, dogging his steps like shadows, and reporting every movement of himself and his friends to the Secretaries of State. Nothing was too insignificant for the curiosity of these exalted magistrates. Every visit he paid or received throughout the day was noted; the persons he chanced to encounter on the streets were not overlooked; it was known where he dined, or went to church, and at what hour he returned home at night.

"In the State trials (England) of 1794, we discover spies and informers in the witness box, who had been active members of political societies, sharing their councils, and encouraging, if not prompting their criminal extravagance. And throughout that period of dread and suspicion, society was every-where infested with espionage.

"Again, in 1817, Government spies were deeply compromised in the turbulence and sedition of that period. Castle, a spy of infamous character, having uttered the most seditious language, and incited the people to arm, proved in the witness-box the very crimes he had himself prompted and encouraged. Another spy, named Oliver, proceeded into the disturbed districts, in the character of a London delegate, and remained for many weeks amongst the deluded operatives, every-where instigating them to rise and arm. He encouraged them with hopes that, in the event of a rising, they would be assisted by a hundred and fifty thousand men in the metropolis; and thrusting himself into their society, he concealed the craft of a spy under the disguise of a traitorous conspirator. Before he undertook this shameful mission he was in communication with the Ministers, and throughout his mischievous progress was corresponding with the Government or its agents. There is little doubt that Oliver did more to disturb the public peace by his malign influence, than to protect it by timely information to the Government. The agent was mischievous, and his principals could not wholly escape the blame of his misdeeds. To the severity of oppressive measures and a vigorous administration of the law, was added the reproach of a secret alliance between the Executive and a wretch who had at once bought and betrayed his victims.

"The relations between the Government and its informers are of extreme delicacy. Not to profit by timely information were a crime, but to retain in Government pay, and to reward spies and informers who consort with conspirators as their sworn accomplices, and encourage while they betray them in their crimes, is a practice for which no plea can be offered. No Government, indeed, can be supposed to have expressly instructed its spies to instigate the perpetration of crimes; but to be unsuspected, every spy must be zealous in the cause which he pretends to have espoused; and his zeal in a criminal enterprise is a direct encouragement of crime. So odious is (and should be) the character of a spy (or informer) that his ignominy is shared by his employers, against whom the public feeling has never failed to pronounce itself, in proportion to the infamy of the agent and the complicity of those whom he served."

It has always been my habit in criminal trials, whatever I may have thought of the probabilities of conviction, to address the jury on the contingent measure of punishment, and at the hazard of misconstruction, I will invite your attention to that question. You, gentlemen, unlike the common law tribunals, are neither limited in the range of your jurisdiction, nor circumscribed in the measure of your punishments. The Constitution of the United States furnishes no guide other than the injunction, that cruel and unusual punishments shall not be inflicted, nor excessive fines imposed—even if this inhibition applies to tribunals organized under the laws of war—upon which there might be great differences of opinion among fair-minded men—since many military punishments are unusual and unknown to the common law courts. The Constitution of the State of Indiana, in a spirit of recognition of, and homage to, the advanced and advancing state of criminal jurisprudence, in the Christian world, provides that "cruel and unusual punishments shall not be inflicted"—and that the "penal code shall be founded on the principles of reformation, not of vindictive justice." All penalties shall be proportioned to the nature of the "offense." These provisions are alike mandatory to courts and legislators, and embrace, if not in their letter, at least in their spirit, all citizens and all tribunals. But it is unworthy of any tribunal, in court or camp, in church or State, to make vindictive justice the measure of punishment. Punishment in the State has the same wise ends in view, and the same restraints and proprieties, upon its indulgence, as in the family circle—not to gratify revenge—not in the spirit of execration, for the kind of crime of which he is convicted—nor to punish the offender in the name of one crime, for a great many other short-comings, for which the law had fixed no penalty

By the act of Congress of July 17, 1862, death—or in the discretion of the Court, imprisonment, for a period of not less than five years, and not less than ten thousand dollars fine—is imposed for the crime of treason.

For the crime of putting on foot insurrection, and giving aid and comfort to rebels, the same act prescribes imprisonment not exceeding ten years, or by fine not exceeding ten thousand dollars, or by both. And for either of these offenses, a confiscation of all property follows. These two offenses are embraced in the accusation against the accused. It is also provided by the act of Congress of July 31, 1861, that the offense of conspiracy shall be punished by a fine of not less than five hundred dollars nor more than five thousand dollars, or by imprisonment, with or without hard labor, as the court shall determine, for a period of not less than six months, nor greater than six years, or by both. This is also one of the offenses embraced in the accusation against all the accused. The other two offenses, of "inciting insurrection," and "disloyal practices," are not defined or punished by any act of Congress, and you must look for the penalties, when you look for the law.

Now, it may be argued, that as this Court derives its jurisdiction to try common law offenses from the laws of war, that you will look to the laws of war for the definition of crimes, and the fixation of their penalties. There is some force in this argument, I admit—but it carries a crushing retroactive stroke of logic against the jurisdiction itself. For if the jurisdiction rests on no law—and all crimes and penalties are to be looked for among the dim and stained repositories of the laws of war, or among the fickle, ubiquitous, but unknown fountains of martial law—then we have lost our foothold on the *terra firma* of law, and have become the sport of the winds and waves that are bearing us, at this time, to an unknown shore. The latitude and longitude of judicial navigation are lost—innocence has no sure protection, and guilt no certain punishment—might gives right—law hides itself, and justice is measured by the strength and will of the tribunal and the defenseless condition of the accused. This is abstract argument, not intended for this Court, whose courtesy and justice, thus far, we have had so much reason to commend. But at least, if conscience demands the conviction of one or more of the accused, it would be a consolation and a shield of justification, hereafter, when our political skies have cleared away, to know, that if you could point to no statute for your *jurisdiction*, that you could for the crime and its penalty.

The true criterion, doubtless, is that medial line, which by its severity—but more by its certainty—deters the incorrigible, and reforms the penitent offender—while its cruelty and vindictiveness do not give a greater shock to the public sense than did the crime for which he is punished—and create a sympathy for the offender and horror for the Court. These are unfavorable times for the admeasurement of punishment, all must admit, where the offense, or the offender, has to stem the sirocco breath of our nation's present heavy breathings. The outside current is strong against the secret order of the Sons of Liberty, and if a defense of the accused necessarily involved a defense of the order, as a political institution, I should despair of the task. Time, and a very limited exercise of reason, will make plain to the popular mind, as it has already to this Court, I trust, the difference between the criminality of the *order*, and the criminality of particular members, at remote distances from each other. And when this mingled pageant of bright bayonets and bloody horrors—of military victories and political defeats—of rival military and civil courts—shall have passed away—and when reason shall dethrone passion, and when this great nation, with garments now bathed in blood, shall lift her head above the clouds, and clothe herself again in the majesty of law—may we have no record of these cases, that we or posterity will blush to read. When the unclouded intellect of the nation is again supreme, in its sway, much of the work, besides that of the Sons of Liberty, to which prejudice and malignity are now devoted, will not receive the sanction, even, of popular approval.

Now, Mr. President, and gentlemen of the Commission, my task is done, whilst yours, in its gravest responsibility, is before you. Humphreys has an unblemished character, the growth of many sacrifices, and the exercise of many virtues—he has a career of honor and usefulness among men, in the future—he has an interesting family, whose fate, fortune and happiness are involved in his own—he has a noble, dauntless, unbroken spirit, which he would not exchange for that of all his accusers—he has life, liberty and happiness—all staked on the issue; and I commit them all to your keeping.

And here is Colonel Bowles, sobered alike by age and the solemnity of the crisis that has overtaken him—with a frame bowed, somewhat, by the storms of life—intimately identified with the past legislative and military history of our State—soon, in the course of nature, nothing will remain of him but his memory—he fondly hopes that his memory is not to be blackened by the stigma of conviction—his family and friends will gather around his grave, and protect that memory, when dead, if you will shield it while living. You might convict and remove him, but great abuses, bad laws, and defective institutions, would still remain. I commend him to your mercy.

ARGUMENT OF JOHN R. COFFROTH,

IN DEFENSE OF

L. P. MILLIGAN.

Mr. President and Gentlemen of the Commission:
I am counsel for Mr. Milligan alone. My argument, therefore, will be more especially directed to matters which concern his defense.

These defendants are on joint trial; their motion for separate trials having been denied them by this Commission. That matter is passed, and I do not wish to refer to it complainingly—propriety forbids it; but, as an act of truth, as well as of simple justice to my client, it is my duty to state, most solemnly, that that refusal has most materially and vitally embarrassed and prejudiced his defense. Evidence of the most vital importance to him was not introduced from the selfish opposition of a co-defendant, induced by the fear that that evidence might remotely affect him. We yielded to that opposition, even to the prejudice of my client's good name, beyond which, in this trial, he has but little concern.

By the common law of practice, a separate trial of persons jointly charged with a felony, has been *rarely* refused, even in cases where the accused were charged with the commission of a single act, committed at the same time and place; while in this, and many other States, the separate trial of persons, jointly indicted for a felony, is expressly guaranteed by statute. I only refer to this matter in explanation of our silence on points upon which we otherwise should have been heard "trumpettongued" by the evidence.

This is a remarkable case, not only in its inception, but in its progress. Strange lights have gleamed in upon us, showing the baleful effects of partisan selfishness and malice; for this cause has assumed in its progress more of a political than a criminal prosecution. You are sitting in judgment upon political opponents for alleged political offenses: let the history of the past admonish you against lending a too willing ear to what may be the perjured tale of accomplices, paid spies or informers. This is a State trial, a political trial; and in all such trials, the tribunal before which the accused are immediately held to answer, is not the only one that sits in judgment. The cause before this tribunal is about to close; but it is continued, for the sober second thought, before that other self-correcting tribunal—public opinion—whose decree frequently reverses the first hasty decision, and whose final judgment is most generally right. It is true that that final judgment may come too late for Mr. Milligan, but his children will reap its advantage. "The mills of the gods grind slowly, but they grind exceedingly fine." I shall be pardoned for this allusion, if it be remembered that it is very difficult to live in a poisoned atmosphere without inhaling a portion of the miasma.

During the whole progress of this trial, partisan hate, with blind and fiendish malignity, has been demanding blood. In many of the public journals, the evidence has been garbled, misrepresented and perverted, and then criticised—begetting a mad fury in the minds of a victorious party, dethroning truth, and making us, at times, tremble for fear of a partial judgment. But, fortunately for the cause of justice, during the lengthy progress of the trial, the storm has, in some measure, spent its fury, and already the truth begins to peep from behind the cloud. The first judgment of that other tribunal is even now undergoing review. The voices that cried "hosannah," afterward shouted "crucify;" and the wild acclaim that welcomed the return of King Charles, and proclaimed the Restoration, came from the same throats that had howled with savage fury for his blood.

> "Hearest thou," he said, "the loud acclaim,
> With which they shout the Douglas' name;
> With like acclaim the vulgar throat
> Strained for King James their morning note;
> With like acclaim they hail'd the day
> When first I broke the Douglas' sway;
> And like acclaim would Douglas greet
> If he could hurl me from my seat."

The first question in order that presents itself, in the consideration of this cause, is as to the jurisdiction of this military tribunal to try these defendants, who are all citizens of Indiana, and in no wise connected with the army or navy of the United States; and, therefore, entitled, by the Federal Constitution, to "a speedy and public trial, by an impartial jury of the State and district wherein the crime shall have been committed," and not by such a tribunal as this Commission, composed, as it is, of citizens of Indiana, Michigan and Massachusetts. But this question of jurisdiction has been so ably and so fully argued by my learned brother, Gordon, (who is counsel for other of the defendants,) that any further elucidation is unnecessary, if not impossible; for the whole subject, to my mind, has been, by him, most learnedly and exhaustively argued.

Allow me, then, at once, to call your attention to the charges, and to the evidence in support of them. The charges are as follows:

1. Conspiracy against the Government of the United States.

2. Affording aid and comfort to rebels against the authority of the United States.

3. Inciting insurrection.

4. Disloyal practices.

5. Violating the laws of war.

The gist of the specification to these charges may be thus stated: That these defendants organized and disseminated, and were members of the "Order of American Knights, or Sons of Liberty," which was both civil and military; that this society was unlawful and treasonable; that it was armed, and was designed to aid the rebels, and to overthrow the Government; that the defendants conspired with Dodd, and others, to seize certain State and United States Arsenals, and to release and arm rebel prisoners. That they counseled and incited resistance to the draft, and attempted to introduce the enemies of the United States within the loyal portions thereof, and held communication with them.

In support of these charges and specifications, the main facts proven against Mr. Milligan are, that he is a member of the "Order of American Knights, or Sons of Liberty;" that he attended two Grand Councils of the society, held at Indianapolis, the one in November, 1863, and the other in June, 1864; and that he was appointed by the order a Major-General thereof. Some minor matters of evidence will be noticed in the course of this argument. We are, therefore, at once led to the inquiry, was the Order of American Knights a conspiracy *per se*, and was it treasonable?

"A conspiracy is a corrupt agreeing together, by two or more, to do, by concerted action, something unlawful, either as a means or an end." 2 *Bishop Crim. Law*, § 149. The legality of the agreement, then, becomes a pertinent question in this branch of our inquiry, or, rather, the illegality of the act or acts that are agreed to be done. It, therefore, becomes necessary to institute a careful examination of the several acts that the "Sons of Liberty" agreed to do; and, first, let us look at the ground work of that society—at its declaration of principles.

And, while reading, I ask you to forget, for the time being, that they are, in any way, connected with the Sons of Liberty, and then let us ask ourselves what part we will condemn.

"DECLARATION OF PRINCIPLES.

"1st. Essence Ethereal, Eternal, Supreme—by us called God—hath created, pervades and controls the universe! dwells in man, and is the DIVINITY within him.

"Sponsors—Amen.

"2d. All men are endowed by the Creator with certain rights, equal only so far as there is equality in the capacity for the appreciation, enjoyment and exercise of those rights, some of which are inalienable, while others may, by voluntary act or consent, be qualified, suspended or relinquished, for the purpose of social governmental organization, or may be taken away from the individual by the supremacy of the law which he himself hath ordained, in conjunction with his fellows, for their mutual protection and advancement toward perfect civilization.

"3d. Government arises from the necessities of a well organized society.

"4th. Right government derives its sole authority from the will of the governed, expressly declared. [*The majority should express such will in the mode which the unanimous voice shall approve, always guaranteeing to each individual, unless he shall have been restrained by the law, the privilege and opportunity to make known his opinion and express his will in regard to all matters relating or pertaining to the Government.*]

"5th. The grand purpose of government is the welfare of the governed; its success is measured by the degree of progress, which the people shall have attained to the most exalted civilization.

"6th. Government founded on the principles enunciated in the foregoing propositions is designated *Democracy*. The division of a Territory, where it exists, is usually called a REPUBLIC, *sometimes a* STATE.

"7th. Reflection, observation and experience seem to have established, in the minds of wise and impartial men, the conclusion that '*Democracy*,' properly organized upon the great principles which our Revolutionary ancestors, *patriots and sages*, held, inculcated and defended, best achieved the grand and munificent end of human government.

"8th. The Government organized and existing in the original thirteen States of North America, when they had severally and unitedly renounced their allegiance to the Government of Great Britain, and dissolved their former colonial relations, we regard as the wisest and best adapted to the nature and character of the people inhabiting the continent of North America at the present day. Under the benign influence of that Government a nation has arisen, and attained a degree of power and splendor which has no parallel in the history of the human race.

"9th. The Government designated 'The United States of America,' which blazons the historic page, and shed its light along the path of future ages, was the transcendent conception and mighty achievement of wisdom, enlightened patriotism and virtue, which appear to have passed from earth amidst the fading glories of the *golden era*, which they illustrated with immortal splendor. That Government was created originally by *thirteen free, sovereign* and independent States, for their mutual benefit, to administer the affairs of their common interest and concern; being endowed with the powers, dignity and supremacy, and no further, or other, which are distinctly specified, and warranted, and conferred by the strict letter of the immortal compact—the Constitution of the United States.

"Sponsors—Amen."

I ask you to read this declaration of principles, and to examine them closely. Are they not, so far as they have any signification, the very principles upon which our Government was administered in the "better days of the

Republic," when it was in the very noontide of its prosperity and glory; and which have canonized their authors as the apostles of civil liberty in America? Which one of those principles is it unlawful to hold, inculcate and defend? But I pass from them as needing no comment.

But, perhaps, the obligations of the order are thought to be objectionable? During the progress of this trial, our attention has been particularly called to the following clause, as the only obnoxious one! by the frequency with which it has been read to the witnesses:

"I do further swear that I will, at all times, if needs be, take up arms in the cause of the oppressed—in my own country first of all—against any *monarch, prince, potentate, power or government* USURPED, which may be found in arms, waging war against a people or peoples, who are endeavoring to establish or have inaugurated a government for themselves, in accordance with, and founded upon, the eternal principles of truth, which I have sworn in the Vestibule, and now in this presence do swear to maintain inviolate and defend with my life."

There is no agreement here to do a particular act; it is a mere promise, upon a given case which may never arise—for we trust that the Government will not adopt the necessity of admitting that any of the contingencies upon which this obligation presupposes the taking up of arms as necessary, have happened or do exist, or that there is even a proximate likelihood of their happening—and which the accused say, by their action and inaction, have not happened. Let us analyze this pledge. And first, who were they to take up arms against? "A monarch, prince, potentate, power, or government usurped." Now, we feel confident that we may, with propriety, dismiss all the objects of this seeming warlike proposition, except the last, for the reason that we can not believe that the Government will insist that in this, our country, "any monarch or prince" has been "found in arms," etc. We will, therefore, confine our remarks to the last proposition, that is, as to a "power or government usurped;" and I here ask the learned Judge Advocate if he is prepared to proclaim to the world that this Government is a usurped one, in order to make this obligation to take up arms apply to it? The declaration would be as startling as any that the defendants are charged with.

I have no purpose to conceal the views of Mr. Milligan, and freely admit that he may have said, what every intelligent man in America knows, that the President, the Congress, and the military authorities, have each and all exercised particular powers that did not belong to them; yet, I submit that he is a gentleman of too much intelligence to entertain or express the opinion that our Federal Government is an usurped one, or that Mr. Lincoln is not the lawful President, elected according to the forms of law, and, as such, entitled to the respect due to his station. True, the defendant has criticised Mr. Lincoln's acts, and so have the American people, as they have claimed and exercised the right

to criticise the acts of all administrations since our existence as a people, Washington's not excepted. The exercise of denied powers, history informs us, has by the people usually been denominated usurpations. But, I trust, this Commission will not lose sight of the distinction between charging a legitimate Government with exercising powers denied to it—using the term "usurp" with reference to the exercise of such powers—and charging a Government with being a usurped one. But, if any one should, unfortunately for the defense, be of opinion that the Government is a usurpation, still I insist that neither the defendants as individuals, nor the Order of American Knights, or Sons of Liberty, ever entertained or expressed such sentiments, but that they have ever treated the Government, including the President, the Courts, the Congress, and the Army, as legitimate, each in its sphere. For the proof of this I appeal to their acts. Where has that order taken up arms or made any preparation to do so, either by organizing, arming or drilling the members? But it is claimed that Mr. Milligan, in public speeches, advised resistance to any encroachment upon the elective franchise. Suppose he did; who would not and be a man? And suppose further that he expressed the opinion that these encroachments would come from the army! Yet, will it be assumed that such encroachments, had they come, would have been the act of the Government? and that resistance to such encroachments would be resistance to the Government? If so, then there are millions of men aspiring to be freemen, who are guilty criminals, deserving the fate now threatened these defendants.

That this obligation did not contemplate the taking up of arms against the Federal Government, is fully shown by the fact that the order did not take up arms; nor was any resolve or movement made in any of its authorized councils, temples, or meetings, to do so, but, on the contrary, the evidence of Mr. Ibach shows, that at the Grand Council of June, 1864, on a resolution being introduced, pledging the order to resist the draft, it was promptly and with great unanimity voted down; and that the belligerent gentleman who introduced the resolution, went away much dissatisfied with the Order. And may he not have been some bosom friend of General Carrington, *a la* Stidger and Zumro? That there may have been persons in the organization who would have gazed with delight upon the torch being applied that should kindle the flames of civil war, and who hoped to find a helping hand in the order, I do not deny; but, from the evidence, I do deny that the order had any such purpose. Nor is the order responsible for the individual acts of its members, any more than a Church, or a lodge of Masons, is responsible for the treasonable acts of any or even all of its members. Mr. Harrison estimates the number of the order in Indiana at 18,000. I respectfully ask the Judge Advocate if he will say, that that mighty host are all responsible for the insane ravings and actions of Dodd & Co., and therefore traitors? If so, why have they not been arrested? Why are they not brought before a military tribunal, and put through the forms of trial and hanged? If they are traitors, they should be. What a grand spectacle it would present! How proud would be the bearing of that *brave* and *gallant* General who has, by his paid spies and informers, been so industriously extending this order, duping innocent men into it, initiating rebel officers, carrying messages between Dodd & Co., and traitors in arms, and facilitating by all possible means the grand carnival of blood that was to have been inaugurated in this city on the 16th of last August! It is true, the accumulated wail of widows and orphans would have risen, even to the threshold of the Courts of Heaven, and what of all that? the strength of the Democratic party would be very much broken, and the soul of John Brown would go "marching on."

We have been informed that the commanders of armies frequently resort to such means. Possibly. But who ever heard of a commander sending out agents to recruit for the ranks of an enemy? What would be thought of General Grant if he should send out agents to recruit for the purpose of filling up the decimated ranks of Lee's army? And yet Carrington paid and encouraged Stidger to extend, as rapidly as possible, an organization that is claimed to be treasonable. And Zumro, another of his infamous spies, inveigled innocent and unsuspecting farmers into it for the purpose of betraying them into peril.

But I must refer, again, to that obnoxious obligation, in order to obtain a fair and rational interpretation of its phraseology, and to ascertain if it is not consistent with patriotism and most devoted *loyalty*, if you please. It is a promise to take up arms, if needs be, against particular forms of Government, "found in arms, waging war against a people or peoples who are endeavoring to establish or have inaugurated a government for themselves, of their own free choice, and in accordance with, and founded upon, the eternal principles of truth." Having shown that no usurped Government exists in this country, and that the order has not found it necessary to take up arms at all; let us endeavor to ascertain if the contingency has happened, upon which they obligated themselves to take up arms for the people or peoples in whose behalf they propose to volunteer. And we inquire where is that people "who have established or inaugurated a government of their own free choice, and in accordance with, and founded upon, the eternal principles of truth?" It will not do to say that the Southern Confederacy is that people, for it would be a eulogy on Jeff Davis' Government more glowing than any Son of Liberty ever uttered. Is their cause that of the oppressed? Is our Government a usurpation? Is the Southern Confederacy founded upon the eternal principles of truth? All this must be admitted in order to make a state of things upon which they agreed to take up arms.

But it is claimed that this obligation has a different meaning, known to and understood by the order. Allow me to invite your attention to the evidence upon that point. There are but three witnesses whose testimony tends to support that view: Tranter, Teney and Robertson. A case must be desperate indeed which relies for support on the testimony of such witnesses—ignorant and stupid beyond comparison. I am at a loss to know how the latter ever found his way from the woods of Randolph county to this Capitol; the other two were drafted and duly escorted here, and no doubt testified under the hope of indulgence from the draft in proportion as their testimony might prove valuable. Tranter and Teney contradict each other in almost every particular, except that they both swear that John W. Stone told them that the Circle of the Mighty Host, and also the Golden Circle, were to "assist Jeff Davis north and south." Tranter swears that this obligation was a part of the Golden Circle, but not of the Mighty Host. Teney, who was not a member of the Golden Circle, says that he was of the Mighty Host. But neither of these pillars of the Government was a member of the American Knights or Sons of Liberty. The evidence further shows that both the defendant, Horsey, and the Government witness, Connell, denied and repudiated the declarations of John W. Stone, who, for aught that appears in the evidence, may have been a Stidger or a Zumro. But in opposition to this *apology* for testimony, we have the evidence of two Government witnesses, Messrs. Bingham and Harrison, and in addition thereto the testimony of the large array of witnesses for the defendants—all of the most honorable character, and many holding the highest social and official positions—coming from various sections of the State, all bearing witness to the fact that the objects of the order were purely political, and intended solely to operate upon the elections by a more systematic organization of the Democratic party; just as the Republican party was doing through the instrumentality of the Loyal League, which it was intended to counteract; and none of them understanding the obligation to mean any thing more than it said, or than the words themselves rationally implied. The testimony of Mr. Bingham is conclusive upon this point; he early became a member, attended Grand Councils, acted on committees, and was in almost daily intercourse with Dodd and other leading members of the order, and yet never knew of any other than its political character until Dodd revealed his insane and hellish proposition, when he immediately took measures to circumvent it. And, I submit, that the conduct of Mr. Bingham is in a commendable contrast to that of the authorities. As soon as he was informed of Dodd's proposed plot, his best efforts were at once directed to paralyze the embryo rebellion; while, on the other hand, the authorities who knew it all, long before Mr. Bingham did, instead of destroying it, were nursing and encouraging it, that it might bring forth the ripe fruit of anarchy, strife, and bloodshed. The evidence of Stidger, their detective and witness, shows that while under the pay and direction of Carrington, and with his consent and approbation, he (Stidger) was extending the order as rapidly as possible, both in Indiana and Kentucky; that with the same approbation he initiated rebel officers, carried messages between Dodd and others and officers in the Confederate service, and afforded every facility to Dodd and his immediate confederates to arrange and perfect the plan for the inauguration of civil war in· Indiana, keeping the authorities here constantly advised of every movement, by regular and frequent reports; and all this for the sole purpose of influencing the then pending elections! History affords no parallel to the dark, malignant designs against peace and good order, on the part of those intrusted with their preservation. They were fully advised of the existence of what they claim to have been a most infernal conspiracy against the peace of the State; they witnessed the maturing of the scheme; they watched the preparation of the brand that was to enkindle civil war, and yet raised not a finger to stop it. Like the tiger, standing at the edge of his jungle, watching the unfortunate traveler as he comes along, springs upon his victim, crushes his bones and laps up his blood; so they looked with savage delight upon the proposed uprising, regarding no other consequence than its probable influence upon the elections. It seemed to matter little to them, though the fire of civil war should desolate our homes, and cause the "shuddering mother to hug her babe more closely to her bosom," so that they could only remain masters of the burnt and blackened field. If Mr. Milligan merits penalties for knowing *nothing* about these alleged conspiracies, what meed of punishment is due to those authorities?

According to the theory of the prosecution, Bingham was a Son of Liberty, and therefore a co-conspirator with Dodd; and yet it is to Bingham, and not to the authorities, that the people of Indiana are indebted for being saved from the woes and horrors of civil war. He quenched the flame that the authorities were fanning. While they were nursing, he was stifling it. This may not unjustly have given rise to the dark suggestion, now current throughout the State, that Dodd was the mere hired tool of Carrington and his co-conspirators against the peace of the State. But it is asked why did not Bingham denounce Dodd to the authorities? My answer is, they knew all about it, long before he did; and in turn, I demand, on behalf of the people of Indiana, whose homes were in jeopardy, why did the authorities suffer Dodd and Walker to remain in this city, unarrested, for weeks after they were apprised of the whole plot? Surely they could not have considered it dangerous. If I am asked why Mr. Milligan did not act as did Bingham; my answer is, that he had no knowledge of the scheme until it was exposed and abandoned.

But I return again to the consideration of that obligation, as it is the only prop upon which the prosecution can reasonably rest its claim that the order is a conspiracy *per se;* and I submit, that its meaning must be ascertained by the same rules by which other writings are construed by the courts—that is, by the import of the words taken in their ordinary or common acceptation, the sense in which they are generally used and received. For, otherwise, how are the members to know the meaning of the obligation, especially in the absence of such lights as Captain Burkebile, Wesley Tranter and John W. Stone? Let it be borne in mind that this order was secret, and, therefore, there could be no motive for making the obligation mean more than, or different from what the language imported. I submit, therefore, that the Commission will not feel called upon to adopt a rule of interpretation heretofore unknown to judicial investigations, in order to make offensive that which is otherwise harmless; and especially against such an array of testimony to the contrary.

If the order of American Knights, or Sons of Liberty, is a conspiracy *per se*, it is only a conspiracy to do what the rational import of the obligations, the ritual, and the declaration of principles imposed upon its members at the time they became such; and therefore, no after agreement of certain of its members, no matter how high in rank, to do a particular thing, not within the purview of the order, can be charged to the order, nor to any of its members not actually a party to such subsequent agreement. This I submit as a legal proposition, and challenge contradiction. To make the act or declaration of a conspirator binding upon another, it must be made or done in pursuance of the originally concerted plan, and with reference to the common object. 1 *Greenl. Ev.*, § 111, *et seq.;* 2 *Stark. Ev.*, 233, *et seq.*

Let us apply this principle. And here I will assume, with all confidence, that it will not be held that any of the obligations of the order proposed that Camps Morton, Douglas, etc., were to be emptied of their prisoners. If that was agreed to, who were the parties to the agreement? From the evidence, if it was agreed to at all, it was simply an open proposition of Dodd's; or, if you choose to give it the latitude claimed by that "mud-sill" of infamy, who, after being on joint trial for three weeks, turned informer, in order to purchase his own release, illustrating the truth of the adage that "it is always the biggest scoundrel that turns State's evidence;"—of that creature—but I will not speak of him; contempt has the property of descending very low, but to even that there is a limit, and it therefore stops far short of Horace Heffren. I repeat, if we adopt his statement, that the parties to the conspiracy to seize the arsenals and liberate the prisoners, consisted of delegates from all the States but two, and that all the delegates were Sons of Liberty; yet, unless that conspiracy comes fairly within the purview of the order, it implicates no one but the parties actually agreeing to the unlawful undertaking. Dodd, Heffren, Wilson, and others, may have conspired, but it was only their own conspiracy, and Mr. Milligan and other of the defendants are not shown to have taken any part in it, or to have had any knowledge of it, and, therefore, are not conspirators with Dodd. Hence, their declarations and admissions are not legitimate evidence against this defendant.

For example: Suppose that A conspires with B to rob the mail, and that, during the existence of that conspiracy, B conspires with C to kill Governor Morton; now, upon the trial of A for the former conspiracy, the declarations of B and C would not be competent, although they are parties with A to another conspiracy. Thus certain persons became members of the Sons of Liberty; a part of them afterward, without the knowledge or consent of the others, conspired to seize arsenals and release rebel prisoners, etc. Can those other members, by any principle of law, be bound by the declaration of those conspirators, or be held to answer for their acts? Why, the evidence shows that Dodd not only contemplated duping and inveigling the Sons of Liberty into his scheme, but also the whole Democratic party. You might, therefore, with as much propriety, hold the individual members of that party responsible, as the individual members of the Sons of Liberty, who, like Mr. Milligan, (I speak by the evidence,) had no knowledge of it whatever. Says Mr. Justice Buller, in Hardy's case: "Before the evidence of the conspiracy can affect the prisoner materially, it is necessary to make out another point, to-wit, *that he consented to the extent that the others did.*" 2 *Stark. Ev.*, 234. And in the course of the same trial, Mr. Roscoe says, "It was said by Eyre, C. J., that in a case of conspiracy, general evidence of the thing conspired is received, and then the party before the Court is to be affected *for his share of it.*" *Ros. Crim. Ev.*, 414.

"The rule," says Mr. Starkie, "that one man is not to be affected by the acts and declarations of a stranger, rests upon the principles of purest justice; and although the courts, in cases of conspiracy, have, out of convenience, and on account of the difficulty in otherwise proving the guilt of the parties, admitted the acts and declarations of strangers to be given in evidence, in order to establish the *fact* of a conspiracy, it is to be remembered that this is an inversion of the usual order for the sake of convenience, and that such evidence is in the result material so far only as the assent of the accused to what had been done by others was proved." 2 *Stark. Ev.*, 235.

If insurrection was one of the purposes of the order, why was not that subject introduced, discussed or suggested in some of its business meetings, when none but those in its secrets were supposed to be present? And yet neither Government detectives nor truckling accomplices ever heard of it. But it is said that there was an inner circle of the order, namely, the military part of it, and that that was treasonable. Harrison states that the order was fully organized at Terre Haute, and a Grand Council appointed. In this organization there was no military feature, and it was not till long afterward that what was termed the "military bill," or military feature of the Order, was introduced; and yet, while all the other proceedings of the order, including reports from county temples, were printed and circulated, this "military bill" was not. In fact, it remained a dead letter, and was not even known to members of the Grand Council,

as we are informed by witnesses of the most honorable character, such as Judge Loughridge, and Messrs. Bird, Ibach and Winters, all members of the Grand Council, and who were never advised of any other than the political character of the order. The military feature, therefore, never formed any part of the order; and if it existed at all, was only a part of an independent conspiracy of Dodd and others.

I come now to the consideration of another inquiry, to which I respectfully ask your attention. Is there any legal evidence of a conspiracy, even on the part of Dodd and others? Do all the acts and declarations proven, make out a conspiracy within the meaning of the law? although I insist that Mr. Milligan is not concerned in this inquiry. "A conspiracy is a corrupt agreement to do, by concerted action, something unlawful." [*Bishop, supra.*] Let us, then, see what, if any thing, was agreed upon; for if what is charged was actually agreed upon, I will admit that it is both corrupt and unlawful.

It is claimed that the meeting at Chicago, of July 20, 1864, conspired to seize certain arsenals, release rebel prisoners, and revolutionize the Government. But what evidence has been given in support of that proposition?

Heffren swears that Wilson told him that this uprising was agreed upon at Chicago. But Wilson, who was there, swears that no business (to his knowledge) was done at that meeting; that Barrett, who had called it, said it was to be a meeting of military men, but that they had not come. Wilson tells us that several plans were talked of; that Dodd's plan seemed to meet with most favor, but was not agreed upon. This is certainly better evidence than the hearsay of Heffren; besides, it is corroborated by the testimony of Harrison and Bingham, and also by the very character of Dodd's plan. What did Dodd tell Harrison? He says: "If it was agreed upon, he (Dodd) was to have charge of releasing the rebel prisoners at this point." Again, Harrison informs us that Dodd told him that it was not finally agreed upon, but depended upon a consultation of prominent individuals, whom he was to summon together for the purpose of determining as to his plan. And here flows in an item of evidence which can not be explained on any other principle than this uprising had not been agreed upon. It is this: Dr. Bowles (as the evidence clearly shows) was at the Chicago meeting. Now, had the uprising been agreed upon there, Dr. Bowles would have understood the whole affair. Why, then, would Dodd send his son to Bowles (as Harrison says) to consult upon the proposition? The evidence also shows that it was for the purpose of consultation that Milligan, Humphreys, Yeakle, Taylor and others were summoned by Dodd. Nor was this call confined to the so-called Major-Generals, but embraced others, to-wit: Yeakle and Taylor. They were not ordered to report to Dodd for duty, but were to consider the propriety of an uprising, and to decide whether or not it should take place.

All of Dodd's declarations show that the uprising was not determined upon by the very parties whose consent and co-operation were necessary to its inauguration. You will remember the fact that the meeting in Chicago was on the 20th of July, when Dodd was in company with Judge Bullitt; that immediately upon his return home, he communicated the matter to Harrison, who fixes the date of that return at the 29th of the same month; and also that the proposed uprising was to take place on the 16th of August. Now, if the scheme had been agreed upon at Chicago, to take place within so short a period, is it rational to suppose that Dodd, who is represented to be an impetuous, hasty man, would have slept until more than one-third of the time had elapsed before he made any move toward that preparation which would necessarily require so much time in maturing? The idea is preposterous; the impetuosity of Dodd would have put the thing in motion at once. But we have the sworn statement of three of the Government witnesses, that the uprising had not been agreed upon, but was awaiting the sanction and co-operation of others, whose concurrence was necessary.

Not only do Wilson and Harrison state that the project was not agreed to, but Bingham (to whom Dodd divulged his whole plan, and who, according to Dodd's statement, was the only person to whom it had been revealed) informs us that Dodd's scheme required his consent as a condition precedent. That he (Bingham) as chairman of the Democratic State Central Committee, must agree to it, and co-operate with him, by calling a mass convention of the Democracy of the State as a part of the programme, without which co-operation on the part of Bingham, the whole scheme would have to be abandoned; as it could not otherwise receive its initiatory impulse. Now this whole thing is consistent with itself, for the Commission will bear in mind Mr. Harrison's testimony, that when Dodd sent him to notify Mr. Milligan to attend this council of the leading men of the order, he instructed him not to inform Milligan of the nature of his errand, but merely to state that business of a very important character would be considered.

I ask here (though for the time digressing) if this looks as though Mr. Milligan knew of the scheme, especially when it is further remembered that he did not attend the proposed council? I respectfully ask the learned Judge Advocate to answer this if he can. If Mr. Milligan was a co-conspirator with Dodd, why must he be kept in ignorance of the project? Why instruct the messenger to observe silence as to the proposed revolution? Does it not show that Dodd considered Mr. Milligan as only belonging to the political, or rather, the *silly* and harmless branch of the order? although he had appointed him a Major General, and hoped to inveigle him into his plots! I earnestly submit to you, as rational and impartial judges, that this one circumstance is a complete refutation of the whole charge that Mr. Milligan was a party to Dodd's proposed conspiracy.

But, to return: what, I inquire, was the purpose of calling these men together, if the plan had already been agreed upon? Why, especially, keep Mr. Milligan in ignorance of the matter? Why instruct the messenger to keep him in the dark? Did Dodd mistrust his messenger? Was he unwilling to intrust so important a secret to him? The evidence informs us, that he had already imparted the whole matter to him; he must, therefore, have regarded his messenger as trusty. Then it will be remembered that the prosecution insists, that, according to the constitution of this order, the members were to implicitly obey the commands of the Grand Commander; I ask, then, if this scheme had been agreed upon, where was the necessity of calling these men together? He could have assigned to each his duty, and implicit obedience *must* be the result.

But, possibly, the prosecution will abandon its theory as to the supreme power of the Grand Commander. Because, if insurrection had been one of the purposes of the order, why try to keep Mr. Milligan ignorant of a fact which, of necessity, he must have known? and why impose secrecy upon the messenger, Mr. Harrison? This, I think, not only shows how the members of the order, but also how the Grand Commander understood that part of the obligation which pledged them to obedience. Thus, when we come to look at the case as judges and lawyers, and not as mere partisans, we find that there has been proven no such complete agreement, as is necessary under the law of conspiracy, even on the part of Dodd, much less on the part of Mr. Milligan, who knew nothing of it until it had died from want of sympathy on the part of those whose approval was to give it vital force.

Were it necessary, I might, without impropriety, refer to the cloud of suspicion through which the testimony of Stidger, Zumro, Heffren and Wilson came to us. The two former stand in the execrable light of informers; the latter, in the equally odious light of accomplices, purchasing their own immunity at the expense of their former alleged confederates; the former have ever been regarded with scorn and abhorrence, while the latter have always, by all honorable minds, been characterized as infamous. Let Heffren pass—"room for the leper, room!" Of Wilson, I scarcely know how to speak—he is self-accused and self condemned. Contrast him, if you please, with the honorable bearing of my client, and it ought to make the "blush of shame" crimson even the check of Wilson. He came to the witness stand with traitors' money under his control, and loaned out to his friends—he came and confessed to the treason, as well as to the ineffable meanness of accepting, from the hands of his country's enemies, the pitiful sum of his expenses to and from Chicago. And yet, this double-dyed traitor—traitor to his own country, according to his own showing, and, for the sake of purchasing his own release, traitor to his former alleged confederates—is to go forth to the world, duly indorsed by the Government as honest and credible; for, I understand, it asks you to believe him. Oh! kind and parental Administration, that allows the confessed traitor to go unpunished, that it may wreak its vengeance upon a mere political opponent!

No Court, either in ancient or modern times, has allowed the conviction of an individual upon the uncorroborated testimony of accomplices. Mr. Greenleaf, in speaking of this kind of evidence, says: "The case of accomplices is usually mentioned under the head of infamy." *Greenl. Ev.*, § 379.

Mr. Starkie says: "With respect to the force and effect of such testimony, it must, from its very nature, be regarded with jealousy and suspicion." "It is hard," Lord Hale observes, "to take away the life of any person upon the evidence of a *particeps criminis*, unless there be very considerable circumstances which may give the greater credit to what he swears.

"In strictness of law, indeed, a prisoner may be convicted on the testimony of a single accomplice, since, where competent evidence is adduced, it is for the jury to determine the effect of that evidence. But in-practice it is usual to direct the jury to acquit the prisoner, when the evidence of an accomplice stands uncorroborated in material circumstances, but this, it is said, is a matter resting entirely within the discretion of the Courts." *2 Stark. Ev.*, p. 12.

"But," says Mr. Phillips, "though accomplices are received as witnesses, their testimony ought to be received by a jury with a sober degree of jealousy and caution, for on their own confession they stand contaminated with guilt, and in the hope of lessening their own infamy, will often be tempted to throw as much guilt as possible upon the prisoner. They may also, in some cases, be entitled to rewards on the prisoner's conviction, and in all cases expected to earn a pardon, and as fear is usually their motive, the same feeling may tempt them to exaggerate their evidence for the purpose of destroying their former associate and securing themselves against his vengeance." *1 Phillips' Ev.*, 20.

"But their testimony alone is seldom of sufficient weight with a jury to convict the offenders, the temptation to commit perjury being so great, where the witness, by accusing another, may escape himself. The practice, therefore, is to advise the jury to regard the evidence of an accomplice only so far as he is confirmed, in some part of his testimony, by unimpeachable testimony." *Ib.*, p. 32.

"The degree of credit," Mr. Greenleaf says, "which ought to be given to an accomplice, is a matter exclusively within the province of the jury. It has sometimes been said that they ought not to believe him unless his testimony is corroborated by other evidence; and, without doubt, great caution in weighing such testimony, is dictated by prudence and good reason. But there is no such rule of law, it being expressly conceded that the jury may, if they please, act on the evidence of the accomplice without any confirmation of his statement. But, on the other hand, judges, in their discretion, will advise a jury not to convict of felony upon the testimony of an accomplice alone, and without corroboration, and it is now so generally the practice to give

them such advice, that its omission would be regarded as an omission of duty on the part of the judge. And, considering the respect always paid by the jury to this advice from the bench, it may be regarded as the settled course of practice not to convict a prisoner, in any case of felony, upon the sole and uncorroborated testimony of an accomplice." *1 Greenl. Ev.*, § 380.

"Judges," observed Lord Ellenborough, "will advise a jury not to believe an accomplice, unless he is confirmed, or only in so far as he is confirmed, but if he is believed, his testimony is unquestionably to establish the facts he deposes. *Jones' case*, 2 *Camp.*, 132. So, where, on an indictment for highway robbery, an accomplice only was called, the Court, though it admitted such evidence was legal, thought it too dangerous to permit a conviction to take place, and the prisoners were acquitted. *Jones & Davis' case*, 1 *Leach*, 479. The practice, therefore, is for the Court to direct the jury in such cases to acquit the prisoner, unless, in some respects, the evidence is confirmed. *Roscoe's Crim. Ev.*, p. 156.

"It is usual for a Court to advise a jury not to regard the evidence of an accomplice, unless he is confirmed in some part of his testimony by unimpeachable testimony. If confirmed in some parts, he may be believed in others." *U. S. vs. Kipler*, 1 *Bald. C. C. R.*, 22

I might stop here and rest the defense with propriety, but some might regard my duty incomplete, and ask if Mr. Milligan's alleged position as a Major General in the order had been satisfactorily disposed of? That is an easy task. For the sake of argument, we will admit that he was appointed a Major General; but where is the evidence that he ever accepted that appointment, or that he other than treated it with merited contempt? I answer, there is none whatever. But perhaps it is proposed to invert the usual order of criminal jurisprudence, and hold him guilty unless he proves himself innocent. Even in that case we are not without the necessary proof; indeed, we are prepared for almost any rule. Mr. Ibach informs us that at the Grand Council, in June, 1864, it was stated that the gentlemen who had been appointed Major Generals, had not accepted, and that it was agreed in Grand Council, that, if they did not accept by the ensuing 4th of July, others should be appointed in their stead. Indeed there is no credible testimony, but only an inference, that he ever knew of his appointment. Mr. Harrison states that the first appointment was in September, 1863, and it is not pretended that Mr. Milligan was at that meeting; nor was he ever informed of it in any official manner, as the Grand Secretary, Mr. Harrison, informs us. The same witness also states that Mr. Milligan was again elected a Major General at the February Grand Council; but this was also during his absence. True, Heffren states that Milligan was at that Grand Council, but this is only another indication of the utter unworthiness of his testimony, for we have the evidence of Messrs. Bingham, Daily, Moses Milligan, Loughridge and Winters, all corroborating Harrison and impeaching Heffren. Can they all be mistaken? Mr. Daily, who is a practicing attorney at Huntington, informs us that the Court at that place was then in session, and that Mr. Milligan was there. Moses Milligan, who was a court bailiff, gives us like testimony. Bingham swears that Mr. Milligan was not there. Judge Loughridge, a delegate to the Council, inquired for him, and found he was not present, and finally, Mr. Winters, a gentleman from Mr. Milligan's town, tells us that they both bought railroad tickets for Indianapolis, but, owing to the crowded state of the cars when they arrived at Huntington, Mr. Milligan refused to go, and did not go. That he (witness) went, and that inquiry was made of him for the reason of Milligan's absence. Stidger states that the roll of Major Generals was called at the June Council; but, Mr. Ibach, the delegate from Huntington, who went there with Milligan, contradicts this, and makes the reasonable statement that if any one from his own town had been named a Major General, he would have observed it. But for the sake of argument, let us suppose that he accepted the sounding title of Major General, yet what was it more than a mere *intended* compliment, or titular dignification? Thus the titles, "Grand Commander," "Sergeant of the Guard," etc., etc., are terms of high import in a lodge of "Sons of Malta," and yet the recipients of these "blushing honors" were never, for that cause, considered traitors, although the order was "military in its character." The title of "King" is one of high signification, and ordinarily means much; and the office of "King" is contrary to the Constitution and laws of the United States; and yet, who ever thought of holding an individual guilty of a crime because of his accepting and exercising the office of King in a Chapter of Royal Arch Masons! It is going back to those days of constructive treason, when a man was hanged for dreaming that he had made his son heir to the crown, although that was the name of his Inn; and another, whose favorite buck had been killed by the King, for wishing that the deer, horns and all, were in the King's belly. 4 *Black. Com., p.* 80. Names do not always signify the same thing—a Major General in the army is a position well understood, and having well defined duties; but tell me, if you please, what were the duties of a Major General in the Sons of Liberty? Where is the evidence of any assigned duties? Mere high-sounding names are not evidence. Men's lives are not to be forfeited by the inconsiderate use of such flimsy stuff.

It is next insisted that Mr. Milligan made a speech at a Democratic mass meeting at Fort Wayne, on the 13th of August last; in which it is claimed that he uttered disloyal sentiments, urged resistance to the draft, and attempted to incite insurrection. When we ask for the proof of all this, we are referred to the testimony of an itinerant news gatherer of the Cincinnati *Gazette* (and which, he says, is not a partisan paper), who was there hunting, at "a penny a line," for some item to be used against the Democratic party, in that political contest. True, he would have you believe that the speech was very disloyal; but against this, we have the testimony of honorable witnesses, Messrs. Bird and Winters, who heard the speech throughout (Mr. Winters having reported it for his paper), who swear there was nothing said in it calculated to incite resistance to the draft, or which counseled insurrection; that the speech was a dry, able, and argumentative one, characterized by moderation and respectful language toward his opponents; that he dealt in no denunciation of the Government, as Mr. Bush would have you believe, but made a broad distinction between the Government and the Administration. No insurrection followed that speech. True, he argued in favor of the doctrine of State Sovereignty. And suppose he did. It is no new doctrine, but is as old as the Constitution. The great and good men of America have advocated the same ideas, and yet were unconscious of committing any crime in doing so. On that very basis our Government was administered for sixty years with most unparalleled success. But suppose the party in power does deem it a political heresy; is heresy of political opinion a crime in this country? Who is to be the judge of the question of what is heresy of opinion? Shall it be the party in power? Then it would be very easy for them to perpetuate that power, by condemning all their political opponents to the halter, as traitors. Liberty of speech would then consist in the right to say, freely, what the Administration dictated. It was a wise remark of Jefferson, that "Error of opinion may well be tolerated as long as reason is left free to combat it."

But it ought not to be expected that gentlemen of the age, firmness, honesty and intelligence of Mr. Milligan, can change their honest convictions upon political questions to suit the views of the Administration, brought into power, perhaps, by a mere changeling mob. But are we to be held criminally responsible for a political speech, addressed to a political meeting in the course of a political campaign, even though it be bitter and denunciatory in its terms? Were it so, half the political speakers in the United States would then deserve hanging. I have only contempt to express for such a proposition. Once admit that principle, and probably at the next change of administration the gentlemen before me would have to change places with Mr. Milligan. If American citizens can not, in a cool, calm and respectful manner, criticise the acts of their public servants, in a canvass for their re-election, it is time they should be informed of the new order of things.

The next thing that claims our consideration is a letter from Mr. Milligan to General Dodd. It is claimed that addressing Dodd as *General*, is an acknowledgment of acquaintance with his military character, and of familiarity with what is termed the military branch of the order. But has it any such significance? Titles are cheap things now-a-days. In this country they do not preclude even the party using them from showing that they are improperly used. Thus, the titles, 'Squire and Judge, are not unfrequently applied to loafers; and how often, indeed, do we hear individuals called Colonel, upon whose shoulders the "Eagle Bird" has never rested; while the prefix of "Hon." has now little or no meaning beyond compliment.

In this letter, Mr. Milligan is writing as a politician, his name having been presented as a candidate for Governor; he was not writing as a Son of Liberty. That the appellation, General, was only used in compliment, is corroborated by the fact that Dodd was not General in, but Grand Commander of, the Sons of Liberty. If Mr. Milligan had been referring to Dodd's official position in the order, he would have addressed him as "Most Eminent Grand Commander." I ask the indulgence of the Commission while I examine this letter a little further. It has been introduced in evidence, and we can not anticipate the uses to which the learned Judge Advocate will attempt to apply it. The letter is a confidential answer to another, in which the writer states his grief on account of the desertion of supposed friends, and the consequent lessening of his political hopes. One or two expressions I will briefly notice. First, he expresses his willingness "to do whatever the cause of the North-west may require;" and then that other sentence, in which he says, "what will those of less pretension do when the real contest comes, when life and property depend upon the issue, when bullets instead of ballots are cast, and when the *halter* is a preamble to our platform? For unless Federal encroachments are arrested in the States by the effort as well of the Legislative as of the Executive, then will our *lives and fortunes* follow where our honors will have gone before." It seems from this that he was looking to legitimate sources, to-wit, the Legislative and Executive authority of the State, for the arrest of apprehended encroachments.

His expressions of sympathy for the North-west, I contend, are shared in, to a great extent, by men of all parties, who have felt that her interests have, by partial legislation, been made to pay tribute to those of New England. Indeed, it was quite a common expression among many members of the party with which Mr. Milligan acted, that the burdens of the war were not equally distributed, and that the Eastern States had not responded to the calls for volunteers with the same alacrity that had distinguished the North-west. Indeed, it will be remembered, that, previous to the date of that letter, public attention was frequently directed by the public journals to the alleged fact, that while Indiana was putting her 118th Regiment into the field, Massachusetts, with a population about equal to that of this State, was recruiting negroes in Indiana to fill up her 54th Regiment. With the justice of these comparisons we have, in the present inquiry, nothing to do, but only with the fact that such complaints were made. Mr. Milligan was then seeking office at the hands of those who uttered them, and the expression meant, simply, that if he was elected Governor, he would only ask Indiana to do her just part; it certainly had no reference to a North-western Confederacy. As to the expression about the halter being a preamble to the platform, etc., it is clearly referable to a reported declaration, said to have been made in a public speech, by our State Executive, shortly before that time, that those leading opponents of the Administration would come to grief, and their families suffer want. Whether or not the declaration was ever made, is unimportant in this inquiry; for, whether true or false, it was so published, and explains the phraseology of this portion of the letter.

And thus closes the last circumstance and the last inquiry, leaving this unhallowed prosecution without a stay or support.

After an investigation, occupying a period of about two months, the prosecution having failed to establish, by evidence, a single one of the inculpatory circumstances charged against Mr. Milligan, I am at a loss to know upon what principle of law, morality, or justice, he is detained in a loathsome prison, under circumstances of extreme hardship. This may, perhaps, be considered strong language, but knowing personally all the circumstances of the case, I must say that his arrest and confinement, considering his character, his physical condition, the health of his family, and the offer of his friends to give bail in any sum that might be asked for his appearance, does not accord with that degree of civilization which should characterize a great people. Never was a citizen more vindictively pursued. Every principle held sacred among honorable men has been violated by those following his track. Professional confidence, ever heretofore held sacred, has been prostituted to manufacture evidence against him. His kindly sympathies were aroused by a villain, who only sought to betray and ruin him. Private and confidential correspondence has been seized and introduced, in the vain hope of finding some inadvertent treason. And yet what has been discovered? What fatal act or word has been found? It is in evidence that, nearly a year ago, Zumro was placed on his track (and I am compelled to give its authors credit for the completeness of their plan)— Zumro, who was his neighbor and acquaintance! In order to more effectually blind Mr. Milligan, Zumro was arrested by the military authorities, and, as a part of the plan, employed his unsuspecting victim, who is a leading lawyer of the State, to defend him; and yet, during all the sacred and confidential intercourse existing between attorney and client, when all restraint is ordinarily thrown off, not a word, not even a murmur against the Government escaped his lips. That ear that was paid to listen with aching interest for some unguarded remark, never caught even a whisper of discontent; until finally, when on a bed of perilous sickness—the bed from which he was dragged to his present dungeon—while delirious with disease and drugs—that spy and informer goes to him in the hopes of hearing some treasonable expression escape him in his wild and incoherent ravings.

And now, forgetting for awhile his terrible impeachment, let us look his evidence full in the face. With insinuating manner, he squats beside that bed of sickness, and asks, "What is the order going to do about the draft?" to which Mr. Milligan replies, "Nothing; there are no fighting men about Huntington." But, unwilling to give it up, for his pay was shining before his greedy vision, with lying tongue he says, "we are going to resist it if we get assistance from here;" to which, he informs us, Mr. Milligan replied, "It is as good a time as any," and that "if he was well and in the woods, he could kill twenty before they could take him." But in this, as in every thing else, he is impeached by Mr. Johnson, a respectable farmer, who was present and heard the whole conversation. Infamous being! May God help you, and never allow your children to know the deep damnation of your infamy; else, from utter shame, they will become vagabonds and outlaws on the earth.

I have done; and now, Mr. President and officers of the Commission, I commit the cause of my client to you. I have known him long and intimately. For fourteen years we have practiced at the same bar, and commingled in its kindly and fraternal intercourse. With his extreme political views I have held no sympathy—for the Sons of Liberty I have had no respect; but I never will believe that Mr. Milligan, either in act or heart, is a traitor. His life has already measured the span of fifty-two years, the last twenty of which have been spent in this State. With "an unblemished reputation" (as the evidence shows,) a good, kind and affectionate wife, a comfortable home, devoted friends, and an enlarged and cultivated mind, he might, in ordinary times, laugh to scorn a charge so preposterous.

To you, gentlemen, I commit his reputation, his liberty and his life; and, higher than all, gentlemen, there is committed to you the duty of respecting that sacred right—the trial by jury. Better let these defendants go, even should you deem them guilty, than to strike at that glorious old bulwark of liberty! It was in defense of it that Hampden fell, that Sidney bled, that Washington fought, and for which the battle fields of our holy Revolution were incarnadined with the best blood of our patriot fathers. Shall we forget the lessons of history? Is the emergency so great? is our nation in such deadly peril? and have we become so insane, as to think we can save its life by cutting out its very vitals? If it can be saved only by the sacrifice of constitutional liberty, and the inalienable rights of our race, I say let it die. But no, no, it is not so. The God of our fathers will not forsake us. True, this nation is sick, very sick— the mailed hand of a foul rebellion has been grappling at its throat, but even now the arm is becoming weak and palsied. Then, while we strike at the fell fiend of treason, let us be careful that our dagger may not, in our blind fury, reach the dear idol of our hopes.

REPLY OF THE JUDGE ADVOCATE.

Gentlemen of the Commission:

In closing this trial, it becomes my duty to reply to the able addresses or arguments made on behalf of the accused by their counsel.

These trials have been in progress now since the nineteenth day of September. It has been one long, continuous labor, exhausting to the Court, to the counsel for the defense, and certainly to myself. The labor that has been required to develop the facts given to this Court, few will ever know, or appreciate. The responsibility of giving to you the facts involved in this issue, and the correct law, so far as I was able, during nearly a three months' struggle, has been solely upon my shoulders, unaided. I beg the Court, therefore, to look charitably upon those efforts wherein I have failed to do the cause of the Government full justice. While I yield to many, to the counsel for the accused, greater experience, learning and ability, I can, and do claim to be the peer of any man in my love of country, love of her glorious institutions, and in my desire and inflexible determination to deal justly with all men.

In discussing this question, I hope to say no word that is not fully warranted by the law and the evidence. There is certainly no bitterness in my heart toward any of these accused; they are all alike strangers to me. Their counsel have, in the conduct of the defense. ever been high-toned, gallant, courteous gentlemen, able advocates, and learned in the law.

In meeting the question of the jurisdiction of this Court, I shall make no plea or apology for the President, or the Commanding General of this District. I shall claim that the President, in issuing his proclamation declaring martial law, suspending the writ of *habeas corpus*. and making this class of offenses punishable by a military tribunal, acted in conformity to the law, and within the provisions of the Constitution; that his acts were warranted and sanctioned by the Constitution; and that had he done less than he has done, he would have performed less than his whole duty—he would not have taken "care that the laws were faithfully executed," and would have been unworthy to be the Chief Executive of this great nation, and the Commander-in-Chief of her armies. Had the Commanding General of this District permitted this conspiracy to ripen, to move forward to its culmination, or even to sleep for the time being, until, Ætna-like, it belched forth upon a sleeping people its glowing, seething, red tide of fire and blood, without grappling it and its leaders with the strong military arm, he would have been an *Arnold*, instead of the brave soldier and patriot he is.

This Court has jurisdiction in these cases, and has a right to hear, and pass sentences.

First. Because it has been expressly clothed with that right and power by the authority competent to give them; and

Second. Because, were no such formal power conveyed, the "laws of war," the military *lex non scripta*, and the necessity of the present crisis, would clothe this Court with jurisdiction to try this class of offenses.

Then as to the express authority. In General Orders No. 141, of the War Department, dated September 25th, 1862, will be found the proclamation of the President, which reads as follows:

War Department, Adjutant General's Office, }
Washington, September 25, 1862. }

General Orders No. 141.

The following proclamation by the President is published for the information and government of the Army, and all concerned:

BY THE PRESIDENT OF THE UNITED STATES OF AMERICA—A PROCLAMATION.

Whereas, It has become necessary to call into service not only volunteers, but also portions of the militia of the States by draft, in order to suppress the insurrection existing in the United States, and disloyal persons are not adequately restrained by the ordinary processes of law from hindering this measure, and from giving aid and comfort in various ways to the insurrection: now, therefore, be it ordered:

First. That during the existing insurrection, and as a necessary measure for suppressing the same, all rebels and insurgents, their aiders and abettors, within the United States, and all persons discouraging volunteer enlistments, resisting militia drafts, or guilty of any disloyal practice. affording aid and comfort to the rebels against the authority of the United States, shall be subject to martial law, and liable to trial and punishment by courts-martial or military commission.

Second. That the writ of *habeas corpus* is suspended in respect to all persons arrested, or who are now or hereafter during the rebellion shall be imprisoned in any fort, camp. arsenal, military prison or other place of confinement, by any military authority, or by the sentence of any court-martial or military commission.

In witness whereof, I have hereunto set my hand, and caused the seal of the United States to be affixed.

Done at the City of Washington, this twenty-fourth day of September, in the year [L. S.] of our Lord one thousand eight hundred and sixty-two, and of the independence of the United States the eighty-seventh.

ABRAHAM LINCOLN.

By the President:

WILLIAM H. SEWARD, *Secretary of State.*

By order of the Secretary of War:

L. THOMAS, *Adjutant General.*

This proclamation, it will be seen, covers many of the offenses set forth in the charges and specifications. It expressly says "that during the existing insurrection, and as a necessary measure for suppressing the same, all rebels and insurgents, their aiders and abettors within the United States, and all persons discouraging volunteer enlistments, resisting militia drafts, or guilty of any disloyal practice, affording aid and comfort to rebels against the authority of the United States, shall be subject to martial law, and liable to trial and punishment by court-martial."

To settle the question of jurisdiction beyond all doubt, this Court has but to determine whether the President had the power and the right, under the Constitution, to issue this proclamation. If he had that right as the executive arm of the Government, or as Commander-in-Chief of her armies, then Congress could in no wise interfere with, or take from a co-ordinate branch of the Government one of its constitutional prerogatives. For it is admitted of all men, that within the limits prescribed by the Constitution, each branch or department of the Government is supreme, and free of control or dictation from either of the others. The question then recurs, had the President the right to suspend the civil law, and put in force martial law, as against the class of offenders designated in the paragraph just quoted? I do not understand that the gentleman contends against, or even questions the authority of a commanding general in the field to declare martial law. In fact, the gentleman who has argued the question of jurisdiction in this case, Mr. Gordon, well stated, in the Dodd case, that the army, wherever it moves, carries martial law with it, without any proclamation. The proclamation, as a general rule, is but the giving notice of a *fact* which already exists. Then, if a commanding general in the field may, within the theater of his military operations, or within the lines of his military command, declare and enforce martial law, who shall be the judge of when and under what circumstances this shall be done? Certainly the military commander himself. It is one of the rights and powers incident to his military position. An army would be powerless could its operations be hindered and stopped by the processes of civil courts. Could the soldiers of an army be taken from its ranks by *habeas corpus,* how long, think you, could any army hold together? If by injunction you could stop the erection of fortifications, or the destruction of private property, of what efficiency would be the movements of your army? The nearer you approach perfect, arbitrary power, in the government of an army, the greater the efficiency and power of that army. To make it effective, it must be as nearly as possible one will, one intelligence, governing and giving direction to the entire physical force under its control; and just in proportion as you distract and divide that will, that intelligence, you distract and divide the strength and efficiency of that army.

The operations of the civil law, of the civil courts, and the full enjoyment of civil rights, are entirely inconsistent with, and opposed to, the operations of an army. The rights of war and the rights of peace are antagonistic, and can not co-exist; one must yield to the other. The laws of war and the laws of peace can not operate at one and the same time upon the same subject-matter; one must take precedence, and the other remain in abeyance. When a war is once *in esse,* the civil courts will take judicial notice of the fact, they should themselves give way, and yield to this new order of things. It is only in great emergencies that the armies of a nation are called into the field, that war is inaugurated; and when war *is* once inaugurated, it is the great, all-absorbing, vital question to that nation. Upon the success of its arms depend its national glory, the full enjoyment of the rights of its people, and, generally, its continuance as a government. Therefore, and for this reason, the civil rights of individuals, the powers and duties exercised by civil courts, for the time being, yield to this greater and more important interest. The commanding general, duly empowered as such, when in the field, has placed upon him great duties and high responsibilities. His power should be adequate to, and coextensive with his duties and responsibilities. He may then, if he deem it necessary for the success of the operations of his army, without its being claimed, it seems to me, by any person, to be a violation of any of the provisions of the Constitution, declare and enforce martial law; he may, at his will, if he deem it necessary, arrest any person within his military limits, or within the theater of his military operations. If he may arrest one, upon the same hypothesis he may arrest a thousand. The number is limited only by the necessity. While the Constitution says no man shall be deprived of life, liberty, or property, without due process of law, yet it can not, and would not be claimed that this would be an unconstitutional exercise of his power. And why? Simply because this clause of the Constitution does not refer to this emergency; it has reference to times of peace, to the normal condition of the country. So while private property, under the Constitution, is to be held inviolate, no man will contend but that a military commander may seize, at his will, all the forage and provisions necessary for the subsistence of his army, and any thing necessary for its transportation, or enter upon any realty necessary for the encampment of his troops, or use any amount of private property necessary for constructing fortifications. He may turn his guns upon the residence of any citizen, loyal though he may be, if it harbor the enemy, or if its removal would render the movements of his army more efficient. He may seize steamers and vessels for transportation; he may blow up bridges and forts; burn and destroy towns and cities; and this power is none the less perfect and unlimited from the fact that the property taken or destroyed is that of a friend, instead of an enemy. Upon this point, Solicitor Whiting, in his pamphlet upon "The War Powers of the President," has well said:

"While war is raging, many of the rights held sacred by the Constitution—rights which can not be violated by any acts of Congress—may and must be suspended and held in abeyance. If this were not so, the Government might itself be destroyed; the army and navy might be sacrificed, and one part of the Constitution would NULLIFY the rest.

"If *freedom of speech* can not be suppressed, spies can not be caught, imprisoned and hung.

"If *freedom of the press* can not be interfered with, all our military plans may be betrayed to the enemy.

"If no man can be *deprived of life without trial by jury*, a soldier can not slay the enemy in battle.

"If *enemy's property* can not be taken without 'due process of law,' how can the soldier disarm his foe and seize his weapons?

"If no person can be arrested, sentenced, and shot, without *trial by jury* in the county or State where his crime is alleged to have been committed, how can a *deserter be shot*, or a *spy be hung*, or an *enemy be taken prisoner?*

"It has been said that '*amidst arms* the *laws are silent.*' It would be more just to say, that while war rages, the *rights* which in peace are sacred, must and do give way to the higher right—the right of *public safety*—the right which the *country, the whole country, claims*, to be protected from its enemies, domestic and foreign—from spies, conspirators, and from traitors. The sovereign and almost dictatorial powers—existing only in actual war; ending when war ends—to be used in self-defense, and to be laid down when the occasion has passed, are, while they last, as *lawful*, as *constitutional*, as *sacred*, as the administration of justice by judicial courts in times of peace. They may be dangerous; war itself is dangerous; but danger does not make them unconstitutional. If the Commander-in-Chief orders the army to seize the arms and ammunition of the enemy; to capture their persons; to shell out their batteries; to hang spies, or shoot deserters; to destroy the armed enemy in open battle; to send traitors to forts and prisons; to stop the press from aiding and comforting the enemy by betraying our military plans; to arrest within our lines, or wherever they can be seized, persons against whom there is reasonable evidence of their having aided or abetted the rebels, or of intending so to do—the pretension that in so doing he is violating the Constitution, is not only erroneous, but it is a plea in behalf of treason. To set up the rules of civil administration, as overriding and controlling the laws of war, is to aid and abet the enemy. It falsifies the clear meaning of the Constitution, which not only gives the power, but makes it the plain duty of the President, to go to war with the enemy of his country. And the restraints to which he is subject *when in war*, are not to be found in the municipal regulations, which can be administered only in peace, but in the laws and usages of nations regulating the conduct of war."

Then, while these powers are conceded to a subordinate military commander in the field, with what consistency can they be denied to his superior, the Commander-in-Chief of all the armies? Is the inferior greater in power than the superior? Is the servant greater than the master? The superior may order the inferior, his junior in rank, to suspend the civil law and declare martial law. He may abrogate and set aside the proclamation of an inferior commander declaring martial law. All the acts of the inferior, the subordinate commander, receive their force, and have vitality only as they are supposed to emanate from and receive the sanction of the military superior, the Commander-in-Chief. Under the Constitution, the Commander-in-Chief appoints all these officers; and when the Constitution says that the President of the United States "shall be Commander-in-Chief of the army and navy," that provision carries with it all the necessary power incident to such office.

Then it having once been admitted that the subordinate military commander can do these acts, the only question that can arise, is, under what *circumstances* can he thus act? First, then, who is to be the judge of when the necessity exists for the Commander-in-Chief to issue his proclamation of martial law, or when he shall declare that martial law does exist?

We have seen that in the field, the subordinate military commander is, and can alone be the sole judge of that necessity; and he will be held to a high accountability for the exercise of a sound discretion in the use of this despotic power. For a wanton, or unwarranted exercise of it, he could be tried before a military tribunal; or on the restoration of peace, he could be held answerable by the aggrieved persons, before a civil tribunal. The only limit to this power in the hands of the subordinate commander, is the existence of the necessity; he being the judge of the necessity within his own military limits. No stronger rules, or greater limitations, of course, would obtain as against the Commander-in-Chief. If, under the existence of a great and overpowering necessity, it is constitutional and lawful for a subordinate commander to declare and enforce martial law, under the same circumstances, and with the same necessity, the Commander-in-Chief can constitutionally and legally declare and enforce martial law. It is not as President of the United States, not as the Chief Executive of a great nation, that he exercises this power, this despotic and arbitrary power, but it is as the Commander-in-Chief of her armies in time of war, made such by the express provisions of the Constitution itself.

In his judgment, that necessity existed in 1862. For a wanton, or unwarranted exercise of that power, he could have been impeached and tried by the Senate. He was the sole judge of that necessity. If he had thought the necessity for it existed, he could have issued his proclamation for the civil law and civil courts to be entirely suspended throughout the land; or in part, only, as the necessity demanded. In these Northern States, where branches of the army were operating, where the civil authorities, though weak, and often needing help from the military arm, were yet dominant, as Commander-in-Chief, the President has said that to "rebel insurgents, their aiders and abettors, and all persons discouraging volunteer enlistments, resisting militia drafts, or guilty of any disloyal practice, affording aid and comfort to rebels against the authority of the United States," the civil law shall be silent, and that, as to them, martial law shall obtain. In all other respects, the civil courts are open and the civil law is in full force.

The counsel, in arguing this question of jurisdiction, has treated the subject, at all times, as though the President, in putting in operation the martial law, must *entirely* subvert and set aside the civil law and its tribunals. This is an error. If he have the right to do it in whole, he can do it in part; the greater includes the less.

His military lines, as Commander-in-Chief of the armies of the United States, and the theater of the military operations of those armies, are coextensive with the geographical lines of the country. Can the gentlemen point to any State or Territory that is not to-day the theater of vast military operations? He has cited this State.

Of the extent of military operations here, of all interests affecting the public welfare, this Court has a right, without proof, to take judicial notice. On that subject, Greenleaf, vol. 1st, page 7, says:

"In like manner, the Law of Nations, and the general customs and usages of merchants, as well as the public statutes and general laws and customs of their own country, as well ecclesiastical as civil, are recognized, without proof, by the courts of all civilized nations. * * * * * * * Neither is it necessary to prove things which must have happened according to the ordinary course of nature; * * * * nor, any matters of public history, affecting the whole people; nor, public matters, affecting the government of the country."

When I say to you, then, that there are to-day in Indianapolis and the vicinity, and have been for the last six months, and the greater portion of the time, ever since 1861, soldiers on duty, preparing for or returning from the field, or passing through your city, *in transitu* from other points, in number more than one-half of the entire army of the United States previous to this war, it will scarcely be denied that this is the theater of military operations. There are here, to say nothing of other portions of the State, nearly 4,000 troops. This Court will recognize the further fact, that upon the streets of this city, to-day, more than one-half of the persons you meet, are either soldiers of the Government, or persons in the military employ and pay of the Gov-

ernment; and more than one-half of the business done in your city is directly, or indirectly, for our army. You are holding in your camps here, within sight of this city, nearly 5,000 prisoners of war, to capture whom probably not less than 5,000 lives of loyal men have been expended;—a force of the enemy as large nearly as either the army of General Scott or General Taylor, when they invaded Mexico.

But, last year, the enemy made a triumphal march through a large portion of this State, and all the available military forces of the State were called out to defend your homes. At what hour this same exigency may happen you again, with the enemy's cannon thundering less than a hundred miles from your border, no man can tell. No year has passed since the inauguration of this rebellion, and scarcely any month, that the commanding officer of this District has not had to send military forces into some portion of this State, to suppress armed insurrection. This is a notorious, public fact. And no month passes, now, but a guerrilla raid is announced from some of the river counties. The theater of military operations is the place where the armies are moving, or operating, where military forces are performing their legitimate duties; tried by this rule, it can scarcely be denied, and certainly not successfully, that your State is the theater of military operations. The condition of things here is paralleled by almost every other State in the Union. It could scarcely be otherwise when the whole country is engaged and taking part in this war; when from an entire population of a little more than twenty millions of people you draw from it, by volunteering and draft, over two millions of able-bodied men. As a general rule in voting, you get but one vote for every six inhabitants, and certainly the proportion of men for the army would not be greater than of votes. This army comes from every township, school district, neighborhood, and almost every family in the land. The whole land, more or less, is making this struggle its chief object. Congress has the right to call into the field, for the sake of maintaining the life of the Government, the entire physical force of this nation. When once in the field, that force is wielded, controlled and molded by but one will, and that, the will of the Commander-in-Chief. How soon it may be necessary to call upon this entire physical force, no one can tell. You certainly have already in the service more than half of those physically able to bear arms; and just in proportion as you obstruct and interfere with the efficiency of that army, as you promote and protect conspirators and conspiracies, here in these States, that must furnish the men for the armies, and the materials of war, just in that ratio will the remaining portion of the able-bodied men be called upon and put into the field, to carry this war successfully through.

As to the extent of this rebellion, its places of operation, etc., Aaron F. Perry, in his admirable argument on the application for a writ of *habeas corpus*, before Judge Leavitt, in the Vallandigham case, says:

"As a matter of course it can not be, and as a matter of fact it is not, limited to places, or described by geographical descriptions. In some parts of the country it dominates society; in other parts it is dominated by the regular civil administration. We hear of no place so dark but that some weak prayers are uttered for the Constitution; and of no place so bright but that lurking treason sometimes leaves its trail, or shows, through all disguises, its sinister unrest.

"The power and wants of the insurrection are not all, nor chiefly, military. It needs not only food, clothing, arms, medicine, but it needs hope and sympathy. It needs moral aid to sustain it against reactionary tendencies. It needs argument to represent its origin and claims to respect favorably before the world. It needs information concerning the strength, disposition, and movements of Government forces. It needs help to paralyze and divide opinions among those who sustain the Government, and needs help to hinder and embarrass its councils. It needs that troops should be withheld from Government, and its financial credit shaken. It needs that Government should lack confidence in itself, and become discouraged. It needs that an opinion should prevail in the world that the Government is incapable of success, and unworthy of sympathy. Who can help it in either particular I have named, can help it as effectually as by bearing arms for it. Wherever in the United States a wish is entertained to give such help, and such wish is carried to its appropriate act, there is the place of the insurrection. Since all these helps combine to make up the strength of the insurrection, war is necessarily made upon them all, when made upon the insurrection. Since each one of the insurrectionary forces holds in check, or neutralizes a corresponding Government force, and since Government is in such extremity as not safely to allow any part of its forces to withdraw from the struggle, it has no recourse but to strike at whatever part of this insurrection it shall find exposed."

In this State the insurrection is dominated by the regular civil authorities; yet it has its existence among you; it has its advocates, its adherents and abettors; those who give it aid and comfort; those who would give it sympathy and encouragement; those who carry that sympathy and encouragement into action. For the keeping of this part of the insurrection, this part of the rebellion in subjection, the Government has deemed it necessary to place troops here, and elsewhere in the State. To that extent, then, certainly, this is the theater of military operations; and, as I have said, this condition of things is paralleled in each of the Northern States. It is a sad fact that we have no State so loyal but that it is found nursing in its bosom some traitors, some who adhere to the enemies of the Government, and give them active sympathy and encouragement.

On the question as to whether the proclamation of the President, cited in this case, was still in full force, the gentleman who has argued this question of jurisdiction has ex-pended much time and labor. I believe this proclamation to be in full force and effect, and to have been in no wise interfered with by act of Congress, or by any subsequent act of the President himself. In this proclamation of September, 1862, he suspends the *habeas corpus*, and puts in operation, or rather declares that martial law is in existence as to a certain class of offenders; saying, in substance, that the necessities of the times demand that this class of cases shall be tried by military courts. He expressly limits the operation of martial law to the offenders, or offenses, therein designated.

It will be remembered by the Court, that at that time there was much cavil and discussion throughout the land, as to whether the power to suspend the writ of *habeas corpus*, under the Constitution, was in the Executive or the Legislative branch of the Government. Congress attempted to put at rest all question upon that subject; and, to strengthen the arms of the President, passed an act, approved March 3d, 1863, authorizing the President to suspend the writ of *habeas corpus*. It has always seemed to me that this act of Congress, to say the best of it, was but a nullity; the Constitution gave this power either to the Executive or to the Legislative department of the Government. If, under the Constitution, it belonged to the Executive, then, certainly, it was simply a work of supererogation for Congress to re-give it to the President: if it was given to the Legislative, it was a power which they could not transfer. If, under the Constitution, it was given to the President, as I before remarked, Congress could not take it from him. The question, then, is simply whether this power to suspend the writ of *habeas corpus* belongs to the President, or to Congress.

The suspension of the writ of *habeas corpus* is not the declaration of martial law; it is more properly one of the incidents of martial law, or of a state of war. This writ is to be suspended when a great public necessity shall demand it. And who shall be the judge as to when that necessity exists?

The Constitution says "the writ of *habeas corpus* shall not be suspended unless in case of rebellion, or invasion, the public safety may require it;" thus placing its suspension upon the contingency of some great public danger or emergency.

Our legislative body, Congress, usually convenes but once a year, never oftener than twice a year: and in times of foreign war, invasion, or rebellion, would we dare to say that the Government should wait the expiration of that year, or until Congress could be convened, to suspend the writ of *habeas corpus* or declare martial law? Such a course would be suicidal, and destructive of the Government itself. The power certainly does rest where it properly should rest, with the Executive of the Government; the Commander-in-Chief of the armies; the power that wields the physical force that must defend the life of the nation, if that life be in danger. It, then, being with the Executive, Congress, by its action, in no wise changed or interfered with this original prerogative of the President. It simply put at rest the discussion as to where this power was vested.

After the passage of this act of Congress, the President again issued a proclamation of September 15th, 1863, entirely suspending the writ of *habeas corpus* throughout the United States as to all classes of persons held by authority of the United States, or charged with offenses against the Government. This was simply making larger and more comprehensive his proclamation of September, 1862. It in no wise abrogated that proclamation, or interfered with its action; it was confined purely to the writ of *habeas corpus*, and was made universal in its operation. Military courts were before given jurisdiction, and martial law was declared as to certain classes of offenses; this, certainly, did not take from those courts that jurisdiction, neither expressly, nor by implication; it did not interfere with the operations of martial law, which had already been declared.

As to the proclamation of the President in Kentucky, on the 5th day of July, 1864, that was simply a proclamation which put into force martial law, and declared that such a state of war existed in that State as to demand the entire silence of civil law; that martial law, without being confined to any particular class of persons or offenses, should there be in existence in all its power and force. It in no wise abrogated, or interfered with, the proclamation of 1862, but simply said that in that State there was a necessity for a more extended operation of martial law than was required in other States, and was perfectly consistent with the proclamation of 1862, and also with that of 1863, suspending the writ of *habeas corpus*. This, I think, sufficiently answers the inquiry of the gentleman as to why the proclamation of July 5th, 1864, was issued.

Finally, as to the formal proclamation of the President, clothing this Court with jurisdiction, I call the attention of the Court to Lawrence's *Wheaton on International Law*, page 522, note, where the author, after reviewing in an extended article the statutory provisions and regulations of the different European Governments in reference to the suspension of the writ of *habeas corpus* and the proclamation of martial law, as to this particular proclamation of September 24th, 1862, says: "But, whatever may be the inference to be deduced, either from constitutional or international law, or from the usages of European Governments, as to the legitimate depository of the power of suspending the writ of *habeas corpus*, the virtual abrogation of the judiciary in cases affecting individual liberty, and the establishment, as *matter of fact*, in the United States, by the Executive alone, of martial law—not merely in the insurrectionary districts or in cases of military occupancy, but throughout the entire Union, and not temporarily, but as an institution as permanent as the insurrection on which it professes to be based, and capable, on the same principle, of being revived in all cases of foreign as well as civil war—are placed beyond question by the President's proclamation of September 24, 1862. It was issued two days after the proc-

lamation for the emancipation of the slaves in the insurgent States," etc.

The counsel for the accused has especially requested me to answer the inquiry, how any department of this Government—each department being limited in its authority by its organic law, the Constitution—can exercise the despotic power of martial law?

I answer him that that department of the Government has that power, which has been expressly clothed, by that organic law, with despotic and perfect arbitrary power, in certain contingencies. I refer to the President when acting as the military chieftain of the armies. As I have before stated, the greatest efficiency of any army is achieved when it approaches nearest the perfection of arbitrary and absolute rule; and that, from time immemorial, has been the aim of all military laws and regulations. Every nation having an army, has felt that there should be but one will to govern that army, to wield the physical force under its command, and that will absolute and untrammeled. In times of war, the power of the President of the United States, as Commander-in-Chief of her armies, is despotic and arbitrary; and must be so, to be of any efficiency whatever—assuming, of course, that the objects to be achieved are legitimate and constitutional. War is defined by Vattel as "that state in which a nation prosecutes its rights by force."

We next come to the consideration of the question of when martial law should obtain, and what the necessity is that will warrant it; whether that necessity has existed in this country during this rebellion; whether that necessity now exists, so as to warrant this Court to proceed in these cases; and whether the operation of martial law is consistent with, and known to the Constitution and laws of our country.

The consideration of these points, and their satisfactory settlement, will also settle the second point upon which we place the jurisdiction of this Court, to wit: that were no such formal power conveyed by the proclamation of the President, yet the "laws of war," the military *lex non scripta*, and the necessity of the present crisis, would clothe this Court with jurisdiction to try this class of offenses. In considering these questions, I do not propose so much to go back to the decisions of the dark ages, nor to untomb the obsolete law of a thousand years ago, nor to rely so much upon English precedents where the forms of that Government are so entirely different from those of our own, as upon the action, the precedents, and opinions of the great and good men of our own nation. The very organizations of those despotic, kingly Governments would preclude and almost make impossible the idea that their action could be quoted as precedents for us. There the King and his faction were at war ever with the aristocracy and the people; the aristocracy and their interests were at war with the King and the people; and the interests of the people, the masses, were always, and ever, adverse to the other two. At one time the King would be so securely enthroned, and so strongly seated upon the arms of his soldiers, that he carried his kingly prerogatives to a cruel and oppressive extent; and again, the aristocracy, the titled few of the nation, the landed nobles would dominate, and their interests would take precedence; and then again the masses, through some noble patriot and champion, would make a struggle once more for their rights. The history of ages and nations that are gone by, are not, therefore, consistent precedents for us; they are not consistent with each other. Here, the great, controlling powers and interests are the rights of the people; no class, no king, nor potentate can maintain interests adverse to them. It can not, however, be said that the action of the English Government, or that the English precedents cited by the gentleman in his argument, are against the enforcement of martial law, as they do recognize its existence and utility in great emergencies. Most of the cases cited in that argument—replete, as it is, with vast research and learning—are instances of the abuse of martial law; of the King using it for carrying out his peculiar and tyrannical notions, for oppressing some particular subject. And I could take the same cases cited by the gentleman himself, to show that in no century has any great emergency arisen, as civil war or rebellion, in that country, but that some department of the Government took upon itself the responsibility of declaring martial law, and permitted the officers of its army to act under its *ægis;*—in some instances Parliament declaring martial law, in others the King claiming it as his peculiar prerogative. Most of the cases cited in which there was an outcry against martial law, were those in which the King, *in time of peace*, had undertaken to enforce martial law in some oppressive manner against some particular subject, from a personal motive. The most prominent to which the gentleman refers is that given by Sir Matthew Hale, in his history of the Common Law, which reads: "The exercise of martial law, whereby any person should lose his life, member, or liberty, may not be permited, *in time of peace*," etc.

And again, in the case of Edmund, Earl of Kent, which was afterward reversed in 1st Edward 3, the language used is as follows: "That whenever any subject of the Lord the King shall be arrested for sedition in time of peace," etc. In the same case, also, the following language occurs: * * * * * "Whence it follows that when it is made known and manifest that all the time during which it is alleged that the crimes were done, on account of which he was arrested, to the time in which he was taken and adjudged to death, was *a time of profound peace*," etc.

I shall not stop now to refer to the circumstances of the suspension of the writ of *habeas corpus*, in these cases in England, but simply cite the gentleman's attention to the fact that it was suspended at the time of the invasion of the Pretender, in 1715, and his son in 1745, in Ireland in 1800, and from 1802 to 1805, from 1807 to 1810, in 1812, and from 1822 to 1824. I desire, however, to call the attention of the gentleman and that of the Court to the action of the British Government in 1848;—the action and speeches of the statesmen of that Government, some of whom are still on the political stage.

The agitation in Ireland began to assume a threatening aspect directly after the continental revolutions of February and March; but in the previous December, Parliament had passed an act forbidding the possession of arms in certain troublesome districts. In April an act called the Felony Bill, was passed, making it felony "for any person to compass, imagine, or intend to depose the sovereign, or to levy war against her." In July, the Whig ministry, through Lord John Russell, introduced a bill into Parliament, empowering the Lord Lieutenant of Ireland, and Deputies, to apprehend and detain till the 1st of March, 1849, such persons as they should suspect of conspiring against Her Majesty's person and government. This was a suspension of the act of *habeas corpus* for all Ireland;—the loyal northern part of the island, as well as the disaffected east, and the rebellious south and west. The bill was introduced, and went through all its stages to its final passage, in one day; on the next day, in like manner it passed the House of Lords, the vote being unanimous in both houses, and on the same day, received the assent of the Queen. Even the Irish members did not vote against it. Lord Brougham, in speaking upon the bill in the House of Lords, said:

"A friend of liberty I have lived, and so I shall die—nor do I care how soon that may be, if I can not be the friend of liberty without being a friend of traitors at the same time, without being a protector of criminals, without being deemed to be the accomplice of foul rebellion and its concomitant civil war, with all its hideous train of atrocious crimes. It is because I am a friend of liberty that I detest the conspiracies which are brewing in the sister isle. The noble Marquis (Lansdowne) has informed us that the danger is imminent. Then let the measure which invests the Government with needful, and no more than needful powers, be immediately adopted."

These words come home to us to-day with peculiar force. Earl Derby, then Lord Stanley, said:

"I think that the Government has asked for the right remedy. I think the remedy for which they have asked is one which will strike the right persons, and strike them within the right time. I am not one of those who would seek for victims among the credulous dupes of the incendiary agitators of Ireland— dupes who will be put forward in the front ranks for the purpose of committing crimes and outrages. I do not desire—God forbid that I should—that upon them the severest penalty of the law should fall. No! I desire it should fall upon those who, well knowing the consequences of their conduct—who, well knowing the falseness of their pretexts—who, well knowing the fatal effects that must flow from the doctrines they preach, evince a readiness to sacrifice every thing to their passions and their sordid interests, and for their own purposes, do not hesitate to involve their friendless and too credulous fellow countrymen in the guilt of treason and the danger of civil war. The persons I wish to see punished are those who have sufficient skill, who have sufficient information and intelligence to keep themselves free from such legal guilt as would bring them under the operation of the law, with the probability of a conviction, but who, nevertheless, are morally guilty in the eye of God and man, of the crime of inciting to treason, murder, rebellion and civil war. I favor the measure now proposed, chiefly because by its means we shall get rid of all doubts and difficulties; we shall have no more of these delays of the war, no more of the chicanery which encourages evil doers to hope for ultimate escape, and which is certain to cause such procrastination that when, at length, the sword of justice falls, the example does not produce half the effect it ought to have."

In the House of Commons, Lord John Russell said:

"I believe in my conscience that this measure is calculated to prevent insurrection, to preserve internal peace, to preserve the unity of this empire, to save the throne of these realms and the free institutions of this country."

Sir Robert Peel, in speaking on this bill, said:

"I, for one, am perfectly prepared to insist on no ordinary powers. I believe that the Government is justified in asking for this measure. I believe the measure itself—the power to apprehend on suspicion, and keep the conspirators in confinement—is necessary. I will not urge on the ministry measures of greater coercion than those their own responsibility demands; but this I say, as nothing but necessity can justify a suspension of the *habeas corpus* act, the same necessity makes immediate action desirable."

Mr. Disraeli thought the House "ought not to hesitate to grant the Government the great and extraordinary powers for which they ask."

And Mr. Joseph Hume, the leader of the Liberals, and always the fast friend of Ireland, said that he should "be sorry to see any division on the measure now before the House."

Martial law in England as completely violates and suspends the Magna Charta as in this country it does our Constitution. Section 39, which has been referred to by the gentleman, provides that "no freeman shall be taken, or imprisoned, or disseized, or outlawed, or banished, or any way injured, nor will we pass upon him, nor send upon him, unless by the lawful judgment of his peers, or by the law of the land."

The Mutiny Act, of 1689—and which has been re-enacted at every session of Parliament for more than 175 years—contains, among others, the following declaration:

"Whereas, no man may be forejudged of life or limb, or subject to any kind of judgment by martial law, or any other matter than by the judgment of his peers, and according to the known and established laws of this realm," etc. There is no doctrine more ineradicably graven upon the Constitution and the civil polity of England, than the writ of *habeas corpus* and the exemption of the subject from martial law; but, notwithstanding this clear provision of the Magna Charta, as often as it has been necessary, martial law has been proclaimed.

In the riots of 1780, after the mob had insulted a member of Parliament, and threatened to attack the residence of the Chief Justice, the King in Council issued his proclamation, as follows:

"We have therefore issued the most direct and effectual orders to all our officers, by an immediate exertion of their utmost force, to suppress the same." After which the Adjutant General issued the following order, to wit:

"In obedience to the order of the King in Council, the military are to act without waiting the direction of the civil magistrate, and to use force for dispersing the illegal and tumultuous assemblages of the people."

In subsequent debates in Parliament, the conduct of the King was approved. Lord Mansfield and Lord Thurlow claimed that it was not a prerogative of the King to declare martial law, or to use the military to suppress riots, but they defended the act on the ground of necessity.

During the Irish rebellion, in 1798, the Lord Lieutenant of Ireland, Lord Camden, proclaimed martial law, which existed a year without any legislative action; and after that, the Irish Parliament sanctioned the act. In 1801, after the Union, this subject was discussed, and a bill was introduced to continue martial law. In this debate, both those who approved and those who opposed the bill conceded the right of the Executive Government to proclaim martial law when necessary. Sheridan, who opposed the bill, said:

"In case of rebellion, or invasion, His Majesty has, by virtue of his prerogative, a right to martial law."

Lord Castlereagh, in defense of the bill, said:

"I perfectly understand that the prerogative of the Crown authorizes this act, in its authority to exercise martial law. I maintain that it is a constitutional mode for the Executive Government to exercise martial law in the first instance, and to come to Parliament for indemnity afterward, and is preferable to applying to Parliament first." This is a somewhat anomalous declaration on the part of Lord Castlereagh; for if it was a prerogative of the Crown, and a constitutional mode of exercising that prerogative, where is the necessity of any subsequent indemnifying act? He goes on to say: "The only circumstance in mind is, whether, if the necessity exists, this is the proper remedy? If it be so, we ought not to take alarm at a departure from principle, which is necessary for the preservation of the Constitution itself."

Sir L. Parsons, in opposing the bill, said he thought "the measure unnecessary. The Executive Government could resort to martial law if it was necessary to suppress rebellion."

Mr. Gray, also one of its opponents, said:

"It was better that the Government should resort to what had been called (he thought not legally) its prerogative of proclaiming martial law. That was no prerogative of the Crown, but rather an act of that power sanctioned by necessity, martial law being a suspension of the King's peace. But it was better that martial law should proceed from the Executive Government, in urgent moments, than be the work of the Legislature, on very slight pretexts."

At the time of the rebellion in Ceylon, in 1848, the Governor proclaimed martial law, and tried and executed many rebels. Here is a case exactly in point. His conduct was severely criticised in England, upon the ground that it was *unnecessary;* and in an able review in the Quarterly, volume 83, page 127, we find the following:

"We shall define martial law to be the law of necessity, or defense. The right which a Governor of a colony has to proclaim martial law over subjects, may be said to bear a close analogy to the right which an individual, in absence of legal protection, has to slay an assailant. In both cases, the evil must be grave. In both cases, all regular means of defense must be exhausted, or beyond reach, before the aggrieved party resorts to extremities. In both cases, the burden of proof lies on him who has ventured on such an expedient; and if he fails to vindicate himself, he is liable to severe punishment.

"Hallam 1, *Constitutional History*, page 240, says:

"'There may, indeed, be times of pressing danger, when the conservation of all demands a sacrifice of the legal rights of a few; there may be circumstances that not only justify, but compel the abandonment of constitutional forms. It has been usual for all Governments, during an actual rebellion, to proclaim martial law, or the suspension of civil jurisdiction. And this anomaly, I must admit, is very far from being less indispensable at such unhappy seasons, in countries where the ordinary mode of trial is by jury, than where the right of decision rests in the judge.'"

In considering the opinions and action of British statesmen upon this question, it should be borne in mind that there is an essential difference between the King of England and the President of the United States, in respect to the prerogatives with which they are clothed by the constitutional laws of the respective nations. The King of England is not the Commander-in-Chief of her army and navy, whereas the President of the United States is, by express provision of our Constitution.

Upon the question of what martial law is, and wherein it differs from military law, there can be no difference of opinion, and need be but little discussion. The rules and regulations, and special acts of Congress existing for the government of those persons in the military service of the country, constitute the military law; and they are as clear and well defined as any statutes of the land. Martial

law, on the contrary, can never be restricted by any defined lines, because it is the law of necessity, the law of self-defense, of self-preservation; it is a law to meet a state of disorder; a law to meet the exigences and necessities of great, unexpected emergencies; and whatever law, or rule of action, becomes necessary to meet those emergencies, is martial law. As, for illustration, martial law, as now being administered, has given these prisoners a fair, impartial hearing, according to the strict rules of the civil law, in all questions of evidence, argument, etc.; it has given them the benefit of counsel, of processes to compel the attendance of witnesses; it has allowed them a clear and public trial, in open day, before their peers, and before just and honorable men. But, under other circumstances, and greater emergencies, it might have demanded that they be shot down in the streets, without trial, and without hearing; as in case they had gone forward in this conspiracy, attacked your camps, undertaken to release your prisoners, and burn your city. In one case, the emergency might have demanded instant and summary punishment, because found in the act of insurrection; the other admits of, and permits, an investigation according to the forms of law, to see whether the accused were actually engaged in, and moving forward to the consummation of an insurrection.

Martial law should obtain, does obtain, and must obtain whenever a state of war exists. Says Vattel, in his *Law of Nations*, page 346: "The whole is deduced from one single principle; from the object of a just war; for, when the end is lawful, he who has a right to pursue that end, has, of course, a right to employ all the means which are necessary for its attainment."

When the fact of war was once established throughout this country, instantly, by reason of that fact, were brought into existence, so far as was necessary, the laws of war; and those laws were in operation wherever the war was being prosecuted. Wherever the army existed, was moving, in part or in whole, or doing battle, there the laws of war took precedence of the civil laws, the laws of peace. In some places, where the clash of arms had made silent all civil avocations, the army was the controlling, the dominant power: the laws of war, martial law, the law of necessity, was the sole law. In other places, where only a branch of the army was operating, existing, or moving in the general purposes of war, some portions of the civil law would continue in operation: those only, however, which were not inconsistent with the existence, movements, or operations of that part of the army. Of the necessity that will warrant the declaration of martial law, or the silencing of the civil law, in part or in whole, the Commander-in-Chief, or his subordinate military commander, can, and must be, the sole judge; and while it is being exercised, it is the dominant law, and is just as much law, just as much constitutional law, as any portion of the civil law. As I have before remarked, the officer or person exercising this high power

17

must be, and always is, held to a high accountability. If the President exercise it, he can be held accountable to the House and Senate on impeachment; if an inferior military commander, he can be held accountable before either a military or a civil tribunal.

It will be recollected by this Court, that in May, 1861, while the courts were open and in full force, one John Merryman, a citizen of Maryland, was arrested by military authority, and held by express sanction and direction of the President. A great outcry was raised throughout the country, by such men as Vallandigham, Voorhees, and others, at this arbitrary arrest, as they called it, and Mr. Vallandigham, in an extra session, in 1861, brought forward in the House a resolution of censure or impeachment of the President, for his unauthorized acts during the war, his proclamations with reference to the blockade, calling out armies to suppress the rebellion, his arbitrary arrests, etc. At this same session, August 6th, 1861, Congress took action upon this subject as follows:

"*And be it further enacted*, That all the acts, proclamations, and orders of the President of the United States after the fourth of March, eighteen hundred and sixty-one, respecting the army and navy of the United States, and calling out or relating to the militia or volunteers from the States, are hereby approved and in all respects legalized and made valid, to the same extent, and with the same effect as if they had been issued and done under the previous express authority and direction of the Congress of the United States." Vol. 12 *United States Statutes at Large*, page 326. Thus says the law by which Congress conveyed to the President their approval of the power then exercised by him, and their opinion of its necessity. When the necessity for its exercise does exist, and the authorities act promptly and vigorously for the good of the Government and the people, and for the preservation of the life of the nation, that action will be justified and commended by all good men; for it can hardly be said that the Constitution did not contemplate and provide for the perpetuity of its own existence, and give to those who were charged with its preservation sufficient power to defend its life in great emergencies; or that it withheld from the Executive, the vital arm of the Government, the power and the right to strike in its own defense, and for its very existence.

Some persons, generally those who have not the best interests of the nation at heart, have been inclined to look upon our Constitution as a cast iron frame, incapable of change or growth; in other words, unfitted to the inevitable growth of the nation; as not framed to be prospective in its operations, nor constructed to meet the wants of an overchanging, increasing, and progressive nation. Or regard it as an iron band placed about the trunk of a living tree, which would girdle it in its growth, or be burst by it. We are inclined to that liberal and seemingly statesmanlike construction of the instrument that believes it to be adopted to meet the exigencos of the nation for which it was brought into existence; we say with Solicitor Whiting:

"By a liberal construction of the Constitution, our Government has passed through many storms unharmed. Slaveholding States, other than those whose inhabitants originally formed it, have found their way into the Union, notwithstanding the guarantee of equal rights to all. The territories of Florida and Louisiana have been purchased from European powers. Conquest has added a nation to our borders. The purchased and the conquered regions are now legally a part of the United States. The admission of new States containing a privileged class, the incorporation into our Union of a foreign people, are held to be lawful and valid by all the Courts of the country. Thus far from the old anchorage have we sailed under the flag of 'public necessity,' 'general welfare,' or 'common defense.' Yet the great charter of our political rights 'still lives;' and the question of to-day is, whether that instrument, which has not prevented America from acquiring one country by purchase, and another by conquest, will permit her to *save herself?*"

It seems to me that our statesmen, heretofore, have been too free to admit the limited and circumscribed powers of that great organic law; but in support of this exercise of the law of necessity—of martial law—some of the prominent writers of our country and many of its ablest statesmen have claimed that a military commander would be authorized to disregard the Constitution and laws themselves, were it necessary to the preservation of the republic; and there is no doubt but that the government *de facto* would be entirely upheld and sanctioned in the exercise of such a power.

It will be remembered that while General Jackson was in command of New Orleans, in 1814, when the British were besieging that city, he declared martial law; believing that the safety of the city, and the safety and welfare of the citizens demanded it, and that it was necessary for his successful defense of the same. While in command of the city, the General arrested a Frenchman named Loualler, on a charge of instigating treason and mutiny, and for conspiring with other treasonable persons in the city, to aid the enemy. Without affidavit, presentment, or indictment, he arrested this man, threw him into prison, and held him. Judge Hall, the United States District Judge for that District, on the 5th day of March, 1815, issued a writ of *habeas corpus* directed to General Jackson, requiring him to answer in person, and bring the person of Louallier before him. General Jackson, instead of obeying the writ, arrested this Judge of the United States Court, and by military force, without hearing or trial, held him for a time as prisoner, and finally sent him beyond his lines. Here was the declaration of martial law, its rigid enforcement, arbitrary arrest, and punishment without any form of trial, by that old patriot General Jackson, whose heroic deeds and name are enshrined in the hearts of all who love their country.

After the city was saved, and that glorious

battle of New Orleans—which will ever make the name of Jackson immortal—was closed, and the enemy had withdrawn from the environs of the city, the necessity for martial law no longer existed, and General Jackson, by public proclamation, abrogated it. Judge Hall then returned to the city; had General Jackson brought before him on a charge of contempt of Court, for refusing to obey the writ of *habeas corpus*, and fined him $1,000. The necessity, as before stated, for martial law having passed away, and the majesty of the civil law having again asserted itself, the General bowed in submission to its mandates. His army, and the loyal citizens of New Orleans, were so indignant and so outraged by this conduct of Judge Hall, that it was only through the efforts of General Jackson himself, that the Judge was saved from personal violence.

In the winter of 1843-4, on a resolution to refund to General Jackson this excessive fine, the whole question of martial law was fully discussed by Congress. On January 7th, Stephen A. Douglas, that clear-headed lawyer, patriot and statesman, reviewed the whole subject in an able speech, from which I propose to make a few extracts. He says:

"To refuse to pass it, [the bill for refunding the fine,] would be an act of the grossest injustice to the American people, and would stamp them with ingratitude to their bravest defender. I am not one to admit that General Jackson violated the Constitution, or the law, at New Orleans. I deny that he violated either. I insist that the General rightfully performed every act that his duty required, and that his right to declare martial law, and enforce it, resulted from the same source, and rested on the same principle, that the gentleman from New York [Mr. Barnard] asserted, from which Judge Hall derived the authority to punish for contempt, without trial, without witnesses, without jury, and without any thing but his own arbitrary will. The gentleman asserted that the power to punish for contempt was not conferred by the statute, or by the common law, but was inherent in every judicial tribunal and legislative body; and he cited the authority of the Supreme Court to support the assertion. He said that this power was necessary to the Courts, to enable them to perform the duties which the laws intrusted to them, and arose from the necessity of the case. Now, it was from the same source that the power to declare martial law was derived—its necessity in time of war for the defense of the country. The defense of the lives and liberties of the people, as well as their property, being all intrusted to the discretion of the commanding General, it became his duty to declare martial law, if the necessity of the case required it. If it became necessary to blow up a fort, he was authorized to do it; if it became necessary to sink a vessel, he was authorized to do it; and if it became necessary to burn a city, he was authorized to do it. The necessity of the case was the law to govern him; and he, on his responsibility, must judge of the existence of that necessity. It was the first law of nature which authorized a man to defend his own person, and his wife and his children at all hazards. It was that law which authorized this body to repel aggression and insult, and protect itself in the exercise of its legislative functions; and it was that law which authorized courts of justice to defend themselves and punish for contempts. He acknowledged that this was a high-handed and despotic power—one that was only to be exercised when necessary, and which ceased when the necessity no longer existed. Such was the power under which General Jackson declared martial law at New Orleans. On this part of the subject he did not intend to go into the history of all the occurrences of that period—they had been detailed in a most faithful and interesting manner, by the gentleman from Louisiana, [Mr. Slidell.] It was sufficient for him to know that General Jackson, who was the commanding General, deemed it necessary to declare martial law in order to defend the city." * * * * * * * * * * *

"These things would not be questioned. The necessity and the glorious effects resulting from the course which that necessity prompted were acknowledged by the whole country, and he would even say by the whole civilized world. Then, as far as this bill was concerned, he [Mr. D.] cared not whether their acts were legal or illegal. He cared not whether General Jackson violated the Constitution or not. He cared not whether General Jackson suspended all civil authority or not. If his acts were necessary to the defense of the country, that necessity was above all law. General Jackson hazarded every thing; he hazarded both life and reputation on that step, which might render him immortal if it saved the country, or, on the contrary, make him ignominious, and a by-word, and a reproach; and the man that dared to do that, deserved the protection and the plaudits of his country. He did not envy the feelings of that man that would get up and talk calmly and coolly under such circumstances, about rules of Court and technicalities of proceeding, and the danger of example, when the city might be in flames and the utmost barbarity might be committed. What were rules of Court but mere cobwebs when they found an enemy with his cannon at the doors of their Courts, and when they saw the flames encircling the cupola? Talk then about rules of Court, and the formality of proceedings! The man that would do this, would fiddle while the capital was burning. He envied not any man the possession of such stoical philosophy. Talk about illegality! Talk about formalities! Why, there was but one formality to be observed; and that was the formality of directing the cannon, and destroying the enemy, regardless of the means whether it be by the seizure of cotton bags, or the seizure of persons, if the necessity of the case required it. The God of nature has conferred this right on men and nations; and therefore let him not be told that it was unconstitutional. To defend the country, let him not be told that it was unconstitutional to use the proper means. The Constitution was adopted for the protection of the country; and under that Constitution the nation had the right to exercise all the powers that were necessary for the protection of the country. *If martial law was necessary to the salvation of the country, martial law was legal for that purpose.* If it was necessary for a judge, for the preservation of order, to punish for contempt, he thought it was necessary for a general to exercise control over his cannon, to imprison traitors, and to arrest spies, and to intercept communications with the enemy. If this was necessary, all this was legal.

"But the ground on which he placed the defense—and he denied that General Jackson did any act which was not justified by rightful and legal authority—was as high and as sacred as self-defense. General Jackson did not exercise any unnecessary arbitrary authority. He did not suspend the civil law nor close the civil tribunals, any farther than was necessary for the carrying out of the military defense of the country. To this extent he did do it, and to this extent it was right that he should do it. In other respects, the civil law, and the courts were in full force. True, General Jackson would not allow them to communicate with the enemy; but they could not surrender aught to the enemy; he deprived them of the power to commit treason; but he deprived them of no power that an honest man would desire to exercise. He imposed no restraint that any man devoted to the country would regret; and the men who instigated proceedings against General Jackson were the men who skulked in the hour of danger." See *Globe* Report of the 28th Congress, first session.

Robert J. Walker, in the Senate, submitted a report upon this subject, in which he said:

"The law which justified this act, was the great law of necessity; it was the law of self-defense. This great law of necessity—of defense of self, of home, and of country—never was designed to be abrogated by any statute, or by any Constitution."

Mr. Payne, of Alabama, also speaking upon this subject, said:

"I shall not contend that the Constitution or laws of the United States authorize the declaration of martial law by any authority whatever; on the contrary, it is unknown to the Constitution or laws." And commenting on the argument that if the Constitution did not authorize it, the General ought not to have declared martial law, he says:

"Who could tolerate this idea? An Arnold might, but no patriotic American could. I may be asked upon what principle a commander can declare martial law, when it is so evident that the Constitution or laws afford him no authority to do so? I answer, upon the principle of self-defense, which rises paramount to all written laws; and the justification of the officer who assumes the responsibility of acting on that principle, must rest upon the necessity of the case."

In a written document submitted by General Jackson to the Court, Mr. Livingston gave his opinion as follows:

"On the nature and effect of the proclamation of martial law by Major General Jackson, my opinion is that such proclamation is unknown to the Constitution and laws of the United States; that it is to be justified only by the necessities of the case;" etc.

With Mr. Payne and Mr. Livingston I can not fully agree. I believe the power exercised by General Jackson, or by any military commander in any great emergency—in the defense of a city, of a people, or the nation itself—is expressly authorized and sanctioned by the Constitution, by that provision which makes the President Commander-in-Chief of the armies, and that other provision which charges him to take care that the laws be faithfully executed. In a lesser degree, the same power may be constitutionally exercised by a subordinate military commander.

And Congress sanctioned this view of the case, by refunding to General Jackson this fine, with full interest; every Democratic member of Congress and many of the Whigs, voting for it. It was passed in the House, January 8th, 1844, by the unparalleled majority of 158 to 28, and in the Senate, by 30 to 16.

Thomas Jefferson, in his letter to Mr. Colvin, dated September 20th, 1810, (see *Jefferson's Complete Works*, volume 5), has also very fully discussed this question. In speaking of the action of General Wilkinson, at New Orleans, he instances cases almost exactly parallel to those in hand. The cases were not as strong as these, for no war was in actual existence, no actual rebellion holding at bay the entire Government, but only the expectancy of an insurrection or rebellion; and yet Jefferson justifies Wilkinson in seizing notorious conspirators within his limits, and sending them beyond his lines, without trial or hearing, to the seat of Government, when they had a right, by the terms of the Constitution, to trial in the district in which their offenses were committed, and says that there can be but two opinions upon this question, that of the guilty and their accomplices, and that of all honest men.

"The question you propose, whether circumstances do not sometimes occur which make it a duty in officers of high trust, to assume authorities beyond the law, is easy of solution in principle, but sometimes embarrassing in practice. A strict observance of the written laws, is doubtless *one* of the high duties of a good citizen, but it is not *the highest.* The laws of necessity, of self-preservation, of saving our country when in danger, are of higher obligation. To lose our country by a scrupulous adherence to written law, would be to lose the law itself, with life, liberty, property, and all those who are enjoying them with us; thus absurdly sacrificing the end to the means. When, in the battle of Germantown, General Washington's army was annoyed from Chew's house, he did not hesitate to plant his cannon against it, although the property of a citizen. When he besieged Yorktown, he leveled the suburbs, feeling that the laws of property must be postponed to the safety of the nation. While the army was before York, the Governor of Virginia took horses, carriages, provisions, and even men, by force, to enable that army to stay together till it could master the public enemy; and he was justified. A ship at sea, in distress for provisions, meets another having abundance, yet refusing a supply; the law of self-preservation authorizes the distressed to take a supply by force. In all these cases, the unwritten laws of necessity, of self-preservation, and of the public safety, control the written laws of *meum* and *tuum.*   *   *   *

"To proceed to the conspiracy of Burr, and particularly to General Wilkinson's situation in New Orleans. In judging this case we are bound to consider the state of the information, correct and incorrect, which he then possessed. He expected Burr and his band from above, a British fleet from below, and he knew there was a formidable conspiracy within the city. Under these circumstances, was he justifiable, 1st, in seizing notorious conspirators? On this there can be but two opinions; one, of the guilty and their accomplices; the other, that of all honest men. 2d. In sending them to the seat of Government, when the written law gave them a right to trial in the territory? The danger of their rescue, of their continuing their machinations, the tardiness and weakness of the law, apathy of the judges, active patronage of the whole tribe of lawyers, unknown disposition of the juries, an hourly expectation of the enemy, salvation of the city, and of the Union itself, which would have been convulsed to its center, had that conspiracy succeeded; all these constituted a law of necessity and self-preservation, and rendered the *salus populi* supreme over the written law. The officer who is called to act on this superior ground, does indeed risk himself on the justice of the controlling powers of the Constitution, and his station makes it his duty to incur that risk. But those controlling powers, and his fellow citizens generally, are bound to judge according to the circumstances under which he acted."

I refer the gentleman to these well digested and unequivocal utterances of the President of the United States—I might say one of the founders of the Government—and one of the most learned expounders of the Constitution, as an answer to why these arrests? and where the jurisdiction of this Court?

In a debate in Congress, on the joint resolutions of distributing rations to the distressed refugees from Indian hostilities, on the 26th of May, 1836, John Quincy Adams, in speaking upon the subject of the war power of Congress and of the President, said:

"Now, the powers incidental to war are derived, not from their internal municipal source, *but from the laws and usages of nations.*

"There are, then, Mr. Chairman, in the *authority of Congress and of the Executive, two classes of powers, altogether different in their nature, and often incompatible with each other—the war power and the peace power.* The peace power is limited by regulations and restricted by provisions prescribed within the Constitution itself. *The war power* is limited only by the laws and usages of nations. This power is tremendous; *it is strictly constitutional, but it breaks down every barrier so anxiously erected for the protection of liberty, of property, and of life.*

"*   *   *   * There are, indeed, powers of peace conferred upon Congress which also come within the scope and jurisdiction of the laws of nations, such as the negotiation of treaties of amity and commerce, the interchange of public ministers and consuls, and all the personal and social intercourse between the individual inhabitants of the United States and foreign nations, and the Indian tribes, which require the interposition of any law. *But the powers of war are all* regulated by the laws of nations, and *are subject to no other limitation.*" Thus it will be seen that all the power claimed for the President as Commander-in-Chief of the armies, or for his subordinate military commanders, is more than conceded by this great statesman. In speaking upon this same subject, Solicitor Whiting, in the pamphlet from which I have already quoted, forcibly says:

"Some persons have questioned whether title passes in this country by capture or confiscation, by reason of some of the limiting clauses of the Constitution; and others have gone so far as to assert that all the proceedings under martial law, such as capturing enemy's property, imprisonment of spies and traitors, and seizures of articles contraband of war, and suspending the *habeas corpus,* are in violation of the Constitution, which declares that no man shall be deprived of life, liberty, or property without due process of law; that private property shall not be taken for public use without just compensation; that unreasonable searches and seizures shall not be made; that freedom of speech and of the press shall not be abridged; and that the right of the people to keep and bear arms shall not be infringed.

"If these rules are applicable to a state of war, then capture of property is illegal, and does not pass a title; no defensive war can be carried on; no rebellion can be suppressed; no invasion can be repelled; the army of the United States, when called into the field, can do no act of hostility. Not a gun can be fired *constitutionally,* because it might deprive a rebel foe of his life without *due process of law*—firing a gun not being deemed a 'due process of law.'   *   *   *   *   * If these rules above cited have any application in time of war, the United States *can not protect* each of the States from invasion by citizens of other States, nor against domestic violence; nor can the army, or militia, or navy be used for any of the purposes for which the Constitution authorizes or requires their employment. If all men have the right to 'keep and bear arms,' what right has the army of the Union to take them away from rebels? If 'no one can constitutionally be deprived of life, liberty, or property without due process of law,' by what right does Government seize and imprison traitors? By what right does the army kill rebels in arms, or burn up their military stores? If the only way of dealing constitutionally with rebels in arms is to go to law with them, the President should convert his army into lawyers, justices of the peace, and constables, and serve 'summonses to appear and answer to complaints,' instead of a summons to surrender. He should send

'GREETINGS' instead of sending rifle shot. He should load his caissons with 'pleas in abatement and demurrers,' instead of thirty-two pound shell and grape shot. In short, he should levy writs of execution, instead of levying war. On the contrary, the Commander-in-Chief proposes a different application of the due process of law. His summons is, that rebels should lay down their arms; his pleas are batteries and gunboats; his arguments are hot shot, and 'always to the point;' and when his fearful execution is 'levied on the body,' all that is left will be for the undertaker.

"The clauses which have been cited from the amendments to the Constitution were intended as declarations of peaceful and loyal citizens, and safeguards in the administration of justice by the civil tribunals; but it was necessary, in order to give the Government the means of defending itself against domestic or foreign enemies, to maintain its authority and dignity, and to enforce obedience to its laws, that it should have unlimited war powers; and it must not be forgotten that the same authority which provides those safeguards, and guarantees those rights, also imposes upon the President and Congress the duty of so carrying on war as of necessity to supersede and hold in temporary suspense, such civil rights as may prove inconsistent with the complete and effectual exercise of such war powers, and of the belligerent rights resulting from them. * * * * * By martial law, loyal citizens may be for a time debarred from enjoying the rights they would be entitled to in time of peace. Individual rights must always be held subject to the exigences of national safety.

"In war, when *martial law is in force*, the laws of war are the laws which the Constitution expressly authorizes and requires to be enforced. The Constitution, when it calls into action martial law, for the time changes *civil* rights, or rights which the citizen would be entitled to in peace, because the rights of persons in one of these cases are totally incompatible with the obligations of persons in the other. Peace and war can not exist together—the laws of peace and war can not operate together; the rights and procedures of peaceful times are incompatible with those of war. It is an obvious, but pernicious error to suppose that in a *state of war*, the rules of martial law, and the consequent modification of the rights, duties and obligations of citizens, private and public, are not *authorized* strictly under the *Constitution*."

Attorney General Bates, on the 5th of July, 1861, transmitted to the House, in answer to a resolution of that body, an opinion based upon certain questions, one of which was as follows: "In the present time of a great and dangerous insurrection, has the President the discretionary power to cause to be arrested and held in custody persons known to have criminal intercourse with the insurgents, or persons against whom there is probable cause for suspicion of such criminal complicity?" In answer to this, and to other questions propounded by the House, he says:

"The argument may be briefly stated, thus: It is the President's bounden duty to put down the insurrection, as (in the language of the act of 1795) the 'combinations are too powerful to be suppressed by the ordinary course of judicial proceedings, or by the powers vested in the marshals.' And this duty is imposed upon the President for the very reason that the courts and the marshals are too weak to perform it. The manner in which he shall perform that duty is not prescribed by any law, but the means of performing it are given in the plain language of the statutes, and they are all means of force—the militia, the army, and the navy. The end, the suppression of the insurrection, is required of him; the means and instruments to suppress it are lawfully in his hands; but the manner in which he shall use them is not prescribed, and could not be prescribed without a foreknowledge of all the future changes and contingencies of the insurrection. He is, therefore, necessarily thrown upon his discretion, as to the manner in which he will use his means to meet the varying exigences as they arise. If the insurgents assail the nation with an army, he may find it best to meet them with an army, and suppress the insurrection in the field of battle. If they seek to prolong the rebellion and gather strength by intercourse with foreign nations, he may choose to guard the coasts and close the ports with a navy, as one of the most efficient means to suppress the insurrection, and if they employ spies and emissaries to gather information, to forward secret supplies, and to excite new insurrections in aid of the original rebellion, he may find it both prudent and humane to arrest and imprison them. And this may be done either for the purpose of bringing them to trial and condign punishment for their crimes, or they may be held in custody for the milder end of rendering them powerless for mischief until the exigency is past."

Upon this same subject—how far a nation may go in the use of power, and the means within its reach, to preserve its own existence—Vattel, in his *Law of Nations*, pp. 5 and 6, well remarks:

"Since, then, a nation is obliged to preserve itself, it has a right to every thing necessary for its preservation. For the law of nations gives us a right to every thing, without which we can not fulfill our obligation; otherwise, it would oblige us to do impossibilities, or rather, would contradict itself in prescribing us a duty, and at the same time, debarring us of the only means of fulfilling it. * * * * *A nation or State has a right to every thing that can help to ward off imminent danger, and keep at a distance whatever is capable of causing its ruin, and that from the very same reasons that establish its right to the things necessary to its preservation.*

Of what martial law is, when it is to be called into existence, and to whom it applies, Benet, in his *Military Law and Courts-Martial*, page 14, has very tersely said:

"*Martial law*, then, is that military rule and authority which exists in time of war, and is conferred by the laws of war, in relation to person and things under and within the scope of active military operations in carrying on the war, and which extinguishes or suspends civil rights, and the remedies founded upon them, for the time being, so far as it may appear to be necessary in order to the full accomplishment of the purpose of the war, the party who exercises it being liable in an action for any abuse of the authority thus conferred. It is the application of military government—the government of force—to person and property within the scope of it, according to the laws and usages of war, to the exclusion of the municipal government, in all respects where the latter would impair the efficiency of military law or military action." See also *North American Review*, October, 1861.

And again, Halleck, in his *International Law and Laws of War*, page 380, says that this right to declare, apply and exercise martial law, is one of the rights of sovereignty, and is as essential to the existence of a State as is the right to declare and carry on war. He says:

"We remark, in conclusion, that the right to declare, apply and exercise martial law, is one of the rights of sovereignty, and is as essential to the existence of a State as is the right to declare or carry on war. It is one of the incidents of war; and, like the power to take human life in battle, results directly and immediately from the fact that war legally exists. It is a power inherent in every government, and must be regarded and recognized by all other governments; but the question of the authority of any particular functionary to exercise this power, is a matter to be determined by local and not by international law. Like a declaration of a siege or blockade, the power of the officer who makes it is to be presumed until disavowed, and neutrals who attempt to act in derogation of that authority, do so at their peril."

We come now to the decisions of our civil tribunals touching these questions. In the case of *Luther* vs. *Borden*, heretofore referred to in the discussion of these principles, Chief Justice Taney, in delivering the opinion of the Court, said:

"It was so understood and construed by the State authorities, and, unquestionably, a State may use its military power to put down an armed insurrection too strong to be controlled by the civil authority. *The power is essential to the existence of every government, essential to the preservation of order and free institutions, and is as necessary to the States of this Union as to any other government.* The State itself must determine what degree of force the crisis demands. And if the government of Rhode Island deemed the armed opposition so formidable, and so ramified throughout the State, as to require the use of its military force, and the declaration of martial law, we see no ground upon which this Court can question its authority. *It was a state of war; and the established government resorted to the rights and usages of war to maintain itself, and to overcome the unlawful opposition.* And in that state of things, the officers engaged in its military service might lawfully arrest any one who, from the information before them, they had reasonable grounds to believe was engaged in the insurrection, and might order a house to be forcibly entered and searched, when there were reasonable grounds for supposing he might be there concealed. *Without power to do this, martial law and the military array of the government would be mere parade, and rather encourage attack than repel it.* No more force, however, can be used than is necessary to accomplish the object. And if the power is used for purposes of oppression, or any injury willfully done to person or property, the party by whom, or by whose order, it is committed, would undoubtedly be answerable."

Here we have the entire question decided by the highest tribunal in the land, as to the right of any government to use its full military power, to resort to the rights and usages of war to maintain itself, and to overcome an unlawful opposition; or, in other words, to put in force the laws of war, and enforce martial law.

As to wherein resides the authority to declare martial law, or in what branch of the Government it resides, this Court does not decide: it does however recognize martial law, as a legitimate means of preserving the Government in great emergencies.

In the same case, Justice Woodbury dissenting, inveighing at great length against the existence of martial law, under any contingency under our Constitution, finally sums up the whole matter by the following admission: "The necessities of foreign war, it is conceded, sometimes impart great powers as to both things and persons, but they are modified by these necessities and subjected to numerous regulations of national law, justice and humanity. These, when they exist in modern times, while laying the persons who conduct war under some necessary authority of an extraordinary character, must limit, control and make its exercise under certain circumstances, and in a certain manner, justifiable or void, with almost as much certainty and clearness as in provisions concerning municipal authority or duty. So may it be in some extreme stages on civil war. Among these my impression is that a state of war, whether foreign or domestic, may exist, in the great perils of which it is competent, under its rights and on principles of national law, for a commanding officer of troops, under the control of the Government, to extend certain rights of war, not only over his camp but its environs, and the near field of his military operations." *6th American Archives*, 186. *Johnson* vs. *Davis et al.*, 3 *Marston*, 535–51.

On this rested the justification of one of the great commanders of this war and the age, in a transaction so well known at New Orleans.

"But in civil strife, they are not to extend beyond the places where insurrection exists." 3 *Marston*, 551. "Nor to portions of the State remote from the scene of military operations, nor after the resistance is over, nor to persons not connected with it, nor even within the scene can they extend to the person or property of citizens against whom no probable cause exists which may justify it." *Sutton vs. Johnson*, 1 *D. & E.*, 549. "Nor to the property of any person without necessity or civil precept."

Here Justice Woodbury himself admits that, in certain contingencies, extraordinary powers may be exercised under the ægis of martial law, limited only by time, place and circumstances. He calls them the "rights of war." I have named the same thing, and the law generally names it the "laws of war." He says, "they" [the rights of war] [the laws of war] "are not to extend beyond the places where insurrection exists, nor to the portions of the State remote from the scene of military operations, nor after the resistance is over, nor to persons not connected with it, nor to persons against whom no probable cause exists." Of course, then, with these limitations, an arrest may be made legally and constitutionally under the exigences contemplated.

The argument to which we have listened on the great danger of too much power being exercised by the President, or the danger of this power being exercised by him, is very ably replied to by Chief Justice Taney, on page 44 of *7th Howard*.

"It is said that this power of the President is dangerous to liberty, and may be abused. All power may be abused if placed in unworthy hands. But it would be difficult, we think, to point out any other hands in which this power would be more safe, and, at the same time, equally effectual. When citizens of the same State are in arms against each other, and the constituted authorities unable to execute the laws, the interposition must be prompt or it is of little value. The ordinary course of proceedings in courts of justice would be utterly unfit for the crisis. And the elevated office of the President, chosen as he is by the people of the United States, and the high responsibility he could not fail to feel when acting in a case of so much moment, appear to furnish as strong safeguards against willful abuse of power as human prudence and foresight could well provide. At all events, it is conferred upon him by the Constitution and laws of the United States, and must, therefore, be respected and enforced in its judicial tribunals."

In a series of Prize cases decided by the Supreme Court, March 10th, 1863, the opinion of the Court was delivered by Mr. Justice Grier. Of the war powers of the President during this rebellion, he says: "By the Constitution, Congress alone has power to declare a national or foreign war. It can not declare war against a State, or any number of States, by virtue of any clause in the Constitution. It confers on the President the whole executive power; he is bound to take care that the laws be faithfully executed. He is Commander-in-Chief of the army and navy of the United States, and of the militia of the several States when called into the active service of the United States. He has no power to initiate or declare war, either against a foreign nation or a domestic State; but by the act of Congress of February 28th, 1795, and March 3, 1861, he is authorized to call out the militia and use the military and naval forces of the United States; in case of invasion by a foreign nation, the President is not only authorized, but bound to resist force by force. He does not initiate a war, but is bound to accept the challenge, without waiting for any special legislative authority. And whether the hostile party be a foreign invader, or States organized in rebellion, it is none the less a war, although the declaration of it be *unilateral*. Lord Stowell (1st *Dodson*, 247) observes that it is none the less a war on that account, for war may exist without a declaration on either side."

Thus we see that under the Constitution, it is the duty of the President to move forward, to enter upon the highway toward the suppression of a rebellion or insurrection, or to meet an invading foe, without any action of Congress, and without any declaration of war; and the route that he shall take, the means that he shall use to meet and suppress that rebellion, or insurrection, are solely in his own discretion.

Again, Justice Grier says, in the same opinion: "Whether the President in fulfilling his duties as Commander-in-Chief, in suppressing an insurrection, has met with such armed hostile resistance, and with civil war of such alarming proportions as will compel him to accord to them a character of belligerents, is a question to be decided *by him;* and this Court must be governed by the decision and acts of the political department of the Government to which this power is intrusted. *It must determine what degree of power the crisis demands.* The proclamation of the blockade is itself official and conclusive evidence to the Court that a state of war existed which demanded and authorized a recourse to such a measure." Thus the Supreme Court of the United States, in the last cases brought before it in which this question was at all discussed, on March 10th, 1863, expressly decided that with the President rests the determination of the degree of power which the crisis demands shall be exercised, and with that determination the Court can not interfere. The President has determined that the degree of power necessary to suppress this rebellion is, to hold this class of offenders amenable to martial law, and to trial by military courts; and his decision in this matter is final. Upon this same question, I find the following: "Moreover, when a military force is called out to repel invasion or suppress a rebellion, it is not placed under the direction of the judiciary, but under that of the executive. Suppose the military force, legally and constitutionally called into service for the purposes indicated, should find it necessary, in the course of its military operations, to occupy a field or garden, or destroy trees, or houses, belonging to some private person, can a court, by injunction, restrain them from committing such waste? It can do so in time of peace, and if its powers are to continue in time of war, the judiciary, and not the executive, will command the army and navy. The taking or destroying of private property in such cases, is a military act, an act of war, and must be governed by the laws of war; it is not provided for by the laws of peace. In the same way, a person taken and held by the military forces, whether before, or in, or after a battle, or without any battle at all, is virtually a *prisoner of war*. No matter what his alleged offense, whether he is a rebel, a traitor, a spy, or an enemy in arms, he is to be held and punished according to the *laws of war*, for these have been substituted for the laws of peace. And for a person so taken and held by the military authority, a writ of *habeas corpus* can have no effect, because, in the words of the United States Supreme Court, 'the ordinary course of justice would be utterly unfit for such a crisis.'" *International and Laws of War, Halleck, p.* 378.

Finally, upon this question, the counsel for the accused, in their argument against the jurisdiction of this Court, rely mainly upon the amendments to the Constitution, articles 5 and 6, which read as follows:

"Art. 5. No person shall be held to answer for a capital or otherwise infamous crime, unless on a presentment or indictment by a grand jury, except in cases arising in the land or naval forces, or in the militia when in actual service in time of war, or public danger; nor shall any person be subject for the same offense to be twice put in jeopardy of life or limb; nor shall be compelled in any criminal case to be a witness against himself, nor be deprived of life, liberty, or property, without due process of law; nor shall private property be taken for public use, without just compensation.

"Art. 6. In all criminal prosecutions, the accused shall enjoy the right to a speedy and public trial, by an impartial jury of the State and district wherein the crime shall have been committed, which district shall have been previously ascertained by law, and to be informed of the nature and cause of the accusation; to be confronted with the witnesses against him; to have compulsory process for obtaining witnesses in his favor; and to have the assistance of counsel for his defense."

Although a strict construction of these articles would seem to give force to such a conclusion, yet in construing the different parts of the Constitution, such a literal interpretation of the amendments must be allowed to give way before the necessity of an efficient exercise of the war power which is vested in Congress by that instrument, and the war powers conveyed to the President when he is designated as Commander-in-Chief of the armies. This more liberal construction of the Constitution has, from a very early period of our history, been recognized by the legislature of the country.

By turning to the 56th and 57th Articles of War, it will be seen—if those articles have any force, and, so far as my knowledge extends, their full power and force have never been questioned—these amendments to the Constitution do not apply to "all persons," nor to "all citizens" of the United States: nor are they applicable to all circumstances and emergencies. Those Articles of War read as follows:

"Art. 56. Whosoever shall relieve the enemy with money, victuals, or ammunition, or shall knowingly harbor or protect an enemy, shall suffer death, or such other punishment as shall be ordered by the sentence of a court-martial.

"Art. 57. Whosoever shall be convicted of holding correspondence with, or giving intelligence to, the enemy, either directly or indirectly, shall suffer death, or such other punishment as shall be ordered by the sentence of a court-martial."

Those articles conferring this jurisdiction, were adopted by the original Congress of the Confederation; and their terms and effect remained unchanged at the time of the formation of the Constitution. In 1806 a slight modification in their language was introduced; the substitution of "whosoever" for "all persons;" and thus a Congress composed of many of the original founders of the Republic, substantially reaffirmed the jurisdiction of military courts as to this class of offenders. This fact, that no alteration has been made in them by any subsequent Congress, either in time of peace, or during any war in which the country has been engaged, may be regarded as an unmistakable indication that the amendments to the Constitution conferring the right of trial by jury, etc., must yield, in a time like the present, to such a vigorous exercise of the war power as may be essential to the preservation of the Government.

Upon the necessity of the declaration and enforcement of martial law in the present cases, I have but a word to say. I believe with the Supreme Court, that this is a matter entirely within the discretion of the commander-in-chief of the armies; that that political department of the Government, to which it properly belongs, must wield the necessary force to suppress this rebellion; what that necessary force is, he alone can determine. I may be permitted to add, however, that in my judgment, and, I believe in the judgment of every man who has carefully and calmly considered the state of the country, and the circumstances of the times when these arrests were made, it was necessary that these parties should be held amenable to martial law, and to trial by a military tribunal. It has been admitted by the counsel for the accused, (Mr. Gordon,) that if martial law does exist here, then these parties may possibly be triable by a military tribunal; without that preceding fact, he says they can not be. In other parts of his argument, he claims that even did the exigences of the time require the arrest of these parties, and the enforcement of martial law, after their arrest they should have been turned over to the civil authorities for trial. To that I answer: all laws—whether they be civil, maritime, or military—have legitimate tribunals for their administration; the common law, by the common law courts; maritime law, by maritime courts; and the military law, by courts-martial. Martial law is as clear and well defined as any other law; and it is but proper that it should have a tribunal by which it shall be administered; the tribunal in this case is a Military Commission. It is better and more in accordance with the progress and tendencies of the age, that this law should be administered by a court governed by all the checks and balances of ordinary courts of justice, than by a military commander, as in former times.

In this case, the accused have had the benefit of an open trial, conducted according to all the known rules of the common law. A majority of the Court is composed of men who have achieved wide reputation in the State as lawyers. There is no right granted to an accused in any civil court in the land, that has not been freely and fully given in the progress of this trial. The questions have been asked and answered orally; all objections have been discussed in open court, and the accused have had the advantage of having every word uttered by the witnesses or by the counsel in discussion, accurately recorded, and to that record they have had full and free access to see that it contains no error or omission that might, in the slightest degree, prejudice their cause. Wherein, then, regarding it as a matter of justice and right, are these accused wronged by this proceeding? They do not complain of the persons who compose this Court; they themselves have passed eulogies upon their high and honorable character; they have made no complaint of the mode of conducting this case; they admit that they have received every courtesy and every right they could justly claim at the hands of the Government; wherein, then, I ask again, is the injustice of trying these accused by this Court, according to all the known rules and principles of the common law?

In considering the question of the necessity of martial law obtaining to the extent of trying this peculiar class of offenders by a military tribunal, we must examine the circumstances as they appeared to the authority who ordered these arrests, and sent these cases before this Court for trial. Upon this question, Chief Justice Taney, in *Mitchell* vs. *Harmony*, 13th *Howard*, page 134, says:

"It is the emergency that gives the right, and the emergency must be shown to exist before the taking can be justified. *In deciding upon this necessity, however, the state of the facts, as they appeared to the officer, at the time he acted, must govern the decision; for he must necessarily act upon the information of others, as well as his own observation.*"

In answer to a question of the accused, through their counsel, Mr. Coffroth, Major General Hovey, in speaking of his action in making these arrests, very pertinently says:

"It was based upon my general knowledge of affairs in Indiana, the condition of the country, and Mr. Milligan's action in regard to it, together with the dangers that surrounded us at that time." The counsel asked him: "To what action do you refer?" The General answered: "To the conspiracy against the authority of the United States." "What particular actions of Mr. Milligan, in the matter?" He answers: "Mr. Milligan, I understood, from reliable authority, was a major general of the organization, and had taken steps to aid it and carry on revolution." And

this answer, the General says, applies to all the accused. Here, then, are the circumstances under which the Commanding General of this District acted in arresting these parties, and sending them before this military tribunal for trial; these are the circumstances, as they appeared to him; and he would certainly have failed in doing his duty, had he acted otherwise. I submit that the facts, as developed before this Court, entirely sustain the opinion formed by General Hovey, as to the necessity for making these arrests, and the necessity for trial before this Commission. It has been proved beyond question, that a conspiracy, more extensive, more perfect in its organization, and more damnable in its designs, never was concocted or brought into existence under any government since governments were first instituted. It has been proved that these parties now on trial, were members of that conspiracy; all, excepting one, holding military positions in this organization; that this conspiracy existed in almost every town and county of the State; and not only in this State, but in the States of Missouri, Kentucky, Illinois and Ohio; that it was thoroughly organized, and partially armed; that all the objects contemplated by the order, were illegal, treasonable and damnable; and that its lurking venom permeated all grades of society. Under such circumstances, would the Government have been safe in issuing a *venire* for a grand or petit jury to investigate and try these cases? Could you have kept from either of these juries a sufficient number of this same organization to have defeated the whole ends of justice? I state what is well known to every lawyer in the land, that no jury could possibly have been convened in this State, by the ordinary process of impanneling a jury, that would not have contained at least one member of this organization; and that one member would have been sufficient to acquit any criminal tried before them. In a land where a conspiracy has so contaminated all classes of society, the ordinary avenues of justice are obstructed, and the Government, under such circumstances, by the ordinary channels, is powerless to punish or to save.

I submit, with all due deference to the opinion of the eminent counsel on behalf of the accused, that at the time these arrests were made, this conspiracy, this intended insurrection *had not been abandoned*. As the evidence in this case, and subsequent events, have most clearly shown, the Order of American Knights, or of the "Sons of Liberty," was never more flourishing, more determined, and more venomous than at that very time.

And had the leaders of this conspiracy, these military chieftains, been arrested, brought before a civil tribunal, and released upon bail, would that have been a sure way of preventing the consummation of this conspiracy? Would it not rather have hastened the catastrophe you are trying to ward off, and simply give them to understand that the Government had some knowledge of their criminal intents? I submit, then, that the danger was imminent; requiring prompt action, and a strong and vigorous arm; that there was an overpowering necessity for military interference on the part of the Government; and the loyal people of this nation would, with one voice, have cried: "Shame, shame," if those who had the power failed to meet the emergency. For this proclamation of martial law, and for this kind of arrests, the President of the United States has been tried by the highest court short of the court of Heaven; he has been tried upon this very issue by a tribunal composed of twenty-five millions of freemen, and the verdict, instead of being condemnation, has been: "Well done, good and faithful servant!" Public opinion, that power which Talleyraud declared to Napoleon was more omnipotent than he and all his armies, has indorsed the necessity for these arrests, and the trial of these parties before courts that can act with a rapidity and vigor unknown to civil tribunals. That power, public opinion, is the court of last resort. Its voice is like the resistless sweep of the arm of Jehovah; before which all powers, governments, statesmanship, and judicial tribunals must yield and change, as it, in its omnipotence, shall direct.

CONSPIRACY PER SE.

We come now to the consideration of whether the Order of American Knights, or Order of Sons of Liberty, was a conspiracy *per se*. And first, we shall direct attention, briefly, to the argument of Mr. Coffroth, counsel for Mr. Milligan, on this point. And in doing so, I deem it my duty to say that it is one of the most singular arguments I have ever met with, or have ever known to be made in the trial of any cause. Its tone is disrespectful, to say the least, to this tribunal, and insulting to the American people, and its statements are frequently at variance with the proofs. Were it not that I see Mr. Coffroth's name signed to this argument, and that I heard him read it as his own production, I would have been strong in the belief that it emanated from the bitter and disloyal heart of the accused, L. P. Milligan, himself.

The counsel starts off with the assertion that this is "more of a political than a criminal prosecution;" and he says to this Court, "you are sitting in judgment upon political opponents, for alleged political offenses." The first assertion is untrue, if he means by the use of the word "political" to class the accused simply as Democrats, because the majority of this Court will tell you that they have never been any thing else. If he means by this political division, to class the accused as against the Government—opposed to its institution, and the Court in favor of them—then they are political opponents. This is no political prosecution. I drew up the charges against these men, and signed my name to them, simply because I had reason to believe they were criminals; I knew nothing of their politics, or of their political standing; no one informed me, before these charges were preferred, what their political standing was; I desired no such information; I desired simply to bring to justice men who were trying to aid traitors in arms against this Government. I next come to the assertion, "During the whole progress of this trial, partisan hate, with blind and fiendish malignity, has been demanding blood." I can not, of course, say what the gentleman may have heard, or determine the source of his information, but I have heard of no partisan demand for blood; I have seen no blind or fiendish malignity exhibited on the part of any citizens of this Republic toward the accused. It is true that when the claims of these traitors, these conspirators, were made known to the people of the land, those who were resting in the peaceful security of their homes, started back appalled at the gulf which was opened to their vision, at their very feet. The cold-blooded villainy of the scheme that these men deliberately discussed in their councils, and proceeded, with premeditation and deliberation, to execute, appalled and shocked the moral sense not only of this entire nation, but of the whole civilized world.

Upon what a conspiracy *per se* is, there can be no difference of opinion; it is a corrupt agreeing together by two or more persons, to do some unlawful thing, either as a means or an end; or, in other words, to do some legal thing in an illegal manner, or directly to commit an illegal act by combination or agreement.

We come next to the parts of this order set out by the gentleman in his argument; and the whole matter can be set at rest by saying that all those parts of the ritual given by the gentleman, are taken from the Vestibule degree. I speak now of the declaration of principles. The gentleman did not go even to the first degree of the order. If he had looked a little further, he would have found that the principles enunciated in the first degree of this Order of American Knights, or Order of Sons of Liberty, are not "the very principles upon which our Government was administered in the better days of the Republic." To understand clearly the ends aimed at by this organization, and whether those ends were legal or illegal, we must place ourselves as nearly as possible at the stand-point of the organization; we must consider the opinions and principles of Government held by its members; we must consider the circumstances of the nation—as this Court has a right judicially to do, without proof—and the attitude of these members of the order toward that nation, during this great crisis.

We find the Government engaged in a struggle for its very existence; calling into requisition all the power and force she can command. She is contending with an enemy so great in numbers, and so powerful, that as yet, after nearly four years' struggle, exerting her utmost strength, she has been unable to overcome it. And where did the men composing this organization stand, upon the vital question of the maintainance of the national integrity? I ask the Court, does the proof show that they were standing by the Government, aiding it cheerfully with their means, with their sympathy, and with their strength? Or does the proof show, on the contrary, that they were opposed to this war waged for the life of the nation; that they were engaged in disseminating the doctrine that such a war was unconstitutional and unauthorized, and giving encouragement and sympathy to the enemies of the Government? This war was begun by those now in arms against the Government, to maintain the doctrine that a State had the right, at will, to secede, and join its fortune to a separate nationality; or, in other words, that this Government of ours is but a combination of separate sovereignties, exercising the special powers delegated by those separate sovereignties, and that at will that compact could be dissolved. This, I believe, is a fair statement of the origin of the contest going on in this nation to-day—what the reasons were of those in arms against the Government for desiring a separate nationality, I do not stop to inquire or discuss. These, then, are the principles that our enemies are attempting to maintain by force of arms.

We have charged in the pleadings in this case, in the first place, "Conspiracy against the Government of the United States;" and under that charge, have set out in Specification 1st, that the accused did join themselves to this secret order "for the purpose of overthrowing the Government and duly constituted authorities of the United States;" and under the Second Specification of that charge, that they did combine with certain parties "to adopt and impart to others the creed or ritual of a secret, unlawful society, or order;" "denying the authority of the United States to coerce to submission certain rebellious citizens of said United States." Specification 3d charges that they did conspire with certain parties "to overthrow and render powerless the Government of the United States" by forming and organizing this unlawful society or order; and that they did assist in extending this order whose purpose was to cripple and render powerless the efforts of the Government in suppressing a then existing and formidable rebellion. Specification 4th sets out the manner by which they were to carry into execution these unlawful schemes. Now, let us see whether, *prima facie*, there is any thing in the principles enunciated by this order, that would support these charges and specifications, outside and entirely separate from any proof in this case.

The Court will bear in mind our statement of the issue upon which the war is being waged in this country to-day. I refer them now to Article 6, in the lesson of the First Degree, of the Order of Sons of Liberty, which says: "The Government designated the United States of America, has no sovereignty, because that is an attribute belonging to the people in their respective State organizations;" is not that really the foundation stone of the present rebellion? Article 7 says, in accordance with this principle, "the Federal Government can exercise only delegated power: hence, if those who shall have been chosen to administer that Government, shall assume to exercise power not delegated, they should be regarded and dealt with as usurpers." This clause of the ritual should be borne in mind while seeking to discover the meaning of the obligation.

It will be remembered by the Court that of all the witnesses who have spoken upon this point, and who have undertaken to explain for the accused their principles, and their understanding of the intent and purposes of this organization, there has not been one but has claimed that the Government was exercising usurped powers, powers not delegated.

The witness Corlew, one of Mr. Milligan's witnesses as to character, and, like nearly all the rest, a member of the order, when the direct question was put to him, whether he considered the Government a usurpation, declared that he did; and it was only after being "doctored" from the evening of one day to the morning of the next, by the astute counsel of Mr. Milligan, that he was brought up to the point of explaining that he did not mean to claim that the Government was a usurpation, but only that there were certain usurpations on the part of the Administration; or, in other words, that the Administration was exercising undelegated powers. The witness Bird, a member of the Legislature, and a member of this order; Judge Loughridge, also a member of the order, and Burton, a witness for Humphreys, also a member of the order, all claimed that the Government was exercising powers not delegated. Having ascertained from the witnesses for the defense their opinion of the acts of the Government, and whether they sympathize with her, or with her enemies, and having found that they believe that the Government is exercising undelegated power, we refer to the ritual of the order to which they have attached themselves by binding oaths—under the penalty of death if violated—to ascertain how they look upon the Government when she is exercising undelegated powers. I refer you again to Article 7. "Hence, if those who shall have been chosen to administer that Government, shall assume (and they say under oath that they have thus assumed) to exercise power not delegated, they should be regarded and dealt with as usurpers."

We proceed to Article 10, which says: "Whenever the officials, to whom the people have intrusted the powers of the Government, shall refuse to administer it in strict accordance with its Constitution, and shall assume and exercise power or authority not delegated, it is the inherent right and imperative duty of the people to resist such officials, and if need be, expel them by force of arms. Such resistance is not revolution, but is solely the assertion of right." Now, with the interests of a great nation resting upon your decision, I ask you, gentlemen of this Court, is it lawful or unlawful for a set of men to combine and agree together that whenever, in their judgment, the Government is exercising powers not delegated, it shall be expelled by force of arms? Gentlemen, what say you? Is it not admitted by all loyal men that the only legal mode of setting aside a Government which may be exercising powers not delegated is, if the President, by impeachment or by ballot; if, then, it is illegal to expel the officials of the Government by force of arms, this organization is a conspiracy *per se.*

Article 11 of the Ritual of the Order of Sons of Liberty says: "It is incompatible with the history and nature of our system of Government, that Federal authority should coerce by arms a sovereign State;" and Art. 12 declares, "Upon the preservation of the sovereignty of the States, depends the preservation of civil and personal liberty." Gentlemen, are these, or are they not the principles enunciated and upheld by those in arms against this Government? Does the dissemination of these doctrines by a large body of men in these Northern States tend to weaken the Government, or to strengthen it? Does it, or does it not tend to encourage and strengthen the rebellion? They are the principles diametrically opposed to those for which our Government is struggling, and for which our armies are fighting. I ask you, is an organization that meets in midnight council, to disseminate these damnable doctrines, loyal or disloyal? Is it legal or illegal?

We come now to the obligation; and in considering that, as I have before remarked, we must do so from their stand-point. In reading the argument of the counsel, (Mr. Coffroth,) I am astonished that he should give this Court credit for so little acumen or judgment. The part of the obligation which the gentleman cites, is as follows: "I do further swear that I will at all times, if needs be, take up arms in the cause of the oppressed—in my own country first of all—against any monarch, prince, potentate, power, or government usurped, which may be found in arms, waging war against a people or peoples, who are endeavoring to establish or have inaugurated a government for themselves, in accordance with, and founded upon, the eternal principles of truth, which I have sworn in the Vestibule, and now in this presence do swear to maintain inviolate, and defend with my life." The sentence following this, and which the gentleman has omitted to quote, is as follows: "This I do promise, without reservation or evasion of mind; without regard to the name, station, condition or designation of the invading or coercing power, whether it shall arise within or come from without!"

In considering the first part of this obligation, the gentleman proceeds to "analyze" it; and says: "We will therefore confine our remarks to the last proposition; that is, as to a power or government usurped; and I here ask the learned Judge Advocate if he is prepared to proclaim to the world that this Government is an usurped one, in order to make this obligation to take up arms apply to it?" Now this is a singular manner of arguing the question; it pre-supposes want of ordinary intelligence on the part of this Court, and all concerned in this trial. When the members of the Order of American Knights, or Sons of Liberty, offer to take up arms against any power or government usurped, we do not ask, what government is really usurped? but what government do they claim to be usurped? And what government do they consider and claim to be exercising undelegated or usurped powers? Messrs. Corlew, Bird, Loughridge and Burton, all witnesses for the defense, have explicitly stated that the Government, or the President, was exercising authority and powers not delegated; and therefore, according to Article 7—to which they have all subscribed—was a usurpation, and should be dealt with as such; and, according to Article 10, should be expelled by force of arms. The obligation but reiterates the doctrines enunciated in Article 10 of the Ritual.

I do not need to go to the statements of the witnesses on the part of the accused, to show that these are their principles, but I will take the statements of the accused himself; for I take it that the accused must be bound by the statements which he submits by his counsel. He says: "I have no purpose to conceal the views of Mr. Milligan; and freely admit that he may have said, what every intelligent man in America knows, that both the President, the Congress and the military authorities have each exercised particular powers, that did not belong to them." The gentleman asserts before this Court, that not only the President, but Congress and the military authorities have exercised undelegated powers; therefore, according to the principles sworn and subscribed to by members of the Order, they are all usurpers, and should be expelled from their places by force of arms; not only the President, but Congress and the army. Mr. Coffroth, it only needs that your client be turned loose to walk in the streets, take up his arms and join the rebel ranks, to carry out the doctrines that you enunciate for him in this Court.

When I stated, at the opening of my review of this organization, that the gentleman had falsified the record, had misrepresented the proof, I said what I stand ready here to prove from the record. But half a page below where the gentleman makes the assertion just quoted, he says: "But if any one should, unfortunately for the defense, be of opinion that the Government is a usurpation, still I insist, that neither the defendants as individuals, nor the Order of American Knights or Sons of Liberty, ever entertained or expressed such sentiments, but that they have ever treated the Government, including the President, the Courts, the Congress, and the Army, as legitimate, each in its own sphere." In reply to this, I simply submit the statement of the accused, Mr. Milligan himself, through his counsel, Mr. Coffroth, and the statements of the witnesses just referred to, and the Ritual of the organization, to which every member of the Sons of Liberty has sworn allegiance. In addition, I quote from the resolution sent up to the Grand Council by Mr. Milligan, by the hand of Mr. Winters, the preamble to which says: "A crisis has arisen in the history of the Federal Government, in relation to the rights of the States, whether delegated or reserved; the manifest usurpations of undelegated powers by the President; the utter disregard of all constitutional guarantees of liberty, looking constantly to the subjugation of States and the establishment of a centralized despotism, already fill us with alarm for the cause of civil liberty in America."

To show that the accused, Mr. Milligan, is

not the saint of submission that he has been pictured by his counsel, I quote the following resolutions: "*Resolved*, That the right to alter or *abolish* their Government, whenever it fails to secure the blessings of liberty, is one of the inalienable rights of the people, that can never be surrendered; nor is the right to maintain a Government that does secure the blessings of liberty, less sacred and inalienable; therefore we declare that patriotism and manhood alike enjoin upon us resistance to usurpation as the highest and holiest duty of freemen." That is the first resolution. Resolution 6 says: "That there is a point at which submission merges the man in the slave, and resistance becomes a duty. Whether that point, in the history of the times, has arrived, may be debated; but we will resist, by force, any attempt to abridge the elective franchise, whether by the introduction of illegal votes, under military authority, or the attempt by Federal officers to intimidate the citizens by threats of oppression." It will be remembered that these resolutions, drawn up by Mr. Milligan, and sent by him to the Grand Council, were published in pamphlet form, and circulated in the county temples. The pamphlet contained also the address of Dodd. These two documents prove the old adage that great minds often think alike. Here are the Grand Commander of the State and a Major General of the Order issuing documents to the world, drawn up at different times, and in different places, but both enunciating substantially the same principles, and, in many instances, using almost precisely the same words and phraseology. I will make but one or two quotations from this address; which has been so frequently referred to, that the Court will remember it: "If these men be prolonged in power, they must either consent to be content to exercise the power delegated by the people, or, by the gods, they must prove themselves physically the stronger. This position is demanded by every true member of this fraternity; honor, life—aye, more than life—the virtue of our wives and daughters demand it; and if you intend to make this organization of any practical value, you will do one of two things—either take steps to work the political regeneration of the party with which we are affiliated, up to this standard, or relying upon ourselves, determine at once our plan of action."

To show the construction put upon the obligation by members of the order, and what they concede were the purposes of the organization, I quote from Dodd's speech, in which he gives what he claims to be the opinions and counsel of the Supreme Commander, Mr. Vallandigham. This document was issued by Dodd for general use in the order. He could not have used Mr. Vallandigham's name in this manner without its having been brought to his notice; we may, therefore, reasonably conclude, that in this publication the views of Mr. Vallandigham were given as Mr. Dodd had received them from him, and that the Supreme Commander of this Order gave the correct exposition of its intents and purposes.

In speaking of Vallandigham, Dodd says:

"He counsels late action on the part of State conventions; thinks Ohio is called too soon—advising that Indiana should have hers, say, first of June. He finally judges that the Washington power will not yield up its power, until it is taken from them by an indignant people, by force of arms. He intimates that parties—men and interests—will divide into two classes, and that a conflict will ensue for the mastery."

Mr. Dodd then continues: "*Sons of Liberty, arise!* The day is rapidly approaching, in the which you can make good your promises to your country.' The furnace is being heated that will prove your sincerity—the hour for daring deeds is not distant—let the watchword be, Onward! And let the result bless mankind with Republican Government, in this, our beloved land, to their latest posterity." Does this utterance of Mr. Dodd send forth any uncertain sound? Can it be said that any member of this order who had taken the obligation, and had heard read the lesson of only the first degree, could not understand what was meant by this manifesto? Harrison swears that copies of this pamphlet were sent to Messrs. Milligan, Humphreys, and he thinks, Bowles. Even if Mr. Milligan had not received one of the documents in which were published his own resolutions, by the ordinary channels of the order; beyond question, he would seek to obtain a copy; and can it well be claimed, that with this document, published soon after the 22d of February, in his hand, he still had no knowledge of the contemplated uprising or insurrection by the members of this order: that he had no idea of its illegal purposes or intents? Can any rational man read these utterances of Mr Milligan himself, or the obligation and oaths of this ritual, and say that he was ignorant of the evil purposes of this organization?

This bitterness appears to culminate in his hatred of General Carrington. I do not wonder that Mr. Milligan should entertain this feeling, for it is mainly due to the General that the evil designs of the order were brought to light and frustrated. Out of justice to a brother officer, who has served his country faithfully and well, and with a singleness of purpose, I am compelled to notice some of the vile slanders and misrepresentations contained in this argument. He says, first, "It may have been some bosom friend of General Carrington *à la* Stidger and Zumro." And again: "What a grand spectacle it would present! How proud would be the bearing of that *brave* and *gallant* General who has, by his paid spies and informers, been so industriously extending this order—duping innocent men into it, initiating rebel officers, carrying messages between Dodd & Co. and traitors in arms, and facilitating by all possible means the grand carnival of blood that was to have taken place at this city on the 16th of last August." The true meaning and effect of which is that General Carrington was aiding this conspiracy; for the counsel explicitly says that he was "facilitating by all possible means the grand carnival of blood that was to have taken place at this city on the 16th of last August." The counsel knew, as he penned those words, that it was a vile slander and a falsehood; he knew that General Carrington's sole purpose was to bring to justice the members of this conspiracy, and that to do this, he had to employ men to become acquainted with their designs and movements, and to apprise him of the same. He neither extended, nor aided in extending the order. The men who joined the order for the purpose of revealing its acts to the Government, did simply what they had to do to keep suspicion from them; they acted the part of members of the order. Again the counsel says: "And yet Carrington paid and encouraged Stidger to extend, as rapidly as possible, an organization that is claimed to be treasonable." Now, the proof shows that Stidger was never in any manner hired, or paid a dollar by General Carrington; that he was never employed to extend the order by any person outside of the organization. Stidger received instructions from Captain Jones, Provost Marshal at Louisville, to keep himself advised of the movements and designs of the members of this order, and by him was employed and paid. He was appointed or elected Grand Secretary of the order, and performed the duties of that office, no more and no less. Dr. Zumro acted in like manner. Why this bitterness toward the men that have revealed the designs and purposes of the order, if it be so pure in its organization and acts? On no single point have the accused attempted to rebut or disprove the statements of Stidger; they have not dared to do so; nor have they questioned the probity of any of Mr. Stidger's statements, but have indulged in bitter, unworthy vituperation against him.

The counsel then proceeds to a consideration of the "obnoxious obligation," to ascertain if it is not "consistent with patriotism and most devoted loyalty." He says: "let us, therefore, examine whether the contingency has happened, upon which they obligated themselves to take up arms, with reference to the subject matter, and the people or peoples for whom and in whose behalf they propose to volunteer. And we inquire, where is that people 'who have established or inaugurated a Government of their own free choice, and in accordance with and founded upon the eternal principles of truth?'" He says further, "It will not do to say that the Southern Confederacy is that people, for it would be a eulogy on Jeff Davis' government more glowing than any son of liberty ever uttered. Is their cause that of the oppressed? Is our Government a usurpation? Is the Southern Confederacy founded upon the eternal principles of truth?" I answer him; the members of this order have said that their cause was that of the oppressed; you have said that our Government, now waging this war against rebellion, is a usurpation; you have said that the Southern Confederacy is founded upon the eternal principles of truth; and therefore we try and judge you by the principles you yourselves have enunciated.

Again, this singular argument says: "and I submit, that the conduct of Mr. Bingham is in commendable contrast to that of the authorities. So soon as he was informed of Dodd's proposed plot, his best efforts were at once directed to paralyze that embryo rebellion; while, on the other hand, the authorities knew it all, long before Mr. Bingham did; and instead of nipping it in the bud, were nursing and encouraging it, so that it might bring forth fully ripe fruit." Does the gentleman think that he can make any fair minded men believe that the Government authorities, whose lives, fortunes and honors are staked on the faithful discharge of their duties, were "nursing and encouraging" this accursed conspiracy? He says further: "The evidence of Stidger, their detective and witness, shows that while under the pay and direction of Carrington, and with his consent and approbation," etc. I here assert, that the evidence of Stidger shows that he never was under the pay or direction of General Carrington; and I appeal to the record; "and with his consent and approbation, that he (Stidger) was extending the order as rapidly as possible, both in Indiana and Kentucky, that with the same approbation he initiated rebel officers, and carried messages between Dodd and others and officers in the Confederate service, and afforded every facility to Dodd and his immediate confederates to arrange, perfect and accomplish the inauguration of civil war in Indiana, keeping the authorities here advised of every movement, by regular and frequent reports—and all this for the sole purpose of influencing the then pending elections." I say to the Court, that there is not one particle of evidence on the part of Stidger, or any other witness, "that while under the pay and direction of Carrington, and with his consent and approbation, he (Stidger) was extending the order .... in Indiana and Kentucky," or that General Carrington knew any thing about it until after the reports had been submitted by Stidger; nor that with the "consent and approbation" of General Carrington, Stidger "carried messages between Dodd ...... and officers in the Confederate service." I ask the gentleman, where, from the first page of the record to the last, there is one particle of evidence to show that any of these things were done for the "purpose of influencing the then pending elections?" And this assertion is repeated again and again. This argument, itself, is the only political thing that I have seen in any way connected with this trial. Referring to the military authorities of the Government, he says: "They were fully advised of the existence of what they claim to have been a most infernal conspiracy against the peace of the State—they witnessed the maturing of the scheme—they saw the preparation of the brand that was to flame into civil war. Yes, they knew it all—and yet raised not a finger to stop it, until it was throttled by the very men who are denounced as its sympathizers. Like the tiger that stands at the edge of his jungle, watching his victim, and as the unfortunate traveler comes along, springs upon him, crushes his bones and laps up his blood, so they looked with savage delight upon the proposed uprising—regarding no other consequence except its probable influence upon the elections." How far in the scale of untruth and want of self-respect must a man have descended, to make these bald, vile, slanderous assertions, without a scintilla of proof to found them upon!

I quote but little more, and then leave this argument—or rather this accumulation of libels—to the fate it deserves. "It seemed to matter little to them even though the fire of civil war should desolate our homes, and cause the 'shuddering mother to hug her babe more closely to her bosom,' so that they could only remain masters of the burnt and blackened field." How false, and infamously slanderous this is, I leave you, gentlemen of the Commission, to decide.

I note the following special instances of misstatements of evidence by the counsel for Mr. Milligan:

Mr. Coffroth states that Mr. Ibach testified that a resolution was introduced at the Grand Council of June, 1864, "pledging the order to resistance to the draft, and that it was promptly and with great unanimity voted down; and that the belligerent gentleman who introduced the resolution, went away very much dissatisfied with the order." There is no such testimony, but simply that the resolution was voted down.

He states:

"And yet Carrington paid and encouraged Stidger to extend, as rapidly as possible, an organization that is claimed to be treasonable." No witness testified to such a statement.

He asserts:

"But the evidence further shows that both the defendant, Horsey, and the Government witness, Connell, denied and repudiated the declarations of John W. Stone." The evidence does not substantiate this assertion.

Again he states that Mr. Bingham "never knew of any other than its political character, until the revelation by Dodd of his 'insane and hellish proposition.'"

Mr. Bingham, on the contrary, testifies that "the first idea I had of its being a military organization" was in hearing Major Conklin's speech at the Grand Council of Feb. 16th and 17th, 1864.

On the same page he asserts:

"The evidence of Stidger, their detective and witness, shows that while under the pay and direction of Carrington, and with his consent and approbation, he extended the order, and perfected arrangements to inaugurate civil war; and all this for the sole purpose of influencing the then pending elections."

Stidger did not so testify. Nothing from which such an inference could have been justly drawn.

On page 10th, he states that Bingham "quenched the flame that the authorities were fanning. While they were nursing, he was stifling." The evidence contradicts that assertion.

Again he says:

Long after "the organization of the Grand Council at Terre Haute, that what was termed 'the military bill,' or military feature of the order, was gotten up." The evidence shows that the Terre Haute meeting was held Aug. 27th, 1863, and the military bill was introduced and adopted Sept. 10th, 1863.

He states that "Dodd's scheme required 'Bingham's' consent as a condition precedent;" and without which, "it otherwise could not receive its initiatory impulse." The evidence shows that Dodd desired Bingham's co-operation; but it also proves that when that co-operation was withheld, Dodd and Walker and their co-conspirators, did not abandon their schemes.

Finally, he states that Harrison testifies "that Dodd instructed him, when he sent him to notify Mr. Milligan to attend this council of the leading men of the order, not to inform Milligan of the nature of the business." Mr. Harrison makes no such statement in his testimony.

One more quotation, and I have done with this argument. I said that this argument looked to me as though it had emanated from the disloyal heart of Mr. Milligan himself; that it contains his bitterness and venom toward all persons connected with the Government, and toward all the institutions of our country. He carries that venom to the extreme of hatred to the people of this nation when exercising the elective franchise. This argument says: "But it is not to be expected that gentlemen of the age, firmness, honesty and intelligence of Mr. Milligan, can change their honest convictions upon political questions to suit the views of the Administration brought into power perhaps by a mere, *changeling mob.*"

This is the culmination of his hatred of our free institutions. When the people in their might assert that great, God-given right of determining by whom they shall be governed, and reiterate the sentiment that just governments are instituted for the benefit of the governed, he calls them, when acting in this noble capacity, a "changeling mob!"

In considering the Ritual and obligations of this order, I have substantially answered the arguments of the counsel for Mr. Humphreys and Dr. Bowles upon those points, and therefore do not refer to them specially.

GENERAL PURPOSES OF THE ORDER.

I come now to the consideration of the general intents and purposes of the order, as shown by the evidence: or, in other words, to the consideration of what the evidence shows was the manner or means by which the members of the order proposed to carry out the purposes enunciated in the Ritual, and to the execution of which they bound themselves by an appeal to Almighty God. The foundation stones of this disloyal structure were: First, that the States were sovereign and independent governments; and that each State, in its sovereign capacity, had a right to secede. That whenever the Government *de facto*, or any department of the Government exercised undelegated powers, it was a usurpation; and that the usurped Government was to be removed by force of arms; and they bound themselves together by oaths to overturn this

Government, which they declared was exercising undelegated and usurped powers. They bound themselves, also, to "assist any people or peoples" who may be waging war in "endeavoring to establish, or have inaugurated, a government for themselves, and to resist any coercing power," whether it shall arise within or come from without the Government. These, then, were the common purposes of the conspiracy, and its ultimate design. How, or by what means these purposes, these designs, were to be carried into execution, was to depend, and must have depended upon the tenor of events, upon certain contingencies of time, place and manner. All these were to be determined upon by the leaders, when a certain set of circumstances should come to pass. In the minds of these leaders it was a question of the time when success would be the most certain.

Then, in the original purpose or purposes of the conspiracy, all were conspirators who joined that organization, who heard that Ritual read, and took that obligation. They united and became one body for the purpose of carrying out these illegal, disloyal and treasonable purposes. I might stop without introducing one particle of evidence as to the means by which they intended to execute these purposes, and rest the case with perfect confidence after I had once proven the nature of this order, that it is disloyal in its inception and in its birth, and that the accused were members of the organization.

"A conspiring together of two or more persons is sufficiently an act, without any step taken in pursuance of the conspiracy." *Bishop's Criminal Law, Par.* 313. *Commonwealth* vs. *Judd,* 2 *Mass.,* 329, 337; *Commonwealth* vs. *Tibbetts,* 2 *Mass.,* 536, 538; *Commonwealth* vs. *Warren,* 6 *Mass.,* 74. *People* vs. *Mather,* 4 *Wend.,* 229; *Commonwealth* vs. *McKisson,* 8 *S. & R.,* 420.

Bishop, *Criminal Law,* Vol. 2, Par. 165, says: "Therefore, in conspiracy, the thing intended need not be accomplished; but the bare combination constitutes the crime." Bishop cites in support of this principle numerous authorities.

No further proof was necessary to warrant this Court in finding every one of the accused guilty under the charges of conspiracy, affording aid and comfort to rebels, inciting insurrection, disloyal practices, and violation of the laws of war. Whether that proof has been clear and conclusive, or not, is for you, gentlemen of the Commission, and not for myself, to determine. I have, however, gone forward, and attempted to bring before this Court the whole truth, to show you how far these parties acted toward the consummation of the common purpose. That proof most clearly demonstrates that the "common design" of the order was to reorganize the Government on the same principles which were the foundation of the present rebellion, and are the cardinal principles of the Confederate Government. The rebels claim that they had a right to dissolve their connection with the old Government. The order conceded that right, and pledged itself to assist, by force of arms, any people found waging war for that

18

right. The order denominates the attempt on the part of the Government to coerce these people into submission, as an act of tyranny and usurpation; claiming that the Government had no right, by force of arms, to coerce a seceding State. The proof of this point is clear and conclusive. They pledged the order, and obligated themselves, to resist this coercion. The order was political in its character only so far as it was intended, and did attempt, to educate the masses of the Democratic party up to this belief. In this attempt, I am glad to say that it signally failed, and I here enter upon this record, and say it to meet the charge made by Mr. Milligan in this Court that this is a political prosecution. The proof has shown that the masses of the Democratic party are loyal and true to their Government, true to the integrity of the Government, and her institutions.

This order, however, in and of itself, was political, if secession, insurrection, disloyal purposes and treason make it political. It did aim to educate the Democratic party up to the disloyal stand-point which it had taken, that it might secure through the ballot-box, by putting its chiefs and leaders in power, the same ends which the Confederacy were fighting to achieve. Failing in this, the order proposed and was pledged to use force of arms to secure these ends. The resort to force was kept constantly in view; and with relation to this, the order was organized, and made military in its character. The details of its military organization were confined to the Grand Council, to a great extent, perhaps, as they were regulated by laws passed at the Grand Council.

The question, then, for the Court to determine, is not so much whether these military details were known to the rank and file of the order, as they were to the members of the Grand Council, of which all the accused have been proven to be members; and further, it is not so material whether the details, and manner, and means by which the purposes of this order were to be carried out, were known to the rank and file of the order, as whether these means, these details, were devised to carry out the common purposes to which the organization, as a body, had originally pledged its members. Just so far as these cardinal principles of the order, which are embodied in the rituals and obligations, warranted the leaders to go in carrying these purposes into execution, just to that extent, the rank and file, including all the members of the organization, were bound by and responsible for their acts.

Roscoe, in his *Criminal Evidence,* says:

"In prosecutions for conspiracies, it is an established rule, that where several persons are proved to have combined together for the same illegal purpose, any act done by one of the party in pursuance of the original concerted plan, and with reference to the common object, is, in the contemplation of law as well as in sound reason, the act of the whole party; and, therefore, the proof of the act will be evidence against any of the others who were engaged in the same general conspiracy, without regard to the question, whether the prisoner is proved to have been concerned in the particular transaction." *Phill. Ev.*, 210, *8th ed.*

The oath taken by the members of this order, bound them to obedience to their superiors as complete and prompt as that of soldiers in the army, or of an inferior to his superior officer. That oath, after the member had assented to the principles enunciated in the rituals, pledged the common members before hand to become *particeps criminis* to whatever insurrectionary purposes, plans, or acts their superior officers might design or execute. As I before said, they became parties to the common conspiracy, the details of which for prudential reasons were confined to the leaders. Then let us see how far the co-operation in this conspiracy moved forward to the consummation of their purposes.

Harrison testifies that on the 10th of September, 1863, when the Military Bill was adopted, it was stated in open council, "that it was necessary to organize in a military capacity, to protect the rights of the members against the encroachments of the Administration." In other words, to prepare to set aside this Government, which was using usurped powers. In his cross-examination, he testifies that the same military feature existed in both the American Knights and the Sons of Liberty. Also, that the military bill was introduced "in pursuance of injunctions received from Mr. Wright, the originator of the organization in this State. * * His instructions were that the order must have a certain number of major-generals." Thus we see, that the ultimate resort to arms, to force, was one of the original, fundamental principles of the order.

Bingham testifies that M. C. Kerr, when he came to this city to see about Dodd's scheme of revolution, and to assist in having it stopped, said that

"The people of Washington, Harrison and Floyd counties have got the idea that a revolution was impending."

Thus it will be seen that this idea of revolution, of resort to arms to set aside the Government, not only permeated the order itself but entire neighborhoods. Its purposes were so generally, so universally known, that people who lived in the sections where this knowledge became prevalent, sold their crops and their personal property that they might save it from the general destruction which, they expected, would follow the contemplated insurrection.

Stidger testifies that on the 6th of May, 1864, "Mr. Heffren told me during the evening that he could call together, within twenty-four hours, from 1,000 to 1,500 armed men in that section in connection with that secret organization." This statement stands unimpeached and uncontradicted, Heffren only saying that he does not recollect the conversation, and that it might have taken place.

Stidger saw Bowles on the 9th of May, 1864, when Bowles told him that he was a 'military chief of the order;" and spoke of the co-operation of the forces of the order in Illinois, Indiana, Missouri and Kentucky with the rebel commands of Price and Buckner.

Here we see that Dr. Bowles, who occupied the same position in the order that Milligan and Humphreys did, had knowledge of these intents and purposes of the order, and declared them to any member of the order who chose to inquire. He had no better means of information, no higher trust than the other major-generals—in fact, he did not receive his appointment until several months after Milligan and Humphreys were appointed. They must have had the same knowledge.

From this time forward, Stidger testifies to details of military plans, purposes and information, given to him by Bowles and others. He also states that in Kentucky, where the order was organized by and through the officers in this State, members "were always instructed regarding the military character of the order." He says that they were instructed "by Judge Bullitt, Dr. Kalfus, or myself, or whoever initiated them, that the order was for the purpose of resisting the Government by force of arms, and for assisting the South."

Heffren makes a distinction between the civil and military parts of the order. This, however, is simply a matter of opinion, and is of no importance one way or the other, so long as it is proven that the order had a military branch, and that the military branch was necessary to the accomplishment of the purposes avowed in the fundamental principles of the order.

Heffren, however, in his testimony, does not say that those to whom arms were to be given belonged solely to the military portion of the order. On the contrary, he says, arming was not confined to the military portion of the order. The military part of the order, he says, "had for its object the separating of the States of Ohio, Indiana, Illinois, Missouri and Kentucky from the Eastern States, and make a North-western Confederacy; and, failing in that, join our fortunes with the South." In pursuance of that object, "that there was half a million dollars sent to Indiana, Illinois, and Kentucky, I think by rebel agents in Canada, for the purpose of procuring arms and ammunition for these Northwestern States to arm themselves with."

"The arms thus bought were to be used to carry out the plans of the military part of the order by arming the order." p. 412.

These military objects were discussed in Grand Council, by members, without reference to their military position. The discussion in the September Council was in open meeting of the order; and the nominations were first made by the delegations from the several military districts. In February, Mr. Heffren says, "The matter (the military objects of the order) was talked of by some of us; perhaps a few of us in a corner, or off to one side."

Even in September, 1864, when the major-generals were appealed to by Heffren to know whether "we," by which word he said, "I mean the members of the Order of American Knights," should submit to Dodd's arrest or fight, it is evident the whole order was expected to co-operate, and that, too, under the direction of the military officers elected by the civil organization of the order. In the Vestibule degree, there is no purpose apparent but a political one; but the moment the oath of the first degree proper is administered, the civil and military parts of the order become blended—one faith, one ritual, one oath, one act, and one supreme head characterizing the unity of the order.

Wilson said Dodd was to be considered the military head of the order in this State; and that the revolution in this State "was to take place by the order of Mr. Dodd; he was to send out couriers to the different commanders of the several districts of the State—the major-generals of the four districts into which the State was divided—and they were to send out couriers into the respective counties composing their several districts; they were to give notice of the uprising in their counties; and then it was expected again that information would be conveyed to certain persons in the county that had been prominent and leading men in the organization, and they were to see that it was conveyed to the different townships in the county."

Wilson also adds that Dodd's plan was "known to all the members of the order in my county." With how much plausibility or reason can it be claimed or argued, that these intents and purposes were unknown to three of the military chieftains of this organization, and yet were known to the entire organization in a county in which the society was fully organized in every township but three.

The defense have attacked with great bitterness the character of Mr. Heffren. They have been unable to say one word as against Dr. Wilson, except that he was an informer. Of Mr. Heffren, I can only say this: In the past history of this State he has been a man of prominence, and a leading member of the Democratic party, and associated as a political co-worker with each of these defendants. For four years he was a member of the Senate of this State, and was the Democratic candidate for Speaker in the House of Representatives at the session of 1861.

He has held a commission as Lieutenant Colonel in our army, which he resigned. The only act of his life that I know of or have heard of against him is, that he became embittered against the Government of the United States, and joined this disloyal and treasonable organization. The accused have been unable to disprove any thing which was uttered upon this stand by him. They had made no attempt to impeach him. Nor have they attempted in any manner to disprove one of the utterances of Dr. Wilson, a man whom every one characterizes as a person of undoubted probity and truthfulness. He now holds the position of Auditor of his county, and has the confidence of the community in which he lives. His evidence, not having been refuted in the slightest particular, and in no respect being improbable, and no impeachment having been attempted, must be given full credit and effect by this Court.

The witnesses introduced by the defense show that the order was not purely political, although they testified with great unanimity that it was designed as an offset to the Union League, as they had heard. But on that point the witnesses stultified themselves by stating that such members as Mr. Milligan had opposed the extension of the order. Why oppose its extension, if it be only designed as a political organization to offset the Union League? Mr. Ibach testifies that the order was political for the purpose of advancing Democratic principles, "as we understood them." He also states that at the June Council, "A young man from the north part of the State was very uneasy about the draft, and thought the order should do something." He thought "we ought to combine." A resolution was offered and voted down, "That the different temples in the counties should organize for the purpose of resisting the Government. * * * It created quite a turbulent time there. Some thought that the order was purely political, and others that there was a military branch to it. The majority of the members did not want any military action, but preferred to wait for a change through the elections." In other words, the dissension was not on the right and duty of resisting the Government, but simply a question of time, means and policy. The relations of the order to the Government came up again, as Mr. Ibach testifies: "They had quite a discussion about the grievances of the Government, but could not come to an understanding about the matter."

The same witness, who has been so often referred to by the counsel for Mr. Milligan, had a muster-roll of a company headed by his own name, which was drawn up within the past eighteen months, whose object was to get State arms, if possible, and to drill—not for State or Government service—but, to use his words, to "protect ourselves * * * against the soldiers that were coming home; * * to guard ourselves against what we called encroachments on our rights."

Judge Wilson B. Loughridge, who has been so often quoted by the defense, another of Mr. Milligan's witnesses, testifies that "it was altogether a political association:" that "it was intended to protect the members of the Democratic party against violence, which it was thought had been used against them in particular quarters; and, in short, to protect the members of the Democratic party, and see that their rights were never trampled upon."

Again he said: "The functions of the organization, as I understood it, were to see that we had a fair election, and maintained our rights. * * To defend ourselves; if we were assailed, to protect ourselves." To do this, "with just such means as were necessary to afford us protection; to exhaust all peaceable means, and if these failed, to exercise the right of self-defense." That "we were to be protected wherever we were assailed. * * The efforts of the members were to be mutual in protecting each other."

Thus it will be seen that the design and purposes of the order were mutual, and were not to be confined to peaceable means, but looked to a final resort to arms.

The same witness identified the tenth section of the Declaration of Principles, read to the candidate for the first degree, as "one of the cardinal principles of the order." He also said he had "never heard members dissent from it;" and that in his paper, and in his speeches, he had expressed the opinion that "the President was assuming powers not delegated;" and that "the order held to that as well." Take this admission in connection with the reading of the tenth section, and out of their own mouths they are convicted of unlawful combination to achieve treasonable purposes.

Stephen G. Burton, a witness for Mr. Humphreys, in his direct examination, testified that the order was political, and "there was nothing more taught in the second or third degree than in the first." In the cross-examination, I read to the witness the tenth section of the Declaration of Principles of the first degree, and asked what those sentences meant. He promptly answered:

"They have reference to counter-revolution. * * Because when one political party assumes power, and begins to trample on the rights of other citizens, these can take their rights in their own hands, and defend them by force of arms. My idea is that it is right for a free American citizen to defend his rights by force when they are trampled upon." I further asked: "Was it one of the purposes of the order, that in case of these encroachments referred to, and the trampling upon their rights, that this order should resist it by force of arms?"

He answered: "Yes, sir."

Thus I need no explanation of the intents and purposes of this order, or its illegal and treasonable designs, by the witnesses for the Government. The defense themselves have made that proof for me. In examining this proof it must be kept in mind what they claim were encroachments, usurpations, and trampling upon their rights or the rights of any people, and in case they deemed them to exist, how, from their stand-point, they proposed to act.

The examination of this witness continued:

"Q. The ritual claims the right of resistance 'whenever the officials assume and exercise power not delegated.' Has not the order claimed that the Government was exercising power not delegated? Have you not so claimed?

"A. I have frequently claimed that it had assumed powers not delegated.

"Q. Has not the order also claimed this?

"A. I suppose it has.

"Q. Was not this one of its principles?

"A. I suppose it was. The Government had assumed too much power.

"Q. In case of such assumption of power, was the remedy contained in these words: 'It is the inherent right and imperative duty of the people to resist such officials, and, if need be, expel them by force of arms?'

"Q. Was that the remedy proposed by the order?

"A. Yes, sir."

Here, gentlemen, is the explanation given by their own witnesses of their own understanding of this combination which they had entered into. This obligation, which they had taken upon themselves, defines whether the purposes of the combination were legal or illegal.

Let us glance for a moment at a few of the overt acts of treason enacted in pursuance of the general purposes of the order. First, as to the drilling and arming of the order.

Teny testifies that, in Martin county, the order "drilled a few times in the township," and "that they were getting arms all the time."

In speaking of the order, I do so without reference to whether it went under the name of the Knights of the Golden Circle, American Knights or Sons of Liberty: for I think I have sufficiently shown that one was but the outgrowth of the other, and that they were all one and the same general conspiracy, actuated by the same motives, and moving forward to the consummation of the same purposes, and as a general rule containing the same members.

Connell and Heffren both testify as to Horsey's having brought ammunition to his own home in Martin county, and Heffren as to its being concealed upon Horsey's premises.

Robertson testifies to the arming and drilling of the order in Randolph county, of its purpose to resist the draft and arbitrary arrests, whenever the emergency arose, or the heads of the order demanded it. He details the military organization of their lodge.

The order in Washington county was generally armed, and $1,000 was placed at the disposal of the order in that county, in June last, by Dr. Bowles, for the purpose of purchasing arms for those unable to arm themselves, as Heffren and Wilson both testify. This was a month nearly before the Confederacy tendered to the order, at the Chicago conclave, $2,000,000 for revolutionary purposes.

In regard to arming the order in this place, Harrison testifies to the arrival of arms, pistols and fixed ammunition, consigned by Walker to J. J. Parsons, a member of the order, and concealed in Dodd's building—which were purchased shortly after the Chicago conclave. Colonel A. J. Warner also testifies to the seizure of these arms.

Stidger testifies that "Bowles made a statement in the Council of the 14th of June, that the organization in his county numbered about 600 men; but that there was a military organization amounting to 900 men, armed and equipped. * * He also stated that he had an arrangement with a man to furnish any number or kind of arms." Also, that in August, Bowles wanted to get arms of Peters, of Cincinnati, and B. C. Kent, of New Albany; and asked Stidger to have "three or four thousand lances made."

Stidger also says: "I was told by Mr. Kern, a member of the order, that Judge Williams, of Kentucky, had given $100, and other members $200 more for organizing the order, and that he had expended that money in the purchase of arms, and that they had sent the men, with the arms, South."

Greek fire was one of the appliances of the order, to be used to destroy Government property, as Stidger, Wilson and Heffren testify, and had been used for that purpose. It is true Bocking attempts to explain and refute some of the evidence of these witnesses; but his story, in and of itself, is so contradictory, improbable and entirely contemptible, that the defense themselves have hardly dared to claim any weight for it. The whole effect of his testimony upon the minds of the members of this Commission, must have been to corroborate Stidger and the statements of the Government witnesses. He admits the receipt of the $200 00. He admits that he was present at the meeting of members of the order at the Louisville Hotel, in Louisville, which was referred to by Stidger. Mr. Bocking stated that he was very much out of health, and went to the Springs, where Dr. Bowles resided, for his health—to recuperate his decaying vital powers—and as the result of this stay, took dinner at these Springs, and left after a long interview with Bowles; and that being entirely out of money, and hard up, he went to the Louisville Hotel, at Louisville. Yet he says he had no business whatever to call him there, nor any thing whatever to do; and that while there, he made and explained to these gentlemen at that Hotel, all about his shells, handgrenades and Greek fire; and that still being hard up, though having received $200 00, he travels to Indianapolis and spends a week, then goes to Detroit and spends a week, thence to Cincinnati, from Cincinnati to Adams county, Ohio, from Adams county to Cincinnati, and from Cincinnati to this city, where he has remained ever since. Concealing the fact that he was at Windsor, Canada, until it is unwillingly drawn from him, he admits that on this trip, in April or May, he stopped for two weeks at the house of the rebel Colonel Steele, in Windsor, Canada, free of charge, without business or employment, or design of any kind, as he swears, in going there. All this is sufficient to give this Commission an understanding of the motives, and bias and weight to be given to Bocking's testimony.

<h3>OPPOSITION TO THE DRAFT.</h3>

This order was pledged, as a body, not to serve in our army. They were sworn not to enter the service of the Government for pay. (See Obligation of the Second Degree.) Its members were even taught that the prosecution of the war was a usurpation of power. Its teachings, as a natural result, led to opposition to the draft. In Wells county, its members, in their temple, discussed opposition to the draft. Joseph Johnson, a witness for the defense, says: "Some said, I will resist; some said, I will fight, or run off, or do something else." The temple in Rock Creek township, Wells county, sent committees to other places, to learn what the order should do about the draft. Milligan counseled resistance, but others of the order thought that impolitic. Zumro and Johnson both testified that they had a military organization in their temple. A flagrant appeal to the people to resist the draft and to discourage enlistment, is the speech of

Mr. Milligan at the gathering of the order, and others, at Fort Wayne, on the 14th of August, 1863. It is a matter of public history that this Convention denounced the draft as the most damnable of all the outrages perpetrated by this Administration. Yet so far from denouncing that resolution and others of kindred disloyalty, Mr. Milligan went into an elaborate defense of the South, denouncing the Government, and the war, and the purpose for which it was waged.

<h3>COMMUNICATION WITH REBELS.</h3>

I come now to consider next the acts of this order, as a body, as to their communication and concert of action with the rebels.

Stidger testifies that he was taken for a rebel commissioner, when he first visited Salem. Heffren corroborates this statement, saying: "It is possible some man played himself off on Stidger, at that time, for me. A great many men about Salem, at that time, were expecting a man from Cumberland Gap, to report rebel movements."

Bowles stated, in the presence of Stidger, "that they had sent a man named Dickerson to Richmond, to have the Confederate authorities send an invading force to act in concert with their order."

Stidger says, that "Bullitt instructed a man to try and get a place appointed for him to meet Colonel Jesse, said to be a rebel colonel in command of the rebel forces in Kentucky; and he instructed this man to go to Colonel Syphert, a rebel colonel, said to be in command of a rebel squad, and have a conference with him about the capture of Louisville." He also states, that in Kentucky, "there was a rebel Col. Anderson, of the 3d rebel Kentucky Regiment of infantry, initiated into the order about the last of June, 1864," by Kalfus; and, also, Captain Van Morgan, Dick Pratt, Jim McCrocklin, and a captain of a squad of guerrillas.

And here let me say, that all that has been said by Mr. Milligan's counsel, or by Mr. Ray in reference to Mr. Stidger's initiating, or assisting in the initiation of those parties, seems to be exceedingly unjust and ill-timed. It certainly can have no weight with this Court, or with any unbiased mind. Mr. Stidger unequivocally states that all he did in the way of initiation of rebel officers, or of any one else, he did in pursuance of instructions from Judge Bullitt, the head of the order in Kentucky, or Dr. Kalfus, or upon his own responsibility. He does not state, and there is not one particle of evidence from the beginning of this trial to its close, to support the allegation, that he ever initiated any person into this order, by the instruction, direction or sanction of General Carrington, or any other officer of the United States, or of the State of Indiana. He was instructed simply to become a member of this order, and learn all he could with reference to its acts and purposes. It is perfectly absurd to claim that there was any desire or design on his part, or on the part of the authorities, to extend or perpetuate this order. All his acts were, weekly and monthly, reported to the United States authorities. They were striving to obtain that degree of information upon which they could act in bringing these conspirators to justice; and the moment they gathered sufficient information to base their action upon, the authorities acted. And you, gentlemen, on the part of the accused, at one moment and in one breath, are bitter beyond degree, in denouncing the authorities because they did not act sooner; and with the same vigor, and in the next breath, you denounce their arrest, finally, as acts of tyranny, unwarranted and unauthorized.

To return to the evidence. Mr. Heffren testifies, that the revolution on the 16th of August hinged on the contingency of the co-operation of the rebels; and that "about the 16th of August, Dr. Bowles had sent a man to General Price, but he had not returned." Rebel communication was also spoken of to Heffren, by Mr. Harris, of Salem. Wilson says, that at the Chicago meeting of July 20th, 1864, he heard communication with the rebels spoken of. He says: "I think Dr. Bowles said, messengers were sent to the rebels. * * I think they were sent into Kentucky and Missouri. * * I inferred it [communication] was to be with Price and Buckner, because they were to be the co-operative forces in case of an uprising." "The general signal for the uprising was to be the appearance of guerrillas or troops in the vicinity of St. Louis or Louisville." The couriers sent, "were to go to Generals Price and Buckner." The Illinois forces of the order were to liberate rebel prisoners in that State, and concentrate at St. Louis, "to co-operate with Price's forces."

Wilson also states that at the Chicago meeting, Dodd represented that he came fresh from a conference with Holcombe, Clay and Sanders, at Niagara Falls, who were duly authorized by the Southern Confederacy to meet them in Chicago, but could not get a safe conduct, through Horace Greeley, from the President. Yet the Southern Confederacy was represented by a Captain Majors, and Mr. Barrett, who said he was authorized to represent the Southern Confederacy.

These men met, according to their own statement, not to destroy the Government, but to save it; and in this work of saving the Government, they boasted of the active sympathy and co-operation of the rebel authorities, who have always maintained the distinctive principles of the order.

Mr. Barrett, of Missouri, in opening the conclave, stated "that his object in calling the meeting was that he thought the Government could be restored, and he was satisfied it could be, if we could get the co-operation of the North with the South—or a portion of the North, Ohio, Indiana, Illinois, Missouri, and Kentucky; he said if the members of the Sons of Liberty in these States, would co-operate with the South, he had no doubt the entire Government could be saved through their action. He also said that it had been contemplated to have an uprising at some time soon, perhaps as early as the 3d of August, but that had failed from some cause; and he thought every thing could be got ready for an uprising, perhaps by the 10th or 15th of the month, and that the South, in order to show her willingness to engage in some movement that would restore the Government, had authorized him to place at the disposal of the members of the organization a large sum of money, amounting to two millions of dollars. * * That the organization could have the use of that amount of money in preparing themselves to rise against the Lincoln Administration; that it would be distributed to the several Grand Commanders of those States, and by them sub-distributed among such persons inside of their order as in their judgment was prudent, and to be expended, by those who received it, for arms and other appliances of war.

"He [Barrett] stated, in speaking of the money, that it had been used for the purpose of paying for the destruction of United States property, arsenals, burning boats," etc. "He said they would pay ten per cent. on Government property so destroyed."

Dr. Wilson said he understood from some source, he thinks from Dr. Bowles, "that Ohio was to be taken care of by Vallandigham * * in the event of a general uprising. He had some forces at his disposal in Canada, and would bring those forces into Ohio to co-operate with other forces at Cincinnati and Louisville."

HOW IT WAS TO BE DONE.

I come next to the consideration of the revolutionary plot, or the plan finally determined upon, by which the purposes of this order were to be carried into execution. The details of the plan of operations matured at Chicago, in July, 1864, involving the release of the rebel prisoners in Ohio, Indiana, and Illinois, and the seizure of Government arsenals, and burning of Northern cities, etc., in this State, in Missouri, and Kentucky, were detailed substantially alike by Harrison, Stidger, Bingham, Wilson and Heffren. Harrison first speaks of it as "a design in progress or in contemplation." Dodd desired to have a Democratic mass meeting called, under cover of which he would carry out his plans. If the meeting was called, Harrison says, "he intended to send out circulars to the members of the order in the various counties, *ordering* the members (not the military members, it should be borne in mind, but all the members) to come up to that meeting *armed*." * * "By the aid of the rebel prisoners, who were to be released through his instrumentality, and that of the persons who came in here to the meeting to be held here on the 16th, they were to have an uprising and overturn the State Government."

"This scheme had its connection not only in this State, but in the State of Illinois." Harrison also stated that Dodd was the proper person to head the uprising. I then asked him:

"Q. Had he the power in an official capacity to order that here?

"A. It was vested entirely in Mr. Dodd.

"Q. Had he the power to order members of the order at will?

"A. He had."

Joseph J. Bingham, in his testimony, states that when Dodd approached him, and asked him for his co-operation in this scheme of revolution, August 2d, he (Dodd) said "that at the Council, a revolution *had been determined* upon. * * Arrangements had been made to release the prisoners on Johnson's Island, at Camp Chase, near Columbus, Ohio, at Camp Morton, and also at Camp Douglas, and that the prisoners at Camp Douglas, after their release, were to go over and release those at Rock Island. At the same time there was to be an uprising at Louisville, at which the Government stores, etc., were to be seized."

This scheme Bingham did not indorse, but did conceal. He did go to Athon and Ristine, as he testifies, and asked them leading questions, and learned nothing, and revealed nothing. Through the instrumentality of Mr. Kerr, who seemed alone faithful to his country among the faithless, a conference of leading Democrats was held to arraign Dodd and Walker. They met at McDonald's offiee. Bingham says: "Colonel Walker and Dodd did not acknowledge or deny, at that interview, that any such scheme was entertained. They both spoke, and very earnestly, about the state of public affairs, and they used about these arguments: 'That the Government could not be restored again under the old state of things, without a forcible revolution. That an appeal to the ballot-box was all folly; that the people were prepared for revolution; that they would not submit to the draft; and that it was better to direct the revolution, than to have the revolution direct us.'"

Every member of that meeting, who heard these speeches uttered by these men, was bound, if he acted in good faith to his country, to have had these men instantly arrested and turned over to the authorities to be punished. And every man who was present on that occasion, failed in his duty to his Government in her hour of sorest need, when he permitted these men to walk abroad maturing their schemes of revolution, of insurrection and treason, or permitted in his hearing the utterances of these sentiments, knowing that they had already matured a scheme for carrying them into execution.

In these brief speeches of Walker and Dodd, as given by Bingham, is outlined the legitimate culmination of the cardinal principles of the order. The order had never doubted the propriety of insurrection and revolution, but only whether the proper time had come for its inauguration. Walker and Dodd believed that period had arrived, and they acted accordingly. They accepted Barrett's offer of rebel co-operation. They counseled with Holcombe, Clay and Sanders, at Niagara Falls, while maturing and arranging the details of revolution. They admitted into their Chicago conclave of July 20th, representatives of the Southern Confederacy. They appointed a meeting with rebel officers in this city, to arrange the details of releasing rebel prisoners.

Bingham says, on the morning of the 11th of August, he met Walker going to the Bates House. "I asked him why he was going?

He said he had to meet these gentlemen by appointment. I understood him to say that they were rebel officers. * * He said that they were on their way to Chicago to take charge of the rebel prisoners when they were released from Camp Douglas. It was necessary that he should see them to tell them that the whole scheme was stopped. He met me afterward, and said that he had seen them, and they had gone on and stopped all operations at that time for the release of the prisoners."

The arrival of the rebel colonels at the Bates House here, from the rebel army, is most conclusive proof of the direct communication and connection of this order with the rebel insurgents. But twenty days elapsed between the time when the plan is agreed upon at Chicago, before that intelligence is transmitted to the rebel authorities, and in pursuance of that intelligence the rebel emissaries arrived at this point to take part in this insurrection. Their couriers must have been swift and sure.

Stidger says that on the 29th of July, he saw Dodd, and Dodd said to him: "He therefore wished me to go home, and get twenty or thirty good runners, so that as soon as Judge Bullitt returned they might have been sent off. He said the programme was arranged, and every thing ready." Bullitt also told Stidger that "the programme was all arranged for this uprising." On the 2d of August, Stidger says Dodd told me "what the programme was, and impressed upon me the importance of secrecy."

Stidger also learned that "their difference at Chicago was whether they should wait until the rebel forces should be sent into Eastern Kentucky to co-operate with them, or to make their uprising now, and co-operate with the rebel forces when Davis could send them." "Bowles at first objected to this uprising until the rebels should invade the eastern part of the State, as he said they would. * * He would consent to the uprising on the 15th or 16th of August, as Dodd had said, provided Colonel Syphert, Colonel Jesse, and Walker Taylor would assist in the capture of Louisville, until the forces of this State could get there."

Piper also told Stidger that "he was carrying orders, or that he had orders from Mr. Vallandigham to Judge Bullitt and Dr. Bowles. They were orders with respect to the time set for the uprising of the order."

Bowles also said to Stidger, that the programme Dodd had given him, "was the programme agreed on at Chicago."

Heffren confirms the statements of other witnesses in regard to this scheme of revolution, and said it failed partly on account of Kerr's exposure, and also, "because the army of the Confederacy did not come through Cumberland Gap, as they had agreed to, or as it was reported they had agreed to do."

The revolutionary purposes of the order were also shown in the speech made at the time of the Chicago Convention, August 29th, 1864, to the conclave of the Sons of Liberty, by Mr. Moss, of Missouri. After describing the indignities suffered by members of the order, in that State, he said: "If this organization was worth any thing, if it was intended to be efficient in the restoration of the Government under the Constitution, that now was the proper time to strike; that these indignities were unbearable; that if they had the true American blood in them, they would not bear it any longer, but would strike now."

These, then, were the chief schemes and purposes of the order, as explained and defined by the acts of its members. These were the means by which they proposed to carry their purposes into execution. These, in brief, are the acts done in pursuance of the original combination; and the culmination of all these acts on the day assigned, was but the natural outgrowth, the proper and natural consummation of the principles and purposes which they had sworn to maintain by force of arms, if necessary. I therefore say that each member of this conspiracy, who took upon himself the oaths of the first, second and third degrees of this order, or of the first degree alone, after fully understanding the lessons and principles of the order, as explained in the Ritual, was responsible for every one of these acts done by the leaders of this order. There is no way by which they can relieve themselves from that responsibility. They must be held accountable for these acts. They were but carrying into practical application the theories and principles they had all sworn to maintain. This organization, as a body, was the gathering together, to be wielded against the Government, of all the bitter and hostile elements in these Northern States. It was truly but a whited sepulcher. To the world it exhibited nothing of its inner corruption, but concealed its acts, principles and purposes. It concealed its very name, its very existence; but within it was filled with dead men's bones, and all manner of corruption. Over the doors of its temples should be inscribed the same maxim that the Roman people used as to their own city, in the days of the Inquisition:

> "Vivere qui sancte vultis discedite Roma,
> Omnia hic esse licent non licet esse probum."

> "He who would live holily, depart from Rome:
> All things are allowed here except to be upright."

All things were allowed in these temples, except to be loyal, true, faithful to the mother who had cherished and nourished them: that dearest mother, our beloved country.

CONNECTION OF THE ACCUSED WITH THIS ORDER.

I now turn to examine briefly the evidence as it applies to the accused individually.

WILLIAM A. BOWLES.

First, then, in the order of their arraignment, I shall consider the proof as it relates to the accused, William A. Bowles. The argument of Mr. Ray, the able counsel for Mr. Bowles and Mr. Humphreys, is an ingenious, courteous, elegant document. I think it puts the evidence in the best possible light for the defendants. But in scanning that argument closely, we see its fallacies and its objects when we come to weigh it by the proof. The counsel puts Mr. Bowles before the public as more sinned against than sinning. This view of the case can only be sustained by a wholesale rejection of the testimony of witnesses of undoubted veracity. While Dr. Bowles has not put himself forward as a public agitator, nor, by speeches to public assemblies, sought to stir up insurrection and dissatisfaction, he has, however, steadily and quietly, in the daily walks of life, in the order and in connection with it, moved forward and labored to secure the overthrow of the Government, even at the expense of insurrection and revolution. That he spent his own time and money freely for this object, there is no doubt. That in his old age, with the span of his life nearly closed, he leagued himself with younger men, and assisted them in their schemes of treason, is clearly proven. There is not, however, a particle of evidence to show that his object, as claimed by his counsel, was simply to effect a compromise between the two sections. All his acts, and those of his co-conspirators, recognize the rebels as friends of civil liberty, and his and their friends; and the Government, and those who administered it, and its supporters, as enemies and usurpers, whom he and they hated with a hatred unutterable and beyond measure.

With these cardinal principles, the accused, William A. Bowles, put himself in communication, and acted in concert with those whose iron hands were grappling at the throat of the Republic.

The testimony shows that William A. Bowles was initiated into the Grand Council Degree of the Order, on the 10th of September, 1863. Mr. Harrison testifies to this positively, and identifies the accused, William A. Bowles, as the person initiated that day. He was a member of the Military Committee appointed at that time. He spoke at considerable length on the features of the military bill. His speech was "approving of the military bill." He was present at the State Council held February 16th and 17th, 1864. The same witness testifies that Bowles was present, and was "elected in the South-east District" as its Major General. Wilson testifies that Dr. Bowles was present at the State Council, which, he thinks, was held about the 6th of November, 1863. A military committee was appointed at that meeting. Wilson says: "I thought from the actions of Dr. Bowles, he must be the chairman of that committee, as he made a verbal report." This was the meeting at which Dodd proposed "to kick down the walls of common decency, and talk treason for awhile;" and spoke of revolution as one of the ulterior plans of the organization, if necessity required it. Here, then, was the explanation of the intents and purposes of the order, in the presence of the accused, boldly and without reserve, to the assembled members of the order, moving forward to its accomplishment. Supreme Councils were held in Chicago, in the latter part of September, 1863, and in New York in October or November, and also in the following February.

Harrison said he understood Bowles was present at the Supreme Council in September, and adds: "I got this information from Dodd." Harrison sent to Dr. Bowles two copies of the printed proceedings of the February Grand Council, with the Constitution of the County and Branch Temples. He says that Dr. Bowles was present at the State Council of June 14th, 1864.

The military bill was changed in the February Council at Bowles' suggestion. Harrison says: "He was elected [Major General] on that occasion. A portion of that bill was changed, and I did not hear him object after the bill was changed."

Heffren states that he made a change in the districts defined by the bill, and then "Dr. Bowles was unanimously elected in place of McGrane."

Mr. Bingham, another witness for the Government, and a member of the order, testifies that "Colonel Bowles, the accused," was present at the February Council. Also, that "about the middle of May, Dr. Bowles, Mr. Dodd, Judge Bullitt, and Barrett were at my office, * * * and supposed that they were all members of the order." Here we find Dr. Bowles moving about, and in close communion with the leading and most venomous and reckless of these conspirators. The Commission will recollect another fact—that this assemblage of these leading conspirators here was in May, and, also, that it was in May of the same year that the leading members of this order were experimenting with this Greek fire in the basement of some building in your city, on Sunday, while your citizens were attending public worship. Undoubtedly these were the men who were superintending those experiments.

Bingham testifies that Bowles was present at Chicago; that Dodd informed him that Dr. Bowles was present at Chicago, where "a revolution had been determined upon."

Stidger says that in his interview with Bowles, "he told me that he was a military chief of the order. * * He said that the forces of Indiana would concentrate in Kentucky, and make Kentucky their battle-ground; that the forces in Illinois would concentrate in St. Louis, and co-operate with the forces in Missouri; that Illinois would furnish 50,000, Missouri 30,000, and Price was to invade the State with 20,000 men, and with that 100,000 men they were to hold and permanently occupy that State; and the troops of Indiana and Ohio concentrate at Louisville.

"He wanted to know how many men Kentucky could furnish, and stated that a rebel force, under Buckner, would come into the eastern part of the State, and with these forces they intended to hold Kentucky.

"He told me that this order was made out of the Knights of the Golden Circle, of which he had been a member; and that he resurrected this order out of it."

Stidger visited Bowles again at French Lick Springs, on the 28th of May. In that interview Bowles "repeated again his revolutionary programme in connection with Price and Buckner."

This evidence of Mr. Stidger stands unimpeached and uncontradicted; and I here venture to say that no witness ever came upon the witness-stand and testified to so many distinct facts, dates, places, and persons—every word being recorded as he stated it—that has been more triumphantly corroborated by all the different witnesses that have testified than Mr. Stidger. While every effort has been made by the defense to break in upon the strength of his testimony, to find some slight variations upon which to base a probability of mistake; yet in every instance the subsequent proof, and the investigation of the facts, have all shown that Stidger was exactly right, and truthful, and triumphantly illustrates the old adage, "Truth is ever consistent."

Stidger goes on to say that, at this same time, "He [Bowles] also told me of the change in the Supreme Commander to Vallandigham, and that he had been appointed a commissioner to visit Vallandigham in Canada."

"Also, that Bowles stated to him, at the same interview, that on Sunday, May 22, himself, Dodd, and a Dutch chemist, experimented with Greek fire, at Indianapolis, and that they had nearly brought it to perfection, and that Bullitt knew how it was made. That they intended to use it for the destruction of Government property; that the Jeff Davis government was to pay them ten per cent. for all the property destroyed, taking the estimate, as given in the Northern papers, of the amount destroyed. He also told me that the two boats burned at the Louisville wharf, last spring, and boats belonging to the Government, that had been destroyed on the Mississippi river and elsewhere, had been burned by the Greek fire."

Here again is a singular corroboration of Stidger's testimony. Wilson testifies that Barrett stated to the members of the order, at Chicago, that he was expressly authorized by the rebel government to pay this ten per cent. for the destruction of Government property. It can not be claimed that there was any collusion between Stidger and Dr. Wilson; the fact is, they have never met.

On the 28th of June, 1864, Bocking exhibited his conical shell, and a diagram of the spherical shell, and explained the principle of the two: Bowles was present. About the 1st of June, "Bullitt and others met at Kalfus' office, in Louisville, and decided that Coffin should be murdered." They sent, by Stidger, a message to Bowles to see that it was done; it was delivered, and Bowles said, "I will put two men on his track." Stidger testifies that, at a meeting of the State Council, held on the 14th of June, 1864, at which Bowles was present, a committee on military affairs was appointed; and that "Milligan, Bowles, McBride, and Dr. Gatling, were four of the military committee. * * * They reported a bill setting forth their views that the order ought to be organized as a military organization at once, and armed." He testifies further, that the list of Major Generals was called over, including Bowles, as "the major-generals, by virtue of their rank, were, ex officio, members of the Supreme Council." The day after the Council, June 15, Bowles, Dodd, and Milligan went to Hamilton, Ohio, to receive an exiled enemy of his country, the Supreme Commander of the Sons of Liberty, C. L. Vallandigham. Bowles stated in the Council, on the 14th of June, as Stidger testifies, that he had "a military organization" in his county, of 900 men, armed and equipped;" and "that he had an arrangement with a man to furnish any number or kind of arms." At another time he stated to Stidger that "they [the order] would go to Kentucky and have a regular understanding with the Confederates, and act in concert with them; and that they had sent a man named Dickerson to Richmond, to have the Confederate authorities send an invading force to act in concert with their order."

In one of the last interviews between Stidger and Bowles, the question of revolution was freely discussed. Stidger says: "Bowles at first objected to this uprising until the rebels should invade the eastern part of the State, as he said they would. * * * * Bowles said he would consent to the uprising on the 15th or 16th of August, as Dodd had said, provided Colonel Syphert, Colonel Jesse, and Walker Taylor would assist in the capture of Louisville, until the forces in this State could get there." "Bowles asked me [Stidger] if I could have three or four thousand lances made; .... he wanted three or four thousand men armed with lances and revolvers; he said he could make them of good service..... He told me that he had spent $2,000 .... for the benefit of the order;" and that "he cared nothing about the election; he was satisfied Lincoln would be elected; he wanted the time spent in perfecting the organization, and getting ready for the uprising."

Piper stated to Stidger that Bowles had charge of the release of the rebel prisoners at Johnson's Island, or Rock Island. This Piper represented himself as having "an appointment on Vallandigham's staff; he said that he was carrying orders, or that he had orders from Mr. Vallandigham to Judge Bullitt and Dr. Bowles. * * They were orders as to the time set for the uprising of the order." Bowles told Stidger, "we" had sent Bocking to Canada, "before he was admitted into the order, to see if he was willing to spend his money in experimenting for the benefit of the Order of Sons of Liberty." This experimenting was to bring to greater destructive perfection those shells, and Bocking's Greek fire. Stidger visited Bowles about the 6th of August, after he had obtained the programme from Dodd, and he says: "I told him the programme as Dodd had given it to me; and he said that was the programme agreed on at Chicago, and that Dodd had no right to change it; that they should have waited the action of the rebel forces; but finally, he had determined he would act without the co-operation of the rebel forces, if he could get the co-operation of three rebel colonels."

Heffren testifies that James B. Wilson, a member of the order, showed him, last summer, $1,000, and remarked, "There was one thousand he had just got from Dr. Bowles to procure arms and ammunition for our county;" that Dodd and Walker had received $100,000 each, and "a portion of it was to go to Dr. Bowles, to be spent in his part of the State in purchasing arms and ammunition." These

arms were to be used for arming the order. He adds, that the military objects were discussed by some members at a State Council, in February, 1864, and that "Dr. Bowles was probably there one morning when we talked about it." He says Wilson told him "that Bowles had made an arrangement to have nine companies of infantry, one of lancers, and one section of artillery, to comprise each regiment in this order." Wilson also stated to Heffren that "about the 16th of August, Dr. Bowles had sent a man to see General Price, but he had not returned. * * * * Dr. Wilson said Dr. Bowles' man had gone to see Price, and another to Richmond, to arrange for troops to come through Cumberland Gap, and when they returned, which they expected would be before the 16th of August, 1864, this uprising would take place."

The cross-examination of Heffren develops the fact that Dr. Bowles was the ranking major-general of the order in this State, and that Dodd stated at the February meeting "that Dr. Bowles was boss of the whole machine of the military part of the order."

James B. Wilson, to whom I have heretofore referred—a man whose candid bearing, deliberation, and evident reluctance to testify, must have convinced every one who heard him, of the unvarnished truth of every word he uttered; who overstated nothing, and only stated that which he was compelled to by his oath and the direct questions propounded to him—testifies that he attended the Chicago conclave of July 20, which Mr. Barrett, of Missouri, said "was to be composed of the military men of the order." Bullitt, of Kentucky, Barrett, of Missouri, Piper, of Illinois, and Dodd and Bowles, of this State, were there. Barrett made a speech, in which he unfolded the programme of the revolution, and asked the co-operation of the order in Ohio, Indiana, Illinois, Missouri, and Kentucky, with the South; and in the name of the South, tendered $2,000,000 to arm the order, and pay for the destruction of Government property. He referred to the destruction of Government property at Louisville, St. Louis, and on the Ohio river, on which the ten per cent. premium had been paid. The witness adds: "I afterward learned from Dr. Bowles that the means employed was Greek fire."

Both Wilson and Heffren testify to a signal flag to be used by the order, in case of a rebel invasion, to protect property, which was mentioned by Bowles to Dr. Wilson.

To gain admittance for Wilson and Greene into the Chicago conclave, Bowles reported them on his staff.

Stidger testifies that the contingency on which Bowles placed the revolution, and his willingness that it should take place, was the co-operation of the rebels. Communication with rebels was spoken of at Chicago.

Wilson says: "I think Dr. Bowles said messengers were sent to the rebels. * * * I think they were sent into Kentucky and Missouri; * * I inferred it was to be with Price and Buckner, because they were to be co-operating forces in case of an uprising.

* * * The forces of Southern Indiana were to be rendezvoused at a place some eight or ten miles from New Albany. * * * It was expected they would he under Dr. Bowles."

Wilson further says: "I was furnished with $1,000 by Dr. Bowles for the purchase of arms for those of the order who were understood to be unable to purchase arms themselves. * * I went to Mr. Kent, of New Albany, to see about the purchase of arms."

R. C. Bocking, now in prison, and awaiting his trial—the only witness introduced in behalf of the accused, Wm. A. Bowles—testified, when put upon the stand by the defense, that Bowles "asked me if I would show him and his friends some of the shells and the Greek fire; I told him yes. * * * * Dr. Bowles said he would see some of his friends, and see if something might not be done so that I might get along with the shells." The result was that Bocking received $200 from Bowles, or through his agency.

Gentlemen of the Commission, I have no comments to make upon this testimony. I leave it to you in all its naked force. I have extracted and collated the evidence in reference to this accused, and I present the results of my examination, verbatim, as it appears upon the record. I leave the evidence thus presented, to answer the truly beautiful and sympathetic appeal of his counsel, Mr. Ray. It is with as deep sorrow and heart-felt regret as the counsel himself can feel, that I submit this conclusive record against this white-haired old man. I look upon him and the crimes he has committed, and those he has contemplated against his country, against the generations that are to come after him—and my heart bleeds that designs so foul and unnatural should ever have existed in any human heart. I pity him. I pity him that he was so constituted, or has so corrupted the spirit with which God endowed him, as to be capable of such crimes. I pity him that his immortal soul—that spark of omniscience—should enter upon its new life in the unknown spirit land, loaded with such infamy and degradation; but while I have sympathy and pity for the man, for what he must suffer in case of conviction, I look about me, and over this wide-spread and once beautiful and peaceful land, and I see *patriots* with whitened locks, and millions of defenseless women and little children, with outstretched hands, appealing to Almighty God for protection from the treason that would plot, and the traitors who would destroy—from the rebels who, with fire and sword, would bring desolation upon all our fair land—from the wicked and misguided men who have caused a wail of anguish and bereavement to ascend from almost every hearth—from those who have sent the maimed, the crippled, and the suffering remnants, of once vigorous manhood to sit ever by your firesides, to be met ever upon your streets—and from all who, from weakness or wickedness, have aided and abetted this monstrous conspiracy. I say that while I look with pity upon the man, and upon his unfortunate condition, there is a broader sympathy and a broader duty that would lead me to sympa-

thize with the suffering that he and such as he have caused, and that he and such as he must cause, if permitted to live and move forward in this work of treason, destruction, desolation and death.

LAMBDIN P. MILLIGAN.

It seems to be admitted by the counsel for the accused that Mr. Milligan was a member of the order, and had attended the Grand Council, and, therefore, a third degree member; also, that he received the appointment of major-general. Upon these points there is no difference of opinion.

Samuel F. Day testifies that Milligan was present at the Grand Council here in September, and states that he made some remarks to their lodge after his return. This Grand Council is the one at which the military bill was adopted, and the major-generals elected. Mr. Harrison testifies as to the appointments of the major-generals at that meeting. Harrison thinks Milligan was absent from one of the State Councils, and thinks it that held on the 16th and 17th of February, 1864. After naming delegates elected at the September State Council to the Supreme Council, Harrison says: "Milligan was elected a delegate to the Supreme Council. I understood Dodd that Milligan was present at the Supreme Council held at Chicago or New York. * * The first meeting was held in Chicago in the latter part of the month of September, 1863."

Here, we see in the very opening of the evidence that Mr. Milligan was one of the prime movers, one of the main spirits in this organization as far back as September, 1863. At that time Mr. Milligan was a prominent leader of the radical peace wing of the Democratic party—that part of the Democratic party so frequently charged with affiliation and sympathy with rebels and traitors. For the Court to understand exactly Mr. Milligan's position in the order, his sentiments in joining it, and what would be his position toward the Government, separate and apart from the order, they must understand his position at the beginning of his connection with it.

The evidence of Mr. Milligan's friends, the witnesses he has introduced upon the stand, have been harmonious upon this one fact, that Mr. Milligan was a bitter partisan, a hater of the Administration, and a leader of the ultra peace wing of the Democratic party. He then enters this organization, that harmonizes with his own sentiments, with his peculiar views as to State rights, State sovereignty, the usurpations of the Administration and the different departments of the Government, and the unconstitutionality of the war, and whose members are the bitter opponents of all the measures to aid in efficiently carrying forward that war.

In considering this evidence, gentlemen, we must look into the surroundings of the men, and the circumstances of the country at that time. Did Mr. Milligan, with these political views, and his undoubted ability, enter this order as one likely to hold back from any of the purposes enunciated in the ritual or the obligation, or from any of the schemes advocated by any of the leaders of the order, as shown by the proof? Were not all these sentiments of the order exactly in consonance with the opinions and principles entertained by Mr. Milligan himself? Indeed, the principles of the order are so much like him, that to him might almost be credited their paternity. With the views which he originally held, and the principles of the order, to which he assented, and which, with his intelligence, he could not have failed to understand, with his nerve and daring, is he not exactly the man to have undertaken to put into practical operation the theories which he and they held?

The only question now, in considering the evidence, is to find the degree of guilt of the accused. That they are all guilty is established the moment you prove that they are members of the order; that they have assented to the principles and taken the obligation of the order. The plea of ignorance, of want of knowledge, and want of assent on the part of the counsel for Mr. Milligan, will not suffice in the case of a man of Mr. Milligan's nerve, energy, and intelligence. It is asking this Court to believe an unreasonable thing, to ask them to believe that this man would enter into any organization, ascend to its highest degrees, and be endowed with its highest honors, without studying thoroughly the cardinal principles upon which it was based. An ignorant man might; an intelligent man never would.

Let us briefly glance at the testimony to see what are the facts in regard to Mr. Milligan's co-operation with the leaders of the order, in carrying into execution its purposes. It has been denied that Mr. Milligan ever accepted the position of a major-general in this order, or that there was any proof to show that he had any knowledge that such an appointment had been made. On the cross-examination of Harrison, his attention was particularly called to the presence of Mr. Milligan, at the September meeting, during that part of the session when the military bill was discussed, and he answers, "I can not say positively whether he was."

Elliot Robertson, of Randolph county, testifies that Nathan Brown was a delegate from their lodge to Indianapolis, in September, 1863; on his return he "spoke of the State being divided into four military districts, and that a man by the name of Milligan commanded our district." Mr. Harrison testifies that at the State Council, of November, 1863, Mr. Milligan was present. At this meeting, Mr. Harrison testifies, nothing was said about the object of the military organization, "except that it was necessary to organize in a military capacity to protect the rights of the members against the encroachments of the Administration." Toward the close of the November Council, Dr. Wilson testifies that Dodd said "that he 'would kick down the walls of common decency,' or some such words, 'and talk treason for awhile.'" I would call the attention of the Court to the fact that supposing Mr. Milligan had been elected a major-general of the order, in September, as

testified to by different witnesses, and not contradicted by any, whether he could have come up to the November Council, and taken part in that meeting, where all the interests and purposes of the order were discussed, without being notified of such appointment. Is it reasonable, or rational, to believe that he could? He was elected by the delegates from the district represented; his election must have been known to all those delegates, and would not some one of them have apprised Mr. Milligan of his appointment? He held one of the four highest offices of the order in this State. Mr. Bingham also testifies that Mr. Milligan was present at this November Council.

Thus it is established beyond question, that Milligan was present at this meeting; it is not denied by the defense. I now desire to call the attention of the Court particularly to what treason it was, as sworn to by Wilson, that Dodd talked at this meeting, at which Milligan was present. Wilson says: "He [Dodd] stated if the purposes of this order could not be carried out, as explained by Mr. Wright, there were other plans that could be resorted to. They could very easily, if their organization was completed, take possession of the railroads, cut the telegraph wires, and throw in, at one time, troops enough at the capital to take the State Government, and have things their own way." Here was the scheme for the uprising, the insurrection, laid down to the members of this order, as early as November, 1863—the same scheme, substantially, that was agreed upon in Chicago, to be carried out on the 16th of August, 1864. If Milligan was present at this November meeting, of which there is no doubt, then he *did* know that these were the ultimate treasonable purposes of the order. The plea of want of knowledge will not avail; it is contrary to reason, and directly contradicted by the evidence.

The testimony of Samuel F. Winters, a witness for the accused, is that Mr. Milligan was not present at the State Council of February 16 and 17, 1864, as he brought down, for Mr. Milligan, a packet of resolutions, which were afterward adopted as part of the platform of the order. Mr. Harrison testifies, that at this meeting the annual election of officers took place, and that Mr. Milligan was elected a major-general of the order in his district. Some weeks after, when the new ritual was printed, Harrison, as Grand Secretary, sent to each branch temple notice of the change, and copies of the proceedings of the State Council, and says that the package for Huntington county he directed to Mr. Milligan.

Mr. Milligan was present at the Council of June 14, as Harrison, Stidger, and Ibach testify; and if Mr. Ibach, who is relied upon fully by the counsel in his argument for Mr. Milligan, is correct, in testifying that Mr. Milligan was not present as a delegate from Huntington temple, he must have been there by virtue of his military position; and this idea would seem to be favored by Section 3 of Article 2 of the Constitution of the Grand Council, which says "The members of the

Grand Commander's staff, and all military officers above the rank of colonel, shall be *ex officio* members of this Grand Council, and entitled to the sign and to participation in its deliberations." Thus, gentlemen, by your own witnesses, you have Mr. Milligan present at this council by virtue of being major-general of this order; he is here exercising the functions of his office.

Mr. Harrison, the Grand Secretary of the order, says: "No person, to my knowledge, ever entered the Grand Council, who was not a member." Stidger testifies that Milligan was present when Bowles reported that "he had 900 men in his county, organized, armed, and equipped;" also, that, "in the afternoon, the list of major-generals was called;" "I do not remember that he [Milligan] made any particular response." * * * "The list of major-generals was called in this way, they being *ex officio* delegates to the Supreme Council. Milligan made no objection to going that I heard." Also, that on the 15th, in pursuance of a resolution of Council, Milligan went to Hamilton, with Bowles and Dodd, to welcome Vallandigham. Here were the three high dignitaries of the order going over to Hamilton, to welcome, in the name of the traitors of Indiana, this returning exile. Can it be claimed, with any show of reason, that Dodd went there as Grand Commander, Bowles as Major General, and Milligan only as a private member of the order? Is it not more reasonable to suppose that that Council sent three of the most prominent, influential men, and the highest officers of the order?

Among the leading men of the order summoned by Dodd to attend a consultation on Tuesday, August 2d, in relation to the revolution, Mr. Harrison testifies that Mr. Milligan was included. He says: "Mr. Dodd informed me that he intended sending for Mr. Milligan, for Dr. Bowles, Mr. Humphreys, and Dr. Yeakle. * * I went to Mr. Milligan."

"Q. Did you see him?

"A. I did.

"Q. Did you tell him your message?

"A. I did.

"Q. What did he say?

"A. He said he did not know whether he could be present, but would try to be."

Here was the Grand Commander summoning his military chieftains about him, to have a council of war, to when and how they should put their forces into the field. The object of this meeting or council of war, as stated by Dodd to Stidger, was to set the time, the exact day, on which the revolution should take place, in this State. Stidger states that Dodd showed and read to him, about the 2d of August, letters from two or three gentlemen; that Dodd's "idea was to go ahead on the 15th or 16th of August, and these letters from these men agreed with him. * * He had sent them word, and they did not come."

It becomes a matter of inquiry here, who these letters were probably from. They were certainly from persons to whom Dodd had imparted his scheme. The evidence justifies this conclusion. Now, who in this State did he probably impart that scheme to, either by letter or in person? Certainly not to more than those whom he summoned to consult with him. Those persons he summoned for consultation, were all Major Generals in the order, or had held that position. Those who did not come, knowing the importance of this meeting, as they must have known of Dodd and Bowles' trip to Chicago and the plan agreed on there, undoubtedly wrote to Dodd, either assenting to or dissenting from his going forward with his scheme of revolution. Then the conclusion is inevitable, that Milligan, after he was sent to as one of those parties for consultation, must have either come in person, or have written to Dodd. If he wrote to Dodd, then no doubt he indorsed his scheme; for it is proven that these letters from those who did not come, agreed with him in his proposed uprising on the 16th.

It is not to be presumed by this Court, that Dodd, with all the hair-brained fanaticism that is claimed against him now, by his then co-workers, fast friends and associates, would have dreamed of going ahead with this revolution without the assent of his military chieftains. The prominent members of the order knew who were Major Generals, who were to command them; and if those Major Generals held back, here was mutiny and insurrection in their own camp, that would have defeated the whole scheme of revolution. Had Milligan made any such attempt at holding back, or refused to co-operate with Dodd in this scheme, it could easily have been shown. If it had been made, either by letter or orally, he could have proven it before this Court. The burden of proof is upon him to show that fact, and if he does not show it— and he has failed to do so—it is to be presumed against him, by this Court, that he acted in concert with Dodd, and assented to all his revolutionary schemes.

Now let us see whether Mr. Milligan's action subsequent to this occasion, was consistent with his knowledge of Dodd's plans and schemes. On the 13th of August, before the action of the State Central Committee had reached Mr. Milligan, he addressed a convention of 5,000 men at Fort Wayne. In that speech, as a witness for the Government, W. S. Bush testifies, he made the following statements:

"He referred to the country as desolated by the war and the oppressions of the Administration. He spoke of the freedom of speech allowed, as simply that granted by a Lincoln mob—as a freedom in name rather than in fact." (Page 575.) "He stated that if the war was right the draft was right, and if they considered the war right, and were good citizens, they would not grumble about the draft." "He denied that the war was right, and proceeded to argue that, under the Constitution, the President had no power to coerce a State; and asked if those who entered the army, would look in the future, for their laurels, to such battles as Bull Run, Chicamauga and Red river. He also appealed to them to consider the condition of their wives and children at home, destitute, and dependent on the charity of their neighbors, if they entered the army;

and asked whether they considered it a duty to make such a sacrifice?" (Page 576.)

"He spoke of him (the President) as a tyrant." (Page 577.) "He held that the war itself was disunion, and that the Union itself could not be restored by war." (Page 577.) That the war "had made the Government a despotism.

"He treated the war itself as a dissolution of the Government.

"He spoke of the Government as a confederation of the several States rather than a unity."

I asked the witness what Mr. Milligan stated "as to the right of the Government of the United States to make war upon rebels, or those in rebellion against the General Government?"

He answered: "He denied that right."

Here we have from Mr. Milligan's own lips, a reiteration, to a public assemblage, of the cardinal principles of the order itself. Here we have him trying to educate the masses of the Democratic party up to the disloyal standard of this order. Here we have him advocating and indorsing the principles avowed by the rebels in arms against the Government. The very principles for which they are fighting to-day, he maintained in public speech before our people. The only difference between Mr. Milligan and the most bitter rebel of them all, was that one was using his arms to enforce his principles, the other by his voice and pen attempted to sustain their armies in that cause, weakening the cause of the Government, and adding numbers to the rebel ranks. What could he do more? What would tend more effectually to stir up to insurrection a brave people, than to teach them that their Government was waging an unjust war, an unconstitutional war; that it was forcing them to fight its battles of tyranny and oppression, against a people who were fighting simply for their just rights, for the right of a State to secede in its sovereign capacity; that this Government was forcing them into her armies by legions, and slaughtering them by thousands, and then citing them to the battle-fields where that Government had been defeated: I ask what more effective mode could have been chosen to give aid and sympathy to the enemy, to weaken the cause of the Government, to stir up the hearts of the people to opposition to this tyranny, oppression and outrage, that he had pictured had been perpetrated upon them by their Government?

I say, then, this speech was in entire keeping with the fact that Mr. Milligan must have known of the intentions and plan of Dodd for revolution. He was aiding that scheme as effectually as he possibly could. He was sowing the seeds of bitterness in the hearts of the masses, the harvest of which was to be the garnering of the dead bodies of the peaceful citizens, defenseless women and little children of your land.

We have heard much argumentation, much special pleading, and many elegant periods, from the counsel for the accused, based upon the action of Mr. Bingham and Mr. Kerr in stopping this revolution of their own will before it had culminated. We have some little light upon this question as evidence that is recorded matter made at the time. This is better evidence than the recollection or the oral explanation of these facts by any witness. It is a letter of Mr. Kerr's, directed to Mr. Bingham, and dated August 8, 1864. In that he says: "I am not content with the result of our conference on Friday. It is not decisive enough." Here was a member of that conference, the man who brought about that meeting, and took more interest in it than any other member, was as honest as any one of them, and yet he states that the meeting was not decisive. He goes on, and says further: "it is enveloped in too much uncertainty." If this whole scheme of revolution had been abandoned by Dodd, and they had all resolved that nothing more was to be done in the matter, as the gentlemen argue and claim, why and wherefore was it enveloped in uncertainty? Further on he says: "There was apparent, on the part of certain *bad* and *reckless* men, too deep a determination to persist in their unlawful and revolutionary purposes." Here is a letter written soon after this meeting, by Mr. Kerr, an honest and upright man, as is admitted by all, to another member of that meeting, in which he not only denies that the scheme had been abandoned and stopped, but affirmatively says, that there has been apparent, on the part of certain bad and reckless men, too deep a determination to persist in their unlawful and revolutionary purposes. Gentlemen, how do you explain this record made at the time?

Then he goes on with this statement: "That they should have been required to come to a more definite and satisfactory abandonment of all such purposes." They should have done what they did not do, Mr. Kerr says. The testimony of Mr. Bingham, the testimony of all the witnesses upon this case, must be explained with this light of Mr. Kerr's letter thrown upon it. Listen a little further to Mr. Kerr: "Ought we not to take further action before the early day to which we adjourned? * * * It *must* not be." What was this that must not be? Let the Court think for a moment, and answer the question. He adds: "It *must* be circumvented, and that speedily, and by us." What was this that must be circumvented speedily, and by us? Here is this letter dated the 8th of August, after this meeting had taken place, at which this witness undertook to say this whole scheme was stopped; urging Bingham to his utmost vigor to unite with him and all good men, in stopping what these gentlemen claim was stopped on the 4th of August, by Mr. Kerr. This is a singular position for Mr. Kerr, that he was appealing by the strongest exhortations, which words could utter, to the brother members of his party, and to his old friend, Mr. Bingham, to join him, and to assist by every means in their power to circumvent these bad men, and to stop this scheme—making these appeals on the 8th to stop, as I before remarked, what he, Mr. Kerr, had stopped on the 4th! Is this true?

The entire proof made during this trial goes to show that the scheme of revolution never was entirely abandoned. On or about the 12th of August, at the identical meeting referred to by Kerr in his letter as necessary to be held, some of the leading loyal Democrats of the State did get promises from Dodd and Walker to abandon their scheme. But that abandonment was simply of the time set for the insurrection; and those men moved forward just as earnestly and vigorously in their organization and purposes, afterward as before. The first lot of Dodd's arms, which Walker had purchased, ten boxes, were brought here and concealed, ready for use, about the 6th of August, two days after this first meeting, when this whole revolution was abandoned, as the defense claims. The next lot came on the 20th of August, two weeks afterward; and yet we are told this whole scheme was abandoned, and nothing was done in pursuance of it. Gentlemen, the proof is against you.

This conspiracy and revolution failed, simply because the hand of the Government was at its throat, and the strong military arm of the Government had fallen upon it; its mailed hand had grappled it, and its giant-like grip was all the more determined in that its dragon-like foe was both subtle and strong.

To rebut the testimony of Mr. Bush in reference to this speech of Mr. Milligan at Fort Wayne, the accused put upon the stand Mr. Winters, the editor of the Huntington *Democrat*, who started out with the assertion, in reply to a question of the accused: "I don't know what you mean by the word loyal." It did seem to me that this was the only unqualified, truthful utterance that the witness gave during his whole testimony. He admitted that in Mr. Milligan's speech, at Fort Wayne, he "denied the power to coerce States, but admitted the power to coerce individual citizens." In his cross-examination he states that Mr. Milligan "has always maintained that a war against sovereign States was an absurdity. * * I have heard him say that the war was unconstitutional, and he was against it;" that he was opposed to the prosecution of the present war; and that "he said at the Fort Wayne meeting that the existing war was an absurdity."

This witness subscribed fully to the obligation of the first degree of the Order of American Knights. I read to him various extracts from Mr. Bush's report of that speech, as published in the Cincinnati *Gazette*, of August 16th, and asked if they were correct. One of the extracts was as follows:

"They (the States) were thirteen nations, and finally formed a Constitution, adopted separately by the several States, Virginia reserving to herself the right at any time to withdraw from the Union. And what Virginia has reserved, all the States had a right to reserve. Their action was based entirely on State rights. The Declaration of Independence states who is to be the judge when the Government shall be subverted. It guarantees to the people the right of revolution when they can no longer tolerate the invasion of their rights. I do not mean that Governor Morton, or the Legislature, or any machinery of office, getting its authority from the people through elections, is the State. But I mean that the free range of all its people is the State. The officers are the mere servants of the people, the mere agents of the Government. Where does sovereignty rest? It is time to settle this question. If you are wrong in your theories, you should change your principles. I know no sovereignty in the Federal Government, or in the State Government, as contra-distinguished from the people of the State. I believe in the doctrine of popular sovereignty, instead of sovereignty in the machinery of the Government."

I then asked the witness, is that a correct statement of what Mr. Milligan said on that point. Mr. Winters answered, "I don't recollect whether those are the exact words: I think that is the substance of what he said on that subject." I read other paragraphs to him, and the whole effect of his testimony was to corroborate Mr. Bush's statement, and to certify to the correctness of his report. He says in answer to one question: "The deduction made from his speech," referring to Mr. Milligan's speech at Fort Wayne, "was that the war was unconstitutional."

Mr. Bird, one of Mr. Milligan's witnesses, and a Son of Liberty, in his cross-examination, admitted that Mr. Milligan in that speech said the war was wrong. Bird's testimony as to that meeting, and what was said there by Mr. Milligan, entirely corroborates the testimony of Mr. Bush. At the time of this speech of Mr. Milligan's at Fort Wayne, the order was still in existence, as is proven by Mr. Harrison, who performed his official duties as Grand Secretary, up to August 20th, 1864, the day Mr. Dodd was still receiving arms for distribution to the members of this order, and the day of Mr. Harrison's arrest. So that this order was in full and vigorous operation up to the day when the Government laid her hands upon it. In fact, it was in full operation up to the session of the Chicago Convention, as proved by Mr. Wilson; up to the time of Dodd's arrest, September 3d, and the arrest of Bowles, September 18th, as testified by Mr. Heffren. Heffren says: "About the time of Dodd's arrest, I wrote a letter to each of the major-generals of the order. * * * Dr. Wilson had come to me and said.....that as I was Deputy Grand Commander, and Dodd was arrested, I must write to Mr. Vallandigham and each of the major-generals. I did not want to do so, but he insisted, and I wrote to Mr. Humphreys, Mr. Milligan, John C. Walker and Mr. Vallandigham. I wrote to Dr. Bowles, but as I understood he was arrested for harboring deserters, I did not send the letter."

"Q. How did you write to Vallandigham?

"A. As Supreme Commander of the Supreme Council of the United States. The substance of the letter was, should we submit or fight?

"Q. Whom did you mean by 'we?'

"A. I meant the members of the Order of American Knights."

This action on the part of Wilson, and Heffren, the Deputy Grand Commander of the order, was sometime after the 3d of September, and shows that the order was in full force at that date.

"Q. Did these gentlemen write back?

"A. None but Mr. Milligan and Mr. Humphreys. Mr. Milligan's letter was signed by some gentleman as his student, as he was sick, and stated that it would not do at the present time, but that we must bide our time." This letter, written by Mr. Milligan's authority—for of course no one would open a letter written to Mr. Milligan, but himself, and whoever answered it must have done so by his instructions—shows that it was not insurrection itself that he was opposed to, but that the time was not propitious. Mr. Milligan was a prominent member of the order, and one of its leaders. The question of his nomination for Governor had been discussed in the February Council, as shown by Mr. Heffren's testimony; it is also shown in the letter of Mr. Milligan to H. H. Dodd, dated May 9th, 1864, in which he declines the nomination of Governor at the hands of McDonald's friends, "because," he says, "I could not represent them; there is no similarity between us. And all this is not so discouraging as the fact that men of the stamp of Judge Hanna, whose profession of principles I could represent, prefer McDonald on account of his supposed availability. It detracts much from my confidence in our ultimate success, when men of so much seeming patriotism, are willing for mere temporary purposes to abandon the great principles of civil liberty. What will those of less pretensions do, when the real contest comes; when life and property all depend on the issue; when bullets instead of ballots are cast, and when the *halter* is a preamble to our platform? For, unless Federal encroachments are arrested in the States by the efforts, as well of the Legislative as the Executive, then will our *lives* and *fortunes* follow where our honors will have gone before." It is an easy matter to get at the motives that actuated Mr. Milligan in his connection with this order, from this piece of record which he has left behind him. The lame manner in which his counsel has undertaken to explain this letter, is simply amusing.

When we recollect that the contest to which Mr. Milligan constantly looked forward, was the contest between the disaffected few of these free States—that class of people whom he represented, malcontents, who believe that the Government is usurping powers, and must be expelled by force—and the Government. Entertaining these principles, he says in his letter, "when the real contest comes; when life and property all depend upon the issue; when bullets instead of ballots are cast, and when the *halter* is a preamble to our platform." For an explanation of what he means by this, he continues: "For unless Federal encroachments"—this was the power with which the contest was to be waged—"are resisted in the States, by the efforts as well of the Legislative as of the Executive, then will our *lives* and *fortunes* follow where our honors

will have gone before." The real meaning and intent of this letter, and the purpose of this man in writing it, was this: every effort was being made by his party to get the machinery of the State Government into their own hands, to obtain control of the Legislature, and to have one of themselves elected Governor; then, with their theories of Government, of State sovereignty, and of State rights, they could plant the State of Indiana against the Federal Government, and make Indiana a second South Carolina, to lead the van in establishing a North-western Confederacy! It was but again laying down an abominable plot of rebellion to be consummated in these Northern States, as it has been in the Southern; to blacken and desolate this beautiful land of ours, as it has blackened theirs; to send up from every hearth the wail of desolation and death that must follow in the wake of this phantom of secession!

To prove his loyalty, Mr. Milligan introduced a number of witnesses, most of whom were fellow-members of the conspiracy. Some of them, by their own showing, were disloyal. John Roach, one of his witnesses, in speaking of Mr. Milligan, said: "I heard him make some remarks, in which he held that some of the officers of the Government were exceeding the authority of law; he complained that they were not acting according to law;" in other words, he was repeating the principles of the Order of Sons of Liberty. Another witness, that Mr. Milligan put upon the stand to support his character for loyalty, etc., M. B. Brant, testified as follows: "Republicans regarded him as connected with a secret organization that is in favor of further secession among the States—a North-western Confederacy." The witness gives one reason why they regarded him as disloyal, in these words: "Mr. Milligan made speeches a year ago last fall, and some persons in the Republican party began to regard him as a man who was opposed to the Government, and was willing and anxious that there should be a North-western Confederacy, and that he was in favor of it."

Thus we see that Mr. Milligan's treason had not confined itself solely to his expressions and actions in connection with the order, but that he was at his work of educating the masses of the Democratic party, and the people of the land, up to his disloyal standard.

Witnesses were also introduced by Mr. Milligan to impeach the reputation for truth and veracity of Dr. Zumro, a witness for the Government. The doubtful loyalty of these men, who themselves indorsed the good character of Mr. Zumro, when they joined the order with him, and the strength of the rebutting testimony of the witnesses in favor of the character of Dr. Zumro for truth and veracity: not only of those of his own political faith, but those opposed to him, and of members of the order, substantiate his truthfulness, and leave his testimony entitled to full credit. Dr. Zumro testifies that he was appointed one of a committee from the temple of the order in his township, to visit Mr. Milligan, in Huntington, and learn what the order proposed to do about resisting the draft. He says: "I asked Mr. Milligan his opinion as to whether we had better resist or not; he said it was as good a time now as any to resist." "He concluded that we should form in companies or squads, just as we could; that ten men were sufficient to start with."

This is the evidence, substantially, in reference to Mr. Milligan, for and against him. It all shows that he was really the right arm of this conspiracy in this State; the active, energetic, and venomous leader. A man of unquestioned ability and determination, and with a heart full of hatred, envy, and malice, he moved forward in this scheme of revolution with a coolness and intensity of purpose, not exceeded by any .other member of the conspiracy. His intelligence and ability gave him a powerful influence for evil, and he used that power to the utmost. I can offer no better comment on the testimony bearing on the case of Mr. Milligan, than by quoting the eloquent words of my friend, Mr. Ray. He says: "It is another and a wicked thing to go bawling about the country, and in flaming speech, and mock patriotism, arraigning the authorities as usurpers, tyrants and despots; poisoning the public heart against those in authority—clamoring for peace in the face of embattled armies—fanning the embers of discord and revolt—kindling, by incendiary appeals, the fires of insurrection and revolution, and finally identifying himself with the cause of rebels and traitors, and lending himself in thought and deed, by night and by day, in secret and in public, giving aid and comfort to the public enemy against his own Government—*this is conspiracy* and treason—it has all the disloyal lineaments of treasonable deformity, and neither eloquence nor art, nor painting, nor poetry, can change it—its office is discord, war, and misery."

The counsel must have had Mr. Milligan in his mind's eye when penning that eloquent description of a conspirator and a traitor.

ANDREW HUMPHREYS.

We come now to the consideration of the evidence in its bearing upon the accused, Andrew Humphreys. It has been conclusively shown that Mr. Humphreys belonged to this conspiracy: that he was, at least, a third degree member, and attended, beyond question, the State Council of the 14th of June last, in the evening. There is no evidence introduced inconsistent with this, and all the evidence introduced by the defense corroborates the Government witnesses, in stating that he was here in the evening of the 14th of June. If the order in his township had been abandoned and the papers destroyed in February or March previously, as Mr. Humphreys has attempted to show, then he must have attended this Grand Council in June, by virtue of his military rank. If the order in his township had been abandoned, he did not come up as a delegate from that temple. This circumstance goes strongly to support the theory that he did accept and hold the position nominally of a major-general in this order. The evidence against Mr. Humphreys, we will briefly review.

19

When Mr. Humphreys became a member of the order, is not definitely proven. A branch temple was organized in Linton, in September, 1863, as W. G. Moss, a witness for the accused, testifies. Mr. Moss and Mr. Heffren, who testify that Mr. Humphreys told them that he had abandoned the order, both establish his membership up to at least February 10th, 1864. His membership, on the 10th of September, is proven by the witness, William M. Harrison, who testifies that the State Council of September 10th, 1863, elected "Andrew Humphreys a major-general under that (the military) bill." Subsequently the witness says: "My understanding of the matter was that appointments were made among members of the order only." He also names the delegates to the Council in Chicago, in September, 1863, and says: "At the meeting in September, John G. Davis and D. R. Eckels were elected delegates to the Council in Chicago, in September, 1863; and, I think, Humphreys also." He adds: "I understood also that Humphreys was present at that meeting, and Yeakle and Dr. Bowles. I got this information from Dodd." Mr. Humphreys was re-elected a major-general at the February Council, while Major Conklin and Dr. Yeakle were superseded in their districts by Dr. Bowles and John C. Walker. He was recognized by the officers of the State Council as retaining his membership, a package of the proceedings of the February Council being addressed to him for the benefit of the order in Green county, some weeks after the session of that Council. The testimony of Stidger and of Harrison is positive as to the presence of Humphreys at the Council of June 14th. Harrison states that Mr. Humphreys was present. In the cross-examination he says: "He came into the meeting in the evening. I saw him in the room, not to exceed one-half or three-quarters of an hour, at that meeting. * * I saw him at the meeting before it adjourned." When asked whether he knew that Mr. Humphreys was a member of the order at all, he answered, "I know it simply from the fact that I saw him at this meeting on the 14th of June. * * I recollect of no person coming in who was not a delegate, and had not become a member * * No person, to my knowledge, entered the Grand Council who was not a member."

Stidger testifies that Mr. Humphreys was present; that "Mr. Dodd told me it was Andrew Humphreys; that Mr. Dodd called over the list of major-generals, on which was the name of Andrew Humphreys, at that session."

To rebut this testimony, Mr. Moss testifies that Mr. Humphreys could not have been present. He states that he carefully examined the account-books to determine that point. When asked, on cross-examination, whether Humphreys came to Indianapolis about that time, he answered: "I am not certain of it. But I think he might have been here." I again asked, "Was he not here in the evening?" He answered: "I can not say; I have tried to find that out by looking at our books."

In the re-examination, the witness strengthens the evidence for the Government. He says:

"The last entry in Humphreys' handwriting, was on the 13th of June, about the last charge entered on the book that day."

"Q. At what time would a man probably arrive here, who left Linton after the time when the last entry must have been made by Humphreys?

"A. It would probably have been 6 or 7 o'clock in the evening * * of June 14th."

His membership in the order, just before the time of the June Council, is confirmed by another portion of Stidger's testimony, in reference to an interview with Bowles, on the 28th of May:

Bowles told me "to say to him [Bullitt] that he had seen Mr. Andrew Humphreys since their meeting at Indianapolis, and Mr. Humphreys had agreed to take the position of a Brigadier, and take charge of the forces in the rear in case of an uprising of the order."

Stidger took that message to Bullitt, and he replied, "It suited him exactly that Humphreys was willing to take that position."

On the 2d of August, when the heads of the order were summoned here by Dodd, to settle the time for the revolution, Mr. Humphreys was sent for. Harrison testifies that "Mr. Dodd informed me that he intended sending for Mr. Milligan, for Dr. Bowles, Mr. Humphreys, and Dr. Yeakle." He was still in the confidence of the leading and active men in the order, in September, 1864, the Deputy Grand Commander, Horace Heffren, addressing an official letter to him, at that time, as a major-general of the order, to know whether the order should submit to Dodd's arrest or fight. He answers against fighting, and in favor of obedience to law, and takes occasion, then, to repudiate his nomination as major-general. This was at a time when the Chiefs of the order were under arrest, and their co-conspirators, all over the State, were trembling with apprehensions of arrest. The repudiation comes too late at that day, and with an ill grace.

In regard to particular acts of disloyalty, the Government has proven, by a witness, whom the accused did not attempt to impeach, Elisha Cowgill, that on the 4th of June, 1863, Mr. Humphreys was, in "Sullivan county, at the head of an army of about 400 men." He says:

"Humphreys talked about a great many things; about the President of the United States, and abused him to the whole crowd. He called him an old tyrant, who was usurping a great deal of power, and wasting the treasure of the United States, and the lives of its citizens."

The spirit of that armed mob, which was following a detachment of United States soldiers, who had impressed a horse for the use of a sick soldier, as though they were enemies of their country, was also shown in their treatment of the officials of the Government. Mr. Cowgill, who was a Deputy United States Marshal, says: "Some said they ought to kill me before I got out of the crowd. Numbers of them swore that they would kill any man who should attempt to enroll Cass township."

He also testifies that Mr. Humphreys made a second speech, "and advised them to go home and mind their own business. * * He also told them, 'Don't sleep too soundly.'"

A few days after the enrolling officer of that township, after partly enrolling the township, was murdered in cold blood, and such was the intensity of the disloyalty of that neighborhood, or the strength of its secret organizations, that a judicial investigation failed to develop the name of the murderer or murderers. This was the state of society in which the Order of American Knights was organized, in 1863, under the auspices and with the co-operation of the accused, Andrew Humphreys.

How he prepared for the extension of that order is shown by the testimony of Nicholas Cochrane, another witness for the Government. He states that he heard Mr. Humphreys speak, about the 5th of September, 1863, in Jackson township. "He criticised the Administration tolerably strongly, * * and he seemed to think that the Democratic party was imposed upon, and ought to stand up for their rights. * * The time had come when Democrats should not appropriate their money, or be willing to spend their means in levity, but should be preparing for self-defense."

At the same meeting a rebel, from Georgia, spoke, advising the audience "to resist the present Abolition Administration at the sacrifice of their lives, their families, and themselves, if necessary."

Cheers were given for the rebel and for Mr. Humphreys.

Mr. Humphreys called two witnesses, as to character for obedience to law. Wm. Wines testified to Humphreys having spoken in favor of the enforcement of the draft, and to his general reputation for loyalty. On cross-examination, he testified:

"Some of my friends down there, of my principles, call him a 'Butternut,' a 'Copperhead,' and a 'traitor,' speaking of him politically."

William Johnson, sr., proved an unfortunate witness as to character. He testifies, that Mr. Humphreys' reputation as a law-abiding citizen "with that party he goes with, is good."

In speaking of a speech, made by Mr. Humphreys, at Linton, in August, this witness states: "He spoke on the right of secession; on the right of a State to secede."

In the cross-examination, I asked:

"In the speech which you heard Mr. Humphreys make, did he argue in favor of the right of a State to secede?

"A. I so understood it.

"Q. Did he say that secession was right?

"A. Yes, sir."

To learn his real *status* with the loyal men of Green county, I asked the witness to state "what his character for loyalty is among the men of unquestioned loyalty in the county where he lives."

He answered: "It is not considered loyal."

In the re-examination, the accused asked:

"Whom do you consider loyal?

"A. The men in favor of the prosecution of the war; I don't understand that any one else is loyal."

From all the evidence in reference to Andrew

Humphreys, I am inclined to believe that he did not, like Dr. Bowles and Mr. Milligan, join this order for the purpose of using it, or assisting in it, to bring about a revolution and insurrection in these Northern States, but, like Mr. Bingham, more, perhaps, for political and personal ends. He used the order to place himself in some political position—to keep on the surface of the wave, that he might, in the ebb and flow of the tide, be placed upon some secure rock of public favor. But while admitting this, we must insist that while his motives might have been less criminal than others in joining it, yet he did take upon himself the responsibility of joining an unlawful, secret organization, treasonable in its intents and purposes, and that having taken upon himself this responsibility, having assisted in placing the Government in great danger of being destroyed by this great combination of treasonable elements, he should be held to a strict accountability for that act. The absence of the *highest* treasonable intent can only be considered in mitigation of the sentence. That he was a conspirator, this Commission must find, if the evidence shows that he belonged to this organization, and if a conspirator, then he is guilty under four of the charges set cut against him. Personal considerations must not weigh with this Court in making up their findings and sentence.

While we have human sympathy, we must rise above human frailty. There must be infused into the hearts of all of this Court a little spark of Divine justice. While weighing in the balance the life of one man, his honor, and his liberty—all of which, I grant you, is as dear to him as yours is to you—we must remember that in the other scale is placed the life, liberty, and well-being of the millions of this nation, and the perpetuity of those institutions that are to give to untold millions yet to come a Government that will secure to its people the highest privileges that citizens can claim, the maintainance of their inalienable rights, and the protection of their lives and liberties.

STEPHEN HORSEY.

We come last to the accused, Stephen Horsey. To the address submitted by him, and drawn up by Mr. Gordon, I have simply to say, that no man is so poor, or so humble, that he can not be a traitor; and no man is so poor and humble but that he may be rich in all the glorious attributes of patriotism, loyalty, and fealty to his Government. If a man becomes so poor, so low, so degraded, as to be a conspirator and traitor, let justice be meted out to him; for *this* is poverty that becomes a crime.

My friend, Mr. Gordon, in drawing up this argument, fell into an error, I fully believe unintentionally, when he asserts that there is no proof that Horsey was ever a member of the Order of American Knights, or Sons of Liberty. The testimony in reference to Stephen Horsey, is briefly as follows:

Wesley Tranter, a witness for the Government, testified that he joined the Circle of Honor, in May, 1863, at the solicitation of Stephen Horsey, and was initiated by Horsey. Horsey presided at a second meeting. In January, 1864, the Circle of Honor was changed to the Knights of the Golden Circle, as Tranter understood, but which Harrison Connell says: "I think they called it the American Knights."

At a meeting held January 27th or 28th, 1864, Stephen Horsey was present. Tranter states: "After we were in, Horsey made a little speech, and said we were to have something different from the other. * * The oath differed from the former oath, but I can not recollect it; there was something about supporting Jeff Davis, North or South. In a speech that John W. Stone made, there was something said about putting Governor Morton out of the way."

It was also stated that, "There was to be a raid made on this place (Indianapolis) about five days from the 1st of April. * * We were to arm ourselves and be ready. We were to take this place, and wear out the soldiers." "When we made the raid on this place, the members of the order in Illinois were to make a raid on Springfield, and those in Missouri on St. Louis. Washington was to be attacked, and Forrest was to make a dash into Kentucky."

The question of arms was discussed, and Horsey spoke of Shirkliff and Coffin having taken off a box of pistols five miles from the Shoals. Horsey "said there would be pistols taken round the country, and any one could have them at cost and carriage."

Stephen Teney, another witness for the Government, testifies that he joined the Circle of Honor at Horsey's solicitation, in the fall of 1863. Teney states: "From what I saw and learned, we were to assist the South if called on."

He says: "We drilled a few times in the township. I was told by one of my brothers, who was a member of the order, that they were getting arms all the time. * * * That they had three hundred pistols in that county."

"Some four or five months since," Teney says, "he (Horsey) told me they were getting along finely with their order."

On cross-examination, Mr. Teney was asked: "Q. Who said you were to support the South?

"A. Mr. Horsey.

"Q. What was his language?

"A. He swore us to support Jeff Davis, North or South.'

The testimony of Tranter and Teney was corroborated by Harrison Connell, who was present at the Gaddis House, where this secret order met, when Stone spoke. On cross-examination he was asked: "Whether or not, on that occasion, those that entered the order, were sworn into the service of Jeff Davis?"

"A. I think the man who initiated the men that night, made a speech to that effect. * * I think he said they might consider themselves sworn into Jeff Davis' army, and the men were very much dissatisfied with his speech."

The accused, Stephen Horsey, is identified as one of the delegates to the State Council of June 14th. Mr. Harrison testifies: "A gentleman by the name of Stephen Horsey was present, but I do not know whether he (the accused) is the man or not; I do not recognize him; at all events he was a delegate from Martin county." Stidger identifies the accused, Stephen Horsey, as present at the June Council, and states that when the case of Coffin was discussed, "they asked him (Horsey) why he was so careless as to initiate such men as Coffin into the order?"

Harrison Connell testifies that in the latter part of July or in August, 1864, "Mr. Horsey told me to meet him about a mile and a half from the Shoals, a certain evening, and we went a piece down the railroad, and we found some ammunition lying at the root of a tree; we put it in a sack and I carried it home." The ammunition consisted of "a keg of powder, a package of lead, and a package of caps." Mr. Connell says that we went with Horsey "according to promise * * made the evening before." That he asked Horsey about the ammunition "when we went back to the railroad. He told me there was some ammunition there he wanted me to take care of." Connell took care of it, by concealing it in his barn.

Mr. Heffren testifies that while confined in prison with Mr. Horsey, the latter admitted that he had ammunition concealed, and stated "where he hid his buckshot, caps and powder; some of it was hid in a manger, to feed horses, and in a barrel the caps were hid, and the horses eat from the top of the manger; and other portions were hid in a stable, and upon the plates in the corn-crib. Shirkliff carried off much of it, and the powder was hid in barrels in his house.

"There were four hundred pounds of lead, and several thousand musket caps; I think some six or seven kegs of powder."

Horsey also "told where the money came from that they got it with. * * From Dr. Bowles."

I desire to call the attention of the Court for a moment to the kind of evidence submitted on behalf of the Government in these cases. Much has been said by the counsel for the accused, in the attempt to bring into disrepute the witnesses for the Government, styling them generally as spies, detectives, and informers. Out of the twenty-eight witnesses introduced by the Government, there were just two who were, as the counsel styles them, spies or detectives. These were Stidger and Zumro. All the other witnesses stood in exactly the same relation to the case as the witnesses introduced by the defense, some of them being members of the order, some had been arrested and released. Why they should be followed by such malignity, hatred, and abuse, I can not conceive. It is not pretended that they swore falsely, or from malice, or hope of reward. They told simply what they were compelled to tell—the truth, and the whole truth, and this, perhaps, is why they hate them.

In using the word "informers," it would seem, the counsel have overlooked the meaning of the term. Burrill's *Law Dictionary* defines an "informer" as "one who informs against another for the violation of some penal statute; one who gives information upon which another may prosecute for the violation of some penal statute." These men who have been called by the Government, gave no information upon which the accused were prosecuted, and only when the cases came up for trial, did they testify, as they were forced to do. And even had they been informers, within the meaning of the law, will the gentlemen show me what crime it is for a man to so love his country, and so earnestly desire its peace and security as to endeavor to bring to justice criminals who were seeking the lives of their fellow men, and the destruction of their Government? Rather would not the counsel have stood in a more enviable light had they stood by and encouraged, by giving the just meed of praise to those who have had the courage and manliness to stand by their Government, and who have done their part in bringing to just punishment those who have sought to destroy it. Think for a moment of the position in which the Government was placed, and consider the difficulties and almost insurmountable obstacles to be overcome in getting at the secrets of this organization, bound together, as this was, by the most solemn and binding of oaths, or get witnesses to publish the secrets of this organization, when they who did so, periled their lives in the act. By what means, gentlemen, could we have developed these facts in a better manner than we have? We have given you the evidence of men who went into the organization for the purpose of revealing their designs; we have added to them those who were among you and of you, and thus out of your own mouths we have made the proof against you.

Finally, may it please the Court, it is for you to consider whether the evidence supports the charges and specifications. That is a matter about which I can give you no opinion. I can only say that if it is proven to your satisfaction that the accused, all of them, or one of them, did join this treasonable Order of American Knights or Sons of Liberty, did assent to the principles of the first degree—and all third degree members must have so assented—and the obligation of that first degree, they are, in contemplation of law, conspirators *per se;* if conspirators *per se*, then, guilty of the first charge, and the first three specifications. The fourth specification under that charge, simply sets out the means by which this order proposed to carry out these unlawful designs.

Charge second, affording aid and comfort to the rebels against the authority of the United States, will be supported if it has been proven that these parties joined themselves to a secret, unlawful organization, whose general principles and purposes were adverse to the Government, and in sympathy and general co-operation with the purposes and principles of the rebel insurgents. The three specifications under that charge simply set out the means, or manner, by which this aid and comfort to rebels was to be given; whether the proof supports these specifications, is alone for you to determine.

Charge third, inciting insurrection, and the two specifications under it, will be supported, if it has been proven to you that by public addresses, by organizing certain societies, and disseminating certain doctrines, the tendencies of which were to embitter and arouse the people to open hostility to the Government. If these parties, or any members of this conspiracy to which they joined themselves, while carrying out the general purposes of the conspiracy, did do any acts, disseminate any sentiments, make incendiary speeches, attempt to arm, or do any thing the tendency of which was to create open revolt, or an effort on the part of the people, by unlawful means, to change their Government, and set aside by force any parts of the Government, then charge third and its specifications are supported.

Charge fourth, disloyal practices, and the five specifications under it, set out substantially, that these accused did join themselves to a secret, unlawful society or order, known as the Order of American Knights, and did, through, and by means of this unlawful combination or order, disseminate principles adverse to the Government of the United States, and did counsel and advise citizens of the United States to disregard the authority of the United States, to resist a call, or draft, designed to increase her armies, and did arm certain citizens of the United States with the intent of resisting said Government; and did attempt to arm, and did arm certain members of this unlawful order, for the purpose of carrying out these unlawful designs; and that these parties did accept and hold offices in the military forces, for the State of Indiana, in this unlawful, secret society, or order; that said offices and military officers were unknown to the Constitution and Laws of the United States. Whether the proof has so connected the accused with this order, with its treasonable purposes and designs, or not, with its efforts to break down and unlawfully set aside the Government, is for you to determine.

Charge fifth, violation of the laws of war, and its two specifications, charge simply that the accused, while pretending to be loyal, peaceable citizens of the United States, did attempt to introduce enemies of the United States into the loyal States, and did thereby violate their allegiance as citizens of said Government; that they did attempt to do this through a certain secret, unlawful combination, or order. Whether the proof supporting these allegations has been made, is a matter for you to determine.

Then, gentlemen of the Commission, in conclusion, permit me to say, that you have, in your hands, the keeping of the dearest rights; in fact, all the rights and privileges of these four men, the accused—that their rights are as sacred and dear to them as are yours to you; that they are possessed of the same attachment to life, its hopes, its fears, its affections, its aspirations, as yourselves; I charge you, therefore, if, in any particular, the evidence has failed to support these charges, or failed to convict these men of these high crimes— the highest crimes known to the law—be proud to acquit them; send them forth to the world, into the broad light of day, free from guilt, untarnished with even the stain of reproach;

let your verdict be not only an acquittal, if these charges are unsustained, but let your action go further, and be a triumphant vindication of their characters.

On the other hand, if the proof does sustain these charges, if these men are guilty, do your duty. Display the manhood and the bravery that I know you all possess; hold down the natural affections and pity of your natures for the men whom you try, and remember only your high duty to your country—to the generations that shall live after you. Remember that each day this war is waged in this country, not four lives, not four hundred, but thousands of patriots must perish, to each one of whose names there is clinging a glorious history; a history of toil, of self-sacrifice, of endurance, of patience and long suffering, of unselfish courage and devotion to their country; think that each day these struggles are prolonged must go down hundreds of these brave men. If you make an example of these men who are prolonging these struggles, you are shortening this desolating contest, and saving the lives of true men. The sacrifice of bad men, of conspirators and traitors, those men that sustain the armed rebellion, that give its cause strength, active sympathy, and encouragement—their sacrifice, I say, saves the good, the true, and the noble of the nation. It is not mercy in you to sit here and acquit the guilty. It is cruelty to the scarred veterans, to the long-suffering patriots, who are fighting your battles. It is cruelty to their lonely wives, who sit with aching hearts and with throbbing pulse, clasping their little ones to their hearts, not knowing what moment the knock at their door shall be the death-knell at their hearts. Your sympathy for traitors and treason makes orphans, makes misery in this land every-where. It makes desolate, and lonely, and sad, the pure, the good, and the true. Therefore, remember that justice in your place is mercy. Nerve your hearts to do fearlessly your duty, let that duty come in what shape it may: sink the frailties of the man, and rise up, grasping a few of the attributes of Omniscience.

Remember, I charge you, that every fiber of this nation is quivering, is strained to its utmost tension, to secure for her people, and for the generations to come, those rights which will give to her people the highest development which mankind can achieve. Remember that while the Revolution gave your nation birth, that from that bloody struggle was achieved national existence, through this second bloody struggle, through this second baptism of fire and sword, she is to achieve immortality. Failing in this struggle, her light goes out in darkness, and with it the hopes, the aspirations, the rights of thirty millions of people. Remember, in this great hour, so to do your duty, that when the Commander-in-Chief of the Universe shall sound the last great reveille, and call from their last, long sleep the unnumbered hosts of the earth, you can point to this day's work as having been well done.

Gentlemen, I have done.

EXPLANATION

INITIAL LETTERS USED IN THE RITUALS.

O. A. K.

K. L.—Knight Lecturer.
W. O. C.—Warden of the Outer Court.
K. C.—Knight Conductor.
N.—Neophite.
A. B.—Ancient Brother.
K. G. N.—Knight Guardian North.
K. G. S.—Knight Guardian South.
G. S.—Grand Seignior.
The above belongs to the First Degree of the Order of American Knights.

E. K. C. W.—Excellent Knight Commander West.

E. K.—Excellent Knight.
E. K. G. C.—Excellent Knight Grand Commander.
O. A. K.—Order of American Knights.
The above belongs to the Second Degree of the Order of American Knights.

M. E. K.—Most Excellent Knight.
M. E. D. O. A. K.—Most Excellent Degree of the O. A. K.
M. E. G. C.—Most Excellent Grand Commander.

O. S. L.

VESTIBULE, OR SON OF LIBERTY LESSON.

V.—Vestibule.
W. O. C.—Warden Outer Court.
L. V.—Lecturer of the Vestibule.
O. C.—Outer Court.
T.—Temple.

FIRST DEGREE.

O. S. L.—Order of the Sons of Liberty.
C. T.—Conductor of the Temple.
W.—Warden.
A. B.—Ancient Brother, (second officer of First Degree).
A. S. L.—A Son of Liberty.
O.—Order.
F. G. N.—Fellow Guardian North.
F. G. S.—Fellow Guardian South.
G. S.—Grand Seignior, (first officer of First Degree).
F. O. S. L.—Fellow in the Order of the Sons of Liberty.

SECOND DEGREE, OR FIRST CONCLAVE DEGREE.

K. O. S. L.—Knight Order Sons of Liberty.
K. C.—Knight Conductor.
K. C. W.—Knight Commander West, (second officer).
I. T.—Inner Temple.
C. C.—Commander Conclave.
T. D.—Temple Degree.
G. C.—Grand Council.
S. C.—Supreme Council.

K. C. C.—Knight Commander Conclave.
I. T. of O.—Inner Temple of the Order.

THIRD DEGREE, OR SECOND CONCLAVE DEGREE.

M. E. K. O. S. L.—Most Excellent Knight Order of the Sons of Liberty.
M. E. K. C. W.—Most Excellent Knight Commander West.
K. C.—Knight Conductor.
M. E. K's.—Most Excellent Knights.
M. E. K. O. S. L.—Most Excellent Knights Order of the Sons of Liberty.
M. E. G. C.—Most Excellent Grand Commander.
I—t T.—Innermost Temple.
C.—Conclave.
G. C. S.—Grand Council of the State.
S. C. O. S. L.—Supreme Council Order Sons of Liberty.
K. C. C.—Knight Commander Conclave.

CONSTITUTION STATE COUNCIL.

G. C.—Grand Council.
G. C.—Grand Commander.
Dep. G. C.—Deputy Grand Commander.
G. C. S. S. C.—Grand Counselor S. Supreme Council.
S. G. C.—Supreme Grand Council.

CONSTITUTION OF THE SUPREME COUNCIL.

S. G. C.—Supreme Grand Council.

RITUAL OF THE KNIGHTS OF THE GOLDEN CIRCLE.

V.

W. O. C. Gives * * *

K. L. Who cometh? Who cometh? Who cometh?

W. O. C. A man! We found him in the dark ways of the sons of folly, bound in chains, and well nigh crushed to death beneath the iron heel of the oppressor. We have brought him hither, and would fain clothe him in the white robes of Virtue, and place his feet in the straight and narrow path which leads to Truth and Wisdom.

K. L. Brothers! The purpose ye have declared touching this stranger is most worthy; let him advance to our altar by the regular steps; instruct him in our chosen, solemn attitude, and let him give testimony of that which is in him.

K. L. Divine Essence! God of our Fathers, whose inspiration moved .them to mighty deeds of valor in the cause of Eternal Truth, Justice and Human Rights. We, their sons, would fain recognize the same presence and inspiration in this V. of the T., consecrated to the principles which they inculcated by precept and by example, and defended with their lives and their sacred honor. With the Divine Presence let holiest memories come, like incense to our souls, and exalt them with emotions worthy of the ceremonies of the Supreme occasion. *Amen!*

Man! Thou art now in the V., and, if found worthy, will hence be ushered into the consecrated T., where Truth dwells amid her votaries; let thy soul be duly conscious of her presence, and go forth in exalted desire for her divine influence. Within those sacred precincts, reverence toward the Supreme Being, Patriotism, Love, Charity and good fellowship are inculcated and cherished. Infidelity to God or our country, nor hatred, nor malice, nor uncharitableness, nor their kindred vices, must enter there. "Love one another," is the *hail* of the order into whose inner circle thou wouldst fain be inducted. Direct thy thoughts within, at this supreme moment, and declare, as thou wouldst answer to a good conscience, is thy soul pure and fitted for the indwelling of Truth?

Answer, "yes," or "no."

Is thy heart quickened with genial emotions toward thy fellow man?

Answer, "yes," or "no."

It is well. If thou hast not answered truly, in obedience to the promptings of thy holier nature, so shalt thou be judged in the last day, when the secrets of thy heart shall be revealed, and the actions and purposes of thy life on earth shall return to thy soul their fruits of bitterness or joy eternal. I charge thee, if thou art impelled hitherward by curiosity; if thou cherish other purposes, in this regard, than the highest and the holiest which thy heart can conceive, it were better for thee that thy feet had never passed the threshold of our outer court. Our faithful and beloved brothers, who have conducted thee hither into this presence, are thy sponsors. A fearful responsibility is upon them! If thou should falsify their assurances to us, betray their trust, or stain thy manhood by unworthy actions, it will be their painful duty to publish thy shame, so that thou art expelled, and ever after excluded from the society of honorable men.

Brothers, explain your obligations as sponsors for the candidate.

OBLIGATION OF THE SPONSORS.

"We do solemnly promise and undertake, amidst the inspiring associations of our sacred V., that the stranger whom we have introduced into this presence, shall in all things prove himself a true man. That from his daily walk and conversation with his fellows, we guarantee his worthiness to be inducted into the sublime mysteries of our beloved order. We do further promise and undertake for him, that he shall faithfully keep secret whatsoever shall transpire in this presence. We do further promise, that if he shall be found worthy thereto, and shall be advanced to the inner T. of our order, that he shall reveal nothing which shall therein be made known to him to be preserved an inviolate secret. We do further promise that, in case he shall betray the confidence which he has inspired in us, we will hold it our bounden duty to see that he is expelled from the association of all honorable men. This we do promise with the approbation of the DIVINE SPIRIT. Amen!

Hast thou heard and considered the words, promises and obligations of thy sponsors?

Answer, "Aye."

Wilt thou, imploring aid from the DIVINITY within thee, perform unto the end that which they have promised in thy behalf?

Answer, "I will."

It is well! God help thee unto the end!

It is now my duty to explain the principles which our order inculcates, holding them for sublime and eternal truths, and which we, as an organized fraternity, and as individuals, aim to illustrate in our lives and conversations, as well in our intercourse with men as in our sacred conclave. Listen to the words of wisdom, and let them sink deep into thy heart.

DECLARATION OF PRINCIPLES.

1st. Essence, Ethereal, Eternal, Supreme—by us called GOD! hath created, pervades and controls the UNIVERSE! dwells in man, and is the DIVINITY within him!

Sponsors. "Amen."

2d. All men are endowed by the Creator with certain rights—equal only so far as there is equality in the capacity for the appreciation, enjoyment and exercise of those rights—some of which are inalienable, while others may, by voluntary act, or consent, be qualified, suspended or relinquished, for the purpose of social governmental organizations, or may be taken away from the individual by the supremacy of the law which he himself has ordained, in conjunction with his fellows, for their mutual protection and advancement toward perfect civilization.

3d. Government arises from the necessities of well-organized society.

4th. Right government derives its sole authority from the will of the governed, expressly declared.

[*The majority should express such will, in the mode which the unanimous voice shall approve; always guaranteeing to each individual, unless he shall have been restrained by the law, the privilege and opportunity to make known his opinions and express his will in regard to all matters relating or pertaining to the government.*]

5th. The grand purpose of the government is the welfare of the governed; its success is measured by the degree of progress which the people shall have attained toward the most exalted civilization.

6th. Government founded upon the principles enunciated in the foregoing propositions, is designated "*Democracy.*" [*The divi-*

sion of Territory where it exists, is called, usually, a "REPUBLIC," *sometimes a* "STATE."]

7th. Reflection, observation and experience, seem to have established in the minds of wise and impartial men, the conclusion that "*Democracy,*" properly organized upon the great principles which our Revolutionary ancestors—*patriots and sages*—held, inculcated and defended, best achieves the grand and benificent ends of human government.

8th. The Government organized and existing in the original Thirteen States of North America, when they had severally and unitedly renounced their allegiance to the Government of Great Britain, and dissolved their former colonial relations, we regard as the wisest, and best adapted to the nature and character of the people inhabiting the Continent of North America at the present day! Under the benign influences of that Government, a nation has arisen and attained a degree of power and splendor, which has no parallel in the history of the human race.

9th. The Government designated "the United States of America," which shall blazon the historic page, and shed its light along the path of future ages, was the transcendent conception and mighty achievement of wisdom, enlightened patriotism, and virtue, which appear to have passed from earth amidst the fading glories of the *Golden Era,* which they illustrated with immortal splendor. That Government was created originally by *thirteen free, sovereign, and independent States,* for their mutual benefit, to administer the affairs of their common interests and concerns; being endowed with the powers, dignity, and supremacy, and no further or other, which are distinctly specified and warranted, and conferred by the strict letter of the immortal compact, "The Constitution of the United States."

Sponsors—Amen!

Man! under the influence of sublime Truth! amid the inspiration of the Divine Presence! which thou didst invoke on thy approach to this Altar, how wilt thou respond to the declarations which thou hast just heard?

Answer as to thy conscience, aye! or no! for so it will be recorded.

Amen!

Place thyself in the solemn attitude of invocation which thou didst first assume before this Altar, and repeat after me:

I ———————, fully comprehending and appreciating the Declaration of Principles which I have just heard pronounced, hold them for truth—to cherish them in my heart of hearts—to inculcate them amongst my fellow men—to illustrate them, as far as in me lies, in my daily walk and conversation, and, if needs be, will defend them with my life. I appeal to that Divine Essence which created and rules the Universe, and dwells in me, to witness the sincerity of my vows. I do solemnly promise, that, should I, from my own volition, or from adjudged unworthiness, advance no further than this V. of the T., consecrated to the rites and mysteries of the brotherhood, to which I purpose to be inducted, I will never reveal, or make known, to any person or persons, by sign or signs, word or words, nor any other manner, the ceremonies in which I have just taken part, nor the names nor persons of those who have participated with me, nor any part, nor any one of them, nor any single word nor thing, which I have heard, or have seen herein; nor any purpose which I have learned or conjectured as the leading purpose of the brotherhood whose *Inner Temple* I desire to enter. To the faithful performance of all which, in presence of these witnesses, my worthy Sponsors, I pledge my most sacred honor! Amen!

Friend! Thou art well and truly informed touching the grand principles of an order, whose highest purpose is to teach, cherish, and inculcate those principles by precept and by example, and to defend them wheresoever assailed; whose other purpose is to love and cherish one another, and to relieve the worthy in their distress, giving our first care to our own brother, and to those who are nearest and dearest to him. Remember, that as a fraternity, we inculcate neither sectarianism or partisanism, only demanding unity in sentiment touching immutable principles.

(*Here endeth the lesson of the V.*)

(*Instruct in the sign.*)

Dost thou now sincerely desire to advance, or shall our worthy brothers conduct thee to the place where thou last saw the light of heaven, and return thee again to the path from which thy feet have been so lately turned aside? Listen to the words of thy Sponsors.

Sponsors. I would advance onward and upward, even to the Temple where Truth dwells serenely. I would fain worship at her shrine through all of life to me on earth.

Friend! Sayest thou so?

Answer. "Aye."

So be it. Thou shalt advance!

Thy Sponsors will deliver thee to the W. of the T., who will conduct thee to the Most Ancient and the Sages, who will instruct thee in wisdom, and will give unto thee a new name.

May not their words fall upon ears which can not hear! Nor their hands fall upon a head that will not learn!

Thou wilt now pass to the sacred precincts, where thou shalt be hailed brother! See that thou return hither a wiser and a better man!

Conduct our Neophyte to the Most Ancient and our Sages. See to it that ye make his pathway smooth. Let the air be redolent with incense, and let it breathe sweetest music upon his ear, so that the pursuit of knowledge shall be to him a continual joy and inspiration.

I.

W. O. C. Gives * * *

K. C. Who cometh? Who cometh? Who cometh?

W. A N., whom our worthy brother L., of the V., commanded us to deliver to the C. of the T. He is from the outer darkness, and would journey east for light and instruction.

K. C. He should have received his first lesson in the V. I would be assured of his proficiency.

Let the N. advance the signs in which he has been instructed.

K. C. 'Tis well. I will conduct thee to the A. B.

A. B. Who cometh? Who cometh? Who cometh?

K. C. A N., whom our worthy brother W. has brought hither by command of our worthy L. of the V. I have proved him, and found him duly proficient in the lesson he has received. He fain would journey east for instruction.

A. B. His desire shall be gratified. But it is my duty to admonish him touching the trials and perils he needs must encounter, and to demand of him a solemn obligation, first giving him assurance that such obligation requires of him nothing inconsistent with his duty to God! to his country! to his family! or to himself. N., with this assurance, are you now willing to take such an obligation?

N. I am.

A. B. Then place yourself in the attitude in which you plighted your solemn vows in the V., holding in your right hand the sacred emblem of our order.

OBLIGATION OF THE N.

I, ——————, in the presence of God! and many witnesses, do solemnly declare, that I do herein, freely, and in the light of a good conscience, renew the solemn vows which I plighted in the V. I do further promise that I will never reveal, nor make known, to any man, woman or child, any thing which my eyes may behold, or any word which my ears may hear, within this sacred T., nor in any other T., nor in any other place where the brotherhood may be assembled. That I will never speak of, nor intimate any purpose or purposes of this order, whether contemplated or determined, to any one except to a brother of this order, whom I know to be such. That I will never exhibit any or either of the emblems or insignia of the order, except by express authority granted to that end, and that I will never explain their use or signification to any one not a brother of this order, whom I know to be such, under any pretense whatsoever, neither by persuasion nor by coercion. That I will never reveal nor make known, to any man, woman or child, any or either of the signs, hails, passwords, watchwords, initials nor initial letters belonging to this order, neither by voice, nor by gesture, attitude or motion of the body, nor any member of the body; nor by intimation through the instrumentality of any thing animate or inanimate, or object in the heavens, or on the earth, or above the earth, except to prove a man if he be a brother, or to communicate with a brother whom I shall have first duly proved or know to be such. That I will never pronounce the name of this order in the hearing of any man, woman or child, except to a brother of this order, whom I know to be such. That I will ever have in my most holy keeping each and every secret of this order, which may be confided to me by a brother, either within or without the T., and rather than reveal which, I will consent to any sacrifice, even unto *death by torture.* I do further promise that I will never recommend for membership to this order any man who is not a citizen of an American State, except by dispensation to that end, by the competent authority of the order—citizenship always resulting from nativity, or from due process of law in such case provided—neither any person who has not attained the age of twenty-one years; neither a man unsound or infirm in body or in mind—such as a cripple or an idiot; neither any one of African descent, whether slave or freeman; neither an avowed and acknowledged atheist; neither a person of bad repute. That I will ever cherish toward each and every member of this order, fraternal regard and fellowship; that I will ever aid a worthy brother in distress, if in my power to do so; that I will never do wrong, knowingly, to a brother, nor permit him to suffer wrong at the hand of another, if it shall be in my power to warn him of danger or prevent the wrong. I do further promise that I will, at all times, if needs be, take up arms in the cause of the oppressed—*in my country first of all*—against any Monarch, Prince, Potentate, Power or Government usurped, which may be found in arms, and waging war against a people or peoples, who are endeavoring to establish, or have inaugurated, a Government for themselves of their own free choice, in accordance with, and founded upon, *the eternal principles of Truth!* which I have sworn in the V., and now in this presence do swear, to maintain inviolate, and defend with my life. *This I* do promise, without reservation or evasion of mind; without regard to the name, station, condition or destination of the invading or coercion power, whether it shall arise

within or come from without! I do further promise that I will always recognize and respond to the hail of a brother, when it shall be made in accordance with the instructions and injunctions of the order, and not otherwise. I do further promise that, with God's help, I will ever demean myself toward my fellow man, and especially toward the brotherhood, as becometh a *true man.* I do further promise that, should I cease to be a member of this order, either of my own volition or by expulsion, I will hold and preserve inviolate my solemn vows and promises herein declared, as well as while I am in full fellowship. All this I do solemnly promise and swear sacredly to observe, perform and keep, with a full knowledge and understanding, and with my full assent, that the penalty which will follow a violation of any or either of these, my solemn vows, *will be a shameful death!* while my name shall be consigned to infamy, while this sublime order shall survive the wrecks of time, and even until the last faithful brother shall have passed from earth to his service in the Temple not made with hands! Divine Essence! and ye men of Earth! witness the sincerity of my soul touching these, my vows!

Amen!

CHARGE.

A. B. Neophyte, thy progress from the outer darkness to this presence, and thy proficiency in the sublime lessons, which have been given thee to learn, gives assurance that there is one more votary to eternal Truth, rescued from the throng which wear the galling chains of Error. Thy journey is well nigh accomplished. Fain would I tell thee that thy trials are passed, but it is not so; yet, I will give thee such caution and admonition as will serve thee much. The Sons of Folly will beset thy path, and aim to turn thee back to thy dark haunts; will scoff and buffet thee; peradventure, will seek thy life. Then put thy trust in God and Truth. Still, thy journey leadeth due East, until thou art hailed by the G. S., who will further instruct thee, welcome thee, brother, in our Inner Court, and give unto thee a new name. Beware, lest thou bear thee toward the North too far, and lose thy way, and perish amid the moaning pines, which crown the rugged hills, sighing ever in rough harmony to the icy blasts, or amid the hoary, moss-clad rocks, whose yawning chasms open wide and bottomless to the hapless wanderer. As well take heed, lest the balmy zephyrs from the golden South entice thee too far thither. There the gentle winds will cool thy fevered temples, and awake thy senses in delirious joy; yet they bear too oft the deadly malaria, and minister to death in his awful revelry. We have a trusty Brother Guardian on either side thy way, who, true and constant at their posts, perchance may hail thee, when thou wilt tarry, should he bid thee, receive what he shall offer, and give thy earnest heed to all his words. Remember, the only path which leads where Truth and Wisdom dwells together, their fairest sister, Virtue, traced. It leadeth onward, upward, straight. It is paved with gems, and pearls, and gold. It is bordered with perennial flowers, whose perfumes all thy senses entrance. Neophyte, be thy watchword—Onward! Onward! Onward!

K. G. N.

K. G. N. Who cometh? who cometh? who cometh? Advance!

K. C. A N., by command of our A. B. in the West, journeying toward the East to receive light and instruction.

K. G. N. Then he has left the straight path, and has lost his way. Danger is in every step he advances. I am from the far North not long since. The barren wastes are white with the bleaching bones of such as he, and the yawning chasms send up an horrid stench from Death's late carnival! Bid him turn back. He has forgotten the instructions of our A. B. Was he not charged to follow the straight and narrow path which Virtue has traced?

K. C. True! We entered upon the straight path, but ere we had proceeded far, the Sons of Folly beset us, and drove us from our course with violence. We were sorely bruised. We were bewildered, and lost our way. Wilt thou direct us hence?

K. G. N. I will; but first I must prove him, that I may know by what right he claims my care and assistance.

K. C. Lo! He hath a sign.

K. G. N. 'Tis well. Hath he a password?

K. C. He has; and will give it.

K. G. N. 'Tis well. Thy watchword?

N. Onward! Onward! Onward!

K. G. N. 'Tis well. Tarry and refresh thyselves; then depart due South. Shouldst thou cross the path thou seekest, and reach the camp of our G. in the South, he will further instruct thee. Thy watchword still—Onward! Onward! Onward!

K. G. S.

K. G. S. Who cometh? Who cometh? Who cometh? Strangers, advance. Declare thy way and purpose.

K. C. I come with this N. from our worthy A. B. in the West, who commanded us to journey due East to the M. E. G. S. and the Sages for light and instruction. He charged us to follow the straight path. We had not journeyed far, when we were beset by the Factionists, Fanatics, and Sons of Error and Folly, who did wound and bruise us sorely, because we would not turn back with them to their dark and devious ways. In brief, we lost our path, and would have perished amid the snows of the icy North,

or sunk into the yawning chasms of the rocks, but that the worthy K. G. N. did hail us as we passed his tent, and gave us wine and bread, instructed us in wisdom, and turned our faces hitherward. Wilt thou show us our path?

K. G. S. I will. But first I would prove thy friend. I know thee well for a true man. Let the Neophyte advance the sign.

K. G. S. 'Tis well. Hath he a password?

K. C. He has.

K. G. S. Bid him give it me. 'Tis well. Thy watchword?

N. Onward! Onward! Onward!

K. G. S. 'Tis well. Tarry and refresh yourselves, and I will instruct you further. Happily, thou didst approach my tent, else thou and thy friend might have perished together in the trackless fen, or perchance thy limbs had wearied, and thy heart become faint in thy weary way under the scorching rays of the meridian sun; or inhaled the rank poison, which, distilled in the cool air of night, swathes the heated brow in the death camp, which no tender hand can wipe away; or, peradventure, the soft gales, laden with perfume, and breathing the syren's entrancing melody, had lulled thy soul to rest in inglorious ease to destruction. Not yet is thy Neophyte fitted for the field of labor. His soul must be attuned to the harmony of great thoughts, to the conception and achievement of mighty deeds and purposes. Our brothers there are doing battle in the cause of eternal Truth. They have no place for Neophytes. When he shall have reached our sacred T., whose spires are glistening in the dawning rays of Truth's resplendent sun; when he shall have drunk deep from the fountains of Wisdom, which send forth their streams to cherish and gladden noble manhood, then shall he don our sacred armor, rush to the deadly breach where faction's darling hosts are gathered, and waiving aloft our holy banner, consecrated to Freedom, Truth and Virtue, shall bear it on to victory, or die beneath its folds. Conduct him again to the straight and narrow path, thence onward due East to our G. S., and the Sages of the T. Cheer his heart; beguile his way with tales of daring deeds. Let the watchword be ever and ever—Onward! Onward! Onward!

G. S.

K. C. We have attained the end of our journey. The W——s of the Eastern Tower have sounded the alarm. Assume the attitude in which thou wert instructed in the V. Fall upon thy knee, in the posture which best expresses humiliation. He that humbleth himself shall be exalted. Thou shalt rise again to welcome the glad light which glows resplendent around our holy place, where Truth, Virtue, Wisdom, dwell together, and their altars ever burn with the incense-offerings of their votaries.

(*Kneels upon his left knee.*)

G. S. Who cometh? Who cometh? Who cometh?

K. C. M. E. G. S., I have brought a N. He is from the West. and hath journeyed East for instruction in Truth and Wisdom. *He is a man.*

G. S. A man! sayest thou? Methinks that posture becometh not a man formed in the image of his Creator. It doth imply debasement—servitude.

K. C. Servitude, M. E. G. S., but not debasement. Two brothers of our sacred order found him bound in chains, and upon his neck a heavy yoke. Our worthy brothers, as is their wont, did break his fetters, cast away his galling yoke, and brought him to our V., where he proved himself a true man. So did our A. B. prove him, and gave to him our sacred watchword. So did our worthy G——s N. and S. prove him by our signs, and by his proficiency in the lessons of our order. Still, M. E. G. S., he serveth.

G. S. Serveth? Whom? What?

K. C. God! and his country!

G. S. 'Tis well. Such service well becometh a man. By the authority vested in me by the C. S. of our order, I give him welcome to our sacred B. Pronounce the name by which he is known amongst his fellow men. I would give him a new name.

[*Instruct.*]

INVOCATION.

OPENING.

Divine Essence! We would recognize Thy Presence in our T., consecrated to Truth! Let holiest memories come, like incense, to our souls; memories of our ancestors' virtues, and their glorious deeds in the holy cause of Truth, Justice, and the Rights of Man! inspiring emotions! holy! exalted! worthy of the ceremonies of this sacred place. May each heart in this presence to other beat in unison, with genial sympathies, while our souls, as one, glow with the emotions of our holy nature. May our cherished brotherhood so live, that when we have done with earthly things, we may be hailed for service in the Temple not made with hands, Eternal, in the heavens. *Amen!*

CLOSING.

'Divine Essence! With grateful hearts we recognize the *Holy Presence, Inspiration, and Guidance,* during the ceremonies and deliberations of the occasion. Deign to go with us to our several homes—to our chambers of repose—so shall gentle slumbers renew our manhood's strength. for better service on earth; the asperities of our grosser nature be subdued and chastened; our souls fitted for the upper sphere, and

welcomed for service in the Inner Temple there by the hail: "Well done." *Amen!*

ORDER OF BUSINESS.

1. Ceremonies of Opening.
2. Reading and approval of minutes of preceding meeting and reports of Secretary and Treasurer.
3. Balloting for Candidates recommended at a former meeting.
4. Induction of Candidates.
5. Reading and consideration of communications from other organizations.
6. Nomination of Candidates and reference to Committee.
7. Propositions for the good of the Order, including immediate purposes and plans, and their consideration and discussion.
8. Lecture.
9. Information concerning the condition of members, whether any one is sick or in distress, requiring aid and sustenance.

S. L.

V.

W. O. C. Gives * * *

L. V. Who cometh?

W. O. C. A citizen we found in the hands of the sons of despotism, bound and well nigh crushed to death beneath their oppressions. We have brought him hither, and would now restore to him the blessings of Liberty and Law.

L. V. Brothers, the purpose ye have declared, touching this stranger, is most worthy. Let him advance to the altar by the regular steps; instruct him in our chosen solemn attitude, and let him give heed to the words which shall be spoken.

INVOCATION.

L. V. God of our Fathers, whose inspiration moved them to deeds of valor, in the cause of Eternal Truth, Justice and Equal Rights; we, their sons, now invoke Thy Divine Presence, in this V. of the T., consecrated to the principles which they inculcated by precept, and by example, and defended with their lives. Bless our country, and restore and protect her liberties. Amen.

L. V. Citizen, thou art now in the V., and if found worthy, will be hence ushered into the consecrated T., within whose precincts, reverence toward the Supreme Being, patriotism, peace, charity and good fellowship are inculcated and cherished. Direct thy thoughts within at this moment, and declare, as thou wouldst answer to a good conscience, art thou ready?

Response. I am.

L. V. It is well! I charge thee that if thou art impelled hitherward by curiosity; if thou cherish other purposes in this regard, than the highest and holiest thy heart can conceive, it were better for thee that thy feet had never passed the threshold of our O. C. Our faithful and well-beloved brothers, who have conducted thee hither into this presence, are thy Sponsors—a fearful responsibility is upon them. If thou shouldst betray their trust, or stain thy manhood by unworthy actions, it will be their solemn duty to publish thy shame, so that thou shalt be expelled, and ever after excluded from the society of honorable men.

Brothers, hear your obligations as Sponsors for the candidate.

OBLIGATION OF SPONSORS.

We do solemnly promise and undertake that the stranger, whom we have introduced into this presence, shall, in all things, prove himself a true man; that from his daily walk and conversation with his brethren, we guarantee his worthiness to be inducted into the mysteries of this society. We do further promise and undertake for him, that he shall faithfully keep secret whatsoever shall transpire in this presence; and that in case he shall betray the confidence which he has inspired in us, we will hold it our bounden duty to aid in his expulsion from all association with honorable men. Amen.

L. V. Hast thou heard and considered the obligation of thy Sponsors?

Answer. I have.

L. V. Wilt thou well and truly perform unto the end, that which they have promised on thy behalf?

Ans. I will.

L. V. It is well. It is now my duty to explain the principles which our society inculcates, and which we, as a fraternity and as individuals, aim to illustrate in our lives and conversation.

DECLARATION OF PRINCIPLES.

1st. God hath created and controls the Universe.

2d. All men are endowed by the Creator with certain rights—equal so far as there is equality in the capacity for the appreciation, enjoyment and exercise of those rights—some of which are inalienable, while others may, by voluntary act or consent, be qualified, suspended, or relinquished, for the purposes of social and governmental organizations.

3d. Government arises from the necessities of society, and rightful government derives its sole authority from the will of the governed, its chief end being their welfare.

4th. The governments organized and existing in the original thirteen States of North America, after they had severally and unitedly renounced their allegiance to the Government of Great Britain, we regard as the wisest and best adapted to the nature and character of the people of the United States.

5th. That government was established originally by *thirteen, free, sovereign and independent States*, "in order to form a more perfect Union, to establish justice, to insure domestic tranquillity, provide for the common defense, promote the general welfare, and secure the blessings of liberty to the people thereof, and their posterity; being intrusted with the powers and supremacy," and no further or other, which are specifically granted in the compact, entitled the *Constitution of the United States*, strictly construed.

L. V. Dost thou assent to the declaration of principles which thou hast just heard?
Ans. I do.

L. V. Present thyself, then, in the attitude of invocation which thou didst first assume before this altar, and receive thy obligation.

OBLIGATION.

I, ——————, fully comprehending the declaration of principles which I have just heard pronounced, hold them for truth—to cherish them in my heart—to illustrate them, as far as in me lies, in my daily walk and conversation, and to defend them with my life. I do solemnly promise, that I will never reveal or make known to any person or persons, by sign or word, or in any manner, the ceremonies in which I have just taken part, nor the names nor persons of those who have participated with me, nor any purpose which I have learned or conjectured as any part of the object of this society; and that I will, without hesitation or delay, perform whatever may be rightfully required of me by the duly constituted authorities of the society. To the faithful performance of all which, in presence of these witnesses, I pledge my most sacred honor. Amen.

(*Instruct, &c.*)

O. S. L.

W. O. C. Gives * * *

C. T. Who cometh?

W. A S. L., whom our worthy brother L. V. commanded us to deliver to the C. T.

C. T. He should have received his first lesson in the V. I would be assured of his proficiency.

Let the S. L. advance the signs in which he is instructed.

C. T. 'Tis well. I will conduct thee to the A. B.

A. B.

A. B. Who cometh?

C. T. A S. L., whom our trusty brother W. has brought hither by command of the L. V. I have proved him, and found him duly proficient in the lesson he has received; he would journey East for instruction.

A. B. His desire shall be gratified; but it is my duty, first, to submit to him the lesson of the T., and then to demand of him a solemn obligation; giving him assurance that such obligation requires of him nothing inconsistent with his duty to his God, his family, or himself. S. L., with this assurance, art thou willing to take such an obligation?

S. L. I am.

LESSON.

1st. A well defined belief in a Creator and Supreme Ruler of the universe, imparts true dignity to man.

2d. The ideas and principles maintained by our O. on the subject of government, are identical with those taught and defended by the founders of American liberty in the original thirteen States of North America.

3d. The liberties of those States were assailed by despotic power, which aimed at their conquest and subjugation; hence they made common cause for their mutual defense, and established friendly relations with each other, in the compact entitled "Articles of Confederation and Perpetual Union between the States."

4th. When those States had maintained their freedom and independence, they severally entered into a compact entitled the Constitution of the United States of America, for the ends and purposes therein distinctly declared and specified; and the government thereby created was intrusted by the States, acting in their several capacities of Free and Independent States, with powers sufficient to the accomplishment of those ends and purposes, and no other; powers not delegated to that government being, by the express letter of the compact, "reserved to the States or to the people respectively."

5th. Sovereignty resides in and with the people of the States respectively, which are parties to the Constitution of the United States. It can not be alienated, neither can it be delegated. Some of its powers may be exercised by delegated authority, while others can not be so exercised, except at the sacrifice, on the part of the constituent, of all that lends dignity to man's relation to government.

6th. The Government designated the United States of America has no sovereignty, because that is an attribute belonging to the people in their respective State organization, and with which they have not endowed that government as their common agent. It was by the terms of this compact, constituted by the States, through the express will of the people thereof severally, such common agent to use and exercise certain specified and limited powers. It was authorized so far as regards its status and relations, as a common agent in the exercise of the powers carefully and jealously delegated to it, to call itself "su-

preme," but not "sovereign." Supremacy, as plainly intended by the tenor and spirit of article VI of the Constitution, was created, defined and limited by the sovereignties themselves.

7th. In accordance with these principles, the Federal Government can exercise only delegated power; hence, if those who shall have been chosen to administer that Government, shall assume to exercise power not delegated, they should be regarded and dealt with as usurpers.

8th. The claim of "inherent power," or "war power," as also "State necessity," or "military necessity," on part of the functionaries of a constitutional government, for sanction of any arbitrary exercise of power, we utterly reject and repudiate.

9th. All power resides in the people, and is delegated always to be exercised for the advancement of the common weal.

10th. Whenever the officials, to whom the people have intrusted the powers of the government, shall refuse to administer it in strict accordance with its constitution, and shall assume and exercise power or authority not delegated, it is the inherent right, and imperative duty of the people, to resist such officials, and, if need be, expel them by force of arms. Such resistance is not revolution, but is solely the assertion of right.

11th. It is incompatible with the history and nature of our system of government, that federal authority should coerce by arms a sovereign State; and all intimations of such power or right, were expressly withheld in the Constitution, which conferred upon the Federal Government all its authority.

12th. Upon the preservation of the sovereignty of the States, depends the preservation of civil and personal liberty.

13th. In a convention of delegates, elected by the people of a State, is recognized the impersonation of the sovereignty of that State. The declaration of such convention upon the subject matter for which it was assembled, is the ultimate expression of that sovereignty. Such convention may refer its action back to its constituents, or the people may reverse the action of one convention by the voice of another. Thus sovereignty resides in the people of each State, and speaks alone through their conventions. S. L., what sayest thou to this lesson? Do its teachings command thy unqualified assent?

S. L. They do.

A. B. Present thyself, then, in the attitude in which thou didst plight thy solemn vows in the V., holding in thy right hand the sacred emblem of our O.

OBLIGATION.

I, ——————, in the presence of God and these witnesses, do solemnly declare that I do herein freely renew the vows which I plighted in the V. I do further promise that I will never reveal, nor make known any thing which my eyes may behold, or any word which my ears may hear in this T., nor in any other T., nor in any other place where this fellowship may be assembled. That I will never speak of, nor intimate, any measure or measures, whether contemplated or determined, of this O., to any one except to a fellow of the O. That I will never explain the use or signification of the emblems or insignia of the O., to any one not a fellow thereof, under any pretense whatsoever, neither by persuasion nor by coercion; that I will never reveal or make known any or either of the signs, hails, passwords, watchwords, nor initial letters belonging to this O., except to prove or communicate with a fellow thereof; that I will never pronounce the name of this O. in the hearing of any man, woman, or child, unless to a fellow thereof; that I will ever have in most holy keeping each and every secret of this O., which may be confided to me by a fellow thereof, either within or without the T.; that I will never recommend, for fellowship in this O., any man who is not a citizen of an American State, except by dispensation to that end by competent authority; neither any person who has not attained the age of eighteen years, neither any one unsound in mind, neither any one of African descent, whether slave or free, neither a person of bad repute; that I will ever cherish toward each and every worthy fellow of this O., fraternal regard and fellowship; that I will ever aid a worthy fellow in distress, if in my power so to do; that I will never wrong a fellow, nor see him wronged if in my power to prevent it; that I will at all times implicitly obey, without question or remonstrance, all rightful commands of the constituted authorities of this O.; that I will always recognize and respond to the hail of a fellow, when it shall be made in accordance with the instructions and injunctions of this O., and not otherwise; and should I cease to be a fellow of this O., either of my own volition or by expulsion, I will hold and preserve inviolate my vows and promises herein declared, as truly as while I am in full fellowship. All this I do solemnly promise sacredly to observe, perform and keep, under such penalties as shall be decreed by the competent authority of this O. Amen.

CHARGE.

A. B. S. L., thy journey is well nigh accomplished. Somewhat yet remains, and the Sons of Despotism will beset thy path and aim to turn thee back—peradventure will seek thy life. Then put thy trust in God and Truth; still thy journey leadeth due East until thou art hailed by the G. S., who will further instruct thee. Beware, lest thou bear thee toward the North too far and lose thy way; as well, also, take heed lest the South entice thee too far thither. We have a trusty F. G., on either side thy way, who, true and constant at his post, perchance may hail thee. Receive what he shall offer, and give earnest heed to all his words. S. L., be thy watchword—Onward!

F. G. N.

F. G. N. Who cometh? Advance.

C. T. A S. L., by command of our A. B. in the West, journeying East for light and instruction.

F. G. N. Then has he left the straight path and lost his way; danger is in every step he advances; bid him turn back; he has forgotten the instructions of our A. B. Was he not charged to follow the straight and narrow path?

C. T. True! we entered upon the straight path, but ere we had proceeded far we were bewildered and lost our way. Wilt thou direct us hence?

F. G. N. I will; but first I must prove him, that I may know by what right he claims my care and assistance.

C. T. Lo! he hath a sign. (*Gives it.*)

F. G. N. 'Tis well. Hath he a password?

C. T. He has, and will give it. (*Gives it.*)

F. G. N. 'Tis well. Thy watchword?

S. L. Onward.

F. G. N. 'Tis well! Now depart due South. Shouldst thou reach the post of our G. in the South, he will further instruct thee. Thy watchword still—Onward!

F. G. S.

F. G. S. Who cometh? Strangers, advance. Declare thy way and purpose.

C T. I come with this S. L. from our worthy A. B. in the West, who commanded us to journey due East to the G. S., for light and instruction, charging us to follow the straight path; we had not journeyed far when we lost our way; but the worthy F. G. N. did hail us as we passed his post, and turned our faces hitherward. Wilt thou show us our path?

F. G. S. I will. But first I would prove this friend; I know thee well for a true man. Let the S. L. advance the sign. (*Gives it.*)

F. G. S. 'Tis well. Hath he a password?

C. T. He has.

F. G. S. Bid him give it me. (*Gives it.*) 'Tis well. Thy watchword?

S. L. Onward.

F. G. S. 'Tis well. Conduct him again to the straight and narrow path; thence onward due East to our G. S. Let thy watchword be ever and ever—Onward!

G. S.

G. S. Who cometh? Advance.

C. T. G. S., I have brought a S. L. He is from the West, and hath journeyed East for instruction. He is a citizen; but he serveth.

G. S. Serveth! Whom—what?

C. T. God and his country.

G. S. 'Tis well. Such service fitly becometh the good citizen. By the authority vested in me, I give him welcome into our T., and pronounce him a worthy F. O. S. L. (*Instruct, &c.*)

INVOCATION.

O God! Creator of all men, we invoke Thy presence. Help us as Thou didst help our fathers. Before Thee we are offenders; but spare us. We pursue Justice—Thou art the author of Justice. We seek Liberty—Thou art the giver of Liberty. We desire Peace—Thou art the God of Peace. Purify our intentions; guide our counsels, and give success to our efforts. Amen.

CLOSING.

O God! from Thee all wise counsels and all good works do proceed. Further Thou our counsels, prosper our works, and grant us Thy peace. Amen.

ORDER OF BUSINESS.

1. Ceremonies of Opening.
2. Reading and approval of minutes of preceding meeting, and reports of Secretary and Treasurer.
3. Balloting for Candidates recommended at a former meeting.
4. Induction of Candidates.
5. Reading and consideration of communications from other organizations.
6. Nomination of Candidates and reference to Committee.
7. Propositions for the good of the O., including immediate purposes and plans, and their consideration and discussion.
8. Lecture.
9. Information concerning the condition of Members, whether any one is sick or in distress, requiring aid and assistance.

INSTALLATION.

The officers elect, being up standing, the Com. T. shall propound to each the following questions:

Com. T. ——— having been duly elected to the office of ———, do you accept the position to which you have been assigned?

Ans. I do.

Com. Brothers, are you content with the choice you have made of ———?

Ans. We are.

The Com. will then administer the following oath of office to each, beginning at the highest, and declare them duly qualified to enter upon their respective duties:

OBLIGATION.

I, ———, having been elected to the office of ———, for the ensuing term, do solemnly swear, in the presence of these witnesses, to support the constitution and laws of the O. S. L., to obey all rightful orders of my immediate G. Com. and the S. Com., and perform the duties of ——— to the best of my ability, so help me God. Amen.

I.

K. O. S. L.

K. C. W. Who cometh?

K. C. A worthy Fellow of the O. S. L., who, having been duly elected, desires induction into the I. T. of our O.

K. C. W. It is well. His desire shall be gratified; but it is my duty first to submit to him the lesson of I. T., and then to demand of him a solemn obligation, giving him assurance that such obligation requires of him nothing inconsistent with his duty to God, to his country, to his family, or to himself. F. S. L., with this assurance, art thou content?

Ans. I am.

LESSON OF THE I. T.

The Kentucky and Virginia Resolutions of 1798, Drafted by Jefferson and Madison.

1. The several States composing the United States of America, are not united on the principle of unlimited submission to the General Government, but by a compact under the style and title of a Constitution for the United States, and of amendments thereto, they constituted a General Government for special purposes, delegated to that Government certain definitive powers, reserving each State to itself the residuary mass of right to their own self-government; and whensoever the General Government assumes undelegated powers, its acts are unauthoritative, void, and of no force; to this compact each State acceded as a State, and is an integral party; that this Government, created by this compact, was not made the exclusive or final judge of the extent of the powers delegated to itself; since that would have made its discretion, and not the Constitution, the measure of its powers; but that, as in all other cases of compact, among powers having no common judge, each party has an equal right to judge for itself as well of infractions as of the mode and measures of redress.

2. It is true as a general principle, and is also expressly declared, by one of the amendments to the Constitution, that the "powers not delegated to the United States by the Constitution, nor prohibited to it by the States, are reserved to the States respectively, or to the people;" and no power over the freedom of religion, freedom of speech, or freedom of the press, being delegated to the United States by the Constitution, nor prohibited by it to

the States, all lawful powers respecting the same, did of right remain, and were reserved to the States or the people; and thus was manifested their determination to retain to themselves the right of judging how far the licentiousness of speech, and of the press, may be abridged, without lessening their useful freedom; and how far those abuses, which can not be separated from their use, should be tolerated, rather than the use be destroyed, and thus also they guarded against all abridgment, by the United States,' of the freedom of religious opinions and exercises, and retained to themselves the right of protecting the same from all human restraint or interference; and in addition to this general principle and express declaration, another and more special provision has been made by one of the amendments to the Constitution, which expressly declares, that "Congress shall make no law respecting an establishment of religion, or prohibiting the free exercise thereof, or abridging the freedom of speech, or the press," thereby guarding in the same sentence, and under the same words, the freedom of religion, of speech, and of the press, insomuch, that whatever violated either, throws down the sanctuary which covers the others, and, therefore, libels, falsehood, and defamation, equally with heresy and false religion, are withheld from the cognizance of Federal tribunals.

3. This O. does explicitly and peremptorily declare that it views the power of the Federal Government, as resulting from the compact to which the States are parties: as limited by the plain sense and intention of the instrument constituting that compact; as no further valid than they are authorized by the grants enumerated in that compact; and that in the case of a deliberate, palpable and dangerous exercise of other powers not granted by the said compact, the States, who are parties thereto, have the right, and are in duty bound, to interpose, for arresting the progress of the evil, and for maintaining, within their respective limits, the authorities, rights and liberties appertaining to them.

K. C. W. F. S. L., what sayest thou to this lesson? Do its teachings command thy unqualified assent?

F. S. L. They do.

K. C. W. Present thyself, then, in the attitude in which thou didst plight thy solemn vows in the T.

OBLIGATION.

I, —————, within the precincts of this I. T., do now freely renew the vows plighted in my progress hither; I do also solemnly swear that I will faithfully keep secret every word that I may hear, and will never, by speech, sign, or intimation, reveal any thing which I may see within or without this I. T., pertaining to the same, unless to a true K.; that I will never explain or exhibit any of the signs, hails, passwords, watchwords, emblems, insignia, initial letters, nor the seal of the I. T., except to prove or communicate with a true K. I do further swear, that I will, as becometh a true K., at all times, and in all places, to the utmost of my ability, respect, perform, and obey, each and every order, command, or request, made to or of me by the K. C. C., or other superior authority, touching any matter or thing which relates or pertains to the purposes or plans of the K. O. S. L.; and I do further swear that I will ever bear in mind the lesson of the I. T., as expounded to me in this presence, and will defend the principles therein laid down, with my life, if need be; that my sword shall ever be drawn in support of the right, and that I will never take up arms in any cause as a mercenary. I do further swear, that I will ever cherish kindly regard and fellowship toward all true K.'s every-where, and will ever aid them in the defense of their rights; that I will ever honor, cherish, and protect woman and the orphan, and especially the mother, widow, sister, or orphan of a deceased K., and will shield them from wrong, insult and oppression; and I do also swear, that I will never induct, nor consent to the induction, of any one into the I. T., who shall not have been duly and well instructed in the T. D., nor then, until he shall have been unanimously approved by a legal conclave of K. O. S. L., nor in any place which has not been appointed and consecrated to that end by the competent authority, nor in the presence of a less number than thirteen true K.'s, each and all of whom shall consent and approve to such induction, nor until I shall have been duly authorized thereto by authority emanating from the G. C.; and, finally, I do solemnly swear, in the presence of these K.'s, my witnesses, to all and singular the foregoing, with full knowledge, and with my full assent, that the penalty declared against any violation of any part of this, my oath, shall be such as may be declared by the G. C., and approved by the S. C. of the O. S. L. Divine presence! approve my truth, and you, ye K.'s, hear and bear witness. Amen!

K. C. W. It is well. The K. C. will now conduct thee to the K. C. C.

K. C. C.

K. C. C. Who cometh? Advance.

K. C. A worthy fellow of the O. S. L., who, having taken the obligation required in this I. T., is, by command of the K. C. W., brought before thee for full induction.

K. C. C. It is well. Let him kneel in token of service to God and his country. * * * Rise, —————, K. O. S. L., and receive thy charge.

CHARGE.

CHARGE.

Brother! Thy presumed worthiness hath secured thy induction into the I. T. of O. Let thy deeds approve thee worthy. Obedience, faith, truth, courage, sincerity, self-denial—these are the virtues of the true K. Make good thy vows. Honor thy God. Love thy country. So shalt thou discharge thy duty on earth, and prepare thyself for the beatitudes of the temple not made with hands. Hear the words of inspiration! then onward! still be thy watchword. Onward!

K. L. [Here reads Isaiah, chap. LIX, verses 14 to 19, inclusive.]

K. C. C. [*Instructs.*]

II.

M. E. K. O. S. L.

M. E. K. C. W. Who cometh? Advance.

K. C. A true K., who, having been duly elected thereto, desires induction in the I—t T. of our most excellent O.

M. E. K. C. W. It is well. Let him present himself in our chosen attitude of invocation.

OBLIGATION.

I, ——————, in the presence of God and these M. E. K.'s, do solemnly swear, that I will never reveal, or make known, directly or indirectly, any thing whatever, pertaining to the M. E. K. O. S. L.; neither will I indicate, by word or intimation, any thing of, or concerning the same, except to a brother thereof, whom I shall have first duly proved. I do further swear, that I will, at all times, and in all places, yield prompt and implicit obedience, to the utmost of my ability, without remonstrance, hesitation or delay, to any and every mandate, order or request, of my immediate M. E. G. C., in all things touching the purposes of the O. S. L., and to defend the principles thereof, when assailed in my own State or country, in whatsoever capacity may be assigned to me by authority of our O.; and I do further swear, that I will never induct, or consent to the induction, of any person into the I—t T., until he shall have first been approved by at least thirteen M. E. K.'s of the local C. to which he is proposed for induction, except by express dispensation to that end from superior authority; and that I will ever faithfully keep secret every counsel of M. E. K.'s, whether in or out of C. To all and singular the foregoing, I do solemnly swear, with full knowledge, and my assent, that the penalty for any violation of any part thereof, shall be whatsoever may be decreed by the G. C. S., and approved by the S. C.—O. S. L.; so help me, God! Amen!

K. C. C. [*Instructs.*]

GENERAL LAWS OF THE S. L.

COUNTY PARENT TEMPLES.

ARTICLE I.

SECTION 1. A Parent County T. may be instituted by an eligible brother who shall be authorized by the Grand Council, or by the G. Com., upon the application of five good and true men, by paying the expenses incurred for books, traveling, etc., and three dollars per day to the person who shall be designated to institute the same.

SEC. 2. Branch County T.'s may be instituted by the mode above, or by the officers of the Parent T. *Provided*, That the Grand Sig. of any Parent T., of this State, be authorized to organize subordinate temples in any township where none have been organized, subject to the constitution and rules of this order, and that until a Parent T. be organized in such county, to which said township belongs, the secretary thereof shall report to the G. Sec. of this State.

SEC. 3. The names and location of Parent and Branches, shall not be changed without permission of the G. Council, or without written consent of the G. Sec.

ARTICLE II.

SECTION 1. Every T. in the State of Indiana shall meet twice in every month, and oftener if they shall deem proper, and shall be opened as near as may be at the time prescribed by the Rules of Order.

SEC. 2. Special meetings may be held, upon the call of G. S., or when requested to do so by five members of the T., general notice of such meeting to be given as far as possible.

SEC. 3. At any regular or special meeting, at which the first and second officers shall be absent, a qualified degree member may be chosen to preside.

SEC. 4. Each T. is empowered to designate what number, not less than five, shall constitute a quorum for the transaction of business.

ARTICLE III.

SECTION 1. The elective officers of the Parent T.'s shall be—M. E. K. C.; M. E. K. C. W.; M. E. K. Sec.; M. E. K. Treas.; M. E. K. Lecturer of the V.; and M. E. K. Rep. to G. C. The officers shall be appointed M. E. K. Cond.; M. E. K. Marshal; M. E. K. W., T.; M. E. K. W., O. C.

SEC. 2. The elective and appointed officers of a Branch County T., shall be those designated in the ritual of the order.

SEC. 3. The election of all officers shall take place annually, on or not to exceed two weeks previous to the 22d day of February in each year.

SEC. 4. At the same time and place the Parent T. shall elect two Representatives to the G. Council, and one additional Representative for every one thousand members in said county.

Sec. 5. All elections shall be by ballot, and a majority of all the votes given be necessary to a choice. *Provided*, That whenever there shall be but one candidate, the election may be by *viva voce.*

Sec. 6. Any elected or appointed officer who shall absent himself from the Temple for three successive stated meetings, unless such absence be satisfactorily accounted for, shall thereby vacate his office, and the vacancy shall be filled by special election, and the member so elected or appointed to fill such vacancy shall, if he serve under such election or appointment, receive all the honors of the station as though he had served the full term.

Sec. 7 All elective officers shall continue to serve until their respective successors are duly elected and qualified.

ARTICLE IV.

Section 1. The duties of the G. S. and M. E. K. C. shall be—

1st. To preside at all meetings of the Temple at which they may be present, and open and close the same in due form; to preserve strict order and decorum, and enforce the Constitution and Laws of the Order.

2d. To decide all questions of order, subject to appeal, by two members, from his decision to the Temple.

3d. To give the casting vote on all questions before the Temple, in which there may be an equal division of members, except in the election of officers and appeals from his decision.

4th. To inspect all ballots on application for membership, degrees, or certificates, and report thereon to the Temple.

5th. To sign all orders drawn on the Treasurer, for the payment of such sums of money as may, from time to time, be voted by the Temple, and also such documents as may require his signature to authenticate them.

6th. To appoint the officers herein before specified, at the time of his installation, and to fill vacancies in the same whenever they may occur.

7th. To appoint, at the same time, such standing committees as the Temple may prescribe, and such other committees, from time to time, as may be required by the Constitution and Laws, or directed by the Temple.

8th. To see that a brother is visited immediately upon being advised of his illness or distress, and to continue to do so at least once per week, during such illness or distress, and see that he is duly provided with attendants.

9th. To install their successors in office.

Sec. 2. Duties of the M. E. K. Sec.

1st. To keep, in suitable books for that purpose, the accounts of the Temple, and the members thereof.

2d. To receive all moneys due the Temple, pay the same to the Treasurer, and take his receipt therefor.

3d. To make out all notices that may be required for special meetings, attendance upon the sick, or distressed.

4th. To furnish the Temple, on the night preceding the expiration of each term of three months, a list of the members thereof, who are delinquent, with the amount due by each.

5th. To make out, at the expiration of each term of three months, a report to the Grand Council, in such form as said Grand Council shall direct, which he shall read in open Temple, and record in a book to be kept for that purpose; and when duly approved by the Temple and signed by the proper officers, he shall forward the same to the Grand Secretary, which shall be done within ten days from the expiration of each term of three months.

6th. To enroll in a book, provided for that purpose, the names of the members of the Temple, age, occupation, and residence thereof, and the degrees taken by each; noting from time to time, in a proper marginal column, the fact of death, suspension, expulsion, or withdrawal, as the same may occur.

7th. To attend the committees appointed to audit the books and accounts of the Temple, and render such assistance as may be necessary.

8th. To deliver up to his successor in office, all books and papers appertaining to his office, which may be in his possession.

9th. Generally to do and perform such other acts as may be required of him by the Temple, and by the laws and usages of the order.

He shall receive for his services such compensation as the Temple may determine.

10th. To keep accurate minutes of the Temple in a book for that purpose.

ARTICLE V.

Section 1. It shall be the duty of the Treasurer—

1st. To receive from the Secretary all moneys due the T.

2d. To pay all orders drawn upon the funds in his hands, when properly attested.

3d. To have his books and accounts ready for settlement at the expiration of his term of office, and open for inspection by the officer of the T., or a committee appointed for that purpose, at all times.

4th. To deliver to his successor in office, at the expiration of his term of office, resignation thereof, or removal therefrom, all moneys remaining in his hands, and all books and papers pertaining to his office.

To give bond with two sureties, conditioned upon the faithful discharge of his duties, as the T. may require.

SEC. 2. The terms of three months shall commence February 22d of each year.

ARTICLE VI.—MEMBERSHIP.

SECTION 1. S. L——. Any white male person, of good moral character, above the age of eighteen years, being proposed by one, and vouched for by two members in good standing, may receive the S. L—— lesson of this order.

SEC. 2. When the name of a candidate is proposed for membership, it shall be referred to a committee of three, appointed by the G. S.; said committee to report on such proposition at the next regular meeting of the Temple, and no balloting for membership to take place until the committee report as aforesaid.

SEC. 3. First degree members must be advanced in accordance with provisions laid down in the ritual of the second and third degrees.

SEC. 4. All candidates for degrees must be balloted for. One negative vote lays the application over one week; two negative votes, for three months; three negative votes disposes of it finally, unless reconsidered.

SEC. 5. A member changing his residence, wishing to withdraw from one T. and unite with another, shall be entitled to receive a certificate of membership, which, being filed with his application, if found worthy, shall be transferred, by vote of the T., at his new residence.

SEC. 6. No T. is permitted to receive applications from persons not residents of the county in which the T. is located, and all applications must be made to the T. nearest to the applicant's residence.—*Res. of G. C.*

SEC. 7. An expelled member can only be reinstated by the consent of the Temple from which he was expelled.

SEC. 8. If a person is proposed for membership and elected, and previous to initiation the Temple obtains information of bad conduct, it may refuse to initiate.

ARTICLE VII.—FEES AND DUES.

SECTION 1. The fee for the first or branch T. degree, shall be one dollar; the fee for the second shall be one dollar and fifty cents; and the fee for the third shall be two dollars and fifty cents.

SEC. 2. The monthly dues for each and every member, shall not be less than ten nor more than fifty cents.

LAWS OF GENERAL APPLICATION.

1st. It shall be the duty of every member of this order, when possessed of any information touching the improper demeanor of a brother, to file written complaint with his immediate G. S. or C., and shall make it known to no other person, and it shall be the duty of such officer specifying the charge in regular meeting of T., withholding name of the informant, appoint committee of five to examine and report upon such charge, and, if upon report of committee, such charge shall be sustained by said T., then said accused shall be notified to appear, and shall be regularly tried by the T., said committee conducting the prosecution, and accused shall have counsel in his behalf, witnesses may be examined, and testimony of those not members of the order may be taken, but not *ex parte.*

Upon fair hearing the T. shall decide upon his guilt and punishment, which shall not be higher than expulsion from the order. The various grades of punishment shall be reprimand, suspension for a time, and expulsion.

2d. It shall be the duty of all T.'s, in case of expulsion of a member or members, to notify the G. Sec. by letter; and it shall be the duty of said G. Sec. to notify all T.'s in this jurisdiction of said fact.

Visiting Brothers.

3d. It shall be the duty of the presiding officer of each and every T., whenever necessary, to appoint two competent brothers an examining committee for the evening; for no visiting brother can be admitted to the T., unless he shall be known, recognized by the officers, vouched for by a brother, or proved by the committee so appointed.

Payment of Assessments.

4th. It shall be the duty of each and every P. T. in the State, to remit to the G. Sec. such amounts as the G. Council shall levy against them, promptly, upon the application of the G. Sec., and in case of failure so to do for a period of three months, such P. T. shall forfeit their organization.

We recommend the Constitution of the Society of the Illini, for all public clubs; and the rules of order, adopted by the G. Council, for the government of all subordinate T.'s in Indiana.

5th. Any additional by-laws may be made by each County Temple, not inconsistent with the laws of the Grand Council, by a two-thirds vote of the members of such temple, four weeks notice being given therefor.

RULES OF ORDER.

1st. When the presiding officer takes the chair, the officers and members shall take their respective seats; and at the sound of the gavel there shall be a general silence, under the penalty of a public reprimand.

2d. The business of the annual meetings shall be taken up in the following order:

Temple opened;

Officers' roll called;

Minutes of last stated and intervening meetings read and passed **upon**;

Certificates of members;

Reports of Temples;

Reports of Committees;

Unfinished business;

New business.

3d. The presiding officer shall preserve order and decorum, and pronounce the decision of the Temple on all subjects; he may speak to points of order in preference to other members, rising from his seat for that purpose; he shall decide questions of order 'without debate, unless entertaining doubts on the point, subject to an appeal to the Temple by any two members, on which appeal no member shall speak more than once.

4th. No member shall disturb another in his speech, unless to call him to order, nor stand up to interrupt him, nor when a member is speaking, pass between him and the chair, or leave the hall.

5th. Every member when he speaks shall rise and respectfully address the chair, and when he has finished shall sit down. Members speaking shall confine themselves to the question under debate, and avoid all personality or indecorous language, as well as any reflection upon the Temple or its members.

6th. If two or more members rise to speak at the same time, the chair shall decide which is entitled to the floor.

7th. No member shall speak until he has been recognized by the chair.

8th. No member shall speak more than once on the same subject or question, until all the members, wishing to speak, shall have had an opportunity to do so, nor more than twice without permission of the T.

9th. If a member, while speaking, be called to order by the chair, he shall cease speaking, and take his seat until the question of order is determined, and permission is given him to proceed.

10th. No motion shall be subject to debate until it shall have been seconded, and stated by the chair, and it shall be reduced to writing if desired by any member.

11th. When a question is before the T., no motion shall be received except for adjournment—the previous question—to lie on the table—to postpone indefinitely—to postpone to a certain time—to divide—to commit or amend; which motions shall severally have preference in the order herein arranged.

12th. On the call of five members, the previous question shall be put. The previous question having been ordered, all further amendments and debates shall be precluded, but the amendments that have been previously offered shall be voted upon in their order before the main question.

13th. When a blank is to be filled, and different sums, numbers, or times shall be proposed, the question shall first be taken upon the highest sum or number, and longest or latest time.

14th. No motion for reconsideration shall be received unless moved by a member who voted in the majority in the first instance.

15th. Any member may excuse himself from serving on any committee at the time of his appointment, if he is then a member of one other committee.

16th. The person first named on a committee shall act as chairman thereof until another is chosen by themselves.

17th. The consequences of a measure may be reprobated in strong terms; but to arraign the motives of those who propose or advocate it, is a personality and against order.

18th. While the chair is putting a question or addressing the Temple, or whilst any other member is speaking, no member shall walk about or leave the Temple, or entertain private discourse.

19th. No motion can be made by one member while another is speaking; and no motion can be made without rising and addressing the chair.

20th. The chair, or any member, doubting the decision of the question, may call for a division of the Temple, and a count of the affirmative and negative vote.

21st. All reports of committees shall be made in writing.

22d. Any member has a right to protest, and to have his protest spread upon the journal.—*C. M.*

23d. Motions for adjournment, the previous question, to lie on the table, and to postpone indefinitely, shall be put without debate.

24th. Any of these rules may be dispensed with by a vote of two-thirds of the members present.

CONSTITUTION OF THE GRAND COUNCIL OF S. L. OF INDIANA.

ARTICLE I.

SECTION 1. This body derives and exercises its power and authority from and by virtue of authority vested in it by the Supreme Grand Council of the United States.

SEC. 2. The members of this G. C. shall consist of Representatives duly elected and commissioned by the various County Temples. Each County Temple shall be entitled to two Representatives; and for each one thousand members one additional Representative.

SEC. 3. The legislative functions of this body shall be vested in such Representatives duly chosen and commissioned, and the elective officers of this G. C.

SEC. 4. All such Representatives and Military Officers, so accredited, shall be entitled to receive the sign of the G. C.

SEC. 5. Representatives shall be elected at any regular meeting, prior to the 22d day of February, in each year, and hold their office during the term of one year, or during the pleasure of the County T.

ARTICLE II.

Sec. 1. The elective officers of this G. C. shall consist of the following, who shall be elected at or prior to the annual meeting, held on the 22d day of February, in each year, viz.: G. C.; Dep. G. C.; G. Sec.; G. Treas.; G. C. to S. C.; one Maj. Gen'l for each military district, prescribed by law.

Sec. 2. The appointed officers of this G. body shall be, one Grand Marshal, one Grand Conductor, one Grand Chaplain, one Grand Warden of the Council, one Grand Warden of the O. C.

Sec. 3. The members of the G. Com. staff, and all military officers above the rank of Colonel, shall be *ex officio* members of this G. C., and entitled to the sign and to participate in its deliberations.

Sec. 4. When upon a call for a vote by counties, all shall be excluded save the duly elected Representatives, and in case of a tie vote the G. Com. presiding shall give the casting vote.

ARTICLE III.

Section I. This G. C. shall have the sole right to determine its own membership, and may exclude any one, representative or otherwise, who shall be convicted of indecorous deportment, or any dishonorable act. *Provided*, That no punishment higher than reprimand shall be inflicted, expulsion from this Order being reserved to the County Temples.

Sec. 2. There shall be chosen, annually, the Grand Commander, and two additional members of this body, delegates to the S. G. C., to whom the G. Secretary shall issue certificates of election, with the seal of the Council.—*Law of S. G. C.*

Sec. 3. The meetings of this G. C., regular and special, shall be held at such time and place as may be fixed by law.

Sec. 4. All elections shall be by ballot, and a majority of all the votes given shall be necessary to constitute a choice. When there are more than two candidates for any office, the lowest of such candidates, at each ballot, after the first, shall be dropped, and all votes that may be given for such candidate or candidates thereafter, shall not be counted. In the event of a tie between two candidates for the same office, for two successive ballotings, the election shall be decided by lot.

ARTICLE IV.—DUTIES OF GRAND OFFICERS.

Section 1. The G. C. shall have and exercise a general supervision of the Order in the State of Indiana. He shall preside at all meetings of the Grand Council, at which he may be present, preserve order, and cause the Constitution and Laws to be strictly observed. His decision on all points not provided for in the Constitution or General Laws, shall be conclusive, unless reversed by the Grand Council of Indiana, or the S. G. C. of the United States, upon appeal thereto. He shall give the casting vote, in case of an equal division, upon all questions arising in the Grand Council, except on appeals from his own decision; and in all elections of officers, he shall be entitled to vote only as other members. He shall not be entitled to participate in any discussions in the Grand Council, except in committee of the whole, or upon questions of order and appeals from his decision. He shall sign all orders drawn on the Grand Treasurer, and all other documents which may require his signature. He shall fill all official vacancies not otherwise provided for. He shall appoint all committees, except when the nomination and appointment thereof shall be reserved by the Grand Council. He shall have power and authority to grant dispensations for conferring degrees in the institution of new Temples, and for the purpose of qualifying officers thereof, during the first six months; and for all other matters unprovided for, wherein immediate action is necessary. He shall have power to call special meetings of the Grand Council, or of any subordinate Temple, whenever he may deem it necessary for the good of the Order so to do. He shall, from time to time, give information, etc.

Sec. 2. The Dep. G. C. shall assist the G. C., and in his absence perform his duties.

Sec. 3. The Grand Secretary shall keep a journal of the proceedings of this body, and money accounts, shall receive all moneys and pay the same to the Treasurer, taking his receipt therefor. He shall attest all dispensations granted, and commissions issued, by the G. Commander. He shall transmit an annual report of the state of the order in Indiana, to the S. G. C. of the United States, in such form as the said S. G. C. may direct. He shall receive all documents for the G. C., and immediately submit the same to the G. Commander. He shall, under the supervision of the G. Com., conduct the correspondence of the G. C. He shall, when so directed, summon the Representatives to attend its special meetings. He shall prepare and procure the signatures of the officers to all charters that may be granted by the G. C. He shall, whenever notified, attend any committee of the Grand Council, and furnish such official papers and documents as may be required. He shall have the custody of the Grand Seal, and perform such other duties as may be prescribed in this Constitution, or the Laws of the Grand Council. He shall receive for his services, annually, the sum of eight hundred dollars; and shall give such bond and security for the faithful performance of his duties, as the Grand Council may require.

Sec. 4. The G. Treasurer shall have charge of the funds, and all other property or evidence of title belonging to, or held in trust by the Grand Council, which may be placed in his hands. He shall keep correct accounts of all moneys which he may receive from the G. Secretary, and from all other sources, and pay all orders drawn upon the funds in his hands, by the Grand Commander, when attested by the G. Secretary. He shall, whenever notified, attend any committee of the Grand Council, and furnish such books and papers in his possession as may be required. At the expiration of his term of office, or after resignation thereof, or removal therefrom, he shall make full settlement with the Finance Committee, and deliver to his successor in office, all moneys, books, bonds, vouchers and documents, and property, belonging to, or held in trust by the Grand Council, which may be in his possession. Before entering upon his duties, he shall give such bond and security as may be required by the Grand Council.

Sec. 5. Other appointed officers shall perform the ordinary duties of their offices, as prescribed by custom or law.

Sec. 6. Any amendment to this Constitution may be made at any regular meeting of this G. C., by giving one day's notice, in writing, and receiving a majority vote of the members present.

Sec. 7. All elective officers shall take the following prescribed oath of office before entering upon their duties, viz.:

Official Oath.

I, ———, having been elected by ——— to the office of ——— in ———, do, in the presence of God and these witnesses, solemnly swear to maintain the Constitution and Laws of this Order; obey all rightful orders emanating from superior authority, and to perform the duties which have been devolved upon me, as ———, to the best of my ability, so help me God.

RULES OF ORDER.

1st. When the presiding officer takes the chair, the officers and members shall take their respective seats; and at the sound of the gavel there shall be a general silence, under the penalty of a public reprimand.

2d. The business of the annual meetings shall be taken up in the following order:

Temple opened;

Officers' roll called;

Minutes of last stated and intervening meetings read and passed upon;

Certificates of members;

Reports of Temples;

Reports of Committees;

Unfinished business;

New business.

3d. The presiding officer shall preserve order and decorum, and pronounce the decision of the Temple on all subjects; he may speak to points of order in preference to other members, rising from his seat for that purpose; he shall decide questions of order without debate, unless entertaining doubts on the point, subject to an appeal to the Temple by any two members, on which appeal no member shall speak more than once.

4th. No member shall disturb another in his speech, unless to call him to order, nor stand up to interrupt him, nor when a member is speaking, pass between him and the chair, or leave the hall.

5th. Every member when he speaks shall rise and respectfully address the chair, and when he has finished shall sit down. Members speaking shall confine themselves to the question under debate, and avoid all personality or indecorous language, as well as any reflection upon the Temple or its members.

6th. If two or more members rise to speak at the same time, the chair shall decide which is entitled to the floor.

7th. No member shall speak until he has been recognized by the chair.

8th. No member shall speak more than once on the same subject or question, until all the members, wishing to speak, shall have had an opportunity to do so, nor more than twice without permission of the T.

9th. If a member, while speaking, be called to order by the chair, he shall cease speaking, and take his seat until the question of order is determined, and permission is given him to proceed.

10th. No motion shall be subject to debate until it shall have been seconded, and stated by the chair, and it shall be reduced to writing if desired by any member.

11th. When a question is before the T., no motion shall be received except for adjournment—the previous question—to lie on the table—to postpone indefinitely—to postpone to a certain time—to divide—to commit or amend; which motions shall severally have preference in the order herein arranged.

12th. On the call of five members, the previous question shall be put. The previous question having been ordered, all further amendments and debates shall be precluded, but the amendments that have been previously offered shall be voted upon in their order before the main question.

13th. When a blank is to be filled, and different sums, numbers, or times shall be proposed, the question shall first be taken upon the highest sum or number, and longest or latest time.

14th. No motion for reconsideration shall be received unless moved by a member who voted in the majority in the first instance.

15th. Any member may excuse himself from serving on any committee at the time of his appointment, if he is then a member of one other committee.

16th. The person first named on a committee shall act as chairman thereof until another is chosen by themselves.

17th. The consequences of a measure may be reprobated in strong terms; but to arraign the motives of those who propose or advocate it, is a personality and against order.

18th. While the chair is putting a question or addressing the Temple, or whilst any other member is speaking, no member shall walk about or leave the Temple, or entertain private discourse.

19th. No motion can be made by one member while another is speaking; and no motion can be made without rising and addressing the chair.

20th. The chair, or any member, doubting the decision of the question, may call for a division of the Temple, and a count of the affirmative and negative vote.

21st. All reports of committees shall be made in writing.

22d. Should any committee be appointed at one session of the Grand Council, to report at the next succeeding session, it shall be the duty of such committee to report in writing, even though they be not Representatives.

23d. Any member has a right to protest, and to have his protest spread upon the journal.—*C. M.*

24th. Motions for adjournment, the previous question, to lie on the table, and to postpone indefinitely, shall be put without debate.

25th. Any of these rules may be dispensed with by a vote of two-thirds of the members present.

CONSTITUTION AND LAWS OF THE S. G. C.

SECTION 1. This organization shall be known as the S. L.

SEC. 2. Its object and purposes are the maintenance of constitutional freedom and State rights, as recognized and established by the founders of our Republic.

SEC. 3. The system of government of this order shall be vested in a Supreme Council of the States, a Grand Council of each State, and Parent and Branch Temples of each county.

SEC. 4. The officers of the Supreme Council shall consist of a Supreme Commander, Secretary of State of the Order, Treasurer, and Clerk of the Council, who shall be annually elected by the Supreme Council, on the twenty-second day of February, and shall hold their offices until their successors are duly elected and qualified.

SEC. 5. The Supreme Council shall be composed of the Grand Commanders of the several States and two delegates, who shall be annually elected by the Grand Councils of the respective States. Each delegate shall be entitled to one vote, and when a full delegation is not in attendance, those present may cast the entire vote of the State, and in all cases of a tie the presiding officer shall have the casting vote.

SEC. 6. The Supreme Council shall meet on the twenty-second day of February, of each year, at such place as may be designated.

SEC. 7. The Supreme Commander or three Grand Commanders of States, may call special sessions of the Supreme Council, at such times and places as he or they may deem expedient.

SEC. 8. The Supreme Commander shall take an oath to observe and maintain the principles of the order, before entering upon the duties of his office, said oath to be prescribed by law. He shall be the presiding officer to the Supreme Council, and charged with the execution of all laws enacted by it. He shall be commander-in-chief of all military forces belonging to the order, in the various States, when called into actual service. He shall deliver a message to each meeting of the Supreme Council, showing the condition of the order, and such recommendations as its interest may demand.

SEC. 9. The Deputy Supreme Commander, in case of death, absence, or resignation of the Supreme Commander, shall exercise all the powers and perform all the duties pertaining to said office; shall take the same oath of office, and be chairman of the Committee on Military Affairs.

SEC. 10. The Secretary of State of the Order shall be the chairman of the Committee on the State of the Order; shall conduct all official correspondence of the Supreme Council, and be the medium of communication between the State and Supreme Councils; he shall ascertain and report at each annual meeting of the Supreme Council, the condition of the order in each State, and make such recommendations as he may deem proper.

SEC. 11. The Treasurer shall be under such regulations as may be prescribed by law; shall be the custodian of all funds belonging to the Supreme Council; shall pay all orders drawn upon him by the Clerk and countersigned by the Supreme Commander, or chairman of the Auditing Committee, and make, at each meeting, reports showing the financial condition of the order, and such recommendations as he may deem expedient.

SEC. 12. All elections shall be by ballot, and a majority of all the votes cast shall be necessary to a choice; *Provided*, That where there is but one candidate, the election may be *viva voce*.

SEC. 13. That the Supreme Commander

administer the oath to all officers; and Councilors take the oath at the Clerk's desk.

GENERAL LAWS.

Section 1. A quorum of the Supreme Council shall consist of a majority of the States, in which State Councils shall have been established.

Sec. 2. Delegates from Territorial Councils shall be entitled to a seat and a right to speak in the Supreme Council, but no vote.

Sec. 3. The ordinance or constitution of the Supreme Council shall be read at the opening of each session, and to all new delegates.

Sec. 4. It shall be the duty of the Clerk to count and announce all votes of the Council, as well when taken by count, as by States or ballot.

CONDITION OF THE ORDER AND REVENUES.

Sec. 5. The Secretaries of the various State Councils are required to report to the Secretary of the Supreme Council, during the month of January of each year, for his report at the annual sessions, the number of brothers in the order, in their respective States, and also the condition of their treasuries.

Sec. 6. The Treasurer of each State Council shall pay over to the Treasurer of the Supreme Council, in January of each year, such sums as may be assessed upon them by the Supreme Council, based upon estimates of the Finance Committee.

Sec. 7. The Standing Committee upon Finance shall be nominated by the Supreme Commander, and confirmed by a vote of two-thirds of the Supreme Council at each annual session; and the two members unprovided for in the Supreme Ordinance, of each of the Committees on the State of the Order and Finance, shall be appointed and confirmed in like manner. These committees shall report and recommend at each annual and extra session.

EXTENSION OF THE ORDER.

Sec. 8. For the purpose of extending the Order into States and Territories, where it does not now exist, it is hereby declared that full authority for this purpose, is vested in the Supreme Commander, or duly qualified Supreme Councilors in the following manner, viz.: They may, at the instance of five good men, in any State or Territory, institute County Temples, and when a sufficient number of such County Temples have been instituted, they may establish a State Council, the duly elected delegates of which shall be admitted to this Supreme Council upon an equality with the organized States or Territories.

FINANCE COMMITTEE.

Sec. 9. It shall be the duty of the Finance Committee, at each meeting, to audit all accounts which shall be presented, and to examine the books and accounts of the Clerk and Treasurer, and report to the Supreme Council.

MILEAGE AND PER DIEM.

Sec. 10. That for the purpose of defraying the expenses of delegates to the Supreme Council, it is hereby left to each State Grand Council to fix, determine, and pay in the manner and to the extent that such State may determine.

Sec. 11. That the Treasurer of the Supreme Council shall, before entering upon the duties of his office, take the oath required, and give bond in a sum double the amount of funds likely to come into his hands.

Sec. 12. The Clerk of the Supreme Council shall keep an accurate journal of all its proceedings, draw orders on the Treasurer for all claims that are presented and properly audited by the Finance Committee; collect all dues from the States, receipt for and pay the same over to the Treasurer, and preserve and keep all records and papers belonging to the Council.

Sec. 13. All laws and resolutions of the Supreme Council shall be signed by the Clerk, countersigned by the Supreme Commander, and attested by the seal of the order.

Sec. 14. The Standing Committees of the Supreme Council shall consist of a Committee on Finance, a Committee on the State of the Order, and a Committee on Military Affairs.

Sec. 15. Delegates to the Supreme Council, before entering upon the duties of their office, shall take an oath to support and maintain the principles of the order.

Sec. 16. The government of the order in the States shall be vested in a Grand Council, composed of not less than one delegate from each county, and a Grand Commander and Deputy Grand Commander, elected by said Councils, in such manner as they may provide.

Sec. 17. The Grand Commanders shall be the presiding officers of the Grand Councils of the States, execute all laws passed by such Councils, and shall be commanders-in-chief of the military forces of their respective States.

Sec. 18. This Constitution shall be the supreme law of the order, and may be amended by a two-thirds vote of the Supreme Council.

PROCEEDINGS

OF THE

GRAND COUNCIL OF THE STATE OF INDIANA,

At their Meeting, held on the 16th and 17th of Feb., 1864.

The within proceedings are published in compliance with the following resolution:

"*Resolved,* That the Grand Secretary prepare and publish, in pamphlet form, the address of the Grand Commander, with such part of the proceedings of the Grand Council, as may be necessary for the information of the County Temples, and send one copy of said publication to each County Temple."

COUNCILORS: For the honor you have done me. in fixing a time to hear my views and suggestions in relation to this organization, and general matters, I feel duly sensible, and am only sorry that I am so illy prepared to meet your expectations.

We are organized for a high and noble purpose, the erection and consecration of Temples to the service of true Republicanism: altars upon which we may lay our hands and hearts with the invocation, "God of our Fathers." Well may we call upon the God of truth, justice, and human rights, in our efforts to preserve what the great wisdom and heroic acts of our fathers achieved.

This, my friends, is no small undertaking—requiring patience, fortitude, patriotism, and a self-sacrificing disposition from each and all, and may require us to hazard life itself, in support and defense of those great cardinal principles which are the foundation stones of the State and Federal Governments. It is the boast of those who, for long centuries, have fostered and kept alive brotherly love and mutual protection, among, not only the civilized, but in some degree the semi-barbarous nations of the earth, that they have attained now apparent great results, through trials, tribulations, long suffering and persecutions. So, too, the worshipers of God, be they Jew or Gentile, claim to more distinctly merit an identity and name, in consequence of the imminent perils and innumerable conflicts, which have been thrown in their way to impede their progress. So may we, and doubtless will, point with pride to our present troubles, in the future, to prove our great worth. This great brotherhood is entitled now to the respect of mankind, for the part it enacted in the period anterior to the Revolution of 1776. Through it the Declaration was made, and the independence of the States achieved. This alone would endear it to every patriot heart, to every lover of republican institutions; if its history should stop here, when its operations were suspended, it were certainly enough—but still more glorious, superlatively brilliant, will be its history, when reinstated as it now is, it shall restore to this great people their *fireside rights, a pure elective franchise, and an untrammeled judiciary;* when fanatical usurpers and would-be tyrants and dictators are swept away with the rubbish that has been thrown to the surface in these extraordinary times; when once more the governing principle shall be the will of the governed expressly declared; when no more power shall be exercised than is or has been de-

rived from the people, the legitimate source of all power.

The great principle now in issue, is the centralization of power, or the keeping it diffused in State sovereignty, as it is by the organic laws, constituting States and forming the General Government.

The creation of an empire, or republic, or the reconstruction of the old Union, by brute force, is simply impossible. The liberation of four million blacks, and putting them upon an equality with the whites, is a scheme which can only bring its authors into shame, contempt and confusion. No results of this enterprise will ever be realized beyond the army of occupation.

It is not the part of wisdom, for those who have in hand the noble work of preserving the States from ruin, and the races from intermixture, to base their action upon any incident or accident, or upon any supposed termination of our present troubles. He who changes his views upon victory or defeat, is but a poor soldier for a long campaign against the mass of error, corruption and crime, now thickly spread over and through the body politic, and to an alarming extent influencing the action of the American mind.

But, shall we stand aloof from political alliances, and seek in our own way to assist in the needful reformation? Shall we rely entirely upon ourselves? By no means—when the great end in view can be in the least degree promoted, we should not hesitate to lend our aid and support; but care should be taken that no uncertain path, or devious ways, be entered upon.

Let me speak plain—our political affinity is unquestionably with the Democratic party, and if that organization goes boldly to the work, standing firmly upon its time-honored principles, maintaining unsullied its integrity, it is safe to presume that it will receive the moral and physical support of this wide extended association.

The great boast of the Democratic party has been, that it has met and beaten back the party of centralization, since the formation of the Union; and, although it has never ordained any principles in regard to the status of the inferior races, it has at all times strictly adhered to the doctrine of making it a purely local matter, and leaving to the States, by the exercise of their reserved powers, to regulate it as a domestic institution; the maintainance of this doctrine, in its intendment and general operations, must be satisfactory to the entire brotherhood. Let no one say we will thus be subservient to a party; rather will we be subservient to the demands of our country, and the cause in which we have enlisted.

There need be no apprehension that a war of coercion will be continued by a Democratic administration. if placed in control of public affairs, for with the experience of the present one, which has for three years, with the unlimited resources of eighteen millions of people, in men, money and ships, won nothing but its own disgrace, and probable downfall, it is not likely that another, if it values public estimation, will repeat the experiment.

Neither have we any reason to fear that the Democratic party, in shaping the canvass of 1864, will go out of its way to insult five hundred thousand of those whose votes are necessary to its success; let us rather incline to the belief that all the elements of opposition can and will be united, with no sacrifice of principle or manhood, to crush out this one now in power.

A mere change of men will avail nothing, without corresponding action. Men, statesmen, and executive officers, exhort people to patience and long suffering, and while condemning Federal usurpation, yield obedience to all its demands. In the estimation of the membership of this organization, such men and such governors, be they of what party they may, must be regarded as enemies to good government. I trust I may be pardoned if I give a few examples to illustrate.

If this people can not excuse the Federal Executive for exercising undue and unwarranted power, toward breaking down their rights, derived from the force of their State Governments, how shall they palliate the offense of Governor Seymour, in violating his obligations in allowing it to be done in the great State of New York? This Governor becomes accessory after the fact, and is alike worthy of public condemnation. Do you tell me it is a necessity to thus subserve the Washington usurpers? In God's name, do not tell me that it is a necessity to be forsworn, to violate the plainest provisions of the Constitution, to consign a people to a slavish subserviency to the will of one man. You may tell me that it is rather a necessity to give up place, aye, to give up life itself. Because the punishment of these crimes against law and the people, being impeachment, and lodged with legislative bodies, that will not execute it, they are nevertheless offenses, and will be so adjudged hereafter, when healthy restraints of law shall be demanded to protect life and property.

The Democracy of Indiana, too, has made a culprit of itself. A Senator, by the mean and contemptible action of a majority of the United States Senate, was wrongfully and maliciously expelled from his seat. The Legislature plainly acquiesced in this insult to the State and the party, by refusing to return him again. Again, our cherished Vallandigham resides in exile, not so much by the power of Lincoln, as the demands of those who are controlling, or did control the Democratic party in that State.

These things are of the past, shall they be repeated in the future? The great fear is, that they will be, so long as this bugbear of civil war shall continue to horrify otherwise sensible people. My advice to you is, look well to the selection of men, upon whom you devolve the functions of leaders. This is no time to put forward men who take counsel of their fears.

Will the exercise of an undoubted right, an inalienable, an inherited, a constitutional right, lead to conflict? Will opposition to usurpers, to dictators, to tyrants, who have broken down the safeguards of life and property, lead to it? Then there is no escape, save in dishonor, and the most potent argument in favor of the permanency and spread of this association lies in the fact, that there are men who desire place and those who desire peace and quiet upon such terms. But who will bring conflict? Who will commence hostilities? Certainly not those who are merely claiming their rights? The conflict must then be commenced by those who are in the wrong. Must a people, therefore, continue to abase themselves, to keep those whom they have placed in authority from committing outrages upon them? This is the strange logic of the times.

This organization is based upon the principle of conserving the government inaugurated by the people, and bound to oppose all usurpations of power. Now it so happens that in the seventh year of its re-establishment, we find our State and Federal Government overturned. Yes, 'tis true. Lincoln's government is an usurpation—Morton's government is an usurpation. Now I know not what others may do, but for myself, I am willing the ballot box shall decide who shall be the officers, under the law and Constitution; but I shall obey them only so far as they exercise their delegated powers. I will not agree to remain passive, under usurped authority, affecting my rights and liberties.

Now, if the present condition can be changed by the ballot, all will rejoice; but how will the ballot decide any thing, when the dominant party of the country appeal from it to force? No one will enter the contest to overturn this party, more cheerfully than will I. But suppose it re-elects itself, will it return to the Constitution and laws? Are all those who do not agree with them to enter upon that delightful future, which has been so often and boastfully predicted by the Executive of this State, and many of his appointees? That future to you and to me is death, confiscation of our property, starvation of our children, the forced marriage of our heirs to their new-made colored brethren in arms.

If these men be prolonged in power, they must either consent to be content to exercise the power delegated by the people, or by the gods they must prove themselves physically the stronger. This position is demanded by every true member of this fraternity, honor, life—aye, more than life, the virtue of our wives and daughters demand it; and if you intend to make this organization of any practical value, you will do one of two things—either take steps to work the political regeneration of the party with which we are affiliated, up to this standard, or relying upon ourselves, determine at once our plan of action.

It might be asked now, shall men be coerced to go to war, in a mere crusade to free negroes, and territorial aggrandizement? Shall our people be taxed to carry forward a war of emancipation, miscegenation, confiscation, or extermination?

It would be the happiest day of my life, if I could stand up with any considerable portion of my fellow men and say, "Not another dollar, not another man, for this nefarious war." But the views and suggestions of exiled Vallandigham will be of greater consequence to you than my own. He says to you, the only issue now is *peace or war*. To the former he is committed, and can not, will not retract. He tells us not to commit ourselves to men. As well as he loves, and much as he admires the little hero McClellan, he would have the Chicago Convention act with untrammeled freedom. He reasons that the spring campaign will be more disastrous to the Federal armies than those heretofore made. That by July the increased call for troops, the certainty of a prolonged war, the rottenness of the financial system, defection of border State troops, the spread and adoption of the principles of this organization, will all tend to bring conservative men to one mind.

He anticipates that the deliberations of the Chicago Convention will no doubt be harmonious, and that its nominees will carry a majority of the adhering States—thinks that Government, by the one-tenth proclamation, will vote all seceded States, and overcome us; and says if this northern people do not inaugurate the men thus duly and legally chosen, they will be wanting in that manhood and spirit that should characterize freemen. He wishes it distinctly understood, although pressed from various quarters, that he will not consent to the use of his name before the convention for a nomination, but thinks, in case we succeed, that he would be entitled to have a place in the cabinet, (may he get it, and not say like General Taylor, that he has "no friends to reward and no enemies to punish.") He counsels late action on the part of State conventions; thinks Ohio is called too soon—advising that Indiana should have hers, say first of June. He finally judges that the Washington power will not yield up its power, until it is taken from them by an indignant people, by force of arms. He intimates that parties—men and interests—will divide into two classes,

and that a conflict will ensue for the mastery.

"*Sons of Liberty*," arise! the day is rapidly approaching in the which you can make good your promises to your country. The furnace is being heated that will prove your sincerity—the hour for daring deeds is not distant—let the watchword be onward! And let the result bless mankind with Republican Government, in this, our beloved land, to their latest posterity.

Your Committee on Platform, having had the subject of a platform to govern the action of the various Councils of the State of Indiana, beg leave to report the following, which they recommend be adopted by this Grand Council:

WHEREAS, A crisis has arisen in the history of the Federal Government in relation to the rights of the States, whether delegated or reserved; the manifest usurpations of undelegated powers by the President; the utter disregard of all Constitutional guarantees of liberty, looking constantly to the subjugation of the States and the establishment of a Centralized Despotism, already fill us with alarm for the cause of civil liberty in America. AND WHEREAS, it is due to those who differ with us in our notions of right, as well as the mode and measure of redress, to know where we stand, we propose to declare to them frankly our convictions and purposes in the premises; therefore,

Resolved, That the right to alter or abolish their Government, whenever it fails to secure the blessings of liberty, is one of the inalienable rights of the people, that can never be surrendered; nor is the right to maintain a Government that does secure the blessings of liberty less sacred and inalienable, therefore we declare that patriotism and manhood alike enjoin upon us resistance to usurpation as the highest and holiest duty of freemen.

2. That the necessity of amendments to the Articles of Confederation was suggested by a prevailing insurrection; its provisions matured amidst the threatening elements of civil war, and the Constitution tendered to the thirteen sovereign and independent States by the wisdom of the age, and accepted by them as a fortress around the liberties of the people, prescribing inflexible limits to the powers of the Government in war as well as in peace, and no necessity, however great, can warrant its violation by any officer of the Government; and every such infraction should be rebuked by the sternest energy of our nature.

3. That the great purpose of the Constitution of the United States was the maintainance of the principles of civil liberty. The Union a means, formed in a spirit of mutual concession, can only be restored and perpetuated by an adherence to the princi-

ples upon which it was founded, the voluntary consent of its members, and a scrupulous observance of the rights of each other under the Constitution; and that "war is disunion, final, irretrievable."

4. That while with just disdain we reject the epithet of "peace at any price" as a slander upon the true Democracy, and with instinctive promptness protest against the brutal doctrine of war for revenge, for plunder, or the debasement of our race to the level of a negro, we do regard the restoration of peace to our country, upon an honorable adjustment of the issues involved in this unholy and unnatural war, without humiliation to either party, as rising above all other considerations, and that in pondering the terms of such settlement we will look only to the peace and welfare of our race.

5. That whatever the theory of the powers of the Federal Government to coerce a State to remain in the Union may be, war as a means of restoring the Union is a delusion, involving a fearful waste of human life, hopeless bankruptcy, and the speedy downfall of the Republic. Therefore we recommend a cessation of hostilities upon existing facts, and a convention of the sovereign States to adjust the terms of a peace with a view to the restoration of the Union, entire if possible; if not, so much and such parts as the affinities of interest and civilization may attract.

6. That there is a point at which submission merges the man in the slave, and resistance becomes a duty. Whether that point, in the history of the times, has arrived, may be debated; but we will resist by force any attempt to abridge the elective franchise, whether by introduction of illegal votes, under military authority. or the attempt by Federal officers to intimidate the citizen by threats of oppression.

7. We reiterate and affirm the Virginia and Kentucky Resolutions of 1798–99, as embodying the true exposition of the Constitution.

8. That we will support and maintain the Constitution of the United States, and of the State of Indiana, and of the laws enacted under the same, as passed by the proper legislative authorities, and as expounded by the proper judicial tribunals.

9. That we will maintain, peaceably if we can, but forcibly if we must, the freedom of speech, the freedom of the press, the freedom of the person from arbitrary and unlawful arrest, and the freedom of the ballot box, from the aggression and violence of every person or authority whatsoever. And to these ends we hereby pledge to each other, and to our brethren throughout the United States and the State of Indiana, our lives, our fortunes, and our sacred honor.

To the Grand Council of Indiana:

Your committee beg leave to submit to this honorable body the following report:

It being of the greatest importance that the Grand Council be amply provided with the necessary means to meet the urgent demands upon it, at this period of its organic existence, and that without sufficient funds in its treasury, no permanent or systematic organization of the State can be effected, would first urge upon every Parent Temple, who has not already responded to the previous assessment of $20 00, made by the Grand Council, on each county or Parent Temple, the necessity of meeting that demand without any further delay. And second, that in order to provide an annual fund for the use of this Grand Council, that each county or Parent Temple be required to pay into the treasury of the Grand Council, on the first Monday in May, 1864, and annually thereafter, until otherwise ordered by the Grand Council, for each member in the county who has received the first degree, the sum of twenty cents. This assessment to include all members of the Sons of Liberty in each county throughout the State, whether members of the Parent Temple or the subordinate Temples throughout the townships. And they would recommend that the demands of the Supreme Council, on this Grand Council, be paid out of the funds to be provided by the foregoing assessment. And they would also recommend that the Grand Treasurer be required to give bond in double the amount of money that may come into his possession, by virtue of his office, conditioned for the faithful performance of his duties—such bond to be given to the Grand Commander, on or before the first day of May, 1864, and afterward upon entering upon the duties of that office.

M. E. Grand Commander:

In compliance with the resolution adopted by this body, I beg leave to submit the following report, showing the number of counties in the State that are organized; the number in process of organization, and the number of members in the organization, so far as I have received reports:

Reports have been received from but seventeen counties. We have organized in the State forty-one counties, and have in process of organization ten additional counties, leaving the number of counties yet to report their membership, thirty-four.

Judging from the reports received, I place the membership in the State, at this time, at least 12,000, not including the membership in the other organizations in the State, that work conjunctly with us. The following is a summary of the reports received: Grant county reports 201 members and 6 branches; Clay county reports 194 members and 3 branches; Blackford county reports 50 members and no branches; DeKalb county reports 34 members and no branches; Harrison county reports 615 members and 11 branches; Marshall county reports 30 members and no branches; Washington county reports 1,100 members and 10 branches; Allen county reports 40 members and no branches; Brown county reports 322 members and 4 branches; Wells county reports 51 members and no branches; Vigo county reports 500 members and 5 branches; Fountain county reports 373 members and 10 branches; Sullivan county reports 600 members and 10 branches; Parke county reports 533 members and 7 branches; Marion county reports 75 members and 1 branch; Vermillion county reports 135 members and 3 branches; Vanderburg county reports 200 members and no branches. Showing a total membership, in the counties reporting, of 5,053.

The above report does not include those counties from whom have been received intelligence, unofficially, of their organization, which would perhaps increase the number of counties organized and in process of organization to—say sixty-one.

The above report is respectfully submitted.

Resolved, That it is the instruction and advice of this Grand Council to the different temples of the State, that they proceed forthwith and perfect a thorough organization of their respective counties, and thereby prepare themselves to carry into effect any and every order of this body.

Resolved, That the delegates present, report the number of subscribers obtained, or that can be obtained for the *Constitutionalist*, the proposed organ of the order.

Reports on the above resolution gave assurance that the subscription lists of the *Constitutionalist* should be immediately taken in hand; and that at least 10,000 subscribers could, and would be obtained.

At this meeting of the Grand Council, thirty-one counties were represented, and there is no doubt, had it not been for the extreme cold, every organized county in the State would have been present through their delegates.

The organization in this State is in its infancy, and when we reflect that we have succeeded in organizing, in the short space of six months, over one-half the counties in the State, and have a membership numbering over 12,000, we have every reason to feel encouraged for the future.

The organization is extending its influence, popularity, and usefulness daily, and is already at work in the States of New York, New Jersey, Pennsylvania, New Hampshire, Connecticut, Ohio, Indiana, Illinois, Michigan, Delaware, Maryland, and Missouri, and numbers in its membership many of the noblest and most devoted champions of civil and religious liberty, remaining in our unhappy and distracted country.

In conclusion, it is urged upon our friends in the counties to work with untiring energy for the purpose of thorough organization. This is the first and only truly national organization the Democratic and Conservative men of the country have ever attempted, and we are assured that through it, and it only, can the peace, harmony and union of these States ever be restored.

OFFICIAL REPORT

OF THE

JUDGE ADVOCATE GENERAL

ON THE

"ORDER OF AMERICAN KNIGHTS,"

OR

"SONS OF LIBERTY."

A WESTERN CONSPIRACY IN AID OF THE SOUTHERN REBELLION.

21

REPORT.

War Department, Bureau of Military Justice,
Washington, D. C., October 8, 1864.

Hon. E. M. Stanton, Secretary of War:

SIR: Having been instructed by you to prepare a detailed report upon the mass of testimony furnished me from different sources in regard to the *Secret Associations and Conspiracies against the Government*, formed, principally in the Western States, by traitors and disloyal persons, I have now the honor to submit as follows:

During more than a year past it has been generally known to our military authorities that a secret treasonable organization, affiliated with the Southern rebellion, and chiefly military in its character, has been rapidly extending itself throughout the West. A variety of agencies, which will be specified herein, have been employed, and successfully, to ascertain its nature and extent, as well as its aims and its results; and, as this investigation has led to the arrest in several States of a number of its prominent members as dangerous public enemies, it has been deemed proper to set forth in full the acts and purposes of this organization, and thus to make known to the country at large its intensely treasonable and revolutionary spirit.

The subject will be presented under the following heads:

I. The origin, history, names, etc., of the order.
  II. Its organization and officers.
  III. Its extent and numbers.
  IV. Its armed force.
  V. Its ritual, oaths, and interior forms.
  VI. Its written principles.
  VII. Its specific purposes and operations.
VIII. The witnesses and their testimony.

I.—THE ORIGIN, HISTORY, NAMES, ETC., OF THE ORDER.

This secret association first developed itself in the West in the year 1862, about the period of the first conscription of troops, which it aimed to obstruct and resist. Originally known in certain localities as the "Mutual Protection Society," the "Circle of Honor," or the "Circle," or "Knights of the Mighty Host," but more widely as the "Knights of the Golden Circle," it was simply an inspiration of the rebellion, being little other than an extension among the disloyal and disaffected at the North of the association of the latter name, which had existed for some years at the South, and from which it derived all the chief features of its organization.

During the summer and fall of 1863 the order, both at the North and South, underwent some modifications as well as a change of name. In consequence of a partial exposure which had been made of the signs and ritual of the "Knights of the Golden Circle," Sterling Price had instituted as its successor in Missouri a secret political association, which he called the "Corps de Belgique," or "Southern League;" his principal coadjutor being Charles L. Hunt, of St. Louis, then Belgian Consul at that city, but whose *exequatur* was subsequently revoked by the President on account of his disloyal practices. The special object of the Corps de Belgique appears to have been to unite the rebel sympathizers of Missouri, with a view to their taking up arms and joining Price upon his proposed grand invasion of that State, and to their recruiting for his army in the interim.

Meanwhile, also, there had been instituted at the North, in the autumn of 1863, by sundry disloyal persons — prominent among whom were Vallandigham and P. C. Wright, of New York—a secret order, intended to be general throughout the country, and aiming at an extended influence and power, and at more positive results than its predecessor, and which was termed, and has since been widely known as the O. A. K., or "*Order of American Knights.*"

The opinion is expressed by Colonel Sanderson, Provost Marshal General of the Department of Missouri, in his official report upon the progress of this order, that it was founded by Vallandigham during his banishment, and upon consultation at Richmond with Davis and other prominent traitors. It is, indeed, the boast of the order in Indiana and elsewhere, that its "ritual" came direct from Davis himself; and Mary Ann Pitman, formerly attached to the command of the rebel Forrest, and a most intelligent witness—whose testimony will be hereafter referred to—states positively that Davis is a member of the order.

Upon the institution of the principal organization, it is represented that the "Corps de Belgique" was modified by Price, and became a Southern section of the Order of American Knights, and that the new name was generally adopted for the order, both at the North and South.

The secret signs and character of the order having become known to our military authorities, further modifications in the ritual and forms were introduced, and its name was finally changed to that of O. S. L., or "Order of the *Sons of Liberty*," or the "Knights of the Order of the Sons of Liberty." These later changes are represented to have been first instituted, and the new ritual compiled, in the State of Indiana, in May last, but the new name was at once generally adopted throughout the West, though in some localities the association is still better known as the "Order of American Knights."

Meanwhile, also, the order has received certain local designations. In parts of Illinois it has been called at times the "Peace Organization," in Kentucky the "Star Organization," and in Missouri the "American Organization;" these, however, being apparently names used outside of the lodges of the order. Its members have also been familiarly designated as "Butternuts" by the country people of Illinois, Indiana, and Ohio, and its separate lodges have also frequently received titles intended for the public ear; that in Chicago, for instance, being termed by its members the "Democratic Invincible Club," that in Louisville the "Democratic Reading Room," etc.

It is to be added that in the State of New York, and other parts of the North, the secret political association known as the "*McClellan Minute Guard*" would seem to be a branch of the Order of American Knights, having substantially the same objects, to be accomplished, however, by means expressly suited to the localities in which it is established. For, as the Chief Secretary of this association, Dr. R. F. Stevens, stated in June last to a reliable witness whose testimony has been furnished, "those who represent the McClellan interest are compelled to preach a vigorous prosecution of the war, in order to secure the popular sentiment and allure voters."

II.—ITS ORGANIZATION AND OFFICERS.

From printed copies, heretofore seized by the Government, of the Constitution of the Supreme Council, Grand Council, and County Parent Temples, respectively, of the Order of Sons of Liberty, in connection with other and abundant testimony, the organization of the order, in its latest form, is ascertained to be as follows:

1. The government of the order throughout the United States is vested in a Supreme Council, of which the officers are a Supreme Commander, Secretary of State, and Treasurer. These officers are elected for one year, at the annual meeting of the Supreme Council, which is made up of the Grand Commanders of the several States *ex officio*, and two delegates elected from each State in which the order is established.

2. The government of the order in a State is vested in a Grand Council, the officers of which are a Grand Commander, Deputy Grand Commander, Grand Secretary, Grand Treasurer, and a certain number of Major Generals, or one for each Military District. These officers also are elected annually by "representatives" from the county temples, each temple being entitled to two representatives, and one additional for each thousand members. This body of representatives is also invested with certain legislative functions.

3. The parent temple is the organization of the order for a county, each temple being formally instituted by authority of the Supreme Council, or of the Grand Council or Grand Commander of the State. By the same authority, or by that of the officers of the parent temple, branch or subordinate temples may be established for townships in the county.

But the strength and significance of this organization lie in its *military* character. The secret constitution of the Supreme Council provides that the Supreme Commander "*shall be commander-in-chief of all military forces belonging to the order in the various States when called into actual service;*" and further, that the Grand Commanders "*shall be commanders-in-chief of the military forces of their respective States.*" Subordinate to the Grand Commander in the State are the "*Major Generals*," each of whom commands his separate district and army. In Indiana the Major Generals are four in number. In Illinois, where the organization of the order is considered most perfect, the members in each congressional district compose a "*brigade*," which is commanded by a "*brigadier general.*" The members of each county constitute a "*regiment*," with a "*colonel*" in command, and those of each township form a "*company.*" A somewhat similar system prevails in Indiana, where also each company is divided into "*squads*," each with its chief—an arrangement intended to facilitate the *guerrilla* mode of warfare in case of a general outbreak or local disorder.

The "McClellan Minute Guard," as appears from a circular issued by the Chief Secretary in New York in March last, is organized upon a military basis similar to that of the order proper. It is composed of companies, one for each election district, ten of which constitute a "brigade," with a "brigadier general" at its head. The whole is placed under the authority of a "commander-in-chief." A strict obedience on the part of members to the orders of their superiors is enjoined.

The first "Supreme Commander" of the order was P. C. Wright, of New York, editor of the New York *News*, who was in May last placed in arrest and confined in Fort Lafayette. His successor in office was Vallandigham, who was elected at the annual meeting of the Supreme Council in February last. Robert Holloway, of Illinois, is represented to have acted as Lieutenant General, or Deputy Supreme Commander, during the absence of Vallandigham from the country. The Secretary of State chosen at the last election was Dr. Massey, of Ohio.

In Missouri, the principal officers were Charles L. Hunt, Grand Commander, Chas. E. Dunn, Deputy Grand Commander, and Green B. Smith, Grand Secretary. Since the arrest of these three persons (all of whom have made confessions which will be presently alluded to), James A. Barrett has, as it is understood, officiated as Grand Commander. He is stated to occupy also the position of chief of staff to the Supreme Commander.

The Grand Commander in Indiana, H. H. Dodd, is now on trial at Indianapolis by a military commission for "conspiracy against the Government," "violation of the laws of war," and other charges. The Deputy Grand Commander in that State is Horace Heffren, and the Grand Secretary, W. M. Harrison. The Major Generals are W. A. Bowles, John C. Walker, L. P. Milligan, and Andrew Humphreys. Among the other leading members of the order in that State are Dr. Athon, State Secretary, and Joseph Ristine, State Auditor.

The Grand Commander in Illinois is —— Judd, of Lewistown, and B. B. Piper, of Springfield, who is entitled "Grand Missionary" of the State, and designated also as a member of Vallandigham's staff, is one of the most active members, having been busily engaged throughout the summer in establishing temples and initiating members.

In Kentucky, Judge Bullitt, of the Court of Appeals, is Grand Commander, and, with Dr. U. F. Kalfus and W. R. Thomas, jailor in Louisville, two other of the most prominent members, has been arrested and confined by the military authorities. In New York, Dr. R. F. Stevens, the chief secretary of the McClellan Minute Guard, is the most active ostensible representative of the order.

The greater part of the chief and subordinate officers of the order and its branches, as well as the principal members thereof, are known to the Government, and, where not already arrested, may regard themselves as under a constant military surveillance. So complete has been the exposure of this secret league, that however frequently the conspirators may change its names, forms, passwords, and signals, its true purposes and operations can not longer be concealed from the military authorities.

It is to be remarked that the Supreme Council of the order, which annually meets on February 22, convened this year at New York city, and a special meeting was then appointed to be held at Chicago on July 1, or just prior to the day then fixed for the convention of the Democratic party. This convention having been postponed to August 29, the special meeting of the Supreme Council was also postponed to August 27,

at the same place, and was duly convened accordingly. It will be remembered that a leading member of the convention, in the course of a speech made before that body, alluded approvingly to the session of the Sons of Liberty at Chicago at the same time, as that of an organization in harmony with the sentiment and projects of the convention.

It may be observed, in conclusion, that one not fully acquainted with the true character and intentions of the order, might well suppose that, in designating its officers by high military titles, and in imitating in its organization that established in our armies, it was designed merely to render itself more popular and attractive with the masses, and to invest its chiefs with a certain sham dignity; but when it is understood that the order comprises within itself a large army of well-armed men, constantly drilled and exercised as soldiers, and that this army is held ready, at any time, for such forcible resistance to our military authorities, and such active co-operation with the public enemy, as it may be called upon to engage in by its commanders, it will be perceived that the titles of the latter are not assumed for a mere purpose of display, but that they are the chiefs of an actual and formidable force of conspirators against the life of the Government, and that their military system is, as it has been remarked by Colonel Sanderson, "the grand lever used by the rebel government for its army operations."

III.—ITS EXTENT AND NUMBERS.

The "temples" or "lodges" of the order are numerously scattered through the States of Indiana, Illinois, Ohio, Missouri, and Kentucky. They are also officially reported as established, to a less extent, in Michigan and the other Western States, as well as in New York, Pennsylvania, New Hampshire, Rhode Island, Connecticut, New Jersey, Maryland, Delaware, and Tennessee. Dodd, the Grand Commander of Indiana, in an address to the members in that State of February last, claims that at the next annual meeting of the Supreme Council (in February, 1865,) every State in the Union will be represented, and adds, "this is the first and only true national organization the Democratic and Conservative men of the country have ever attempted." A provision made in the constitution of the Council for a representation from the *Territories* shows, indeed, that the widest extension of the order is contemplated.

In the States first mentioned, the order is most strongly centered at the following places, where are situated its principal "temples." In Indiana, at Indianapolis and Vincennes; in Illinois, at Chicago, Springfield and Quincy, (a large proportion of the lodges in and about the latter place having been founded by the notorious guerrilla chief, Jackman;) in Ohio, at Cincinnati, Dayton, and in Hamilton county (which is proudly termed by members "the South Carolina of the North;") in Missouri, at St. Louis; in Kentucky, at Louisville; and in Michigan, at Detroit, (whence communication was freely had by the leaders of the order with Vallandigham during his banishment, either by letters addressed to him through two prominent citizens and members of the order, or by personal interviews at Windsor, C. W.) It is to be added that the regular places of meeting, as also the principal rendezvous and haunts of the members in these and less important places, are generally well known to the Government.

The actual *numbers* of the order have, it is believed, never been officially reported, and can not, therefore, be accurately ascertained. Various estimates have been made, by leading members, some of which are no doubt considerably exaggerated. It has been asserted by delegates to the Supreme Council of February last, that the number was there represented to be from eight hundred thousand to one million; but Vallandigham, in his speech last summer at Dayton, Ohio, placed it at five hundred thousand, which is probably much nearer the true total. The number of its members in the several States has been differently estimated in the reports and statements of its officers. Thus, the force of the order in Indiana, is stated to be from seventy-five to one hundred and twenty-five thousand; in Illinois, from one hundred to one hundred and forty thousand; in Ohio, from eighty to one hundred and eight thousand; in Kentucky, from forty to seventy thousand; in Missouri, from twenty to forty thousand; and in Michigan and New York, about twenty thousand each. Its representation in the other States above mentioned does not specifically appear from the testimony; but, allowing for every exaggeration in the figures reported, they may be deemed to present a tolerably faithful view of what, at least, is regarded by the order as its true force in the States designated.

It is to be noted that the order, or its counterpart, is probably much more widely extended at the South even than at the North, and that a large proportion of the officers of the rebel army are represented by credible witnesses to be members. In Kentucky and Missouri the order has not hesitated to admit as members, not only officers of that army, but also a considerable number of guerrillas, a class who might be supposed to appreciate most readily its spirit and purposes. It is fully shown that as lately as in July last, several of these ruffians were initiated into the first degree by Dr. Kalfus, in Kentucky.

A review of the testimony in regard to the *armed* force of the order, will materially aid in determining its real strength and numbers.

Although the order has from the outset partaken of the military character, it was not till the summer or fall of 1863 that it began to be generally organized as an armed body. Since that date its officers and leaders have been busily engaged in placing it upon a military basis, and in preparing it for a revolutionary movement. A general system of drilling has been instituted and secretly carried out. Members have been instructed to be constantly provided with weapons, and in some localities it has been absolutely required that each member should keep at his residence, at all times, certain arms and a specified quantity of ammunition.

In March last, the entire armed force of the order, capable of being mobilized for effective service, was represented to be three hundred and forty thousand men. As the details, upon which this statement was based, are imperfectly set forth in the testimony, it is not known how far this number may be exaggerated. It is abundantly shown, however, that the order, by means of a tax levied upon its members, has accumulated considerable funds for the purchase of arms and ammunition, and that these have been procured in large quantities for its use. The witness Clayton, on the trial of Dodd, estimated that *two-thirds* of the order are furnished with arms.

Green B. Smith, Grand Secretary of the order in Missouri, states in his confession of July last: "I know that arms, mostly revolvers and ammunition, have been purchased by members in St. Louis, to send to members in the country where they could not be had;" and he subsequently adds that he himself alone clandestinely purchased and forwarded, between April 15th and 19th last, about two hundred revolvers, with five thousand percussion caps and other ammunition. A muster-roll of one of the country lodges of that State is exhibited, in which, opposite the name of each member, are noted certain numbers, under the heads of "Missouri Republican," "St. Louis Union," "Anzeiger," "Miscellaneous Periodicals," "Books," "Speeches," and "Reports;" titles which, when interpreted, severally signify *single-barreled guns, double-barreled guns, revolvers, private ammunition, private lead, company powder, company lead*—the roll thus actually setting forth the amount of arms and ammunition in the possession of the lodge and its members.

In the States of Ohio and Illinois the order is claimed, by its members, to be unusually well armed with revolvers, carbines, etc.; but it is in regard to the arming of the order in Indiana that the principal statistics have been presented, and these may serve to illustrate the system which has probably been pursued in most of the States. One intelligent witness, who has been a member, estimates that in March last, there were in possession of the order in that State six thousand muskets and sixty thousand revolvers, besides private arms. Another member testifies that at a single lodge meeting of two hundred and fifty-two persons, which he attended early in the present year, the sum of $4,000 was subscribed for arms. Other members present statements in reference to the number of arms in their respective counties, and all agree in representing that these have been constantly forwarded from Indianapolis into the interior. Beck & Brothers are designated as the firm in that city, to which most of the arms were consigned. These were shipped principally from the East; some packages, however, were sent from Cincinnati, and some from Kentucky, and the boxes were generally marked "pick-axes," "hardware," "nails," "household goods," etc.

General Carrington estimates that in February and March last nearly thirty thousand guns and revolvers entered the State, and this estimate is based upon an actual inspection of invoices. The true number introduced was, therefore, probably considerably greater. That officer adds, that on the day in which the sale of arms was stopped by his order, in Indianapolis, nearly one thousand additional revolvers had been contracted for, and that the trade could not supply the demand. He further reports that after the introduction of arms into the Department of the North had been prohibited in General Orders of March last, a seizure was made by the Government of a large quantity of revolvers and one hundred and thirty-five thousand rounds of ammunition, which had been shipped to the firm in Indianapolis, of which H. H. Dodd, Grand Commander, was a member; that other arms about to be shipped to the same destination were seized in New York city; and that all these were claimed as the private property of John C. Walker, one of the Major Generals of the order in Indiana, and were represented to have been *"purchased for a few friends."* It should also be stated that at the office of Hon. D. W. Voorhees, M. C., at Terre Haute, were discovered letters which disclosed a correspondence between him and ex-Senator Wall, of New Jersey, in regard to the purchase of twenty thousand Garibaldi rifles, to be forwarded to the West.

It appears in the course of the testimony that a considerable quantity of arms and ammunition were brought into the State of Illinois from Burlington, Iowa, and that ammunition was sent from New Albany, Indiana, into Kentucky; it is also represented that, had Vallandigham been arrested on his return to Ohio, it was contemplated furnishing the order with arms from a point in Canada, near Windsor, where they were stored and ready for use.

There remains further to be noticed, in this connection, the testimony of Clayton upon the trial of Dodd, to the effect that arms were to be furnished the order from Nassau, N. P., by way of Canada; that, to defray the expense of these arms or their transportation, a formal assessment was levied upon the lodges, but that the transportation into Canada was actually to be furnished by the Confederate authorities.

A statement was made by Hunt, Grand Commander of Missouri, before his arrest, to a fellow member, that shells and all kinds of munitions of war, as well as infernal machines, were manufactured for the order at Indianapolis; and the late discovery in Cincinnati of samples of hand-grenades, conical shells, and rockets, of which one thousand were about to be manufactured, under a special contract, for the Order of the Sons of Liberty, goes directly to verify such a statement.

These details will convey some idea of the attempts which have been made to place the order upon a war footing and prepare it for aggressive movements. But, notwithstanding all the efforts that have been put forth, and with considerable success, to arm and equip its members as fighting men, the leaders have felt themselves still very deficient in their armament, and numerous schemes for increasing their armed strength have been devised. Thus, at the time of the issuing of the general order in Missouri requiring the enrollment of all citizens, it was proposed in the lodges of the Order of American Knights, at St. Louis, that certain members should raise companies in the militia, in their respective wards, and thus get command of as many Government arms and equipments as possible, for the future use of the order. Again it was proposed that *all* the members should enrol themselves in the militia, instead of paying commutation, in this way obtaining possession of United States arms, and having the advantage of the drill and military instruction. In the councils of the order in Kentucky, in June last, a scheme was devised for disarming all the negro troops, which it was thought could be done without much difficulty, and appropriating their arms for military purposes.

The despicable treachery of these proposed plans, as evincing the *animus* of the conspiracy, need not be commented upon.

It is to be observed that the order in the State of Missouri has counted greatly upon support from the enrolled militia, in case of an invasion by Price, as containing many members and friends of the Order of American Knights; and that the "Paw-Paw Militia," a military organization of Buchanan county, as well as the militia of Platte and Clay counties, known as "Flat-Foots," have been relied upon, almost to a man, to join the revolutionary movement.

V.—ITS RITUAL, OATHS, AND INTERIOR FORMS.

The ritual of the order, as well as its secret signs, passwords, etc., has been fully made known to the military authorities. In August last one hundred and twelve copies of the ritual of the Order of American Knights were seized in the office of Hon. D. W. Voorhees, M. C., at Terre Haute, and a large number of rituals of the Order of the Sons of Liberty, together with copies of the constitutions of the councils, etc., already referred to, were found in the building at Indianapolis, occupied by Dodd, the Grand Commander of Indiana, as had been indicated by the Government witness and detective, Stidger. Copies were likewise discovered at Louisville, at the residence of Dr. Kalfus, concealed within the mattress of his bed, where Stidger had ascertained that they were kept.

The ritual of the Order of American Knights has also been furnished by the authorities at St. Louis. From the ritual, that of the Order of the Sons of Liberty does not materially differ. Both are termed "progressive," in that they provide for *five* separate *degrees* of membership, and contemplate the admission of a member of a lower degree into a higher one only upon certain vouchers and proofs of fitness, which, with each ascending degree, are required to be stronger and more imposing.

Each degree has its commander or head; the fourth or "grand" is the highest in a State; the fifth or "supreme" the highest in the United States; but to the first or lower degree only do the great majority of members attain. A large proportion of these enter the order, supposing it to be a "Democratic" and political association merely; and the history of the order furnishes a most striking illustration of the gross and criminal deception which may be practiced upon the ignorant masses by unscrupulous and unprincipled leaders. The members of the lower degree are often for a considerable period kept quite unaware of the true purposes of their chiefs. But to the latter they are bound, in the language of their obligation, "*to yield prompt and implicit obedience to the utmost of their ability, without remonstrance, hesitation or delay*," and meanwhile their minds, under the discipline and teachings to which they are subjected, become educated and accustomed to contemplate with comparative unconcern the treason for which they are preparing.

The oaths, "invocations," "charges," etc., of the ritual, expressed as they are in bombastic and extravagant phraseology, would excite in the mind of an educated person only ridicule or contempt, but upon the illiterate they are calculated to make a deep impression, the effect and importance of which were doubtless fully studied by the framers of the instrument.

The *oath* which is administered upon the introduction of a member into any degree, is especially imposing in its language; it prescribes as a penalty for a violation of the obligation assumed "a shameful death," and further, that the body of the person guilty of such violation shall be divided in four parts and cast out at the four "gates" of the temple. Not only, as has been said, does it enjoin a blind obedience to the commands of the superiors of the order, but it is required to be held of *paramount obligation* to any oath which may be administered to a member in a court of justice or elsewhere. Thus, in cases where members have been sworn by officers empowered to administer oaths to speak the whole truth in answer to questions that may be put to them, and have then been examined in reference to the order, and their connection therewith, they have not only refused to give any information in regard to its character, but have denied that they were members, or even that they knew of its existence. A conspicuous instance of this is presented in the cases of Hunt, Dunn, and Smith, the chief officers of the order in Missouri, who, upon their first examination under oath, after their arrest, denied all connection with the order, but confessed, also under oath, at a subsequent period, that this denial was wholly false, although in accordance with their obligations as members. Indeed, a deliberate system of deception in regard to the details of the conspiracy is inculcated upon the members, and studiously pursued; and it may be mentioned, as a similarly despicable feature of the organization, that it is held bound to injure the Administration and officers of the Government, in every possible manner, by misrepresentation and falsehood.

Members are also instructed that their oath of membership is to be held paramount to an oath of allegiance, or any other oath which may impose obligations inconsistent with those which are assumed upon entering the order. Thus, if a member, when in danger, or for the purpose of facilitating some traitorous design, has taken the oath of allegiance to the United States, he is held at liberty to violate it on the first occasion, his obligation to the order being deemed superior to any consideration of duty or loyalty prompted by such oath.

It is to be added that where members are threatened with the penalties of perjury, in case of their answering falsely to questions propounded to them in regard to the order before a court or grand jury, they are instructed to refuse to answer such questions, alleging, as a ground for their refusal, that their answers may *criminate* themselves. The testimony shows that this course has habitually been pursued by members, especially in Indiana, when placed in such a situation.

Besides the oaths and other forms and ceremonies which have been alluded to, the ritual contains what are termed "Declarations of Principles." These declarations, which are most important as exhibiting the creed and character of the order, as inspired by the principles of the rebellion, will be fully presented under the next branch of the subject.

The *signs, signals, passwords,* etc., of the order are set forth at length in the testimony, but need only be briefly alluded to. It is a significant fact, as showing the intimate relations between the Northern and Southern sections of the secret conspiracy, that a member from a Northern State is enabled to pass without risk through the South by the use of the signs of recognition which have been established throughout the order, and by means of which members from distant points, though meeting as strangers, are at once made known to each other as "brothers." Mary Ann Pitman expressly states in her testimony that whenever important dispatches are required to be sent by rebel generals beyond their lines, members of the order are always selected to convey them. Certain passwords are also used in common in both sections, and of these, none appears to be more familiar than the word "Nu-oh-lac," or the name "Calhoun" spelt backward, and which is employed upon entering a temple of the first degree of the Order of American Knights—certainly a fitting password to such dens of treason.

Beside the signs of recognition, there are *signs of warning and danger,* for use at night, as well as by day; as, for instance, signs to warn members of the approach of United States officials seeking to make arrests. The order has also established what are called *battle-signals,* by means of which, as it is asserted, a member serving in the army may communicate with the enemy in the field, and thus escape personal harm in case of attack or capture. The most recent of these signals represented to have been adopted is a five-pointed copper star, worn under the coat, which is to be disclosed upon meeting an enemy, who will thus recognize in the wearer a sympathizer and an ally. A similar star of German silver, hung in a frame, is said to be numerously displayed by members or their families in private *houses* in Indiana, for the purpose of insuring protection to their property in case of a raid or other attack; and it is stated that in many dwellings in that State a portrait of John Morgan is exhibited for a similar purpose.

Other signs are used by members, and especially the officers of the order in their *correspondence.* Their letters, when of an official character, are generally conveyed by special messengers, but when transmitted through the mail are usually in cipher. When written in the ordinary manner, a character at the foot of the letter, consisting of a circle with a line drawn across the center, signifies to the member who receives it that the statements as written are to be understood in a sense directly the opposite to that which would ordinarily be conveyed.

It is to be added that the meetings of the order, especially in the country, are generally held at night and in secluded places; and that the approach to them is carefully guarded by a line of sentinels, who are passed only by means of a special *countersign,* which is termed the "picket."

VI.—ITS WRITTEN PRINCIPLES.

The "*Declaration of Principles,*" which is set forth in the ritual of the order, has already been alluded to. This declaration, which is specially framed for the instruction of the great mass of members, commences with the following proposition:

"All men are endowed by the Creator with certain rights, equal as far as there is equality in the capacity for the appreciation, enjoyment, and exercise of those rights." And subsequently there is added: "In the Divine economy no individual of the human race must be permitted to encumber the earth, to mar its aspects of transcendent beauty, nor to impede the progress of the physical or intellectual man, neither in himself nor in the race to which he belongs. Hence, a people, upon whatever plane they may be found in the ascending scale of humanity, whom neither the divinity within them nor the inspirations of divine and beautiful nature around them can impel to virtuous action and progress onward and upward, should be subjected to a just and humane servitude and tutelage to the superior race until they shall be able to appreciate the benefits and advantages of civilization."

Here, expressed in studied terms of hypocrisy, is the whole theory of human bondage—the right of the strong, because they are strong, to despoil and enslave the weak, because they are weak! The languages of earth can add nothing to the cowardly and loathsome baseness of the doctrine, as thus announced. It is the robber's creed sought to be nationalized, and would push back the hand on the dial plate of our civilization to the darkest periods of human history. It must be admitted, however, that it furnishes a fitting "corner-stone" for the government of a rebellion, every fiber of whose body and every throb of whose soul is born of the traitorous ambition and slave-pen inspirations of the South.

To these detestable tenets is added that other pernicious political theory of State sovereignty, with its necessary fruit, the monstrous doctrine of secession—a doctrine which, in asserting that in our federative system a part is greater than the whole, would compel the General Government, like a Japanese slave, to commit hari-kari whenever a faithless or insolent State should command it to do so.

Thus, the ritual, after reciting that the States of the Union are " free, independent, and sovereign," proceeds as follows:

"The government designated 'The United States of America' has no *sovereignty*, because that is an attribute with which the people, in their several and distinct political organizations, are endowed, and is inalienable. It was constituted by the terms of the *compact*, by all the States, through the express will of the people thereof, respectively—a common agent, to use and exercise certain named, specified, defined, and limited powers which are inherent of the sovereignties within those States. It is permitted, so far as regards its status and relations, as common agent in the exercise of the powers carefully and jealously delegated to it, to call itself 'supreme,' but not '*sovereign*.' In accordance with the principles upon which is founded the *American theory*, government can exercise only delegated power; hence, if those who shall have been chosen to administer the government shall assume to exercise powers not delegated, they should be regarded and treated as *usurpers*. The reference to 'inherent power,' 'war power,' or 'military necessity,' on the part of the functionary for the sanction of an arbitrary exercise of power by him, we will not accept in palliation or excuse."

To this is added, as a corollary, "it is incompatible with the history and nature of our system of government, that Federal authority should coerce by arms a sovereign State."

The declaration of principles, however, do s not stop here, but proceeds one step further, as follows:

"Whenever the chosen officers or delegates shall fail or refuse to administer the Government in strict accordance with the letter of the accepted Constitution, it is the inherent right and the solemn and imperative duty of the people to *resist* the functionaries, and, if need be, to *expel them by force of arms!* Such resistance is not revolution, but is solely the assertion of right—the exercise of all the noble attributes which impart honor and dignity to manhood."

To the same effect, though in a milder tone, is the platform of the order in Indiana, put forth by the Grand Council at their meeting in February last, which declares that "the right to alter or *abolish* their government, whenever it fails to secure the blessings of liberty, is one of the inalienable rights of the people that can never be surrendered."

Such, then, are the principles which the new member swears to observe and abide by in his obligation, set forth in the ritual, where he says: "I do solemnly promise that I will ever cherish in my heart of hearts the sublime creed of the E. K., (Excellent Knights,) and will, so far as in me lies, illustrate the same in my intercourse with men, and will defend the principles thereof, if need be, with my life, whensoever assailed, in my own country first of all. I do further solemnly declare that I will never take up arms in behalf of any government which does not acknowledge the sole authority or power to be the will of the governed."

The following extracts from the ritual, may also be quoted as illustrating the principle of the right of revolution and resistance to constituted authority insisted upon by the order:

"Our swords shall be unsheathed whenever the great principles which we aim to inculcate and have sworn to maintain and defend are assailed."

Again: "I do solemnly promise, that whensoever the principles which our order inculcates shall be assailed in my own State or country, I will defend these principles with my sword and my life, in whatsoever capacity may be assigned me by the competent authority of our order."

And further: "I do promise that I will, at all times, if need be, take up arms in the cause of the oppressed—in my own country first of all—against any power or government usurped, which may be found in arms and waging war against the people or peoples who are endeavoring to establish, or have inaugurated, a government for themselves of their own free choice."

Moreover, it is to be noted that all the addresses and speeches of its leaders breathe the same principle, of the right of the forcible resistance to the Government, as one of the tenets of the order.

Thus P. C. Wright, Supreme Commander, in his general address of December, 1863, after urging that "the spirit of the fathers may animate the free minds, the brave hearts, and still unshackled limbs of the *true democracy*," (meaning the members of the order,) adds as follows: "To be prepared for the crisis now approaching, we must catch from afar the earliest and faintest breathings of the spirit of the storm; to be successful when the storm comes, we must be watchful, patient, brave, confident, organized, *armed*."

Thus, too, Dodd, Grand Commander of the order in Indiana, quoting, in his address of February last, the views of his chief, Vallandigham, and adopting them as his own, says:

"He (Vallandigham) judges that the Washington power will not yield up its power until it is taken from them by an indignant people *by force of arms.*"

Such, then, are the written principles of the order in which the neophyte is instructed, and which he is sworn to cherish and observe as his rule of action, when, with arms placed in his hands, he is called upon to engage in the overthrow of his Government. This declaration—first, of the absolute right of slavery; second, of State sovereignty and the right of secession; third, of the right of armed resistance to constituted authority on the part of the disaffected and the disloyal, whenever their ambition may prompt them to revolution—is but an assertion of that abominable theory which, from its first enunciation, served as a pretext for conspiracy after conspiracy against the Government on the part of Southern traitors, until their detestable plotting culminated in open rebellion and bloody civil war. What more appropriate password, therefore, to be communicated to the new member upon his first admission to the secrets of the order could have been conceived, than that which was actually adopted—"Calhoun!"—a man who, baffled in his lust for power, with gnashing teeth turned upon the Government that had lifted him to its highest honors, and upon the country that had borne him, and down to the very close of his fevered life labored incessantly to scatter far and wide the seeds of that poison of death now upon our lips. The thorns which now pierce and tear us are of the tree he planted.

VII.—ITS SPECIFIC PURPOSES AND OPERATIONS.

From the principles of the order, as thus set forth, its general purpose of co-operating with the rebellion may readily be inferred, and, in fact, those principles could logically lead to no other result. This general purpose, indeed, is distinctly set forth in the personal statements and confessions of its members, and particularly of its prominent officers, who have been induced to make disclosures to the Government. Among the most significant of these confessions are those already alluded to, of Hunt, Dunn, and Smith, the heads of the order in Missouri. The latter, whose statement is full and explicit, says: "At the time I joined the order I understood that its object was to aid and assist the Confederate Government, and endeavor to restore the Union as it was prior to this rebellion." He adds: "The order is hostile in every respect to the General Government, and friendly to the so-called Confederate Government. It is exclusively made up of disloyal persons—of all Democrats who are desirous of securing the independence of the Confederate States with a view of restoring the Union as it was."

It would be idle to comment on such gibberish as the statement that "the independence of the Confederate States" was to be used as the means of restoring "the Union as it was;" and yet, under the manipulations of these traitorous jugglers, doubtless the brains of many have been so far muddled as to accept this shameless declaration as true.

But proceeding to the *specific* purposes of the order, which its leaders have had in view from the beginning, and which, as will be seen, it has been able, in many cases, to carry out with very considerable success, the following are found to be the most pointedly presented by the testimony:

1. *Aiding Soldiers to Desert and Harboring and Protecting Deserters.*—Early in its history the order essayed to undermine such portions of the army as were exposed to its insidious approaches. Agents were sent by the Knights of the Golden Circle into the camps to introduce the order among the soldiers, and those who became members were instructed to induce as many of their companions as possible to desert, and for this purpose the latter were furnished by the order with money and citizens' clothing. Soldiers who hesitated at desertion, but desired to leave the army, were introduced to lawyers who engaged to furnish them some *quasi* legal pretext for so doing, and a certain attorney of Indianapolis, named Walpole, who was particularly conspicuous in furnishing facilities of this character to soldiers who applied to him, has boasted that he has thus aided five hundred enlisted men to escape from their contracts. Through the schemes of the order in Indiana whole companies were broken up— a large detachment of a battery company, for instance, deserting on one occasion to the enemy with two of its guns—and the camps were imbued with a spirit of discontent and dissatisfaction with the service. Some estimate of the success of these efforts may be derived from a report of the Adjutant General of Indiana, of January, in 1863, setting forth that the number of deserters and absentees returned to the army through the post of Indianapolis alone, during the month of December, 1862, was nearly two thousand six hundred.

As soon as arrests of these deserters began to be generally made, writs of *habeas corpus* were issued in their cases by disloyal judges, and a considerable number were discharged thereon. In one instance in Indiana, where an officer in charge of a deserter properly refused to obey the writ, after it had been suspended in such cases by the President, his attachment for contempt was ordered by the Chief Justice of the State, who declared that "the streets of

Indianapolis might run with blood, but that he would enforce his authority against the President's order." On another occasion certain United States officers who had made the arrest of deserters in Illinois were themselves arrested for kidnapping, and held to trial by a disloyal judge, who at the same time discharged the deserters, though acknowledging them to be such.

Soldiers upon deserting, were assured of immunity from punishment and protection on the part of the order, and were instructed to bring away with them their arms, and, if mounted, their horses. Details sent to arrest them by the military authorities, were in several cases forcibly resisted, and, where not unusually strong in numbers, were driven back by large bodies of men, subsequently generally ascertained to be members of the order. Where arrests were effected, our troops were openly attacked and fired upon on their return. Instances of such attacks occurring in Morgan and Rush counties, Indiana, are especially noticed by General Carrington. In the case of the outbreak in Morgan county, J. S. Bingham, editor of the Indianapolis *Sentinel*, a member or friend of the order, sought to forward to the disloyal newspapers of the West false and inflammatory telegraphic dispatches in regard to the affair, to the effect that cavalry had been sent to arrest all the Democrats in the county, that they had committed gross outrages, and that several citizens had been shot; and adding "ten thousand soldiers can not hold the men arrested this night. Civil war and bloodshed are inevitable." The assertions in this dispatch were entirely false, and may serve to illustrate the fact heretofore noted, that a studious misrepresentation of the acts of the Government and its officers is a part of the prescribed duty of the members of the order. It is proper to mention that seven of the party in Morgan county, who made the attack upon our troops, were convicted of their offense by a State court. Upon their trial it was proved that the party was composed of members of the Knights of the Golden Circle.

One of the most pointed instances of protection afforded to deserters occurred in a case in Indiana, where seventeen intrenched themselves in a log cabin with a ditch and palisade, and were furnished with provisions and sustained in their defense against our military authorities for a considerable period by the order or its friends.

2. *Discouraging Enlistments and Resisting the Draft.*—It is especially inculcated by the order to oppose the re-enforcement of our armies, either by volunteers or drafted men. In 1862 the Knights of the Golden Circle organized generally to resist the draft in the Western States, and were strong enough in certain localities to greatly embarrass the

Government. In this year and early in 1863 a number of enrolling officers were shot in Indiana and Illinois. In Blackford county, Indiana, an attack was made upon the court-house, and the books connected with the draft were destroyed. In several counties of the State a considerable military force was required for the protection of the United States officials, and a large number of arrests were made, including that of one Reynolds, an ex-Senator of the Legislature, for publicly urging upon the populace to resist the conscription—an offense of the same character, in fact, as that upon which Vallandigham was apprehended in Ohio. These outbreaks were no doubt, in most cases, incited by the order and engaged in by its members. In Indiana nearly two hundred persons were indicted for conspiracy against the Government, resisting the draft, etc., and about sixty of these were convicted.

Where members of the order were forced into the army by the draft, they were instructed, in case they were prevented from presently escaping, and were obliged to go to the field, to use their arms against their fellow-soldiers rather than the enemy, or, if possible, to desert to the enemy, by whom, through the signs of the order, they would be recognized and received as friends. Whenever a member volunteered in the army he was at once expelled from the order.

3. *Circulation of Disloyal and Treasonable Publications.*—The order, especially in Missouri, has secretly circulated throughout the country a great quantity of treasonable publications, as a means of extending its own power and influence, as well as of giving encouragement to the disloyal and inciting them to treason. Of these, some of the principal are the following: *Pollard's Southern History of the War, Official Reports of the Confederate Government, Life of Stonewall Jackson*, pamphlets containing articles from the *Metropolitan Record, Abraham Africanus, or Mysteries of the White House, The Lincoln Catechism, or a Guide to the Presidential Election of 1864, Indestructible Organics*, by Tirga. These publications have generally been procured by formal requisitions drawn upon the grand commander by leading members in the interior of a State. One of these requisitions, dated June 10th last, and drawn by a local secretary of the order at Gentryville, Missouri, is exhibited in the testimony. It contains a column of the initials of subscribers, opposite whose names are entered the number of disloyal publications to be furnished, the particular book or books, etc., required being indicated by fictitious titles.

4. *Communicating with, and Giving Intelligence to, the Enemy.*—Smith, Grand Secretary of the order in Missouri, says, in his confession: " Rebel spies, mail-carriers, and emis-

saries have been carefully protected by this order ever since I have been a member." It is shown in the testimony to be customary in the rebel service to employ members of the order as spies, under the guise of soldiers furnished with furloughs to visit their homes within our lines. On coming within the territory occupied by our forces, they are harbored and supplied with information by the order. Another class of spies claim to be deserters from the enemy, and at once seek an opportunity to take the oath of allegiance, which, however, though voluntarily taken, they claim to be administered while they are under a species of duress, and, therefore, not to be binding. Upon swearing allegiance to the Government, the pretended deserter engages, with the assistance of the order, in collecting contraband goods or procuring intelligence to be conveyed to the enemy, or in some other treasonable enterprise. In his official report of June 12th last, Colonel Sanderson remarks: "This department is filled with rebel spies, all of whom belong to the order."

In Missouri regular mail communication was for a long period maintained through the agency of the order from St. Louis to Price's army, by means of which private letters, as well as official dispatches between him and the Grand Commander of Missouri, were regularly transmitted. The mail-carriers started from a point on the Pacific railroad, near Kirkwood station, about fourteen miles from St. Louis, and, traveling only by night, proceeded (to quote from Colonel Sanderson's report) to "Mattox Mills, on the Maramee river, thence past Mineral Point to Webster, thence to a point fifteen miles below Van Buren, where they crossed the Black river, and thence to the rebel lines." It is, probably, also by this route that the secret correspondence, stated by the witness Pitman to have been constantly kept up between Price and Vallandigham, the heads of the order at the North and South, respectively, was successfully maintained.

A similar communication has been continuously held with the enemy from Louisville, Kentucky. A considerable number of women in that State, many of them of high position in rebel society, and some of them outwardly professing to be loyal, were discovered to have been actively engaged in receiving and forwarding mails, with the assistance of the order and as its instruments. Two of the most notorious and successful of these, Mrs. Woods and Miss Cassell, have been apprehended and imprisoned.

By means of this correspondence with the enemy, the members of the order were promptly apprised of all raids to be made by the forces of the former, and were able to hold themselves prepared to render aid and comfort to the raiders. To show how efficient for this purpose was the system thus established, it is to be added that our military authorities have, in a number of cases, been informed, through members of the order employed in the interest of the Government, of impending raids and important army movements of the rebels, not only days, but sometimes weeks, sooner than the same intelligence could have reached them through the ordinary channels.

On the other hand, the system of *espionage* kept up by the order, for the purpose of obtaining information of the movements of our own forces, etc., to be imparted to the enemy, seems to have been as perfect as it was secret. The Grand Secretary of the order in Missouri states, in his confession: "One of the especial objects of this order was to place members in steamboats, ferry-boats, telegraph offices, express offices, department headquarters, provost marshal's office, and, in fact, in every position where they could do valuable service;" and he proceeds to specify certain members who, at the date of his confession, (August 2d last,) were employed at the express and telegraph offices in St. Louis.

5. *Aiding the Enemy, by Recruiting for them, or assisting them to Recruit, within our lines.*—This has also been extensively carried on by members of the order, particularly in Kentucky and Missouri. It is estimated that two thousand men were sent South from Louisville alone during a few weeks in April and May, 1864. The order and its friends at that city have a permanent fund, to which there are many subscribers, for the purpose of fitting out with pistols, clothing, money, etc., men desiring to join the Southern service; and, in the lodges of the order in St. Louis and Northern Missouri, money has often been raised to purchase horses, arms, and equipments for soldiers about to be forwarded to the Southern army. In the latter State, parties empowered by Price, or by Grand Commander Hunt as his representative, to recruit for the rebel service, were nominally authorized to "*locate lands,*" as it was expressed, and in their reports, which were formally made, the number of acres, etc., located represented the number of men recruited. At Louisville, those desiring to join the Southern forces were kept hidden, and supplied with food and lodging until a convenient occasion was presented for their transportation South. They were then collected, and conducted at night to a safe rendezvous of the order, whence they were forwarded to their destination, in some cases stealing horses from the United States corrals on their way. While awaiting an occasion to be sent South, the men, to avoid the suspicion which might be excited by their being seen together in any considerable number, were often employed on farms in the vicinity of

Louisville, and the farm of one Grant in that neighborhood, (at whose house, also, meetings of the order were held,) is indicated in the testimony as one of the localities where such recruits were rendezvoused and employed.

The same facilities which were afforded to recruits for the Southern army were also furnished by the order to persons desiring to proceed beyond our lines for any illegal purpose. By these Louisville was generally preferred as a point of departure, and, on the Mississippi river, a particular steamer, the Graham, was selected as the safest conveyance.

6. *Furnishing the rebels with Arms, Ammunition, etc.*—In this, too, the order, and especially its female members and allies, has been sedulously engaged. The rebel women of Louisville and Kentucky are represented as having rendered the most valuable aid to the Southern army, by transporting large quantities of percussion caps, powder, etc., concealed upon their persons, to some convenient locality near the lines, whence they could be readily conveyed to those for whom they were intended. It is estimated that at Louisville, up to May 1st last, the sum of $17,000 had been invested by the order in ammunition and arms, to be forwarded principally in this manner to the rebels. In St. Louis several firms, who are well known to the Government, the principal of which is Beauvais & Co., have been engaged in supplying arms and ammunition to members of the order, to be conveyed to their Southern allies. Mary Ann Pitman, a reliable witness, and a member of the Order of American Knights, who will hereafter be specially alluded to, states in her testimony that she visited Beauvais & Co. three times, and procured from them on each occasion about $80 worth of caps, besides a number of pistols and cartridges, which she carried in person to Forrest's command, as well as a much larger quantity of similar articles which she caused to be forwarded by other agents. The guerrillas in Missouri also receive arms from St. Louis, and one Douglas, one of the most active conspirators of the Order of American Knights in Missouri, and a special emissary of Price, was arrested while in the act of transporting a box of forty revolvers by railroad to a guerrilla camp in the interior of the State. Medical stores in large quantities were likewise, by the aid of the order, furnished to the enemy, and a "young doctor" named Moore, said to be now a medical inspector in the rebel army, is mentioned as having "made $75,000 by smuggling medicines"—principally from Louisville—through the lines of our army. Supplies were, in some cases, conveyed to the enemy through the medium of professed loyalists, who, having received permits for that purpose from the United States military authorities, would forward their goods as if for ordinary purposes of trade, to a certain point near the rebel lines, where, by the connivance of the owners, the enemy would be enabled to seize them.

7. *Co-operating with the Enemy in Raids and Invasions.*—While it is clear that the order has given aid, both directly and indirectly, to the forces of the rebels, and to guerrilla bands, when engaged in making incursions into the border States, yet because, on the one hand, of the constant restraint upon its action exercised by our military authorities, and, on the other, of the general success of our armies in the field over those of the enemy, their allies at the North have never thus far been able to carry out their grand plan of a general armed rising of the order, and its co-operation on an extended scale with the Southern forces. This plan has been twofold, and consisted, first, of a rising of the order in Missouri, aided by a strong detachment from Illinois, and a co-operation with a rebel army under Price; second, of a similar rising in Indiana, Ohio, and Kentucky, and a co-operation with a force under Breckinridge, Buckner, Morgan, or some other rebel commander, who was to invade the latter State. In *this* case the order was first to cut the railroads and telegraph wires, so that intelligence of the movement might not be sent abroad and the transportation of Federal troops might be delayed, and then to seize upon the arsenals at Indianapolis, Columbus, Springfield, Louisville, and Frankfort, and, furnishing such of their number as were without arms, to kill or make prisoners of department, district, and post commanders, release the rebel prisoners at Rock Island, and at Camps Morton, Douglas, and Chase, and thereupon join the Southern army at Louisville or some other point in Kentucky, which State was to be permanently occupied by the combined force. At the period of the movement it was also proposed that an attack should be made upon Chicago by means of steam-tugs mounted with cannon. A similar course was to be taken in Missouri, and was to result in the permanent occupation of that State.

This scheme has long occupied the minds of members of the order, and has been continually discussed by them in their lodges. A rising, somewhat of the character described, was intended to have taken place in the spring of this year, simultaneously with an expected advance of the army of Lee upon Washington; but the plans of the enemy having been anticipated by the movements of our own generals, the rising of the conspirators was necessarily postponed. Again, a general movement of the Southern forces was expected to occur about July 4, and with this the order was to co-operate. A speech to be made by Vallandigham at the Chicago Convention was, it is said, to be the signal for the rising; but the postponement of the convention, as well as the failure of the rebel armies to engage in the anticipated movement, again operated to disturb the programme of the order. During the summer, however, the grand plan of action above set forth has been more than ever discussed throughout the order, and its success most confidently predicted, while, at the same time, an extensive organization and preparation for carrying the conspiracy into effect have been actively going on. But, up to this time, notwithstanding the late raids of the enemy in Kentucky, and the invasion of Missouri by Price, no such general action on the part of the order as was contemplated has taken place—a result, in great part, owing to the activity of our military authorities in strengthening the detachments at the prisons, arsenals, etc., and in causing the arrest of the leading conspirators in the several States, and especially in the seizure of large quantities of arms which had been shipped for the use of the order in their intended outbreak. It was doubtless on account of these precautions that the day last appointed for the rising of the order in Indiana and Kentucky (August 16) passed by with but slight disorder.

It is, however, the inability of the public enemy, in the now declining days of the rebellion, to initiate the desired movement which has prevented the order from engaging in open warfare; and it has lately been seriously considered in their councils whether they should not proceed with their revolt, relying alone upon the guerrilla bands of Syphert, Jesse and others, for support and assistance.

With these guerrillas the order has always most readily acted along the border, and in cases of capture by the Union forces of Northern members of the order engaged in co-operating with them, the guerrillas have frequently retaliated by seizing prominent Union citizens and holding them as hostages for the release of their allies. At other times our Government has been officially notified by the rebel authorities that if the members of the order captured were not treated by us as ordinary prisoners of war, retaliation would be resorted to.

An atrocious plan of concert between members of the order in Indiana and certain guerrilla bands of Kentucky, agreed upon last spring, may be here remarked upon. Some two thousand five hundred or three thousand guerrillas were to be thrown into the border counties, and were to assume the character of refugees seeking employment. Being armed they were secretly to destroy Government property wherever practicable, and subsequently to control the elections by force, prevent enlistments, aid deserters, and stir up strife between the civil and military authorities.

A singular feature of the raids of the enemy remains only to be adverted to, viz.: that the officers conducting these raids are furnished by the rebel Government with quantities of United States Treasury notes for use within our lines, and that these are probably most frequently procured through the agency of members of the order.

Mary Ann Pitman states that Forrest, of the rebel army, at one time exhibited to her a letter to himself from a prominent rebel sympathizer and member of the order in Washington, D. C., in which it was set forth that the sum of $20,000 in "greenbacks" had actually been forwarded by him to the rebel Government at Richmond.

8. *Destruction of Government Property.* — There is no doubt that large quantities of Government property have been burned or otherwise destroyed by the agency of the order in different localities. At Louisville, in the case of the steamer Taylor, and on the Mississippi river, steamers belonging to the United States have been burned at the wharves, and generally when loaded with Government stores. Shortly before the arrest of Bowles, the senior of the major generals of the order in Indiana, he had been engaged in the preparation of "Greek Fire," which, it was supposed, would be found serviceable in the destruction of public property. It was generally understood in the councils of the order in the State of Kentucky that they were to be compensated for such destruction by the rebel Government, by receiving a commission of ten per cent. of the value of the property so destroyed, and that this value was to be derived from the estimate of the loss made in each case by Northern newspapers.

9. *Destruction of Private Property and Persecution of Loyal Men.*—It is reported by General Carrington that the full development of the order in Indiana was followed by "a state of terrorism" among the Union residents of "portions of Brown, Morgan, Johnson, Rush, Clay, Sullivan, Bartholomew, Hendricks, and other counties" in that State; that from some localities individuals were driven away altogether; that in others their barns, hay and wheat-racks were burned; and that many persons, under the general insecurity of life and property, sold their effects at a sacrifice and removed to other places. At one time in Brown county, the members of the order openly threatened the lives of all "Abolitionists" who refused to sign a peace memorial which they had prepared and addressed to Congress. In Missouri, also, similar outrages committed upon the property of loyal citizens are attributable in a great degree to the secret order.

Here the outbreak of the miners in the coal districts of Eastern Pennsylvania, in the autumn of last year, may be appropriately referred to. It was fully shown in the testimony adduced, upon the trials of these insurgents, who were guilty of the destruction of property and numerous acts of violence, as well as murder, that they were generally members of a secret treasonable association, similar in all respects to the Knights of the Golden Circle, at the meetings of which they had been incited to the commission of the crimes for which they were tried and convicted.

10. *Assassination and Murder.*—After what has been disclosed in regard to this infamous league of traitors and ruffians, it will not be a matter of surprise to learn that the cold-blooded assassination of Union citizens and soldiers has been included in their devilish scheme of operations. Green B. Smith states in his confession that "the secret assassination of United States officers, soldiers, and Government employes, has been discussed in the councils of the order and recommended." It is also shown in the course of the testimony that at a large meeting of the order in St. Louis, in May or June last, it was proposed to form a secret police of members for the purpose of patrolling the streets of that city at night and killing every detective and soldier that could be readily disposed of; that this proposition was coolly considered, and finally rejected, not because of its fiendish character—no voice being raised against its criminality—but because only it was deemed premature. At Louisville, in June last, a similar scheme was discussed among the order for the waylaying and butchering of negro soldiers in the streets at night; and in the same month a party of its members in that city was actually organized for the purpose of throwing off the track of the Nashville railroad a train of colored troops and seizing the opportunity to take the lives of as many as possible. Again, in July, the assassination of an obnoxious provost marshal, by betraying him into the hands of guerrillas, was designed by members in the interior of Kentucky. Further, at a meeting of the Grand Council of Indiana at Indianapolis on June 14th last, the murder of one Coffin, a Government detective, who, as it was supposed, had betrayed the order, was deliberately discussed and unanimously determined upon. This fact is stated by Stidger in his report to General Carrington of June 17th last, and is more fully set forth in his testimony upon the trial of Dodd. He deposes that at the meeting in question, Dodd himself volunteered to go to Hamilton, Ohio, where Coffin was expected to be found, and there "dispose of the latter." He adds that prior to the meeting, he himself conveyed from Judge Bullitt, at Louisville, to Bowles and Dodd, at Indianapolis, special instructions to have Coffin "put out of the way"—"murdered"—"at all hazards."

The opinion is expressed by Colonel San-derson, under date of June 12th last, that "the recent numerous cold-blooded assassinations of military officers and unconditional Union men throughout the military district of North Missouri, especially along the western border," is to be ascribed to the agency of the order. The witness Pitman represents that it is "a part of the obligation or understanding of the order" to kill officers and soldiers "*whenever it can be done by stealth*," as well as loyal citizens when considered important or influential persons; and she adds, that while at Memphis, during the past summer, she *knew* that men on picket were secretly killed by members of the order approaching them in disguise.

In this connection may be recalled the wholesale assassination of Union soldiers by members of the order and their confederates at Charleston, Illinois, in March last, in regard to which, as a startling episode of the rebellion, a full report was addressed from this office to the President, under date of July 26th last. This concerted murderous assault upon a scattered body of men, mostly unarmed—apparently designed for the mere purpose of destroying as many lives of Union soldiers as possible—is a forcible illustration of the utter malignity and depravity which characterize the members of this order in their zeal to commend themselves as allies to their fellow-conspirators at the South.

11. *Establishment of a North-western Confederacy.*—In concluding this review of some of the principal specific purposes of the order, it remains only to remark upon a further design of many of its leading members, the accomplishment of which they are represented as having deeply at heart. Hating New England, and jealous of her influence and resources, and claiming that the interests of the West and South, naturally connected as they are through the Mississippi valley, are identical, and actuated further by an intensely revolutionary spirit as well as an unbridled and unprincipled ambition, these men have made the establishment of a Western or North-western Confederacy, in alliance with the South, the grand aim and end of all their plotting and conspiring. It is with this steadily in prospect that they are constantly seeking to produce discontent, disorganization, and civil disorder at the North. With this in view, they gloat over every reverse of the armies of the Union, and desire that the rebellion shall be protracted until the resources of the Government shall be exhausted, its strength paralyzed, its currency hopelessly depreciated, and confidence every-where destroyed. Then, from the anarchy which, under their scheme, is to ensue, the new Confederacy is to arise, which is either to unite itself with that of the South, or to form therewith a close and permanent alli-

ance. Futile and extravagant as this scheme may appear, it is yet the settled purpose of many leading spirits of the secret conspiracy, and is their favorite subject of thought and discussion. Not only is this scheme deliberated upon in the lodges of the order, but it is openly proclaimed. Members of the Indiana Legislature, even, have publicly announced it, and avowed that they will take their own State out of the Union, and recognize the independence of the South. A citizen captured by a guerrila band in Kentucky last summer, records the fact that the establishment of a new confederacy as the deliberate purpose of the Western people was boastfully asserted by these outlaws, who also assured their prisoner that in the event of such establishment there would be "a greater rebellion than ever!"

Lastly, it is claimed that the new confederacy is already organized; that it has a "provisional government," officers, departments, bureaus, etc., in secret operation. No comment is necessary to be made upon this treason, not now contemplated for the first time in our history. Suggested by the present rebellion, it is the logical consequence of the ardent and utter sympathy therewith which is the life and inspiration of the secret order.

VIII.—THE WITNESSES AND THEIR TESTIMONY.

The facts detailed in the present report have been derived from a great variety of dissimilar sources, but all the witnesses, however different their situations, concur so pointedly in their testimony, that the evidence which has thus been furnished must be accepted as of an entirely satisfactory character.

The principal witnesses may be classified as follows:

1. Shrewd, intelligent men, employed as detectives, and with a peculiar talent for their calling, who have gradually gained the confidence of leading members of the order, and in some cases have been admitted to its temples and been initiated into one or more of the degrees. The most remarkable of these is Stidger, formerly a private soldier in our army, who, by the use of an uncommon address, though at great personal risk, succeeded in establishing such intimate relations with Bowles, Bullitt, Dodd, and other leaders of the order in Indiana and Kentucky, as to be appointed Grand Secretary for the latter State, a position the most favorable for obtaining information of the plans of these traitors and warning the Government of their intentions. It is to the rare fidelity of this man, who has also been the principal witness upon the trial of Dodd, that the Government has been chiefly indebted for the exposure of the designs of the conspirators in the two States named.

2. Rebel officers and soldiers voluntarily or involuntarily making disclosures to our military authorities. The most valuable witnesses of this class are prisoners of war, who, actuated by laudable motives, have of their own accord furnished a large amount of information in regard to the order, especially as it exists in the South, and of the relations of its members with those of the Northern section. Among these, also, are soldiers at our prison camps, who, without designing it, have made known to our officials, by the use of the signs, etc., of the order, that they were members.

3. Scouts employed to travel through the interior of the border States, and also within or in the neighborhood of the enemy's lines. The fact that some of these were left entirely ignorant of the existence of the order, upon being so employed, attaches an increased value to their discoveries in regard to its operations.

4. Citizen prisoners, to whom, while in confinement, disclosures were made relative to the existence, extent, and character of the order by fellow-prisoners who were leading members, and who, in some instances, upon becoming intimate with the witness, initiated him into one of the degrees.

5. Members of the order, who, upon a full acquaintance with its principles, have been appalled by its infamous designs, and have voluntarily abandoned it, freely making known their experience to our military authorities. In this class may be placed the female witness, Mary Ann Pitman, who, though in arrest at the period of her disclosures, was yet induced to make them for the reason that, as she says, "at the last meeting which I attended they passed an order which I consider as utterly atrocious and barbarous; so I told them I would have nothing more to do with them." This woman was attached to the command of the rebel Forrest, as an officer under the name of "Lieutenant Rawley;" but, because her sex afforded her unusual facilities for crossing our lines, she was often employed in the execution of important commissions within our territory, and, as a member of the order, was made extensively acquainted with other members, both of the Northern and Southern sections. Her testimony is thus peculiarly valuable, and, being a person of unusual intelligence and force of character, her statements are succinct, pointed, and emphatic. They are also especially useful as fully corroborating those of other witnesses regarded as most trustworthy.

6. Officers of the order of high rank, who have been prompted to present confessions, more or less detailed, in regard to the order and their connection with it. The principals of these are, Hunt, Dunn, and Smith, Grand Commander, Deputy Grand Commander, and Grand Secretary of the

22

order in Missouri, to whose statements frequent reference has been made. These confessions, though in some degree guarded and disingenuous, have furnished to the Government much important information as to the operations of the order, especially in Missouri, the affiliation of its leaders with Price, etc. It is to be noted that Dunn makes the statement in common with other witnesses that, in entering the order, he was quite ignorant of its ultimate purposes. He says: "I did not become a member understandingly; the initiatory step was taken in the dark, without reflection and without knowledge."

7. Deserters from our army, who, upon being apprehended, confessed that they had been induced and assisted to desert by members of the order. It was, indeed, principally from these confessions that the existence of the secret treasonable organization of the Knights of the Golden Circle was first discovered in Indiana in the year 1862.

8. Writers of anonymous communications, addressed to heads of departments or provost marshals, disclosing facts corroborative of other more important statements.

9. The witnesses before the grand jury at Indianapolis, in 1863, when the order was formally presented as a treasonable organization, and those whose testimony has been recently introduced upon the trial of Dodd.

It need only be added that a most satisfactory test of the credibility and weight of much of the evidence which has been furnished is afforded by the printed testimony in regard to the character and intention of the order, which is found in its National and State constitutions and its ritual. Indeed, the statements of the various witnesses are but presentations of the logical and inevitable consequences and results of the principles therein set forth.

In concluding this review, it remains only to state that a constant reference has been made to the elaborate official reports, in regard to the order, of Brigadier General Carrington, commanding District of Indiana, and of Colonel Sanderson, Provost Marshal General of the Department of Missouri. The great mass of the testimony upon the subject of this conspiracy has been furnished by these officers; the latter acting under the orders of Major General Rosecrans, and the former co-operating, under the instructions of the Secretary of War, with Major General Burbridge, commanding District of Kentucky, as well as with Governor Morton, of Indiana, who, though at one time greatly embarrassed, by a Legislature strongly tainted with disloyalty, in his efforts to repress this domestic enemy, has at last seen his State relieved from the danger of a civil war.

But, although the treason of the order has been thoroughly exposed, and although its capacity for fatal mischief has, by means of the arrest of its leaders, the seizure of its arms, and the other vigorous means which have been pursued, been seriously impaired, it is still busied with its plottings against the Government, and with its perfidious designs in aid of the Southern rebellion. It is reported to have recently adopted new signs and passwords, and its members assert that foul means will be used to prevent the success of the Administration at the coming election, and threaten an extended revolt in the event of the re-election of President Lincoln.

In the presence of the rebellion and of this secret order—which is but its echo and faithful ally—we can not but be amazed at the utter and widespread profligacy, personal and political, which these movements against the Government disclose. The guilty men engaged in them, after casting aside their allegiance, seem to have trodden under foot every sentiment of honor and every restraint of law, human and divine. Judea produced but one Judas Iscariot, and Rome, from the sinks of her demoralization, produced but one Catiline; and yet, as events prove, there has arisen together in our land an entire brood of such traitors, all animated by the same parricidal spirit, and all struggling with the same relentless malignity for the dismemberment of our Union. Of this extraordinary phenomenon—not paralleled, it is believed, in the world's history—there can be but one explanation, and all these blackened and fetid streams of crime may well be traced to the same common fountain. So fiercely intolerant and imperious was the temper engendered by slavery, that when the Southern people, after having controlled the national councils for half a century, were beaten at an election, their leaders turned upon the Government with the insolent fury with which they would have drawn their revolvers on a rebellious slave in one of their negro quarters; and they have continued since to prosecute their warfare, amid all the barbarisms and atrocities naturally and necessarily inspired by the infernal institution in whose interests they are sacrificing alike themselves and their country. Many of these conspirators, as is well known, were fed, clothed, and educated at the expense of the nation, and were loaded with its honors at the very moment they struck at its life with the horrible criminality of a son stabbing the bosom of his own mother while impressing kisses on his cheeks. The leaders of the traitors in the loyal States, who so completely fraternize with these conspirators, and whose machinations are now unmasked, it is as clearly the duty of the Administration to prosecute and punish as it is its duty to subjugate the rebels who are openly in arms against the Government. In the performance of this duty, it is entitled to expect, and will doubtless receive, the zealous co-operation of true men everywhere, who, in crushing the truculent foe ambushed in the haunts of this secret order, should rival in courage and faithfulness the soldiers who are so nobly sustaining our flag on the battle-fields of the South. Respectfully submitted,

J. HOLT, *Judge Advocate General.*

The history of the exposure of the Northwestern Conspiracy would be incomplete without the insertion of the following letter:

HEADQUARTERS NORTHERN DEPARTMENT, }
Columbus, Ohio, October 1, 1864. }

Major-General Halleck, Chief of Staff, Washington, D. C.:

GENERAL: Soon after my arrival here, to take command of this Department, I was informed, from the War Department, of secret organizations then forming in some of the States of my command, and instructions to try and ferret them out. I placed the papers in the hands of Brigadier-General H. B. Carrington, stationed at Indianapolis, Indiana, through whom I have been enabled to keep the War Department fully informed of the measures being taken by the disloyal. Through his energy, perseverance and good judgment, I am indebted for all the information I have been able to transmit. Through the information thus obtained, and the measures taken in consequence thereof, we are indebted, mainly, to being saved from the horrors of civil war in these States.

I can not be relieved from the duties of this Department, without putting on record my testimony in General Carrington's favor.

I have the honor to be, General,

Very respectfully,

Your obedient servant,

S. P. HEINTZELMAN,
Major-General.

C. H. POTTER, Assistant Adjutant-General.

REPLY OF H. H. DODD.

Editors of the Cincinnati Enquirer:

Gentlemen: In your issue of yesterday, in an editorial article, I notice the following language:

"By the way, it would be instructive to learn where the money came from with which Mr. Dodd's pistols were purchased; and furthermore, how Mr. Dodd—crowded as Indiana is with spies and secret policemen, every one of whom know him, or had his portrait in possession—contrived to escape to Canada, with his pockets full of the effigies of the President and Secretary of the Treasury."

The only force and effect of which is to convey the idea that I have been acting in the interest of the Administration party, and have been paid for my services, and allowed to escape through their instrumentality.

This unfounded assault upon my character, originated with some irresponsible correspondent of the Chicago *Times*, at Indianapolis, and which has since been made the basis of editorial comments, in the *Sentinel* and *Enquirer*, and thus, intentionally or otherwise, you are giving credence and publicity to the "*complicity with Morton*" dodge, gotten up by a *coterie* of "*Sons*," who have seen fit to take the benefit of the "baby act."

I certainly have no objection to your whipping your Abolition contemporaries, or to your censuring and condemning the men in power or their measures; but I must enter my solemn protest against the use of my sore back as a medium to do the one or the other. Neither do I complain of comments upon my public or private acts, political principles, combinations or associations, as against abolitionism, terrorism, despotism, usurpation, oppression and military dictation; nor upon any sins of commission or omission in this direction. I am ready to hear "charges and specifications," of attempted assassinations, of estimates upon my ability, intentions or purposes, and this sort of thing; make me out an enemy to society from either weakness or ambition; call me a revolutionist, or what not, I am willing to leave to time to prove that "*The worst enemy to the peace of mankind is he who renders a revolution necessary.*"

But to charge me with being a "*spy and informer*," that I would become a *decoy* to lure unsuspecting associates into the boiling cauldron of "crime, hatred and malice," all for the "effigies of the President and Secretary of the Treasury," is to charge me with a heinous crime against mankind, that I can not permit to be laid at my door—and I may not remain silent, when the editor of the *Enquirer*, from personal knowledge, knows me incapable of playing such a *role*.

Do you wish sincerely to know in regard to the pistols? You will recollect that a gentleman in New York claimed them as his individual property, and by reference to my card, published on the 5th day of September last, you will find further explanation as to my connection with the said pistols. It was not then considered even a crime by Democratic journals, to buy and sell, or to keep and bear arms. The amount involved was not so large as to raise the inquiry, "*Where the money came from?*"

My escape was no great exploit; not sufficiently so, at least, to raise the question of "*How it was contrived?*" A little affair of this sort could be managed as well as the purchase of a few hundred pistols, without the intervention of the Government or any of its agents. You do me great injustice when you speak of me as some notorious criminal, personally known to all thief-catchers, and whose picture every detective in the country carried about with him. The fact that I have safely arrived in a country where the "*majesty of the law*" is respected, fully proves the contrary; for how could I pass through a perfect forest of detectives, secret policemen, spies, soldiers in uniform, soldiers in citizens' dress—in female attire, dressed as hod carriers, as peddlers, as white-washers, teamsters, wood-choppers, spread all through the county of Marion and adjoining counties; swarming in the cities of Indianapolis, Cincinnati, Cleveland, Toledo and Detroit, and upon every railway train; yet simply because I was unknown to them, and because they did not have my picture in their pockets, I passed through them all unnoticed.

It is no longer necessary to attack my honor, to prove the Democratic "*leaders*" in no way connected with the "Dodd conspiracy." They are no more responsible for my acts than I am for theirs, and I am perfectly willing that the acts of some of them, in this case, should be the standard if the rest of them will assent.

But the simple object of this note, however, was to have you give my denial to the charge of "*complicity with Morton*." This is all I ask, so that the Democratic masses can see it over my own signature. I care not who avers it. I am satisfied to risk the question of veracity. If you are incredulous, just inquire of Major Burnett, General Hovey or Colonel Warner, and methinks the energetic replies will be entirely satisfactory.

It may be that I committed an error in abandoning the "Commission." Be this as it may, I regret exceedingly to have made any plea either to the jurisdiction or to the indictment, or to have, in any manner, recognized the tribunal.

The charge that I violated a parole is, like all the rest, utterly false. I was in solitary confinement every moment from the time of my arrest until the escape.

Respectfully yours, etc.,

H. H. DODD.

6786-ج
96